THE MORAL DOMAIN

Guided Readings in Philosophical and Literary Texts

NORMAN LILLEGARD

University of Tennessee at Martin

New York   Oxford
OXFORD UNIVERSITY PRESS
2010

Oxford University Press, Inc., publishes works that further Oxford University's
objective of excellence in research, scholarship, and education.

Oxford New York
Auckland   Cape Town   Dar es Salaam   Hong Kong   Karachi
Kuala Lumpur   Madrid   Melbourne   Mexico City   Nairobi
New Delhi   Shanghai   Taipei   Toronto

With offices in
Argentina Austria Brazil Chile Czech Republic France Greece
Guatemala Hungary Italy Japan Poland Portugal Singapore
South Korea Switzerland Thailand Turkey Ukraine Vietnam

Published by Oxford University Press, Inc.
198 Madison Avenue, New York, New York 10016
http://www.oup.com

Library of Congress Cataloging-in-Publication Data

The moral domain: guided readings in philosophical and literary texts/
   [compiled by] Norman Lillegard.
       p. cm.
   Includes bibliographical references (p.   ) and index.
   ISBN 978-0-19-514808-4
   1. Ethics. I. Lillegard, Norman, 1938–
   BJ1012.M6323 2010
   170--dc22

                                                2009014278

Printing number: 9 8 7 6 5 4 3 2 1

Printed in the United States of America
on acid-free paper

CONTENTS

CHAPTER TEN * 295

Virtues, Narrative and Community: Some Recent Discussions

FURTHER DISCUSSION AND APPLICATIONS

Works Cited · 317

PREFACE

Principal Aims

This text has three principal aims. First it provides substantial selections from some of the major figures in the history of Western ethics. The assumption is that these "classical" texts still deserve careful and extensive treatment and are not beyond the reach of most undergraduates. Fairly extensive readings from Plato, Aristotle, Aquinas, Hobbes, Hume, Kant and Mill form a core anthology that enables a more thorough treatment of these figures than do many anthologies. There are also selections from Butler and Nietzsche, from some Eastern sources and religious texts and from some 20th century writers, resulting in an anthology of over 25 selections (with portions of several works by Plato and Aquinas).

The second aim is to present these writings in a way that will enable typical contemporary undergraduates to navigate them with some success. I measure "success" in terms of comprehension, at a fairly elementary level, but also in terms of an appreciation for the importance and contemporary relevance of these works. Three things have been done in an attempt to achieve this second goal.

1. All of the principal readings contain explanatory commentary wherever it is almost certainly needed and quite a few questions designed to promote thoughtfulness about the main texts. "Thoughtfulness" includes thoughtfulness about exegetical matters but also about applications. Orienting Questions at the beginning of each chapter are also dedicated to this end, and those questions are referred to in the texts and questions within the selections that follow.

2. Selections are included from nonphilosophical works, such as novels, traditional narratives and drama. The vividness and immediacy of such texts can often prompt ethical reflection more readily than can difficult philosophical texts treated in isolation. These works also provide some of the "thick description" of ethical life that has been particularly valued in recent philosophy with an "Aristotelian" bent. The literary selections serve to introduce some of the human issues that provoke philosophical work.

3. There is some thematic coherence to the chapters. A quick look at the chapter titles will show the prominence of *reason* as a unifying topic. The chapters are organized topically, but with at least a bow to historical order. Students need help in recognizing that the major figures anthologized here were engaged in something like historically extended conversations.

The third principal aim is the basis for the section of each chapter titled "Further Discussions and Applications" and is really an extension of the second. Some exegetical and evaluative issues are treated in the guides within the main selections, but some of those issues that have been treated in an interesting way in the secondary literature get further development in the "Further Discussions" sections. I tried to select issues that seem to me most in need of further elaboration or of most intrinsic interest or both. In the course of discussing the major works, I have also introduced discussions of the kinds of issues typically treated in anthologies of "applied ethics." However, the selected issues are just that, selected. Their treatment is not unified, and instructors will naturally pick what parts of the "Further Discussions" they find interesting or helpful. Thus Aquinas' discussion of double effect may need to be complemented by Matthew's discussion, and the abstract passages from Kant's work receive further illustration and applications in the writings of Singer and Regan.

Richard Hare remarked that many philosophers seem to forget "their peculiar art" when they turn from ethical theory to applied ethics. To see what that "peculiar art" is, students need exposure to metaethics. But they may also need to see something of where the theoretical views of the major ethicists go. Feminist and environmental ethics, abortion and euthanasia, just war, murder, international rights, feeding the hungry, sexual morality, moral education, the treatment of animals and specific virtues and vices, such as courage and generosity, folly and cruelty, are all treated in this text, some of them from several perspectives. Some of them are of course a focus of attention within the principal readings. But the "Further Discussions" sections provide a kind of second-level anthology, in which students can work through summaries of well-known essays in applied ethics. This second-level anthology attempts to find a middle ground between large anthologies with numerous complete or nearly complete essays (but usually with shorter selections from the major figures) and a straight text that summarizes current discussions.

The classical tradition, as represented by Aristotle in particular, has been deliberately highlighted. Typical "Aristotelian issues" (but they are certainly not issues only for Aristotle), such as moral education, get treated in more than one chapter. Frequent references throughout to Aristotle, and much of the material in the last chapter, also reflect that priority. Nonetheless I believe Aristotle's main competitors get fair and extensive treatment.

Some Ways to Use This Text

Some of the questions interspersed throughout the readings test for minimal comprehension; some require more thought and imagination; some are difficult and require an ability to keep track of the ways issues are unfolding through the chapters. The more difficult questions are starred. Questions that are both difficult and require more extended discussion get two stars. Some instructors may want to supply questions of their own or to collect or grade only selected questions, such as those that test for minimal comprehension. There are some cross-references in the text and the study questions to related chapters or works, but I have tried to keep them to a minimum so that instructors can make independent use of whatever parts of the text appeal most to them.

Sample Syllabi

As with any text that is primarily an anthology, it is unlikely that the entire text will be used. Here are a few suggestions for syllabi that have some thematic unity. The first syllabus is slanted toward metaethics and theory and skips Chapters 5 and 10 and some of the fictional works. The second syllabus has a perhaps more Aristotelian accent, stresses the extent of the "moral domain," skips Chapter 6, omits much of the exegetical and metaethical discussions in the "Further Discussions" and exploits all of the fictional selections. There are of course many other possibilities, both within and across chapters.

Acknowledgments

I would like to dedicate this book to my wife, Diane, and my daughter Sigrid, with thanks for their patience and support during its production.

I also am indebted to my daughter Kirsten, whose literary advice informs the choice of fictional selections, particularly the selection from Edith Wharton in Chapter 10, and my son, Hans, with whom I have often discussed Russian literature and who supplied the translation of the story by Tolstoy in Chapter 1.

I cannot catalog my debts to all those who have tried to improve my grasp, and presentation, of the topics treated in this book, but I cannot omit mention of the importance to me of the conversations, over many years, with Jim Fieser and Chris Brown, my colleagues at the University of Tennessee—Martin. Both of them have influenced my thinking on those topics in a multitude of ways.

I am also very indebted to the careful reviews given to earlier versions of this text by the following

Christina Bellon, *California State University, Sacramento*

Christopher M. Brown, *University of Tennessee, Martin*

Chai-sik Chung, *Boston University*

David E. Cooper, *Northern Michigan University*

Scott A. Davison, *Morehead State University*

James G. Hanink, *Loyola Marymount University*

John D. Jones, *Marquette University*

Robert B. Kruschwitz, *Baylor University*

Glen Mazis, *Penn State, Harrisburg*

Marshall Missner, *University of Wisconsin, Oshkosh*

David M. Parry, *Penn State, Altoona*

Gaile Pohlhaus, *Miami University*

Williams J. Prior, *Santa Clara University*

David Vogel, *University of California, Berkeley*

While I have learned a great deal from all of the above, the responsibility for such shortcomings as may remain lies solely with me.

The Moral Domain

The words *ethics* and *morals* often conjure up accounts of cheating CEOs, court decisions relating to abortion and euthanasia, the morally heated rhetoric of antiwar demonstrations and other matters that feature in daily newspapers and Internet blogs. Even this brief list shows something about how much we are preoccupied with morality. But it is also misleading. Most of us will never be in a position to bilk a huge company of millions (though we all have plenty of opportunities for dishonesty), and even people who consider themselves "activists" will probably not spend much of their life protesting a war (though unfortunately many of us may be involved in some form of violence against others!).

Moreover, this brief list of "moral" matters may obscure how pervasive moral matters are in any life. In fact virtually everyone is constantly involved in moral assessment of themselves, other people and the situations they are in. That fact (it is a fact) may be denied only by forgetting what actually goes on. I may think of an acquaintance as cowardly, another as reliable, another as lacking integrity. Even when I am trying to be "nonjudgmental" I may find myself assessing those I think are *too* judgmental in moral terms. I may insist that it is *wrong* or *insensitive* to be so judgmental! I have promises to keep, chances to be either kind or indifferent, temptations to dishonesty that must be dealt with. There is honor even among thieves, and those who claim to be "above" morality are frequently caught blaming or praising people for what amount to moral reasons. When I watch a film or play, I find myself inevitably thinking about the characters as having or lacking traits many of which are moral in character. Some are vengeful, some are, perhaps, justly vengeful, some are unscrupulous, some are kind, some brave, some are deceivers who seek their own benefit at the expense of others. Just as inevitably, I react to these character traits with praise or blame, contempt or admiration. Many admired the character of William Wallace as represented in the film *Braveheart* and loathed the unscrupulous and self-seeking elder Bruce, and the cruel King Edward. Film and novelistic portrayals of Hitler's cruelties and the characters that carried out his will evoke contempt and moral revulsion from most and admiration from a few. At a more subtle level, stories and novels evoke questions about what sorts of motivation are good or bad, what sorts of things might be regretted or induce remorse or when guilt is or is not appropriate. Stories and narratives, including biographies, can often enhance our appreciation for "moral psychology." There would not be much subject matter for films, novels or biographies if matters of moral interest were excluded.

The omnipresence of moral concerns and judgments in daily life are what philosopher Mary Midgley refers to as "the sheer size of morality." There are factors at work in contemporary culture that encourage us to ignore, forget, evade or misconstrue the presence, the importance, the sheer size, of moral concerns. Some of those factors are the focus of Chapter 1.

Philosophers have sometimes underrated the pervasiveness of moral phenomena by focusing all their analytic skills on a few clear examples of what are widely considered to be good or bad conduct. Thus the contemporary literature on abortion alone is enormous, for it is a discrete conduct that evokes moral judgment and controversy. On the other hand the long tradition of moral philosophy or ethics that focuses on character has sometimes gone in the opposite direction, seeing matters of moral interest everywhere. We do not ordinarily think of the ability to throw a good party as a moral or ethical trait, but some such trait is treated in Aristotle's character ethics. Thus one question that invites philosophical treatment is this: Just what are the boundaries of the ethical? What distinguishes moral praise or blame from other kinds? If I blame someone for being impolite, does that involve ethical judgment, or is it more like the disapproval we may feel toward someone whose way of dressing shows bad taste? Many people reacted very negatively to a work of art titled "Piss Christ" that showed a crucifix submerged in a container filled with urine. Was that a moral reaction or a religious one, or do moral and religious reactions overlap completely in such a case?

The wide extent of the moral domain is probably most evident when we think of an entire life as a "failure." The character Lily Bart in Wharton's *The House of Mirth* (see Chapter 10) may seem to have lived a failed life, yet she has not led a particularly immoral life and in fact is quite upright in many respects. Is the claim that a life is a failure an ethical or moral claim or perhaps a religious claim? Or are these kinds of considerations always entangled with one another? Philosophers have reflected on such questions for millennia, and their answers have often conflicted.

1. *Give an example of
a concern that is certainly a moral concern,
a concern that might be moral, and
a concern that certainly is not, in your view,
moral at all.*

Philosophers have sometimes tried to offer specific advice or views on what sorts of conduct or character traits should be counted as good or bad, morally praiseworthy or blameworthy. *Normative ethics* addresses such matters. But it is perhaps more typical of philosophers in particular that they should expend a lot of energy trying to answer such questions as the following when doing ethics.

1. What is the basis for moral claims?
2. Are moral judgments expressions of knowledge or of mere opinion?
3. Do disagreements in ethics prove that there can be no "right views" in ethics?

These and related questions belong to what is sometimes called *metaethics*. They arise in attempts to reflect systematically *about* ethics, rather than within it, so to speak. Answers to them do not necessarily help us in our quest for moral advice.

Although normative and metaethical questions can be separated in discussion, they do not come apart so easily in practice, and even much of ethical theorizing moves easily from one to the other without marking the change. No attempt is made in this book to separate the two neatly. Nonetheless a good deal of space is devoted to the most typically philosophical issues, the "metaethical" issues. The following question is particularly central:

What is the role of reason and knowledge in morality or the good life?

I encourage readers to peruse the Table of Contents to see some of the ways in which that question recurs throughout.

CHAPTER ONE

Relativism, Skepticism and the Possibility of Moral Judgment

Introduction

Why have books on ethics? Why teach, or take, courses in ethics? Many people today have views about ethics or morals that imply that a book on ethics is a waste of time. Consider remarks like this one:

Who am I (or you) to judge the way anyone else acts?

This question is often prompted by the notion that when I judge others, I in effect oppress them, try to force them into my own mold. Or it may arise from the conviction that moral beliefs are private, individual matters. People's private lives should, of course, be left alone, so moral "judgments" should be avoided.

Or consider this remark:

It's all relative. People have different ideas on right and wrong. Who is to decide?

This last question may arise from honest puzzlement. It seems to many people that there is no "truth" about morality or ethics, or if there is any "truth" it is only "for the individual" and does not apply generally.

If these popular views are correct, then it might be pointless, and even impolite, to discuss ethical matters in a way that tries to get at the *truth* about them, which is what most philosophers have done. It

is thus appropriate to start right out by investigating the claims that morality is "merely subjective," that moral beliefs are strictly "relative to" individuals or particular cultures or socially accepted standards or that making moral judgments about others always amounts to unwarranted interference in people's privacy and freedom, if not actual oppression of those who have the misfortune of being "different."

ORIENTING QUESTIONS, INITIAL REACTIONS
1. Do you think it is wrong to judge other people's conduct? Your own conduct?
2. Is there something about moral judgments or claims that makes them "subjective" or "just a matter of opinion?" Does it follow that we should keep our moral judgments to ourselves?
3. Do you believe there are any "moral universals," that is, moral claims or judgments that apply to all people at all times? For example, is it always, at all times and places, wrong to kill an innocent person just for the fun of it? Discuss other possible examples.
4. To some extent it seems that beliefs about morality are passed on through families and other cultural institutions. Is it possible for a person to rise above his or her environment and to arrive "on his or her own" at moral beliefs, or to develop moral attitudes, that conflict with the cultural environment? If so, how?

5. Apparently the Aztecs thought that human sacrifice was permissible and perhaps even a duty. Do you think the Aztecs were wrong? Immoral? Or were they simply different? Explain your view, and relate your answer to question 3.

Note your answers to these questions, and go back to them at the end of this chapter.

LEO TOLSTOY

Count Leo Tolstoy was born into a wealthy Russian family in 1828, was educated in oriental languages and the law, joined the military and eventually settled down to manage his vast estates. He married in 1862 and raised a large family. He began to write fiction while still in the military and quickly established a reputation as a leading Russian writer. He is now widely regarded as one of the greatest writers of fiction in any language. His writings show an intense concern with ethical and "existential" questions and eventually with religious questions. He died in 1910 amidst personal turmoil resulting from religious concerns and family struggles.

Society and Moral Knowledge

In the following story, written late in Tolstoy's life, he presents a character, Ivan Vasilievich, whose sense of good and evil is purportedly *not* simply a reflection of his social environment. It is clear that Ivan's moral beliefs and attitudes are not his simply because he is accustomed to "doing the done thing" or reflecting the culture around him. A direct experience of cruelty changes Ivan so that he is able to live a life that is a kind of judgment on the moral (or immoral) attitudes that are prevalent in his society.

Here is a brief glossary of terms that may be unfamiliar.

Shrovetide: The time just before Lent. Preparation for Lent is supposed to include being "shriven," or given absolution from sin, but in fact it became a time of excessive celebration, or "carnival"; the irony in that fact is relevant to the themes of this story.

quality: Used here to refer to rank or social position.

rubicund: Of the face, complexion, etc.: reddish, flushed, highly colored, especially *as the result of good living.*

References to **Nicholas** are to the Russian czar, who as the most elite of the elite set the standard for manners and style in Tolstoy's day.

After the Ball: A Tale

So you say that a man may not understand on his own what is good and what is bad. That it is all a matter of the social environment, and the environment determines everything. But I think that it is all a matter of coincidence. But here, I will speak personally . . .

This is what the highly respected Ivan Vasilievich said to us, after a conversation about whether it was necessary to change the conditions in which people live before personal improvement is possible. None of us actually said that a man may not understand on his own what is good and what is bad, but Ivan Vasilievich had a way of responding to thoughts of his own provoked by a conversation, and relating a story from an episode of his own life suggested by those thoughts. Often he completely forgot what led him to the story he related, so absorbed was he in it, and all the more so in that he told the story sincerely and honestly.

So he did now.

"I will tell you myself what happened. All of my life has been molded in this way, and no other; not by the environment; but by something completely different."

"From what, then?"—we asked.

"It's a long story. There is a lot to tell if you are going to understand it."

"Well then tell us."

Ivan Vasilievich frowned in thought, and nodded his head.

"Yes"—he said—"All my life changed in one night, or rather; in one morning."

"Yes? What happened?"

"The fact was that I was deeply in love. I had fallen in love many times, but this was my deepest love. It was a long time ago; she already has married daughters. That was B. . . , yes, Varenka B. . . ,"—Ivan Vasilievich gave her surname. "Even at fifty years of age she was a remarkably beautiful woman. But in youth, at eighteen years of age, she was incredible: tall and shapely, gracious and majestic; especially majestic. She held herself very erect, as though she wasn't able to do otherwise, and tipped her head back a little, and that gave her, with both her beauty and her tall stature (and regardless of her thinness and boniness) a queenly air that would have been intimidating, if it had not been for her gay and playful smile and mouth, her glittering eyes and her overall charm and youthfulness."

"How Ivan Vasilievich describes her!"

"No description I could give would tell you what she was really like, but that isn't the point: What I want to tell you happened in the 1840s. I was a student at the provincial university. I don't know if it was a good or bad thing, but we had at that time in our university no circles, no theories, but we lived as do youth, full of themselves. I was very happy and boyish as a youth, and yes, even rich. I had a good horse and went tobogganing with the young ladies (skating at that time was not in style.) I imbibed with companions (at that time we drank nothing but champagne, and when there wasn't the money, we drank nothing. We didn't drink vodka like they do these days.) My main pleasures consisted in mixers and balls. I danced well, and looked pretty good."

"—Well, no need to be modest," broke in one woman. "We all know, after all, what you looked like from your daguerreotype. You did not just look pretty good; you were quite handsome."

"—That's as it may be, but that isn't the point. For at the time when my love for her was deepest, there was a Shrovetide ball at the mansion of the Marshall of nobility, a good-souled old man and a rich host to grand social events. His wife also received us, in as good-spirited a way as he; she wore a velvet gown, with a diamond tiara on her head, and her old, plump shoulders and breast were exposed as in the portraits of Empress Elizabeth Petrovna. The ball

was extraordinary; and the main hall was beautiful, with singers, and an orchestra composed of serfs of one of the land owners—well known by the music lovers at court. The buffet was enormous with a small ocean of champagne. I liked champagne, but I didn't drink, because I was drunk already without wine, drunk with love for Varenka; but for all of that I danced till I dropped; danced quadrilles and waltzes and polkas, as many as there were, with Varenka. She wore a white dress with a rose-colored silk belt and white kid gloves that stretched to her large, bony elbows, and white satin slippers. Only the mazurka they took from me: Fate opposed me with the engineer, Anisimov, whom I will not forgive; have not forgiven to this day—he had asked her for this dance at the moment she arrived. I had gone around to the men's groom for gloves and was late to the event. I danced that mazurka, not with her, but instead with a German girl I had gone in for previous to that. I fear I was not very considerate that evening, for I didn't speak with her, didn't look at her, and my eyes were all for the tall and statuesque figure in the white dress with the rose belt, her flushed and dimpled face and her kind, tender eyes. And I was not alone; for all looked at her and loved her, both men and women loved her, she enchanted them all.

"By law of fate, so to speak, I didn't dance the mazurka with her, but in truth, I danced with her most of the time. She, unembarrassed, came to me, and I would jump up, not waiting for her invitation, and she would bless me with a smile for my interest. When my party was formally introduced to her, and she did not guess my quality, she shrugged her bony shoulders at me in a sign of sympathy and quieted me, smiling at me. When the figure of the mazurka became the waltz, I danced long with her, and she, breathing lightly, said to me, 'Encore.' I waltzed and waltzed until I was no longer conscious of my body."

"Oh you were conscious of it, I think; when your arm encircled her waist, you must have been very conscious of both her body and your body," said one of the guests.

Ivan Vasilievich blushed and almost angrily cried out:

"Yes, that is you; today's youth. Except for the body, you see nothing. In our time it wasn't so. The stronger my love for her grew, the less bodily she became for me. These days you see feet, ankles, and sometimes a little more. You unclothe the woman with whom you are in love, but for me and my time (Alphonse Karr—a good writer—said it all), on the object of my love are bronzed vestments. For us it was not to unclothe, but to cover nakedness as did the good son of Noah. You just don't understand . . ."

"Don't listen to that. What further?"—said one of us.

"Yes. I danced with her more and more, so that I didn't note the time. The musicians, exhausted, were strumming away at the same mazurka theme; you know how it is at the end of a ball; and from the sitting room all the papas and mamas rose from the card tables; the servants were running back and forth carrying what-not. It was the third hour of the morning. I had to make the most of every minute. I took her again, and we, for the hundredth time, moved across the hall."

"Then I will have an after-dinner quadrille with you?"

"It is understood; if they don't take me home first," she said, smiling.

"I won't allow it," I said.

"Give me back my fan," she said.

"It breaks my heart to do so,"—I said, giving her the white, inexpensive fan.

"Here is something for you, so that your heart does not break"—she pulled a feather from the fan and gave it to me.

I took the feather and only with my gaze could I express my joy and thankfulness. I was not only happy and satisfied, but was fortunate, blessed; I overflowed with goodness; I wasn't myself, but some unearthly, higher creature, without knowledge of evil and capable only of good. I hid the feather in my glove and stood there, unable to summon up the strength to go from her.

"Look, they want papa to dance" she said to me, pointing at the tall, stately figure of her father, a colonel with silver epaulettes, standing in the door with the hostess and other noble ladies.

"Varenka, come here,"—we heard the loud voice of the hostess with the diamond tiara and the Elizabeth-Petrovnian shoulders.

Varenka went to the door, and I behind her.

"Convince your father, my dear, to take a round with you. Well, please Peter Vladislavich,"—the hostess said, turning to the colonel.

Varenka's father was very handsome; stately, tall, and fresh in appearance even as an old man. His face was rubicund with a white, à la Nicholas I mustache, white sideburns that met with the mustaches, with the hair on the side of his head combed forward, and an affectionate and joyful smile, like his daughter's, on his glittering eyes and lips. His posture was perfect, with a wide, tasteful decoration of medals pinned on a soldier's chest, with strong shoulders above elegant legs. He was a military leader of the old type from the campaigns of Nicholas I.

When we first went up to the doors, the colonel first refused, saying that he barely remembered how to dance, but turning, he smiled and, bending his left arm, took his sword from its scabbard, handed it to an obsequious young man, and putting a glove on his right hand—"Everything according to regulations," he said, smiling—took the arm of his daughter, made a quarter turn, and waited for the mazurka to begin.

When it did, he smartly pounded one foot on the floor and then leaned into the other, his tall, grave figure now quietly floating, and then storming loudly, with the neat tap of feet, making a complete circuit around the hall. The gracious figure of Varenka floated near him, the shortening or lengthening of her step imperceptible in the small white satin slippers. The entire hall followed every movement of the pair. I not only loved them, but looked at them with gentle amazement. His boots especially caught my attention; they were fastened by foot straps; good calf-skin martial boots, though not the pointed modern kind, but with the old four-cornered toes without heels. It was obvious that they had been made by the battalion boot maker. "He brings out and dresses his daughter, but doesn't buy modern boots himself and wears the previous fashion," I thought, and the four pointed toes of those boots especially moved me. It was evident that at one time he danced expertly, but now was weighted down with age, and his feet were no longer lively enough for the beautiful and quick dance steps which he attempted to perform. He nevertheless performed two entire circuits of the floor.

When he planted his feet apart and then brought them back together, and then sank, although a little heavily, to one knee, and she, smiling, straightened her dress and circled him once as if chained, everyone burst into thunderous applause. Standing again, with some effort, he kissed his daughter on the forehead, affectionately embracing her behind the ears, and led her to me, thinking that I would dance with her. I said that I was not her escort.

"Well, nevertheless, go with her," he said, smiling kindly and returning his saber to its scabbard.

After dinner I danced with her the promised quadrille and regardless of the fact that I was, it appeared, eternally happy, my happiness grew more and more. We didn't say anything about love. I didn't ask her, or myself, whether she loved me. It was enough for me that I loved her. I feared only one thing: that something would ruin my happiness.

When I went home, undressed and thought about sleep, I found that it was utterly impossible. I had in my hand the feather from the fan and one of her gloves that she had given me as she left (I helped first her mother and then her into their carriage). I looked at those things, not closing my eyes; saw her in that moment when she, choosing between two other escorts, *did* guess my quality and I heard her gentle voice saying "Pride? Yes?"—and had joyfully given me her hand, saw how after dinner, when she touched the champagne glass with her lips she looked at me with affectionate mistrust. But more than any other thing, I saw her dancing with her father, when she smoothly moved near him ,with pride and joy for herself and for him, surveying the adoring spectators. I unconsciously linked him and her in one humble, gentle emotion.

It had been about 4 a.m. when I left the ball; I sat about for two hours, so that when I went out onto the street it was already light. When I went out into the field where their house was and looked to its end near the fairground, I saw a large patch of black, like encroaching darkness, and heard coming from there the sounds of fife and drum. All of that time my head was full of music and now and then the tune of the mazurka. But this was some other, harsh, music that boded ill.

"What is that?" I thought, when I'd traveled through half of the field on the slippery road, as if directed by the sounds of the music. Walking 100 paces, I began to make out the black forms of people through the fog. Obviously soldiers. "Now, this is something I should learn about," I thought, and I, following along behind a smith's assistant in a soiled shirt and smock who was carrying something, went closer. Soldiers in black outer jackets stood in two rows, one opposite the other, holding the butts of their long-barreled rifles at rest, unmoving. Behind them stood a drummer and a flute player, repeating the same harsh melody.

"What are they doing?" I asked the smith's assistant who had stopped next to me.

"Punishing a tartar for desertion," the smith's assistant said angrily, training his eyes on the further end of the rows of soldiers.

I followed his gaze and saw, approaching between the rows, a fearful sight. There was a man stripped to the waist and tied to the rifles of two soldiers who led him. Alongside of them came a tall colonel in a military jacket and peaked hat, a figure that looked familiar. The man being punished, his feet dragging though the wet piles of snow, moved towards me beneath a rain of blows from both sides. When he fell back, the subordinate officers knocked him forward with their rifles, and when he fell because of it, they would yank him back with the ropes. Beside him, the colonel moved with a firm pace. It was her father, with his rubicund face and white mustache and sideburns.

With every blow the man being punished turned his face, contorted with suffering, toward that side of the row from which the blow fell, and, grimacing, kept repeating the same phrase. Only when he was passing could I hear the words. They weren't spoken, but sputtered: "Brothers, have mercy. Brothers, have mercy." But the brothers were not merciful, and when the terrible procession drew even with me, I saw a soldier opposite heft a wooden rod so that it whistled in the air, and slam it into the back of the Tartar. The Tartar stumbled forward, but the NCOs held him up, and a like blow fell on him from the other side, and again from this side, and again from that side. The colonel went next to him and looked at his feet occasionally and then at the Tartar; and holding in his breath, puffed out his cheeks and slowly blew it through his protruding lips. When the ugly procession had passed the place where I stood, I caught a glimpse of the Tartar's back. It was a splotch mark, blackened, wet and red, unearthly, so that I found it hard to believe that it was the back of a human being.

"*Jesus,*"—said the smith's assistant who was standing next to me.

The procession started to draw further away, and nevertheless blows fell always from either side of the formation on the writhing, stumbling man, and all the while the drum pounded and the fife whistled, and all the while the tall, stately figure of the general with his firm step moved alongside the Tarter. Suddenly the general stopped, and then quickly approached one of the soldiers.

"I'll teach you to miss the mark"—I heard his wrathful voice. "Going to miss the mark, were you!? Going to miss it, you!?"

I saw how he slapped a frightened, puny soldier in the face because he had not swung his wooden rod hard enough at the back of the Tartar.

"Give them fresh rods!" he shouted, and as he looked around he saw me. Pretending not to know me, he frowned evilly and quickly turned away. At that point it became too embarrassing for me; I did not know where to look; I felt caught in the most shameful of crimes. I lowered my eyes and attempted frantically to get home. All along the road the drumbeat throbbed and the fifes whistled in my ears, and I heard the words "Brothers. Have mercy," or then I heard the self-confident, wrathful voice of the general shouting "Going to miss the mark, were you!? Were you!?" And all the while I was filled with an almost physical agony, rising to the point of nausea, so that several times I slowed to a stop, and it seemed to me as if I would have to vomit up all the horror I had experienced. I don't remember how I managed to get home and lie down. But the moment I started to drift off, I would hear and see it all again, and I would leap out of bed.

"It is obvious he knows something I don't—If I only knew what he knows, I would understand, and that which I've seen wouldn't torture me." And the more I thought the more I was unable to understand that which the Colonel knew. I barely slept until eve-

ning and even then only after I went to a friend's and proceeded to get very drunk.

"And do you think I then decided that there was something bad in the thing which I saw? Not at all. If it was done with such conviction and admitted by all to be necessary, then it goes to say they knew something which I didn't know; I thought and tried to find out what it was. But however many times I tried I was then unable to understand it. And not being able to understand, I could not rationally serve in the military as I had wanted to previously, and I couldn't find a place for myself anywhere in society, and ended up being good for nothing, as you can see."

"Well, we know how good for nothing you are," said one of us—"But tell us, how many would be good for nothing if it were not for the likes of you?"

"Well, that is perfectly stupid," said Ivan Vasilievich with unfeigned irritation.

"And what of love?" we asked.

"My Love? From that day it faded away. When she, as she often happened to do, grew pensive, with that smile on her face, I'd immediately remember the general on the field, and I would feel awkward and it became unpleasant for me, and I started to see her less often. Love fell away to nothing. That's the way it is with some things, they change and rule over the entire life of a man. But you say . . . ," he concluded.

1911

Tolstoy's story is a harsh indictment of the conventional morality of his time. There are many aspects to that indictment. For example, the story reveals that there is a kind of hypocrisy built into conventional mores. A man can be a "loving father" one moment and a brutal sadist the next, and there is not supposed to be any inconsistency. Ivan *feels* that there is, but assumes, or at least pretends, that he must be missing something that others know.

1. *Is the inconsistency in the character of the colonel believable? Does it matter whether or not it is?*

One main topic of this chapter is *cultural relativism*. We can define it, tentatively, in the following way:

cultural relativism: The view that there are no standards for moral conduct that are independent of the particular moral conventions that hold in various societies or "cultures."

On the relativist view, if it is in accord with the standards of a particular society to X, then it is permissible or required to X, since each society's standards are the highest standards there can be.

Ivan reflects on the cruel punishment he witnessed in a way that suggests he really cannot completely separate himself from the "conventional" view: "If it was done with such conviction and admitted by all to be necessary, then it goes to say they knew something which I didn't know; I thought and tried to find out what it was. But however many times I tried I was unable to understand it. And not being able to understand, . . . I couldn't find a place for myself anywhere in society, and ended up being good for nothing, as you can see." There are ironies here. Tolstoy implies that "they" did not really know anything, other than "what the conventions are," and that it is in fact Ivan who has acquired some real knowledge. Moreover, Ivan's self-description as being "no good for anything" *because he does not fit into society and its norms* is taken to be the reverse of the truth, even by Ivan's conformist companions, whose remarks imply that he is widely regarded as an exemplary person, someone worth imitating.

> 2. *Find a remark toward the end of the story that shows that Ivan's friends have high regard for his character. Look for and comment on any irony.*

One feature of moral "conformism" is that, like other forms of conformism, it is often motivated by fear of loss, and it enables a person to feel comfortable, secure, even happy. At one point Ivan confesses a fear that "something might spoil my happiness." He does not immediately know what that something is. But as the story unfolds, it becomes clear that his "happiness" can be spoiled by moral criticism, moral attitudes that put him in conflict with convention and with superficial ways of evaluating people. Even romantic love can be spoiled when someone recognizes that it depends on conventional ideas of beauty and charm that have no particular connection to real goodness.

> 3. *A charming young man, Scott Petersen, was convicted of murdering his wife and unborn child. The couple had been described as "the perfect couple" on the basis of their fulfilling many conventional notions of "perfection" (good looks, charm, pleasant personalities) and on the basis of an apparently happy relationship (they were having a ball, you might say). Relate this event to Tolstoy's story.*

If, despite Ivan's statements, *he* is the one who has real knowledge and understanding, how did he acquire it? Did he simply *feel* that the cruelty he witnessed was a terrible thing? And if so, did that feeling put him in touch with some important moral *fact*?

> 4. *How would you answer the last question?*

The story ends this way:

"But you say . . . ," he concluded.

You should be able to fill in the dots.

> 5. *"You" (Ivan's friends) say that a person cannot **"on his own"** distinguish _____ from _____. They apparently believe that such distinctions depend on a person's _____.*

Ivan says, "The whole of my life's been like this; it hasn't been influenced by my environment, but by something else entirely." But he does not say what the "something else" is. We can guess what it would be for Tolstoy, however. As he grew older he became very passionate about the Christian gospels, which emphasize such things as mercy, not returning evil for evil, and the need to struggle to achieve a very high ideal that transcends mere rules, particularly socially accepted rules.

> 6. *Reconsider your answers to Orienting Question 4. Has reading Tolstoy's story had any impact on the way you would answer that question? Explain.*
> 7. *Would you call Ivan "judgmental" in the light of his reaction to the cruelty of the general? Recall your answer to Orienting Question 1.*
> *8. *Write down some reasons why Tolstoy might have chosen "Shrovetide" as the time for the "ball."*

Relativism

The idea that the environment sets the standard for what we must think about good and evil, right and wrong, is a "relativistic" idea. The "environment" in this case probably means the cultural environment, the religious, ethical, economic, political (and the like) setting for a person's life.

There can be no doubt that there are many differences between cultures, and even between individuals, respecting how to behave and live. Some of those differences do not appear to be suitable topics for reasoning or arguments respecting right or wrong. For example, differences in manners or in ways of dressing are simply a fact of life. Generally most of us would not say that the way Amish people dress is "wrong" just because it differs from the dressing habits of the majority. Some people consider it bad manners not to include salad forks in a table setting, placed on the outside; others do not. It hardly seems to be a matter that has a universal right or wrong to it that everyone should agree on, provided they are reasonable and know the facts. Would there be something very unreasonable about putting the salad fork on the inside, by the plate, or in lots of other places, or not having one at all?

On the other hand, differences about scientific matters, such as whether the earth is orbiting the sun rather than standing still relative to the sun, seem to be differences that can be settled by reason, where "reason" includes collecting evidence, making good inferences, putting theories to the test.

But what about moral and religious differences? Are they more like differences over how to dress (where there is no "right or wrong" or that cannot be settled by reason, it seems), or are they more like scientific differences? That question has been discussed vigorously for thousands of years. For example, Protagoras (c. 490–c. 420 BC), the first and most eminent of the Greek Sophists, is perhaps best known for the following remark:

A human being is the measure of all things;
of the things that are, that they are, and of the
things that are not, that they are not.

To say that a human being is the measure of all things could be to say that each individual person is the measure (**standard or norm**) for what is true or right. That would be individual relativism. Protagoras pointed out that if something is sweet to me, then it is sweet (to me), and if the same thing is sour to you, then it is sour (to you). There does not seem to be any truth of the matter beyond the truth "for the individual" or "relative to" the individual. Can we extend that way of thinking to moral differences also? Could it be that child abuse is right for me (since I have a "taste" for it) and wrong for you (who find it repellent)?

It is also possible that Protagoras wanted to say that human *groups or cultures* provide the measure or standard for what is right or wrong. In that case he would have been following his Greek predecessor, the historian Herodotus, who declared that "custom is King." Herodotus appears to have accepted a form of cultural relativism, the view that standards of right and wrong are simply matters of custom, which vary from one culture or historical period to another, and that these differences are on the same level as differences in dress or table manners.

Two thousand years after Herodotus we find the French thinker Michel de Montaigne proposing a very similar view. Montaigne (1533–92) was a French skeptic who tried to think honestly about human capacities and particularly about the capacity to know anything for sure. The ancient Greek philosopher Socrates was famous for his ability to create doubts in people about what they thought they knew. Montaigne thus became known as the "French Socrates." He lived during the wars between Roman Catholics and Protestants in France and was a friend and adviser to important representatives of both sides of the conflict, including Henry of Navarre, a Protestant who turned Catholic and became King of France. Montaigne witnessed first hand the suffering caused by religious dogmatists who were sure they were absolutely right. He became a strong advocate of religious tolerance. Henry's promulgation of an edict of religious toleration in 1591 was very much in the spirit of Montaigne, and it put a stop to the wars. It is likely that Montaigne was motivated by his skepticism to be untypically tolerant. When a person is not sure that he is right in his beliefs, he is less likely to try to force anyone to accept them.

Montaigne lived in an age of world exploration (the 16th century) and was aware of differences in morals among remote peoples. He thought that those differences supported his skepticism about the possibility of *knowing* moral truths that apply to all cultures. It is only a short step from that skepticism to the claim that there *are* no moral truths that apply to all cultures. That is cultural relativism. In his *Essays* he reports on some of those differences.

> In one place, men feed upon human flesh. In another, it is reputed a holy duty for a man to kill his father at a certain age. Elsewhere, the fathers dispose of their children while yet in their mothers' wombs, some to be preserved and carefully brought up, and others to be abandoned or made away. Elsewhere the old husbands lend their wives to young men; and in another place they are in common, without offence. In one place particularly, the women take it for a mark of honor to have as many gay fringed tassels at the bottom of their garment as they have lain with several men.
>
> To conclude, there is nothing, in my opinion, that she [i.e., custom] does not, or may not do; and, therefore, with very good reason it is, that Pindar calls her the queen, and empress of the world. He that was seen to beat his father, and reproved for so doing, made answer, that it was the custom of their family: that, in like manner his father had beaten his grandfather, his grandfather his great-grandfather, "and this," says he, pointing to his son, "when he comes to my age, shall beat me." The laws of conscience, which we pretend to be derived from nature, proceed from custom; everyone, having an inward veneration for the opinions and manners approved and received amongst his own people, cannot, without very great reluctance, depart from them, nor apply himself to them without applause. [From *Essays*, "Of Custom"]

Given the sorts of differences mentioned by Montaigne, what should we infer? Montaigne inferred that morality "proceeds from custom," and that appears to imply that what is moral "truth" for me might be falsehood for you. Perhaps it would make more sense simply to deny that the notions *true* and *false* have any application to moral utterances. Even if I feel strongly that the colonel's beating of the Tartar was cruel, perhaps it is just a custom in his profession or not at all frowned on by the Russian culture of his time. Customs are human inventions that can be changed anytime. In this view, beating one's father is on the same level as wearing whatever style of clothing is customary or as keeping the salad fork on the outside or as driving on the right side of the road. "Custom" includes manners, all sorts of local traditions and, on this view, moral (or "immoral") practices as well.

There are also indications of individual relativism in Montaigne. He claims that he has found in himself a "ruling pattern" according to which he lives. He does not suppose that his pattern should fit anyone else. Another person might guide his or her life according to a very different "pattern."

If Montaigne and Protagoras are right, it follows that any attempt to inquire into ethics, in an attempt to find correct answers to questions about the best way to live or act, must be a waste of time, *unless* it is relativized to an individual or to a particular culture or set of customs. There could be no generally correct answer, no best way. There are simply lots of different ways, and there is no way to compare them, no single measure to use in determining which "measures up" or constitutes "the best." Each human, or each culture, is itself the measure for itself. Another way to put this view is as follows: Morality is *relative to* particular individuals or to particular societies or historical eras.

Though this view, called, naturally enough, *cultural relativism*, has been around for thousands of years, in recent years various versions of it have become very popular, partly for reasons discussed later. further in this chapter

> 9. *Do you consider yourself a relativist? If yes, why? If no, why?*

In the following selection, American philosopher James Rachels attacks relativism.

JAMES RACHELS

James Rachels (b. 1941) was University Professor of Philosophy at the University of Alabama. He is the author of several books on applied ethics. He has held the position that philosophy can give genuine guidance in dealing with ethical dilemmas.

Against Relativism

Rachels argues that the initial plausibility of relativism disappears upon closer examination.

From *Elements of Moral Philosophy*, 3rd ed. (1999), Ch. 2.

Cultural Relativism, as it has been called, challenges our ordinary belief in the objectivity and universality of moral truth. It says, in effect, that there is no such thing as universal truth in ethics; there are only the various cultural codes, and nothing more. Moreover, our own code has no special status; it is merely one among many.

As we shall see, this basic idea is really a compound of several different thoughts. It is important to separate the various elements of the theory because, on analysis, some parts turn out to be correct, while others seem to be mistaken. As a beginning, we may distinguish the following claims, all of which have been made by cultural relativists.

1. Different societies have different moral codes.
2. There is no objective standard that can be used to judge one societal code better than another.
3. The moral code of our own society has no special status; it is merely one among many.
4. There is no "universal truth" in ethics; that is, there are no moral truths that hold for all peoples at all times.
5. The moral code of a society determines what is right within that society; that is, if the moral code of a society says that a certain action is right, then that action is right, at least within that society.
6. It is mere arrogance for us to try to judge the conduct of other peoples. We should adopt an attitude of tolerance toward the practices of other cultures.

Although it may seem that these six propositions go together naturally, this is in quoted text they are independent of one another, in the sense that some of them might be false even if others are true. In what follows, we will try to identify what is correct in cultural relativism, but we will also be concerned to expose what is mistaken about it.

THE CULTURAL DIFFERENCES ARGUMENT

Rachels next presents—then attacks—a standard argument for relativism.

Cultural Relativism is a theory about the nature of morality. At first blush it seems quite plausible. However, like all such theories, it may be evaluated by subjecting it to rational analysis; and when we analyze Cultural Relativism we find that it is not so plausible as it first appears to be.

The first thing we need to notice is that at the heart of Cultural Relativism there is a certain form of argument. The strategy used by cultural relativists is to argue from facts about the differences between cultural outlooks to a conclusion about the status of morality. Thus we are invited to accept this reasoning:

> (1) The Greeks believed it was wrong to eat the dead, whereas the Callatians believed it was right to eat the dead.
> (2) Therefore, eating the dead is neither objectively right nor objectively wrong. It is merely a matter of opinion, which varies from culture to culture.

Or, alternatively:

> (1) The Eskimos see nothing wrong with infanticide, whereas Americans believe infanticide is immoral.
> (2) Therefore, infanticide is neither objectively right nor objectively wrong. It is merely a matter of opinion, which varies from culture to culture.

Clearly, these arguments are variations of one fundamental idea. They are both special cases of a more general argument, which says:

> (1) Different cultures have different moral codes.

(2) Therefore, there is no objective "truth" in morality. Right and wrong are only matters of opinion, and opinions vary from culture to culture.

We may call this the Cultural Differences Argument. To many people, it is persuasive. But from a logical point of view, is it sound?

It is not sound. The trouble is that the conclusion does not follow from the premise—that is, even if the premise is true, the conclusion still might be false. The premise concerns what people believe: In some societies, people believe one thing; in other societies, people believe differently. The conclusion, however, concerns what really is the case. The trouble is that this sort of conclusion does not follow logically from this sort of premise.

Consider again the example of the Greeks and the isn't this a change to Rachel's text that we are quoting? Callatians. The Greeks believed it was wrong to eat the dead; the Callatians believed it was right. Does it follow, from the mere fact that they disagreed, that there is no objective truth in the matter? No, it does not follow, for it could be that the practice was objectively right (or wrong) and that one or the other of them was simply mistaken.

To make the point clearer, consider a different matter. In some societies, people believe the earth is flat. In other societies, such as our own, people believe the earth is (roughly) spherical. Does it follow, from the mere fact that people disagree, that there is no "objective truth" in geography? Of course not; we would never draw such a conclusion because we realize that, in their beliefs about the world, the members of some societies might simply be wrong. There is no reason to think that if the world is round everyone must know it. Similarly, there is no reason to think that if there is moral truth everyone must know it. The fundamental mistake in the Cultural Differences Argument is that it attempts to derive a substantive conclusion about a subject from the mere fact that people disagree about it.

This is a simple point of logic, and it is important not to misunderstand it. We are not saying (not yet, anyway) that the conclusion of the argument is false. It is still an open question whether the conclusion is true or false. The logical point is just that the conclusion does not follow from the premise. This is important, because in order to determine whether the conclusion is true, we need arguments in its support. Cultural relativism proposes this argument, but unfortunately the argument turns out to be fallacious. So it proves nothing.

10. *The Cultural Differences Argument is unsound, according to Rachels, because it mistakenly assumes that if individuals or cultures disagree with each other about some claim, such as "the earth is flat" or "one should not eat dead relatives," then it follows that there is no objective or transcultural truth about these matters. But it does not follow. What shows that it does not follow?*

THE CONSEQUENCES OF TAKING CULTURAL RELATIVISM SERIOUSLY

Although Rachels believes that we should reject the Cultural Differences Argument as invalid, he feels that it is important to note additional problems with cultural relativism. In particular, he notes some absurd consequences that result if we take the arguments for cultural relativism seriously.

Even if the Cultural Differences Argument is invalid, Cultural Relativism might still be true. What would it be like if it were true?

William Graham Sumner summarizes the essence of Cultural Relativism. He says that there is no measure of right and wrong other than the standards of one's society: "The notion of right is in the folkways. It is not outside of them, of independent origin, and brought to test them. In the folkways, whatever is, is right."

Suppose we took this seriously. What would be some of the consequences?

1. We could no longer say that the customs of other societies are morally inferior to our own. This, of course, is one of the main points stressed by Cultural Relativism. We would have to stop condemning other societies merely because they are "different." So long as we concentrate on certain examples, such as the funerary practices of the Greeks and Callatians,

this may seem to be a sophisticated, enlightened attitude.

However, we would also be stopped from criticizing other, less benign practices. Suppose a society waged war on its neighbors for the purpose of taking slaves. Or suppose a society was violently anti-Semitic and its leaders set out to destroy the Jews. Cultural Relativism would preclude us from saying that either of these practices was wrong. We would not even be able to say that a society tolerant of Jews is better than the anti-Semitic society, for that would imply some sort of transcultural standard of comparison. The failure to condemn these practices does not seem enlightened; on the contrary, slavery and anti-Semitism seem wrong wherever they occur. Nevertheless, if we took Cultural Relativism seriously, we would have to regard these social practices as also immune from criticism.

2. We could decide whether actions are right or wrong just by consulting the standards of our society. Cultural Relativism suggests a simple test for determining what is right and what is wrong: All one need do is ask whether the action is in accordance with the code of one's society. Suppose in 1975 a resident of South Africa was wondering whether his country's policy of apartheid—a rigidly racist system—was morally correct. All he has to do is ask whether this policy conformed to his society's moral code. If it did, there would have been nothing to worry about, at least from a moral point of view.

This implication of Cultural Relativism is disturbing because few of us think that our society's code is perfect; we can think of ways it might be improved. Yet Cultural Relativism would not only forbid us from criticizing the codes of other societies; it would stop us from criticizing our own. After all, if right and wrong are relative to culture, this must be true for our own culture just as much as for other cultures.

3. The idea of moral progress is called into doubt. Usually, we think that at least some social changes are for the better. (Although, of course, other changes may be for the worse.) Throughout most of Western history the place of women in society was narrowly circumscribed. They could not own property; they could not vote or hold political office; and generally they were under the almost absolute control of their husbands. Recently much of this has changed, and most people think of it as progress.

If Cultural Relativism is correct, can we legitimately think of this as progress? Progress means replacing a way of doing things with a better way. But by what standard do we judge the new ways as better? If the old ways were in accordance with the social standards of their time, then Cultural Relativism would say it is a mistake to judge them by the standards of a different time. Eighteenth-century society was, in effect, a different society from the one we have now. To say that we have made progress implies a judgment that present-day society is better, and that is just the sort of transcultural judgment that, according to Cultural Relativism, is impermissible.

Our idea of social reform will also have to be reconsidered. Reformers such as Martin Luther King, Jr., have sought to change their societies for the better. Within the constraints imposed by Cultural Relativism, there is one way this might be done. If a society is not living up to its own ideals, the reformer may be regarded as acting for the best: The ideals of the society are the standard by which we judge his or her proposals as worthwhile. But the "reformer" may not challenge the ideals themselves, for those ideals are by definition correct. According to Cultural Relativism, then, the idea of social reform makes sense only in this limited way.

These three consequences of Cultural Relativism have led many thinkers to reject it as implausible on its face. It does make sense, they say, to condemn some practices, such as slavery and anti-Semitism, wherever they occur. It makes sense to think that our own society has made some moral progress, while admitting that it is still imperfect and in need of reform. Because Cultural Relativism says that these judgments make no sense, the argument goes, it cannot be right.

11. *Of the three "absurd consequences" that Rachel's claims follow from relativism, which best fits the issues portrayed in Tolstoy's story? Explain.*

WHY THERE IS LESS DISAGREEMENT THAN IT SEEMS

Rachels continues his attack on cultural relativism by claiming that relativists overstate the moral differences between cultures. They do that partly because they misconstrue the character of many of the cultural differences that do exist.

The original impetus for Cultural Relativism comes from the observation that cultures differ dramatically in their views of right and wrong. But just how much do they differ? It is true that there are differences. However, it is easy to overestimate the extent of those differences. Often, when we examine what seems to be a dramatic difference, we find that the cultures do not differ nearly as much as it appears.

Consider a culture in which people believe it is wrong to eat cows. This may even be a poor culture, in which there is not enough food; still, the cows are not to be touched. Such a society would appear to have values very different from our own. But does it? We have not yet asked why these people will not eat cows. Suppose it is because they believe that after death the souls of humans inhabit the bodies of animals, especially cows, so that a cow may be someone's grandmother. Now do we want to say that their values are different from ours? No; the difference lies elsewhere. The difference is in our belief systems, not in our values. We agree that we shouldn't eat Grandma; we simply disagree about whether the cow is (or could be) Grandma.

The point is that many factors work together to produce the customs of a society. The society's values are only one of them. Other matters, such as the religious and factual beliefs held by its members and the physical circumstances in which they must live are also important. We cannot conclude, then, merely because customs differ, that there is a disagreement about values. The difference in customs may be attributable to some other aspect of social life. Thus there may be less disagreement about values than there appears to be.

Consider again the Eskimos, who often kill perfectly normal infants, especially girls. We do not approve of such things; a parent who killed a baby in our society would be locked up. Thus there appears to be a great difference in the values of our two cultures. But suppose we ask why the Eskimos do this. The explanation is not that they have less affection for their children or less respect for human life. An Eskimo family will always protect its babies if conditions permit. But they live in a harsh environment, where food is in short supply. A fundamental postulate of Eskimo thought is: "Life is hard, and the margin of safety small." A family may want to nourish its babies but be unable to do so.

As in many "primitive" societies, Eskimo mothers will nurse their infants over a much longer period of time than mothers in our culture. The child will take nourishment from its mother's breast for four years, perhaps even longer. So even in the best of times there are limits to the number of infants that one mother can sustain. Moreover, the Eskimos are a nomadic people; unable to farm, they must move about in search of food. Infants must be carried, and a mother can carry only one baby in her parka as she travels and goes about her outdoor work. Other family members help whenever they can.

Infant girls are more readily disposed of because, first, in this society the males are the primary food providers—they are the hunters, according to the traditional division of labor—and it is obviously important to maintain a sufficient number of food providers. But there is an important second reason as well. Because the hunters suffer a high casualty rate, the adult men who die prematurely far outnumber the women who die early. Thus if male and female infants survived in equal numbers, the female adult population would greatly outnumber the male adult population. Examining the available statistics, one writer concluded that "were it not for female infanticide . . . there would be approximately one-and-a-half times as many females in the average Eskimo local group as there are food-producing males."

So among the Eskimos, infanticide does not signal a fundamentally different attitude toward children. Instead, it is a recognition that drastic measures are sometimes needed to ensure the family's survival. Even then, however, killing the baby is not the first option considered. Adoption is common; childless couples are especially happy to take a more fertile couple's "surplus." Killing is only the last resort. I emphasize this in order to show that the raw data of the anthropologists can be misleading; it can make the differences in values between cultures appear greater than they are. The Eskimos' values are not all that different from our values. It is only that life forces upon them choices that we do not have to make.

How All Cultures Have Some Values in Common

Rachels argues further against cultural relativism by noting that all societies actually have some common values.

It should not be surprising that, despite appearances, the Eskimos are protective of their children. How could it be otherwise? How could a group survive that did not value its young? It is easy to see that, in fact, all cultural groups must protect their infants:

(1) Human infants are helpless and cannot survive if they are not given extensive care for a period of years.
(2) Therefore, if a group did not care for its young, the young would not survive, and the older members of the group would not be replaced. After a while the group would die out.
(3) Therefore, any cultural group that continues to exist must care for its young. Infants that are not cared for must be the exception rather than the rule.

Similar reasoning shows that other values must be more or less universal. Imagine what it would be like for a society to place no value at all on truth telling. When one person spoke to another, there would be no presumption at all that he was telling the truth, for he could just as easily be speaking falsely. Within that society, there would be no reason to pay attention to what anyone says. (I ask you what time it is, and you say, "Four o'clock." But there is no presumption that you are speaking truly; you could just as easily have said the first thing that came into your head. So I have no reason to pay attention to your answer; in fact, there was no point in my asking you in the first place.) Communication would then be extremely difficult, if not impossible. And because complex societies cannot exist without communication among their members, society would become impossible. It follows that in any complex society there must be a

presumption in favor of truthfulness. There may of course be exceptions to this rule: There may be situations in which it is thought to be permissible to lie. Nevertheless, these will be exceptions to a rule that is in force in the society.

Here is one further example of the same type. Could a society exist in which there was no prohibition on murder? What would this be like? Suppose people were free to kill other people at will, and no one thought there was anything wrong with it. In such a "society," no one could feel secure. Everyone would have to be constantly on guard. People who wanted to survive would have to avoid other people as much as possible. This would inevitably result in individuals trying to become as self-sufficient as possible—after all, associating with others would be dangerous. Society on any large scale would collapse. Of course, people might band together in smaller groups with others that they could trust not to harm them. But notice what this means: They would be forming smaller societies that did acknowledge a rule against murder. The prohibition of murder, then, is a necessary feature of all societies.

There is a general theoretical point here, namely, that there are some moral rules that all societies will have in common, because those rules are necessary for society to exist. The rules against lying and murder are two examples. And in fact, we do find these rules in force in all viable cultures. Cultures may differ in what they regard as legitimate exceptions to the rules, but this disagreement exists against a background of agreement on the larger issues. Therefore, it is a mistake to overestimate the amount of difference between cultures. Not every moral rule can vary from society to society.

12. *Give two reasons for thinking that the Eskimo practice of infanticide does not show that Eskimos have moral views very different from those who find infanticide morally repugnant.*
13. *Why, according to Rachels, does the fact that it is considered wrong to eat cows in one culture and right to eat them in another not show that the cultures in question have different moral beliefs? What sorts of different beliefs might*

they have, if the differences are not moral differences?

14. *Having read Rachels, are you inclined to change any of your answers to the Orienting Questions? If so, how? If not, why not?*

Relativism seems naturally to suggest to many people that there is something wrong or logically amiss in making moral judgments.

If cultural relativists are right, then moral judgments directed toward the beliefs and practices of those from other cultures are nonsense.

If individual relativism is correct, then all moral judgments applied to anyone but oneself are nonsense.

But Rachel's arguments should make it a bit more difficult to hold to such positions.

Moral Skepticism, Judgmentalism and Antimoralism

Relativism is distinct from *moral skepticism*, which is, roughly, the view that we cannot have real moral knowledge. And it is distinct from the view that it is an imposition on the freedom and right to privacy of others when we make moral judgments about their behavior. Finally, it is distinct from *amoralism,* or *antimoralism,* which is the stance of those who think it is possible to do away with morality altogether and who (try to) positively reject all moral thinking and judgments.

Although these are distinct views, they overlap and reinforce each other. For example, the apparent relativity of many moral claims might encourage moral skepticism. That may have been the case with Montaigne. Moral skepticism might support the view that we should not make judgments about the behavior of other people, since we cannot *know* enough to be in a position to make such judgments. And it might support the view that morality is unimportant and that it can be abandoned (amoralism or antimoralism). But do these relativistic and skeptical ideas take account of what we have referred to as the

size of the moral domain? These matters are taken up in the next section.

MARY MIDGLEY

Contemporary philosopher Mary Midgley taught for many years at the University of Newcastle upon Tyne, England. During her retirement she produced the book excerpted here and other books designed for general audiences.

Can't We Make Moral Judgments?

People everywhere commonly make such judgments as the following: "That was wrong," "That just was not right," "That was courageous," "You must be honest in all your dealings," "That was vicious," "How *could* you (cheat on me, lie about me), you louse?," "She is wonderfully generous," "It is evil to kill an innocent child" and so on for a great variety of remarks that we will lump together here as *moral judgments*. These are clearly *moral* judgments. We find this sort of thing in all ancient and modern literatures from all over the world, and we find it in our daily lives. It should seem odd, then, that many people, especially in recent times, feel so much sympathy for the following sort of remark:

> "But surely it's always wrong to make moral judgments?"

How can something that is so common be so wrong?

The quoted remark serves as a sort of epigram to the book by Mary Midgley excerpted here. It is in fact a quote from one of her students. She tries here to reflect philosophically on very ordinary difficulties that many people have come to experience, difficulties having to do with the very possibility of moral judgment. There are a couple of sources of those difficulties.

1. There are "problems of false universality." People will claim something very general or universal, such as that we can get along without

morality altogether, when what they are really claiming has a much narrower application.

2. There is a widespread desire to protect the freedom of others.

The Problem of False Universality

Midgley illustrates how the first problem gets started with excerpts from a detective story by P. D. James (*Devices and Desires*). Some of the main characters present themselves as "amoralists," that is, people who supposedly refuse to make moral judgments and who, in fact, think they can throw out morality altogether. Alice is one of those characters. Midgley recounts some conversations from the novel.

From *Can't We Make Moral Judgments?* (1993), Chs. 1–2

In the third [conversation], Alice, the actual murderess (seen throughout as a sympathetic, though damaged character) is explaining to her friend Meg why she did the murder. Meg protests:

> "Nothing Hilary Roberts did deserved death."
>
> "I'm not arguing that she deserved to die. It doesn't matter whether she was happy, or childless, or even much use to anybody but herself. What I'm saying is that I wanted her dead."
>
> "That seems to me so evil that it's beyond my understanding. Alice, what you did was a dreadful sin."
>
> Alice laughed. The sound was so full-throated, almost happy, as if the amusement were genuine. "Meg, you continue to astonish me. You use words which are no longer in the general vocabulary, not even in the Church's, so I'm told. The implications of that simple little word are beyond my comprehension."

The same device recurs often in the conversation in this novel (and in others), with this same implication that the moral language others speak is a foreign one, something "no longer in the general vocabulary"—a language that the more sophisticated speaker finds senseless, naive and (most damning of all) out of fashion. Since it is unnerving to be sneered at, this tactic is often successful in silencing people,

both in fiction and real life. But that is quite another thing from saying that it makes sense.

Virtually always, the sense of the tactic is annulled by its context. Again there is false universality. The characters who talk like this are in general quite as ready as other people to live most of their lives by existing standards, to pass judgments about others, and to invoke morality. They still feel high-minded, and this is not an accident, but a necessary consequence of their wish to be seen as reformers. They are "immoralists" in the sense that they want to back and recommend actions currently taken to be immoral. But this backing and recommending is itself unavoidably a moral stand. It is not possible to sneer at other people's standards without committing yourself to rival standards of your own.

Nietzsche, who patented the word *immoralist*, spent a great deal of his time protesting in this way against current standards by recommending different ones. He also tried, and sometimes very seriously, to get rid of the notion of moral standards altogether. The word *amoralist* has since been coined to name this more radical campaign. However, it faces serious difficulties, which will occupy us a good deal in this book.

In P. D. James's novel, both Alex and Caroline are noticeably self-righteous people, contemptuous of others. Caroline in particular habitually shows priggish contempt for people whom she thinks are lacking in quite traditional values such as courage and honesty. Moreover she at once goes on to appeal—successfully—to Jonathan's sympathy and consideration to make him lie for her, which he would scarcely have done if he had accepted the amoralist manifesto she has just pronounced. Again, the murder Alice commits is altruistic, indeed, by her account to Meg, quite incredibly high-principled. I have the impression that P. D. James takes these amoralist manifestos fairly seriously, and that she is anxious to get them a serious hearing by showing the people who speak them as honorable and high-principled characters. The trouble is that this only suggests that they can't mean exactly what they say.

Tom Stoppard puts this point sharply at the end of his play *Professional Foul*, where two philosophers are returning by air from an Ethics Congress in Prague [when Prague was still part of a communist state with lots of censorship]. McKendrick, the younger, who has been advancing some dramatic amoralist views about the flexibility of moral principles, is rather surprised to find that his fuddy-duddy companion has managed to smuggle something out at the airport:

McKENDRICK. What was it?
ANDERSON. A thesis. Apparently rather slanderous from the State's point of view.
McKENDRICK. Where did you hide it?
ANDERSON. In your briefcase. (Pause)
McKENDRICK. You what?
ANDERSON. Last night. I'm afraid I reversed a principle. (McKendrick opens his briefcase and finds Hollar's envelope. Anderson takes it from him. McKendrick is furious.)
McKENDRICK. You utter bastard!
ANDERSON. I thought you would approve.
McKENDRICK. Don't get clever with me. (He relapses, shaking.) Jesus. It's not quite playing the game, is it?
ANDERSON. No. I suppose not. But they were very unlikely to search you.
McKENDRICK. That's not the bloody point.
ANDERSON. I thought it was. But you could be right. Ethics is a very complicated business. That's why we have these congresses.
(Tom Stoppard, 1978, p. 179)

McKendrick has been making amoralist claims. But in the practical context of this conversation, it turns out that he has strong moral beliefs, and makes judgments according to them.

DIFFICULTIES OF THE EXTRATERRESTRIAL POSITION

The point I am making here is not just a petty one, about chance inconsistencies of particular characters or particular authors. It is a point about the sheer size of morality. People who talk about opting out of it are thinking of it as a mere local set of restrictions—often sexual restrictions—something comparable to a district one might leave, or a set of by-laws that one might repeal or decide to ignore. But in fact this community of standards and ideals is something much wider, much more pervasive, more enclosing—much more like the air we breathe. It is not even comparable with a particular language that we might decide to stop speaking, though that could itself be traumatic enough. It is more like the condition of speaking—and thinking—in any language at all. Getting right outside morality would be rather like getting outside the atmosphere. It would mean losing the basic social network within which we live and communicate with others, including all those others in the past who have formed our culture. If we can imagine this deprived state at all, it would be a solitary condition close to that of autism or extreme depression—a state where, although intelligence can still function, there is no sense of community with others, no shared wishes, principles, aspirations or ideals, no mutual trust or fellowship with those outside, no preferred set of concepts, nothing agreed on as important. People whom we sometimes call amoral are not actually in this extraterrestrial condition. They are merely using standards somewhat different from our own. Their distinctiveness often looks much greater than it is, because a shared moral background is so important to us that even quite a slight difference of standards—even a small shift of emphasis—can make an impression of great strangeness. Sometimes it is refreshing, making change and development possible. But just as often it causes alarm and gives both sides the impression that they are divided by something as vast as the difference between being inside and outside morality. The charge of senselessness which Alice brings is often used to express this sense of shock. "I simply can't understand it," we complain, and this remark is well known to count, not as a request for explanation, but as a serious criticism, sometimes a declaration of war. Reformers who want to stress individual liberty have therefore often accepted and returned this incredulous repudiation, and have claimed to be what other people have called them—outside morality. But this no more has to be literally true than most of the other wild claims that are generated in controversy.

UNPACKING THE PARCEL

It should be becoming clear that the moral skepticism, the incredulity about all moral judgments that I am talking of, is not a simple thing, but a whole complex of varying attitudes. As we unpack it, we shall find many different elements in it, among them some of great value. But we shall find great difficulty in making sense of it as a single whole. It may seem rather confusing to open the subject at this everyday level, by starting from extreme, everyday pronouncements and pointing out the clashes between what they seem to say and the intentions of the people who make them. I have chosen to do this because I think it is often easier to understand current confusions by starting from the familiar forms in which they are expressed in our own lives than by using the less familiar, more carefully guarded formulations of moral theorists. Besides, it is the ideas we actually live by that we most need to understand. I think it is important to notice how very negative these everyday manifestos are. It is much clearer what they are attacking than why they are attacking it and what they are proposing instead. On these points they vary enormously, which is why I am stressing the false universality that conceals their differences.

This approach from the confusions of everyday thought does not at all mean that I simply want to shoot down the whole attitude behind the incomplete statements. The difficulties about moral judgment are real. They are not due to chance pieces of incompetence on the part of people who discuss this sort of thing. They spring from major value-conflicts—clashes and gaps between the various ideals and principles we live by—which are deeply rooted in our culture today and affect us all. Indeed, more generally it is hardly ever sensible to refute any argument just by pointing out an inconsistency in it. What is needed is to trace the considerations on both sides that have led us to hold clashing views, and to rethink them somehow so as to do justice to all these elements.

THE INDIGNANT REFORMERS

We must start by looking more fully at the context in which this sort of conflict arises, before turning to the small print of the arguments that are used. A very important point about that context is surely the one already touched on—that explicit, skeptical attacks on moral judgment are not usually made (as we might perhaps expect) by lotus-eating cynics anxious to save themselves the trouble of thinking whether anything is right or wrong at all. (These people seldom bother with argument.) Often, as we have seen, antijudgmentalists are people seriously concerned to protect the victims of moral intrusion. Often, too, they are thinkers concerned with the value of the inner life—eager to save us from spoiling our lives by imposing mistaken moral standards on ourselves. Again, they sometimes want education changed and society reshaped in a way that will make this kind of inner oppression less likely.

Both these last kinds of consideration were very powerful with Nietzsche, which is why, though he called himself an "immoralist," he was also in a very important sense a moralist. He desperately wanted to change the world; he was thoroughly confident that the changes he proposed were the right ones, and the chief tool that he used to promote these was not hesitation or doubt but burning moral indignation.

15. *What, in your own words, is the problem of false universality?*
16. *Antijudgmentalists, according to Midgley, are often anxious to do what?*

ARE AMORALISTS MORALISTS?

Thus the campaign against "moral judgment" seems often to spring from, and to rely on, strong and confidently held moral positions—decisions both about what is important and about the way in which these important things should be changed, or not changed. All these positions, if taken seriously, have clear and specific implications about what actually ought not to be done. The question then is what is the standing of these new and innovative judgments? Are they armored in some way against the skeptical solvent that is invoked to destroy all the others? Or are they perhaps not to be classed as moral judgments at all?

THE BACKGROUND: WHY FREEDOM MATTERS

Before plunging into detailed discussion of this, it may be helpful to sketch hastily what I think our main difficulty is—to outline briefly the range of topics that we must later go into more fully.

In our history, two quite different moral insights seem to have become entangled, forming a plausible argument which in our time has so dazzled people that it has seemed to transform the whole moral scene. One is a tremendous exaltation of individual freedom. The other is a skeptical or incredulous approach to knowledge, designed to weed out all inadequate forms of it in order to make room for modern science. Both these insights stem from the Enlightenment, and both are still extremely powerful in our lives.

These two ideas have been combined to form the claim that respect for freedom is founded on people's ignorance of each other. On this principle, the reason why we ought to leave other people free is simply that we do not know anything about them which could justify us in interfering. The formula of freedom is then close to our manifesto, and runs something like this: It is always wrong to interfere with other people's actions, because we can never know that any action is wrong.

Until you notice the internal conflict in it, this formula seems to resolve in one stroke two very difficult and disturbing questions. The first is: Why is freedom so important? This is a pressing question because freedom does sometimes clash with other ideals, and when it does, we need to know whether it ought to prevail. The second is about the standing of nonscientific reasoning generally. In an age where science reigns, what sort of validity can nonscientific forms of thought, including moral judgment, possibly have? Puzzled people have hoped to have found an answer to the first question by simply answering "none" to the second. Freedom then becomes a supreme value; it has to be infinite because nobody ever knows enough to be in a position to restrict it.

This rum [strange] solution involves some obvious confusions. It looks attractive because there is a range of important cases where our ignorance of other people's lives and standards actually does provide a good reason for not interfering with them. These cases arise especially between groups with different classes or cultures, and they can be disastrous politically where one group is trying to rule the other. Thus imperialist powers have often done great harm by putting down religious or marital customs that they simply did not understand.

But could there be reason to suggest that this ignorance—so obvious in particular situations—is something which extends over the whole field of mo-rality? Are we just as ignorant about more familiar matters, where we seem to know so much more? And even if we are indeed so ignorant, can this ignorance possibly be the only reason, or even the main reason, why we ought to respect freedom?

Ignorance, after all, provides only a reason for indifference, for detachment, for not caring about what other people do or suffer. That is the attitude we might have to have towards alien beings if a set of them came to live somewhere on earth, and were so totally incomprehensible to us that we could form no opinion at all about what they did or suffered. That indifference would indeed often stop us interfering with them. But it is hard to imagine a detachment so total, so far beyond the range of anything attempted in science fiction. And it is not an attitude that we could possibly take for our social relations with those around us.

Ignorance plainly is not the kind of reason that we normally have in mind when we say that we should respect other people's freedom. The reasons why we respect it are different and much more positive. They arise out of the fact that we honor and trust other people, that we think them capable of acting independently, and that we believe independent, self-chosen action to have in general a special kind of value.

This strong positive moral judgment—now so familiar and acceptable to most of us—explains the reason why we should respect the freedom, not only of those about whom we are ignorant, but also of the people we know well. It operates, too, not only where we think we cannot judge the rightness or wrongness of their actions, but also where we think we can judge it, and have judged that these actions are not wrong. (That, too, is of course a moral judgment.) When we do think other people's actions wrong—for instance, in cases such as murder or child abuse—we do not usually believe that we ought not to interfere. Toleration is a complex issue. But virtually nobody thinks it our duty to tolerate every kind of conduct in others.

SORTING OUT THE MORAL ISSUES

What we mainly need to notice here is that this exaltation of individual freedom apparently is itself a moral judgment, and that the arguments supporting it are moral arguments. This is as true of the principles requiring respect for freedom as it is of other principles equally fundamental to our life today, for instance: that it is wrong to punish people by burning them to death, however gravely they may have offended. When propositions like these are questioned, we support them by moral arguments.

17. *What two moral insights have become "entangled" according to Midgley?*

Skepticism and Relativism

Midgley goes on to argue in more detail against moral skepticism. Most of us would agree that we should not make judgments or claims in situations where we simply do not know what we are talking about. For example, it is all too common for people to make pronouncements about, say, particular foreign policy initiatives, even though they lack much, or any, knowledge of the relevant facts.

Now, the moral skeptic denies, in one way or other, that it is possible for *anyone ever* to know what they are talking about when it comes to morals! Morality is nothing more than a matter of personal opinion or guesses, they claim. Many of the moral theories discussed in this book are, among other things, attempts to defeat such skepticism. One of the main hurdles antiskeptics must overcome is of course *relativism*, the way of thinking described earlier in this chapter, for relativism probably makes most sense when interpreted as a kind of skepticism.

18. *People like Alice or McKendrick claim to be outside of morality altogether and to find moral concerns "senseless." According to Midgley, what are they actually doing? Is Midgley right? Argue pro and con.*

19. *What is legitimate, and what is not, in the idea that we should not judge people's conduct, according to Midgley?*

The UN Universal Declaration of Human Rights

In 1948 the United Nations approved as part of its charter a declaration of human rights. This declaration was set forth as an enumeration of moral rights applicable to all people at all times and places. Clearly such a document is thoroughly antirelativist.

20. *Why is it antirelativist?*

The following is the full text of the declaration. When it was adopted in 1948 the General Assembly called on all member countries to publicize the text of the declaration and "to cause it to be disseminated, displayed, read and expounded principally in schools and other educational institutions, without distinction based on the political status of countries or territories." The document is available in many translations at http://www.unhchr.ch/udhr/.

Preamble

Whereas recognition of the inherent dignity and of the equal and inalienable rights of all members of the human family is the foundation of freedom, justice and peace in the world,

Whereas disregard and contempt for human rights have resulted in barbarous acts which have outraged the conscience of mankind, and the advent of a world in which human beings shall enjoy freedom of speech and belief and freedom from fear and want has been proclaimed as the highest aspiration of the common people,

Whereas it is essential, if man is not to be compelled to have recourse, as a last resort, to rebellion against tyranny and oppression, that human rights should be protected by the rule of law,

Whereas it is essential to promote the development of friendly relations between nations,

Whereas the peoples of the United Nations have in the Charter reaffirmed their faith in fundamental human rights, in the dignity and worth of the human person and in the equal rights of men and women and have determined to promote social progress and better standards of life in larger freedom,

Whereas Member States have pledged themselves to achieve, in cooperation with the United Nations, the promotion of universal respect for and observance of human rights and fundamental freedoms,

Whereas a common understanding of these rights and freedoms is of the greatest importance for the full realization of this pledge,

Now, therefore, THE GENERAL ASSEMBLY proclaims THIS UNIVERSAL DECLARATION OF HUMAN RIGHTS as a common standard of achievement for all peoples and all nations, to the end that every individual and every organ of society, keeping this Declaration constantly in mind, shall strive by teaching and education to promote respect for these rights and freedoms and by progressive measures, national and international, to secure their universal and effective recognition and observance, both among the peoples of Member States themselves and among the peoples of territories under their jurisdiction.

ARTICLE 1.

All human beings are born free and equal in dignity and rights. They are endowed with reason and conscience and should act towards one another in a spirit of brotherhood.

ARTICLE 2.

Everyone is entitled to all the rights and freedoms set forth in this Declaration, without distinction of any kind, such as race, color, sex, language, religion, political or other opinion, national or social origin, property, birth or other status. Furthermore, no distinction shall be made on the basis of the political, jurisdictional or international status of the country or territory to which a person belongs, whether it be independent, trust, non-self-governing or under any other limitation of sovereignty.

ARTICLE 3.

Everyone has the right to life, liberty and security of person.

ARTICLE 4.

No one shall be held in slavery or servitude; slavery and the slave trade shall be prohibited in all their forms.

ARTICLE 5.

No one shall be subjected to torture or to cruel, inhuman or degrading treatment or punishment.

ARTICLE 6.

Everyone has the right to recognition everywhere as a person before the law.

ARTICLE 7.

All are equal before the law and are entitled without any discrimination to equal protection of the law. All are entitled to equal protection against any discrimination in violation of this Declaration and against any incitement to such discrimination.

ARTICLE 8.

Everyone has the right to an effective remedy by the competent national tribunals for acts violating the fundamental rights granted him by the constitution or by law.

ARTICLE 9.

No one shall be subjected to arbitrary arrest, detention or exile.

ARTICLE 10.

Everyone is entitled in full equality to a fair and public hearing by an independent and impartial tribunal, in the determination of his rights and obligations and of any criminal charge against him.

ARTICLE 11.

(1) Everyone charged with a penal offense has the right to be presumed innocent until proved guilty according to law in a public trial at which he has had all the guarantees necessary for his defense.

(2) No one shall be held guilty of any penal offense on account of any act or omission which did not constitute a penal offense, under national or international law, at the time when it was committed. Nor shall a heavier penalty be imposed than the one that was applicable at the time the penal offense was committed.

ARTICLE 12.

No one shall be subjected to arbitrary interference with his privacy, family, home or correspondence, nor to attacks upon his honor and reputation. Everyone has the right to the protection of the law against such interference or attacks.

ARTICLE 13.

(1) Everyone has the right to freedom of movement and residence within the borders of each state.

(2) Everyone has the right to leave any country, including his own, and to return to his country.

ARTICLE 14.

(1) Everyone has the right to seek and to enjoy in other countries asylum from persecution.

(2) This right may not be invoked in the case of prosecutions genuinely arising from non-political crimes or from acts contrary to the purposes and principles of the United Nations.

ARTICLE 15.

(1) Everyone has the right to a nationality.

(2) No one shall be arbitrarily deprived of his nationality or denied the right to change his nationality.

ARTICLE 16.

(1) Men and women of full age, without any limitation due to race, nationality or religion, have the right to marry and to found a family. They are entitled to equal rights as to marriage, during marriage and at its dissolution.

(2) Marriage shall be entered into only with the free and full consent of the intending spouses.

(3) The family is the natural and fundamental group unit of society and is entitled to protection by society and the State.

ARTICLE 17.

(1) Everyone has the right to own property alone as well as in association with others.

(2) No one shall be arbitrarily deprived of his property.

ARTICLE 18.

Everyone has the right to freedom of thought, conscience and religion; this right includes freedom to change his religion or belief, and freedom, either alone or in community with others and in public or private, to manifest his religion or belief in teaching, practice, worship and observance.

ARTICLE 19.

Everyone has the right to freedom of opinion and expression; this right includes freedom to hold opinions without interference and to seek, receive and impart information and ideas through any media and regardless of frontiers.

ARTICLE 20.

(1) Everyone has the right to freedom of peaceful assembly and association.

(2) No one may be compelled to belong to an association.

ARTICLE 21.

(1) Everyone has the right to take part in the government of his country, directly or through freely chosen representatives.

(2) Everyone has the right of equal access to public service in his country.

(3) The will of the people shall be the basis of the authority of government; this will shall be expressed in periodic and genuine elections which shall be by universal and equal suffrage and shall be held by secret vote or by equivalent free voting procedures.

ARTICLE 22.

Everyone, as a member of society, has the right to social security and is entitled to realization, through national effort and international cooperation and in accordance with the organization and resources of each State, of the economic, social and cultural rights indispensable for his dignity and the free development of his personality.

ARTICLE 23.

(1) Everyone has the right to work, to free choice of employment, to just and favorable conditions of work and to protection against unemployment.

(2) Everyone, without any discrimination, has the right to equal pay for equal work.

(3) Everyone who works has the right to just and favorable remuneration ensuring for himself and his family an existence worthy of human dignity, and supplemented, if necessary, by other means of social protection.

(4) Everyone has the right to form and to join trade unions for the protection of his interests.

ARTICLE 24.

Everyone has the right to rest and leisure, including reasonable limitation of working hours and periodic holidays with pay.

ARTICLE 25.

(1) Everyone has the right to a standard of living adequate for the health and well-being of himself and of his family, including food, clothing, housing and medical care and necessary social services, and the right to security in the event of unemployment, sickness, disability, widowhood, old age or other lack of livelihood in circumstances beyond his control.

(2) Motherhood and childhood are entitled to special care and assistance. All children, whether born in or out of wedlock, shall enjoy the same social protection.

ARTICLE 26.

(1) Everyone has the right to education. Education shall be free, at least in the elementary and fundamental stages. Elementary education shall be compulsory. Technical and professional education shall be made generally available and higher education shall be equally accessible to all on the basis of merit.

(2) Education shall be directed to the full development of the human personality and to the strengthening of respect for human rights and fundamental freedoms. It shall promote understanding, tolerance and friendship among all nations, racial or religious groups, and shall further the activities of the United Nations for the maintenance of peace.

(3) Parents have a prior right to choose the kind of education that shall be given to their children.

ARTICLE 27.

(1) Everyone has the right freely to participate in the cultural life of the community, to enjoy the arts and to share in scientific advancement and its benefits.

(2) Everyone has the right to the protection of the moral and material interests resulting from any scientific, literary or artistic production of which he is the author.

ARTICLE 28.

Everyone is entitled to a social and international order in which the rights and freedoms set forth in this Declaration can be fully realized.

ARTICLE 29.

(1) Everyone has duties to the community in which alone the free and full development of his personality is possible.

(2) In the exercise of his rights and freedoms, everyone shall be subject only to such limitations as are determined by law solely for the purpose of securing due recognition and respect for the rights and freedoms of others and of meeting the just requirements of morality, public order and the general welfare in a democratic society.

(3) These rights and freedoms may in no case be exercised contrary to the purposes and principles of the United Nations.

ARTICLE 30.

Nothing in this Declaration may be interpreted as implying for any State, group or person any right to engage in any activity or to perform any act aimed at the destruction of any of the rights and freedoms set forth herein.

*21. *Do you think the UN simply made a mistake when it tried to produce a universal declaration of rights? Relate your answer to what you said about Orienting Question 3.*

*22. *Are any of the rights listed in the declaration not really "rights" at all? For example, we can perhaps all agree that education for all would be a good thing. But does it follow that everyone has a "right" to it? Discuss.*

Further Discussion and Applications

Relativism, skepticism, antijudgmentalism and antimoralism are in the main negative views or positions that tell us what we should avoid or not do. But they link up with some very popular positive views, including the following.

a. We should always accept others even when they are very different from ourselves.
b. We must be tolerant of people with different ways of life.
c. We should learn to appreciate diversity and be open to alternative ways of life.
d. We should try to be "multicultural."

It is probably obvious how some of these might get linked to relativism or antijudgmentalism. To the extent that those ideas are suspect, these popular positive views require some critical scrutiny.

Accepting Differences

Although Rachel's discussion focuses on relativism exclusively, it has implications for other views and attitudes. For example, there is a very widespread conviction that a willingness to accept differences is a good thing, a virtue. And surely it can be.

However, clearly not all differences should be accepted! (*Think*!) But which ones should be accepted and which should not? That needs discussion. Unfortunately many people tend to deny there could be any point to such discussions, because they have been brought up in a relativist culture in which they are constantly exhorted to " accept one another's differences" but are seldom explicitly reminded that some differences should not be accepted. At the very least, which ones should or should not be accepted needs to be kept open as a matter for discussion. Someone might claim that no one would infer from the exhortation "be accepting of differences" that we should therefore accept as just "different" Nazis who have been conditioned by a whole, longstanding culture, to think it is right to incinerate Jews en masse. Unfortunately, people do make such an inference or simply fail to think the matter through.

It is, in fact, very difficult to be a consistent "accepter," as Midgley shows through her fictional excerpts. People who are extremely emphatic about the importance of accepting differences often get very heated up morally about cases like the tribal practices of clitorectomies that have been in the news in recent years. Nonetheless some anthropologists and others inclined toward relativism do try to "accept" all such differences and deny that anyone has grounds for objecting to any of them. Thus some anthropologists have claimed that the UN Universal Declaration of Human Rights is merely a product of white male Western imperialist ethnocentrism and should not be used as a general standard for judging people. (See the UN Declaration and the later discussion). One of the founders of the discipline of anthropology in the United States, Franz Boas, who was originally a German Jew, claimed that cultural relativism was the only respectable view. When Boas learned what the Nazis were doing, he came to doubt his own relativist views.

23. *Why would he have started to doubt in that way?*

Accepting people who are "different" might be interpreted to mean simply accepting people who are different with respect to race, religion, intelligence, looks, social graces or the lack thereof. That seems fine until you start thinking about Aztec child sacrifice or an old Hindu practice of burning widows alive on their husband's funeral pyres, often against their will (called *sati*). Should the religious or social differences that explain those practices be accepted? Or should we try to talk such people out of their beliefs or prohibit them from acting on them if we are able?

On the other hand, accepting people who are "different" might be interpreted to mean "continuing to believe in the dignity and worth of all people, even those who are wrong, immoral, etc." That, it can be argued, would be a very good thing. We will return to this point in our discussion of Kant (Chapter 8).

24. *State in your own words the two meanings of "accepting differences" just mentioned. Which seems more "sensible" to you, and why?*

Tolerance

Since tolerance is often equated with "acceptance," much of what was just said about accepting differences applies here also. Tolerance is also widely considered to be a very important virtue, and intolerance one of the worst of vices. That it can be a very important virtue is illustrated in the life of Montaigne, described briefly earlier in the chapter.

There is, however, a widespread semantic confusion about the notion of tolerance. If I accept what you believe or do (in the sense of agreeing with it or being indifferent toward it), then I cannot "tolerate" you or your beliefs. It would not make sense to say that I tolerated a belief or kind of behavior I found unobjectionable or that did not matter to me one way or the other. These are facts about the meaning of *tolerance*. It is necessary for genuine, morally worthy tolerance that I actually disagree with those I tolerate. Moreover it is consistent with tolerance that I think it necessary to argue with some of the people I tolerate in an attempt to convince them that they are mistaken. It is not difficult to see the value of tolerance in the historical situation of Montaigne. There was no chance, at that time in France, that Protestants and Catholics would come to theological agreement, but there was a chance that they might stop killing each other and settle for tolerance as just defined. Few would dispute that tolerance in such cases is a very good thing.

However, even in cases where tolerance is a real possibility, it is far from clear that it is always a good thing. Should we tolerate the burning of widows or the holding of slaves? One probably should for the most part tolerate those with differing religious beliefs (depending on what behavior those beliefs involve), even where one considers those beliefs to be foolish or superstitious. Likewise for many other differences. But tolerance is not always a virtue.

In many cases where we do think tolerance is required, we may still want to look for a respectful and nuanced way of expressing disagreement. That would make tolerance a matter of style, so to speak. But the notion that tolerance, in a substantive sense, is always a good thing is manifestly false. On the other hand, the notion that we should respect other people simply because they are fellow human beings might well be true. These two things, tolerance and respect, are by no means equivalent. It is arguable that there is a sense in which we should respect even an axe murderer. He or she is a human being and should not be treated like dirt, like a mere animal. But we certainly should not tolerate axe murderers.

25. *Why is the view that tolerance is always a good thing "manifestly false"? Illustrate with some examples.*
26. *Can you be tolerant of someone who has views or behaves in ways that make no difference to you? Explain.*

The Possibility of Real Moral Disagreement

When we have culled through all the differences of the sorts mentioned by relativists as support for their view, will there be any real *moral* differences left over, any that are not due to the sorts of factors mentioned by Rachels, such as the harsh environmental circumstances that explain Eskimo infanticide? Perhaps. In one area of China, where cats are often part of the menu, they are sometimes immersed in boiling water, while still conscious, and then skinned alive, in the process of preparing them as food. Most Westerners find this inexcusably cruel. It is not clear that this difference in moral assessment can be traced back to any of the sorts of differences mentioned by Rachels. Perhaps this is a case where there are genuinely incommensurate modes of moral evaluation. If there are such cases, Rachels would still argue that they are few and far between and that they are relatively peripheral. Agreement on central cases will still exist across cultures and historical periods. In fact most Chinese do not condone cruelty to cats, but in any case certainly no Chinese would condone boiling human beings and skinning them alive in preparation for eating them or for any other purpose! Relativists, on the other hand, stress the differences that do exist and interpret many moral differences simply as cases of moral incommensurabilities. The cat cookers do pose a problem for the antirelativist.

27. *Connect the concept of moral incommensurability to Protagoras' remark about man being the measure of all things. Remember, to say that two conflicting claims are incommensurable is to say that there is no common measure, no general standard, for determining which is right or true.*

Rachels and Midgley have argued that relativism and related views or attitudes are often incoherent. As the preceding discussions indicate, people who stress the relativity of moral beliefs are often anxious to advocate tolerance and acceptance of those who are "different." However, to "advocate" in that way is to take up a moral stance or make a moral claim and to insist that it is right for all people. But relativism is the view that there are no moral stances or claims that are right for all people! So many relativists insist in one breath that there are no moral absolutes and in the next give us a moral absolute!

Nonetheless the relativist may be on to something. As we will see, the worries generated by relativism and those generated by skepticism go hand in hand. Skeptics and relativists may be claiming any or all of the following.

1. There is no moral truth.
2. Moral claims are not objective, in the sense that there is any "reasonable" way of settling moral differences between cultures.
3. Moral claims are not about something that exists "outside the head" or "out there in the real world."
4. There is no such thing as moral knowledge.

These are not equivalent claims, though they are often confused with one another. The cultural relativist certainly agrees with (2) and often makes the mistake of supposing that (2) implies (1), (3) and (4). The skeptic insists on (4) but does not have to hold to any of (1) through (3). These points will be discussed further in later selections. However, something like (2) might itself be true, and by itself that may pose a problem for the antirelativist.

Thin and Thick Moral Concepts (Williams)

Contemporary philosopher Bernard Williams agrees that relativism is often mistaken or even incoherent.

Nevertheless he asks us to consider the difference between what are called *thin* and *thick* moral concepts. *Cruelty*, which is what some people would see in the Chinese treatment of those cats, is an example of a *thick* moral concept. That means it has lots of descriptive content. I do not say "*x* is cruel" simply to indicate that *x* makes me feel a certain way. If I did, saying "*x* is cruel" would be like saying "*x* is nauseating." But it is not. To say that *x* is nauseating is just to say how it makes me feel. A great many different *x*'s could make a person feel nauseated, and an *x* that makes one person nauseated might have no effect on another person. To say that *x* is cruel is not to simply say how *x* makes me feel, but to say how *x* is, whether it makes me feel a certain way or not. Of course, I would not likely say of *x* that it is cruel if it did not make me feel something quite negative. In using a word like *cruel* I bring together a claim about how things are with how I feel about them. But I *am* claiming something about how the world is, as I do in knowledge claims. So "*x* is cruel" is not a subjective claim, even though feelings of certain kinds belong to it.

Now contrast "*x* is cruel" with "*x* is wrong." The latter doesn't give much information about *x* or the sort of thing that was done. *Wrong* is a *thin* ethical concept. If it gives information about something in the world, it gives very little.

So, if I say that what A did is "cruel," that tells a good deal about A and the nature of her act. If I merely say that what she did was wrong, I express what seems to be little more than a negative response. It is not surprising, then, that virtually all peoples at all times have concepts of *right* and *wrong*. That fact might looks promising to the antirelativist, but at the same time it has a subjective quality, as though it were merely an expression of a very general negative attitude

Cruel seems different from *wrong,* in these respects. It seems to be anchored to objective facts in some way. It seems to express a kind of knowledge about how things are as well as negative feelings. Oddly enough, however, on further examination it may seem to be more "relative" than thinner concepts. Even if the concept is used in some alien culture, might it not be used to describe actions that we think are not cruel, and vice versa? Might it not be used at all?

In the course of pondering the possibility and nature of moral knowledge, Williams considers the case of moral advisers in our lives. Obviously if morality were "just a matter of opinion" there would be no point in looking for moral advice. But in fact people do seek out moral advice. What do we look for in an adviser? Williams suggests that *we seek someone who skillfully uses thick moral concepts.*

From "Ethics" in *Philosophy*, ed. A. C. Grayling (1995), pp. 463–464.

A more recognizable picture (which has an Aristotelian provenance) is that of a person who is good at understanding situations which raise moral questions, can helpfully suggest the moral light in which a problem can be seen, and so forth. This is the model of ethical knowledge in terms of a person who can be a good ethical adviser (which he or she will assuredly be only if a good practical adviser more generally). This model respects a general feature of knowledge, that a principal interest we have in using it is to locate informants, people who can help us to come to know the answers to questions we have. In the ethical case the idea of an informant yields rather to that of an adviser; to become convinced of an ethical conclusion involves more than one's being authoritatively informed of it (which is why the idea of a theoretical expert about morality is so unconvincing). However, an informant and an adviser importantly share the feature that we seek them because we want to resolve some question, and we think that in virtue of things that they know or understand they can help us do so. This model ties up helpfully with the idea of knowledge under thick concepts, since one of the most helpful activities of ethical advisers is to suggest ways in which a situation falls or fails to fall under such concepts.

However, such an adviser will be no help to someone who does not share the same thick ethical concepts. This is just one aspect of a general point about these concepts, that they are by no means constant across cultures or times (it is instructive to reflect what has happened in the past century or so to the concept of *chastity*). Assured and shared use of thick concepts in a given culture may well provide, to a greater extent than anywhere else in ethics, examples of truth, objectivity and knowledge, but that advantage is rarely shared by discussions between cultures, groups, traditions or generations on questions of what thick concepts to use. That is why it does not go far enough to point out that, relative to a given concept such as *cruelty*, there may be "no alternative" to thinking that a given act was cruel; this overlooks the alternative of not thinking in terms of cruelty at all.

It might well be that the Chinese cat cooker simply does not think in terms of cruelty at all, nor do his customers, which may include sweet little children and kind grandmothers. They are sitting in the restaurant waiting for their cooked cat. The children may even have been given the opportunity to pick out which live cat they should have cooked for dinner! If we suppose that there is simply "no alternative" to thinking such acts cruel, we may be mistaken.

If Williams is right, then there is an important difference between how most people think about science and how we should think about ethics. Many people, scientists included, think that scientists must be able to come to agreement on what concepts to use in describing the world. Such agreement would seem to be required by the idea that scientists get at how things "really are." Perhaps no similar agreement is possible in ethics. Perhaps there would be no way to convince Chinese cat cookers that their actions are rightly described using the thick ethical concept *cruel*. Perhaps they do not use that concept at all. Can we show that they are making a mistake? If not, perhaps the lack of similarity between "knowledge" in ethics and knowledge in science does undercut the claim that there can be moral knowledge, Midgley's objections notwithstanding.

Consider Williams' remark about chastity. How many people still use the concept *chastity* in their moral thinking? Is it possible that people might cease to use that concept entirely? If the answer is "yes," does that support relativism?

28. *Which of the following would you classify as "thick" ethical concepts and which as "thin"?*

Kind. Dutiful. Treacherous. Good. Wrong. Nasty. Vicious. Rude. Put them on a "thickness" continuum.

29. *Do you ever use the concept chastity? Do you hear it mentioned in any way in popular entertainment (TV, movies, popular music)? How might it matter whether you do or do not?*

30. *In order for A to be a good moral adviser to B, A must share some thick ethical concepts with B, according to Williams. Give an example to illustrate this idea.*

Origins of the UN Universal Declaration of Human Rights (Glendon)

The use of the term *rights* is very common ("I have a right to that," "You have no right to do that"), but the notion is not so clear. One question that naturally arises is "Where do rights come from?" When Jefferson penned the Declaration of Independence he claimed that all "men" are "endowed by their creator with certain inalienable rights." He thereby provided an answer to the question "Where do such rights come from?" They come from the "creator," or God. Jefferson was an enlightenment thinker who was certainly no orthodox Christian, but he apparently had a generalized belief in God as creator and as a source of moral law.

In the United Nations Universal Declaration there is no reference to God or a creator, so the questions "Where do such rights come from?" and "What grounds these claimed rights?" become pressing. Probably the authors hoped that most people would find their claims intuitively obvious. However, the American Association of Anthropology condemned the Declaration as "ethnocentric." They claimed that it reflected the moral standpoint of Western Europe and the United States, while at the same time betraying a lack of respect for cultural differences. They in effect answered the question "Where do these rights come from?" with the answer "from the particular customs of the modern West." It is evident that some anthropologists think "custom is king" and thus that any declaration of rights would *have* to reflect particular customs. Thus it could not be a truly "universal" declaration.

Was their view correct, even if we assume that morality amounts to nothing more than custom? That signatories to the Declaration included peoples from all over the world suggests otherwise. Or it might be taken to suggest that there is not as much difference between the "customs" of the West and the customs of other parts of the world as the anthropologists supposed. Nonetheless it is fairly clear that parts of the Declaration derive from the U.S. Constitution and very similar documents. Here are some items from the Declaration.

Article 3 states, "Everyone has the right to life, liberty and security of person."

Article 7 states, "All are equal before the law and are entitled without any discrimination to equal protection of the law."

Article 18 states, "Everyone has the right to freedom of thought, conscience and religion."

These articles will look familiar to Americans who know a little about the Declaration of Independence and their own constitution, such as the First Amendment. There are, however, parts of the Declaration that have no counterpart in the U.S. Constitution. Mary Ann Glendon, currently a professor in the Harvard Law School, comments:

> Several features [of the Universal Declaration of Human Rights] set it apart from both Anglo-American and Soviet-bloc documents, and these should be kept in mind as contests over the meanings of the Declaration's provisions continue. Consider the following: its pervasive emphasis on the "inherent dignity" and "worth of the human person"; the affirmation that the human person is "endowed with reason and conscience"; the right to form trade unions; the worker's right to just remuneration for himself and his family; the recognition of the family as the "natural and fundamental group unit of society" entitled as such to "protection by society and the State"; the prior right of parents to choose the education of their children; and a provision that motherhood and childhood are entitled to "special care and assistance."
>
> Where did those ideas come from? The immediate source was the 20th century constitutions of

many Latin American and continental European countries. But where did the Latin Americans and continental Europeans get them? The proximate answer to that question is: mainly from the programs of political parties, parties of a type that did not exist in the United States, Britain, or the Soviet bloc, namely, Christian Democratic and Christian Socialist parties.

And where did the politicians get their ideas about the family, work, civil society and the dignity of the person? The answer is: mainly from the social encyclicals *Rerum novarum* (1891) and *Quadragesimo anno* (1931) [documents of the Roman Catholic Church]. And where did the church get them? The short answer is that those encyclicals were part of the process through which the church had begun to reflect on the Enlightenment, the 18th century revolutions, socialism, and the labor question in the light of Scripture, tradition, and her own experience as an "expert in humanity." (*Commonweal*, 10/12/2001)

31. *According to Glendon, not all of the provisions of the Declaration derive from the kinds of norms endorsed by the U.S. Constitution and related documents. List three that do not.*

The sources of the Declaration are in fact quite diverse. But what is most interesting in Glendon's remarks is the way they end: They suggest an answer to the question "Where do these rights come from?" that is like Jefferson's in one respect. As we track down the sources of at least parts of the moral thinking in the Declaration, we discover that the notion that God is the ultimate source of moral rights is hovering in the background. We will return to the idea of a divine source for morality in Chapter 4. Theists have typically resisted relativism and have insisted that there are universal moral principles that apply to all people, principles that derive from the God who created all people and gave them a common nature, or at least a God who issued universal commands. Nontheists who reject relativism seek other grounds for morality, though they may also assume something like a common human nature. The principal nontheistic accounts will be discussed in subsequent chapters.

32. In your opinion, is it possible that the rights that are enumerated in the U.S. Constitution and other such documents actually require some kind of religious grounding?

At this point you should return to the Orienting Questions and see how, if at all, your answers to them may have changed or been modified.

In the course of attempts to overcome skepticism and relativism, the philosophers we will study in the remaining chapters usually propose answers, or ways to get answers, to the most practical questions of all:

What is the best kind of life, and how do I achieve it?
How should I act in particular situations? What particular action would be right, or wrong, in a given situation?

The *first* of these questions is the main focus of the next two chapters. There the second question is usually subordinated to the first.

CHAPTER TWO

The Good Life, Reason and Tragic Conflict

Introduction

Whole industries, professions and institutions are dedicated to improving people's lives. Even exercise equipment is sold with the promise that it will produce a *new*, and of course more complete and satisfied, you. These are surface symptoms of a very basic fact: For most people, perhaps for all, the most fundamental question, *the* question, is:

> What is the best kind of life, and how do I achieve it?

At first sight this looks like a question that has moral bearings, and it suggests that the sheer size of morality, the size of the moral domain, is very great. It is difficult to imagine any intact human being who does not give *some* thought to *the* question, whether the answers proposed are silly or not. Someone who insisted that it did not matter to him whether his life was good rather than wretched, or totally uninteresting, or degraded in some way, would be, at the least, very puzzling. Everyone wants a good life, and the concern to achieve it pervades life, even when *the* question is not consciously entertained. Some people may have despaired or given up on the possibility of a good life, but even they must have some views on what such a life is like. Nonetheless the more thought people give to *the* question, the more likely they are

to run into difficulties. Is a good life one filled with secure pleasures? Must the best life also be a moral life? Can you have the best kind of life "by yourself," apart from a good community?

There are plenty of conflicting views around, and plenty of people are prepared to give advice on how to live. Some of those views are based in pop psychology and some on religious or moral ideals; and there are many such ideals. Some can be traced back to philosophical teachings. Some are nothing more than surmises by the latest gurus or advice mongers, out to make a quick buck by selling their opinions on how to live. The demand for advice on this matter must be heavy, since many of those advice mongers have evidently found a way to make a living. The list of "best sellers" that focus on some version of *the* question is very long.

The question certainly also invites a lot of philosophical reflection, as we shall see.

1. *Mention or briefly sketch three different views that you have heard expressed on what makes up a good life (include your own view if you like).*

Whatever the best answer to the question may be, most people would probably agree that there are obstacles of many sorts to a good life. External factors, such as accidents, disease, war, unhappy childhoods, bad luck of all sorts, seem to be among them. The novelist Thomas Hardy, in his novel *Tess of the d'Urbervilles,* remarked on how often it happens that marriages, which we hope will be sources of happiness, make people miserable, simply because of bad luck, a bad match into which people may be drawn for all sorts of reasons or for no reason at all. And he denied that any philosophy had ever been able to account for this recurrent fact of human life.

Similar sorts of facts were certainly on the minds of those ancient Greeks whose writings we will now consult. Many Greek thinkers were very conscious of tensions and defects within people that lead to lives that are miserable or at best merely endurable. In addition, many of them had the conviction that life is ruled by fate, a fate that is often unkind. Although people may have some control over their own destinies, they nonetheless often find themselves trapped in patterns of misfortune that go on from generation to generation.

ORIENTING QUESTIONS

1. Must a good life be just or morally good? Could a murderer or thief or crooked CEO have a truly good life, the "best kind of life"?

2. Must moral goodness be based in some transcendent source (such as God), or can an account be given of it that refers only to human desires and reason?

3. If we are perfectly reasonable, think clearly and don't get carried away by our desires, shouldn't we be able to figure out what is the best kind of life *and also be able to live it*? Will good or bad luck play a role no matter how smart we are?

4. What do we get from living in communities (clubs, churches, sororities, civic communities such as the city or state) ? Do these communities have to be "ethical" in some sense in order to contribute to a good life?

5. In connection with question 4, do communal norms sometimes need to be violated in order to avoid a loss of self or integrity? If so, is there some higher standard (higher than the community) by which to justify those violations (compare your answer to that to question 2)?

SOPHOCLES

Sophocles lived long (90 years, from 495 to 405 BCE) and was the most successful of all the great Greek playwrights. He lived through great upheavals in Greek life, both political and more narrowly intellectual. His themes include challenges to the old order of beliefs and ideas and the price of change. The Athenians loved his work and must have loved him. They made him a treasurer and general in 443 and 441 and a principal adviser after the disaster in Sicily, in which two Athenian expeditionary forces were totally destroyed (413). His plays consistently explore the limits imposed on human life and happiness by misfortune, "fate" and personal failure, including failures of character.

We begin this chapter with a typical dramatic representation of the obstacles to happiness that confront even very strong people and the tensions within them that lead to disaster. The following play is one part of a longer story about Oedipus, king of Thebes, and his descendants. It is a story full of tragic conflicts, seemingly dictated by a cruel and heedless fate. The main characters are beset by conflicting loyalties and obligations. They are also confronted by deep limitations in human nature itself, or so it certainly seems. Some of their actions are self-destructive. There are disagreements about right and wrong, vice and virtue, and those disagreements sometimes generate violent conflict.

One feature of the cultural background to this play should be noted: It was widely believed by the Greeks that the dead belong to Hades (also called *Pluto*), god of the underworld, and that the way to honor Hades' rightful claim is to provide a proper burial, including appropriate rituals, for a dead person.

The play begins just after the two sons of the deceased King Oedipus, Eteocles and Polyneices, have killed each other in a war over succession to the throne of Thebes. Although it was indeed Polyneices' turn to take the throne, the boys' uncle, Creon (a name that means "ruler" in Greek) has sided with Eteocles, who had remained in Thebes, and against Polyneices, who left the city to form an alliance with the Argives in order to take by force what was rightfully his. With both sons dead, the rule has fallen to

Creon. In the opening scene one of the sisters of the dead brothers, Antigone (a name that means "in opposition" in Greek), describes the most recent results of the war to her sister, Ismene.

(Before you begin reading the play itself, it may be helpful to look at the list of "themes" at the end of this play and even to jot down a few key words.)

From *Antigone* (translated by R. C. Jebb, revised and edited on the basis of the Greek text by N. Lillegard)

ANTIGONE: Sister, my own dear sister, do you know of any misfortune, of all fated to us by Oedipus, that is not fulfilled by Zeus for us two while we live? There is nothing painful, nothing fraught with ruin, no shame, no dishonor, that I have not seen in your woes and mine.

And now what new edict is this of which they tell, that our Captain [Creon] has just published to all Thebes? Do you know of it? Have you heard? Or is it hidden from you that our friends are threatened by doom from our foes?

ISMENE: No word of friends, Antigone, gladsome or painful, has come to me, since we two sisters were bereft of both our brothers, killed in one day by twofold blow; and since in this last night the Argive host has fled, I know no more, whether my fortune be brighter, or more grievous.

ANTIGONE: I knew it well, and therefore sought to bring you beyond the gates of the court, that you might hear when we are alone.

ISMENE: What is it? It is plain that you are brooding on some dark tidings.

ANTIGONE: Haven't you heard that Creon has destined one of our brothers to honored burial, the other to unburied shame? Eteocles, they say, he has laid in the earth, with due observance of right and custom, for his honor among the dead below. But as to the hapless corpse of Polyneices, rumor has it that it has been published to the town that none shall entomb him or mourn, but leave him unwept, unsepulchred, a welcome store for the birds, when they see him, to feast on at will. Such, it is said, is the edict that the good Creon has set forth for you and for me, yes, for

me, and he is coming here to proclaim it clearly to those who know it not; nor does he take the matter lightly, but, whoever disobeys in any respect, will have as his doom death by stoning before all the folk. Now you know; and you will soon show whether you are nobly bred, or the base daughter of a noble line.

ISMENE: Poor sister, if things stand thus, what could I help to do or undo?

ANTIGONE: Consider whether you will share the toil and the deed.

ISMENE: In what venture? What is your meaning?

ANTIGONE: Will you aid this hand to lift the dead?

ISMENE: Aid you? You would bury him, when it's forbidden to Thebes?

ANTIGONE: I will do my part, and yours, if you will not, to a brother. I will never be found false to him.

ISMENE: Ah, overbold! when Creon has forbidden it?

ANTIGONE: He has no right to keep me from my own.

Ismene recalls the tragic history of their family, the power they are subject to as women, the pointlessness of trying to defy the state. Antigone responds by arguing that there is a higher law than that of the state, which they are bound to obey. The idea that there is a law higher than the law of specific communities is one we shall encounter again in this text.

Antigone now moves to act against Creon's edict.

ANTIGONE: I will bury him: well for me to die in doing that. I shall rest, a loved one, with him whom I have loved, sinless in my crime; for I owe a longer allegiance to the dead than to the living: in that world I shall abide forever. But if you will not help me you will be guilty of dishonoring laws which the gods have established in honor.

ISMENE: I do them no dishonor; but to defy the State, I have no strength for that.

ANTIGONE: Such be your plea: I, then, will go to heap the earth above the brother whom I love.

ISMENE: Oh, unhappy one! How I fear for you!

ANTIGONE: Fear not for me: guide your own fate rightly.

ISMENE: At least, then, disclose this plan to none, but hide it closely, and so, too, will I.

ANTIGONE: Oh, denounce it! You will be far more hateful for your silence, if you do not proclaim these things to all.

ISMENE: You have a hot heart for chilling deeds.

ANTIGONE: I know that I please where I am most bound to please.

ISMENE: Yes, if you can; but you would do what you cannot do.

ANTIGONE: Why, then, when my strength fails, I shall have done.

ISMENE: A hopeless quest should not be made at all.

ANTIGONE: If that is how you speak, you will have hatred from me, and will justly be subject to the lasting hatred of the dead. But leave me, and the folly that is mine, alone, to suffer this dread thing; for I refuse to suffer anything so dreadful as an ignoble death.

ISMENE: Go, then, if you must; and of this be sure, that, though your errand is foolish, to your dear ones you are truly dear.

(Exit ANTIGONE on the spectators' left. ISMENE retires into the palace by one of the two side doors. When they have departed, the CHORUS OF THEBAN ELDERS enters.)

The chorus describes the victory of Thebes over the Argives in glowing terms, and proclaims that Zeus has aided them in battle. They confidently assume the justice of their own side in the war.

CHORUS: For Zeus utterly abhors the boasts of a proud tongue; and when he beheld them [the Argives] coming on in a great stream, in the haughty pride of clanging gold, he smote with brandished fire one who was on his way to shouting "victory" upon our ramparts.

. . . But look, the king of the land comes yonder, Creon, son of Menoeceus, our new ruler by the new fortunes that the gods have given; what counsel is he pondering, that he has proposed this special conference of elders, summoned by his general mandate?

(Enter CREON, from the central doors of the palace, in the garb of king, with two attendants.)

CREON: Sirs, the vessel of our State, after being tossed on wild waves, has once more been safely steadied by the gods: and you, out of all the folk, have been called apart by my summons, because I knew, first of all, how true and constant was your reverence for the royal power of Laius; how, again, when Oedipus was ruler of our land, and when he had perished, your steadfast loyalty still upheld their children. Since, then, both his sons have fallen in one day by a twofold doom, each smitten by the other, each stained with a brother's blood, I now possess the throne and all its powers, by nearness of kinship to the dead. No man can be fully known, in soul and spirit and mind, until he has been seen versed in rule and lawgiving. For if any, being supreme guide of the State, does not cleave to the best counsels, but, through some fear, keeps his lips locked, I hold and have ever held him most base; and if anyone cares more for anything else than his fatherland, that man has no place in my regard. For I—be Zeus my witness, who sees all things always—would not be silent if I saw ruin, instead of safety, coming to the citizens; nor would I ever deem the country's foe a friend to myself; remembering this, that our country is the ship that bears us safe, and that only while she prospers in our voyage can we make true friends. Such are the rules by which I guard this city's greatness. And in accord with them is the edict which I have now published to the folk touching the sons of Oedipus; that Eteocles, who has fallen fighting for our city, in all renown of arms, shall be entombed, and crowned with every rite that follows the noblest dead to their rest. But for his brother, Polyneices, who came back from exile, and sought to consume utterly with fire the city of his fathers and the shrines of his fathers' gods, sought to taste of kindred blood, and to lead the remnant into slavery; touching this man, it has been proclaimed to our people that none shall grace him with burial or lament, but leave him unburied, a corpse for birds and dogs to eat, a spectacle of shame.

Creon goes on to warn the chorus (the elders of the community) that they must not be tempted to disobey his edict. At that point a messenger enters, bringing news that he fears to tell, since it will make Creon angry.

(A GUARD enters from the spectators' left.)
GUARD: My liege, I will not say that I come breathless from speed, or that I have plied a nimble foot; for often did my thoughts make me pause, and wheel round in my path, to return. My mind was holding large discourse within me; "Fool, why do you go to certain doom?" "Wretch, tarrying again? And if Creon hears this from another, won't you be sorry for it?" So debating, I went on my way with lagging steps, and thus a short road was made long. At last, however, it carried the day that I should come here to you; for I come with a good grip on one hope, namely that I can suffer nothing but what is my fate.
CREON: And what is it that troubles you?
GUARD: I wish to tell you first about myself. I did not do the deed. I did not see the doer. It is not right that I should come to any harm.
CREON: You have a shrewd eye for your mark; well do you fence yourself round against the blame; clearly you have some strange thing to tell.
GUARD: Aye, truly; dread news makes one pause long.
CREON: Then tell it, will you, and then leave?
GUARD: Well, this is it. The corpse; someone has just given it burial, and gone away, after sprinkling thirsty dust on the flesh, with such other rites as piety enjoins.
CREON: What are you saying? What living man has dared this deed?
GUARD: I know not; no stroke of pickaxe was seen there, no earth thrown up by mattock; the ground was hard and dry, unbroken, without track of wheels; the doer was one who had left no trace. And when the first day watchman showed it to us, extreme wonder fell on all. The dead man was veiled from us; not shut within a tomb, but lightly strewn with dust, as by the hand of one who shunned a curse. And no sign met the eye as though any beast of prey or any dog had come nigh to him, or torn him. . . . At last, when all our searching was fruitless, one spake, who made us all bend our faces on the earth in fear; his counsel was that this deed must be reported to you, and not hidden. And this seemed best; and the lot doomed poor me to win this prize. So here I stand, as unwelcome as unwilling, I certainly believe; for no one likes the person who brings bad news.
LEADER: O king, my thoughts have long been whispering, can this deed, by any chance, even be the work of gods?
CREON: Cease, before your words fill me utterly with wrath, so that you not be found both old and foolish. For in saying that the gods have care for this corpse you say something unbearable. Was it for high reward of trusty service that they sought to hide his nakedness, that one who came to burn their pillared shrines and sacred treasures, to burn their land, and scatter its laws to the winds? Or did you behold the gods honoring the wicked? It cannot be. No! From the first there were certain in the town that muttered against me, chafing at this edict, wagging their heads in secret, and kept not their necks under the yoke of justice, contented with my rule. It is by them, well I know, that these have been beguiled and bribed to do this deed. But all the men who brought this thing about for hire have made it sure that, soon or late, they shall pay the price. Now, as Zeus still has my reverence, know this, I say it on my oath: If you find not the very author of this burial, and produce him before my eyes, death alone shall not be enough for you, till first, hung up alive, you have revealed this outrage . . .
(CREON goes into the palace.)
CHORUS (singing) strophe 1:
   Many things inspire awe and wonder, but none is more wonderful and terrifying than man; the power that crosses the white sea, driven by the stormy south wind, making a path under surges that threaten to engulf him; he wears out Earth, the eldest of the gods, the immortal, the unwearied, turning the soil with the offspring of horses, as the ploughs go to and fro from year to

year . . . And speech, and swift thought, and all the moods that mould a state, has he taught himself; and how to flee the arrows of the frost, when it's hard lodging under the clear sky, and the arrows of the rushing rain; yes, he has resources for everything; only against Death shall he call for aid in vain; but from baffling maladies he has devised escapes. Cunning beyond fancy's dream is the fertile skill which brings him, now to evil, now to good. When he honors the laws of the land, and that justice which he has sworn by the gods to uphold, his city stands proudly: but no city has he who, due to rashness, dwells with sin. Never may he share my hearth, never think my thoughts, who does these things!

(Enter the GUARD on the spectators' left, leading in ANTIGONE.)

LEADER OF THE CHORUS: What portent from the gods is this? My soul is amazed. I know her. How can I deny that this maiden is Antigone? O unhappy one, and child of an unhappy sire, of Oedipus! What means this? You a prisoner? You, disloyal to the king's laws, and taken in folly?

GUARD: Here she is, the doer of the deed: I caught this girl burying him: but where is Creon?

(CREON enters hurriedly from the palace.)

LEADER: Here he comes out again from the house, at our need.

CREON: What is it? What has happened, that makes my coming timely?

GUARD: O king . . . , I have come . . . bringing this maid; who was taken showing grace to the dead. This time there was no casting of lots; no, this luck has fallen to me, and to no one else. And now, sire, take her yourself, question her, examine her as you will; but I have a right to be completely free and free of this trouble.

CREON: And your prisoner here. . . . How and from where have you taken her?

GUARD: She was burying the man; you know all.

CREON: Do you mean what you say? Do you speak correctly?

GUARD: I saw her burying the corpse that you had forbidden to bury. Is that plain and clear?

CREON: And how was she seen? How taken in the act?

GUARD: [The guard describes how Antigone came to cover the body of Polyneices, which the guards had uncovered.] We rushed forward when we saw it, and at once closed upon our quarry, who was not at all dismayed. Then we confronted her with her past and present doings; and she, to both my joy and to my pain, denied nothing. To have escaped from ills one's self is a great joy; but it is painful to bring friends to ill. In any case, all such things are of less account to me than my own safety.

CREON: You whose face is bent to earth, do you admit or not admit to this deed?

ANTIGONE: I admit it; I make no denial.

CREON (to GUARD): Go where you want, free and clear of a grave charge. (Exit GUARD) (To ANTIGONE) Now, tell me, not in many words, but briefly, did you know that an edict had forbidden this?

ANTIGONE: I knew it: could I help it? It was public.

CREON: And you did indeed dare to transgress that law?

ANTIGONE: Yes; for it was not Zeus that had published me that edict; not such are the laws set among men by the justice who dwells with the gods below; nor did I think that your decrees were of such force, that a mortal could override the unwritten and unfailing statutes of heaven. For their life is not of today or yesterday, but from all time, and no man knows when they were first put forth.

Not through dread of any human pride could I answer to the gods for breaking the decrees of heaven. I must die, I knew that well (how should I not?) even without your edicts. But if I am to die before my time, I count that a gain: for when any one lives, as I do, compassed about with evils, can such a one find anything less than gain in death? So for me to meet this doom is trifling grief; but if I had suffered my mother's son to lie in death as an unburied corpse, that would have grieved me; for this action against your decree, I am not grieved. And if my present deeds are

foolish in your sight, it may be that a foolish judge arraigns my folly.
LEADER OF THE CHORUS: The maid shows herself to be a passionate child of a passionate sire, and knows not how to bend before troubles.

Creon threatens to force Antigone to bend to his will. He also believes that Ismene is involved in the crime. And he confidently claims that all Thebans support his edict. But Antigone continues to debate with him the rightness of his edict by questioning whether it could have divine approval. For the rule "treat the dead with respect" was generally thought to derive from the Gods.

ANTIGONE: Nevertheless, Hades [God of the Dead and the underworld] desires these rites.
CREON: But the good desires not a like portion with the evil.
ANTIGONE: Who knows but this seems blameless in the world below?
CREON: A foe is never a friend, not even in death.
ANTIGONE: It is not my nature to join in hating, but in loving.
CREON: Pass, then, to the world of the dead, and, if you must love, love them. While I live, no woman shall rule me.

Ismene enters, led in by two attendants. She now wishes, out of personal love for her sister, to share in the blame. But Antigone proudly refuses, and Creon makes it clear that Antigone is as good as dead. Then Ismene reminds him that Antigone is betrothed to his own son, Haemon (a name that means "blood" in Greek).

ISMENE: But will you slay the betrothed of your own son?
CREON: There are other fields for him to plough.
ISMENE: But there can never be such love as bound him to her.
CREON: I like not an evil wife for my son.
ANTIGONE: Haemon, beloved! How your father wrongs you!
CREON: Enough, enough of you and of your marriage!

LEADER OF THE CHORUS: Will you indeed rob your son of this maiden?
CREON: It is Death that shall stay these bridals for me.
LEADER: It is determined, it seems, that she shall die.
CREON: Determined, yes, for you and for me. (To the two attendants) Delay no longer, servants, take them within! Henceforth they must be women, and not range at large; for verily even the bold seek to fly, when they see Death now closing on their life.
   (Attendants exit, guarding ANTIGONE and ISMENE. CREON remains.)
CHORUS (singing): Blest are they whose days have not tasted of evil. For when a house has once been shaken from heaven, there the curse fails nevermore, passing from life to life of the race . . . Your power, O Zeus, what human trespass can limit? That power which neither Sleep, the all ensnaring, nor the untiring months of the gods can master; but you, a ruler to whom time brings not old age, dwellest in the dazzling splendor of Olympus. And through the future, near and far, as through the past, shall this law hold good: Nothing that is vast enters into the life of mortals without a curse. . . . For with wisdom has some one given forth the famous saying, that evil seems good, sooner or later, to him whose mind the god draws to mischief.
LEADER OF THE CHORUS: But lo, Haemon, the last of your sons. Does he come grieving for the doom of his promised bride, Antigone, and bitter for the baffled hope of his marriage?
   (Enter HAEMON)
CREON: We shall know soon, better than seers could tell us. My son, hearing the fixed doom of your betrothed, do you come in rage against your father? Or have I your good will, no matter how I act?
HAEMON: Father, I am yours; and you, in your wisdom, trace for me rules which I shall follow. No marriage shall be deemed by me a greater gain than your good guidance.
CREON: Yes, this, my son, should be your heart's fixed law, in all things to obey your father's will.

Do not, my son, at pleasure's beck, dethrone your reason for a woman's sake; knowing that this is a joy that soon grows cold in clasping arms, an evil woman to share your bed and your home. For what wound could strike deeper than a false friend? Nay, with loathing, and as if she were your enemy, let this girl go to find a husband in the house of Hades. For since I have caught her, alone of all the city, in open disobedience, I will not make myself a liar to my people I will slay her.

. . . Disobedience is the worst of evils. This it is that ruins cities; this makes homes desolate; by this, the ranks of allies are broken into headlong rout; but, of the lives whose course is fair, the greater part owes safety to obedience. Therefore we must support the cause of order, and in no wise suffer a woman to worst us. Better to fall from power, if we must, by a man's hand than to be called weaker than a woman.

LEADER: To us, unless our years have stolen our wit, you seem to say wisely what you say.

HAEMON: Father, the gods implant reason in men, the highest of all things that we call our own. Not mine the skill—far from me be the quest!—to say wherein you speak not aright; and yet another man, too, might have some useful thought. At least, it is my natural office to watch, on your behalf, all that men say, or do, or find to blame. For the dread of your frown forbids the citizen to speak such words as would offend yours ear; but they can hear these murmurs in the dark, these moanings of the city for this maiden; "no woman," they say, "ever merited her doom less, none ever was to die so shamefully for deeds so glorious as hers; who, when her own brother had fallen in bloody strife, would leave him unburied, to be devoured by carrion dogs, or by any bird: Does not she deserve the reward of golden honor?" Such is the darkling rumor that spreads in secret. For me, my father, no treasure is so precious as your welfare. What, indeed, is a nobler ornament for children than a prospering sire's fair fame, or for sire than son's? Wear not, then, one mood only in yourself; think not that your word, and yours alone, must be right. For if any man thinks that he alone is wise, that in speech, or in mind, he has no peer, such a soul, when laid open, is ever found empty. No, though a man be wise, it is no shame for him to learn many things, and to bend in season. Do you see, beside the wintry torrent's course, how the trees that yield to it save every twig, while the stiff necked perish root and branch? And even thus he who keeps the sheet of his sail taut, and never slackens it, upsets his boat, and finishes his voyage with keel uppermost. Give up your wrath; permit yourself to change.

LEADER: Sire, it is proper that you should profit by his words, if he speaks in season, and you, Haemon, by your father's; for on both parts there has been wise speech.

CREON: Men of my age, are we indeed to be schooled, then, by men of his?

HAEMON: In nothing that is not right; but if I am young, you should look to my merits, not to my years.

CREON: Is it a merit to honor the unruly?

HAEMON: I could wish no one to show respect for evildoers.

CREON: Then is she not tainted with that malady?

HAEMON: Our Theban folk, with one voice, deny it.

CREON: Shall Thebes prescribe to me how I must rule?

HAEMON: See, there you have spoken like a youth indeed.

CREON: Am I to rule this land by other judgment than my own?

HAEMON: That is no city which belongs to one man.

CREON: Is not the city held to be the ruler's?

HAEMON: You would make a good monarch of a desert.

CREON: This boy, it seems, is the woman's champion.

HAEMON: If you are a woman; indeed, my care is for you.

CREON: Shameless, at open feud with your father!

HAEMON: No, I see you offending against justice.

CREON: Do I offend, when I respect my own prerogatives?

HAEMON: You do not respect them, when you trample on the gods' honors.

CREON: O dastard nature, yielding place to woman!

HAEMON: You will never find me yielding to baseness.

CREON: All your words, at least, plead for that girl.

HAEMON: And for you, and for me, and for the gods below.

CREON: You can never marry her, on this side of the grave.

HAEMON: Then she must die, and in death destroy another.

CREON: How! does your boldness run to open threats?

HAEMON: What threat is it, to combat vain resolves?

CREON: You shall rue your witless teaching of wisdom.

HAEMON: Were you not my father, I would have called you unwise.

CREON: You woman's slave, don't use wheedling speech with me.

HAEMON: You would speak, and then hear no reply?

CREON: Say you so? Now, by the heaven above us, be sure of it, you shall smart for taunting me in this wicked manner. Bring forth that hated thing, that she may die forthwith in his presence—before his eyes at her bridegroom's side!

HAEMON: No, she shall not perish at my side—never; nor shall you ever again set eyes upon my face: rave, then, with such friends as can endure you.

(Exit HAEMON)

LEADER: The man is gone, O king; a youthful mind, when stung, is fierce.

CREON: Let him do, or dream, more than man—good speed to him!—But he shall not save these two girls from their doom.

LEADER: Do you indeed purpose to slay both?

CREON: Not her whose hands are pure: you say well.

LEADER: And by what doom do you intend to slay the other?

CREON: I will take her where the path is loneliest, and hide her, living, in a rocky vault, with so much food set forth as piety prescribes, that the city may avoid a public stain. And there, praying to Hades, the only god whom she worships, perchance she will obtain release from death; or else will learn, at last, though late, that it is lost labor to revere the dead.

(CREON goes into the palace.)

CHORUS (singing): Love, unconquered in the fight, Love, who makes havoc of wealth, who keeps your vigil on the soft cheek of a maiden; you roam over the sea, and among the homes of dwellers in the wilds; no immortal can escape you, nor any among men whose life is for a day; and he to whom you have come is mad. The just themselves have their minds warped by you to do wrong, for their ruin: It is you that have stirred up this present strife of kinsmen; victorious is the love-kindling light from the eyes of the fair bride; it is a power enthroned in sway beside the eternal laws; for there the goddess Aphrodite is working her unconquerable will.

(ANTIGONE is led into the palace by two of CREON'S attendants, who are about to conduct her to her doom.)

But now I also am carried beyond the bounds of loyalty, and can no more keep back the streaming tears, when I see Antigone thus passing to the bridal chamber where all are laid to rest.

A responsive chant between Antigone and the chorus follows, in which Antigone's terrible fate is described and placed in the context of mythological stories and the miseries of her family's incestuous history. The fact that she will never marry is prominent in her lament, and the chorus shows considerable ambivalence toward her. The chant ends thus:

CHORUS: Reverent action claims a certain praise for reverence; but an offence against power cannot be allowed by him who has power in his keeping. Your self-willed temper has brought your ruin.

ANTIGONE: Unmourned, friendless, without marriage song, I am led forth in my sorrow on this journey that can be delayed no more. No longer, unhappy one, may I behold yon daystar's sacred eye; but for my fate no tear is shed, no friend makes moan.

(CREON enters from the palace.)

CREON: Do you not know that songs and wailings before death would never cease, if it profited to utter them? Away with her, away! And when you have enclosed her, according to my word, in her vaulted grave, leave her alone, forlorn, whether she wishes to die, or to live a buried life in such a home. Our hands are clean as touching this maiden. But this is certain—she shall be deprived of her sojourn in the light.

ANTIGONE: . . . But I cherish good hope that my coming will be welcome to my father, and pleasant to you, my mother, and welcome, brother, to you; for, when you died, with my own hands I washed and dressed you, and poured drink offerings at your grave; and now, Polyneices, it is for tending your corpse that I win such recompense as this. And yet I honored you, as the wise will deem, rightly.

And now he leads me thus, a captive in his hands; no bridal bed, no bridal song has been mine, no joy of marriage, no portion in the nurture of children; but thus, forlorn of friends, unhappy one, I go, living, to the vaults of death. And what law of heaven have I transgressed? Why, hapless one, should I look to the gods anymore, what ally should I invoke, when by piety I have earned the name of impious? No, if these things are pleasing to the gods, when I have suffered my doom, I shall come to know my sin; but if the sin is with my judges, I could wish them no fuller measure of evil than they, on their part, wrongfully inflict on me.

The Chorus compares the fate of Antigone to various legends and myths, until Antigone is led away. Then the old blind Tiresias is led in by his guide. Tiresias is a seer (soothsayer, fortune teller) who uses various traditional methods for augury, or discerning the future, such as observing the flights of birds.

TEIRESIAS: Princes of Thebes, we have come with linked steps, both served by the eyes of one; for thus, by a guide's help, the blind must walk.

CREON: And what, aged Teiresias, are your tidings?

TEIRESIAS: I will tell you; and do you hearken to the seer.

CREON: Indeed, I have not been accustomed to ignore your counsel.

TEIRESIAS: Thus did you steer our city's course aright.

CREON: I have felt, and can attest, your benefits.

TEIRESIAS: Mark that now, once more, you stand on fate's fine edge.

CREON: What does this mean? How I shudder at your message!

TEIRESIAS: You will learn, when you hear the warnings of my art. As I took my place on my old seat of augury, where all birds have been wont to gather within my ken, I heard a strange voice among them; they were screaming with dire, feverish rage, that drowned their language in jargon; and I knew that they were rending each other with their talons, murderously; the whirr of wings told no doubtful tale. Forthwith, in fear, I essayed burnt sacrifice on a duly kindled altar: but from my offerings the Fire god showed no flame; a dank moisture, oozing from the thigh-flesh, trickled forth upon the embers, and smoked, and sputtered; the gall was scattered to the air; and the streaming thighs lay bared of the fat that had been wrapped round them. Such was the failure of the rites by which I vainly asked a sign, as I learned from this boy; for he is my guide, as I am guide to others. And it is your counsel that has brought this sickness on our State. For the altars of our city and of our hearths have been tainted, one and all, by birds and dogs, with carrion from the son, the hapless corpse, the son of Oedipus: and therefore the gods no more accept prayer and sacrifice at our hands, or the flame of meat-offering; nor does any bird give a clear sign by its shrill cry, for they have tasted the fatness of a slain man's blood. Think, then, on these things, my son. All men are liable to err; but when an error has been made, that man is no longer witless or unblest who heals the ill into which he has fallen, and remains not stubborn. Self-will, we know, incurs the charge of folly. Nay, allow the claim of the dead; stab not the fallen; what prowess is it to slay the slain anew? I have sought your good, and for your good I speak: and never is it sweeter to learn from a good counselor than when he counsels for your own gain.

CREON: Old man, you all shoot your shafts at me, as archers at the targets; You must needs practice on me with seer-craft also; aye, the seer-tribe has long trafficked in me, and made me their merchandise. Gain your gains, drive your trade, if you will, in the silver-gold of Sardis and the gold of India; but you shall not hide that man in the grave, no, though the eagles of Zeus should bear the carrion morsels to their Master's throne—no, not for dread of that defilement will I permit his burial: for well I know that no mortal can defile the gods. But, aged Teiresias, the wisest fall with shameful fall, when they clothe shameful thoughts in fair words, for money's sake.

TEIRESIAS: Alas! Does any man know, does any consider . . .

CREON: About what? What general truth do you announce?

TEIRESIAS: How precious, above all wealth, is good counsel.

CREON: As folly, I think, is the worst mischief.

TEIRESIAS: Yet you are tainted with that distemper.

CREON: I would not answer the seer with a taunt.

TEIRESIAS: But you do, in saying that I prophesy falsely.

CREON: Well, the prophet-tribe was ever fond of money.

TEIRESIAS: And the race bred of tyrants loves base gain.

CREON: Do you not realize that your speech is spoken of your king?

TEIRESIAS: I know it; for through me you have saved Thebes.

CREON: You are a wise seer; but you love evil deeds.

TEIRESIAS: You will rouse me to utter the dread secret in my soul.

CREON: Out with it! Only do not speak it for profit.

TEIRESIAS: Indeed, methinks, I shall not, as touching you.

CREON: Know that you shall not trade on my resolve.

TEIRESIAS: Then know you, yes, know it well, that you shall not live through many more courses of the sun's swift chariot, before one begotten of your own loins shall have been given by you, a corpse for corpses; because you have thrust children of the sunlight to the shades, and ruthlessly lodged a living soul in the grave. At the same time you keep in this world one who belongs to the gods below, a corpse unburied, unhonored, all unhallowed. In such a one you have no part, nor have the gods above, but this is a violence done to them by you. Therefore the avenging destroyers lie in wait for you, the Furies of Hades and of the gods, that you may be taken in these same ills. And mark well if I speak these things as a hireling. A time not long to be delayed shall awaken the wailing of men and of women in your house. And a tumult of hatred against you stirs all the cities whose mangled sons had the burial rite from dogs, or from wild beasts, or from some winged bird that bore a polluting breath to each city that contains the hearths of the dead.

Such arrows for your heart, since you provoke me, have I launched at you, archer-like, in my anger, sure arrows, which you shall not escape. Boy, lead me home, that he may spend his rage on younger men, and learn to keep a tongue more temperate, and to bear within his breast a better mind than now he bears.

(The Boy leads TEIRESIAS out.)

LEADER OF THE CHORUS: The man has gone, O King, with dread, awe-filled prophecies. And, since the hair on my head, once dark, has turned white, I have never known him to be a false prophet to our city.

CREON: I, too, know it well, and am troubled in soul. It is terrible to yield; but, by resistance, to smite my pride with ruin, this, too, is a dreadful choice.

LEADER: Son of Menoeceus, it is proper for you to take wise counsel.

CREON: What should I do, then? Speak and I will obey.

LEADER: Go, and free the maiden from her rocky chamber, and make a tomb for the unburied dead.

CREON: And this is your counsel? You would have me yield?

LEADER: Yes, King, and with all speed; for swift harms from the gods cut short the folly of men.

CREON: Ah, it is hard, but I resign my cherished resolve, I obey. We must not wage a vain war with destiny.

LEADER: Go, you, and do these things; leave them not to others.

CREON: I'll go just as I am. Go on, my servants, each and all of you, take axes in your hands, and cut to the ground what you see yonder! Since our judgment has taken this turn, I will be present to unloose her, as I myself bound her. In my heart I doubt my own actions, it is best to keep the established laws, even to life's end.

CREON and his servants exit on the spectators' left and the chorus joins in a hopeful chant. Then a messenger enters, bearing news of Haemon.

(Enter MESSENGER, on the spectators' left.)
MESSENGER: Dwellers by the house of Cadmus and of Amphion, there is no estate of mortal life that I would ever praise or blame as settled. Chance (*tuche*) raises and Chance humbles the lucky or unlucky from day to day, and no one can prophesy to men concerning those things which are established. For Creon was blest once, as I count bliss; he had saved this land of Cadmus from its foes; he was clothed with sole dominion in the land; he reigned, the glorious sire of princely children. And now all has been lost. For when a man has forfeited his pleasures, I count him not as living, I hold him but a breathing corpse. Heap up riches in your house, if you will; live in kingly state; yet, if there be no gladness

there, I would not give the shadow of a vapor for all the rest, compared with joy.

LEADER OF THE CHORUS: And what is this new grief that you have to tell for our princes?

MESSENGER: Death; and the living are guilty for the dead.

LEADER: And who is the slayer? Who the stricken? Speak.

MESSENGER: Haemon has perished; his blood has been shed by no stranger.

LEADER: By his father's hand, or by his own?

MESSENGER: By his own, in anger at his father for the murder.

LEADER: O prophet, how true, then, have you proved your word!

MESSENGER: These things stand thus; you must consider the rest.

LEADER: Lo, I see unhappy Eurydice, Creon's wife, approaching; she comes from the house by chance, perhaps, or because she knows the tidings of her son.

(Enter EURYDICE from the palace.)
EURYDICE: People of Thebes, I heard your words as I was going forth, to salute the goddess Pallas with my prayers. Even as I was loosing the fastenings of the gate, to open it, the message of a household woe smote on my ear: I sank back, terror stricken, into the arms of my handmaids, and my senses fled. But say again what the tidings were; I shall hear them as one who is no stranger to sorrow.

MESSENGER: Dear lady, I will witness of what I saw, and will leave no word of the truth untold. Why, indeed, should I soothe you with words which must presently be found false? Truth is ever best. I attended your lord as his guide to the furthest part of the plain, where the body of Polyneices, torn by dogs, still lay unpitied. We prayed the goddess of the roads, and Pluto, in mercy to restrain their wrath; we washed the dead with holy washing; and with freshly plucked boughs we solemnly burned such relics as there were. We raised a high mound of his native earth; and then we turned away to enter the maiden's nuptial chamber with rocky couch, the caverned mansion of the bride of Death. And, from afar off, one of us heard a voice of loud wailing at that bride's unhallowed bower; and came to tell our master Creon. And as the king drew nearer, doubtful sounds of a bitter cry floated around him; he groaned, and said in accents of anguish, "Wretched that I am, can my foreboding be true? Am I going on the most woeful way that ever I went? My son's voice greets me. Go, my servants, and when you have reached the tomb, pass through the gap, where the stones have been wrenched away, to the cell's very mouth, and look. and see if it is Haemon's voice that I know, or if my ear is cheated by the gods." This search, at our despairing master's word, we went to make; and in the furthest part of the tomb we saw her hanging by the neck, slung by a thread-wrought halter of fine linen: while he was embracing her with arms thrown around her waist, bewailing the loss of his bride who is with the dead, and his father's deeds, and his own ill-starred love. But his father, when he saw him, cried aloud with a dread cry and went in, and called to him with a voice of wailing: "Unhappy one, what deed have you done! What thought has come to you? What manner of mischance has marred your reason? Come forth, my child! I pray you! I implore you!" But the boy glared at him with fierce eyes, spat in his face, and, without a word of answer, drew his crosshilted sword: as his father rushed forth in flight, he missed his aim; then, wroth with himself, he straightway leaned with all his weight against his sword, and drove it, half its length, into his side; and, while sense lingered, he clasped the maiden to his faint embrace, and, as he gasped, sent forth on her pale cheek the swift stream of the oozing blood. Corpse enfolding corpse he lies; he has won his nuptial rites, poor youth, not here, yet in the halls of Death; and he has witnessed to mankind that, of all curses which cleave to man, ill counsel is the sovereign curse.

(EURYDICE retires into the house.)
LEADER: What would you foretell from this? The lady has turned back, and is gone, without a word, good or evil.

MESSENGER: I, too, am startled; yet I nourish the hope that, at these painful tidings of her son, she cannot bear to show her sorrow openly, but in the privacy of the house will set her handmaids to mourn the household grief. For she is not untaught of discretion, that she should err.
LEADER: I know not; but to me, at least, a strained silence seems to foretell peril, no less than vain abundance of lament.
MESSENGER: Well, I will enter the house, and learn whether indeed she is not hiding some repressed purpose in the depths of a passionate heart. You say well: excess of silence, too, may have a perilous meaning.

(The MESSENGER goes into the palace. Enter CREON, on the spectators' left, with attendants, carrying the shrouded body of HAEMON on a bier. The following lines between CREON and the CHORUS are chanted responsively.)
CHORUS: Behold, yonder the king himself draws near, bearing that which tells too clear a tale, the work of no stranger's madness, if we may say it, but of his own misdeeds.
CREON: Woe for the sins of a darkened soul, stubborn sins, fraught with death! Ah, you behold us, the sire who has slain, the son who has perished! Woe is me, for the wretched blindness of my counsels! Oh my son, you have died in your youth, by a timeless doom, woe is me!—your spirit has fled,—not by your folly, but by mine!
CHORUS: Oh, how all too late you seem to see the right!
CREON: Ah me, I have learned the bitter lesson! But then, I think, oh then, some god smote me from above with crushing weight, and hurled me into ways of cruelty, woe is me, overthrowing and trampling on my joy! Woe, woe, for the troubled toils of men!

(Enter MESSENGER from the house.)
MESSENGER: Sire, you have come, I think, as one whose hands are not empty, but who has store laid up besides; you bear yonder burden with you, and you are soon to look upon the woes within your house.
CREON: And what worse ill is yet to follow upon ills?

MESSENGER: Your queen has died, true mother of that corpse, ah, poor lady, by blows newly dealt.

CREON: Oh Hades, whom no sacrifice can appease! Have you, then, no mercy for me? O you herald of evil, bitter tidings, what word do you utter? Alas, I was already as dead, and you have smitten me again! What say you, my son? What is this new message that you bring, woe, woe is me! Of a wife's doom, of slaughter headed on slaughter?

CHORUS: You can behold: It is no longer hidden within.

(*The doors of the palace are opened, and the corpse of EURYDICE is disclosed.*)

CREON: Ah me, yonder I behold a new, a second woe! What destiny can yet await me? I have but now raised my son in my arms, and there, again, I see a corpse before me! Oh weep, weep, for the unhappy mother! Weep for my child!

MESSENGER: There, at the altar, self-stabbed with a keen knife, she allowed her darkening eyes to close, when she had wailed for the noble fate of Megareus who died before, and then for his fate who lies there, and when, with her last breath, she had invoked evil fortunes upon you, the slayer of your sons.

CREON: Woe, woe! I thrill with dread. Is there none to strike me to the heart with two-edged sword? O miserable that I am, and steeped in miserable anguish!

MESSENGER: Yes, both this son's doom, and that other's, were laid to your charge by her whose corpse you see.

CREON: And what was the manner of the violent deed by which she passed away?

MESSENGER: Her own hand struck her to the heart, when she had learned her son's sorely lamented fate.

CREON: Ah me, this guilt can never be fixed on any other of mortal kind for my acquittal! I, even I, was your slayer, wretched that I am I own the truth. Lead me away, O my servants, lead me hence with all speed, whose life is but as death!

CHORUS: Your counsels are good, if there can be good with ills; briefest is best, when trouble is in our path.

CREON: Oh, let it come, let it appear, that fairest of fates for me, that brings my last day, aye, best fate of all! Oh, let it come, that I may never look upon tomorrow's light.

CHORUS: These things are in the future; present tasks claim our care: the ordering of the future rests where it should rest.

CREON: All my desires, at least, were summed in that prayer.

CHORUS: Pray you no more; for mortals have no escape from destined woe.

(*As CREON is being conducted into the palace, the LEADER OF THE CHORUS speaks the closing verses.*)

LEADER: Wisdom is the supreme part of happiness*; and reverence towards the gods must be inviolate. Great words of prideful men are ever punished with great blows, and, in old age, teach the chastened to be wise.

THE END

There are many ways to read this play. It may evoke feminist concerns or reflections on the nature of sex and family. Freudian psychologists and Hegelian philosophers have had quite a bit to say about this play. The themes that are of particular relevance to our concerns in this chapter, and to themes in subsequent chapters, include the following.

1. The law of the community must be honored, or chaos will result. Moreover duties to one's family must also be fulfilled. Creon confidently states: "He who does his duty in his own household will be found righteous in the State also." Thus Creon supposes that there need be no deep conflicts between the laws of the state, duties to family, and duty to God or the Gods. He has an optimistic view of harmony among our ethical obligations.

*2. *Do you believe that deep and serious conflicts between duties are possible? For example, might you have a duty to care for your own*

---

*The Greek word for "happiness" here is very central for ancient ethics. It is *eudaimonia*, a term that signifies a good life overall, rather than transitory feelings. The idea that wisdom is necessary for *eudaimonia* is developed at great length by Plato, Aristotle and others.

child that would conflict with a duty to help an unfortunate child who is not your own? Give examples in your answer.

2. Antigone, on the other hand, easily supposes that divine law can override civil law and that obligations to the family can conflict with positive laws or edicts of the state. She supposes that these conflicts necessarily disrupt life. She is much less of an optimist about harmony than is Creon. Antigone does not tell us how she knows what the divine law requires or whether the God or Gods could change that law.

*3. Do you ever think that you should do something because it is required by God? Would such a requirement override all others? Is there some way you can be sure about what God requires?

Both 1 and 2 bring to mind a saying of the philosopher Heraclitus (540–480 BCE), a predecessor of Sophocles: "One must fight for the law as for the city wall." Heraclitus supposed that the law of the community was enormously important. At the same time it is evident from other sayings of his that he thought the laws of a particular community could sometimes be foolish. Antigone and Creon are initially simpleminded, or at any rate insist on seeing things in an oversimplified way. They can only see one side of the dispute. Antigone is like some youthful protestor who is very confident of having an inside track to ultimate, even divine, wisdom, which trumps mere human law. Creon is equally confident of his position, in which the laws of the particular community trump all individual insight or conscience. Many philosophers and others have taken one side or the other in this age-old dispute, and many have tried to work out mediating positions, as we shall see.

3. Human beings are portrayed by Sophocles as torn by very powerful passions that lead to bad judgment. One of the most notable is love, understood as erotic desire. But the love Antigone feels extends to family in general, including her brother. The chorus proclaims,

> Love, unconquered in the fight, Love, who makes havoc of wealth, who keeps your vigil on the soft cheek of a maiden; you roam over the sea, and

among the homes of dwellers in the wilds; no immortal can escape you, nor any among men whose life is for a day; and he to whom you have come is mad. The just themselves have their minds warped by you to do wrong, for their ruin: It is you that have stirred up this present strife of kinsmen; victorious is the love-kindling light from the eyes of the fair bride; it is a power enthroned in sway beside the eternal laws; for there the goddess Aphrodite is working her unconquerable will.

4. Can "love" make you do crazy things? Could it make you do something vicious or cruel?

4. Human life is complex and baffling. It is *deinos*, terrible, awe inspiring, uncanny. Humans are unlike anything else in nature, and they exercise great power over nature. This is both a blessing and a curse. It brings with it the possibility of great suffering. The chorus claims,

> Nothing that is vast enters into the life of mortals without a curse.

5. What do you make of the last quote?

5. There appears to be confidence in reason to solve dilemmas, but at the same time the reasonable result is seldom within the grasp of a single mind. Those who insist on those limits may insist on the need for "counsel." Haemon declares,

> Father, the gods implant reason in men, the highest of all things that we call our own. Wear not, then, one mood only in yourself; think not that your word, and yours alone, must be right.

Later, when he finds his father unbending, Haemon declares,

> You would make a good monarch of a desert.

In these comments we see the conflict between more democratic and more autocratic ideals of government as well as a dispute about the nature of reason and its exercise in relation to the state and to conduct generally.

6. Does being reasonable require a willingness to consult with other people? Aren't "other people" sometimes foolish?

6. There does not seem to be any correspondence between service to God and reward or recognition from God. Antigone says,

> And what law of heaven have I transgressed?
> Why, unfortunate, should I look to the gods
> anymore, what ally should I invoke, when by piety
> I have earned the name of impious?

Socrates, whose ideas are explored briefly next in this chapter, was condemned to death for "impiety" partly as the result of exercising a certain *kind* of piety. There have been many other such cases.

7. There is a pervading sense that even those who do their best and act nobly may be subject to forces over which they have little or no control. They may be the victims of divine fate or simply of bad luck. The result will be that their lives will be unhappy in the long run. They will fail in the struggle to achieve what the Greeks call *eudaimonia*, the best kind of life. The Chorus proclaims,

> For Creon was blest once, as I count bliss; he had saved this land of Cadmus from its foes; he was clothed with sole dominion in the land; he reigned, the glorious sire of princely children. And now all has been lost. For when a man has forfeited his pleasures, I count him not as living, I hold him but a breathing corpse. Heap up riches in your house, if you will; live in kingly state; yet, if there be no gladness therewith, I would not give the shadow of a vapor for all the rest, compared with joy.

Later it is said:

> Dwellers by the house of Cadmus and of Amphion, there is no estate of mortal life that I would ever praise or blame as settled. Chance (*tuche*) raises and Chance humbles the lucky or unlucky from day to day.

> *7. You may have discussed the issues raised here in a general way in connection with Orienting Question 3. Does the fate of Antigone and Creon in this play result entirely from their own actions, or does luck play a role? Cite relevant text.*

Every one of the themes mentioned will surface repeatedly in the stories and reflections that follow throughout this book. Keep an eye out for them, and note them as you go along. They certainly are center stage in the concerns of Plato.

SOCRATES

Socrates (469–399 BC), an Athenian Greek, wrote no philosophical works but had a major influence on the history of philosophy. He was concerned exclusively with ethics and the conduct of life, topics he discussed publicly with prominent Athenians both young and old. He attracted many followers, among them Plato, who wrote dialogues in which he recalled Socrates' teachings and personality. The extent to which Plato makes Socrates a spokesman for his own ideas is still debated, but the view that Plato's early dialogues reflect Socrates' own thinking has long been popular. Socrates was prosecuted for corrupting the youth and for impiety, was convicted and executed. His association with the brilliant but traitorous Alcibiades and the tyrant Critias no doubt had something to do with his conviction, even though he could hardly be blamed for the faults of those men.

Socrates is usually portrayed in Plato's dialogues as a questioner who does not propose views of his own on ethical issues. However, in the *Apology* he does express some definite views on what is required for a worthy life. This dialogue includes a description of Socrates' trial and his "defense" (that is what *apology* means here) against various charges.

Apology

The most important charges against Socrates were brought by Meletus and Anytus, who accused him of corrupting the youth and denying the Gods and bringing in religious innovations. Socrates' defense includes the following claims about how any worthy person should live and act.

WHAT IS AND IS NOT TRULY HARMFUL AND TRULY FEARFUL

Men of Athens, do not interrupt, but hear me; there was an agreement between us that you should hear me out. And I think that what I am going to say will do you good: for I have something more to say, at which you may be inclined to cry out; but I beg that you will not do this. I would have you know that, if you kill such a one as I am, you will injure yourselves more than you will injure me. Meletus and Anytus will not injure me: they cannot; for it is not in the nature of things that a bad man should injure a better than himself. I do not deny that he may, perhaps, kill him, or drive him into exile, or deprive him of civil rights; and he may imagine, and others may imagine, that he is doing him a great injury: but in that I do not agree with him; for the evil of doing as Anytus is doing—of unjustly taking away another man's life—is greater far.

8. *What does Socrates think constitutes real injury?*

Socrates explains his behavior (going about questioning people) in terms of something like a divine call. He also argues that he has never taken public office because he does not believe that a person can be honest and also be in politics! His accusers are of course unmoved, and he is found guilty by a majority of the jury (consisting of 500 Athenian men). Socrates goes on to argue that he should be penalized by being given a pension by the state! The penalty proposed, however, is death.

And so he proposes death as the penalty. And what shall I propose on my part, O men of Athens? Clearly that which is my due. And what is that which I ought to pay or to receive? What shall be done to the man who has never had the wit to be idle during his whole life; but has been unconcerned about what the many care about—wealth, and family interests, and military offices, and speaking in the assembly, and magistracies, and plots, and parties. Reflecting that I was really too honest a man to follow in this way and live, I did not go where I could do no good to you or to myself; but where I could do the greatest good privately to every one of you, thither I went, and sought to persuade every man among you that he must look to himself, and seek virtue and wisdom before he looks to his private interests, and look to the state before he looks to the interests of the state;

and that this should be the order which he observes in all his actions. What shall be done to such a one? Doubtless some good thing, O men of Athens, if he has his reward; and the good should be of a kind suitable to him. What would be a reward suitable to a poor man who is your benefactor, who desires leisure that he may instruct you? There can be no more fitting reward than maintenance in the Prytaneum, O men of Athens, a reward which he deserves far more than the citizen who has won the prize at Olympia in the horse or chariot race, whether the chariots were drawn by two horses or by many. For I am in want, and he has enough; and he only gives you the appearance of happiness, and I give you the reality. And if I am to estimate the penalty justly, I say that maintenance in the Prytaneum is the just return.

Perhaps you may think that I am braving you in saying this, as in what I said before about the tears and prayers. But that is not the case. I speak rather because I am convinced that I never intentionally wronged anyone, although I cannot convince you of that—for we have had a short conversation only; but if there were a law at Athens, such as there is in other cities, that a capital cause should not be decided in one day, then I believe that I should have convinced you; but now the time is too short. I cannot in a moment refute great slanders; and, as I am convinced that I never wronged another, I will assuredly not wrong myself. I will not say of myself that I deserve any evil, or propose any penalty. Why should I? Because I am afraid of the penalty of death which Meletus proposes? When I do not know whether death is a good or an evil, why should I propose a penalty which would certainly be an evil? Shall I say imprisonment? And why should I live in prison, and be the slave of the magistrates of the year—of the Eleven? Or shall the penalty be a fine, and imprisonment until the fine is paid? There is the same objection. I should have to lie in prison, for money I have none, and I cannot pay. And if I say exile (and this may possibly be the penalty which you will affix), I must indeed be blinded by the love of life if I were to consider that when you, who are my own citizens, cannot endure my discourses and words, and have found them so grievous and odious that you would gladly have done with them, others are likely to endure me. No, indeed, men of Athens, that is not very likely. And what a life should I lead, at my age, wandering from city to city, living in ever-changing exile, and always being driven out! For I am quite sure that into whatever place I go, as here so also there, the young men will come to me; and if I drive them away, their elders will drive me out at their desire: and if I let them come, their fathers and friends will drive me out for their sakes.

Someone will say: Yes, Socrates, but cannot you hold your tongue, and then you may go into a foreign city, and no one will interfere with you? Now I have great difficulty in making you understand my answer to this. For if I tell you that this would be a disobedience to a divine command, and therefore that I cannot hold my tongue, you will not believe that I am serious; and if I say again that the greatest good of man is daily to converse about virtue, and all that concerning which you hear me examining myself and others, and that the life which is unexamined is not worth living—that you are still less likely to believe.

Here are two things that Socrates strongly affirms:

A good man cannot be harmed.
The unexamined life is not worth living.

9. *What does Socrates mean by the first of these?*
10. *What kind of examination of life does Socrates have in mind? Psychological examination? Moral examination?*

Socrates was sentenced to death and imprisoned. When the day of execution arrived, some of his friends and followers gathered round him for final conversations and then watched as he administered to himself the poison used in executions. The death scene is impressively described in Plato's dialogues *Crito* and *Phaedo*. The latter dialogue concludes with these words:

Then holding the cup to his lips, quite readily and cheerfully he drank off the poison. And hitherto most of us had been able to control our sorrow; but

now when we saw him drinking, and saw too that he had finished the draught, we could no longer forbear, and in spite of myself my own tears were flowing fast, so that I covered my face and wept over myself, for certainly I was not weeping over him, but at the thought of my own calamity in having lost such a companion. Nor was I the first, for Crito, when he found himself unable to restrain his tears, had got up and moved away, and I followed. And at that moment, Apollodorus, who had been weeping all the time, broke out in a loud cry which made cowards of us all. Socrates alone retained his calmness: What is this strange outcry? he said. I sent away the women mainly in order that they might not offend in this way, for I have heard that a man should die in peace. Be quiet, then, and have patience. When we heard that, we were ashamed, and refrained our tears. He walked about until, as he said, his legs began to fail, and then he lay on his back, according to the directions, and the man who gave him the poison looked at his feet and legs now and then; and after a while he pressed his foot hard and asked him if he could feel; and he said, no; and then his leg, and so upwards and upwards, and showed us that he was cold and stiff. And he felt them himself, and said: When the poison reaches the heart, that will be the end. He was beginning to grow cold about the groin, when he uncovered his face, for he had covered himself up, and said (they were his last words)—he said: Crito, I owe a cock to Asclepius; will you remember to pay the debt? The debt shall be paid, said Crito; is there anything else? There was no answer to this question, but in a minute or two a movement was heard, and the attendants uncovered him. His eyes were set, and Crito closed his eyes and mouth. Such was the end, Echecrates, of our friend, whom I may truly call the wisest, and justest, and best of all the men whom I have ever known.

It is worth noting that Socrates' last words were a request that a religious ritual be performed, the offering of a cock to the God Asclepius. Asclepius was the God of healing and was even credited with raising a man from the dead. Socrates' participation in the cult of Asclepius is striking in view of the fact that he was condemned for impiety!

PLATO

Plato (427–347 BC) was an Athenian Greek of aristocratic family, the author of brilliant "dialogues," in most of which Socrates is the dominating character. Some of his earliest dialogues defend Socrates and his philosophical mission against the foolish prejudices and envy that—in the view of his friends—had brought about Socrates' death. Several of the dialogues pit Socrates against sophists, such as Protagoras, or supposed experts on religion, such as Euthyphro.

Later dialogues develop powerful philosophical theories in ethics, the philosophy of language, political philosophy, metaphysics (theories about ultimate reality) and theory of knowledge. In some of these dialogues Plato presents very powerful criticisms of his own views, which is a testimony to his intellectual honesty. Plato's thinking in all of these areas has been extraordinarily influential.

The Good Life and Reason

Plato was particularly concerned to find a single rational solution to the quest for the good life. Of the seven themes in *Antigone*, which were set out earlier, pay attention to number 6 in particular as you study Plato's views. During part of his career Plato thought that a good community should get rid of the "poets" (meaning primarily dramatists like Sophocles). For the poets, as we have seen, portray life as complex, not fully rational, beset by passions that can overcome reason and by a fate that is inscrutable. Moreover, they often suggest or imply that there is not always a best way to act, that some situations are "tragic," in the sense that, no matter how we act, we will be filled with regrets. As a result Sophocles implies that even the wisest persons may have a kind of sadness, as does the seer Teiresias.

Plato wants to reject such a tragic vision of life. He wants to show that reason at its best ensures a good life. He is certainly aware, however, that questions about how to live, how to conduct ourselves, generate conflict in a way that questions about theoretical science, or even some practical matters, do not.

Euthyphro (tr. B. Jowett)

In these short excerpts from the early dialogue *Euthyphro*, Socrates is questioning Euthyphro, a young man who is prosecuting his own father in the courts. Euthyphro defends his action by claiming that it is "pious" or "holy," that is, approved by the Gods. Socrates examines Euthyphro's reasoning and shows that he is a pretentious fool. In the course of their discussion Socrates questions him about the sorts of disagreements that create conflict between people.

[SOCRATES:] And what sort of difference creates enmity and anger? Suppose, for example, that you and I, my good friend, differ about a number; do differences of this sort make us enemies and set us at variance with one another? Do we not go at once to arithmetic, and put an end to them by calculating?

[EUTHYPHRO:] True.

[SOCRATES:] Or suppose that we differ about magnitudes, do we not quickly end the differences by measuring?

[EUTHYPHRO:] Very true.

[SOCRATES:] And we end a controversy about heavy and light by resorting to a weighing machine?

[EUTHYPHRO:] To be sure.

[SOCRATES:] But what differences are there which cannot be thus decided, and which therefore make us angry and set us at enmity with one another? I dare say the answer does not occur to you at the moment, and therefore I will suggest that these enmities arise when the matters of difference are the just and unjust, good and evil, honorable and dishonorable. Are not these the points about which men differ, and about which, when we are unable satisfactorily to decide our differences, you and I and all of us quarrel, when we do quarrel?

[EUTHYPHRO:] Yes, Socrates, the nature of the differences about which we quarrel is such as you describe.

Socrates is here pointing out a feature of what we would call *moral disagreement*, namely, that there seems to be no generally agreed-on way of settling such disagreement. On the other hand, on many factual matters there are such agreed-on ways.

> 11. *Give an example of a moral disagreement. Give an example of a factual disagreement, and show how it could be resolved to everyone's satisfaction. If you cannot think how to answer this, look at Socrates' examples, given earlier.*

This feature of moral disagreements, namely, that there seems to be no agreement on methods for resolving them, has troubled philosophers for millennia. It supports skeptical views about ethics, as Midgley pointed out in Chapter 1. It has led some to claim that moral opinions do not bear on any facts at all but are mere expressions of personal taste! (I like chocolate, you like vanilla. What is there to argue about?)

> *12. *Try to think of an example of a moral disagreement that could* not *be just a matter of taste. Argue.*

Protagoras

In the *Protagoras* Socrates is debating with the sophist Protagoras (see Chapter 1) about the objective truth of justice and morality generally. Socrates attempts to show that there is a single method that can be used to arrive at agreement on right and wrong. By following this method a reasonable person can avoid tragic dilemmas and moral conflict. Clearly Sophocles would have been very surprised to learn that there could be such a method. Judging by the discussion in the *Euthyphro,* one might expect that Socrates would have been surprised also. Yet it is Socrates that speaks here.

Another question treated in this dialogue is this: Does a person every *knowingly* do evil? That is a question that Plato continues to treat in later dialogues.

The first issue (the objective nature of moral truth) is also treated in later dialogues, but in a very different way. Probably the way explored here is simply an experiment, not a view that Plato (or Socrates) ever held.

The Good and Calculation of Pleasure/Pain (tr. Benjamin Jowett)

Socrates: "And do you not pursue pleasure as a good, and avoid pain as evil?" He assented, "Then you think that pain is an evil and pleasure is a good: and even pleasure you deem an evil, when it robs you of greater pleasures than it gives, or causes pains greater than the pleasure. If, however, you call pleasure an evil in relation to some other end or standard, you will be able to show us that standard. But you have none to show."

I do not think that they have, said Protagoras.

"And have you not a similar way of speaking about pain? You call pain a good when it takes away greater pains than those which it has, or gives pleasures greater than the pains: then if you have some standard other than pleasure and pain to which you refer when you call actual pain a good, you can show what that is. But you cannot."

True, said Protagoras.

Suppose again, I said, that the world says to me: "Why do you spend many words and speak in many ways on this subject?" Excuse me, friends, I should reply; but in the first place there is a difficulty in explaining the meaning of the expression "overcome by pleasure"; and the whole argument turns upon this. And even now, if you see any possible way in which evil can be explained as other than pain, or good as other than pleasure, you may still retract. Are you satisfied, then, at having a life of pleasure which is without pain? If you are, and if you are unable to show any good or evil which does not end in pleasure and pain, hear the consequences: If what you say is true, then the argument is absurd which affirms that a man often does evil knowingly, when he might abstain, because he is seduced and overpowered by pleasure; or again, when you say that a man knowingly refuses to do what is good because he is overcome at the moment by pleasure. And that this is ridiculous will be evident if only we give up the use of various names, such as pleasant and painful, and good and evil. As there are two things, let us call them by two names: first, good and evil, and then pleasant and painful. Assuming this, let us go on to say that a man does evil knowing that he does evil.

But someone will ask, Why? Because he is overcome, is the first answer. "And by what is he overcome?" the enquirer will proceed to ask. And we shall not be able to reply, "By pleasure," for the name of pleasure has been exchanged for that of good.

13. *Fill in the blank: Suppose that*
    i. *a man does evil knowing he does evil.*
    ii. *the reason for i is that he is overcome by pleasure*
    iii. *pleasure is the good, pain is (the) evil.*
    iv. *It follows that a man who does evil knowing he does evil does so because he is overcome by pleasure (ii) and thus he does evil because he is overcome by the _____ (iii)*

If you fill in the blank correctly, you end up with something, iv, that is pretty silly. But iv *follows from* i–iii. If i–iii are true, iv *must* be true. *So* there must be something wrong with one or more of i–iii. Socrates thinks i is the culprit. It can't be the case that people do evil knowing that they do evil.

In our answer, then, we shall only say that he is overcome. "By what?" he will reiterate. By the good, we shall have to reply; indeed we shall. Nay, but our questioner will rejoin with a laugh, if he be one of the swaggering sort, "That is too ridiculous, that a man should do what he knows to be evil when he ought not, because he is overcome by good. Is that," he will ask, "because the good was worthy or not worthy of conquering the evil?" And in answer to that we shall clearly reply, "Because it was not worthy; for if it had been worthy, then he who, as we say, was overcome by pleasure, would not have been wrong. "But how," he will reply, "can the good be unworthy of the evil, or the evil of the good?" Is not the real explanation that they are out of proportion to one another, either as greater and smaller, or more and fewer? This we cannot deny. And when you speak of being overcome, "What do you mean," he will say, "but that you choose the greater evil in exchange for the lesser good?" Admitted. And now substitute the names of pleasure and pain for good and evil, and say, not as before, that a man does what is evil knowingly, but that he does what is painful

knowingly, and because he is overcome by pleasure, which is unworthy to overcome. What measure is there of the relations of pleasure to pain other than excess and defect, which means that they become greater and smaller, and more and fewer, and differ in degree? For if any one says: "Yes, Socrates, but immediate pleasure differs widely from future pleasure and pain" To that I should reply: And do they differ in anything but in pleasure and pain? There can be no other measure of them. And do you, like a skillful weigher, put into the balance the pleasures and the pains, and their nearness and distance, and weigh them, and then say which outweighs the other. If you weigh pleasures against pleasures, you of course take the more and greater; or if you weigh pains against pains, you take the fewer and the less; or if pleasures against pains, then you choose that course of action in which the painful is exceeded by the pleasant, whether the distant by the near or the near by the distant; and you avoid that course of action in which the pleasant is exceeded by the painful. Would you not admit, my friends, that this is true? I am confident that they cannot deny this.

Socrates is proposing a solution to several problems here. First, he is trying to provide a single "measure" on which all can agree, that will make the resolution of moral disagreements possible. He is thus trying to show a way to answer the first main question raised in the passages from the *Euthyphro* quoted earlier.

Secondly, he is doing this by equating what is good with the result of a correct weighing up of pleasures and pains, so as to get the best overall balance between them. Thus he explicitly takes up a way of solving moral differences that he had rejected in the *Euthyphro*, for there he had *contrasted* moral disagreements with disagreements over quantitative properties (whether pleasures can indeed be treated quantitatively is of course debatable). The idea that there might be such a single "measure" is prophetic (see later)

14. *Fill in the blanks:*
    i. *Pleasures and pains come in degrees or amounts or different "weights."*

ii. *A pleasure that is immediately available (or "nearer") often seems to be greater in _____ than one that is "farther away."*

iii. *A man will mistakenly do evil (do evil without knowing he is doing evil) if he thinks that a certain pleasure "weighs more" than it actually does, which he might do if that pleasure is, or seems to be, _____.*

iv. *Therefore one must be sure to weigh pleasures properly in order to avoid doing _____.*

Third, he is trying to show that the kind of rationality he is describing could never properly be said to be overcome by pleasure (or pain). If you look at the argument you just filled out, you will see that a truly rational person, that is, one who weighs things properly, will not do evil, since evil simply *is* a failure to weigh or measure pleasures and pains properly. We do evil when we pursue some pleasure because we think it is more valuable, or "weighs more," than it really is or does. Evil results from a kind of stupidity and irrationality or, at the very least, inattentiveness. If our arithmetic were not so bad, we would be morally good people!

It follows, doesn't it, that the Sophoclean claim made in *Antigone* that love, for example, can overcome *reason* is false? A perfectly rational person *could* not be overcome by love; only a person who is ignorant and irrational can be "pushed around" by love. Socrates expands on these points in what follows.

Socrates pictures the man who does evil as *ignorant*. Ignorant of what? Ignorant of how much "weight to give" to various pleasures and pains. Suppose, for example, that I give great weight to the pleasures of sex. The problem is not that sexual pleasure is not a good, since all pleasure is good. The problem is that I might make a mistake in "weighing" it. Just as I can be mistaken in thinking that *x* is larger than *y* because *x* is closer, so I can be mistaken in thinking *x* is more pleasant than *y* because of its immediate availability, or the seeming remoteness of *y*, or for many other bad reasons.

Socrates makes it sound as though any pleasure (pain) can be assigned a unit value. To simplify, suppose sexual pleasure with a spouse gets three units. Suppose sex with an office mate gets four units. And suppose the pleasures of family stability get five units. If I stick to sex with a spouse, I might end up with eight units. But I may opt for sex with the office mate because she or he is "nearer" or readily available more of the time, or because I have lost sight of, or assigned too low a unit value to, family stability. I am not mistaken about what things are pleasant. The mistake arises when I don't pay attention to all relevant values or make a mistake in assignment of unit value or am simply lousy at addition.

15. *Do you think that all pleasures can be "weighed on the same scale," so to speak? Can you compare the pleasure of enjoying a hot fudge sundae and the pleasure of a good conversation with a friend, so that one of these gets, say, ten units and the other six units? Can they be compared that way?*

If you answered "yes" to the last question, then you think that all pleasures are "commensurable." "Co-measurable" so to speak. If you said "no," then you think pleasures can be incommensurable. Make sure you are able to define these terms.

*16. *If some pleasures are incommensurable, then even if we agree that all pleasures are good, we might still be unable to resolve a moral dispute or dilemma in the way Socrates suggests. Explain why, using an example.*

On the view argued for in the *Protagoras,* the fully rational person, who is also the person with real knowledge, will not be subject to any tragic dilemmas, such as the dilemma posed by Sophocles' *Antigone.* He will always be able to give an answer to any question about how to behave or about what is right or just. His answer will be as precise as an answer to questions about how much something weighs or how much a column of numbers adds up to. He has, so to speak, a single unambiguous scale for weighing or measuring alternative courses of action.

17. *Judging by* Antigone, *how would Sophocles respond to Socrates?*

The view attributed to Socrates in this dialogue is very similar to that taken by a later Greek, Epicurus, and by Jeremy Bentham and J. S. Mill, whose views we will examine later (Chapter 9). Notice that it is a fundamentally optimistic position, one that rejects the inevitability of tragic conflicts in life.

The Republic (tr. Benjamin Jowett)

In Plato's most famous dialogue, the *Republic* (tr. Benjamin Jowett in the following selections), he attempts to show that reason can discover what the true good is and follow it. But Plato has something quite different in mind from that expressed in the *Protagoras*. He thinks of reason as something other than a faculty for calculating the balance of pleasures and pains. Rather, reason is understood as a faculty that can grasp a truth, such as what true justice is, by reaching beyond this life to something permanent. That would be something that is above all human feelings, pleasures or pains and every normal "worldly" idea of what could count as happiness. True justice, for example, is beyond this life, or is something "transcendent." Plato calls true justice, or "justice itself," the *form* of justice. Forms do not exist in this world with its various pleasures and pains. Thus Plato completely rejects the idea that the good might be based on calculations of pleasure and pain.

In the following selections from the *Republic*, Plato tries to illustrate the great difficulty of arriving at any knowledge of such a transcendent good. He compares the process of coming to such knowledge to escaping from a cave. The cave symbolizes the ignorance that traps people generally and keeps them "in the dark" about the most important matters. In this dialogue Socrates is conversing with a friend, Glaucon, and with the sophist Thrasymachus. Glaucon sometimes takes the position of Thrasymachus for the sake of argument.

Book VII: The Allegory of the Cave; the Struggle for Knowledge of the Good

[SOCRATES:] And now, let me show in a figure how far our nature is enlightened or unenlightened:—Behold! human beings living in a underground den, which has a mouth open towards the light and reaching all along the den; here they have been from their childhood, and have their legs and necks chained so that they cannot move, and can only see before them, being prevented by the chains from turning round their heads. Above and behind them a fire is blazing at a distance, and between the fire and the prisoners there is a raised way; and you will see, if you look, a low wall built along the way, like the screen which marionette players have in front of them, over which they show the puppets.

[GLAUCON:] I see.

[SOCRATES:] And do you see, men passing along the wall carrying all sorts of vessels, and statues and figures of animals made of wood and stone and various materials, which appear over the wall? Some of them are talking, others silent.

[GLAUCON:] You have shown me a strange image, and they are strange prisoners.

[SOCRATES:] Like ourselves; and they see only their own shadows, or the shadows of one another, which the fire throws on the opposite wall of the cave?

[GLAUCON:] True,; how could they see anything but the shadows if they were never allowed to move their heads?

[SOCRATES:] And of the objects which are being carried in like manner they would only see the shadows?

[GLAUCON:] Yes.

[SOCRATES:] And if they were able to converse with one another, would they not suppose that they were naming what was actually before them?

[GLAUCON:] Very true.

[SOCRATES:] And suppose further that the prison had an echo which came from the other side, would they not be sure to fancy when one of the passersby spoke that the voice which they heard came from the passing shadow?

[GLAUCON:] No question.

[SOCRATES:] To them, the truth would be literally nothing but the shadows of the images.

[GLAUCON:] That is certain.

[SOCRATES:] And now look again, and see what will naturally follow if the prisoners are released and disabused of their error. At first, when any of them is liberated and compelled suddenly to stand up and turn his neck round and walk and look towards the light, he will suffer sharp pains; the glare will distress him, and he will be unable to see the realities of which in his former state he had seen the shadows. Next imagine someone saying to him, that what he saw before was an illusion, but that now, when he is approaching nearer to being and his eye is turned towards more real existence, he has a clearer vision,—what will be his reply? And you may further imagine that his instructor is pointing to the objects as they pass and requiring him to name them,—will he not be perplexed? Will he not fancy that the shadows which he formerly saw are truer than the objects which are now shown to him?

[GLAUCON:] Far truer.

[SOCRATES:] And if he is compelled to look straight at the light, will he not have a pain in his eyes which will make him turn away and take in the objects of vision which he can see, and which he will conceive to be in reality clearer than the things which are now being shown to him?

[GLAUCON:] True.

[SOCRATES:] And suppose once more, that he is reluctantly dragged up a steep and rugged ascent, and held fast until he's forced into the presence of the sun himself, is he not likely to be pained and irritated? When he approaches the light his eyes will be dazzled, and he will not be able to see anything at all of what are now called realities.

[GLAUCON:] Not all in a moment.

[SOCRATES:] He will require to grow accustomed to the sight of the upper world. And first he will see the shadows best, next the reflections of men and other objects in the water, and then the objects themselves; then he will gaze upon the light of the moon and the stars and the spangled heaven; and he will see the sky and the stars by night better than the sun or the light of the sun by day?

[GLAUCON:] Certainly.

[SOCRATES:] Last of all he will be able to see the sun, and not mere reflections of him in the water, but he will see him in his own proper place, and not in another; and he will contemplate him as he is.

[GLAUCON:] Certainly.

[SOCRATES:] He will then proceed to argue that this [the Sun] is he who gives the season and the years, and is the guardian of all that is in the visible world, and in a certain way the cause of all things which he and his fellows have been accustomed to behold?

[GLAUCON:] Clearly, he would first see the sun and then reason about him.

[SOCRATES:] And when he remembered his old habitation, and the wisdom of the den and his fellow prisoners, do you not suppose that he would be happy with the change in himself, and pity them?

[GLAUCON:] Certainly, he would.

[SOCRATES:] And if they were in the habit of conferring honors among themselves on those who were quickest to observe the passing shadows and to remark which of them went before, and which followed after, and which were together, and who were therefore best able to draw conclusions as to the future, do you think that he would care for such honors and glories, or envy the possessors of them? Would he not say with Homer, "Better to be the poor servant of a poor master," and to endure anything, rather than think as they do and live after their manner?

[GLAUCON:] Yes, I think that he would rather suffer anything than entertain these false notions and live in this miserable manner.

[SOCRATES:] Imagine once more such a one coming suddenly out of the sun to be replaced in his old situation; would he not be certain to have his eyes full of darkness?

[GLAUCON:] To be sure.

[SOCRATES:] And if there were a contest, and he had to compete in measuring the shadows with the prisoners who had never moved out of the den, while his sight was still weak, and before his eyes had become adjusted (and the time which would be needed to acquire this adjustment might be very considerable), would he not be ridiculous? Men would say of him that up he went and down he came without his eyes, and that it was better not even to think of ascending. And if anyone tried to release another and lead him up to the light, let them only catch the offender, and they would put him to death.

[GLAUCON:] No question.

[SOCRATES:] This entire allegory, you may now append, dear Glaucon, to the previous argument; the prison-house is the world of sight, the light of the fire is the sun, and you will not misapprehend me if you interpret the journey upwards to be the ascent of the soul into the intellectual world according to my poor belief, which, at your desire, I have expressed, whether rightly or wrongly God knows.

But, whether true or false, my opinion is that in the world of knowledge the idea of good appears last of all, and is seen only with an effort; and, when seen, is also inferred to be the universal author of all things beautiful and right, parent of light and of the lord of light in this visible world, and the immediate source of reason and truth in the intellectual; and that this is the power upon which he who would act rationally, either in public or private life, must have his eye fixed.

*18. *Most modern people tend to think of ethics as having to do with good and bad, moral and immoral. They do* not *think of it as having anything to do with the truths of mathematics or physics, for instance. Thus a "good" proof*

in mathematics has nothing to do with moral goodness. Do you think Plato would agree?

It is clear from the cave allegory that Plato thinks that acquisition of knowledge requires discipline and is painful. "No pain, no gain" is even more true in the realm of knowledge than it is in the realm of physical training and improvement. So if you find studying painful sometimes, do not be surprised!

Plato thinks that bodily life, with all its appetites, makes us forget truths that are deeply implanted in us even before birth. We tend to focus on what is perceptible and satisfies bodily desires. It is very difficult to turn away from the body, and someone who prodded people into making that turn or conversion might not be too popular. Moreover such a person might be thought a crackpot by some, since he claims that the familiar world is not fully real or worthy of our attention. Socrates was such a person, and in this dialogue Plato may be referring to Socrates when he speaks of the unpopularity of those who try to help people out of the cave.

19. *A notable feature of this allegory is the status of the Sun. The Sun is being compared to what?*

It may still be far from clear why Plato would accord the form of the Good such preeminent status. He does not give a clear account of it, but he thinks that knowledge of that form, that is, of pure goodness, would enable a person to understand, and thus have true knowledge of, everything. Of course, some things may be good instrumentally, that is, good for something else. For example, money may be good, but not in itself (it is just paper) but for the sake of something else (a new Lexus, perhaps). Even the new Lexus might not be good in itself, but merely good as a means to getting from one place to another or, perhaps, getting from one place to another while impressing the neighbors. But Plato thinks there must be something that is *entirely* good in itself. All instrumental goods would ultimately be intelligible in the light of that "Good-in-Itself." It is what Plato calls "the Form of the Good." Plato apparently thinks that all explanations, thus all understanding and knowledge, must be guided by familiarity with a pure goodness that completely transcends this world. The standard and the source of all good lies outside the world. Knowledge of that Good would be completely general, like knowledge in mathematics. It would not be knowledge about any particular thing, just as knowledge that $2 + 2 = 4$ is not knowledge about any particular thing or things! In fact there is no 'knowledge' of any particulars, only, at best, opinion.

What Is the Advantage of Being Just?

The *Republic* is concerned with the nature of justice in individuals and in communities. But this matter of justice raises an interesting question that is at the heart of much of the discussion in the *Republic*. The sophist Thrasymachus argues that justice is nothing but the interest of the stronger. In his view, if I am strong enough to get away with cheating and murder, then I should cheat and murder whenever it is to my advantage to do so. I would come out ahead. There would be no advantage in being consistently "just" in the conventional sense. According to Thrasymachus, a strong person could be a person in whom the appetites dominated, but that would not lead to any harm to himself, since he is, by hypothesis, strong enough to get away with crimes of all sorts in the pursuit of his desires. In the following passage Glaucon is voicing the views of Thrasymachus.

FROM BOOK II

[GLAUCON:] Now that those who practice justice do so involuntarily and because they have not the power to be unjust will best appear if we imagine something of this kind: Having given both to the just and the unjust the power to do what they will, let us watch and see whither desire will lead them. Then we shall discover the just man to be resorting to the same conduct as the unjust man, proceeding along the same road, grasping for their own advantage, which all natures deem to be their good. Only by the force of law do they honor equality.

The liberty which we are supposing may be most completely given to them in the form of such a power as is said to have been possessed by Gyges, the ancestor of Croesus the Lydian. According to the tradition, Gyges was a shepherd in the service of the king of Lydia. There was a great storm, and an earthquake made an opening in the earth at the place where he was feeding his flock. Amazed at the sight, he descended into the opening, where, among other marvels, he beheld a hollow brazen horse having doors, at which he, stooping and looking in, saw a dead body of more than human stature, as appeared to him, and having nothing on but a gold ring. He took this ring from the finger of the dead and went back up.

Now the shepherds met together, according to custom, that they might send their monthly report about the flocks to the king. Gyges came into their assembly with the ring on his finger, and as he was sitting among them he chanced to turn the collet of the ring inside his hand. Instantly he became invisible to the rest of the company and they began to speak of him as if he were no longer present. He was astonished at this, and again touching the ring he turned the collet outwards and always with the same result—when he turned the collet inwards he became invisible, when outwards he reappeared. Whereupon he contrived to be chosen one of the messengers who were sent to the court. As soon as he arrived he seduced the queen, and with her help conspired against the king and slew him, and took the kingdom.

Suppose now that there were two such magic rings, and the just put on one of them and the unjust the other; no man can be imagined to be of such an iron nature that he would stand fast in justice. No man would keep his hands off what was not his own when he could safely take what he liked out of the market, or go into houses and lie with any one at his pleasure, or kill or release from prison whom he would, and in all respects be like a God among men. Then the actions of the just would be as the actions of the unjust; they would both come at last to the same point. And this we may truly affirm to be a great proof that a man is just, not willingly or because he thinks that justice is any good to him individually, but of necessity, for wherever anyone thinks that he can safely be unjust, there he is unjust. For all men believe in their hearts that injustice is far more profitable to the individual than justice, and he who argues as I have been supposing, will say that they are right. If you could imagine anyone obtaining this power of becoming invisible, and never doing any wrong or touching what was another's, he would be thought by the onlookers to be a most wretched idiot.

20. *Why are just people (for example, honest people) just, according to Glaucon?*
21. *If you had the ring of Gyges, do you think you would have any reason not to be immoral? Explain your answer.*

Glaucon/Thrasymachus is in effect proposing the following argument:

(i) Everyone wants to be happy. (That seems like a pretty fair assumption!)
(ii) Therefore it would be irrational to act in any way that would not contribute to one's own happiness.
(iii) Therefore if someone could be happy through injustice, it would be irrational for that person to stick to being just. People would rightly think such a person to be an "idiot."

Certainly Thrasymachus' position is still a popular one. There is in fact a widespread tendency to picture good people as being rather stupid, whereas evil people are often portrayed as very clever and shrewd.

22. *Can you think of an example from a film or story or novel of a person who is portrayed as very smart and also as very evil or very good and very stupid? Mention any examples you can think of.*

Many would agree with Thrasymachus that the person who tries to be just is indulging in "high-minded foolishness" or some other form of stupidity. Consider just the following points.

FROM BOOK II
[THRASYMACHUS:] First of all, in private contracts: wherever the unjust is the partner of the just you will find that, when the partnership

is dissolved, the unjust man has always more and the just less. Secondly, in their dealings with the State: when there is an income tax, the just man will pay more and the unjust less on the same amount of income; and when there is anything to be received, the one gains nothing and the other much. Observe also what happens when they take an office: there is the just man neglecting his affairs and perhaps suffering other losses, and getting nothing out of the public, because he is just; moreover he is hated by his friends and acquaintances for refusing to serve them in unlawful ways.

23. *Is there anything familiar sounding in that? Mention a contemporary example that in your opinion illustrates what Thrasymachus is talking about.*

Plato wants to refute Thrasymachus' position. But he agrees with (i) and (ii) in the preceding argument! So he must show that being just pays, that it leads to greater happiness. He must show that someone with the ring of Gyges would actually be better off if she did *not* rob, murder, etc., even when doing so would get her what she "wants" without any risk.

Being Just (Being Good) Does Pay

Plato uses various strategies in tackling Thrasymachus' challenge. One of them consists in asking what would become of a community (any group of people trying to live together) if justice was completely ignored.

FROM BOOK I
[SOCRATES:] . . .would you have the goodness also to inform me, whether you think that a state, or an army, or a band of robbers and thieves, or any other gang of evildoers could act at all if they injured one another?
[THRASYMACHUS:] No indeed, they could not.
[SOCRATES:] But if they abstained from injuring one another, then they might act together better?
[THRASYMACHUS:] Yes.
[SOCRATES:] And this is because injustice creates divisions and hatreds and fighting, and

justice imparts harmony and friendship; is not that true, Thrasymachus?

[THRASYMACHUS:] I agree, because I do not wish to quarrel with you.

[SOCRATES:] How good of you, ; but I should like to know also whether injustice, having this tendency to arouse hatred, wherever existing, among slaves or among freemen, will not make them hate one another and set them at variance and render them incapable of common action.

[THRASYMACHUS:] Certainly.

[SOCRATES:] And even if injustice be found in two only, will they not quarrel and fight, and become enemies to one another and to the just?

[THRASYMACHUS:] They will.

[SOCRATES:] And suppose injustice abiding in a single person, would your wisdom say that she loses or that she retains her natural power? Let us assume that she retains her power. Yet is not the power which injustice exercises of such a nature that wherever she takes up her abode, whether in a city, in an army, in a family, or in any other body, that body is, to begin with, rendered incapable of united action by reason of sedition and distraction? And does it not therefore become its own enemy and at variance with all that opposes it, and with the just? Is not this the case?

[THRASYMACHUS:] Yes, certainly.

[SOCRATES:] And is not injustice equally fatal when existing in a single person? For in the first place it renders him incapable of action because he is not at unity with himself, and in the second place it makes him an enemy to himself and the just? Is not that true, Thrasymachus?

[THRASYMACHUS:] Yes.

[SOCRATES:] And O my friend, surely the gods are just?

[THRASYMACHUS:] Granted that they are.

[SOCRATES:] But if so, the unjust will be the enemy of the gods, and the just will be their friend?

[THRASYMACHUS:] Feast away in triumph, and take your fill of the argument; I will not oppose you, lest I should displease the company.

24. *What does Plato think will happen when any group of people ignores the rules of justice?*

25. *Do you agree with Plato about this?*

Thrasymachus' grouchy retort may indicate that he feels Socrates has scored a point against him. But has he? Socrates' argument is this:

(i) Injustice creates conflict and strife.
(ii) Justice enables harmony and peace.
(iii) Harmony and peace are preferable to conflict and strife.
(iv) Therefore, Justice is preferable to Injustice.

Is this a good argument? Try to imagine a case where injustice would not create conflict (that is, a world where (i) is false). The problem is to imagine people living peacefully together without anyone following any rules, without any agreement as to how to live. It is indeed difficult to imagine such a possibility. (Recall here your discussion of Orienting Question 1). A later philosopher, Thomas Hobbes (17th century CE) argued that a condition in which everyone did as he pleased would be "nasty, brutish and short." But Hobbes thought the necessary order could be imposed by force by a sufficiently powerful monarch. Even such a monarch, however, would have to impose something like the traditional rules of justice. If he made it a rule that people should kill other people whenever they thought it would be to their advantage, he might soon be without a community to rule (for more on Hobbes, see Chapter 5).

However, even if Plato's argument shows the impossibility of a peaceful or thriving community in which there is no heed paid to justice, has he also succeeded in showing that an *individual* might not be better off by ignoring the requirements of justice? Part of the difficulty in answering this question may be due to lack of clarity in the notion of justice itself.

What Is Justice? The Just Individual and the Just Community

Notice that Plato claims that the same argument does in fact apply to an individual. But does it? In Plato's view, to know what justice is you have to grasp the *form* of Justice. You might expect that doing this is connected in some way with the use of "reason." We have already seen the idea expressed in the *Protagoras* that goodness consists in knowledge and that evil people are always ignorant, that is, don't really *know* what they are doing. In *The Republic* Plato continues to hold that same view, though on the basis of somewhat different reasoning. Justice is a matter of knowledge, knowledge requires the use of reason, or having wisdom "in control." Even though Plato rejects the focus on pleasure that he proposed in the *Protagoras,* he continues to insist that there is a fundamental connection between reason, or rationality, and goodness and thus justice. He develops this view by arguing that individual souls are complex, consisting of reason, "spirit" and appetite. He thinks that communities or states have a similar complex structure, with certain people playing the role of reason (an educated intellectual elite), others representing "spirit" (the military or police class) and ordinary laborers representing appetite.

FROM BOOK IX

[SOCRATES:] . . . the individual soul . . . has been divided by us into three principles. . . . It seems to me that to these three principles three pleasures correspond; also three desires and governing powers.

[GLAUCON:] How do you mean?

[SOCRATES:] There is one principle with which, as we were saying, a man learns, another with which he is angry; the third, having many forms, has no special name, but is denoted by the general term *appetitive,* from the extraordinary strength and vehemence of the desires of eating and drinking and the other sensual appetites which are the main elements of it; also money-loving, because such desires are generally satisfied by the help of money.

[GLAUCON:] That is true.

[SOCRATES:] If we were to say that the loves and pleasures of this third part were concerned with gain, we should then be able to fall back on a single notion, and might truly and intelligibly describe this part of the soul as loving gain or money.

[GLAUCON:] I agree with you.

[SOCRATES:] Again, is not the spirited element wholly set on ruling and conquering and getting fame?

[GLAUCON:] True.

[SOCRATES:] Suppose we call it the *contentious* or *ambitious*—would the term be suitable?

[GLAUCON:] Extremely suitable.

[SOCRATES:] On the other hand, every one sees that the principle of knowledge is wholly directed to the truth, and cares less than either of the others for gain or fame.

[GLAUCON:] Far less.

[SOCRATES:] "Lover of wisdom," "lover of knowledge" are titles that we may fitly apply to that part of the soul?

[GLAUCON:] Certainly.

[SOCRATES:] One principle prevails in the souls of one class of men, another in others, as may happen?

[GLAUCON:] Yes.

[SOCRATES:] Then we may begin by assuming that there are three classes of men—lovers of wisdom, lovers of honor, lovers of gain?

In Plato's view it is the function of reason in the individual to rule, the function of the appetites to obey and the function of spirit to assist reason. In the community it is the function of the reasonable element, the educated (especially the philosophers!) to rule, the function of the great masses of people (the craftspeople, workers, farmers,) to follow the commands of the rulers and the function of the spirited types, or "lovers of honor," to assist the rulers in carrying out their reasonable commands. The following brings out the comparison:

- just individual: just state
- reason rules: the educated rule
- spirit assists reason: soldiers assist the educated rulers
- appetites obey: the masses of ordinary people willingly follow the rules set down by the educated elite

You should be able to guess why Plato thinks that reason should rule in the community. He certainly thinks that only through reason can anyone discover or know what is real. Without reason people are chained down like the inhabitants of the cave, not really knowing what is what. Would you want such ignorant, deluded people in charge of the community in which you live? Similarly, reason must rule in the individual. Otherwise a person is simply batted around by her or his competing and chaotic desires and fears.

26. *Why must reason rule in the state? In the individual?*

Just why Plato thinks the various "parts" of the state or community have the functions he claims they have will not be treated here, but you can get the flavor of his thinking from the following passage.

FROM BOOK IV

[SOCRATES:] But when the cobbler or any other man whom nature designed to be a trader, having his heart lifted up by wealth or strength or the number of his followers, or any like advantage, attempts to force his way into the class of warriors, or a warrior into that of legislators and guardians, for which he is unfitted, and either to take the implements or the duties of the other, or when one man is trader, legislator, and warrior all in one, then I think you will agree with me in saying that this interchange and this meddling of one with another is the ruin of the State.
[GLAUCON:] Most true.
[SOCRATES:] Seeing then, that there are three distinct classes, any meddling of one with another, or the change of one into another, is the greatest harm to the State, and may be most justly termed evildoing?
[GLAUCON:] Precisely.
[SOCRATES:] And the greatest degree of evil doing to one's own city would be termed by you injustice?
[GLAUCON:] Certainly.
[SOCRATES:] This, then, is injustice; and on the other hand when the trader, the auxiliary, and the guardian each do their own business, that is justice, and will make the city just.

So the answer to the question "What is justice?" is this:

In the state (or "city"), justice is each person performing his proper function.

We have all heard complaints about politicians trying to do the work of soldiers. There have also been complaints about soldiers trying to be politicians, as when Gen. Douglas MacArthur tried to defy the orders of President Harry Truman during the Korean war. Some people also worry when businesspeople become too prominent in political leadership, for fear they will bend government to their own private profit. And so on.

27. *Give an example of your own of harm done to a community when someone does not tend to her own business but, even with the best of intentions, tries to do someone else's job.*
*28. *If businesspeople have excessive influence over government, might that be bad simply because they are not performing their "proper function"? Or might it be bad because they are dishonest or selfish? What does Plato suggest? What is your view?*

Though we may not agree with all the details of Plato's view, we can probably feel some sympathy with the general point that a good and just community will be one in which each person fulfills that role for which he or she is best suited. But we may wonder about the suggestion made in the passage just quoted that some people "by nature" have a certain function, so that someone who is "naturally" a cobbler should stick to making shoes and keep his nose out of politics or police work. It is not clear that anyone is by nature a cobbler, and most of us probably think that there might be cobblers (or electricians or librarians) out there who would make good presidents. It does seem that some people might not be fit by nature to do certain jobs (for instance, someone with an IQ of 70 is by nature not a good candidate for doing the work of a rocket scientist). It does not follow that a librarian might not make a good president.

*29. *Nor does it follow that lawyers, even though familiar with the law, are likely to make the best legislators. Why not?*

Further Discussion and Applications

Why Go Back to the Cave? (Annas)

The cave allegory is puzzling, in a way. Plato supposes that most people are trapped in darkness, subject to manipulation, unable to distinguish what is real from what is not. The cave allegory is quite vivid. The film director Bernardo Bertolucci drew on Plato's allegory to portray people deluded into acceptance of a manipulative dictator (like Mussolini, the fascist dictator of Italy during WWII) as a source of truth. Plato's allegory invites such an application.

Now, normally we would think that escape from such a condition would involve increased self-knowledge. In realizing that I am "being had," I come to realize something about myself, my susceptibility to illusion and seduction. But Plato does not claim that release from the cave involves self-knowledge, though his mentor, Socrates, certainly would have. Plato's model for genuine knowledge is mathematics. In mathematics we can have certain knowledge that does not change with circumstances. All knowledge is like that according to Plato, for real knowledge (as opposed to mere opinion) consists in the grasp of "forms" that are absolute (absolute beauty, absolute justice, absolute goodness). The forms transcend this world and everything individual, including oneself. Genuine knowledge, or understanding, is theoretical. It is never knowledge of particulars of any kind, including oneself or other particular human beings. That being the case, it is difficult to understand what would *motivate* a person ever to leave the cave or what the dynamics of being "released" or "unchained" amount to.

This problem dovetails with another. Plato supposes that at least some of those who, by a rigorous education, escape the cave will return in order to govern those who remain. They are what he calls the "Guardians" of the state. Those "returnees" will be uniquely qualified to lead, since they really know what is good. But why would they return? The best kind of life for a human, in Plato's view, is life outside the cave, where one is able to behold pure goodness. Why would anyone want to be a Guardian at all? The

question is particularly pressing since, as we have seen, Thrasymachus/Glaucon challenges Socrates on just this point and puts forth the myth of the "ring of Gyges" to argue that it could not be in anyone's interest to be just or moral. Socrates replies by trying to show that it is in a person's *interest* to be just. But how could that be, given that true justice has nothing to do with individuals? Julia Annas puts the matter this way:

> The Guardians are not just a fanciful idea; they are what just people in a perfectly just society are supposed to be like. But now we see that justice demands that I retreat to a point of view from which I can judge my own happiness and interests in exactly the same impersonal way as everybody else's. I must come to cease to care about my own happiness. But why ever should it be in my interests to want to do that?
>
> . . . it is far from clear that anyone has a reason to be just if that implies taking the viewpoint on one's own interests that the Guardians do.
>
> The Guardians' return to the Cave has always been recognized as a major problem in the *Republic,* for the results are very ugly, whether the Guardians suffer real loss by doing it or not. If they suffer real loss, because their own prospects of happiness are sacrificed, then justice is not in their interests—and yet they are the paradigms of justice in a just society, and Plato set out to show that justice was in the agent's interests. But if they do not suffer real loss, because they view their own happiness as rationally and impersonally as they do everybody else's, then justice seems to demand an ideal, impersonal viewpoint that is not in the interests of any actual people to adopt. We thought that Plato's account had the virtue of taking seriously the claims of justice on us as we are; now justice demands that we positively stop being human.
>
> He will not allow that the functions of reason might ever be divided . . . the reason that made just decisions for me and for others becomes identified with the reason that studies what is absolutely just, just unqualified and not just for me or for anyone. Plato does not see that such

a notion of reason is bound . . . to threaten the coherence of his argument for the worthwhileness of justice. This is not, however, a simple mistake. There is a grandeur in the way that Plato makes the wise ruler be an intellectual genius as well, refusing to allow that the detached study of eternal truths is not an extension of the same thing as the just person's powers of practical judgment. (from "Understanding and the Good: Sun, Line and Cave")

*30. *In what sense does justice require that I "stop being human" according to Annas' account of Plato?*

*31. *(a) Do you think that the kind of reasoning required to do geometry and the kind of reasoning required to deal with a rowdy roommate are basically, at bottom, the same kind of reasoning?*

   (b) Do they require "reason" in completely different senses?

   (c) Partly different, partly the same?

   Explain and illustrate your answer.

Most of us are likely to think of goodness as a quality that can be found right here, in particular actions or institutions or persons. At the same time, many of us would like to believe that goodness here is somehow supported by, or made possible by, some transcendent source.

32. *For many people, that transcendent source would be _____.*

But can we have it both ways? How can what is totally beyond this world connect to what is in the world? That is a problem for anyone, not just Plato, who thinks that goodness is grounded in something transcendent. But Plato has a particular problem rooted in his notion that only theoretical reason is worthwhile. His own discussion of the ring of Gyges and of the value of justice for a community does not fit with that notion of theoretical reason.

Simplification and Purity (Murdoch)

Despite the problems pointed out by Annas, there is a way of reading Plato that reconnects his thought

to individuals "as they are" and that points the way toward higher human development.

We have seen that Sophocles regards any tendency to oversimplify moral life as itself a source of tragedy. Plato on the other hand thinks that reasoning about the good is like mathematical reasoning. There cannot be more than one right answer to any problem in math, and neither can there be more than one right answer about how to live. The right answer to the question about the good life may not be "simple" in the sense of "easy," just as math is not always easy. But it should be simple in the sense that the person who has seen the "good" will not be troubled by tragic dilemmas or confused by the possibility that he "added things up" incorrectly.

We have seen, with Annas, that Plato's way of thinking leads to a kind of paradox. Perhaps there is a kind of sense to Plato's view nonetheless. We asked, "Why go back to the cave?" What motive could there be? If there is none, than there is no reason for being good in this world, whether we have the ring of Gyges or not. But perhaps the problem is that we are thinking of this matter in terms of what will satisfy us personally, make our lives better at the individual level. Plato can be taken as rejecting that idea. By his account, those who know pure goodness will be without desires for personal gain of any kind. Iris Murdoch, a British novelist and moralist, puts it this way:

A genuine mysteriousness attaches to the idea of goodness and the Good. This is a mystery with several aspects. The indefinability of Good is connected with the unsystematic and inexhaustible variety of the world and the pointlessness of virtue. In this respect there is a special link between the concept of Good and the ideas of Death and Chance. A genuine sense of mortality enables us to see virtue as the only thing of worth; and it is impossible to limit and foresee the ways in which it will be required of us. That we cannot dominate the world may be put in a more positive way. Good is mysterious because of human frailty, because of the immense distance which is involved. If there were angels they might be able to define Good but we would not understand the definition. We are largely mechanical creatures, the slaves of relentlessly strong selfish forces the lure of which we scarcely comprehend. At best, as decent persons, we are usually very specialized. We behave well in areas where this can be done fairly easily and let other areas of possible virtue remain undeveloped. There are perhaps in the case of every human being insuperable psychological barriers to goodness. The self is a divided thing and the whole of it cannot be redeemed any more than it can be known. And if we look outside the self what we see are scattered intimations of Good. There are few places where virtue plainly shines: great art, humble people who serve others.

It is in the context of such limitations that we should picture our freedom. Freedom is, I think, a mixed concept. The true half of it is simply a name of an aspect of virtue concerned especially with the clarification of vision and the elimination of selfish impulse. The false and more popular half is a name for the self-assertive movements of deluded selfish will which because of our ignorance we take to be something autonomous. We cannot then sum up human excellence for these reasons: the world is aimless, chancy, and huge, and we are blinded by self. (from *The Sovereignty of Good*)

Although Plato thinks of the Good in this austere way, he also supposes that it has in it a strong magnetic force, something that draws the soul. We will not examine this further feature of Plato's thinking here, but those who are interested should read the dialogue *Ion*.

33. *We raised the question "How could it be in the interest of the Guardians to return to the cave?" According to Murdoch, the answer is that the Guardians are people who have learned to disregard their own _____.*

34. *Murdoch thinks that even quite good people are "divided," in the sense that their goodness is not complete. Parts of them remain under the rule of selfish impulse. Part is pulled toward the good. Illustrate her point with respect to someone you know (it could be yourself).*

*35. *True goodness, by Murdoch's account, is not _____. It is pure, unmixed with any-*

thing selfish. Does this ideal of goodness seem unrealistic to you?*

*36. *Since Plato stressed that knowledge of the good is indeed knowledge, a kind of deep comprehensive grasp of all truth about what is good, would he accept the distinction commonly made nowadays between "facts" and "values"?*

Whatever we may think of Plato's "transcendentalism," most of us are naturally likely to have the view that personal goodness is something "here and now." Aristotle thought that Plato was confused about the good. He argued that there is no such thing as simply "the Good." There are varying criteria for goodness. What makes a car a good car is quite different from what makes a salad a good salad. And what makes a person a good person is of course different from both. He might agree with Annas that an ideal such as that described in *The Republic* is in some sense inhuman. As we shall see in the next chapter, he seeks for a more "practical" and "mundane" account of the Good.

Plato's Basis for "Strong Evaluation" (Taylor)

When we judge that an action is cruel or that a person is kind or that a life has been worthless, we do not think of our judgments or claims as expressions of mere gut reactions, comparable to feelings of nausea. If someone does not feel nausea when required to eat a piece of smelly, gory roadkill dumped on his dinner plate, we might think it odd, but we are not likely to think that he has made a mistake. His reactions are different from mine, perhaps different from most people's or even from all others, but not mistaken. The absence of nausea might signal a defect in, say, his olfactory nerves, but it signals no defect in his understanding, his powers of judgment. (If he actually eats the roadkill, that would be another matter, of course.)

In contrast, consider the Nazi guard who forces a mother to choose which of her sons should be executed (see Chapter 5 for further description of this case). A person who fails to see the wanton cruelty in such an act is not just different. Rather, he is deficient, he has failed to see that such actions *deserve* to be described as cruel, *deserve* to be condemned, even if no one reacts in the way that such actions require. It is this feature of moral judgments that Canadian philosopher Charles Taylor is referring to when he calls such judgments "strong evaluations." They are judgments that are grounded in "how things are," not simply in how people may react to how things are or how people happen to feel.

Strong evaluations thus require an account of "how things are" at some very deep level. The action of the Nazi guard does not have some obvious *empirical* property that earns it the label *cruel*. The guard could have spoken his order in a loud voice or in a soft voice, for example. It hardly matters which, and the same would be true for any other empirical properties of "what he did." So there must be something else about such an action that warrants the label *cruel* and that warrants us in thinking of the guard as deeply defective, out of touch with important realities. But what are those important realities?

Plato provides a definite answer to the last question. There is, by his account, an objective moral order, accessed through reason, to which in fact reason is naturally attuned. If all humans suddenly turned into irrational or nonrational animals, so that no one grasped that objective moral order, it would still be there. In the actual world, where possession of some measure of rationality is definitive of humanity, there will always be people who grasp that moral order through reason. Those people are the ones in whom, according to Plato's description in *The Republic*, reason is the ruling part. Reason rules over desire or appetite and over spirit (*thumos*) in the just man. Reason can be attuned to that objective order because that order is itself an eminently reasonable order. Taylor remarks:

> The vision of the good is at the very centre of Plato's doctrine of moral resources. The good of the whole, whose order manifests the Idea of the Good, is the final good, the one which englobes all partial goods. It not only includes them but confers a higher dignity on them, since the Good is what commands our categorical love and allegiance. It is the ultimate source of strong evaluation, something which stands on its own as worthy of being desired and sought, not just desirable given our existing goals and appetites. It provides the standard of the desirable beyond the variation of de facto desire. In the light of the Good, we can see that our good, the proper order in our souls, has this categoric worth, which it enjoys as a proper part of the whole order.
>
> Thus the good life for us is to be ruled by reason, not just as the vision of correct order in our souls, but also and more fundamentally, as the vision of the good order of the whole. And we cannot see one of these orders without the other. For the right order in us is to be ruled by reason, which cannot come about unless reason reaches its full realization, which is in the perception of the Good; and at the same time, the perception of the Good is what makes us truly virtuous. (*Sources of the Self*, p. 122)

Taylor emphasizes that Plato's account does not locate the capacity for goodness *in* individuals, but rather in the alignment between individual reason and an objective rational order. In that respect, he argues, it contrasts with many later views on morals that locate moral capacity in personal feelings or desires, in individual calculations of benefit or in reason by itself, apart from its connection to an objective moral order. Thus Plato's account does abundant justice to the ordinary intuition that there is something *objective* that grounds moral judgments. Perhaps it also does justice to our sense that we can just "see" that the Nazi guard is cruel and that his failure to see that himself can only be corrected by a kind of *conversion* to the good. He needs to be converted to seeing his own actions "in the light of the good," we might say. That is also Plato's language, as Taylor points out. *Convert* is derived from a Latin word that means "to turn around." The soul must be turned around to face in the right direction, as the allegory of the cave shows. The prisoners in the cave are unable to turn around, to see the light of the fire, or to move out of the cave to see the fire of the sun. Only when the chains are broken, only when the soul is converted, is it able to see everything in the light of the Good.

However, Plato's quite exclusive stress on *reason* as the capacity to "see" the Good might not seem so intuitively obvious. Is it obvious that the Nazi guard is somehow irrational or stupid? These questions have already been raised in the readings, and they will continue to come up in various contexts.

> 37. *If the capacity for goodness is not in individuals, then where is it, by Taylor's account of Plato?*

The Good Life, Community and Plato's "Totalitarianism" (Popper)

Plato's *The Republic* deals with a wide range of philosophical issues. Obviously issues in political philosophy are among them, as the very title of the book suggests. Political philosophy and ethics are closely connected for both Plato and Aristotle. Both argue that any answer to *the* question worth considering will take account of the way life is organized at the political or social level. The good life, the best kind of life, both argue, is only possible in a good community. You cannot have the good life "by yourself." (cf. Orienting Question 4)

What, then, makes for a good community? When contemporaries think about that question they may be thinking about clubs, churches and local communities as well as the state or the national government. For Plato and Aristotle, on the other hand, "community" (their word was *polis,* from which *political* comes) meant primarily one thing. They lived most or all of their lives in "city states," in particular, Athens. Greece in the 5th and 4th centuries was not a "nation" under one government. It consisted of independent cities that governed themselves. They were tied together only by a shared language, some other aspects of culture and occasional alliances. Some of them, Athens included, achieved power over other cities, but generally the fundamental unit of government was the city. Athens was notable for its development of a direct democracy. All the adult male citizens had an equal voice in deciding matters pertaining to the community. Citizenship was not confined to those who owned land or were materially wealthy or educated. Craftsmen had the same voting rights as rich men. All of them fought in the army, and they elected their generals. They decided on

taxes and entertainment, on rules for the market place and what buildings should be built. And they built the buildings themselves, aided by slaves. They took turns serving in the courts as jurymen, and it was a jury of the Athenian democracy that condemned Socrates to death. Although their democracy did not give women the same rights as men (neither did American "democracy" until the 20th century!), they succeeded more or less in developing a model of communal organization that was unique for its time and that has inspired many people right up to the present.

Democracy did not inspire Plato, however. Our brief selections from the *Republic* should make that clear. Plato does not think that most people are wise enough to govern themselves. They need an educated elite, the "Guardians," to rule them. Cobblers should stick to being cobblers. The masses are ignorant and easily swayed by demagogues. They live in "the cave." Therefore they need to be told what to do or how to live by those elites who have a secure grasp of "the good."

Plato's notion that people are by nature fit for certain roles and that some are fit to rule and others only fit to obey is definitely antidemocratic. His antidemocratic ideas go further than that, however. He advocates a kind of communism, in which the "private" is entirely eliminated. Here are a few more remarks from a later dialogue, *The Laws (Book V).*

> The first and highest form of the state and of the government and of the law is that in which there prevails most widely the ancient saying, that "Friends have all things in common." Whether or not there is anywhere now, or will ever be, this communion of women and children and of property, in which *the private and individual is altogether banished from life*, and things which are by nature private, such as eyes and ears and hands, have become common, and in some way see and hear and act in common, in which, in a word, everything has become one, no better criterion of excellence could be found. (emphasis added)

Plato literally means that women and children are to be held in common. He means that traditional family life will be eliminated in the best state. He means that everyone should see, think, act "as one." Such a state will be administered according to strict

Platonic principles. For example, in order to ensure that the citizens are encouraged to virtue, the Guardians impose strict censorship. Plato has this to say to such tragic poets as Sophocles:

> Do not then suppose that we shall all in a moment allow you to erect your stage in the agora, or introduce the fair voices of your actors, speaking above our own, and permit you to harangue our women and children, and the common people, about our institutions, in language other than our own, and very often the opposite of our own. For a state would be mad which gave you this license, until the magistrates had determined whether your poetry might be recited, and was fit for publication or not.

In the light of such remarks it is not difficult to understand why one 20th century philosopher, Karl Popper (in his book *The Open Society and Its Enemies*), listed Plato as one of the sources of totalitarian thinking in Western culture. In Plato's view the state comes first, the individual second. In Plato's view the state is to control everything, family life, sexual conduct, the kind of entertainment people witness, the kind of art an artist is allowed to produce, and so on. This has quite a chilling sound to people today who have seen similar ideas enacted in fascist Germany or in the communist Soviet Union. Austrian and British philosopher Karl Popper remarks:

> Because of his radical collectivism, Plato is not even interested in those problems which men usually call the problems of justice, that is to say, in the impartial weighing of the contesting claims of individuals. Nor is he interested in adjusting the individual's claims to those of the state. For the individual is altogether inferior . . . Justice, to him, is nothing but the health, unity, and stability of the collective body. (from *The Open Society and Its Enemies,* vol. I, 1962)

It is important, however, not to misjudge Plato. He does not think that the individual's happiness does not count. Rather, the community or state needs to be ordered so that all the members of the community together have the best possible life. He is convinced that "the individual" cannot live a good life alone. The best kind of life is communal life, and the best communal life is run by the wise, in a paternalistic manner. They should treat ordinary citizens not as means to their own ends, not as a means to power and glory or wealth, but as loving parents treat children. "We should consider," he says, "whether the laws of states ought not to have the character of loving and wise parents, rather than of tyrants and masters, who command and threaten."

Another notable feature of Plato's conception of the best community is that in it women can assume positions of complete equality with men. Women can be Guardians. That fact has led some to claim that Plato was a kind of early feminist. But many feminists point to conflicting views about women expressed in Plato's dialogues.

38. *Suppose that your conception of the best life includes having the ability to decide for yourself how you shall live. Would your conception be compatible with Plato's?*

*39. *Make a list of ethical qualities that assume life in community. Include at least five items. For example, honoring promises, being reliable in that sense, could not exist unless there were others to whom the promisor binds herself (a born and permanent Robinson Crusoe could not have that ethical quality of reliability.)*

*40. *It is fairly obvious that much of what we value in people has to do with the way they behave in society. Is it also obvious that much of what we value in a "good" society is the way in which it encourages and nurtures "good" people? Argue for your view.*

CHAPTER THREE

The Good Life, Reason and Virtue

Introduction

It is worth remembering again, as we did at the be-ginning of Chapter 2, how much effort and money are spent in the attempt to help people to a better life. If you are overweight, there are programs and drugs to fix that. If you get angry too easily or are addicted to harmful pleasures, then therapy, drugs or a self-help book may fix that. If you are depressed and feel life is meaningless, there may be a drug or a therapy to fix that. If you can't perform sexually, there are all sorts of drugs and remedies for that. Poor people can get rich by following any number of prescriptions, and even fame is available at bargain rates. Rarely does anyone raise the question "Would any of this *in fact* contribute to a good, or at least a better, life?" People seem to think that there are objective, rational answers to questions about how to acquire pleasures, health, and wealth and that it follows as a matter of course that there are objective answers to questions about how to achieve happiness. Otherwise it seems likely that very few would pay attention to mental and physical health gurus, get-rich-quick schemes or the omnipresent ads from drug companies.

Plato and Aristotle were also concerned with the difficulties involved in living well and were look-ing for a route to happiness, in some sense, but they wanted an account that could withstand rigorous philosophical criticism. We have seen that the quest for an objective, rational answer to *the* question (What is the best life, the good life, and how does one achieve it?) led Plato from a denial of relativism to a view based on his belief in a transcendent Good that somehow provides whatever meaning and reality our lives might have. That belief of Plato's was based in part on some rather difficult philosophical doctrines. Aristotle was also concerned to answer *the* question, but to a large extent he wanted an answer that takes its starting point in, and honors, common sense. Aristotle's approach has been and continues to be influential enough to warrant an entire chapter and copious excerpts from his main work in ethics.

ORIENTING QUESTIONS FOR DISCUSSION
1. Could a person have a "good" life and not be happy?
2. Would being famous, or popular, or rich, or healthy, be crucial to being happy? (Would being poor, or sick, ensure unhappiness?)
3. How important are each of the following to achiev-ing a good life?
    - a good upbringing
    - a good community
    - friends
    - good luck
    - avoiding bad luck
    - being virtuous

(You could try rating each on a scale of 1–10.)

4. Ideas about the good life, or happiness, seem to vary quite a bit from culture to culture and even from person to person. Could some of those ideas simply be mistaken and others more or less correct? If not, why not, and if so, what might make some of them more correct?

5. What role does knowledge play in achieving a good life? Could a person know what makes a life good and nonetheless not act consistently with her knowledge?

Aristotle: The Nichomachean Ethics

ARISTOTLE (384–322 BCE)

Aristotle of Stagira, in Macedonia, was certainly one of the most important philosophers of the ancient world, and probably one of the four or five most important to date. Though not an Athenian, he spent most of his life in Athens as a student and teacher of philosophy. For 20 years he was a member of Plato's Academy. Though critical of various Platonic doctrines, he did not simply rebel against his great teacher. Eventually he set up his own philosophical school, the Lyceum. Most of his extant works are probably derived from the lectures he gave in the Lyceum.

Aristotle established the idea of philosophy as a discipline with distinct areas or branches, and he denied that the standards of argumentation, proof and evidence that apply in one area must apply in all. Thus he insists that the kind of precision found in logic or mathematics should not be expected in ethics. You should know by now that Plato would have disagreed.

Aristotle made important contributions to areas we now think of as distinct from philosophy, particularly biology. He was for a time the tutor of Alexander ("the Great"), the young Macedonian prince who conquered the Greek cities of Europe as well as much of Asia and Persia, and he continued to be a friend of Alexander's during the latter's adult life. After the death of his first wife, Aristotle formed an attachment to Herpyllis, and they had a son, Nicomachus, to whom his chief work on ethics (excerpted in this chapter) is inscribed.

When Alexander the Great died in 323, Aristotle left Athens due to anti-Macedonian sentiments that put him in danger. He is said to have remarked that he did not want Athens to sin twice against philosophy (remember Socrates?). He went to Chalcis, on the island of Euboea, where he died in 322.

The Nichomachean Ethics is a sustained examination of the concepts of happiness, the good life, self-fulfillment, moral virtue, choice and many related topics. Aristotle's text is divided into 10 books composed of short chapters, and those divisions are kept here. The chapter headings or brief introductions given here are *not* part of his text, however.

Book I: The Goal of Living

CHAPTER I: *THE GOOD AS THE AIM OF ALL ACTION.*

Every art and every scientific inquiry, and similarly every action and purpose, may be said to aim at some good. Hence the good has been well defined as that at which all things aim. But it appears that there is a difference in the ends; for the ends are sometimes activities, and sometimes results beyond the mere activities. Also, where there are certain ends beyond the actions, the results are naturally superior to the activities.

1. *Don't some actions aim at what is bad?*

As there are various actions, arts, and sciences, it follows that the aims or ends are also various. Thus health is the aim of medicine, a vessel of shipbuilding, victory of strategy, and wealth of domestic economy. It often happens that there are a number of such arts or sciences which fall under a single discipline, as the art of making bridles, and all such other arts as make the instruments of horsemanship fall under horsemanship, and this again as well as every military action under strategy, and in the same way other arts or sciences under other disciplines. But in all these cases the ends of the higher arts or sciences, whatever they may be, are more desirable than those of the subordinate arts or sciences, as it is for the sake of the former that the latter themselves are sought. It makes no difference to the argument whether the activities themselves are the ends of the actions, or something else beyond the activities as in the above-mentioned sciences.

CHAPTER II: *THE SCIENCE OF THE HIGHEST GOOD IS "POLITICAL."*

Political science is knowledge of what is required for a good community. It includes more than "politics" as we may understand that word.

If it is true that

a. in our actions there is an end which we wish for its own sake, and on account of which we wish everything else, and

b. that we do not desire all things for the sake of something else (for, if that were so, the process would go on ad infinitum, and our desire would be idle and futile), then

c. it is clear that this [end, goal] will be the good or the supreme good.

Does it not follow then that the knowledge of this supreme good is of great importance for the conduct of life, and that, if we know it, we shall have a better chance of attaining what we want, like archers who have a target to aim at? But, if this is the case, we must endeavor to understand, at least in outline, its nature, and the branch of knowledge or the discipline to which it belongs.

It would seem that it would be the most authoritative or overarching science or discipline, and such is evidently the political; for it is political science or the discipline of politics which determines what sciences are necessary in states, and what kind of sciences should be learnt, and who in the state should learn them and to what extent. We perceive too that the most honored disciplines, e.g., generalship, domestic economy, and rhetoric, are subordinate to it. But as it makes use of the other practical sciences, and also legislates upon the things to be done and to be avoided, it follows that its end will include the ends of all other sciences, and will therefore be the true good of humans. For although the good of an individual is identical with the good of the state, it is evidently greater and more perfect to attain and preserve the good of the state. Though it is worth something to do

this for an individual, it is nobler and more divine to do it for a nation or state. These then are the objects at which the present inquiry aims, and so it is in a sense a political inquiry.

> **2. Some commentators have thought that Aristotle confuses the claim that there is some one goal that all people strive for with the claim that each and every person strives for some one goal (which could be different for different people). Which claim would be easier to defend, in your view, and why?*

Suppose Aristotle thinks there is some one goal that all people strive for, provided they know what they are doing. In what sense might that one goal be *one*? Most people want many things in their lives, an interesting job, family, friends, some pleasures. Would all of those together, perhaps in a certain optimal arrangement, be *one* goal? On this matter, too, students of Aristotle have disagreed.

Aristotle does believe that politics, in the sense of legislating, should contribute to individual realization of the good. For example, legislators could make laws requiring certain kinds of moral education. Aristotle might be thought of as advocating absorption of the individual into the state. But that can hardly be his thought. Rather, he sees that the chances of individual happiness are much greater in a state that has good laws, in the positive sense that they encourage moral development, not just in the negative sense in which they deter or prohibit evil.

Unlike most of us, who live in modern liberal democracies, he does not think of the legislator primarily as someone who ensures the "rights" of citizens against one another. The primary function of the statesman is to bring about the good of the citizens as such, just as the primary aim of the parents may be the good of the family as such. The parents' own good is included; knowing what one's own good is and knowing what the good of the family is consists in knowing the same kind of thing. The way of thinking, common among us, in which individuals pursue their own happiness while the state merely prevents other people from interfering in that pursuit is foreign to Aristotle.

CHAPTER III: *THE METHODS FOR THIS INQUIRY.*
Ethical reasoning is not like many other sorts of reasoning, such as that required for geometry or the construction of a watch.

But our statement of the case will be adequate, if it be made with all such clearness as the subject matter admits; for it would be wrong to expect the same degree of accuracy in all reasonings just as it would with respect to the products of the various crafts. Noble and just things, which are the subjects of investigation in political science, show so much variety and uncertainty that they are sometimes thought to have only a conventional, and not a natural, existence. There is the same sort of uncertainty in regard to good things, as it often happens that injuries result from them; thus people have been ruined by wealth, or lost their lives dues to courage. As our subjects then and our premises are of this nature, we must be content to indicate the truth roughly and in outline; and as our subjects and premises are true generally but not universally, we must be content to arrive at conclusions which are generally true. It is right to receive the particular statements which are made in the same spirit; for an educated person will expect accuracy in each subject only so far as the nature of the subject allows; he might as well accept probable reasoning from a mathematician as require demonstrative proofs from a rhetorician.

But everyone is capable of judging the subjects which he understands, and is a good judge of them. It follows that in particular subjects it is a specialist who is a good judge. Hence the young are not proper students of political science, as they have no experience of the actions of life which form the premises and subjects of [practical] reasonings. Also it may be added that from their tendency to follow their emotions they will not study the subject to any purpose or profit, for the purpose of ethical science is not knowledge but action.

It makes no difference whether a person is young in years or youthful in character; for the defect of which I speak is not one of time but is due to the emotional character of his life and pursuits. Knowledge is as useless to such a person as it is to an in-

temperate person. But where the desires and actions of people are regulated by reason the knowledge of these subjects will be extremely valuable. But having said so much by way of preface as to the students of political science, the spirit in which it should be studied, and the object which we set before ourselves, let us resume our argument as follows.

CHAPTER IV: *COMMON BELIEFS ABOUT THE HIGHEST GOOD ARE INACCURATE.*
Aristotle takes everyday beliefs about ethics seriously, but he also is critical of them.

As every knowledge and moral purpose aspires to some good, what is in our view the good at which the political science aims, and what is the highest of all practical goods? As to its name, there is, I may say, a general agreement. The masses and the cultured classes agree in calling it happiness (*eudaimonia*), and conceive that "to live well" or "to do well" is the same thing as "to be happy." But as to the nature of happiness, they do not agree, nor do the masses give the same account of it as the philosophers. The former describe it as something visible and palpable, e.g., pleasure, wealth or honor. People give various definitions of it, and often the same person gives different definitions at different times; for when a person has been ill, it is health, when he is poor, it is wealth.

If someone is conscious of his own ignorance, he envies people who use grand language above his own comprehension. Some philosophers on the other hand have held that, besides these various goods, there is an absolute good which is the cause of goodness in them all

It would perhaps be a waste of time to examine all these opinions; it will be enough to examine such as are most popular or as seem to be more or less reasonable.

But we must not fail to observe the distinction between the reasonings which proceed from first principles and the reasonings which lead up to first principles. For Plato was right in raising the difficult question whether the true way was from first principles or to first principles, as in the race course from the judges to the goal , or vice versa. We must begin with such facts as are known. But facts may be known in two ways, i.e., either relatively to ourselves or absolutely. It is probable then that we must begin with such facts as are known to us, i.e., relatively. It is necessary therefore, if a person is to be a competent student of what is noble and just and of politics in general, that he should have received a good moral training. For the fact that a thing is so is a first principle or starting point, and, if the fact is sufficiently clear, it will not be necessary to go on to ask the reason of it. But a person who has received a good moral training either possesses first principles, or will have no problem in acquiring them. But if he does not possess them, and cannot acquire them, he had better lay to heart Hesiod's lines:

> Far best is he who is himself all wise,
> And he, too, good who listens to wise words;
> But whoever is not wise nor lays to heart
> Another's wisdom is a useless man.

3. Does it follow that people with a bad upbringing cannot understand the good for humans?

Keep in mind Orienting Question 2 as you study the following section.

CHAPTER V
Aristotle sets out some objections to common views on what constitutes that good, or those goods, at which all our actions aim.

But to return from our digression: It seems not unreasonable that people should derive their conception of good or of happiness from men's lives. Thus ordinary or vulgar people conceive it to be pleasure, and accordingly approve a life of enjoyment. For there are exactly three prominent lives, the sensual, the political, and, thirdly, the speculative.

Now, the mass of men present an absolutely slavish appearance, as choosing the life of brute beasts, but they meet with consideration because so many persons in authority share the tastes of Sardanapalus [a mythical Assyrian king whose epitaph was supposed to include the words "eat, drink, play, for all else is worthless"].

Cultivated and practical people, on the other hand, identify happiness with honor, as honor is the general end of political life. But this appears too su-

perficial for our present purpose; for honor seems to depend more on the people who pay it rather than upon the person to whom it is paid, and we have an intuitive feeling that the good is something that is proper to a man himself and cannot be easily taken away from him. It seems too that the reason why men seek honor is that they may be confident of their goodness. Accordingly they seek it at the hands of the wise and those who know them well, and they seek it on the ground of virtue; hence it is clear that in their judgment at any rate virtue is superior to honor.

It would perhaps be right then to look upon virtue rather than honor as being the end of the political life. Yet virtue again, it appears, lacks completeness; for it seems that a man may possess virtue and yet be asleep or inactive throughout life, and, not only so, but he may experience the greatest calamities and misfortunes. But nobody would call such a life a life of happiness, unless he were maintaining a paradox. It is not necessary to dwell further on this subject, as it is sufficiently discussed in the popular philosophical treatises. The third life is the "theoretic," which we will investigate hereafter.

The life of money making is in a sense a life of constraint, and it is clear that wealth is not the good of which we are in quest; for it is useful in part as a means to something else. It would be a more reasonable view therefore that the things mentioned before, namely sensual pleasure, honor and virtue, are ends, rather than wealth, since they are things that are desired on their own account. Yet these too are apparently not ends, although much argument has been employed to show that they are.

CHAPTER VI
A philosophical theory or "science" of the highest good; a critique of the Platonic view that there is a single absolute goodness (see Chapter 2, discussion ii.)

In the following chapter Aristotle begins a discussion of happiness, which is fundamental to his account. The Greek word that is translated as "happiness" is *eudaimonia*. There is little agreement on how to translate that word. We will use "happiness," but it is important to realize that that is not quite right. In particular, it makes sense to us to say that someone is happy today but was not yesterday. It would never make sense to Aristotle to say that someone is *eudaimon* today but was not yesterday but will be again tomorrow. *Eudaimonia* is a long-term feature, and it differs from "happiness" in other ways as well.

CHAPTER VII: *MAKING MORE PRECISE THE IDEA OF A HIGHEST GOOD.*

Aristotle now attempts to develop an account of the good that can withstand the kinds of objections he has brought against some popular accounts.

But leaving this subject for the present let us revert to our question about the good, and consider what its nature might be. . . .

As it appears that there are more ends than one and some of these, e.g., wealth, flutes, and instruments generally we desire as means to something else, it is evident that they are not all final ends. But the highest good is clearly something final. Hence if there is only one final end, this will be the object we are looking for, and if there are more than one, it will be the most final of them. We speak of that which is sought after for its own sake as more final than that which is sought after as a means to something else; we speak of that which is never desired as a means to something else as more final than the beings which are desired both in themselves and as a means to something else; and we speak of a thing as absolutely final if it is always desired in itself and never as a means to something else.

It seems that happiness preeminently answers to this description, as we always desire happiness for its own sake and never as a means to something else, whereas we desire honor, pleasure, intellect, and every virtue, partly for their own sake (for we should desire them independently of what might result from them) but partly also as being means to happiness, because we suppose they will prove the instruments of happiness. Nobody desires happiness, on the other hand, for the sake of these things, nor indeed as a means to anything else at all.

We come to the same conclusion if we start from the consideration of self-sufficiency, if it may be assumed that the final good is self-sufficient. . . . We define the self-sufficient as that which, taken by itself, makes life desirable, and wholly free from want, and this is our conception of happiness.

Again we conceive happiness to be the most desirable of all things, and that not merely as one among other good things. If it were one among other good things, the addition of the smallest good would increase its desirableness; for the accession makes a superiority of goods, and the greater of two goods is always the more desirable. It appears then that happiness is something final and self-sufficient, being the end of all action.

4. *Why is happiness the supreme good?*

Perhaps, however, no one would ever disagree with the claim that happiness is the supreme good; what is wanted is to define its nature a little more clearly. The best way of arriving at such a definition will probably be to ascertain the function of a human being. For, as with a flute player, a statuary, or any artisan, or in fact anybody who has a definite function and action, his goodness, or excellence , seems to lie in his function, so it would seem to be with a human being, if indeed he has a definite function. Can it be said then that, while a carpenter and a cobbler have a definite function and action, a human being, unlike them, is naturally functionless? The reasonable view is that, as the eye, the hand, the foot, and similarly each several part of the body has a definite function, so a human being may be regarded as having a definite function apart from these.

What, then, can this function be?

It is not life; for life is apparently something which a human being shares with the plants; and it is something unique to man that we are looking for. We must exclude therefore the life of nutrition and increase.

There is next what may be called the life of sensation. But this too is apparently shared by humans with horses, cattle, and all other animals.

There remains what I may call the practical life of the rational part of human being. But the rational part is twofold; it is rational partly in the sense of being obedient to reason, and partly in the sense of possessing reason and intelligence. The practical life too may be conceived in two ways, namely, either as a moral state, or as a moral activity: but we must understand by it the life of activity, as this seems to be the truer form of the conception.

The function of a human being then is the activity of soul in accordance with reason, or not independently of reason.

Now the function of any *x* and of a good *x* will be the same (thus the function of a harpist and of a good harpist are the same, and likewise for all classes of things). This being so, if we

a. define the function of a human being as a kind of life, and

b. this life as an activity of soul or a course of action in conformity with reason, and

c. if the function of a good human being is to perform such activities well and finely, and

d. if a function is performed well and finely when it is performed in accordance with its proper excellence [virtue, *arete*], then it follows that the good of human beings is an activity of soul [or a course of action] in accordance with [human beings'] proper excellence or virtue or, if there are more virtues than one, in accordance with the best and most complete virtue. But it is necessary to add the words "in a complete life." For as one swallow or one day does not make springtime, so one day or a short time does not make a blessed or happy human being.

This may be taken as a sufficiently accurate sketch of the good; for it is right, I think to draw the outlines first and afterwards to fill in the details.

Aristotle's discussion here and in what follows seems to waver between treating the supreme good as a *good life* and treating it as some element within that life. In the latter case it is a central *value* that gives shape to everything else in that life. There may be many things needed for a good life, including some things that are valuable in themselves (such as bodily health), but that are not central to a good life. Moreover none of those things (health, for example) will be important if the central value is missing. Happiness, in *some* sense, seems to be such a central value. Health without happiness would hardly be optimal.

But what is happiness? In brief, Aristotle argues that it is "functioning well." So what is *that*? Operating in accordance with a proper excellence. Item (d)

tells you that a *good* human being is one that operates in accordance with a human's proper excellence. That comes rather close to saying that a good human being is a good human being. Not very informative, right? What we need to know is what the proper excellence of a human being *is*. The term for "excellence" here is "virtue" (the Greek word *arete* could be translated either way). So we need to know what the human virtues are.

Aristotle's view that there is a "function" common to all humans, or at any rate to all "men," is quite crucial to his argument. Yet the fact that the few things he mentions (a cobbler, an eye, etc.) have functions doesn't provide much reason for thinking a person has one. Moreover, the idea seems odd. People can generally "function" in so many ways, fill so many roles, that it seems odd to suggest that there is one function that all people have in common. Even though we can ask a quarterback in football what his function is, it almost seems insulting to ask someone what his or her "function" is simply *as a human being*. A doorknob has a function. A human being does not. Or so it might seem. However, in Aristotle's view just about everything has a function, that is, some natural, built-in purpose that will be fulfilled when it is "functioning" properly.

*5. *We are inquiring into the good life for human beings. For Aristotle that comes to inquiring into what a good human being is. You might disagree. Perhaps you know someone who seems quite happy, who has a "good life," but is not a good (honest, etc.) person. Discuss.*

*6. *Aristotle determines the function of human beings by asking what is unique about people. Consider the following comparison. Suppose I wonder what the function of the quarterback in football is. I notice that he contributes to winning the game, so perhaps that is his function. But so do the others players. If I want to know what his _____ _____ is, the function that distinguishes him from all other players, I must learn what his _____ contribution to playing and winning is. Right? That is, those actions, roles or tasks that distinguish him from others will tell me what his function is. So we* *might determine what trait or characteristic distinguishes human beings from other beings in order to see what the function of human beings is. Aristotle thinks that _____ is the distinguishing trait.*

7. *Does that seem like a good suggestion to you? Try coming up with an alternative distinguishing trait.*

Some people think that what is unique about humans is their use of language. Some think what is unique in them is the possibility of a conscious relation to God. There are lots of other views. It is worth noting that Aristotle includes quite a bit under "reason." For example, language is impossible without reason. So his view is not so narrow as might at first appear. But it is not immediately evident that Aristotle has good arguments for claiming that a life lived in accord with reason is *the* kind of life that fulfills the function of a human being. Further arguments for his view emerge in what follows.

*8. *In any case, if you mean by "good person" a person who is* functioning *optimally, and if you think that "happiness" consists precisely in functioning optimally, then of course you will have to conclude that a good person is a happy person. Would you also have to conclude that a happy person is a good person? Explain.*

CHAPTER VIII: *THIS ACCOUNT OF THE GOOD SQUARES WITH COMMON BELIEFS.*
Although Aristotle has criticized common ideas about the good (see Chapter v), he still thinks them important. They derive from experiences that all people have.

In considering the first principle we must pay regard not only to the conclusion and the premises of our argument, but also to such views as are popularly held about it. For while all experience harmonizes with the truth, it is never long before truth clashes with falsehood.

Goods have been divided into three classes, namely, external goods as they are called, goods of the soul and goods of the body. Of these three classes we consider the goods of the soul to be goods in the strictest or most literal sense. But it is to the soul that we ascribe psychical actions and activities. Thus our definition is a good one, at least according to this theory, which is not only ancient but is accepted by students of philosophy at the present time. It is right too, insofar as certain actions and activities are said to be the end; for thus it appears that the end is some good of the soul and not an external good. It is in harmony with this definition that the happy man should live well and do well, since happiness, as has been said, is in fact a kind of living and doing well [or a kind of optimal functioning].

It appears too that the requisite characteristics of happiness are all contained in the definition; for some people hold that happiness is virtue, others that it is practical wisdom, others that it is wisdom of some kind, others that it is these things or one of them conjoined with pleasure or not dissociated from pleasure, others again include external prosperity. Some of these views are held by many ancient thinkers, others by a few thinkers of high repute. It is probable that neither side is altogether wrong, they are both right.

Now, the definition is in harmony with the view of those who hold that happiness is virtue or excellence of some sort; for activity in accordance with virtue implies virtue. But it would seem that there is a considerable difference between taking the supreme good to consist in a moral state (a disposition to be moral or a capacity to be so) or in an activity. For a moral state, although it exists, may produce nothing good, e.g., if a person is asleep, or has in any way become inactive. But this cannot be the case with an activity, since activity implies action and good action. As in the Olympian games it is not the most beautiful and strongest persons who receive the crown but they who actually enter the lists as combatants—for it is some of these who become victors—so it is they who act rightly that attain to what is noble and good in life, and their life is pleasant in itself. For pleasure is a psychical fact, and whatever a man is said to be fond of is pleasant to him, e.g., a horse to one who is fond of horses, a spectacle to one who is fond of spectacles, and similarly just actions to a lover of justice, and virtuous actions in general to a lover of virtue. Now, most men find a sense of discord in their pleasures, because their pleasures are not such as are naturally pleasant.

But to the lovers of nobleness natural pleasures are pleasant. It is actions in accordance with virtue that are naturally pleasant both relatively to these people and in themselves.

Nor does their life require that pleasure should be attached to it as a sort of amulet; it possesses pleasure in itself. For it may be added that a person is not good, if he does not take delight in noble actions, as nobody would call a person just if he did not take delight in just actions, or generous if he did not take delight in generous actions and so on. But if this is so, it follows that actions in accordance with virtue are pleasant in themselves. But they are also good and noble, and good and noble in the highest degree, if the judgment of the virtuous man upon them is right (his judgment being such as we have described). Happiness then is the best and noblest and most pleasant thing in the world, nor is there any such distinction between goodness, nobleness, and pleasure as the epigram as Delos suggests:

"Justice is noblest, Health is best,
To gain one's end is most pleasant."

For these are all essential characteristics of the best activities, and we hold that happiness consists in these or in one and the noblest of these.

Still it is clear that happiness requires the addition of external goods, as we said; for it is impossible, or at least difficult, for a person to do what is noble unless he is furnished with external means. For there are many things which can only be done through the instrumentality of friends or wealth or political power, and there are some things the lack of which must mar felicity, e.g., noble birth, a prosperous family, and personal beauty. For a person is incapable of happiness if he is absolutely ugly in appearance, or low born, or solitary and childless, and perhaps still more so, if he has exceedingly bad children or friends and has lost them by death. As we said, then, it seems that prosperity of this kind is an indispensable addition to virtue. It is for this reason that some persons identify good fortune, and others, virtue, with happiness.

*9. *Some may think of happiness as a condition in which good things are happening, in which* "everything is going my way," *perhaps just because of good luck. Cite remarks from the previous passage that show Aristotle rejects this idea of happiness, and evaluate his view. Relate your discussion to Orienting Questions 2 and 3.*

10. *We may think that "doing what is right" is usually unpleasant in some way. For example, keeping a promise may involve giving up certain pleasures and telling the truth may get you grounded! Would Aristotle agree that doing what is right is typically unpleasant?*

11. *Mention two pleasures, one of which would clash with the other.*

*12. *The last text paragraph contains claims that many people will deny. Pick out two, and criticize them.*

CHAPTER IX: *HAPPINESS IS ACQUIRED PRIMARILY THROUGH EFFORT OF SOME SORT, RATHER THAN THROUGH CHANCE OR "GOOD LUCK."*

We see, as the discussion continues in this section, that Aristotle is ambivalent about the role of luck in the good life.

The question is consequently raised whether happiness is something that can be learnt or acquired by habit or discipline of any other kind, or whether it comes by some divine dispensation or even by chance.

Now, if there is anything in the world that is a gift of the Gods to men, it is reasonable to suppose that happiness is a divine gift, especially as it is the best of human things. This, however, is perhaps a point which is more appropriate to another investigation than the present. But even if happiness is not sent by the Gods but is the result of virtue and of learning or discipline of some kind, it is apparently one of the most divine things in the world, for it would appear that that which is the prize and the end of virtue is the supreme good and is in its nature divine and blessed. It will also be widely extended; for it will be capable of being produced in all persons, except such as are morally deformed, by a process of study or care. And if it is better that happiness should be produced in this way than by chance, it may reasonably be supposed that it is so produced, since everything is ordered in the best possible way in Nature and so too in art, and in causation generally and most of all in the highest kind of causation. But it would be altogether inconsistent to leave what is greatest and noblest to chance.

But the definition of happiness itself helps to clear up the question; for happiness has been defined as a certain kind of activity of the soul in accordance with virtue or excellence. Of the other goods, i.e., of goods besides those of the soul, some are necessary as antecedent conditions of happiness, others are in their nature cooperative and serviceable as instruments of happiness.

The conclusion at which we have arrived agrees with our original position. For we laid down that the end of political science is the supreme good; and political science is concerned with nothing so much as with producing a certain character, that is, with making people good, and capable of performing noble actions.

It is reasonable then not to speak of an ox, or a horse, or any other animal as happy; for none of them is capable of participating in activity as so defined.

For the same reason no child can be happy; as the age of a child makes it impossible for him to display this activity at the present, and if a child is ever said to be happy, the grounds for saying so is his potential, rather than his actual performance. For happiness demands, as we said, a complete virtue and a complete life. For there are all sorts of changes and chances in life, and it is possible that the most prosperous of men will, in his old age, fall into extreme calamities, as is told of Priam in the heroic legends. But if a person has experienced such chances, and has died a miserable death, nobody calls him happy.

*13. *Try to think of a case where* luck *played a role in a person's becoming a good person, and describe it. Then try to think of and describe a case where bad luck played an important role in a person's becoming a bad person. Are there any cases where bad luck played a role in a person's becoming a* good *person?*

Aristotle is saying that if happiness consists in an activity, as he originally claimed, then it cannot be something that simply "happens to you" but must rather be more like an achievement, something that depends on your own agency.

Animals and children cannot be happy. To which we might say, "Why not?" If happiness is a kind of optimal functioning (activity in accord with excellence), then why can't a horse or dog or child be "happy" as so defined? A happy horse, we might say, is an optimally functioning horse, exercising to the full those capacities that make a horse a horse.

14. *Has Aristotle simply defined happiness in such a way as to exclude animals? Try to defend his definition.*

15. *We do of course speak of children as being "happy." That would be a quite typical use of that English word* happy. *But if we stick with the idea that happiness, or* eudaimonia, *is optimal (human) functioning and that optimal functioning involves developed reason, then perhaps we can appreciate Aristotle's point, since children are thought of as not yet arrived at the age of reason (but why not?). Critically discuss Aristotle's claim.*

16. *Aristotle mentions Priam, the king of Troy, apparently a man of virtue. His last few months of life were terrible, everything that mattered most to him was destroyed. It looks as though the world does not always cooperate with "virtue" in such a way that "happiness" always goes with virtue. Is Aristotle brushing off this tragic fact too quickly, in your opinion?*

CHAPTER X: *UNDER WHAT CONDITIONS CAN SOMEONE BE CALLED HAPPY? MUST THEY BE IMMUNE TO CHANGES OF FORTUNE?*
Once again Aristotle is ambivalent (check again Chapters vii and ix). To his puzzlement so far he adds questions about the extent to which a person's happiness will be affected by the fortunes of her descendants after she dies.

If a person has lived a fortunate life up to old age, and has died a good death, it is possible that he may experience many vicissitudes of fortune in the persons of his descendants. Some of them may be good and may enjoy such a life as they deserve; others may be good and may have a bad life. It is clear, too, that descendants may stand in all sorts of different degrees of relationship to their ancestor. It would be an extraordinary result, if the dead man were to share the vicissitudes of their fortune and to become happy or miserable when they are. But it would be equally extraordinary, if the fortune of future descendants should not affect their ancestors at all or just for a certain time.

. . . It is clear that if we follow the changes of fortune, we shall often call the same person happy at one time and miserable at another, representing the happy man as "a sort of chameleon" and "a temple on rotting foundations."

It cannot be right to follow the changes of fortune. It is not upon these that good or evil depends; they are necessary accessories of human life, as we said; but it is a man's activities in accordance with virtue that constitute his happiness and the opposite activities that constitute his misery. The difficulty which has now been discussed is itself a witness that this is the true view. For there is no human function so constant as activities in accordance with virtue; they seem to be more permanent than the sciences themselves. Among these activities, too, it is the most honorable which are the most permanent, as it is in them that the life of the fortunate chiefly and most continuously consists. For this is apparently the reason why such activities are not liable to be forgotten.

The element of permanency which is required will be found in the happy man, and he will preserve his character throughout life; for he will constantly or in a preeminent degree pursue such actions and speculations as accord with virtue; nor is there anybody who will bear the chances of life so nobly, with such a perfect and complete harmony, as he who is truly good and "foursquare without a flaw."

Now, the events of chance are numerous and of different magnitudes. It is clear then that small incidents of good fortune, or the reverse, do not turn the scale of life, but that such incidents as are great and numerous augment the felicity of life if they are fortunate, since they tend naturally to embellish it where the use of them is noble and virtuous, but frequent reversals can hem in and mar our happiness both by causing pains and by hindering various activities. Still even in these circumstances nobility shines out, when a person bears the weight of accumulated misfortunes with calmness, not because he does not really feel them, but from innate dignity and magnanimity.

But if it is the activities which determine the life, as we said, nobody who is fortunate can become miserable; for he will never do what is hateful and mean. For our conception of the truly good and sensible man is that he bears all the chances of life with decorum and always does what is noblest in the circumstances. If this is so, it follows that the happy man can never become miserable; I do not say that he will be fortunate if he meets such chances of life as Priam. Yet he will not be variable or liable to frequent change, as he will not be moved from his happiness easily or by ordinary misfortunes but only by such misfortunes as are great and numerous, and after them it will not be soon that he will regain his happiness, but, if he regains it at all, it will be only in a long and complete period of time and after attaining great and noble results.

We may safely then define a happy man as one whose activities accord with perfect virtue and who is adequately furnished with external goods, not for a brief period of time but for a complete or perfect lifetime. But perhaps we ought to add that he will always live so, and will die as he lives; for it is not given us to foresee the future. But we take happiness to be an end, and to be altogether perfect and complete, and, this being so, we shall call people fortunate during their lifetime, if they possess and will possess these characteristics, but fortunate only so far as men may be fortunate. So much for the determination of this matter.

17. *Could you be happy now if you knew that your children or grandchildren would live in misery, due, let us say, to environmental disasters?*

Aristotle is once again addressing what might be called the "problem of moral luck." We have encountered this before (v. theme 7 in the list of themes following *Antigone*). The problem for Aristotle is: How can fortune, good or bad, determine the goodness of a life when the best kind of life has already been described as activity in accordance with reason, or optimal human functioning? Yet we can hardly say that when terrible things happen, even to the best person, that that has no effect on her "happiness."

> 18. *In the previous paragraphs Aristotle suggests a sort of solution to this problem; discuss his solution and try to defend it.*

Aristotle does not want to deny the importance of luck, but he does wants to resist the idea that personal goodness is just a function of luck or fortune. Can you appreciate the difficulty here? In speaking of the good person as "fortunate only so far as men may be fortunate," does Aristotle suggest that there are real limits to ethical endeavor, that no matter how hard we try and how well we act, our lives may still go down in defeat?

> **19. *Compare the vision of life found in Sophocles, Plato and Aristotle. Would Aristotle be more open to Sophocles' tragic vision than Plato? Are both more optimistic than Sophocles? Explain your answer.*

CHAPTER XIII: *AN INTRODUCTION TO THE CONCEPT OF VIRTUE.*
The notion of a virtue as Aristotle and the Greeks generally employed it is the notion of an excellence (some trait necessary for optimal functioning). In human beings it would be a trait of the soul. He first reiterates his claim that statesmen must be able to produce virtue in citizens. Doing that requires knowledge of the soul. The more cultivated doctors take a great deal of trouble to acquire knowledge of the body, and likewise the statesman must make a study of the soul. He then goes on to discuss the nature of the soul.

There are some facts concerning the soul which we have adequately stated in our popular works as well, and these we may rightly use. It is stated, for example, that the soul has two parts, one irrational and the other possessing reason.

Again, it seems that of the irrational part of the soul one part is common, i.e., shared by man with all living things; I mean the part which is the cause of nutrition and growth. . . . It is clear then that the virtue or excellence of this faculty is not distinctively human but is shared by man with all living things;

for it seems that this part and this faculty are especially active in sleep, whereas good and bad people are never so little distinguishable as in sleep . . . the principle of nutrition possesses no natural share in human virtue.

It seems that there is another natural principle of the soul which is irrational and yet in a sense partakes of reason. It appears that the irrational part of the soul is itself twofold; for the vegetative faculty does not participate at all in reason but the faculty of desire participates in it more or less, insofar as it is submissive and obedient to reason. But it is obedient in the sense in which we speak of paying attention to a father or to friends, but not in the sense in which we speak of paying attention to mathematics. All correction, rebuke and exhortation is a witness that the irrational part of the soul is in a sense subject to the influence of reason. But if we are to say that this part too possesses reason, then the part which possesses reason will have two divisions, one possessing reason absolutely and in itself, the other listening to it as a child listens to its father.

Virtue or excellence again admits of a distinction which depends on this difference. For we speak of some virtues as intellectual and of others as ethical; thus wisdom, intelligence and practical wisdom are intellectual virtues, while liberality and temperance are moral or ethical virtues. For when we describe a person's character, we do not say that he is wise or intelligent but that he is gentle or temperate. Yet we praise a wise man too in respect of his disposition, and such dispositions as deserve to be praised we call virtuous.

Many people tend to think of the soul as a separable thing. It is clear that Aristotle does not think of it that way. The immediately preceding passage amounts to a little introduction to his concept of the soul. Here he speaks of the soul as having a "vegetative part." What that means is that a human being has capacities for taking in nutrients, digesting them, and the like, which are similar in important ways to "vegetative" capacities found in plants and nonhuman animals.

> 20. *Vegetative capacities are clearly not "rational." Reason is not required for digestion. You do*

not have to think about or plan your digesting in order to digest well. Mention here some capacities that you think are rational.

It seems natural to say of certain desires, or emotions, that they are themselves rational or irrational. For example, the desire for pain, except in very unusual circumstances, would seem to be irrational. Fear of being in a crowd would seem to be irrational. Yet our desires and emotions do not belong to reason per se, in Aristotle's view, but are capable of being organized or trained by reason. They can become "obedient" to reason in varying degrees.

21. *If you woke up one morning and found yourself with an inexplicable yearning for a bowl of mud for breakfast, would that desire seem irrational to you, or rational, or neither? What is Aristotle's view? Defend his view.*

A disposition is a habit-like tendency. For example, a person who has a tendency to get angry easily has an angry disposition. Many dispositions can be acquired. You may have been trained to study a lot, and find it natural and easy to do so, in which case you have a studious disposition. Dispositions make up your character. If you are easily angered and accustomed to studying, those are two facets of your character, for better or worse.

22. *Name two other dispositions or character traits, good or bad.*
23. *Aristotle is interested in "character." He thinks that good character is acquired through a training in which reason plays a fundamental role. Our emotions and feelings are also part of our character and so must be able to be reasonable in some sense. His way of putting this has been to say that there must be a part of the _____ which is subject to _____.*

Try now to fill out the following summary of Aristotle's argument so far.

The concern of "ethics" is with determining what is the best kind of life for a human being. A "good" person will be one who has achieved that kind of life, the "good life."

1. All actions aim at some _____.
2. There must be a highest good, which is the ultimate _____ of all our actions, which is desired for its own sake, not merely as a _____ to something else.
3. Knowledge of this supreme _____ will obviously be important for the conduct of life, if we wish to lead a good life, or live in such a way as to achieve the highest goal.
4. Common opinion holds that this highest good is _____ and that seems correct insofar as _____ is desired for ___ ___ _____, not for the sake of something else.
5. But there is no common agreement on the correct _____ of happiness. Some common notions are that happiness is _____ or _____ or _____. But all of these are open to strong objections as definitions of happiness.
6. Since happiness is universally agreed to be equivalent to the good for humans, we can arrive at a good definition of happiness by considering what the specific good of humans might be, and we can do that by discovering the _____ of humans, since a "good *x*" is one that is _____ well, i.e., works and develops according to its own inmost nature.
7. We can determine the function of humans by considering what makes them different from other beings.
8. Thus we can see that the unique function of humans is to act in accord with _____, since the ability to so act is what distinguishes humans from other _____.
9. Now, a good thing of any kind (and, thus, a good human being) is one that performs its particular function well.
10. It follows from 6 through 9 that a happy person will be a good person, i.e., a person who is performing his particular function well.
11. Thus the end of human life, the _____ at which all human actions ultimately aim, is excellent activity in accordance with _____.

Something that functions optimally or operates in an excellent way is said to have a virtue or virtues, since a *virtue* is, in the Greek conception, simply a trait required for excellent operation. So to be a good person is to be a virtuous person, and vice versa.

*24. *Now, can you think of some objections to all of this? For instance, can you imagine a person who is using reason to guide all of his actions, who is doing an excellent job of it, but who is nonetheless not "good" or virtuous and might even be evil? Try to describe such a case.*

Here is an objection that you *cannot* have to Aristotle's account. You may think that it is sometimes important to sacrifice happiness in order to do your duty. The soldier might even give up his life, which might have included many happy days with loved ones, in order to do his duty. So you might say that for that reason duty is a higher end or aim than happiness.

Why can't you make that objection? Because what Aristotle *means* by happiness is a life lived virtuously. So it would not make sense to say, in his view, that a dutiful action could trump happiness. If you are doing your duty, you *are* happy, even if you are getting killed or opening yourself to criticism or other harms by doing it!

We will examine the concept of duty further in later chapters. The task now is to examine more closely the concept of virtue and a virtuous life.

Book II: The Concept of a Virtue

Chapter I: *VIRTUE, CHARACTER AND TRAINING.*
Aristotle now provides an analysis of the concept of a virtue or excellence (arete *in Greek*).

Virtue or excellence being twofold, partly intellectual and partly moral, intellectual virtue is both originated and fostered mainly by teaching; it therefore demands experience and time. Moral virtue, on the other hand, is the outcome of habit, and accordingly its name is derived, by a slight variation of form, from "habit." From this fact it is clear that no moral virtue

is implanted in us by nature; a law of nature cannot be altered by habituation. Thus a stone naturally tends to fall downwards, and it cannot be habituated or trained to rise upwards, even if we were to [try to] habituate it by throwing it upwards 10,000 times; nor again can fire be trained to sink downwards, nor anything else that follows one natural law be habituated or trained to follow another. It is neither by nature then nor in defiance of nature that virtues are implanted in us. Nature gives us the capacity of receiving them, and that capacity is perfected by habit.

Again, if we take the various natural powers which belong to us, we first acquire the proper faculties and afterwards display the activities. It is clearly so with the senses. It was not by seeing frequently or hearing frequently that we acquired the senses of seeing or hearing; on the contrary it was because we possessed the senses that we made use of them, not by making use of them that we obtained them.

In contrast, we acquire the virtues by first exercising them, as is the case with all the arts, for it is by doing what we ought to do when we have learnt the arts that we learn the arts themselves; for example, we become builders by building and harpists by playing the harp. . . . The case of the virtues is the same. It is by acting in such transactions as take place between person and person that we become either just or unjust. It is by acting in the face of danger and by habituating ourselves to fear or courage that we become either cowardly or courageous. It is much the same with our desires and angry passions. Some people become temperate and gentle, others become intemperate and angry, according as they conduct themselves in one way or another way in particular circumstances.

To sum up then, states of character are the results of repeated acts corresponding to those states. So it is necessary for us to produce on demand those activities which will produce the corresponding [ethical] states. It makes no small difference then how we are trained up from our youth; rather it is a serious, even an all-important matter.

In thinking about habit and training into "virtues," consider what we might call a "nonmoral" example:

If you were brought up in a messy home and repeatedly left things in a mess everywhere you went in the house, without getting scolded, you will probably be a messy person, no matter what your "natural" tendencies may be.

> *25. Does Aristotle's account imply that if you have not been brought up properly you have very little or no chance of becoming a good (i.e., properly habituated and optimally functioning, virtuous, and thus happy) person? Discuss and defend your own view on this matter.*

CHAPTER II

Aristotle introduces the notion of a virtue as a kind of mean state, in which excess or deficiency is avoided.

. . . The first point to be observed then is that in such matters as we are considering deficiency and excess are equally fatal. It is so, as we observe, in regard to health and strength; for we must judge of what we cannot see by the evidence of what we do see. Excess or deficiency of gymnastic exercise is fatal to strength. Similarly an excess or deficiency of meat and drink is fatal to health, whereas a suitable amount produces, augments and sustains it. It is the same then with temperance, courage, and the other virtues. A person who avoids and is afraid of everything and faces nothing becomes a coward; a person who is not afraid of anything but is ready to face everything becomes foolhardy. Similarly he who enjoys every pleasure and never abstains from any pleasure is licentious; he who eschews all pleasures like a boor is an insensible sort of person. For temperance and courage are destroyed by excess and deficiency but preserved by the mean state.

Again, not only are the causes and the agencies of production, increase and destruction in the ethical states the same, but the sphere of their activity will be proved to be the same also. It is so in other instances which are more conspicuous, e.g., in strength; for strength is produced by taking a great deal of food and undergoing a great deal of labor, and it is the strong man who is able to take the most food and to undergo the most labor.

The same is the case with the virtues. It is by abstinence from pleasures that we become temperate,

and, when we have become temperate, we are best able to abstain from them. So too with courage; it is by habituating ourselves to despise and face alarms that we become courageous, and, when we have become courageous, we shall be best able to face them.

> 26. *Aristotle makes a point at the beginning of this chapter that he treats in considerable detail in later chapters of this book and that is thought by some to be his most characteristic idea, namely, that virtues are midpoints between extremes. For example, courage is midway between being cowardly and being rash. Would generosity be a mean between two extremes? If so, what would they be?*

CHAPTER III: *VIRTUE, PLEASURE AND PAIN.*

Aristotle shows that virtues are traits that are connected in some way with our ability to manage pleasures and pains in a reasonable way.

The pleasure or pain that follows upon actions may be regarded as a test of a person's moral state. He who abstains from physical pleasures and feels delight in so doing is temperate but he who feels pain at so doing is licentious. He who faces dangers with pleasure, or at least without pain, is courageous; but he who feels pain at facing them is a coward.

For moral virtue is concerned with pleasures and pains. [This can be seen from the following facts:]

1. It is pleasure which makes us do what is base, and pain which makes us abstain from doing what is noble. Hence the importance of having had a certain training from very early days, as Plato says, namely such a training as produces pleasure and pain at the right objects; for this is the true education.
2. Again, if the virtues are concerned with actions and emotions, and every action and every emotion is attended by pleasure or pain, this will be another reason why virtue should be concerned with pleasures and pains.
3. There is also a proof of this fact in the use of pleasure and pain as means of punishment; for punishments are in a sense medical measures, and the means employed as remedies are natu-

rally the opposites of the diseases to which they are applied.

4. Again, as we said before, every moral state of the soul is in its nature relative to, and concerned with, the thing by which it is naturally made better or worse. But pleasures and pains are the causes of vicious states of character when we pursue and avoid the wrong pleasures and pains, or pursue and avoid them at the wrong time or in the wrong manner, or in any other of the various ways in which it is logically possible to do wrong. Hence it is that people actually define the virtues as ways of being unaffected and undisturbed [by pleasures and pains]; but they are wrong in using this absolute language, and not qualifying it by speaking of being affected in the right or wrong manner, time and so on.

It may be assumed then that moral virtue tends to produce the best action in respect of pleasures and pains, and that vice is its opposite. But the same points will be evident from the following considerations:

5. There are three things which influence us to desire them, namely the noble, the expedient, and the pleasant; and three opposite things which influence us to avoid them, namely the shameful, the injurious and the painful The good man then will be likely to take a right line, and the bad man to take a wrong one, with respect to all these, but especially in respect to pleasure; for pleasure is felt not by humans only but by the lower animals, and is associated with all things that are matters of desire, as the noble and the expedient alike appear pleasant.

6. Pleasure too develops in us all from early childhood, so that it is difficult to get rid of the emotion of pleasure, as it is deeply ingrained in our life.

7. Again, we make pleasure and pain in a greater or less degree the standard of our actions. So our entire study should be concerned from first to last with pleasures and pains; for right or wrong feelings of pleasure or pain have a material influence upon actions.

8. Again, it is more difficult to contend against pleasure than against anger, as Heraclitus says, and both art and virtue are constantly concerned with what is more difficult. For a good result [or product] is even better by virtue of this [the difficulty involved in producing it]. So for this reason pleasure and pain are the whole business of both virtue and politics, since the one who makes good use of them is good, the one who makes a bad use is evil.

27. *Pick two of Aristotle's eight reasons for his claim that virtue (excellence) has to do with pleasures and pains that you think are especially important, and say why.*

28. *Consider your own assessments of other people. Do you tend to think badly of people who are addicted to certain pleasures? Give one example.*

29. *Are any of the sorts of things people do to avoid pain what you would call "immoral"? Give an example.*

CHAPTER IV: *THE DISTINCTION BETWEEN A VIRTUOUS ACT AND A VIRTUOUS PERSON.*
A difficulty may be raised as to what is meant by saying that in order to become just we must do just actions, and in order to become temperate we must do temperate actions. For [someone might argue], if they do such actions they must be just already, just as, if they spell correctly or play in tune they are already scholars or musicians.

Aristotle's solution is as follows: Suppose I do a courageous act, but (1) I do not fully understand the situation I am in (do not fully understand the danger, for instance, or do not have an accurate idea of my own abilities to handle the situation); and/or (2) I cannot be said to have deliberately chosen to so act (since perhaps I did not have enough knowledge to deliberate) and thus, since I do not fully appreciate what I am doing, cannot be said to have chosen this act "for its own sake"; and/or (3) I have not become accustomed or habituated to acting in this way. Where any of these three conditions hold, then we should not say that I was a virtuous person, even though my act was a virtuous act. But where I do understand the situation, deliberately choose, and am properly habituated, then my courageous action is the action of a virtuous person. It is the action of a person who actually is courageous, as opposed to someone who happens to do a courageous thing now and then, even though he is generally cowardly.

CHAPTER V: *THE GENUS OF VIRTUE.*

Virtue is a "state of the soul." Exactly what kind of state?

We have next to consider the formal definition of virtue.

A state of the soul is either an emotion, a capacity, or a disposition; virtue must be one of these three then. By emotions I mean desire, anger, fear, confidence, envy, joy, friendship, hatred, longing, jealousy, pity; and such states of mind accompanied by pleasure or pain. The capacities are the faculties in virtue of which we can be said to be liable to emotions, e.g., capable of releasing anger or pain or pity. Dispositions are formed states of character in virtue of which we are well or badly disposed in respect of the mentioned; for instance, we have a bad disposition in regard to anger if we are disposed to get angry too violently or not enough, a good disposition if we habitually feel moderate anger [in the right situations]; and similarly with respect to other emotions.

Now, virtues and vices are not identical with emotions because we are not called good or bad according to our emotions; nor are we praised or blamed for our emotions—no one is praised for being frightened or angry, or blamed for being angry merely, but only for being angry in a particular way—but we *are* praised or blamed for our virtues and vices. Again, we are not angry or afraid from choice, but the virtues are certain modes of choice, or involve choice.

The same considerations show that virtues and vices are not capacities, since we are not called good or bad, praised or blamed, because of our capacity for emotion.

If then the virtues are neither emotions nor capacities, it remains that they are dispositions. Thus we have said what the genus of virtue is [it is a disposition].

CHAPTER VI. *THE SPECIES OF VIRTUE.*

A virtue is a disposition (a tendency). But what specific kind? Remember, to be good is to be functioning well (excellently) and that is what happiness is. And excellence in human living requires the use of Reason.

By the mean in respect of the thing itself, or the absolute mean, I understand that which is equally distinct from both extremes; and this is one and the same thing for everybody. By the mean considered relative to ourselves I understand that which is neither too much nor too little; but this is not one thing, nor is it the same for everybody.

Thus if 10 be too much and 2 too little we take 6 as a mean in respect of the thing itself; for 6 is as much greater than 2 as it is less than 10, and this is a mean in arithmetical proportion. But the mean considered relative to ourselves must not be ascertained in this way. It does not follow that if 10 pounds of meat be too much and 2 too little for a man to eat, a trainer will order him 6 pounds, as this may itself be too much or too little for the person who is to take it; it will be too little, e.g., for Milo [a very big Greek athlete], but too much for a beginner in gymnastics. It will be the same with running and wrestling; the right amount varies with the individual.

This being so, everybody who understands his business avoids alike excess and deficiency; he seeks and chooses the mean, not the absolute mean, but the mean considered relative to himself.

Every science then performs its function well, if it regards the mean and refers the works which it produces to the mean. This is the reason why it is usually said of successful works that it is impossible to take anything from them or to add anything to them, which implies that excess or deficiency is fatal to excellence but that the mean state ensures it. . . . Virtue therefore will aim at the mean.

I speak of moral virtue, as it is moral virtue which is concerned with emotion and actions, and it is these which admit of excess and deficiency and the mean. Thus it is possible to go too far, or not to go far enough, in respect of fear, courage, desire, anger, pity, and pleasure and pain generally, and the excess and the deficiency are alike wrong; but to experience these emotions at the right times and on the right occasions and towards the right persons and for the right causes and in the right manner is the mean or the supreme good, which is characteristic of virtue.

Similarly there may be excess, deficiency, or the mean, in regard to actions. But virtue is concerned with emotions and actions, and here excess is an error and deficiency a fault, whereas the mean is successful and laudable, and success and merit are both characteristics of virtue. It appears then that virtue is a mean state, so far at least as it aims at the mean.

> 30. *The mean is a midpoint. Courage is a mean, since it is midway between cowardice and rashness. Now illustrate what is meant by "the mean considered relative to oneself."*
>
> *31. *Aristotle claims that having a virtue is not just having a disposition to act in a certain way, but it is also having dispositions to feel in certain ways. And of course the two are closely connected. Give an example from your own life of a tendency to feel in inappropriate ways, which leads you to act badly (you will be unable to answer this question only if you are a perfect person).*

Aristotle's view is sometimes equated with the saying, "moderation in all things." But that is not his view. Sometimes it is appropriate to get extremely angry or to do something very dangerous, thus putting one's own life at risk. What puts an action "in the mean" is that it is *appropriate* to the situation, *for the person involved.*

> 32. *Try to think up a case where extreme anger would be appropriate and would thus express the "mean" in feeling.*

Again, error is many formed (for evil is a form of the unlimited and good of the limited, as the Pythagoreans imaged it), while success is possible in only one way, which is why it is easy to fail and difficult to succeed, as it is easy to miss the mark and difficult to hit it. This is another reason why excess and deficiency are marks of vice, and observance of the mean a mark of virtue:

Goodness is simple, badness is manifold.

Virtue then is a disposition with respect to choice, i.e. the disposition to choose a mean that is relative to ourselves, the mean being determined by reasoned principle, that is, as a prudent man would determine it.

Virtue is a mean state lying between two vices, the vice of excess on the one hand, and the vice of deficiency on the other, and whereas the vices either fall short of or go beyond what is proper in the emotions and actions, virtue not only discovers but embraces the mean. Accordingly, virtue, if regarded in its essence or theoretical conception, is a mean state, but, if regarded from the point of view of the highest good, or of excellence, it is extreme.

But it is not every action or every emotion that admits of a mean state. There are some whose very name implies wickedness, as, e.g., malice, shamelessness, and envy, among emotions, or adultery, theft, and murder, among actions. All these, and others like them, are censured as being intrinsically wicked, not merely the excesses or deficiencies of them. It is never possible then to be right in respect of them; they are always wrong. Right or wrong in such actions as adultery does not depend on our committing them with the right person, at the right time or in the right manner; on the contrary it is wrong to do anything of the kind at all. It would be equally wrong then to suppose that there can be a mean state or an excess or deficiency in unjust, cowardly or licentious conduct. For, if it were, there would be a mean state of an excess or of a deficiency, an excess of an excess and a deficiency of a deficiency [which is nonsense].

Aristotle's definition of virtue as a "disposition to choose the *mean*" is not practically useful. Actions "in the mean" are simply those actions that a virtuous person will produce. There is no point in trying to find the mean or "midpoint" in action and then trying for that. There is no such midpoint existing independent of the virtuous agent. Extreme anger, violent actions, fleeing from a battle, all of these could be virtuous, depending on the agent and the circumstances. Moreover, there are some actions that a virtuous person would not even consider. To choose the mean is, practically, to do what is right.

The notion of the mean does suggest an interesting way to think about the virtuous life, however, for it suggests that virtuous responses are a small selection out of many possibilities. There are, as Aristotle states, many ways of going wrong, but the right way is "narrow."

> 33. *State Aristotle's full definition of virtue, beginning with "virtue then is a disposition . . . "*

CHAPTER VII: *A CATALOGUE AND CHART OF THE VIRTUES.*

What follows is an outline of some of the main virtues and vices. We can imagine Aristotle pointing to a chart with three divisions, one for excesses, one for virtues and one for defects.

But it is not enough to lay this down as a general rule; it is necessary to apply it to particular cases, as in reasonings upon actions generally, statements, although they are broader are less exact than particular statements. For all action refers to particulars, and it is essential that our theories should harmonize with the particular cases to which they apply.

We must take particular virtues then from the catalogue of virtues. In regard to feelings of fear and confidence, courage is a mean state. On the side of excess, he whose fearlessness is excessive has no name, as often happens, but he whose confidence is excessive is foolhardy, while he whose timidity is excessive and whose confidence is deficient is a coward.

In respect of pleasures and pains, although not indeed of all pleasures and pains, and to a less extent in respect of pains than of pleasures, the mean state is temperance, the excess is licentiousness. We never find people who are deficient in regard to pleasure; accordingly such people again have not received a name, but we may call them insensible [dull, listless].

As regards the giving and taking of money, the mean state is liberality, the excess and deficiency are prodigality and illiberality [stinginess]. Here the excess and deficiency take opposite forms; for while the prodigal man is excessive in spending and deficient in taking, the illiberal man is excessive in taking and deficient in spending.

(For the present we are giving only a rough and summary account of the virtues, and that is sufficient for our purpose; we will hereafter determine their character more exactly.)

In respect of money there are other dispositions as well. There is the mean state, which is magnificence;

for the magnificent man, who is one who deals with large sums of money, differs from the liberal man, who has to do only with small sums; and the excess corresponding to it is bad taste or vulgarity, the deficiency is meanness. These are different from the excess and deficiency of liberality; what the difference is will be explained hereafter.

When modern people hear the word *ethics* they may think of such questions as whether it is ever right to tell a lie or to cheat, whether it is ever right to remove a respirator from a terminally ill person, and so forth. Many of us do not typically think about "character traits" when we hear *ethics*, but even if we do, we would probably not include all the traits Aristotle is discussing here, such as being a big (and vulgar) spender on the one hand, or stingy on the other, as opposed to being "just right" (knowing how to spend, buy presents or throw a party with just the right degree of opulence). So not only is Aristotle more concerned with character traits than with criteria for right actions, he is also concerned with character traits that we might not think of as having anything to do with ethics.

> 34. *But remember, he is raising the question of what the _____ kind of life is, or what the _____ is of all our actions, and he has concluded that the answer is* happiness. *And surely all sorts of character traits have a bearing on how _____ we are, not just the "ethical" ones, as we tend to think of* ethics. *For example, how clever or pleasant or artistic a person is can obviously have a bearing on the quality of his or her life. Aristotle discusses some of these next, along with many other such traits.*

In respect of honor and dishonor the mean state is *high-mindedness*, the excess is what is called *vanity*, the deficiency *little-mindedness*.

Corresponding to liberality, which, as we said, differs from magnificence as having to do not with great but with small sums of money, there is a moral state which has to do with petty honor and is related to high-mindedness, which has to do with great honor; for it is possible to aspire to honor in the right way, or in a way which is excessive or insufficient, and if a person's aspirations are excessive, he is called *ambitious*, if they are deficient, he is called *unambitious*, while if they are between the two, he has no name. The dispositions too are nameless, except that the disposition of the ambitious person is called *ambition*. The consequence is that the extremes lay claim to the mean or intermediate place. We ourselves speak of one who observes the mean sometimes as ambitious and at other times as unambitious; we sometimes praise an ambitious, and at other times an unambitious person. The reason for our doing so will be stated in due course, but let us now discuss the other virtues in accordance with the method which we have followed hitherto.

> 35. *Aristotle is evidently having some difficulty getting all of the virtues (vices) mapped onto his scheme of the _____, the_____ (the virtue) and the _____. This again suggests that this scheme is not so central to his aims as his discussion seems to indicate.*

There are also mean states in the emotions and in the expression of the emotions. For although modesty is not a virtue, yet a modest person is praised as if he were virtuous; for here too one person is said to observe the mean and another to exceed it, as, e.g., the bashful man, who is never anything but modest, whereas a person who has insufficient modesty or no modesty at all is called *shameless*, and one who observes the mean *modest*.

Righteous indignation, again, is a mean state between envy and malice. They are all concerned with the pain and pleasure which we feel at the fortunes of our neighbors. A person who is righteously indignant is pained at the prosperity of the undeserving; but the envious person goes further and is pained at anybody's prosperity, and the malicious person is so far from being pained that he actually rejoices at misfortunes. We shall have another opportunity, however, of discussing these matters.

Notice again that Aristotle's discussion of virtues and vices includes much that we might include under the emotions or temperament. But of course such an emotion as envy tends to go with certain dispositions

to act in ignoble ways. So Aristotle's claim that the species of virtue is dispositions not only to act but to *feel* certain ways looks quite defensible.

> 36. *Is the presence of envy and malice in the world at least as responsible for the miseries of life as what we call immoral actions, such as lying and murder and theft?*
> 37. *Are the people who have these vices as likely to be unhappy as the people who are their victims? Explain your view briefly.*

There are then three dispositions, two being vices, namely one the vice of excess and the other that of deficiency, and one virtue, which is the mean state between them; and they are all in a sense mutually opposed. . . . Thus the courageous man appears foolhardy as compared with the coward, but cowardly as compared with the foolhardy. Similarly, the temperate person appears licentious as compared with the insensible person but insensible as compared with the licentious, and the liberal man appears prodigal compared to the stingy man, but stingy compared to a prodigal one.

Again, while some extremes exhibit more or less similarity to the mean, as foolhardiness resembles courage [more than cowardice does] and prodigality resembles liberality [more than stinginess does], there is the greatest possible dissimilarity between the extremes themselves. But things that are furthest removed from each other are defined to be opposites; hence the further things are removed, the greater is the opposition between them. It is in some cases the deficiency and in others the excess which is the more opposite to the mean. Thus it is not foolhardiness (the excess), but cowardice (the deficiency) which is the more opposed to courage, nor is it insensibility (the deficiency), but licentiousness (the excess) which is the more opposed to temperance.

There are two reasons why this should be so. One lies in the nature of the thing itself; for as one of the two extremes is the nearer and more similar to the mean, it is not this extreme, but its opposite, that we chiefly set against the mean. For instance, as it appears that foolhardiness is more similar and nearer to courage than cowardice, it is cowardice that we chiefly set against courage; for things which are further removed from the mean seem to be more opposite to it.

There is a second reason, which lies in our own nature. It is the things to which we ourselves are naturally more inclined that appear more opposed to the mean. Thus we are ourselves naturally more inclined to pleasures than to their opposites, and are more prone therefore to licentiousness than to decorum. Accordingly we speak of those things, in which we are more likely to run to great lengths, as being more opposed to the mean. Hence it follows that licentiousness, which is an excess, is more opposed to temperance than dullness.

It has now been sufficiently shown that moral virtue is a mean state, and in what sense it is a mean state; it is a mean state as lying between two vices, a vice of excess on the one side and a vice of deficiency on the other, and as aiming at the mean in the emotions and actions.

That is the reason why it is so hard to be virtuous; for it is always hard work to find the mean in anything. For example, it is not everybody, but only a man of science, who can find the mean or center of a circle. So too anybody can get angry, that is an easy matter, and anybody can give or spend money, but to give it to the right persons, to give the right amount of it and to give it at the right time and for the right cause and in the right way, this is not what anybody can do, nor is it easy. That is the reason why it is rare and laudable and noble to do well. Accordingly one who aims at the mean must begin by departing from that extreme which is the more contrary to the mean . . . and this we shall best do in the way that we have described, i.e., by steering clear of the evil which is further from the mean.

We must also observe the things to which we are ourselves particularly prone, as different natures have different inclinations, and we may ascertain what these are by a consideration of our feelings of pleasure and pain. And then we must drag ourselves in the direction opposite to them; for it is by removing ourselves as far as possible from what is wrong that we shall arrive at the mean, as we do when we pull a crooked stick straight.

But in all cases we must especially be on our guard against what is pleasant and against pleasure, as we are not impartial judges of pleasure. Hence our attitude towards pleasure must be like that of the elders of the people in the Iliad towards Helen, and we must never be afraid of applying the words they used; for if we dismiss pleasure as they dismissed Helen, we shall be less likely to go wrong.

It is by action of this kind, to put it summarily, that we shall best succeed in hitting the mean. It may be admitted that this is a difficult task, especially in particular cases. For example, it is not easy to determine the right manner, objects, occasions, and duration of anger. There are times when we ourselves praise people who are deficient in anger, and call them gentle, and there are other times when we speak of people who exhibit a savage temper as spirited. It is not, however, one who deviates a little from what is right, but one who deviates a great deal, whether on the side of excess or of deficiency, that is censured; for he is sure to be found out.

Again, it is not easy to decide theoretically how far and to what extent a man may go before he becomes blamable, but neither is it easy to define theoretically anything else within the region of perception; such things fall under the head of particulars, and our judgment of them depends upon our perception.

*38. *Briefly, why is it that we tend to think of certain extremes as being closer to the right and virtuous actions (or dispositions) than others? For example, why do we think rashness closer to courage than cowardice, even though courage is supposed to be a "midpoint"? Remember, there are two reasons. Give both.*

*39. *Some people, in Aristotle's day and ever since, have thought that the best life is one of excess (eat drink and be merry, . . . a lot). Mention a few things here that you might say against such a view to someone, including possibly yourself, who believes it.*

40. *(a) Do Aristotle's concerns with pleasure show that he has puritanical and repressive tendencies? (b) Mention some examples of your own of people who have made themselves miserable through their inability or refusal to manage and control their desires for pleasure (you do not need to mention names). Try to make your answers to (a) and (b) consistent.*

Aristotle is claiming something in the last sentence that is quite central to his way of thinking about ethics. He is saying that in order to achieve a good life, a life of virtue and thus of happiness, we must have something like what we would now call *perceptiveness*. We use this word to describe a sensitivity to particular persons and particular situations.

> ****41.** *But couldn't a person still be a good person who lacked perceptiveness, provided only that the person followed such rules as "Do not lie, do not cheat, do not inflict unnecessary pain, be kind" and so forth? If you can think of a reason why such a person might not succeed in being, or at any rate doing, good, state it here. If you cannot, think about it a little more.*

Some philosophers have suggested that we can enrich and broaden our understanding of what is involved in being perceptive (or imperceptive) by reading certain kinds (but not just any kinds!) of novels and other literature. The novels of Jane Austen, for instance, constantly explore successes and failures in perception on the part of the main characters.

> ***42.** *Does what Aristotle says about rearing and training at the end of II, i and the beginning of II, iii have any bearing on this matter of perceptiveness? Try producing some examples of such training from some nonethical domain (e.g., sports, the arts). For example, you might have to learn to notice things about your golf swing, and someone might have to teach you to notice those things (be perceptive).*

Book III: "Free Will," the Voluntary and Choice

In Book III, Aristotle is discussing a topic that may seem an essential preliminary to ethics. If people are not capable of voluntary acts, then there would be no room for ethical evaluation. Today we speak of heredity and environment, operating in a "law like" way, as "determining" behavior, and if a person's actions turn out to be the inevitable result of such "laws of nature," we may refuse to blame or praise him or even to think of those actions in ethical terms. If a

rock falls on someone and kills him, we don't blame the rock. If natural forces beyond a person's control lead her to kill someone, we do not blame her either.

It is important to understand that Aristotle does *not* think about voluntary or chosen actions, as opposed to actions that are somehow "determined" or "beyond our control," in ways that connect up simply with modern ways of thinking. He does not think of bodies as governed by "laws of nature." In his thinking, all bodies or physical things, including humans, have certain "natures," and their actions follow from those natures, unless impeded in some way. But of course he recognizes that our bodies can be "forced" in various ways. I could grab your arm and push it into someone's (let's say, Dan's) face. You would not be blamable for hitting Dan. Aristotle calls such a case *compulsion*. There are also cases where I act without fully realizing what I am doing. I act "through ignorance." Usually we do not blame or praise those who so act. These are ordinary distinctions that we use pretty much as Aristotle did.

Aristotle's concept of virtue requires an account of choice. Choice, you may remember, was essential to his definition of virtue; "virtue is a disposition to choose *the mean. . . ."*

CHAPTER I: *CHOSEN ACTIONS ARE A SUBSET OF VOLUNTARY ACTIONS.*
So Aristotle first discusses the distinction between voluntary and involuntary actions.

But if someone were to say that pleasant and noble objects have a compelling power, forcing us from without, *all* acts would be for him compulsory; for it is for these objects that all men do everything they do. And those who act under compulsion and unwillingly act with pain, but those who do acts for their pleasantness and nobility do them with pleasure; it is absurd to make external circumstances, rather than oneself, responsible, when easily caught by the attractions of pleasures, and on the other hand to make oneself responsible for noble acts, but the pleasant objects responsible for base acts. The compulsory, then, seems to be that whose moving principle is outside, while the person who is compelled contributes nothing.

An act done through ignorance is never voluntary, but it is involuntary by virtue of its causing pain and regret; for someone who acts through ignorance and feels no regret . . . cannot be said to have acted involuntarily, since he acts without distress. . . . We may call him a *nonvoluntary* agent.

. . . What, then, or what kind of thing is choice, since it is none of the things we have mentioned? It seems to be voluntary, but not all that is voluntary seems to be an object of choice. Is it, then, what has been decided on by *previous* deliberation [about various possibilities]? At any rate choice involves a rational principle and thought. Even the name seems to suggest what is chosen *before* other things. [The Greek word translated as "choice" can be taken to mean "to take before," in the sense of thinking ahead of time, as in thoughtfully choosing to eat only vegetables or thoughtfully choosing which guy to date out of all that have asked].

Aristotle claims that any view that makes *all* actions "compulsory" is "absurd." Only when the "moving principle" comes from outside can I be said to be compelled. In Chapter i he makes commonsense distinctions between actions that are forced from "outside," those that are clearly chosen, those done through ignorance and those we perform even though we would not normally choose them. The last category would include telling a lie because a dictator will kill my family if I do not, or throwing goods overboard to save a ship from sinking. Aristotle concedes that in one sense I act unwillingly in such instances, my action is involuntary, but in another way the source of movement still comes from "within," from myself, and so is voluntary.

Acting through ignorance is different. Aristotle has in mind ignorance about particular circumstances of an action. If I switch on the light, not knowing the switch will short out and start a fire, then my burning down my house was not something I chose. However, the action of burning down the house is said to be involuntary only if I regret the fact that the house was burned down or feel distressed about it. However, suppose I wanted the house burned down, even though I didn't know the switch was wired so as to start a fire! Why not call such an action involuntary?

But since it got me what I wanted, Aristotle gives it a separate name, i.e., *nonvoluntary.*

Aristotle also notes that actions done "*in* ignorance" are not rightly called involuntary. They are classed with voluntary acts. For instance, a drunken person may act in ignorance, where his ignorance is the result of being drunk. He could have avoided getting drunk. So such actions are blamable.

Here is his scheme so far:

a. voluntary acts (source is in me, and I chose it)
b. involuntary acts (source comes from outside, and I did not want the result)
c. acts that are voluntary but not ones I would normally choose
d. nonvoluntary acts (acting through ignorance, I didn't realize what I was doing, but I like the result)
e. acting in ignorance

Aristotle's discussion is complex, and perhaps not entirely consistent. In any case it largely conforms to common sense and legal reasoning regarding actions that are done by a person under external duress, or through ignorance, or "in" ignorance.

43. *Does it seem to you that a person who throws cargo overboard to save a ship is acting voluntarily, or is that person, rather, "forced" by circumstances, just as when I force your hand into someone's face? Defend your view.*

*44. *By Aristotle's account, actions done "through" ignorance are not involuntary, but nonvoluntary, since there is no regret. Should there be a similar distinction for compelled acts? Suppose someone forces my fist into Dan's face, when in fact I was wanting to punch Dan anyway. Shouldn't that make that compelled act nonvoluntary too, instead of involuntary? What is Aristotle's view, or isn't it clear?*

Chapter iii: *what choice is. choice and deliberation.*

We do not deliberate about what is impossible (for example, whether or not to jump 500 feet into the air from a standing position on the earth) or about other matters that are not under our control. His positive account follows.

. . . Things that are brought about by our own efforts, but not always in the same way, are the things about which we deliberate, e.g., questions of medical treatment or of moneymaking. And we do so more in the case of the art of navigation than in that of gymnastics, inasmuch as the art of navigation has been less exactly worked out, and again about other things in the same ratio, and more also in the case of the arts than in that of the sciences; for we have more doubt about the former. Deliberation is concerned with things that happen in a certain way for the most part, but in which the event is obscure, and with things in which it is indeterminate.

We call on others to aid us in deliberation on important questions, distrusting ourselves as not being equal to deciding. We deliberate not about ends but about what pertains to the end.

It seems, then, as has been said, that man is a moving principle of actions. Now, deliberation is about the things to be done by the agent himself, and actions are for the sake of things other than themselves. For the end cannot be a subject of deliberation, but only what promotes the end; nor indeed can the particular facts be a subject of it, as whether this is bread or has been baked as it should; for these are matters of perception. If we are to be always deliberating, we shall have to go on to infinity.

The same thing is deliberated upon and is chosen, except that the object of choice is already determinate, since it is that which has been decided upon as a result of deliberation that is the object of choice. For everyone ceases to inquire how he is to act when he has brought the moving principle back to himself and to the ruling part of himself; for this is what chooses. . . . The object of choice being one of the things in our own power which is desired after deliberation, choice will be deliberate desire of things in our own power; for when we have decided as a result of deliberation, we desire in accordance with our deliberation. We may take it, then, that we have described choice in outline, and stated the nature of its objects and the fact that it is concerned with means.

Here is Aristotle's definition of *choice*:

choice = deliberate desire of things in our power

This definition is notable for the way in which it postulates a *combining* of reason and desire. Choice is not construed as the exercise of a raw faculty of will, nor as the output of pure rationality.

45. *If without thinking you simply grabbed something because you desired it, Aristotle would deny that you had made a choice. Do you agree? Why?*

Aristotle's account implies that, when we are genuine choosers, rather than people moved by various forces outside our control, we are motivated to act by reason-with-desire. Reason by itself will not move us to act, but reason combined with desire is essential to acts that are really chosen. There are two claims here: Reason by itself will not produce any actions at all; actions that arise out of pure desire or feeling (gobbling down something tasty, panic attacks, etc.) hardly even count as actions, and certainly will never be ethically good. Both these claims have been the subject of discussion and controversy in the history of ethics, so they are worth noting now for future reference.

Write down:

claim 1
claim 2

Aristotle's general definition of choice may still leave us wondering whether there is some standard for distinguishing good from bad choice, correct from incorrect. Here is his answer.

. . . The excellent man judges each class of things rightly, and in each the truth appears to him. For each state of character has its own ideas of the noble and the pleasant, and perhaps the excellent man differs from others most by seeing the truth in each class of things, for he is as it were the norm and measure of [what is true] in them. In most things the error seems to be due to pleasure; for it appears a good when it is not. We therefore choose the pleasant as a good, and avoid pain as an evil.

The excellent man is not so swayed by love of plea-sure or fear of pain that he chooses badly or foolishly. He is "serious," in the sense of appreciating the true qualities of things and knowing what to take seri-ously. Pleasures and pains are not per se to be taken seriously in the way that, for example, honesty is.

> 46. *Can you think of a case where you took pleasure, or fear of pain, more seriously than honesty? Describe such a case.*

CHAPTERS IV, V
Aristotle expands his account of choice. Choice reveals character, i.e., virtue or vice. Now Aristotle insists that virtue and vice are "up to us," or are voluntary, just as much as particular acts may be "up to us." Aristotle mentions the idea that character might be "innate" and dismisses it, since if it were innate, praising and blam-ing people for their character or acts (and all people do praise and blame in that way) would be pointless.

These claims may seem to be in tension with Aristo-tle's stress on the importance of upbringing and train-ing. If my character depends on who brought me up, then how can it truly depend on me or be entirely "up to me"? Aristotle's reply, in part, is that training only works where persons voluntarily submit to directions. So the result of the training, which is their "character," is thus up to them to an extent. Aristotle seems to claim that it is entirely up to them, however.

> 47. *If character were "innate" it would be pointless to blame someone for being a coward, say, or praise her for being courageous. Why?*

CHAPTERS VI, VII, VIII, IX
Aristotle expands on his discussion of particular vir-tues begun in Book I, with a focus on courage and tem-perance. Many distinctions are made between actions and persons that may appear virtuous but are not. For example, the highly trained and experienced soldier may appear courageous compared to some less experi-enced recruit, but in fact the difference between them may be that the recruit overestimates a danger that the veteran has learned to estimate more accurately as be-ing not so great. So the difference in their behavior is not necessarily a difference due to lack of courage on the part of the recruit.

Book IV
An examination of generosity (Chapter i), magnificence (great expenditure on great and important matters) (Chapter ii), being "great souled" (something like pride and concern with great honor) (Chapter iii), honor itself (Chapter iv), gentleness (Chapter v), something like "considerateness" (Chapter vi), truthfulness about oneself (as opposed to being a braggart, for instance) (Chapter vii). Chapter viii has an interesting discus-sion of what might be called good taste in humor.

Book V
Book V is a detailed discussion of Justice. Aristotle ac-knowledges that there is more than one concept of jus-tice. Sometimes justice *is used to refer to virtue in gen-eral. Sometimes it has mainly political bearings. Often it has to do with "equity" of some sort in our dealings with others. Aristotle's views on justice and egoism, or self-interest, issues raised in our selections from Plato's* The Republic, *are discussed later, in the* Further Dis-cussions *section of Chapter 6 of this book.*

Book VI: Some Points About Practical Wisdom
The Greek word Phronesis, *which is translated in the following excerpts and discussions as "practical wis-dom," has often been translated as "practical judgment" or as "prudence." The concept is absolutely central to Aristotle's thinking about ethics, and his discussion of it, as you will see, brings together many of the most im-portant points made in earlier books. The themes an-nounced in Book VI invite comparison to other writers in this anthology, and thus may require more extensive commentary.*

CHAPTER V
Regarding practical wisdom we shall get at the truth by considering what sort of people we suppose have it. Now, it is thought to be the mark of a man of practical wisdom to be able to deliberate well about what is good and expedient for himself, but not just in some particular respect, for example, about what sorts of thing conduce to health or to strength, but rather about what sorts of thing conduce to the good life in general. This is shown by the fact that we credit men with practical wisdom in some particular re-

spect when they have calculated well with a view to some good end which is one of those that are not the object of any art. It follows that in the general sense also the man who is capable of deliberating has practical wisdom.

These remarks bring us back to the idea that all actions aim at happiness, which would be "the good life in general." Happiness (*eudaimonia*) is the target, the goal, the "end" of all action. To be able to have such an end and to act on it, a person must be more than a "technician" who knows how to get particular results. A loan officer at a bank, for instance, aims at making "good" loans, that is, loans that will be repaid. In order to do that he follows certain rules and collects certain data. His procedure could be written down in a manual and followed by someone else or even put into a computer!

But insofar as my aim is happiness or a *good life*, I cannot possibly put down in a manual the steps to be taken in reaching that goal or end. Why not? Because *everything* that I do bears on that goal. How could I formulate all of that? I do not even know what sorts of things I may need to be doing tomorrow, not to mention five years from now.

> 48. *Are there any people today who seem to pass themselves off as "technicians" of the good life, by writing "manuals" on how to live well? Give an example of a type of book that seems to fit that description (think about the self-help section of a bookstore). Take a look at your answer to Orienting Question 5.*

There are disputes about how to interpret some of Aristotle's claims here. Does he mean that the practically wise person has formulated some very complex overarching conception that contains in it all the principles needed for a good life? That would be a conception that could, at least in theory, be stated or articulated.

On the other hand, perhaps he thinks of the practically wise man as having no such statable end. Suppose I am deliberating whether to go to a party or stay at home to study. Must I review my idea of happiness first and then apply the results of that review to the particular situation, or do I (normally) not think of happiness at all but simply think about this particular situation, my particular goals, and how, and whether, to strive for them in this situation? Let us develop the example further.

One particular goal of mine might be to graduate from college. What does that goal require in the particular situation I am in? Suppose it is Friday, all midterm exams are completed, and I've been invited to a party by someone whose friendship matters to me. Perhaps, then, I should skip studying. Or suppose that pursuing that goal (graduating) now and in the future, would mean ignoring a big problem that has just arisen in my family. Perhaps, then, I should tend to my family and not pursue graduation at all! The practically wise person knows how to get through such tangled situations. She sees how best to reach certain goals, how some goals must be modified or given up in some circumstances but not in others, and how various goals relate to each other. She acts well since she is attuned to those features of her situation at any moment that are relevant to living and acting well. *But she could not possibly codify or articulate what those features are or what that notion of acting and living well is.* That notion "falls out" of her actions as her life proceeds.

If we think of "happiness" as a single (though perhaps complex) stable goal, we might confuse Aristotle's view with the view that some goal is so important that it should be pursued *no matter what,* for happiness is *always* pursued, and rightly so.

It would not make sense, though, to think of happiness as pursued *no matter what.* The practically wise person may decide, about *any* goal, that *in a certain situation*, it is not a worthy goal, even though there are no "technical" obstacles to achieving it and doing so would be pleasing to everyone. (It is worth noting this, since it may show that Aristotle's view contrasts with *utilitarianism*, a view that is the topic of Chapter 9.) It follows that "happiness" cannot be a particular, stable goal in the way that "graduating" is, for there is no *situation* in which happiness is not pursued by the practically wise person, whereas there may be a situation in which a practically wise person does not pursue graduating. It does not make sense to think that in a certain situation happiness might not be a worthy goal. The person who pursues happiness well *is* precisely the person who modifies his actions, and even his particular *statable* goals, in the light of each situation in which he finds himself and in the light of his trained desires and acquired principles.

> *49. Suppose I think "happiness = being rich." It makes sense to suppose that someone could pursue the goal of being rich "no matter what" that required (it might even require murdering someone!). But in Aristotle's view the person who wisely pursues happiness would always be able to give up such a goal as "being rich." On the other hand, no wise person gives up the pursuit of happiness. So it follows logically, in Aristotle's view, that it cannot be the case that _____ = _____.*

The remaining alternative, then, is that [practical wisdom] is a true and reasoned state or capacity to act with regard to the things that are good or bad for man. For while making has an end other than itself [for example, a house or an artwork], action cannot have such an external end; for good action itself is its end. It is for this reason that we think Pericles and men like him have practical wisdom, namely because they can see what is good for themselves and what is good for men in general. . . . This is why we call temperance by this name *(sophrosune)* [this Greek term for "temperance" suggests "saving or preserving practical wisdom"]. Now, what it preserves is a judgment of the kind we have described. For not any and every judgment is destroyed and perverted by pleasant and painful experiences. For example, the judgment that the triangle has or has not its angles equal to two right angles will not be affected by pain, but judgments about what is to be done will be so affected. For the originating causes of the things that are done consist in the end at which they are aimed; but the man who has been ruined by pleasure or pain forthwith fails to see any such originating cause—that is, he fails to see that for the sake of or because of this originating cause he ought to choose and do whatever he chooses and does; for vice is destructive of the originating cause of action.

Let us say that when I fly, rather than drive, to New York, I achieve the end, getting to New York, *through* (by means of) flying. In contrast, suppose that my end or goal is to have pleasant taste experiences, and eating Boston cream pie is pleasant to me. Then we will say that I achieve my goal *in* (not *through*) eating that pie. Eating the pie is not an "external" means to my goal. It *is* the goal, or one specification of it. Now answer this question;

> *50. "Good action itself is its end." Suppose one of my ends or goals is to graduate. Suppose that I must act to achieve that end by doing either A (say, studying all day Friday), B (studying now, even though my friend George needs my help now) or C (studying during the NBA playoffs on Saturday, which I want to watch). In this situation doing B would be wrong, and doing C would conflict with some other goal I have (i.e., the goal of watching the playoffs). Then, other things being equal, I will do A if I am practically wise. Doing A is a means to graduating. But in this situation doing A is itself the best way to act, by Aristotle's account. It is best because it doesn't violate any moral requirements, the way B does, or have other problems. So it too is something I aim at, it is part of the goal of living well, or happily. Thus acting in the best way is itself the supreme goal for a practically wise person. Thus in doing A I am pursuing two ends, namely graduation and _____. The first of these is achieved through doing A, the second in doing A.*
>
> 51. *Theoretical reason deals with questions in "theoretical" disciplines, such as math. Such reasoning is not usually going to go wrong because of desires for various pleasures or fears of various pains. Right? Why? But when I reason about how to _____, my reasoning may very well "go wrong" because of such desires or fears. So such reasoning is unlike theoretical reasoning in an important way.*

CHAPTER XIII: *SOCRATES' MISTAKE.*

. . . Socrates in one respect was on the right track while in another he went astray. In thinking that all the virtues were forms of practical wisdom he was wrong, but in saying they implied practical wisdom he spoke well. This is confirmed by the fact that even now all men, when they define virtue, after naming the state of character and its objects add "that (state) which is in accordance with right reason." Now, what is right is that which is in accordance with practical wisdom. But we must go a little further. For it is not merely the state in accordance with right reason, but the state that really involves right reason, that is virtue; and practical wisdom is right reason about such matters. Socrates, then, thought the virtues were rational principles (for he thought they were, all of them, forms of scientific knowledge), while we think they involve a rational principle. It is clear, then, from what has been said, that it is not possible to be good in the strict sense without practical wisdom, nor practically wise without moral virtue.

But in this way we may also refute the dialectical argument whereby it might be contended that the virtues exist in separation from each other. The same man, it might be said, is not best equipped by nature for all the virtues, so that he will have already acquired one when he has not yet acquired another. This is possible so far as the natural virtues go, but not with respect to those for the sake of which a man is called good without qualification; for with the presence of the one quality, practical wisdom, all the virtues will be given.

Moral virtue makes the end to be enacted, practical wisdom makes the things pertaining to that end to be enacted.

The preceding passages are rich in significance and invite extensive commentary. One of Aristotle's points can perhaps be summarized using an example. Suppose my conception of living well includes helping friends in trouble. I notice (what not just anyone might notice) that a friend is in trouble. Do I then immediately step in and help? Not necessarily. Perhaps I also see that this friend brought his trouble on himself and really needs reproof. That might be a case of "equitable" judgment, which is a virtue. Moreover, acting on that judgment might require courage, another virtue, since I might risk losing my friend. What to do on any occasion is determined by practical wisdom, but practical wisdom operates on a combination of virtues, determining their relations

or interactions. In that sense it is a master virtue, required to keep other virtues from turning into something bad. But the other virtues are not reducible to practical wisdom (Socrates seemed to think that they are reducible to wisdom; see earlier). Practical wisdom is not a science that absorbs all of conduct into the grasp of sure principles. It is a sort of balancing act, drawing on a fund of experience out of which the wise person has developed an understanding of and desire for the best way of life and which at the same time rebounds on his understanding and the kinds of desires he has.

The claim that practical wisdom comes with all the virtues amounts to a claim about the unity of the virtues. They cannot exist in separation from one another. That seems to be false. Why couldn't someone have some virtues and also some vices? What about the courageous thief or the person who patiently plots a murder? This issue is discussed in Chapter 10. But something can be said at this point.

Aristotle rightly thinks of any action as "facing in many directions at once." That is, what I do at any moment can be described in many ways; for example, the actions of the courageous thief can be described as "courageous actions" and also as "dishonest actions" and also as "actions harmful to innocent persons" and so forth. Now, in Aristotle's view the virtuous person "acts well" under every description of his actions. But under some descriptions the courageous thief does not act well. Aristotle concludes that the actions of such a person are not truly courageous. They are not the actions of one who is acting well. But all virtuous actions *are* cases of acting well.

52. *What is the problem with the claim that the virtues cannot exist "in separation from one another"? Give an apparent counterexample to that claim.*

A CRUCIAL POINT; FACTS VS. VALUES

The entire discussion in Book VI makes one thing very clear. Aristotle is claiming something that conflicts with a common modern view. That view could be summarized as follows: **There is a gulf separating facts from values.** Facts, we may suppose, are dealt with by reasoning, in some broad sense. Since reason is "objective," it is possible, at least in principle, for us to come to agreement about factual matters. We simply find more evidence or make better inferences or think more clearly or refine our calculations, in order to take care of disagreements (cf. Socrates in the *Euthyphro* and in the *Protagoras* [Chapter 2]). Values, on the other hand, may seem to us to be subjective, perhaps just a matter of feeling, rather than a matter of reason. So there would not be much point in arguing about which values are "right." Now, Aristotle is *denying* such a view. He thinks that ethical matters *are* matters of reason. Feeling is certainly involved, but that does not make values "subjective." Of course, in his own time sophists held a view similar in some respects to modern views, so he is denying their view also.

53. *To summarize, by Aristotle's account, there is no sharp contrast between _____ and _____. Try to refute his view.*

Aristotle's view is rejected by many modern philosophers, some of whom are indebted to Hume for their ways of approaching ethics. Hume is the subject of Chapter 7 in this book. Here it may suffice to say just this much: On Hume's view two separate, independently definable faculties or aspects of a person are involved in action. We are moved to act by desires or feelings of various kinds (what he calls *sentiments*). So, if I desire a hot fudge sundae, the desire may move me to get one. But, in order to get one, I may need something else, namely, reason. Reason will inform me about facts (such as where the Dairy Queen is located and how to get there easily and efficiently). So my desiring self may put reason to use in order to get what is desired. Now, in Hume's view there is nothing either rational or irrational about the desire itself. I just have it. Nor is there anything intrinsically rational or irrational, stupid or foolish, about acting on it, not even if doing so led to my death or the destruction of the whole world! When I act on a desire, no matter how "crazy" the desire might be, my action cannot be assessed as rational or irrational, except insofar as the means I choose to fulfill my desire are more or less sensible, efficient, "logical."

Aristotle, in contrast, insists that some desires are themselves "right" and that acting on them is intrin-

sically reasonable, or practically wise, whereas others are not right, and only a fool, someone who is not fully rational, would act on them. In Hume's view, reason cannot be *practical* at all, whereas for Aristotle there is a kind of reason that is precisely practical, like theoretical reason in some respects but unlike it by virtue of its involvement in action and changes in the world.

It should be noted here that some translations of the last sentence in the preceding quote have "moral virtue makes the end of action right, practical wisdom makes the means to the end right." Such translations obscure the differences between Aristotle and Hume respecting the nature of "reason." They make it sound as though reason is concerned only with the means to an end but has nothing to do with the end itself. That is not Aristotle's view. That it is not can be seen from the following considerations, among others.

In terms taken from Chapter ii, earlier, that which is desirously pursued in rational choice and that which is affirmed by reason (or "thinking") in that same rational choice are the *same*. In contrast, in Hume's view, even if reason tells me that having a hot fudge sundae will harm me, perhaps kill me, still there is nothing irrational in eating one or in the desire to eat one. In Hume's view what a person *does* is the causal result of what they desire or prefer, and desires and preferences are neither rational nor irrational. So what reason affirms and what desire pursues need not be the *same* for a rational person. Aristotle says they must be the same for a practically wise person. *Both* reason (or thinking) *and* desire say "Yes, do it!" with respect to a rational choice. For Hume, on the contrary, reason never says "do *x*" for *any x*, even though it might say *x* is the most efficient thing as a means to an end or the thing most conducive to survival in the circumstances.

Hume's view isn't perfectly clear. But Aristotle's may seem even more obscure. What does he mean? Can he possibly be right in claiming that reason and desire "affirm" together and that desire or feeling can thus be "right" or "true?"

Roughly, the answer, or part of it, goes like this: The agent, in reviewing the "facts" of his situation, scans those facts with a view to *what is to be done*.

That is, the fact-collecting aspect of "reason" is already "infected," so to speak, with desire or practical import. In Aristotle's view there is no such thing as a totally disengaged reason of the sort postulated by Hume, except in purely theoretical contexts (when doing geometry, for example).

Here is one further forward-looking consequence of Aristotle's view. Kant (see Chapter 8) held that certain types of actions are per se wrong. Lying is one example of a type of act that is wrong in itself (per se). Aristotle also affirms that some types of actions (or inactions) are virtually never permissible. But the mere fact that a certain action can be described as "lying" does not take care of the question of whether to do it or not, in Aristotle's view. Rather, deliberation will be required. And even if deliberation never came up with the result "go ahead and tell a lie," that would be so only because no circumstances ever warranted a rational person in doing such a thing. You couldn't come to that conclusion just by thinking about what lying in general is like. Kant thought (more or less) that you could.

> ****54.** *Roughly, what is the main contrast between Aristotle and Hume? Aristotle and Kant?*
> ***55.** *Would the contrast between Aristotle and Hume have anything in common with the contrast between Aristotle and the sophists? Explain. Be careful.*

Book VII: The Problem of Incontinence (Lack of Self-Control)

CHAPTER I.
Aristotle distinguishes between vice, lack of self-control and animal-like behavior. The desires of a person who lacks self-control are not bad per se, and such a person knows that. The aim is not to get rid of them entirely but to control them and eventually to combine them with reason in the way typical of a virtuous person. The vicious person, on the other hand, has actually chosen to follow various desires whenever opportunity presents itself and has no interest in controlling them where good reasoning would require controlling them.

Consider this case: Smith is an M.D. specializing in heart conditions. He is overweight and has problems with high cholesterol and arterial plaque. He desires to lose weight, *and he has chosen to diet, in the full Aristotelian sense of "choice." He knows all of the purportedly relevant facts about his condition, and he also knows that the delicious-looking piece of chocolate cake before him is very fattening and very high in cholesterol and that there is every good reason to avoid eating it. But he eats it anyway. He knows he should not, but he acts against his knowledge.*

It is a plain fact, as Aristotle points out, that there are such cases. Socrates had denied that there were, since he believed that knowledge included virtue, so that no one could actually knowingly act intemperately, for instance. Aristotle sticks with the "plain fact" but finds it puzzling. His attempt to unscramble that puzzle is the topic of Chapters ii and iii of Book VII, to which the student is referred.

Book VIII: Friendship
Aristotle argues that friendship is essential to personal and communal life. He discusses different kinds of friendship, and stresses how people depend on one another.

CHAPTER I
Not a few things about friendship are matters of debate. . . . Let us examine those which . . . involve character and feeling, e.g., whether friendship can arise between any two people or whether people cannot be friends if they are wicked, and whether there is one kind of friendship or more than one. . . .

CHAPTER III
Aristotle discusses three kinds of friendship. Some people may be our "friends" for what we can get out of them. Some people may be our friends just because they are a lot of fun, good partygoers, and so forth. But these two forms are "easily dissolved," he argues. For example, the first form dissolves when someone "ceases to be useful." Only the third kind, perfect friendship, is true and enduring.

. . . Perfect friendship is the friendship of men who are good, and alike in virtue; for these wish well alike to each other qua good, and they are good themselves. Now those who wish well to their friends for their sake are most truly friends; for they do this by reason of their own nature and not incidentally; therefore their friendship lasts as long as they are good, and goodness is an enduring thing. And each is good without qualification and to his friend, for the good are both good without qualification and useful to each other. So too they are pleasant; for the good are pleasant both without qualification and to each other, since to each his own activities and others like them are pleasurable, and the actions of the good are the same or like. And such a friendship is, as might be expected, permanent, since there meet in it all the qualities that friends should have.

. . . All the qualities we have named belong to a friendship of good men in virtue of the nature of the friends themselves; for in the case of this kind of friendship the other qualities also are alike in both friends, and that which is good without qualification is also without qualification pleasant, and these are the most lovable qualities. Love and friendship therefore are found most and in their best form between such men.

But it is natural that such friendships should be infrequent; for such men are rare. Further, such friendship requires time and familiarity; as the proverb says, men cannot know each other till they have "eaten salt together"; nor can they admit each other to friendship or be friends till each has been found lovable and been trusted by each. Those who quickly show the marks of friendship to each other wish to be friends, but they are not friends unless they both are lovable and know the fact; for a wish for friendship may arise quickly, but friendship does not.

CHAPTER IV: *FRIENDSHIP WITH THOSE WHO ARE BAD AND THOSE WHO ARE GOOD.*
For the sake of pleasure or utility, then, even bad men may be friends of each other, or good men of bad, or one who is neither good nor bad may be a friend to any sort of person, but for their own sake clearly only good men can be friends; for bad men do not delight in each other unless some advantage come of the relation. The friendship of the good too and this alone is proof against slander; for it is not easy to trust anyone who talks about a man who has long been tested by oneself; and it is among good men that trust and the feeling that "he would never wrong me"

and all the other things that are demanded in true friendship are found. In the other kinds of friendship, however, there is nothing to prevent these evils arising. For men apply the name of friends even to those whose motive is utility. . . .

In the film *Donny Brasco* (based on an actual case), an FBI informant (Donny) becomes friends with a gangster who routinely steals, murders and commits other crimes. It seems like a genuine friendship, based partly on a kind of sympathy that Donny comes to have for the difficult life of his "friend." Aristotle apparently denies that this relationship could be a real friendship.

> 56. *Why? Do you think such a friendship would really be possible? Give reasons pro and con.*

Aristotle includes much under friendship that we might not. Relations between husbands and wives, children and parents, and between citizens of a community who are in merely contractual relations with each other are included, and some of these are regarded as inevitably unequal in various ways (for example, that between husband and wife, since the husband "rules in virtue of fitness"!).

Book IX: Friendship and Self-Knowledge.
Aristotle argues that even though there is a kind of self-sufficiency enjoyed by a virtuous person, it is not such that friends are not essential. One reason is that we are essentially reflective, conscious beings and interaction with friends is one of the forms in which consciousness is exercised and increased.

CHAPTER IX.
. . . If perceiving that one lives is in itself one of the things that are pleasant (for life is by nature good, and to perceive what is good present in oneself is pleasant); and if life is desirable, and particularly so for good men, because to them existence is good and pleasant (for they are pleased at the consciousness of the presence in them of what is in itself good); and if as the virtuous man is to himself, he is to his friend also (for his friend is another self): if all this be true,

as his own being is desirable for each man, so, or almost so, is that of his friend.

Now, his being was seen to be desirable because he perceived his own goodness, and such perception is pleasant in itself. He needs, therefore, to be conscious of the existence of his friend as well, and this will be realized in their living together and sharing in discussion and thought; for this is what living together would seem to mean in the case of man, and not, as in the case of cattle, feeding in the same place. If, then, being is in itself desirable for the supremely happy man (since it is by its nature good and pleasant), and that of his friend is very much the same, a friend will be one of the things that are desirable. Now that which is desirable for him he must have, or he will be deficient in this respect. The man who is to be happy will therefore need virtuous friends.

57. *Could you be happy even though you had no* virtuous *friends? Explain.*

Book X

In Book X, the last book of this work, Aristotle continues the discussion of pleasure begun in Book VII. He then goes on to discuss the place of theoretical reason or intellectual "contemplation" in the good life.

Aristotle's ethics sometimes takes on an "antipleasure" appearance, since he is alert to the way in which people fall into vices as the result of the attractions of various pleasures. But at the same time he insists on the importance of pleasure to the best kind of life. However, we must avoid confusion in our thinking about what pleasure is.

CHAPTER IV

Pleasure brings activity to completion, not, like a fixed disposition, by being already in the agent, but as something that supervenes upon the activity, like the bloom of health upon the healthy. It might be held that all seek pleasure because all desire life. Life is a kind of activity, and each person is active in relation to those objects and with those capacities which he likes most; a musical person by hearing and with melodies, a lover of learning in thinking and with topics from theoretical wisdom.

If we think of the pleasures of eating something tasty, it may seem natural to think of pleasure as something that is caused in us by some *external* factor. Aristotle has quite a different view of pleasure, as the preceding quote shows. First, he associates pleasure with activity, rather than with passive reception of sensations of some kind. The music lover takes pleasure in an active kind of hearing. She must have an active interest in the music itself; if she does, the pleasure "supervenes," that is, it is not caused by the music as something external to the pleasure, but follows from the activity, the way the "bloom of health" follows from being healthy (obviously, the bloom of health does not *cause* health). If the pleasure I get from listening to Bach's *Goldberg Variations* were simply caused by the sounds that impact my eardrums, we would think that everyone with normal hearing would get pleasure, and indeed the same pleasure, from listening to that piece by Bach; but clearly that is not how it is. Some people get practically no pleasure from any music, and some people get no pleasure from listening to Bach. Aristotle might have argued that the latter have not learned to listen well. They are not good at that activity.

If we think of pleasure as something intrinsic to well-performed activities, then we can appreciate Aristotle's view that pleasure goes with virtuous activity. The virtuous person is the person who leads an active life in the most excellent way. The athlete takes pleasure in doing something well (throwing a good pass, sinking a hole-in-one). The courageous person takes pleasure in acting courageously. Pleasure supervenes on, or varies with, the quality of my "performance" in particular specialties, but, most importantly, in my performances simply as a human being.

58. *If you have absolutely no horse-riding skills, that is, are simply no good at that kind of activity, are you likely to get much pleasure from riding a horse?*

59. *Does it seem plausible to think of the courageous person whose life is being threatened in a battle as experiencing* pleasure *during the fight? Discuss pro and con.*

Aristotle's analysis of pleasure anticipates in some respects the discussion in Butler (Chapter 6).

From Chapter vi onwards Aristotle discusses the place of theoretical wisdom, or "contemplation." in the happy life.

Aristotle seems to claim that the contemplation of theoretical truth is the highest happiness and that it makes a person completely self-sufficient. Thus it seems that the highest happiness does not even require friendship. It is not clear how these sorts of claims hang together with the other things Aristotle has been saying about happiness. If there is such a thing as practical wisdom and if the best kind of life consists in virtuous activity of many kinds, then the reduction of happiness to one kind of thing, namely, contemplation of theoretical or unchanging truth, seems out of character with the rest of this work. Interpreters differ over the place and importance of these claims in Book X. But many discussions of Aristotle's ethics take it to be his view that the best kind of life includes more than contemplation and that the kind of "self-sufficiency" attributed to contemplation is not necessary for human well-being. It may even be incompatible with it.

60. *The claim that happiness consists in _____ seems to conflict with the idea that happiness is optimal practical functioning.*

Further Discussion and Applications

Ethical "Science," Tragic Conflict and Human Vulnerability (Kraut, Nussbaum)

Plato's tendency to deny any place to practical (as opposed to theoretical) reason in the best life goes hand in hand with a tendency to seek a single "science" of the ethical. We have seen how this puts him at odds with "poets" like Sophocles and with much common opinion. Aristotle on the other hand wants to credit, at least to some extent, what people generally believe about the good life. But those common beliefs may conflict with one another. For example, common beliefs about the good of the family might sometimes conflict with beliefs about the good of the state (cf. *Antigone*). Practical wisdom, as we have

seen in Aristotle's account, is nuanced judgment that cannot be reduced to a single set of reliable rational principles. Maybe practical wisdom is just what we need for dealing with such conflicts as are found in *Antigone*!

Just how it might do that was discussed in NE VI. As mentioned in the guide there and in Book X, some interpreters believe that Aristotle has a "scientific" ethics after all, one not so different from Plato's. In this view, Aristotle "presents the reader with a systematic and unified vision of how life should be lived," which supplies "a single rule, standard or goal to bear on every situation."(Richard Kraut, "Aristotle on the Human Good: An Overview" in Sherman, p. 97). These interpretative issues will not be debated here. But the view that there is no such single "rule, standard or goal" is of intrinsic interest in any case and will be discussed here as one plausible construal of Aristotle.

American philosopher Martha Nussbaum is a prominent exponent of this "antiscientific" reading of Aristotle. She points out that the interest in a "scientific" ethics is still with us. It is at one end of a spectrum that has noncognitivism at the opposite end. But Aristotle would oppose both extremes. Nussbaum writes:

> Aristotle's position is subtle and compelling. It seems to me to go further than any other account of practical rationality I know in capturing the sheer complexity and agonizing difficulty of choosing well. But whether we are in the end persuaded by it or not, the need to study it is urgent. Even more in our time than in his, the power of "scientific" pictures of practical rationality affects almost every area of human social life, through the influence of the social sciences and the more science-based parts of ethical theory on the formation of public policy. We should not accept this situation without assessing the merits of such views against those of the most profound alternatives. . . .
>
> In this essay the word *scientific* will he used as Aristotle used it, to designate a family of characteristics that were usually associated with the claim that a body of knowledge had the status

of an *episteme* [systematic knowledge]. Aristotle's attack [on "scientific ethics"] has three distinct dimensions, closely interwoven. These are: (1) an attack on the claim that all valuable things are commensurable; (2) an argument for the priority of particular judgments to universals; and (3) a defense of the emotions and the imagination as essential to rational choice. (Martha Nussbaum, *Love's Knowledge*, p. 55)

61. *Again, illustrate what it means to say that two valuable things are (or are not) "commensurable" (pick your own two things, or use some from the text).*

The idea that all valuable things are "commensurable" has been discussed in connection with Plato. One way to defend that idea, as we saw in Plato's *Protagoras*, is to claim that there is a single value, for example, pleasure, that can be quantified and that the ethical person seeks to maximize that value. But Aristotle denies that pleasure is one single quantifiable thing. He argues that pleasures often differ in kind from each other and cannot be compared (they cannot always be measured by a single standard). Nussbaum claims that none of the other candidates, popular or philosophical, for a single dominating value are accepted by Aristotle as the key to ethics.

Nussbaum's Aristotle could not endorse utilitarianism, either in its older forms (see discussion, Chapter 9), which emphasized maximization of pleasure, or in more recent forms that stress maximizing preferences, whatever they may be. Some people's preferences, Aristotle would argue, are not worth considering. The wise and virtuous person provides the standard for what preferences carry ethical weight.

Utilitarian reasoning and closely related approaches (rational choice theory, for example) are very influential in debates about public policy and social ethics (cf. text Chapters 6 and 9.) But Aristotle may offer an alternative to those debates, as some of the following discussion may indicate.

Another consequence of the rejection of commensurability stressed by Nussbaum is that it opens the door to tragic conflicts. There may be situations where I must give up a good, for example, the good of my family, for the sake of another good, such as the good of my country, even though both are ethically valued and perhaps even require my attention. In such a situation a person is bound to feel regret, remorse, perhaps even guilt, due to the loss, or violation, of some ethical good or requirement. If that is Aristotle's view, it would help to explain why he shows a favorable attitude toward the tragic poets, for they present these tragic conflicts unflinchingly and in an instructive way. It is nonetheless pretty clear that Aristotle is basically optimistic when compared, e.g., to Sophocles.

*62. *Try to give your own example of the sort of tragic conflict just described, in which you must give up something ethically good in order to achieve something else that is ethically good.*

Moral Education (Sher and Bennett)

It is clear (see NE I, II) that Aristotle stresses upbringing. No one can become good just by studying a "goodness" manual, nor can people be expected to hit on the best way to live just by thinking about it on their own or by learning through "experience" without any guidance. So, in his view, children and other immature people need moral educators and good examples.

Many modern thinkers, on the other hand, are suspicious of the very idea of "directive" moral education. They fear that it amounts to indoctrination, i.e., filling young people with dogmas about right and wrong. That is thought to be a bad thing because it interferes with autonomy. *Autonomy* refers to the ability to govern one's own self rather than just acting out of habits or ideas instilled by others. Some people think autonomy is essential to genuine morality, since someone who just does what he or she has been told or conditioned to do is hardly better than the Nazi prison guard who excuses his actions on the grounds that he is following orders. A good person should act on (moral) reasons that he or she can see to be good reasons.

George Sher and William Bennett argue that early training need not conflict with autonomy. Even when that training involves "nonrational" means (such as encouraging a child's good behavior with candy or a movie), the child can grow into an autonomous adult.

> Even if an adult is motivated by a desire that was originally produced by nonrational means, it still seems possible for his action to be done for good, moral reasons. In particular, this still seems possible if his nonrationally produced desire is precisely [a desire] to act in accordance with such reasons. But it is surely just this desire which the sensitive practitioner of directive moral education seeks to instill. (Sher and Bennett, "Moral Education and Indoctrination," 1982)

Sher and Bennett argue that even if, for example, an adult's desire to act courageously was produced by a kind of conditioning rather than by reasoning, the adult may still understand why the courageous act is rational and do it because it is rational. This accords perfectly with Aristotle's account in NE Book II, Chapter iv, as well as with his entire account of practical wisdom. Practical wisdom includes a desire and disposition to act in accordance with good, "moral" reasons. But practical wisdom is produced by early training. Early training may indeed involve rewards and punishments but not much appeal to reasoning. Nonetheless Aristotle insists that it leads to good reasoning later in life. Thus it need not interfere with autonomy.

But the opponent of directive moral education may insist that a person is only truly autonomous when motivated by reason, rather than by early training. Sher and Bennett reply by arguing that directive moral education does not have to violate autonomy in that sense either. But they go even further and argue that moral education that instills good habits (for example, the habit of persevering in the face of difficulties) can serve to eliminate the sorts of things that distract people from acting on good, moral reasons. For example, obstinate resistance on the part of others to considerations of justice can distract a person from acting on good reasons of justice. In such cases the just person must "persevere," and to do that he must have "picked up the habit of perseverance" from early training. To the extent that directive moral education frees people so as to enable them to act on reasons that they themselves see to be morally im-

portant, directive moral education does not interfere with autonomy. Instead it sometimes actually makes it possible!

Sher and Bennett are aiming their defense of directive moral education at Kantians in particular (see Chapter 8), but their arguments can be used to show that Aristotle's account of moral upbringing encourages the kind of "autonomy" that he considers important, namely, the kind that resides in the operation of "deliberative desire"(See NE III). Sher and Bennett and Aristotle would agree that in order to become good, I need to be shaped and educated through the instruction and examples of good people.

> 63. *In your own words, explain what is meant by autonomy.*
> *64. *Might there still be something to the objections of those who oppose directive moral education? Try to imagine a case in which my upbringing by good representatives of my community might make me into a person with prejudices. Describe it here. Would such a case show a flaw in Sher and Bennett's position?*

Community and Friendship (Cooper)

We have seen how Aristotle insists that humans are social beings and that human flourishing requires a good community in which to live. It is not just that people need each other for getting specialized tasks taken care of, such as effective defense and good medical care. Aristotle thinks of the community (*polis*) as constitutive for genuinely human life. It is not a mere means to an end, a convenient arrangement for those who are already fully human, designed to ensure that their lives will not be too "mean, brutish and short"(cf. Hobbes, text Chapter 6). Rather, they become fully human only in the "polis."

Aristotle's stress on community is particularly prominent in his discussion of friendship. Friends are essential to humans because of the sort of beings humans essentially are. First, we are reasoning, conscious beings concerned to know truth. That fact about us is clearly essential to Aristotle's account of virtue and happiness. And it is precisely in relations with others that the most important truths, truths about character or virtue, come to be known most securely.

American philosopher John Cooper argues that this is especially so for self-knowledge. He bases his view partly on a passage from Aristotle's *Magna Moralia* , where it is stated that self-knowledge requires friends. This is striking, since one might think self-knowledge requires simply thinking honestly about oneself. But Aristotle makes the point that our partiality to ourselves is largely what prevents us from knowing ourselves. It is much easier, on the other hand, to see faults, including ones we have but do not acknowledge, in someone else. As we have seen, Aristotle conceives a friend as "another self." But we can see faults (including our own) more clearly in others. It follows that in coming to see the faults of a friend, we may come to see ourselves in a truer light.

But could we not learn more from a mere acquaintance? Wouldn't we have the same partiality to our friends that we have for ourselves and thus be as easily deceived about them as we are about ourselves? Though there is that possibility, there is plausibility in thinking that we have less of a tendency to be mistaken even about a friend than we do about ourselves. And a relation to a mere acquaintance might not supply the needed knowledge because of the lack of depth in the relation and the lack of extensive familiarity that is made possible through sustained friendships.

65. *What are two reasons for thinking that self-knowledge might be increased through friendship?*

Cooper gathers some further evidence for the necessity of friendship from Aristotle's remarks on the importance of joint activities. Even intellectual activities, which *could* be pursued alone, acquire greater interest, life and longevity when carried out in consort with others. That is generally true, but especially true for friends, for we "live with them" and thus are able to sustain and develop "conversation" (see earlier, NE Book IX, Chapter ix). And since what qualifies them as (true) friends is that they are virtuous, then the things we most need to know and practice (the virtues) are most likely to be known and practiced with them. Cooper sums up his discussions in this way:

> Aristotle argues, first, that to know the goodness of one's [own] life, which he reasonably assumes to be a necessary condition of flourishing, one needs to have intimate friends, . . . since one is better able to reach a sound and secure estimate of the quality of a life when it is not one's own. Secondly, he argues that the fundamental moral and intellectual activities that go to make up a flourishing life cannot be continuously engaged in with pleasure and interest, as they must be if the life is to be a flourishing one, unless they are engaged in as parts of shared activities, rather than pursued merely in private; and given the nature of the activities that are in question, this sharing is possible only with intimate friends who are themselves morally good persons.
>
> Three points about these arguments should be noted. First, in a certain way they both emphasize human vulnerability and weakness. If human nature were differently constituted we might very well be immune to the uncertainties and doubts about ourselves that, according to Aristotle, make friendship such an important thing for a human being. As it is, we cannot, if left each to his own devices, reach a secure estimate of our own moral character; nor by ourselves can we find our lives continuously interesting and enjoyable, because the sense of the value of the activities which make them up is not within the individual's power to bestow. The sense of one's own worth is, for human beings, a group accomplishment. Hence we need each other because as individuals we are not sufficient—psychologically sufficient—to sustain our own lives. (Sherman, *Aristotle's Ethics: Critical Essays,* p. 293)

Thus, reflection on friendship also brings us back to a theme we have already found prominent in Aristotle, namely, the theme of human vulnerability, as the thing that sets the stage for ethical living and thinking. Aristotle, it seems increasingly clear, accepts this vulnerability. Any other kind of life would not be a human life and thus not something a human could want. Otherwise put, wanting to be free of such limitations is wanting some nonhuman, perhaps godlike, status. But if we achieved it, what then would have become of *us*?

*66. *What, according to Cooper, is the connection between friendship and acceptance of one's own vulnerability?*

The Virtue of Generosity (Wallace)

Nearly any list of virtues might be expected to include generosity. Aristotle discusses it in Book IV of *The Nichomachean Ethics* and says that it has to do with giving and taking of things with monetary value. Contemporary American philosopher James Wallace agrees with Aristotle so far and argues that generosity should include the following three characteristics.

1. The agent [generous person], because of his direct concern for the good of the recipient, gives something with the intention of benefiting the recipient, not with the intention of getting something in return.
2. The agent gives up something of his that has a market value and that he has some reason to value and, therefore, to keep.
3. The agent gives more than moral requirements or custom would lead anyone to expect.

These characteristics seem intuitively obvious. For example, if someone gave a great deal of money to some charity, but that money meant nothing to him (perhaps because he was extremely rich), he would not be thought of as generous. Such a case would violate characteristic 2. Where an agent gives primarily because of an expectation of receiving as much back, she would not be considered generous. That would violate characteristic 1. The intention would not be to benefit the recipient, or that would not be the primary intention. If someone gave a very great gift at a wedding but lived in a culture where such great gifts were expected at weddings, that would not be generosity. Characteristic 3 would be violated. Of course the usual conditions for ascribing a virtue also obtain. Someone who gives in a way that meets characteristics 1–3 but does it only once and otherwise is stingy is not a generous person, however generous that particular act may be. Virtues are, as Aristotle says, dispositions, settled tendencies. Moreover the

agent must know what she is doing, must understand the circumstances in which the gift is made, and so forth.

There may, however, appear to be cases of generosity that do not have all of characteristics 1–3. Wallace asks us to consider a woman whose social Darwinist beliefs include opposition to helping out starving people. She normally thinks, "Let the weak die off! Survival of the fittest!" But on a particular occasion she is moved by pity for a starving family that she has personally encountered. She makes an average-sized contribution to feeding them, one that most people would consider their *duty* to make. Is she generous? It might seem that she violates characteristic 3, since she is giving no more than is expected. But since she does not share the beliefs on which the usual expectation is based, namely, that one ought to help out starving people, from her perspective she is fulfilling characteristic 3. Similarly, the very rich person who makes a large donation to a charity might seem to meet all three conditions, but only if he places some value on the gift. These are borderline cases. Wallace comments:

> In these cases involving unusual beliefs or attitudes, one is pulled simultaneously in two different directions. The way the agent sees the situation and the way one expects him to see the situation diverge. Crucial conditions are satisfied from one way of regarding the case and unsatisfied from the other. (from Wallace, *Virtues and Vices*, 1978)

Consideration of such details leads to the conclusion that generosity, like the other virtues, is not an all or nothing matter. There are degrees. But a case of unqualifiedly generous action would always have characteristics 1–3, in Wallace's view.

There are of course ways of being generous that may not involve anything of monetary value. A person might be generous with her or his time. Time in a certain circumstance might not have market value, but it is still valuable to the person. So the parent who spends lots of time with a child might seem to have characteristics 1–3 in all other respects.

Wallace considers another form of generosity, namely, being generous-minded. The generous-minded person, by his account, should not be confused with someone who overestimates other people, complementing them where they clearly do not deserve it, for instance. That seems more like a case of bad judgment than a virtue. Nowadays some people might disagree, since so much emphasis is placed on building esteem. In Wallace's view such "esteem builders" are simply undiscriminating. But how then should we characterize the generous-minded person? Wallace suggests that such a person gives the benefit of the doubt where there is reasonable room to do so. Such a one avoids derogatory judgments where they are not clearly called for and seeks to discern merit in another where there really is a possibility of finding it. But couldn't such tendencies lead people to make incorrect judgments, whereas a tendency to simply make accurate judgments about others would not? And is not such a tendency nonvirtuous? Wallace admits this possibility and concludes that generous-mindedness should not be considered a primary virtue of persons. It is simply part of general benevolence, a concern for others and for fair treatment.

67. *Do you think of generosity as a virtue? If you think you are generous, offer some evidence that you are that is* consistent *with Wallace's account of what generosity is.*
68. *Do you think that the social Darwinist is not truly generous, in the case imagined earlier? Why?*
*69. *Why does Wallace think that generous-mindedness is not a primary virtue?*

Confucian Parallels (and Differences) (The Confucian School)

Aristotle's ideas about virtue and community are certainly not completely peculiar to the civilization of 4th century Greek city-states. Not only are there many contemporary applications, but we can find some striking similarities, for example, in enduring civilizations of the Far East. Confucius proposed that personal virtues, centering around familial and other relationships, are essential to a good life in a good community. Like Plato and Aristotle, his views are in many respects agent centered, rather than centered on the search for impersonal norms to guide the conduct of any person. He too emphasized education and training into a moral condition. He stresses the need for the governing class to know what the aim of life

is, much as Aristotle does in the first chapters of NE. The school Confucius founded even propounded a doctrine of the mean that is like Aristotle's in some respects. Some of these points are very evident in the "Two Books."

TWO BOOKS
The Four Books (*shu*) of Confucianism include two short works that originally appear in the *Book of Rites* but were extracted from this because of their unique philosophical content. They are *The Great Learning* (Ta Hsio) and *The Doctrine of the Mean* (Chung Yung).

The Great Learning (Ta Hsio) is a brief text on the subject of good government. A passage from Confucius' *Analects* on the subject of good government states that "He who exercises government by means of his virtue may be compared to the north polar star, which keeps its place and all the stars turn towards it" (2:1). Confucius advised rulers to live virtuously, since doing so will result in goodness transferring down the social hierarchy to the people. This is also the message of *The Great Learning*. Tradition attributes this work either to Confucius's disciple or to his grandson. However, scholars contend that the work was written during the 3rd century BCE.

The path of learning to be great consists of exhibiting clear character, loving people, and resting in the highest good. If we know the point in which we are to rest, we can determine the object of pursuit. When we determine that, we can attain a calmness, and from that will follow tranquility. In tranquility we can carefully deliberate, and that deliberation will be followed by the attainment of the desired end.

Things have their roots and their branches. Affairs have their beginnings and ends. To know what is first and what is last will lead us near the path of learning to be great.

The ancients who wished to exhibit their clear character to the world first brought order to their states. Wishing to order their states, they first regulated their families. Wishing to regulate their families, they first cultivated their personal lives. Wishing to cultivate their personal lives, they first corrected their minds. Wishing to correct their minds, they first sought to be sincere in their thoughts. Wishing to be sincere in their thoughts, they first extended their knowledge.

From the son of heaven down to the common people on earth, all must consider the cultivation of one's personal life as the root of everything else. When the root is neglected, what springs from it will not be well ordered. No one has ever taken slight care of greatly important things, and no one has greatly cared for slightly important things.

70. *Mention one thing in the preceding passage that you think Aristotle would endorse.*

The Doctrine of the Mean (Chung Yung) is traditionally attributed to Confucius's grandson, although scholars place authorship of the text in the 2nd century BCE. The opening section of the text is the heart of the work, which advocates maintaining a mental state of equilibrium between extreme emotions, such as pleasure and pain, sorrow and joy. If we abide by the mean between extreme mental states, then harmony and order will come to the world. The text distinguishes between the path of equilibrium and the path of harmony. The first involves the elimination of emotions, and the second involves a moderate and balanced expression of emotions.

> We say that the mind is in a state of equilibrium when it has no stirrings of pleasure, anger, sorrow, or joy. When these feelings are stirred, and they act in their proper degree, we call the results a "state of harmony." . . . This harmony is the universal path that they all should pursue. When the states of equilibrium and harmony exist in perfection, a happy order will prevail throughout heaven and earth, and all things will be nourished and flourish.

The Confucian "state of harmony" is similar in some respects to Aristotelian ideas about "proper" or correct degrees of feeling that are ingredients of, or required for, virtue. At the same time, Aristotle does not place value on the moderating of emotion per se, but only relative to circumstances.

It is in the concept of virtue itself that the most interesting similarities and differences appear. Confucian virtue (*de*) is associated with power, just as the word "virtue" (*arete*) is in Aristotle (and in the English and Greek languages), and with character traits. Good character traits are like powers to act in fitting ways. As in Aristotle, there is no theoretical way to acquire virtue, although in Confucius the contrast "theoretical/practical" hardly exists. The Confucian (or perhaps simply Chinese) focus is almost entirely practical. Aristotle's insistence on the nonsystematic character of practical wisdom thus fits in with Confucianism, as does his stress on context in thinking about human living. And for both, the existence of paradigmatic figures, wise men who serve as guiding examples, is crucial to the building and preserving of viable community.

The long Confucian tradition is certainly not homogenous (nor is the long Aristotelian tradition), but certain parts of it at least remind a Western reader of Aristotle. Nonetheless there is one thing that does not seem prominent in Aristotle, despite his stress on politics as the highest art. He does not stress the handing down of traditions in the way that the Confucians have. Even religious traditions seem to be important to Confucius, though he has been construed, especially of late, as a purely secular thinker. It is arguable that the references to "heaven" are genuinely religious, and there seems to be little similar to that in Aristotle. It is interesting, however, to see the way in which Aristotelian ideas have been combined with an account of social and religious traditions in recent years; that theme is taken up in the last chapter of this book. There is, in any case, a pattern of similarities that puts in question the extreme relativism or perspectivalism advocated by some sophists. Even if custom sometimes seems to be king, there also seem to be recurring themes in geographically and temporally disparate customs.

*71. *Discuss one similarity between Confucius and Aristotle that would distinguish both of them from Plato. (Recall Plato's views on theoretical knowledge in relation to ethics.)*

72. *Both Aristotle and Confucius think that "the cultivation of the personal life" is fundamental and has priority over abstract principles and ideals. Would either of them say that that cultivation is possible for individuals acting on their own? Discuss.*

CHAPTER FOUR

Morality and Religion

Introduction

We have seen in Chapters 2 and 3 attempts to ground morality in a transcendent impersonal good (Plato) or in a developmental, teleological conception of human nature (Aristotle). Neither of them appeal specifically to a divine source for morality, if what we mean by *divine* is a personal God. But many people do think there is a divine source for morality. Many people in the past, and many people today, believe that moral requirements and rules exist and have the authority they have because they are expressions of God's will or God's design or are directly commanded by God. Such views are quite typical of monotheistic traditions such as Judaism, Christianity and Islam, but the idea that there is some kind of religious bases for morality can be found all over the world. The following selections and discussions indicate some of the ways in which ethics and religious belief have interacted.

ORIENTING QUESTIONS FOR DISCUSSION

1. Do you think that the wrongness of, say, torturing an innocent child is grounded in the will or intention of God for human life? Would it be wrong even if there were no God?
2. If there is a God and God has created everything that exists, including human beings, would you expect that God would also have certain rules or laws according to which everything is meant to function? Why or why not?
3. It certainly seems that some atheists are exceptionally moral people. How could someone who believes that morality is grounded in God or God's commands account for that fact?
4. Is there some connection between what is *natural* and what is *right or wrong*? For example, is murder unnatural, and does a murderer do something which he at some level knows is unnatural or "not how things were meant to be"?
5. If moral truths are grounded in or depend for their truth on God's commands, would it not follow that anything that God commanded would be moral? If so, would it be morally right to murder an innocent child if God commanded it?

Natural Law

Natural law theory has taken many forms, but all natural law theories agree that there are standards of right conduct or virtuous living that are above and independent of "positive" (actually enacted) human laws and conventions. Thus there are at least hints of the idea of a "higher law of nature" wherever, as in Sophocles' *Antigone*, communal norms are challenged by reference to a "law of heaven." Typical natural law theories hold that the fundamental principles or laws of morality can be grasped by reason and can transcend humans laws or communal norms. Plato and Aristotle thus have something in common with natural law theorists, but they do not typically emphasize *law* in their ethics.

Natural law theories refuse to unify ethical ideas through some single principle, in contrast to some of the ethical theories that are discussed in later chapters of this book. Rather, there are several basic laws or principles that govern all of life, such as the principle that humans should be sociable or should confine sexual activity to acts that are reproductive in type, within a marriage.

The concept of natural law can be found in the Stoics and other non-Christian thinkers, but it has had a special appeal to Christians and other religious thinkers who believed that ethical requirements are based in, or are, the commands or "law" of a personal God. In the "Old Testament," or the "TANAK" (Torah, prophets, etc), God is often portrayed as proclaiming or promulgating laws. If we think of God as a supremely rational being and his laws as reflecting that rationality, then obeying them would be the intrinsically reasonable thing to do. Moreover there is sometimes a strong connection made in the TANAK between keeping God's law and prospering and flourishing. Thus it is possible to think that there is a strong connection between being reasonable and flourishing. One can hardly help thinking of Aristotle, who held that the virtuous life is intrinsically rational and is a flourishing life.

Those who fail to keep the natural law, on the other hand, are fools. In the natural law conception they are more than that, however. Even Aristotle would agree that a person who fails to promote her own well-being is a fool. But he would not have described such a person as being guilty of sin or as a "transgressor" or as "perishing" or certain to be punished. But that is typically how the person who ignores God's law is described. These ideas are expressed clearly in Ps. 1, a psalm that is a preface to many of the psalms that follow, such as Psalm 19, and that anticipates many other statements in the Judeo-Christian scriptures.

Psalm 1

1: Blessed is the man who walks not in the counsel of the wicked, nor stands in the way of sinners, nor sits in the seat of scoffers;

2: but his delight is in the law of the LORD, and on his law he meditates day and night.

3: He is like a tree planted by streams of water, that yields its fruit in its season, and its leaf does not wither. In all that he does, he prospers.

4: The wicked are not so, but are like chaff which the wind drives away.

5: Therefore the wicked will not stand in the judgment, nor sinners in the congregation of the righteous;

6: for the LORD knows the way of the righteous, but the way of the wicked will perish.

Psalm 19

7: The law of the LORD is perfect, reviving the soul; the testimony of the LORD is sure, making wise the simple;

8: the precepts of the LORD are right, rejoicing the heart; the commandment of the LORD is pure, enlightening the eyes;

9: the fear of the LORD is clean, enduring forever; the ordinances of the LORD are true, and righteous altogether.

10: More to be desired are they than gold, even much fine gold; sweeter also than honey and drippings of the honeycomb.

11: Moreover by them is thy servant warned; in keeping them there is great reward.

12: But who can discern his errors? Clear thou me from hidden faults.

13: Keep back thy servant also from presumptuous sins; let them not have dominion over me! Then I shall be blameless, and innocent of great transgression.

One of the most influential proponents of natural law theory among Christians was Thomas Aquinas.

He argued that the law of God is such that those who follow it will flourish as human beings. He brings together Aristotelian ideas about happiness with the idea that God, through his laws, has established precisely that pattern of living that is necessary for a good and fulfilled life.

THOMAS AQUINAS (ca. 1225–1274 CE)

Aquinas was born at Roccasecca, near Naples, Italy, the youngest son of a large aristocratic Italian family. He was a student at the Benedictine abbey at Monte Cassino (1231–1239) and from 1239 to 1244 studied at the University of Naples. In 1244 he joined the Dominican friars, a religious order devoted to study and preaching. This did not please his family, who hoped that he might rise to a powerful position in the church, so they had him abducted while he was on a journey to Paris and kept him at home for two years. However, his determination to lead a life as a Dominican finally won out, and he returned to the order, which sent him to Paris in 1245 for further study. There he encountered the philosopher/theologian Albert the Great, who was impressed by this large (perhaps overweight?), modest and humble student who, though apparently referred to by some as a "dumb ox," in fact outshone the brightest and best of them.

Aquinas became a regent master (professor) in theology at Paris, and he produced perhaps the most impressive body of work in theology and philosophy in the high medieval era.

Aquinas' personal piety is especially evident in the hymns he composed, some of which are still used in the worship of many Christian communities.

Aquinas argued that knowledge of natural law is implanted in humans by God. God has created according to a "design plan" and that plan is expressed by the natural law, a law that all people do or can know, at least in part. Now, for a thing to fulfill its design plan or purpose is for it to achieve its proper good, that which is good for it by nature. Aquinas shares with Aristotle the notion that there is such a thing as "human nature," which can be fulfilled or not

fulfilled, depending on whether we live according to the intrinsic requirements of that nature. Like Aristotle, he closely identifies that nature with reason. Reason, when it is not corrupted, directs us to act justly, temperately and, in general, virtuously, for only then do we fulfill ourselves, that is, realize our true nature. Moreover, that fulfillment amounts to "happiness," or *eudaimonia*, so Aquinas' ethical views are to be classified as eudaimonistic views. However, Aquinas argues that the ultimate goal or purpose of human life is a religious one, which cannot be grasped by reason unaided by God's revelation of his will for humans. Only the godly can reach complete happiness.

Summa Theologica: **The Treatise on Law**

Aquinas discusses natural law most fully in his "Treatise on Law," which is part of his *Summa Theologica* (Summary of Theology). There he presents his views in a debate format, in which various controversial claims or "questions" (indicated by "Q") are examined pro and con. Here is the typical format he uses (it reflects the debate style in some classes in the universities of his day)

He begins by considering objections (numbered 1, 2, 3, etc.) to the view that he will try to uphold.

Next he says "on the contrary" and states his own view. He often supports it with quotations from Scripture, from Augustine, from Aristotle (whom he refers to as *the* philosopher, and whose Nichomachean Ethics are referred simply as *Ethic*), from Isadore of Seville and from other authoritative sources.

Finally he gives replies to the objections. He frequently refers to other parts of his *Summa* in stating his views and replies. The "questions" are themselves divided up into "articles" (indicated by *Art.*). In both the questions and the replies Aquinas frequently refers to other, earlier questions and articles not cited here.

In reading the following treatise, should keep in mind that the word *end* means the same thing as *goal* or *aim*.

The first question of the Treatise on Law, Q. 90, examines the relationship between law and reason. This relationship is fundamental to understanding Aquinas' ethics and connects his thinking to the stress on reason in Aristotle. The first article of Q. 90 is given here only in part.

Article 1: Whether Law Is Something Pertaining to Reason

Objection 1 (omitted)

Objection 2 (omitted)

Objection 3: Further, the law moves those who are subject to it to act aright. But it belongs properly to the will to move to act, as is evident from what has been said above (Question [9], Article [1]). Therefore law pertains, not to the reason, but to the will; according to the words of the Jurist (Lib. i, ff., De Const. Prin. leg. i): "Whatsoever pleaseth the sovereign has force of law."

On the contrary, It belongs to the law to command and to forbid. But it belongs to reason to command, as stated above (Question [17], Article [1]). Therefore law is something pertaining to reason.

I answer that, Law is a rule and measure of acts, whereby man is induced to act or is restrained from acting: for "lex" [law] is derived from "ligare" [to bind], because it binds one to act. Now the rule and measure of human acts is the reason, which is the first principle of human acts, as is evident from what has been stated above (Question [1], Article [1], ad 3); since it belongs to the reason to direct to the end, which is the first principle in all matters of action, according to the Philosopher (Phys. ii). Now that which is the principle in any genus, is the rule and measure of that genus: for instance, unity in the genus of numbers, and the first movement in the genus of movements. Consequently it follows that law is something pertaining to reason.

Reply to Objection 3: Reason has its power of moving from the will, as stated above (Question [17], Article [1]): for it is due to the fact that one wills the end, that the reason issues its commands as regards things ordained to the end. But in order that the volition of what is commanded may have the nature of law, it needs to be in accord with some rule of reason. And in this sense is to be understood the saying that the will of the sovereign has the force of law; other-wise the sovereign's will would savor of lawlessness rather than of law.

As Aristotle also argued, reason directs us toward our good. The good is the "end," or goal, of all our actions. A person may be mistaken about what the good is, but all people act to realize or bring about what they believe to be their own good, and there would be something utterly unreasonable (crazy?) about someone who said, "I see that doing so and so will be absolutely bad for me, but I will do it anyway." Right reason directs people to their true good. Corrupted reason may lead to self-harm, but even then the corrupted individual *thinks* that what he or she is doing is reasonable and will lead to good.

Aristotle argued that we can "measure" or assess anyone's actions in terms of how well that person tends to achieve what is objectively good and, thus, reasonable. Similarly Aquinas says that "The rule and measure of human acts is the reason, . . . since it belongs to reason to direct to the end." But *laws* are also measures or standards for actions, so we can assess actions in terms of their conformity to laws or rules. Perhaps then good actions conform to law or a rule, bad ones do not. Think of the rules in sports, for example. A pass is not a good pass if the quarterback throws it when ahead of the line of scrimmage, because doing so violates a rule.

But is there some strong connection between laws and reason? Are laws and rules anything more than conventions and thus not intrinsically reasonable or unreasonable? In that case, actions that conform to them would not be *intrinsically* good. For example, could we not change the rule about forward passes without being unreasonable? It seems obvious that we could. However, the question before us is this; could we change *moral* rules or laws without being unreasonable? Aquinas' answer is "no." Moral rules are in fact rules that direct us to our proper end. Human beings are created or constituted in such a way that they cannot get to the goal (happiness) unless they follow moral laws. Moral laws show us *the* way to our goal. Since they show *the* way, not to follow them would be unreasonable. Thus moral laws are "dictates of reason" and not mere conventions.

Now, here is an obvious problem, which Aquinas deals with in the reply to objection 3. Suppose someone (a ruler, a legislator) makes a *bad* law, one that, if followed, will not lead to the good. For example, laws permitting the sterilization of people judged to be handicapped in various ways seem to most people to be rationally indefensible, bad, not conducive to the good. Doesn't that show that there is no connection between law and reason? Aquinas admits that rulers sometimes pass laws that "savor of lawlessness." Laws that require immoral acts would be such laws, and they would lack genuine rationality.

Aquinas assumes that rulers or legislators are doing, for the whole community over which they rule, what a reasonable individual does for himself when he tries to shape his own conduct so as to achieve happiness. That is, they are seeking happiness, but they seek it for the whole community. Moreover, even the individual takes into account the good of the whole community when he acts, since individuals are "political animals" who cannot achieve their *own* good apart from the good of the community to which they belong. These issues are discussed in the next article.

ARTICLE 2 (IN PART): WHETHER THE LAW IS ALWAYS SOMETHING DIRECTED TO THE COMMON GOOD

Objection 1: Omitted.
Objection 2: Omitted.
Objection 3: Further, Isadore says (Etym. v, 3): "If the law is based on reason, whatever is based on reason will be a law." But reason is the foundation not only of what is ordained to the common good, but also of that which is directed to private good. Therefore the law is not only directed to the good of all, but also to the private good of an individual.

On the contrary, Isadore says (Etym. v, 21) that "laws are enacted for no private profit, but for the common benefit of the citizens."

I answer that, as stated above (Article [1]), the law belongs to that which is a principle of human acts, because it is their rule and measure. Now as reason is

a principle of human acts, so in reason itself there is something which is the principle in respect of all the rest: wherefore to this principle chiefly and mainly law must needs be referred. Now the first principle in practical matters, which are the object of the practical reason, is the last end: and the last end of human life is bliss or happiness, as stated above (Question [2], Article [7]; Question [3], Article [1]). Consequently the law must needs regard principally the relationship to happiness. Moreover, since every part is ordained to the whole, as imperfect to perfect; and since one man is a part of the perfect community, the law must needs regard properly the relationship to universal happiness. Wherefore the Philosopher, in the above definition of legal matters mentions both happiness and the body politic: for he says (Ethic. v, 1) that we call those legal matters "just, which are adapted to produce and preserve happiness and its parts for the body politic": since the state is a perfect community, as he says in Polit. i, 1.

Since the law is chiefly ordained to the common good, any other precept in regard to some individual work, must needs be devoid of the nature of a law, save insofar as it regards the common good. Therefore every law is ordained to the common good.

Reply to Objection 3: Just as nothing stands firm with regard to the speculative reason except that which is traced back to the first indemonstrable principles, so nothing stands firm with regard to the practical reason, unless it be directed to the last end which is the common good: and whatever stands to reason in this sense, has the nature of a law.

> *1. *Reason, as Aristotle stresses, directs people to their proper "end." To say that the proper end is the "last" end is simply to say that there is nothing more complete by reference to which we decide how to act. So if my end in going to school is to graduate, that could not be my final end. Why not?*

When we think of law, we usually think of something that has been voted into effect by a legislature or proclaimed or "promulgated" by a legitimate ruler. A law that has never been declared to be law is no law at all. That being so, does it follow that the laws of *God* must have been explicitly declared or promulgated somewhere, and if so, where? Aquinas is working on an answer to this question in Q. 90, Art. 4. Notice in particular the reply to Objection 1.

ARTICLE 4: WHETHER PROMULGATION IS ESSENTIAL TO A LAW

Objection 1: It would seem that promulgation is not essential to a law. For the natural law above all has the character of law. But the natural law needs no promulgation. Therefore it is not essential to a law that it be promulgated.

Objection 2: Further, it belongs properly to a law to bind one to do or not to do something. But the obligation of fulfilling a law touches not only those in whose presence it is promulgated, but also others. Therefore promulgation is not essential to a law.

Objection 3: Further, the binding force of a law extends even to the future, since "laws are binding in matters of the future," as the jurists say (Cod. 1, tit. De lege et constit. leg. vii). But promulgation concerns those who are present. Therefore it is not essential to a law.

On the contrary, It is laid down in the Decretals, dist. 4, that "laws are established when they are promulgated."

I answer that, as stated above (Article [1]), a law is imposed on others by way of a rule and measure. Now a rule or measure is imposed by being applied to those who are to be ruled and measured by it. Wherefore, in order that a law obtain the binding force which is proper to a law, it must needs be applied to the men who have to be ruled by it. Such application is made by its being notified to them by promulgation. Wherefore promulgation is necessary for the law to obtain its force.

Thus from the four preceding articles, the definition of law may be gathered; and it is nothing else than

> an ordinance of reason for the common good, made by him who has care of the community, and promulgated.

Reply to Objection 1: The natural law is promulgated by the very fact that God instilled it into man's mind so as to be known by him naturally.

Reply to Objection 2: Those who are not present when a law is promulgated, are bound to observe the law, insofar as it is notified or can be notified to them by others, after it has been promulgated.

Reply to Objection 3: The promulgation that takes place now, extends to future time by reason of the durability of written characters, by which means it is continually promulgated. Hence Isadore says (Etym. v, 3; ii, 10) that "lex [law] is derived from legere [to read] because it is written."

> *2. Does Aquinas hold that a law is promulgated only when it is written down or spoken out loud by somebody with authority? Does his view seem plausible to you? Discuss.*

So far Aquinas has been discussing the essence, or definition, of law in general. But he is particularly concerned to clarify God's law and to what he refers to earlier, in the reply to objection 1, as the "natural law." His thinking about God's law shows the same debt to Aristotle that we noted several times already.

Aristotle and Aquinas both hold that living things develop according to built-in purposes or goals. An acorn develops into an oak tree because it has built into it tendencies and capacities that will cause it to develop or mature in that way, provided no obstacles arise, such as lack of moisture or being eaten by a squirrel. The development of the acorn is lawlike, or follows a law. It cannot develop into a birch tree or a dog, obviously. If it could develop in any way whatsoever, that would amount to its not having any "law" at all for its development. But it does, and according to Aquinas that law is grounded in or expresses God's intentions or purposes.

Like other natural things, humans too have built-in purposes that are reflected in laws of nature. In order to develop properly, in order to mature and flourish as human beings, we must follow those laws. To name a few, we must be rational, we must be social and we must maintain some kind of connection between sex and procreation. These natural laws express the way things were "meant to be" (by God) or the way they ought to be and thus how we ought to behave. So irrational behavior, asocial behavior and sexual behavior that is completely disconnected from a desire for procreation would be contrary to natural law.

3. *Does it seem to you that in Aquinas' view biochemical "laws," such as those that determine the growth of an acorn, would be among God's laws and thus not so different from the Ten Commandments? Assuming the answer is "yes," would that show he is confused? Explain.*

The Various Kinds of Law

There are four kinds of law: eternal law, natural law, human law and divine law. Eternal law, the broadest type of law, is the unchanging divine governance over the universe. This covers the "laws of nature" and both general moral rules of conduct, such as "Murder is wrong," and particular cases, such as, "People should not poison their rich aunts." Natural law is a subset of eternal law that can be discovered by humans through reflection, but it includes only general rules of conduct. Human law (the laws passed by state legislatures, for instance) is derived from natural law in various ways. Finally, divine law (contained in the Bible) is a specially revealed subset of the eternal law. All moral laws are general principles either known by all rational beings or derived from those principles or found in the scriptures. All of them are ultimately grounded in an objective, universal and unchanging eternal law, the law of God.

In Q. 91 Aquinas discusses the different kinds of law.

ARTICLE 1 (IN PART): IS THERE AN ETERNAL LAW?

. . . A law is nothing else but a dictate of practical reason emanating from the ruler who governs a perfect community. Now it is evident, granted that the world is ruled by Divine Providence, as was stated in I, 22, A1, 2, that the whole community of the universe is governed by Divine Reason. Wherefore the very idea of the government of things in God the Ruler of the universe, has the nature of a law. And since the Divine Reason's conception of things is not subject to time but is eternal, according to Prov. 8:23, therefore it is that this kind of law must be called eternal.

ARTICLE 2: IS THERE A NATURAL LAW IN US?

Objection 1: It would seem that there is no natural law in us. Because man is governed sufficiently by the eternal law: for Aug. says (De Lib. Arb. i) that "the eternal law is that by which it is right that all things should be most orderly." But nature does not abound in superfluities as neither does she fail in necessaries. Therefore no law is natural to man.

Objection 2: Further, by the law man is directed, in his acts, to the end, as stated above (90, 2). But the directing of human acts to their end is not a function of nature, as is the case in irrational creatures, which act for an end solely by their natural appetite; whereas man acts for an end by his reason and will. Therefore no law is natural to man.

4. *Pay special attention to objection 2 and the next one and the replies. They seem to imply that there is a fundamental difference between physical "laws," such as laws of chemistry, physiology or psychological laws of conditioning and the like, that determine the behavior of plants and nonrational animals, on the one hand, and a law such as "Do not commit adultery" that applies only to humans. What is the difference?*

Objection 3: Further, the more a man is free, the less is he under the law. But man is freer than all the animals, on account of his free will, with which he is endowed above all other animals. Since therefore other animals are not subject to a natural law, neither is man subject to a natural law.

On the contrary, A gloss on Rm. 2:14: "When the Gentiles, who have not the law, do by nature those things that are of the law," comments as follows: "Although they have no written law, yet they have the natural law, whereby each one knows, and is conscious of, what is good and what is evil."

I answer that, As stated above (90, 1, ad 1), law, being a rule and measure, can be in a person in two ways: in one way, as in him that rules and measures; in another way, as in that which is ruled and measured, since a thing is ruled and measured, insofar as it partakes of the rule or measure. Wherefore, since all things subject to Divine providence are ruled and measured by the eternal law, as was stated above (1); it is evident that all things partake somewhat of the eternal law, insofar as, namely, from its being imprinted on them, they derive their respective inclinations to their proper acts and ends. Now among all others, the rational creature is subject to Divine providence in the most excellent way, insofar as it partakes of a share of providence, by being provident both for itself and for others. Wherefore it has a share of the Eternal Reason, whereby it has a natural inclination to its proper act and end: and this participation of the eternal law in the rational creature is called the natural law. Hence the Psalmist after saying (Ps. 4:6): "Offer up the sacrifice of justice," as though someone asked what the works of justice are, adds: "Many say, Who shows us good things?" in answer to which question he says: "The light of Your countenance, O Lord, is signed upon us": thus implying that the light of natural reason, whereby we discern what is good and what is evil, which is the function of the natural law, is nothing else than an imprint on us of the Divine light. It is therefore evident that the natural law is nothing else than the rational creature's participation of the eternal law.

Reply to Objection 1: This argument would hold, if the natural law were something different from the eternal law: whereas it is nothing but a participation thereof, as stated above.

Reply to Objection 2: Every act of reason and will in us is based on that which is according to nature, as stated above (10, 1): for every act of reasoning is based on principles that are known naturally, and every act of appetite in respect of the means is derived from the natural appetite in respect of the last end. Accordingly the first direction of our acts to their end must needs be in virtue of the natural law.

Reply to Objection 3: Even irrational animals partake in their own way of the Eternal Reason, just as the rational creature does. But because the rational creature partakes thereof in an intellectual and rational manner, therefore the participation of the eternal law in the rational creature is properly called a law, since a law is something pertaining to reason, as

stated above (90, 1). Irrational creatures, however, do not partake thereof in a rational manner, wherefore there is no participation of the eternal law in them, except by way of similitude.

Aquinas uses the expression "participation of the law in" to refer to actions or features of something that do instantiate some (eternal) law. Thus a plant leaf that turns toward light (phototropism) participates in law, that is, in the divine order established by God in creating that plant in such a way that it will grow and flourish, that is, achieve its "proper end." But the plant does not "know what it is doing" and therefore is not in a sense "following a law." Only where creatures "know what they are doing" in following a law is it strictly proper to say that there is a "participation of the eternal law in them." So even though eternal law determines the movements of the plant's leaves, the plant is related to eternal law and reason in a way that is merely similar in some respects to the way in which human actions can be related to eternal law. Only in the case of rational creatures is there, strictly speaking, a following of eternal law. Rational beings can themselves understand to some extent what their proper end is and act so as to achieve it. When they do that they are following the law of nature.

Aquinas argues next that there must be human law (passed by legislatures, for instance) even though divine law "covers everything" in a sense.

ARTICLE 3: WHETHER THERE IS A HUMAN LAW

Objection 1: It would seem that there is not a human law. For the natural law is a participation of the eternal law, as stated above (2). Now through the eternal law "all things are most orderly," as Augustine states (De Lib. Arb. i, 6). Therefore the natural law suffices for the ordering of all human affairs. Consequently there is no need for a human law.

Objection 2: Further, a law bears the character of a measure, as stated above (90, 1). But human reason is not a measure of things, but vice versa, as stated in Metaph. x, text. 5.

Therefore no law can emanate from human reason.

Objection 3: Further, a measure should be most certain, as stated in Metaph. x, text. 3. But the dictates of human reason in matters of conduct are uncertain, according to Wis. 9:14: "The thoughts of mortal men are fearful, and our counsels uncertain." Therefore no law can emanate from human reason.

On the contrary, Augustine (De Lib. Arb. i, 6) distinguishes two kinds of law, the one eternal, the other temporal, which he calls human.

I answer that, as stated above (90, 1, ad 2), a law is a dictate of the practical reason. Now it is to be observed that the same procedure takes place in the practical and in the speculative reason: for each proceeds from principles to conclusions, as stated above (De Lib. Arb. i, 6). Accordingly we conclude that just as, in the speculative reason, from naturally known indemonstrable principles, we draw the conclusions of the various sciences, the knowledge of which is not imparted to us by nature, but acquired by the efforts of reason, so too it is from the precepts of the natural law, as from general and indemonstrable principles, that the human reason needs to proceed to the more particular determination of certain matters. These particular determinations, devised by human reason, are called human laws, provided the other essential conditions of law be observed, as stated above (90, A2,3,4). Wherefore Tully says in his Rhetoric (De Invent. Rhet. ii) that "justice has its source in nature; thence certain things came into custom by reason of their utility; afterwards these things which emanated from nature and were approved by custom, were sanctioned by fear and reverence for the law."

When we bring someone to court, we "measure" or assess their actions in light of the law. So the law is a measure. If it is a good law, one that reflects God's law, it tells us what is both right and good.

5. *Would you say that the law "Do not murder" determines what is reasonable to do as well as what is right or wrong to do? Or do such laws*
tell us what is right or wrong but not what is according to reason?

6. *Aquinas' remarks here (note objection 2) should remind you of a famous statement by the ancient Greek philosopher Protagoras: "Man is the measure of all things." How is Aquinas responding to the Protagorean claim?*

Once again the notion of *custom* (what people customarily believe to be right and wrong) is said to be rooted in nature, where *nature* means the way things are or are meant to be, independent of custom, in which case custom (*nomos* in Greek) is *not* king, despite what some Greek relativists had claimed. Rather, nature is king. Customs derive from what is "natural." Could that be right?

It is clear that some laws or customs (e.g., "Drive on the right-hand side of the road") are simply a matter of convention (nomos). We could change that to "Drive on the left-hand side" and no one would be any worse off. There is nothing particularly "natural" about driving on the right-hand side of the road. (However, it is a fact of nature that there needs to be some coordination of traffic flow in order to avoid accidents and disruptions of all sorts. So in that sense even "Drive on the right-hand side of the road" is based on nature and is a reflection of reason, which infers human laws from general reasonable principles.) Now, what about laws against murder or theft? Are they somehow rooted in nature also, or, to put it another way, are they rooted in the way things were "meant to be"? (And if so, who "meant them to be that way"?)

7. *What is your own view on the relation of law to custom and nature? If you think laws prohibiting murder are rooted in nature or "the way things were meant to be," you may be close to Aquinas' view.*

8. *Try to give some other account of such laws as those prohibiting murder and theft that does not rely on the idea of a natural order of some sort. What might account for the wrongness of murder or theft or lying, if not that they violate God's design, or will, or intention? In this connection you might recall your answer to Orienting Question 3.*

ARTICLE 4: WHETHER THERE WAS ANY NEED FOR A DIVINE LAW

Objection 1: It would seem that there was no need for a Divine law. Because, as stated above (2), the natural law is a participation in us of the eternal law. But the eternal law is a Divine law, as stated above (1). Therefore there was no need for a Divine law in addition to the natural law, and human laws derived therefrom.

Objection 2: Further, it is written (Sirach 15:14) that "God left man in the hand of his own counsel." Now counsel is an act of reason, as stated above (14, 1). Therefore man was left to the direction of his reason. But a dictate of human reason is a human law as stated above (3). Therefore there is no need for man to be governed also by a Divine law.

Objection 3: Further, human nature is more self-sufficing than irrational creatures. But irrational creatures have no Divine law besides the natural inclination impressed on them. Much less, therefore, should the rational creature have a Divine law in addition to the natural law.

On the contrary, David prayed God to set His law before him, saying (Ps. 118:33): "Set before me for a law the way of Your justifications, O Lord."

I answer that, Besides the natural and the human law it was necessary for the directing of human conduct to have a Divine law. And this for four reasons. First, because it is by law that man is directed how to perform his proper acts in view of his last end. And indeed if man were ordained to no other end than that which is proportionate to his natural faculty, there would be no need for man to have any further direction of the part of his reason, besides the natural law and human law which is derived from it. But since man is ordained to an end of eternal happiness which is disproportionate to man's natural faculty, as stated above (5, 5), therefore it was necessary that, besides the natural and the human law, man should be directed to his end by a law given by God.

Secondly, because, on account of the uncertainty of human judgment, especially on contingent and particular matters, different people form different judgments on human acts; whence also different and contrary laws result. In order, therefore, that man may know without any doubt what he ought to do and what he ought to avoid, it was necessary for man to be directed in his proper acts by a law given by God, for it is certain that such a law cannot err.

Thirdly, because man can make laws in those matters of which he is competent to judge. But man is not competent to judge of interior movements, that are hidden, but only of exterior acts which appear: and yet for the perfection of virtue it is necessary for man to conduct himself aright in both kinds of acts. Consequently human law could not sufficiently curb and direct interior acts; and it was necessary for this purpose that a Divine law should supervene.

Fourthly, because, as Aug. says (De Lib. Arb. i, 5, 6), human law cannot punish or forbid all evil deeds: since while aiming at doing away with all evils, it would do away with many good things, and would hinder the advance of the common good, which is necessary for human intercourse. In order, therefore, that no evil might remain unforbidden and unpunished, it was necessary for the Divine law to supervene, whereby all sins are forbidden.

And these four causes are touched upon in Ps. 118:8, where it is said: "The law of the Lord is unspotted," i.e., allowing no foulness of sin; "converting souls," because it directs not only exterior, but also interior acts; "the testimony of the Lord is faithful," because of the certainty of what is true and right; "giving wisdom to little ones," by directing man to an end supernatural and Divine.

In the Judeo-Christian scriptures such expressions of "divine law" as the following can be found: 1. You shall have no other Gods before you (none other than the God of Israel, who is identified by his deeds, etc.); 2. Whoever looks on a woman lustfully has already committed adultery in his heart; 3. Turn the other cheek, do not return violence with violence.

9. *Try to associate each of the scriptures just cited with one of Aquinas' four reasons for his claim that there is a need for divine law. So, for example, if you think his first reason would go with number 2, write "I, 2."*

Three Points About Human and Divine Law

In Question 93 Aquinas discusses the nature of the eternal law, which is the ultimate source of all moral laws. First, he argues that eternal law is instituted by God as God's way of governing all things, including human actions. Second, when considering whether the knowledge of the eternal law is available to everyone, Aquinas argues that the complete list of eternal laws is known only to God. However, humans have access to a subset of eternal law that is discovered through reflection (i.e., natural law). Third, Aquinas considers whether all laws, including human laws of governments, are derived from eternal law. He argues that so long as governing bodies derive their laws carefully and rationally from natural law, then these laws will also be part of eternal law. However, even the slightest error of reasoning may result in an improper human law. Moreover, human law does not cover everything covered by divine law. In this connection refer to the previous question.

In Question 94 Aquinas addresses the concept of natural law directly. First, when considering whether natural law is the same in all people, he argues that the more general or primary principles of natural law are common to all, such as "Do not harm others." However, more particular or secondary derivations from these, such as "Do not sell dangerous toys" might not be common to all. Second, as to whether the natural law can be changed, Aquinas argues that, although new primary principles may be added, none which are already there can be subtracted. Further, the formulation of secondary principles, as noted earlier, may not be consistently derived by all people in the same way or at all times and in that sense may change.

ARTICLE 4: WHETHER THE NATURAL LAW IS THE SAME IN ALL PEOPLE

Objection 1 (omitted)

Objection 2: Further, "Things which are according to the law are said to be just," as stated in Ethic. v. But it is stated in the same book that nothing is so universally just as not to be subject to change in regard to some men.

Therefore even the natural law is not the same in all men.

Objection 3: Further, as stated above (2, 3), to the natural law belongs everything to which a man is inclined according to his nature. Now different men are naturally inclined to different things; some to the desire of pleasures, others to the desire of honors, and other men to other things. Therefore there is not one natural law for all.

Objection 3 relates to Aquinas' claim that all rational creatures are "naturally inclined" toward their true end, which is happiness. The objector (the author of Objection 3) says in effect, "Hey, wait a minute, people are 'naturally inclined' toward all sorts of things. Some might even be 'naturally inclined' toward the pleasures of sadism, for instance. So how can you say that all are naturally inclined toward the *same* end and that there is therefore *one* law for all?" See Aquinas' reply to objection 3 in this "Question."

On the contrary, Isidore says (Etym. v, 4): "The natural law is common to all nations."

I answer that, as stated above (2, 3), to the natural law belongs those things to which a man is inclined naturally: and among these it is proper to man to be inclined to act according to reason. Now the process of reason is from the common to the proper, as stated in Phys. i. The speculative reason, however, is differently situated in this matter, from the practical reason. For, since the speculative reason is busied chiefly with the necessary things, which cannot be otherwise than they are, its proper conclusions, like the universal principles, contain the truth without fail. The practical reason, on the other hand, is busied with contingent matters, about which human actions are concerned: and consequently, although there is necessity in the general principles, the more we descend to matters of detail, the more frequently we encounter defects.

Accordingly then in speculative matters truth is the same in all men, both as to principles and as to conclusions: although the truth is not known to all as regards the conclusions, but only as regards the principles which are called common notions. But in matters of action, truth or practical rectitude ("rectitude"= "rightness or correctness") is not the same for all, as to matters of detail, but only as to the general principles: and where there is the same rectitude in matters of detail, it is not equally known to all.

It is therefore evident that, as regards the general principles whether of speculative or of practical reason, truth or rectitude is the same for all, and is equally known by all. As to the proper conclusions of the speculative reason, the truth is the same for all, but is not equally known to all: thus it is true for all that the three angles of a triangle are together equal to two right angles, although it is not known to all. But as to the proper conclusions of the practical reason, neither is the truth or rectitude the same for all, nor, where it is the same, is it equally known by all. Thus it is right and true for all to act according to reason: and from this principle it follows as a proper conclusion, that goods entrusted to another should be restored to their owner. Now this is true for the majority of cases: but it may happen in a particular case that it would be injurious, and therefore unreasonable, to restore goods held in trust; for instance, if they are claimed for the purpose of fighting against one's country. And this principle will be found to fail the more, according as we descend further into detail, e.g., if one were to say that goods held in trust should be restored with such and such a guarantee, or in such and such a way; because the greater the number of conditions added, the greater the number of ways in which the principle may fail, so that it be not right to restore or not to restore.

Consequently we must say that the natural law, as to general principles, is the same for all, both as to rectitude and as to knowledge. But as to certain matters of detail, which are conclusions, as it were, of those general principles, it is the same for all in the majority of cases, both as to rectitude and as to knowledge; and yet in some few cases it may fail, both as to rectitude, by reason of certain obstacles (just as natures subject to generation and corruption fail in some few cases on account of some obstacle), and as to knowledge, since in some the reason is perverted by passion, or evil habit, or an evil disposition of nature; thus formerly, theft, although it is expressly contrary to the natural law, was not considered wrong among the Germans, as Julius Caesar relates (De Bello Gall. vi).

Reply to Objection 2: The saying of the Philosopher is to be understood of things that are naturally just, not as general principles, but as conclusions drawn from them, having rectitude in the majority of cases, but failing in a few.

Reply to Objection 3: As, in man, reason rules and commands the other powers, so all the natural inclinations belonging to the other powers must needs be directed according to reason. Wherefore it is universally right for all men, that all their inclinations should be directed according to reason.

Speculative reason deals with such things as mathematics. The principles of speculative reason include such truths as that the interior angles of a triangle sum to 180 degrees, a truth grasped by that kind of reason. That truth is true for anyone, no matter where or when he was born or what the people around him happen to think. But of course not everyone knows that truth. For example, you did not know it when you were 2 years old, and people ignorant of geometry do no know it. So its "rectitude," or correctness, is the same for all, but it is not equally known to all, as Aquinas puts it.

Practical reason, on the other hand, deals with such matters as how to act in everyday life. It includes such truths as "You should usually warm up before running a race" and "You should return borrowed goods." Are these truths also the same for everyone, and does everyone know them?

10. *Aquinas claims that the general principles of practical reason are the same for all and known by all. Give an example of such a general principle.*

11. *He also claims that the conclusions or inferences drawn from the general principles of practical reason are not always the same for all and are not known by all. Give an example of a conclusion or inference from the general principle that you stated in the previous question.*

*12. *It is according to practical reason that we restore to the rightful owner anything we have borrowed, and so this principle is part* *of natural law. Suppose we borrowed a gun from a friend and then discovered that he had become suicidal. (a) Should we return the gun? (b) What would Aquinas say? (c) How does his answer bear on the general question whether the natural law is the same for all? (d) How does it bear on the issue of relativism, if at all?*

13. *Sometimes people fail to know the general and particular principles of natural law because their reason has been corrupted. Illustrate how that might happen, using an example from Aquinas. Try to add one of your own.*

Someone who believes, as Aquinas does, that all genuine law is rooted in the eternal and unchanging will of God must give an account of the way in which actual human laws, which are supposed to be somehow based in or derivable from the eternal law of God, seem to change and vary with time and circumstance. He discusses this further in Art. 5.

ARTICLE 5: WHETHER THE NATURAL LAW CAN BE CHANGED

Objection 1: It would seem that the natural law can be changed. Because on Sirach 17:9, "He gave them instructions, and the law of life," the gloss says: "He wished the law of the letter to be written, in order to correct the law of nature." But that which is corrected is changed. Therefore the natural law can be changed.

Objection 2: Further, the slaying of the innocent, adultery, and theft are against the natural law. But we find these things changed by God: as when God commanded Abraham to slay his innocent son (Gn. 22:2); and when he ordered the Jews to borrow and purloin the vessels of the Egyptians (Ex. 12:35); and when He commanded Osee to take to himself "a wife of fornications" (Osee 1:2). Therefore the natural law can be changed.

Objection 3: Further, Isidore says (Etym. 5:4) that "the possession of all things in common, and universal freedom, are matters of natural law." But these things are seen to be changed by hu-

man laws. Therefore it seems that the natural law is subject to change.

On the contrary, It is said in the Decretals (Dist. v): "The natural law dates from the creation of the rational creature. It does not vary according to time, but remains unchangeable."

I answer that, A change in the natural law may be understood in two ways. First, by way of addition. In this sense nothing hinders the natural law from being changed: since many things for the benefit of human life have been added over and above the natural law, both by the Divine law and by human laws.

Secondly, a change in the natural law may be understood by way of subtraction, so that what previously was according to the natural law, ceases to be so. In this sense, the natural law is altogether unchangeable in its first principles: but in its secondary principles, which, as we have said (4), are certain detailed proximate conclusions drawn from the first principles, the natural law is not changed so that what it prescribes be not right in most cases. But it may be changed in some particular cases of rare occurrence, through some special causes hindering the observance of such precepts, as stated above (4).

Reply to Objection 1: The written law is said to be given for the correction of the natural law, either because it supplies what was wanting to the natural law; or because the natural law was perverted in the hearts of some men, as to certain matters, so that they esteemed those things good which are naturally evil; which perversion stood in need of correction.

Reply to Objection 2: All men alike, both guilty and innocent, die the death of nature: which death of nature is inflicted by the power of God on account of original sin, according to 1 Kgs. 2:6: "The Lord kills and makes alive." Consequently, by the command of God, death can be inflicted on any man, guilty or innocent, without any injustice whatever. In like manner adultery is intercourse with another's wife; who is allotted to him by the law emanating from God. Consequently intercourse with any woman, by the command of God, is neither adultery nor fornication. The same applies to theft, which is the taking of another's property. For whatever is taken by the command of God, to Whom all things belong, is not taken against the will of its owner, whereas it is in this that theft consists. Nor is it only in human things, that whatever is commanded by God is right; but also in natural things, whatever is done by God, is, in some way, natural, as stated in I, 105, 6, ad 1.

Reply to Objection 3: A thing is said to belong to the natural law in two ways. First, because nature inclines thereto: e.g., that one should not do harm to another. Secondly, because nature did not bring in the contrary: thus we might say that for man to be naked is of the natural law, because nature did not give him clothes, but art invented them. In this sense, "the possession of all things in common and universal freedom" are said to be of the natural law, because, to wit, the distinction of possessions and slavery were not brought in by nature, but devised by human reason for the benefit of human life. Accordingly the law of nature was not changed in this respect, except by addition.

Aquinas' concern to establish the unchangeableness of natural law is to be expected, for several reasons, one of them being that if it were changeable even with respect to its first principles, that would imply that there is no fixed human nature with a built-in purpose by reference to which we can determine right and wrong, virtue and vice.

Aquinas makes some remarkable claims in art. 5. For example, he claims that what would normally be called stealing or murder might be compatible with natural law. One way to think about Aquinas' position is this: Actions can be described in many ways. Thus, not every act of intentionally deceiving a person automatically gets described as "lying." It might be described as "deceiving a tyrant to save an innocent life." We could not consistently hold both that all acts of lying are wrong and that some act of lying is right, but we could consistently hold both that all acts that are correctly described as "acts of lying" are wrong, but that some acts of intentionally deceiving come under more morally relevant descriptions than the description "acts of lying." In fact, Aquinas argues that the Israelite "theft" of Egyptian gold was not rightly described as "theft" after all, since it was done by the command of God, who ultimately owns all things. You

cannot be said to have "stolen" *x* when the owner of *x* told you to take it. This is Aquinas' way out of the problem posed in Art. 5, Objection 2.

14. *Does this "redescription" maneuver seem to you like a "cheap way out"? Discuss it in connection with theft and argue pro and con.*
15. *Aquinas also seems to argue (in the last reply) that slavery might be justified in terms of its benefit for human life. Does this imply that it is consistent with natural law, and thus with God's eternal law, that there be slavery?*
16. *Would Aquinas' reply to objection 2 leave it open to someone to justify any act whatsoever, no matter how horrible, by simply claiming that God has commanded it? Why or why not? Check your discussion of Orienting Question 5.*

Aquinas discusses various moral issues in other places in the *Summa Theologica* and in other works. One that is obviously of great importance has to do with the permissibility or impermissibility of killing.

Summa Theologica and De Malo: Killing and the Principle of Double Effect

Summa Theologica: On Wisdom and Folly

Aquinas, like Aristotle, allots a central place to wisdom among the virtues. Aristotle distinguishes practical wisdom (*phronesis*) from theoretical wisdom and seems to think that theoretical wisdom, which deals with the highest topics in metaphysics, such as the "first cause," has no direct bearing on conduct. It seems possible, at least on first sight, that, by Aristotle's account, Hitler or a "mad scientist" could have theoretical wisdom. If this is a correct account of Aristotle, then at this point Aquinas parts company with Aristotle, for Aquinas considers that the highest cause, the origin of the universe, is in fact God, the same God that has written the law in human hearts and ordered everything in the universe. So we might guess that Aquinas thinks that something like theoretical wisdom *does* have a bearing on conduct. Someone like Hitler could *not* have had theoretical wisdom of the highest kind, in Aquinas' view. If he did he would have believed in God and understood that all conduct must accord with God's will. The knowledge of God includes knowledge of how to live. That is in fact Aquinas' view. He does not think, however, that the "godless" are incapable of any kind of practical wisdom. He distinguishes between wisdom proper and prudence. The latter can be found among unbelievers. But true wisdom is in fact a gift of the Holy Spirit and is thus reserved for believers.

Summa IIaIIae Q. 45

ARTICLE 1: WHETHER WISDOM SHOULD BE RECKONED AMONG THE GIFTS OF THE HOLY GHOST

Objection 1: It would seem that wisdom ought not to be reckoned among the gifts of the Holy Ghost. For the gifts are more perfect than the virtues, as stated above (FS, Question [68], Article [8]). Now virtue is directed to the good alone, wherefore Augustine says (De Lib. Arb. ii, 19) that "no man makes bad use of the virtues." Much more therefore are the gifts of the Holy Ghost directed to the good alone. But wisdom is directed to evil also, for it is written (James 3:15) that a certain wisdom is "earthly, sensual, devilish." Therefore wisdom should not be reckoned among the gifts of the Holy Ghost.

Objection 2: Further, according to Augustine (De Trin. xii, 14) "wisdom is the knowledge of Divine things." Now that knowledge of Divine things which man can acquire by his natural endowments, belongs to the wisdom which is an intellectual virtue, while the supernatural knowledge of Divine things belongs to faith which is a theological virtue, as explained above (Question [4], Article [5]; FS, Question [62], Article [3]). Therefore wisdom should be called a virtue rather than a gift.

On the contrary, It is written (Is. 11:2): "The Spirit of the Lord shall rest upon Him; the spirit of wisdom and of understanding."

I answer that, According to the Philosopher (Metaph. i: 2), it belongs to wisdom to consider the highest cause. By means of that cause we are able to form a most certain judgment about other causes, and according thereto all things should be set in order. Now the highest cause may be understood in two ways, either simply or in some particular genus. Accordingly he that knows the highest cause in any particular genus, and by its means is able to judge and set in order all the things that belong to that genus, is said to be wise in that genus, for instance, in medicine or architecture, according to 1 Cor. 3:10: "As a wise architect, I have laid a foundation." On the other hand, he who knows the cause that is simply the highest, which is God, is said to be wise simply, because he is able to judge and set in order all things according to Divine rules.

Now man obtains this judgment through the Holy Ghost, according to 1 Cor. 2:15: "The spiritual man judgeth all things," because as stated in the same chapter (1 Cor. 2:10), "the Spirit searcheth all things, yea the deep things of God." Wherefore it is evident that wisdom is a gift of the Holy Ghost.

Reply to Objection 1: A thing is said to be good in two senses: first in the sense that it is truly good and simply perfect, secondly, by a kind of likeness, being perfect in wickedness; thus we speak of a good or a perfect thief, as the Philosopher observes (Metaph. v, text. 21). And just as with regard to those things which are truly good, we find a highest cause, namely the sovereign good which is the last end, by knowing which, man is said to be truly wise, so too in evil things something is to be found to which all others are to be referred as to a last end, by knowing which, man is said to be wise unto evil doing, according to Jer. 4:22: "They are wise to do evils, but to do good they have no knowledge." Now whoever turns away from his due end, must needs fix on some undue end, since every agent acts for an end. Wherefore, if he fixes his end in external earthly things, his "wisdom" is called "earthly," if in the goods of the body, it is called "sensual wisdom," if in some excellence, it is called "devilish wisdom" because it imitates the devil's pride, of which it is written (Job 41:25): "He is king over all the children of pride."

Reply to Objection 2: The wisdom which is called a gift of the Holy Ghost, differs from that which is an acquired intellectual virtue, for the latter is attained by human effort, whereas the latter is "descending from above" (James 3:15). In like manner it differs from faith, since faith assents to the Divine truth in itself, whereas it belongs to the gift of wisdom to judge according to the Divine truth. Hence the gift of wisdom presupposes faith, because "a man judges well what he knows" (Ethic. i, 3).

ARTICLE 3: WHETHER WISDOM IS MERELY SPECULATIVE, OR PRACTICAL ALSO

Objection 1: It would seem that wisdom is not practical but merely speculative. For the gift of wisdom is more excellent than the wisdom which is an intellectual virtue. But wisdom, as an intellectual virtue, is merely speculative. Much more therefore is wisdom, as a gift, speculative and not practical.

Objection 2: Further, the practical intellect is about matters of operation which are contingent. But wisdom is about Divine things which are eternal and necessary. Therefore wisdom cannot be practical.

Objection 3: Further, Gregory says (Moral. vi, 37) that "in contemplation we seek the Beginning which is God, but in action we labor under a mighty bundle of wants." Now wisdom regards the vision of Divine things, in which there is no toiling under a load, since according to Wis. 8:16, "her conversation hath no bitterness, nor her company any tediousness." Therefore wisdom is merely contemplative, and not practical or active.

On the contrary, It is written (Col. 4:5): "Walk with wisdom towards them that are without." Now this pertains to action. Therefore wisdom is not merely speculative, but also practical.

I answer that, As Augustine says (De Trin. xii, 14), the higher part of the reason is the province of wisdom, while the lower part is the domain of knowl-

edge. Now the higher reason according to the same authority (De Trin. xii, 7) "is intent on the consideration and consultation of the heavenly," i.e., Divine, "types"; it considers them, insofar as it contemplates Divine things in themselves, and it consults them, insofar as it judges of human acts by Divine things, and directs human acts according to Divine rules. Accordingly wisdom as a gift, is not merely speculative but also practical.

Reply to Objection 1: The higher a virtue is, the greater the number of things to which it extends, as stated in De Causis, prop. x, xvii. Wherefore from the very fact that wisdom as a gift is more excellent than wisdom as an intellectual virtue, since it attains to God more intimately by a kind of union of the soul with Him, it is able to direct us not only in contemplation but also in action.

Reply to Objection 2: Divine things are indeed necessary and eternal in themselves, yet they are the rules of the contingent things which are the subject matter of human actions.

Reply to Objection 3: A thing is considered in itself before being compared with something else. Wherefore to wisdom belongs first of all contemplation which is the vision of the Beginning, and afterwards the direction of human acts according to the Divine rules. Nor from the direction of wisdom does there result any bitterness or toil in human acts; on the contrary the result of wisdom is to make the bitter sweet, and labor a rest.

17. *According to Aquinas, a "perfect thief" would be someone who knew everything he needed to know in order to pursue the goal of getting the property of others unjustly but who did not know what goals are worth pursuing. Is that what you might mean by "a perfect thief?" Would you agree that such a person does not know what goals are worth pursuing?*

18. *Aquinas claims here that the highest form of virtue, true wisdom that orders all actions rightly, is only available to those gifted by God. It is therefore not true that the use of natural human faculties (reason) can achieve the highest kind of human goodness. Is this view in conflict with Aquinas' account of natural law? Why or why not?*

On Folly

WHETHER FOLLY IS CONTRARY TO WISDOM

Objection 1: It would seem that folly is not contrary to wisdom. For seemingly unwisdom is directly opposed to wisdom. But folly does not seem to be the same as unwisdom, for the latter is apparently about Divine things alone, whereas folly is about both Divine and human things. Therefore folly is not contrary to wisdom.

Objection 2: Further, one contrary is not the way to arrive at the other. But folly is the way to arrive at wisdom, for it is written (1 Cor. 3:18): "If any man among you seem to be wise in this world, let him become a fool, that he may be wise." Therefore folly is not opposed to wisdom.

Objection 3: Further, one contrary is not the cause of the other. But wisdom is the cause of folly; for it is written (Jer. 10:14): "Every man is become a fool for knowledge," and wisdom is a kind of knowledge. Moreover, it is written (Is. 47:10): "Thy wisdom and thy knowledge, this hath deceived thee." Now it belongs to folly to be deceived. Therefore folly is not contrary to wisdom.

Objection 4: Further, Isidore says (Etym. x, under the letter S) that "a fool is one whom shame does not incite to sorrow, and who is unconcerned when he is injured." But this pertains to spiritual wisdom, according to Gregory (Moral. x, 49). Therefore folly is not opposed to wisdom.

On the contrary, Gregory says (Moral. ii, 26) that "the gift of wisdom is given as a remedy against folly."

I answer that, Stultitia [Folly] seems to take its name from "stupor"; wherefore Isidore says (Etym. x, under the letter of S): "A fool is one who through dullness [stuporem] remains unmoved." And folly differs from fatuity, according to the same authority (Etym. x), in that folly implies apathy in the heart and dullness in the senses, while fatuity denotes entire privation of the spiritual sense. Therefore folly is fittingly opposed to wisdom.

For "sapiens" [wise] as Isidore says (Etym. x) "is so named from sapor [savor], because just as the taste is quick to distinguish between savors of meats, so is a wise man in discerning things and causes." Wherefore it is manifest that "folly" is opposed to "wisdom" as its contrary, while "fatuity" is opposed to it as a pure negation: since the fatuous man lacks the sense of judgment, while the fool has the sense, though dulled, whereas the wise man has the sense acute and penetrating.

Reply to Objection 1: According to Isidore (Etym. x), "unwisdom is contrary to wisdom because it lacks the savor of discretion and sense"; so that unwisdom is seemingly the same as folly. Yet a man would appear to be a fool chiefly through some deficiency in the verdict of that judgment which is according to the highest cause, for if a man fails in judgment about some trivial matter, he is not for that reason called a fool.

Reply to Objection 2: Just as there is an evil wisdom, as stated above (Question [45], Article [1], ad 1), called "worldly wisdom," because it takes for the highest cause and last end some worldly good, so too there is a good folly opposed to this evil wisdom, whereby man despises worldly things: and it is of this folly that the Apostle speaks.

Reply to Objection 3: It is the wisdom of the world that deceives and makes us foolish in God's sight, as is evident from the Apostle's words (1 Cor. 3:19).

*19. "That judgment which is according to the highest cause" (reply to Objection 1) would be judgment concerning the deep purposes of human life, which are what they are by virtue of God's (the highest cause's) will. Now answer the following:
a. If I mistakenly, perhaps carelessly, judge that the shortest route from one town to another is a route that is in fact not the shortest route but actually five miles out of the way, would that show that I am a fool?
b. If I judge that the best kind of life is one spent watching the soaps on TV, would Aquinas classify me as a fool?

Just what makes (a) and (b) so different, if they are so different?

Sometimes a concept can be more easily grasped by considering a contrasting concept. That may be the case when trying to grasp what is distinctive in Aquinas' account of the concept of *wisdom*. The contrasting or opposed concept is *folly*. Folly, he argues, is marked by a kind of dullness or apathy. The fool is not merely stupid, someone who is unable, for example, to correctly relate means to ends or to make correct judgments about such things as what sort of behavior is offensive or rude. Rather, he is unresponsive where we expect otherwise. A stupid person might make a rude remark and then be surprised to discover that it was considered rude. Moreover when the rudeness is pointed out, a stupid person might well feel bad, be embarrassed or ashamed, and try to "make things right."

A fool, on the other hand, might well know that he or she had been rude but would be indifferent, unembarrassed, not inclined to do anything about it. Aquinas quotes Isadore of Seville: "A fool is one who through dullness [stuporem] remains unmoved." A further quote from Isadore, from objection 4 of Ques.46 (earlier), is apropos: "A fool is one whom shame does not incite to sorrow, and who is unconcerned when he is injured." Although this last remark is from an objection, Aquinas in effect endorses it in his reply, though not the implications drawn from it. The "injury" that is relevant here might include condemnation from other people for bad behavior. The fool does not feel such an injury or is "unconcerned" with it. For further discussion and examples, see the Further Discussion section.

20. *List the main features of folly as given by Aquinas. Give an example of folly that satisfies Aquinas' account.*

Aquinas: Killing, Consequences and Double Effect

A "law" ethics such as we have in Aquinas consists in the claim that right actions are those that conform to a law. Following a law requires doing what the law demands no matter what the consequences. But most people probably think that we cannot act morally unless we *do*, at least some of the time, take account of consequences. So if Aquinas' "law" ethics

never allows consideration of consequences, then his view conflicts with many ordinary intuitions about morality. There seems to be a defect in Aquinas' position here, and perhaps the same defect would attach to any "law" ethics.

It seems obvious that a morally responsible person will sometimes consider the consequences of her actions when deciding how to behave, although some, for example, Kant (Chapter 7), appear to deny it. Mill (Chapter 9) goes so far as to make the calculation of consequences central to morality. Would it be possible to allot an important place to consequences in moral reasoning *without* assuming that consequences themselves (or reasonably expected consequences) *determine* what is moral? Aquinas explicitly claims that on some occasions it would be right to perform an action, *X*, that would normally be forbidden by natural law, on the grounds that the consequences of not doing *X* are worse than the consequences of doing *X*. So he is not a "rigorist" who claims that every right action must conform to law in some obvious way, even where the law is God's law. His discussion of killing illustrates his position on consequences vs. law in morality.

Aquinas discusses the question of whether killing is ever permissible. It is clear that he assumes constraints on killing that not all of us would accept and that are not reflected in the laws of every community. He takes killing very seriously. Almost all killings are morally forbidden in his view, with the exception of those committed in the name of legitimate governmental authority, such as that exercised by the police, and even then strict limits apply. In the following question, however, he notes an exception, which depends on the idea that the intended effect of an act of self-defense may be exceeded by a further effect. Thus there is a "double effect," the one intended and the other not. An "effect" is one kind of consequence, so Aquinas is claiming that sometimes, in attempting to act morally, we may need to consider consequences.

Whether It Is Lawful to Kill a Man in Self-Defense (Q. 64, Art. 7)

Objection 1: It would seem that nobody may lawfully kill a man in self-defense. For

Augustine says to Publicola (Ep. xlvii): "I do not agree with the opinion that one may kill a man lest one be killed by him; unless one be a soldier, exercise a public office, so that one does it not for oneself but for others, having the power to do so, provided it be in keeping with one's person." Now he who kills a man in self-defense, kills him lest he be killed by him. Therefore this would seem to be unlawful.

Objection 2: Further, he says (De Lib. Arb. i, 5): "How are they free from sin in sight of Divine providence, who are guilty of taking a man's life for the sake of these contemptible things?" Now among contemptible things he reckons "those which men may forfeit unwillingly," as appears from the context (De Lib. Arb. i, 5): and the chief of these is the life of the body. Therefore it is unlawful for any man to take another's life for the sake of the life of his own body.

Objection 3: Further, Pope Nicolas [*Nicolas I, Dist. 1, can. De his clericis] says in the Decretals: "Concerning the clerics about whom you have consulted Us, those, namely, who have killed a pagan in self-defense, as to whether, after making amends by repenting, they may return to their former state, or rise to a higher degree; know that in no case is it lawful for them to kill any man under any circumstances whatever." Now clerics and laymen are alike bound to observe the moral precepts. Therefore neither is it lawful for laymen to kill anyone in self-defense.

Objection 4: Further, murder is a more grievous sin than fornication or adultery. Now nobody may lawfully commit simple fornication or adultery or any other mortal sin in order to save his own life; since the spiritual life is to be preferred to the life of the body. Therefore no man may lawfully take another's life in self-defense in order to save his own life.

Objection 5: Further, if the tree be evil, so is the fruit, according to Mt. 7:17. Now self-defense itself seems to be unlawful, according to Rm. 12:19: "Not defending [Douay: "revenging"] yourselves, my dearly beloved." Therefore its result, which is the slaying of a man, is also unlawful.

On the contrary, It is written (Ex. 22:2): "If a thief be found breaking into a house or undermining it, and be wounded so as to die; he that slew him shall not be guilty of blood." Now it is much more lawful to defend one's life than one's house. Therefore neither is a man guilty of murder if he kill another in defense of his own life.

I answer that, Nothing hinders one act from having two effects, only one of which is intended, while the other is beside [or beyond] the intention. Now moral acts take their species according to what is intended, and not according to what is beside [beyond] the intention, since this is accidental as explained above (Question [43], Article [3]; FS, Question [12], Article [1]). Accordingly the act of self-defense may have two effects, one is the saving of one's life, the other is the slaying of the aggressor. Therefore this act, since one's intention is to save one's own life, is not unlawful, seeing that it is natural to everything to keep itself in "being," as far as possible.

And yet, though proceeding from a good intention, an act may be rendered unlawful, if it be out of proportion to the end. Wherefore if a man, in self-defense, uses more than necessary violence, it will be unlawful: whereas if he repel force with moderation his defense will be lawful, because according to the jurists [*Cap. Significasti, De Homicid. volunt. vel casual.], "it is lawful to repel force by force, provided one does not exceed the limits of a blameless defense." Nor is it necessary for salvation that a man omit the act of moderate self-defense in order to avoid killing the other man, since one is bound to take more care of one's own life than of another's. But as it is unlawful to take a man's life, except for the public authority acting for the common good, as stated above (Article [3]), it is not lawful for a man to intend killing a man in self-defense, except for such as have public authority, who while intending to kill a man in self-defense, refer this to the public good, as in the case of a soldier fighting against the foe, and in the minister of the judge struggling with robbers, although even these sin if they be moved by private animosity.

Reply to Objection 1: The words quoted from Augustine refer to the case when one man intends to kill another to save himself from death. The passage quoted in the Second Objection is to be understood in the same sense. Hence he says pointedly, "for the sake of these things," whereby he indicates the intention. This suffices for the Reply to the Second Objection.

Reply to Objection 3: Irregularity results from the act, though sinless, of taking a man's life, as appears in the case of a judge who justly condemns a man to death. For this reason a cleric, though he kill a man in self-defense, is irregular, albeit he intends not to kill him, but to defend himself.

Reply to Objection 4: The act of fornication or adultery is not necessarily directed to the preservation of one's own life, as is the act whence sometimes results the taking of a man's life.

Reply to Objection 5: The defense forbidden in this passage is that which comes from revengeful spite. Hence a gloss says: "Not defending yourselves—that is, not striking your enemy back."

21. *Aquinas considers that it is legitimate under certain circumstances for police officers and others acting in a public capacity, such as soldiers, to intend to kill another human being, such as a criminal or aggressor. But he insists that even they may not be moved by "private animosity" or "revengeful spite." In a famous film,* Dirty Harry, *a police officer shoots a repulsive criminal and clearly enjoys doing it. Do you think Aquinas would have considered this officer morally blameworthy? Would you? Discuss pro and con.*

22. *Fill in the third condition in the following. Aquinas is claiming that even for a private citizen an act of killing an attacker is permissible where*
   1. *The intention was only to defend oneself, or to preserve ones own life.*
   2. *The intention was* not *to kill the attacker.*
   3.

For example, suppose that Jack is coming at me with a knife, displaying all the signs of intending to stab me to death (and let us suppose he has a motive too). Suppose that I have a handgun and I have no skills or sufficient strength to defend myself against such an attack. I cannot reasonably hope to prevent my own death in any other way than by shooting Jack. I aim at his legs, with the intention of stopping him but not with the intention of killing him. The bullet hits him square in the femoral artery, and he bleeds to death quickly, before help arrives. This case fits the three conditions Aquinas sets forth.

23. *Argue that it fits the third condition.*

At this point you may wonder: Is any person (other than a government official), according to Aquinas, excusable for killing in self-defense if that person uses means to self-defense that he or she believes and foresees *will* kill the attacker? Or is a person excusable only if he or she does not believe and foresee that what is done will kill the attacker (as in the example of Jack, who presumably shoots the attacker in the legs because he believes he will not in that way kill him)? Another way to put the question is this: If Jack grabs a bazooka and aims it straight at his attacker, he must certainly foresee that he will kill him. In that case can we really say that he did not *intend* to kill him? Aquinas rules out unnecessary violence. But suppose the bazooka was the only means of self-defense available that had any chance of succeeding?

In any case, if I act in a way that invariably has a certain result, then it seems I should not be excused from responsibility for that result even though I did not intend it. Thus, if it were the case that every time I shoot someone that person dies, no matter whether I shoot him in the leg, the foot or the toe, then what can we make of the claim that in shooting him I did not intend for him to die? It looks like sophistry to say that I did not intend a certain effect or result even though it always or invariably follows or is a concomitant of a given act. Aquinas discusses this matter in another work, *De Malo.* Here a distinction is drawn between a "per se" effect and an accidental effect.

(from QDM 1.3 ad15. Cited in Matthews, pp. 72–73)

Sometimes an accident of some effect is joined to it in a few cases and rarely, and then it is reasonable to presume that the agent in intending the *per se* effect in no way intends the accidental effect. But sometimes an accident of this kind always or in most cases accompanies the effect principally intended, and then the accidental effect is not separated from the agent's intention. If then in a few cases some evil is joined to the good that the will intends, the sin is excusable, for example, if someone cutting timber in a woods through which people rarely pass, in felling a tree should kill a man. But if always or for the most part evil is connected with the good that is *per se* intended, it does not excuse from sin, even if that evil is not *per se* intended. Now an evil is always joined to the pleasure that is connected with adultery, namely, a privation of the order of justice; hence there is no excuse from sin, because from the very fact that a person chooses a good to which evil is always joined, even if he does not will the evil in itself, nevertheless he is more willing to fall into this evil than to be without such a good.

With this qualification we might generalize Aquinas' idea in the following way (call this formulation of the *principle of double effect* "Aq," for "Aquinas' formulation"). The exception for government officials is assumed:

Aq

Where an action has two effects one of which is good, the other bad, the act is morally permissible if and only if

1. The *per se* intention was to produce only the good effect.
2. The bad effect would not be an invariable concomitant of the good effect
3. The means to the good effect are proportional to the good to be achieved.

*24. *Try to apply Aq to an abortion. Assume that killing a fetus is indeed killing a human being and that the reason for the abortion is to protect the pregnant woman from a dangerous delivery. Make sure you carefully take account of all three conditions or constraints.*

Divine Commands

At first glance much of religious ethics, particularly of the kind associated with Judaism, Christianity and Islam, appears to be determined by the commands of God. In both the "Old Testament" (the Torah etc.) and the new, God and, in some cases, Jesus issue commands to the people of Israel or to the disciples or to all humans. The most comprehensive command, one that is said to sum up all the particular commandments, is a command to love God and one's neighbor as oneself. The very notion that love, which is naturally thought to be an emotion and connected with desire, could be commanded may seem paradoxical. I can of course issue verbal commands to someone to feel a certain way or to desire something, but doing so seems pointless. What this suggests is that the love command and all divine commands have little or nothing to do with feelings or desires. Those commands could just as well conflict with any of our feelings and desires, including our supposedly natural desire to be happy or to achieve a fulfilled life. These apparent facts about divine commands are in tension with some of Aquinas' natural law views.

Recall that Aquinas and some other natural law theorists hold that moral rules are indeed grounded in the will of God. However, they do not hold that a person must know that such a command as "Do not commit murder" has been issued by God in order to know that it is a correct principle. Rather, any person, even an atheist, has certain built-in inclinations, such as the inclination to do good and to avoid evil or to be sociable, and everyone is able to see by use of natural intelligence that committing murder goes against such principles and thus against what he knows. To say that a human being has these built-in inclinations is to say something about how people feel or what they desire, provided they have not been corrupted somehow. In Aquinas' view, the commands of God thus enforce what humans most deeply feel and desire as their good. The good for a human being determines the content of morality. Aquinas is an Aristotelian who understands the good in terms of self-fulfillment, or *eudaimonia,* and who believes that the use of reason is essential to self-fulfillment. He differs from Aristotle in that he believes that the ultimate happiness for humans consists in something unattainable in this life, namely, the contemplation of a personal God. Nonetheless Aquinas is still a *eudaimonist.*

Some religious thinkers have rejected *eudaimonism,* however. They have claimed two things:

1. Humans are obligated by divine law or commands.
2. There is no necessary connection between following those commands and human happiness.

These claims seem to square with the idea that the commands of God need not have anything to do with our feelings and desires for what is *good.* According to many divine command moralists, we must obey God's commands because it is *right* to do so, not because it is *good* (even though it might in fact turn out to be good). One version of such a view consists in holding that what makes God's commands obligatory, and thus what makes it *right* to obey them, is simply that they come from God's will.

It pays here to look at Plato's dialogue *Euthyphro,* part of which was discussed in Chapter 2. The question raised by Socrates was in effect this: Is *x* right only because God commands *x,* or does God command *x* because it is right? Euthyphro's attempt to define or elucidate what is *pious* (or morally right) leads to a difficulty that Socrates exposes through a dilemma, one that may cast doubt on any attempt to connect morals and religion via divine commands.

The Euthyphro

[EUTHYPHRO:] Yes, I should say that what all the gods love is pious and holy, and the opposite which they all hate, impious.
[SOCRATES:] Ought we to enquire into the truth of this, Euthyphro, or simply to accept the mere statement on our own authority and that of others? What do you say?
[EUTHYPHRO:] We should enquire; and I believe that the statement will stand the test of enquiry.
[SOCRATES:] We shall know better, my good friend, in a little while. The point which I should first wish to understand is this:

Is the pious or holy beloved by the gods because it is holy, or,
Is it holy because it is beloved of the gods?

The dilemma Socrates states here has been much discussed throughout the history of ethics. Since it is first stated clearly in this dialogue, it is often referred to as the *Euthyphro dilemma.* The dilemma could be restated this way:

Either (1) God loves or commands what is right (holy, etc.) because it is right, or (2) what is right (holy) is right because God commands (loves) it.

Suppose that (1) is correct. In other words, suppose that God wills what is right because it is right. That would imply that there is a standard of rightness that even God must observe and that in a sense is thus above God. But how could anything be above God?

On the other hand, suppose that (2) is correct, that is, that what is right (holy, etc.) is right because God loves it or proclaims it right. Then, it seems, anything that God loves or proclaims as right would be right. It seems to follow that if God loved the torture of innocent children or proclaimed it to be right on some occasion to murder one's child (cf. the story of Abraham and Isaac in the Hebrew scriptures, which is presented later in this chapter), then such torture or murder would be right. But how could torturing or killing innocent people be right? But either (1) is correct or (2) is. This dilemma poses a difficulty for anyone who believes that morality is grounded in the commands of God. And that is exactly what many people do believe. It may also pose a problem for the belief in a personal God.

It is worth noting a variation on the Euthyphro dilemma. Suppose that (1) is correct. That might be because of facts about human nature that make doing *X* best for humans, where *X* is one of the things God commands. (For example, it might be that humans cannot live long or satisfying lives without following the command "Do not murder." See the discussion of Hobbes in Chapter 6.) If that were so, then presumably God commands *X* because he sees that doing so will be best for humans. But then the rightness of doing *X* does not depend on God at all. It would be just as right to do *X* even if there were no God. It is the facts about human nature that make *X* right, not God's will. So this conclusion runs contrary to any attempt to show that morality is dependent on God. Recall in this connection your discussion of Orienting Question 5.

This dialogue provides no answers to two of the main questions Socrates raises: (1) How can moral disagreement be resolved? (2) How can morality depend on the will of God? But Plato, with Socrates as his mouthpiece, did attempt to provide answers in other dialogues, such as the *Protagoras*.

> 25. *Are right and wrong determined by God's commands? Or can ethics get along better without reference to God? Argue for your answer.*

Some divine command theorists argue that it is not because murder is wrong that God commands us not to murder, but, rather, murder is wrong simply because God says so. If God were to "change his mind" and command murder, then it would, in this view, automatically become right to commit murder. Some stories from the bible seem to support such a view. Perhaps the best known is the following.

The Story of Abraham and Isaac: Gen. 22. (IV)

1 Some time later God tested Abraham. He said to him, "Abraham!" "Here I am," he replied.

2 Then God said, "Take your son, your only son, Isaac, whom you love, and go to the region of Moriah. Sacrifice him there as a burnt offering on one of the mountains I will tell you about."

3 Early the next morning Abraham got up and saddled his donkey. He took with him two of his servants and his son Isaac. When he had cut enough wood for the burnt offering, he set out for the place God had told him about. 4 On the third day Abraham looked up and saw the place in the distance. 5 He said to his servants, "Stay here with the donkey while I and the boy go over there. We will worship and then we will come back to you."

6 Abraham took the wood for the burnt offering and placed it on his son Isaac, and he himself carried the fire and the knife. As the two of them went on together, 7 Isaac spoke up and said to his father Abraham, "Father?"

"Yes, my son?" Abraham replied.

"The fire and wood are here," Isaac said, "but where is the lamb for the burnt offering?"

8 Abraham answered, "God himself will provide the lamb for the burnt offering, my son." And the two of them went on together.

9 When they reached the place God had told him about, Abraham built an altar there and arranged the wood on it. He bound his son Isaac and laid him on the altar, on top of the wood.

10 Then he reached out his hand and took the knife to slay his son.

11 But the angel of the LORD called out to him from heaven, "Abraham! Abraham!"

"Here I am," he replied.

12 "Do not lay a hand on the boy," he said. "Do not do anything to him. Now I know that you fear God, because you have not withheld from me your son, your only son."

13 Abraham looked up and there in a thicket he saw a ram [a] caught by its horns. He went over and took the ram and sacrificed it as a burnt offering instead of his son.

14 So Abraham called that place The LORD Will Provide. And to this day it is said, "On the mountain of the LORD it will be provided."

15 The angel of the LORD called to Abraham from heaven a second time 16 and said, "I swear by myself, declares the LORD, that because you have done this and have not withheld your son, your only son, 17 I will surely bless you and make your descendants as numerous as the stars in the sky and as the sand on the seashore. Your descendants will take possession of the cities of their enemies, 18 and through your offspring all nations on earth will be blessed, because you have obeyed me."

> 26. *Abraham is being tested or tried, according to v. 1. Does that mean he doesn't really have to kill Isaac? If Abraham knew or was certain that he would not really have to kill Isaac, would it have been a real test?*
>
> 27. *Is it clear that Abraham is about to commit murder? Keep your answer to the previous question in mind.*

This story has been much discussed in both Jewish and Christian theological and devotional literature. The larger context of the story is the promise made by God to Abraham that he will be the father of a great nation. Since Isaac is his only son, it would seem that he is being tested for his confidence in God's ability to keep God's promises no matter how much the facts, particularly the fact of not having any descendants at all when Isaac is dead, go against those promises. But it is also the case that the story seems on the face of it to commend Abraham for being prepared to obey a direct command of God to do what would normally be considered murder. Earlier we saw how Aquinas deals with this story so as to escape having to say that acts of murder could *generally* be right or moral. But some theologians and philosophers even in the medieval period actually claimed that God *could* command murder and that then it *would* be generally right to commit murder.

One example of such a thinker was Duns Scotus, whose life overlapped with Aquinas'.

JOHN DUNS SCOTUS

Scotus was born about 1266, perhaps in Scotland, as his name suggests, or elsewhere in the British Isles. He was a student at Oxford and Paris and became a regent in theology at Paris, as had Aquinas. He was a Franciscan and, like other members of that order, less devoted to Aristotle than was Aquinas, who was a Dominican. He became famous for his careful and subtle style of analysis, and he greatly influenced late medieval thought. His name provides the origin for the word dunce, *which usually means "stupid person." In fact his reasoning was so detailed and intricate that many of his readers became impatient with his "hair-splitting" and the "duns-men" began to be held in contempt by later thinkers. It is clear, however, that Scotus was no more a "dunce" than was Aquinas a "dumb ox." He died in Germany in 1308. All of his very substantial and complex writings must have been produced in about the space of 10 years.*

Scotus makes all contingent things or states of affairs directly dependent on the will of God. Contingent things are things that could be otherwise. Dogs are contingent things. There are dogs, but it is surely logically *possible* that there never have been any or that there could cease to be any. Unicorns are contingent beings also. There are no unicorns, but logically there could be. All that means is that the assumption that there are does not lead to a contradiction. Contrast dogs and unicorns with round squares. The assumption that there are round squares does lead to a contradiction (more than one, in fact), so the nonexistence of round squares is necessary, not contingent. It does not just happen to be the case that there are no round squares. There *could* not be such things. Even God could not will into existence a round square, according to Scotus, since he would be willing the existence of something that is both round and not round, and that is a contradiction. Even God cannot will contradictions to exist. But since there is no contradiction in supposing that unicorns exist, the *only* reason there are none is simply that God did not will there to be any. There is no other reason. If God changes his mind or wills otherwise, there may eventually be plenty of unicorns around.

It follows that some of God's commands are contingent. The most basic statement of God's commands from the Tanak is the "Ten Commandments," which are usually divided into two "tables." The first contains commands relating directly to God, such as "You shall have no other Gods before Me (i.e., the true God, identified in relation to the acts recorded in the Tanak). This command is *not* contingent, since a person who knows the meaning of "God" (or "true God") understands that it is impossible that there should be any other God or any other thing that is before God or more important or more worthy of worship than God, just as a person who understands "square" understands that a square cannot be round. In either case, to suppose otherwise is to land in contradiction.

The commands of the "second table" are, however, contingent. Thus the commands "You shall *not* commit murder" and "You shall not commit adultery" are contingent. Their denials are no more self-contradictory than are the denials of "You *shall* commit murder" or "You shall lie," so God could have commanded any of them. And if he had, humans would be obliged to murder, commit adultery, etc. It would have been *right* for humans to do those things.

Scotus' emphasis on God's will makes him a *voluntarist* (*voluntas* = will, in Latin). There is ongoing controversy about the extent and significance of his voluntarism, but the following passages support the view that Scotus thought God could have given a general command to commit adultery (to take but one example).

It follows from Scotus' position that human reason cannot determine the content of the moral law, for God does not need or have reasons for the commands he issues. Other than God's will itself, which is changeable, there is no basis for the moral law, so there is nothing from which to infer it. However, Scotus believes that God has supplied human beings with a kind of direct intuition of right and wrong, so they can know what is moral without the use of reason. Interestingly, he cites in favor of his view the same passage of scripture that natural law theorists cite in favor of their view that the moral law can be known by reason, namely, Romans 2:15, which states that the law is "written in the hearts" of the gentiles (non-Jews).

The following references are from Latin editions of Scotus' works, the Wadding edition and the Vatican critical edition. The translations are all by Thomas Williams.

Everything other than God is good because it is willed by God, and not vice versa. (*Ordinatio*, Book Three, Distinction 19)

Since the divine will has no rectitude inclining it determinately to anything but its own goodness, as if to another—for to any other object it is related only contingently, in such a way that it can [tend] equally to that object and to its opposite—it follows that [God] has no justice except in rendering to his own goodness or will what befits it. (*Ordinatio* 4, d. 46, q. 1, n. 7)

The truth is that nothing external to God is determinately just except in a certain respect, i.e., with the qualification "so far as it is on the part of a creature." The only thing that is just in an unqualified sense is whatever is related to the first justice, i.e., because it is actually willed by the divine will. (*Ordinatio* 4, d. 46, q. 1, n. 12)

In virtue of the fact that something agrees with the divine will, it is right. . . . But nothing that does not involve a contradiction is absolutely repugnant to the divine will. Therefore, whatever God causes or does will be right and just, and so God's justice will

be every bit as extensive as his power. . . . This justice of God does not restrict him to one possibility more than another, as justice in you and me restricts us to doing this or that, for instance, to perform the acts that God has commanded. For it would be unjust [for us] not to perform the commanded acts, but the divine justice is not restricted to one thing or another. (*Reportatio* 4, d. 46, q. 4, nn. 8, 11)

And if you ask why the divine will is determined to one of a pair of contradictories rather than to the other, I must reply that "It is characteristic of the untutored to look for causes and proof for everything." . . . There is no cause why the will willed, except that the will is the will, just as there is no cause why heat heats, except that heat is heat. There is no prior cause. (*Ordinatio* 1, d. 8, pars 2, n. 299)

Some general laws dictating rightly are preestablished by the divine will, and not by the divine intellect as it precedes an act of the divine will. . . . When the intellect offers the divine will such a law, for instance, "Whoever is to be glorified must first be given grace," if it pleases his will, which is free, it is a correct law; and so it is for the other laws. (*Ordinatio* 1, d. 44, n. 6)

The last quotation stresses the precedence of will over intellect in God. In contrast, Aquinas claimed that intellect is primary, in the sense that God cannot will what his intellect does not approve.

Someone might think that even though God can will anything noncontradictory, God must command humans to do what will lead to their final or ultimate end or goal. Aquinas certainly thought that God's commands, and the natural law, must be conducive to the highest human end. But even that is denied by Scotus.

For in the things that they [the commandments of the second table] prescribe there is no goodness necessary for the goodness of the ultimate end that turns one towards the ultimate end, and in the things they prohibit there is no badness that necessarily turns one away from the ultimate end. So even if that good were not commanded, the ultimate end could be loved and attained; and if that evil were not prohibited, the attainment of the ultimate end would be consistent with that evil. With the commandments of the first table, however, it is otherwise, since they have to do immediately with God as their object. (*Ordinatio* 3, d. 37, n. 5)

> 28. *This last quotation amounts to this: If I believe that by telling the truth I am doing something necessary for my ultimate _____ (namely, eternal life), then I am mistaken. Telling lies would not turn me away from that _____.*

Many subsequent medieval, Renaissance and early modern thinkers accepted Scotist voluntarism and divine command ideas and even took them further than Scotus himself had. Descartes, for instance, argued that God could create logically contradictory things, such as square circles (WW 75). As we have seen, Scotus would not go that far.

What motivates the strict voluntarist views? Certainly one motivation is to protect the majesty, power, sovereignty and transcendence of God. Nothing must be allowed to be higher than God. The Reformation leader Martin Luther argued:

> He is God, and for his will there is no cause or reason that can be laid down as a rule or measure for it, since there is nothing equal or superior to it, but it is itself the rule and measure of all things. For it is not because he is or was obliged so to will that what he wills is right, but on the contrary, because he himself so wills, therefore what happens [is commanded] must be right. Cause and reason can be assigned for a creature's will, but not for the will of the Creator, unless you set up over him another creator. (from *Bondage of the Will,* in E. G. Rupp and P. S. Watson, eds., *Luther and Erasmus: Free Will and Salvation,* pp. 236–237)

Another major Reformation figure, John Calvin, insisted that "God's will is so much the highest rule of righteousness, that whatever he wills, by the very fact that he wills it, must be considered righteous." (Institutes 3.22.2)

However, even people who insist on the majesty and complete transcendence of God may find voluntarism implausible and even repulsive. There is a widely shared intuition that the mere fact that something is *willed and commanded* by someone (whether it be God or Hitler) cannot by itself be a sufficient reason for obeying the command. There must be something in the content of what is willed or commanded that makes it right to obey. But that intuition is apparently rejected by Scotus, Luther and many other theists.

> 29. *Suppose that somehow you came to believe that God had commanded you to murder the next infant you encountered. But you decide that that belief must be erroneous, since no God worthy of the name could possibly command such a terrible thing. What is wrong with your reasoning, according to Scotus? Do you see any way out of the problem that he points out? Review you answer to Orienting Question 5.*

THE BHAGAVAD GITA

This Hindu scripture is contained in an epic poem, the Mahabharata (c. 200 BC to AD 200, traditionally attributed to Vyasa). This poem or song (the title means "the song of God") includes a dialogue between Krishna, an incarnation of the Supreme Being, Vishnu, and the warrior Arjuna (accent is on the first syllable). The concepts employed in these ancient scriptures are not easily represented in English, so translations vary. The reader must try to understand the parts, or particular statements that employ Hindu concepts, by becoming familiar with the whole.

The *Bhagavad Gita* is widely considered to be the single most important Indian text relating to ethics. The ethical teachings and religious concepts are intertwined. It attempts to combine competing ideals in Hindu ethics and religion, namely, the ideals of duty and renunciation. Duty (*dharma*) had been understood as, for example, the requirements of correct performance of rituals, but here it has come to refer more generally to actions that are simply required, with no view to results. "You have a right to action alone, not the fruits [of action]" (2.47). This requirement to act obtains even for the God, Krishna. Moreover, renunciation (of, for example, sensual pleasures) is internalized here; the one who refrains in action but still desires those pleasures in his mind is a hypocrite (3.6).

Arjuna wonders whether he should participate in a great battle about to take place in which he would have to fight against his own relatives. They are despots who have deprived him and his brothers of their share of the kingdom, but Arjuna feels that to kill them would be a violation of duty. As in Sophocles' *Antigone* there is a conflict between duties, but in this case the conflict is not simply between duties to family and duty to the state. Arjuna's situation is morally complex. The solution proposed by Krishna is *yoga,* a discipline that will transform a person so that the forces of nature, and ultimately God, work through him or her. The resolution of ethical dilemmas requires, in the final analysis, proper devotion to God. The *Gita* can thus describe right actions as a sacrifice to God and finally as part of a great drama of life directed by God.

> [NARRATOR:] . . . Standing there in both armies were uncles and grandfathers, teachers, mother's brothers, cousins, sons and grandsons, comrades, fathers-in-law, and benefactors. Seeing all these kinsmen standing in line, Arjuna was deeply moved to pity, said this in sadness:
> [ARJUNA:] Krishna, seeing my kinsmen lined up and eager to fight, my limbs fail, my mouth is parched, my body quivers, my hair stands on end, my bow slips from my hand, my skin burns all over, I am not able to stand, my mind is spinning, and I see omens of evil. I see no advantage in slaying kinsmen in battle. For I desire neither victory, nor kingdoms, nor pleasures. What are kingdoms to us, what is enjoyment, or even what is life? Those for whose sake we desire kingdoms, enjoyment, and pleasures stand here in battle, abandoning life and riches. They are our teachers, fathers, and sons. They are also our grandfathers, mother's brothers, fathers-in-law, grandsons, brothers-in-law, and other relatives. Though I may be slain myself, I do not wish to kill these people, even for the sake of the kingship of the three worlds. How then can I wish this for earth? . . .

> [NARRATOR:] After saying these things on the battlefield, Arjuna sank down on the seat of his chariot, throwing aside his bow and arrow. His mind was overcome by grief. [*Bhagavad Gita,* Sect. 1]

> [KRISHNA:] You grieve, Arjuna, for those that should not be grieved for, yet you speak words of wisdom. The wise grieve neither for the living nor for the dead. There was never a time at which I truly did not exist, nor you, nor these princes. Nor truly will there ever be a future time in which we cease to exist. Just as the dweller in this body goes through childhood, youth, and age, so too does he pass on to another body at death. The wise do not grieve at this. The experiences of cold and heat, pleasure and pain [which result from contact with material things], they come and go, and are impermanent. You must bravely endure them. A person is fit for immortality who is not tormented by these things, is balanced in pain and pleasure, and is steadfast. The unreal has no existence, and the real never ceases to exist. Those who see the essence of things understand the truth about both existence and nonexistence. That which pervades everything is indestructible. No one can do anything to destroy that which is imperishable. Bodies are known to be finite. But that which possesses the body is eternal, indestructible and immeasurable. Therefore, Arjuna, you must fight. Those who distinguish between the slayer and the slain are ignorant of them both. No one slays, and no one is slain. No one is born, and no one dies. No one who once existed ceases to exist. They are unborn, perpetual, eternal and ancient, and are not slain when their bodies are slaughtered. If we understand a person to be indestructible, perpetual, unborn, undiminishing, how can that person slay, or be slain? [*Bhagavad Gita,* Sect. 2]

The doctrine set forth here will be somewhat familiar to many under the term *reincarnation*. But it is clear that there is something that "pervades everything" that is fundamental to this Hindu idea, so reincarnation should not be thought of independently of a certain way of conceiving God. That way has ethical implications. In particular, it implies getting rid of certain kinds of self-concern. The disciplined person, the yogi, is concerned only with the *atman*, which is the true self, devoid of what we might call *ego*.

[KRISHNA:] The foolish utter flowery speech, and rejoice in the letter of the Vedas [i.e., Hindu scriptures]. For them there is nothing but a desire for the self with only the intent on reaching heaven. They prescribe many ceremonies to attain pleasure and power, but rebirth is the fruit of their actions. The Vedas deal with three attributes. You must be above these three attributes, Arjuna, and beyond the pair of opposites. You must be consistently pure, unconcerned with possessions, and full of the Atman. All the Vedas are about as useful to a Priest (*Brahmin*) who understands as a pond is useful in a place covered all over with water.

Your business is with actions only, and never with the fruits of your actions. So do not let the fruit of your actions motivate you, and do not be attached to inaction. Perform action, Arjuna, dwelling in the union of the divine. Renounce attachments, and balance yourself evenly between success and failure. Equilibrium is called Yoga. Action is inferior to discrimination; so take refuge in the intellect. People are pitiable who work only for its fruits. By disciplining one's intellect, one abandons both good and evil deeds. Therefore you should cling to [*karma*] Yoga, which is skill in action. The wise disciplined their intellect, renounced the fruits of their actions, released (*moksha*) themselves from the bonds of birth, and attained a state of bliss. When your intellect escapes from the tangle of delusion, then you too will be indifferent about what you had heard and will hear [in the Vedas].

[ARJUNA:] What is the mark of the person who is stable of mind and steadfast in contemplation, Krishna? How does the stable-minded person talk, sit, or walk?

[KRISHNA:] When a person abandons all the desires of his heart and is satisfied in the Self and by the Self, then he is called "stable in mind." A sage of stable mind is free from anxiety when surrounded by pains, is indifferent when surrounded by pleasures, and is freed from passion, fear, and anger. He is without attachments on every side, whether desirable or undesirable, and neither likes nor dislikes. The person of understanding is well poised. Just as a tortoise pulls in all its limbs, the sage withdraws his senses from the objects, and his understanding is well poised. [*Bhagavad Gita*, Sect. 2]

*30. *Is there one word that describes the main characteristic of the person who is "stable of mind"? Try to find one, and say why you think it picks out what is central.*

The ideal of detachment from the fruits (or consequences) of action and of indifference to pain and pleasure sounds quite similar to the ethical ideal propounded by the Greek and Roman Stoics. So does the emphasis on "duty." These similarities are discussed briefly in "Further Discussions."

[KRISHNA:] He who performs his actions as a duty, independent of the fruit of the action, is an ascetic. He is a Yogi, and not the person who intentionally avoids actions such as lighting the sacred fire and performing the sacred rites. Understand that "Yoga" is renunciation, and no one becomes a Yogi without renouncing his will. . . . The Yogi should constantly engage himself in Yoga, staying in a secret place by himself, subduing his thoughts and self, and freeing himself from hope and greed. He should set up a fixed seat for himself in a pure place, which is neither too high nor too low, made of a cloth, a black deerskin, and kusa grass, one over the other. Once there he should practice Yoga for the purification of the self; he should make his mind one-pointed, subduing his thoughts and the functions of his senses. He should hold his body, head, and neck erect, immovably steady, looking at the point of his nose with an unseeing gaze. His heart should be serene, fearless and firm in the vow of renunciation. His mind should be controlled as he sits in harmony. In this manner he will think on me and aspire after me.

Yoga is not for the person who eats too much or too little, or who sleeps too much or too little. Yoga kills all pain for the person who is moderate in eating, amusement, performing actions, sleeping, and waking. When his subdued thought is fixed on the Atman and free from desiring things, then we can say that he is harmonized. Just as a lamp in a windless place does not flicker, so too will the subdued thought of the Yogi be absorbed in the Yoga of the self. . . . The Yogi who harmonizes the self and puts away evil will enjoy the infinite bliss of unity with the eternal Brahman. The self, harmonized by Yoga, sees the Atman abiding in all beings, and all beings in the Atman. Everywhere he sees the same thing. I will never lose hold of the person who sees me everywhere, and sees everything in me, and that person will never lose hold of me. Regardless of how else he may live, the Yogi lives in me who is established in unity and worships me abiding in all things. The perfect Yogi is the one who, established in unity, sees equality in everything, whether pleasant or painful.

The dutiful yogi does not get "heaven as a reward" for his good life after death. Rather, he enjoys "unity with the eternal Brahman." We might say that he is one with God. That is not a reward for righteousness, but a condition that goes with renunciation or nonattachment, subdued thought, seeing equality in everything. It is achieved through meditative disciplines.

[ARJUNA:] You describe this Yoga as a unity. However, Krishna, I see no basis for it given the impermanence of thought. The mind is very restless. Indeed, it is impetuous, strong, and difficult to bend. Perhaps it is as hard to control as the wind.
[KRISHNA:] Undoubtedly, Arjuna, the mind is restless and hard to control. But it may be controlled with constant practice and dispassion. I think Yoga is hard to attain by an uncontrolled self. But for a controlled Atman, it is attainable by properly directing energy.
[ARJUNA:] Suppose that a person has faith, but his mind is still uncontrolled and wanders away from Yoga, thus failing to attain perfection in

Yoga. What is in store for him? He fails in his quest for Brahman, and thus fails both his earthy and spiritual quest. Please dispel my doubts, since only you are able to do this.

[KRISHNA:] No, he will not be lost in this life or the next. No one who does what is right will walk the path of destruction. [*Bhagavad Gita,* Sect. 6]
[KRISHNA:] There are four kinds of righteous people who worship me. They are those who suffer, those who seek knowledge, those who seek wealth, and those who seek wisdom. . . All of these [kinds of people] are noble, but I hold the wise as truly my own. They are harmonized and fixed on me, the highest path. At the close of many births the wise come to me knowing that I am all there is. It is very difficult to find such a great soul. [*Bhagavad Gita,* Sect.7]

[KRISHNA:] I am the creator of everything. Everything comes from me. Understanding this, the wise adore me in a state of rapture. They are mindful of me, and their life is hidden in me. They illuminate each other, continually talking about me, and they are content and joyful. I give the Yoga of discrimination (*buddhi Yoga*) to these people who are harmonious and worship in love. By means of this they come to me. Out of pure compassion for them, dwelling within their hearts, I shine the lamp of wisdom and destroy the darkness born of ignorance. [*Bhagavad Gita,* Sect.10]

The *Bhagavad Gita* belongs to that version of Hindu piety that stresses worship and adoration of God, devotion to God. God is conceived as the creator and the source of all wisdom for the conduct of life. In these respects this Hindu theology and ethics does not sound so different from some common Western ideas about God and ethics. Yet there is something quite different or a quite different emphasis.

31. *Try to describe that different conception or emphasis, using some expressions from the preceding texts.*
32. *Does natural law, á la Aquinas, or divine commands, play any role in the thinking on ethics and religion in the Gita? Argue.*

Further Discussion and Applications

Further Points About Natural Law and Double Effect

The notion of natural law as found in Aquinas and others has several appealing features.

1. He shows how to base law and all of morality on the will of God, *without* assuming that people who are not religious cannot know the difference between right and wrong. By his account, even atheists and religiously ignorant people have the natural law instilled in them and can know it naturally by reason, without consulting religious texts or authorities.

2. He provides various ways of overcoming relativism. He show that differences over what the law requires and what morality requires can be explained without giving up the basic idea that there is one unchanging eternal law that applies to everyone. For example, differences about morals may arise because some people make mistakes in deriving particular conclusions from the general principles of natural law or because their reason may have become corrupted by "evil habits" and the like so that they are no longer thinking clearly.

His account also has some problematic features.

1. His claims about the basis of natural law all assume that there is a creator God who orders all things to their proper end. Is it reasonable to believe there is such a God? Many have denied it.

2. The general principles of natural law may seem so general that they could license all sorts of conflicting inferences. Someone might argue, "Of course people should seek good and avoid evil. So robbing banks would be good, since it might make a comfortable life possible." Aquinas' reply to this objection would be that robbing banks is not in fact reasonable since it does not in fact conduce to the best sort of life. But his proof of that claim involves disputable claims about human nature and the purpose of human life as created.

What is natural for one person might seem unnatural for another. The purpose for one life might differ from the purpose for another. A further way to put this is as follows in point 3.

3. The notion of what is "natural" and known naturally is problematic. For example, it may seem perfectly natural and reasonable to some people to be hermits, even though the principle that one should be sociable is a part of natural law. And even though Aquinas claims that sexual behavior is naturally connected to procreation and thus condemns homosexual intercourse as unnatural, such intercourse purportedly seems perfectly natural to some people, namely, people with "same-sex orientations." This point is developed further later. The notion of the "natural" also may run into a kind of cultural relativism. Aristotle thought that a kind of pride and desire for prestige is "natural," and there is much in the Greek culture of his day that reinforces that idea. But Christians have explicitly denied that such desires are natural and affirmed that humility, even the kind of self-abasement found in Christ, reflects the truth about human nature.

Aquinas' idea of double effect also seems useful at first. Surely there should be some morally significant distinction between, say, bombing an entire city and thus indiscriminately slaughtering the civilian population, on the one hand, and bombing a munitions factory in a city and accidentally killing some civilians living close by the factory. The principle of double effect proposes a way to make such a distinction.

But there are difficulties with the principle. It may not be very useful. If doing some action, *X*, has both good and bad effects, we must intend only the good. That does not amount to much of a guide to action. Also, the means chosen to bring about the good effect must be "proportional" so as not to increase the balance of evil in the world, so to speak. Thus the principle employs inherently vague notions. How do we determine what is "proportionate" when deciding that the means to a good effect is proportionate to the effect? Suppose that in bombing the munitions factory 500 innocent civilians are likely to be killed even though the aim or intention is not to kill any of them. Would that be a proportionate means to the end (which is, say, the defeat of an evil aggressor)? How about 1,000? 10,000? Further discussion of double effect and its possible applications can be found later in this chapter.

Further Points About Divine Commands

The idea that morality is grounded in commands that proceed from the will of God (where God can will anything that is not logically inconsistent) also has certain appeals.

1. It seems to comport well with the notion that moral requirements are categorical, not to be argued with. The duties to keep promises and to refrain from lying seem to be strict duties. They are what must be done or must not be done, regardless of whether doing or refraining would lead to fulfillment or happiness or good states of affair or would "make sense" in some other way. What would account for such duties? One answer is that they are commanded by an absolute authority who is not to be questioned.

2. The notion of absolute authority fits with a common theistic conception of God. God is above human understanding, transcendent, a being whose nature is unknowable. The relation of humans to God is something like the relation of a little child to a parent. The parent says, "Do X." The child says, "Why should I do X?" The answer: "Because I said so." Would that ever be a good answer? It would be if the child was unable to understand the parent's reasons. It appears though that in the case of God there need be no reasons for his commands. God's commands come from God's will, not God's intellect, and the intellect is the source of "reasons." So the analogy has limited value.

However divine command ethics also runs into difficulties.

1. The most obvious one has been discussed. In the voluntarist view, God could command murder of the innocent or the telling of lies, for example, and it would then be right and even obligatory to murder some innocent person or to tell lies. That idea seems extremely counterintuitive.

2. Furthermore, if it could be right to tell lies, then there is no reason to think that God himself does not tell lies. In the voluntarist view, God could not be *essentially* truthful or just or faithful. But then the idea that we should do what God commands simply because God commands it breaks down. Suppose that God commands Albert to X (murder someone, for instance). Could Albert know that God was not being deceitful when God commanded him to do X? No, for in the voluntarist view God is not essentially truthful. So Albert cannot know whether it is right to do X. So voluntarism seems potentially self-defeating.

3. A related problem is the following: Let us grant that the source of our obligation to keep promises, refrain from murder and so forth is that God has commanded us to keep our promises, not commit murder and so forth. The following question can still be raised: "What obligates us to keep God's commands?" The answer could not be that God commands us to keep his commands. If there were such a command, it would be just one more command, and we would have to raise the same question about what obligates us to keep *that* command.

When commands are issued, whether by a human being in authority, such as a parent or government official, or even by God, it does not seem correct to say that what obligates us to keep those commands is simply that they have been willed. There must be some *prior obligation* to obey the one giving the commands, perhaps based in their position of authority. But what gives anyone authority?

33. *Here is a small list of commands:*
    a. *Tell the truth.*
    b. *Help those in need of your help where possible, other things being equal.*
    c. *Do not shed innocent blood.*
    d. *Keep God's commands.*
    Suppose we are obligated to obey (a)–(c) simply because God commands or wills that we

obey them. Now consider (d). What problem arises in supposing that we are obligated to obey (d) simply because God commands (d)?

The problem with divine command theory referred to in the last question could perhaps be solved in the following way. The divine command moralist could argue that we are not in fact *morally* obligated to keep God's commands. Rather, we might have nonmoral reasons for obeying God. For example, the goodness of God might be a reason for obeying God. Similarly, I might have as a reason for obeying my mother the fact that she is good. Perhaps that is a "moral" reason in a broad sense, but it does not morally *obligate* me. Not everything that is good or even morally good need be morally *obligatory*. For example, it might be morally good for me to devote my entire life to helping the poor, but it seems incorrect to say that I am morally *obligated* to do that. If I were obligated to spend my whole life that way, then I could not, for instance, be obligated to spend my life trying to find a cure for cancer. But why should the first be obligatory and not the second? The sensible thing to say, it seems, is that both would be good ways to spend a life and even morally good ways, but neither is morally obligatory.

Can the divine command moralist solve problem 3 in this way? It seems that he or she cannot without giving up the strict voluntarist's idea that there is no essential goodness or essential anything else in God. For if there is no essential goodness in God, then, given the dependence of everything else on God, there could not be anything essentially good about helping the poor or finding a cure for cancer. Those things would become good, in the voluntarist conception, only when God commands them, and then they would be *obligatory also*. What is good would collapse into what is required. The good would be subordinate to the right, as it is sometimes put.

So perhaps the divine command theorist needs to give up voluntarism. Could there be a divine command ethics that is *not* voluntarist in the sense discussed here? This possibility is discussed further in the later section "A Revised Divine Command Theory."

Folly and the Death Camp Doctors (Stump)

American philosopher Eleonore Stump describes some striking cases of persons who would count as fools according to Aquinas' account of folly. They are not stupid people, and in fact some are quite intelligent, if we think of intelligence as the sort of thing that is measured by IQ tests. But they seem to be missing a whole range of normal concerns and self-reflective emotions. Stump mentions Ike Turner, as presented in the film *What's Love Got to Do With It?* Ike is portrayed as treating his beautiful and talented wife, Tina, shamefully and abusively and being frequently unfaithful to her. The film version of Ike was thoroughly repulsive to most people. After the film's release, Ike was questioned about its accuracy. He did not deny that he did the things attributed to him. He had beaten Tina, for instance, but then sometimes she really made him mad! His reaction boiled down to "I did it, but so what?" He was not unaware of what he was doing, but he was apparently "unmoved," dull to the criticism that he evoked, incapable of shame or of any motivation to change or improve. No doubt the film did injury to Ike, but he remained "unconcerned." He certainly was not "incited to sorrow" when his bad conduct came to the attention of many people. He fits the description of a fool given by Aquinas.

Similar remarks apply to some of the perpetrators of Nazi crimes, such as Adolph Eichmann, who showed no remorse when convicted as a mass murderer. Another striking example was the camp doctor at Auschwitz, Johan Paul Kremer, who personally murdered many people while performing ghastly "medical" experiments on them. Kremer continued to think of himself as a good and upright person even when his crimes were exposed to public view. Cases like these raise questions about how people can get into a condition where they are unresponsive, "dull" and "apathetic" with respect to their own moral deformities. How do people become fools?

Stump considers in more detail the case of Franz Stangl, another Nazi death camp commandant. Stangl was initially repelled by the euthanasia practiced in a clinic he was assigned to (the Nazis euthanatized people with various mental and physical defects). But he "adjusted" or dulled his own thinking so as not to lose his job. Gradually he moved from thinking of euthanasia as a necessary evil to thinking of it as a favor bestowed on the victims! In order to do that, he had to direct his attention to certain things and away from others. By Aquinas' account, a person cannot will an action unless his intellect approves of it. And a particular intellect only approves of things that appear to it to be good, or at least good under some description. Stangl focused particularly on the comment of a Roman Catholic nun about a severely disabled 16-year-old; Stangl reported her as saying "How could they refuse to deliver him from this miserable life?" That is to say, one does a favor to disabled persons by killing them! By reflecting on this statement by a person normally thought of as being a moral authority and by directing his attention away from the evident evil of his actions, Stangl was gradually able to dull himself to the character of his own acts.

What all of these examples show is that in a broad sense folly is a moral condition. A person is not a fool because she produces a wretchedly bad proof in geometry or stumbles around and hurts herself when changing a tire. We might think less of some people on account of their lack of various theoretical or practical skills, but we do not tend to think of them as *fools*. Here our intuitions correspond pretty well to Aquinas'. The word *fool* connotes something more than mere stupidity or practical ineptness.

34. *Do you think of a person who does not know when to shut up as a fool? Why or why not? Would Aquinas?*

On the other hand, the term *fool* might not come to mind immediately when thinking of Ike Turner or Kremer or Stangl. They seem morally debased or morally monstrous, but why should they be called fools? A fool is lacking in wisdom. These people seem much worse than that. They do not merely lack something; they are positively evil. However, the brief description of Stangl's progress may show that Aquinas is on to something. In order to do evil, these people had to misprogram their own intellects. They had to

deceive themselves into thinking that what they were doing was dutiful and right or at least justified by circumstances, which is to say that they had to *think* in a way that was manifestly distorted. Thus they were guilty of intellectual as well as moral vice. Since wisdom is a virtue of the intellect and its opposing vice is folly, Aquinas' account speaks to an issue raised by Socrates, who thought that no one could knowingly do evil. Aquinas would not entirely disagree. A distorted intellect, a way of thinking that takes something to be good that is not, is a necessary condition for folly, he argues. But his account of folly helps to explain something that puzzled Socrates, Aristotle and Plato. The road to folly is littered with corrupt motives, such as Stangl's, who wanted the security and prestige of his position even when the job involved doing evil. What these corrupt motives need in order to produce evil actions is a kind of *thinking* that gradually gets more and more distorted. Ike Turner apparently came to believe that beating Tina was justified so long as she made him mad enough. Stangl came to believe that euthanasia for the handicapped was good for them, even though he initially was repelled by such actions.

Now, Plato and Aristotle tended to the view that passions and appetites (such as anger and greed) cannot overcome intellect, since intellect is intrinsically superior to them. Aquinas tries to show that the intellect can cooperate with passions and appetites. It does not need to be overcome by them in order to function badly. It merely needs to be selective, partial, dull to the most salient facts, but alive to facts that support what the greedy or angry person wants.

Of course Aquinas also disagrees with Plato and Aristotle regarding what is required in order to achieve wisdom. Divine grace is essential in his view. The theistic character of his ethics is particularly pronounced when he discusses wisdom and folly.

*35. *Was Stangl not thinking about what he was doing, or was he thinking about what he was doing while paying attention to only some descriptions of what he was doing? Explain.*

36. *Would Aquinas think that anyone, through honest effort, could achieve wisdom? Why or why not?*

Religious Worship and Moral Agency Are Incompatible (Rachels)

Philosopher James Rachels (see his bio in Chapter 1) argues that no one could be *both* a moral person and a worshipper of God. Moral distinctions and norms could not be *based* in the commands or law of God, since they are not even *logically compatible* with the *existence* of God. Morality and God cancel each other out, so to speak.

Rachels cites the story of Abraham and Isaac to illustrate his point. Rachels assumes that Abraham does not have an unusual or peculiar conception of God. Abraham apparently thinks of God as creator of the universe and thus of all human beings, governor of all that exists, all-knowing, all-powerful, and perfectly good, and in all of these respects infinitely above all created things. Believers in God always believe that they are infinitely inferior to God, in a way that they are not to even the most superior human being. Moreover Abraham evidently thought of himself as in a personal relationship with God; he was, so to speak, a child of God. Now, nobody could believe that such a being as God exists without feeling awe and reverence or without feeling the need to submit humbly to it. If, for example, I claimed to believe in God but at the same time thought that I knew better than God how I should live, that would simply show that I did not believe in *God* at all. I might use the word *God* for whatever it is that I believe in, but I could not mean by it what most religious believers mean. I could not mean, obviously, that I thought of God as all-knowing and in that respect infinitely above any human being, including myself.

37. Why not?

The importance of worship in religion is a reflection of these facts. To worship is to express my awe of God, to submit to God, to make and renew my commitment to follow any commands that God might issue. To worship is to enforce the thought of myself as under God, a child of God, duty bound to follow God no matter what. If I should have the thought that I could defy God in some way or that I might know better than God what is right and what is wrong, that would show that I no longer understood what the word *God* means. (The following quotes are from "God and Human Attitudes" in *Religious Studies* 7, 1971).

> That God is not to be judged, challenged, defied or disobeyed, is at bottom a truth of logic; to do any of these things is incompatible with taking him as One to be worshipped. . . .In admitting that a being is worthy of worship we would be recognizing him as having an unqualified claim on our obedience.

Yet the worship of God, as described here, is incompatible with being a moral person. Why? Rachels continues:

> There is a long tradition in moral philosophy according to [which] to be a moral agent is to be an autonomous or self-directed agent. The virtuous man is therefore identified with the man of integrity, i.e., the man who acts according to precepts which he can, on reflection, conscientiously approve in his own heart. On this view, to deliver oneself over to a moral authority for directions about what to do is simply incompatible with being a moral agent.

It might be helpful at this point to compare someone who believes in and worships God to a child who trusts in a parent. Children are generally not thought to be, or fully be, moral agents, since they rightly rely on their parents for moral direction. If a child were accused of stealing and we learned that the child had been told by her parents to steal, we would not hold the child responsible. The child lacks autonomy, and thus "My Mom told me to do it" is a perfectly good reason for the child to give for stealing. We could even say that it is the responsible thing for the child to do. It would not be a good reason for an adult, however. That is what it means to say that an adult is a moral agent, or is morally autonomous, or is able to act on precepts he or she sees to be right in themselves, no matter what someone else says.

What, then, must be said about religious worshippers? By saying "God told me to do it," do they get moral justification for what they do? We should, rather, conclude, according to Rachels' argument, that adult religious believers who do that are acting like little children when in fact they ought to take responsibility for themselves as self-governing moral agents.

It follows that one cannot be both a moral agent and a worshipper of God.

38. *Fill in the blanks in the following argument.*
   a. *A moral person never does something simply because he or she has been _____ to do it.*
   b. *A worshipper of God must believe that he or she must obey God no matter what.*
   c. *Therefore a worshipper of God must be prepared to do something simply because he or she has been _____ to do it.*
   d. *Therefore a worshipper of God could never be a _____ person.*

Rachels considers several possible replies to his argument. One of them comes from Aquinas and the natural law tradition. Aquinas, as we have seen, argues that when a person acts on precepts that reason and conscience tell him to be morally right, he is already conforming to divine law, even though he might not think of it that way.

Rachels objects: "If, in speaking to us through the voice of conscience, God is informing us of what is right, then there is no reason to think that we could not discover this for ourselves—the notion of 'God informing us' is eliminable." That is not much of a response, since Aquinas agrees that the notion of "God informing us" is in a sense eliminable. Here Rachels seems to ignore Aquinas' claim that a person can know right from wrong without any reference to God whatsoever, even though moral distinctions are in fact grounded in divine law. Rachels thinks it is relevant to point out that "in acting from conscience we are acting under the view that our actions are right and not merely that they are decreed by a higher power." He then goes on to cite the Euthyphro dilemma, which we discussed earlier. Rachels thinks that the believer in God must be stuck on the second horn of the dilemma. Rachels thus seems to think of Aquinas as a divine command voluntarist, for the voluntarist does claim that what is right is right "merely" because God commanded it (that is the "second horn").

*39. Aquinas is not a divine command voluntarist. What is his view?

Even if Rachels' response to the natural law tradition misfires, his argument might still be very telling against divine command ethics, particularly in its extreme voluntarist form, for the voluntarist does seem to portray the moral person as one who abdicates autonomy and simply "does what he is told" without having any further reasons or motivation. Suppose that the voluntarist way is the correct way to think of morality from a theistic perspective. It follows that *if* autonomy is central to moral agency, then Rachels may indeed have shown that a person cannot worship God, on the one hand, and at the same time be a moral person. The theist's only response, it seems, would be to deny that autonomy is central to moral agency.

A Revised Divine Command Theory (Adams)

The basic idea in divine command theory as presented so far is this: moral right and wrong are constituted by being commanded by God. Otherwise put, if it is morally *obligatory* to do X (or refrain from doing X), then what makes it so, or constitutes X as morally obligatory (or refraining from X as morally obligatory), is that X is commanded (forbidden) by God.

At first glance this seems to leave no room for any other *motive* for right action than blind obedience to the arbitrary will of a powerful ruler. And that seems incompatible with genuine morality, as Rachels argued. It seems to conflict with how we think of moral obligation. But how *do* we think of it? American philosopher Robert Adams offers the following account (all quotes are from *Finite and Infinite Goods*, 1999):

> The obligatory, we may say, is what we *have* to do. There are things it would be good to do that we don't have to do. The most important difference between the right, or obligation, and the good, in my opinion, is that right and wrong, as matters of obligation, must be understood in relation to a *social* context.

For example, a pain is something bad quite apart from any particular context. If I run my foot through with a nail, the resulting pain is bad, quite apart from what anyone else thinks or says or does or expects. But it is meaningless to say that breaking a promise is bad (wrong) apart from what anyone else says or thinks or does or expects. Promises only exist where there are people relating to each other, and the badness of breaking one is a function of relationships between people. It is that fact that accounts for the *wrongness* (as opposed to the badness) of breaking a promise.

> *40. *Give an example of something that it would be good to do that you do not have to do. What does this suggest about the relation between the good and the obligatory? the good and the right?*

The social nature of obligation and "rightness" shows up in our attitudes toward obligations and violations of them. It turns out that what other people think and do is essential to those attitudes. Adams continues:

> What must be true of anything that is to count as moral obligation? One main point is that we should *care* about complying with it. Likewise it is important that it be something one can be motivated to comply with; a related point is that the nature of obligation should be such as to ground *reasons* for compliance.
>
> Part of taking moral obligation seriously is our response to violations of it. If an act is morally wrong, then it is appropriate for the agent to be blamed, by others and himself.
>
> The nature of moral obligation cannot be understood apart from its relation to guilt. If I voluntarily fail to do what I am morally obliged to do, I am guilty. I may appropriately be blamed by others for my omission, and ought normally to reproach myself for it.

It turns out then that a full analysis of moral obligation requires a discussion of guilt. Guilt is social, that is, the word *guilt* refers to a moral condition (and also to feelings that go with that condition) that I am in when I have *let others down*, failed them by

not doing what they rightly expected and also, often, harmed them. For example, I have failed to obey a legitimate command or to keep a promise.

People sometimes talk about feeling guilt because they have let *themselves* down. We also speak of forgiving ourselves. But it seems that the feeling involved in such cases is shame, not guilt. I can certainly be ashamed of myself even when I have not harmed anyone or let anyone down other than myself. But the original situation in which we acquire notions of guilt is a situation *with others* whose *reactions to us we value*. It is a *social* situation. Parents and valued peers are perhaps the most important "others" in our formative years.

These facts about obligation and guilt, along with others not discussed here, can help us to understand what motivates people to do what is obligatory or right and to refrain from doing what is wrong. A main motive would be that we value our relations to others, our "social bonds." It is because I value the relationships I have to my parents that I feel guilty when I fail to do what they rightly expect or do something that harms them. (It is, unfortunately, possible to have pathological guilt. Some people feel guilty because they failed to do something for a parent that the parent had no right to expect them to do. But that does not show that there is no such thing as normal guilt.)

How does this social conception of moral obligation, with its stress on guilt and other social feelings and statuses, help us to understand divine command ethics? The answer begins with reminders about the limits and frequent defects in many social relationships. The demands put on a person by his family, peers and wider social groups may well be less than moral and in some cases may even be immoral. Consider the strong sense of obligation rooted in "family" ties that a mafia "soldier" might have, even when what he is commanded to do by his "father" or "godfather" is to murder some innocent person. Failure to carry out the obligation might carry a strong sense of guilt. Yet surely we would not want to call the obligation in question a "moral" obligation. The problem is that the social bonds in question are not good ones. Adams wants to explain moral obligation in terms of social relations, but he recognizes that some social obligations cannot be *moral* obligations because the social bonds in question are themselves morally corrupt in some way.

There is a further problem: In some societies the problem is not that the social requirements that actually exist are themselves evil, but that there are no social requirements at all where, it seems, there morally ought to be. For example, in many societies there has been no prohibition, legal or moral, against the enslavement of some people.

It is precisely at this point that the relevance of a relation to God comes into the picture. If a person's social bonds include bonds to God, then, by Adam's analysis, an incorruptible source of obligation enters the picture. The mafia godfather's commands might not be a source of *moral* obligations, but the commands of God surely would be, for God is good, morally and in other ways. To suppose otherwise is to be confused about the concept *God*. It turns out, then, that in Adam's view what motivates a believer to obey God's commands is not blind obedience to a powerful ruler, but valued social bonds to a God with whom the believer has a long history, to whom he or she is indebted in a multitude of ways (as with an earthly parent, but infinitely more so) *and who is regarded as the highest exemplar of goodness.*

Adams has developed a view according to which the fact that *X* is commanded by God makes *X* obligatory. But the God in question cannot be any God but only a good God.

> When I say that an action's being morally obligatory consists in its being commanded by God, I assume that they [God's commands] are consistent with the divine nature having properties that make God an ideal candidate, and the salient candidate, for the semantically indicated role of the supreme and definitive Good.

That is to say, what we *mean* by *good* is in the highest sense ideally illustrated by God. The notion of moral obligation, and rightness, is thus subordinate to a certain notion of goodness.

To sum up: The notion of moral obligation is grounded in and presupposes social relations and bonds. That fact explains what motivates people to keep their obligations or to feel guilty when they do

not. But many forms of social life are corrupt in various ways (see the selection from Twain, Chapter 7, for further illustration of this point). Thus social obligations will not always be fully *moral* obligations. For that we need social bonds to a being who is perfectly good. Adams argues at length that our notions of goodness are best understood in relation to a perfect goodness, God. Thus, fully moral obligations will be rooted in the commands of God.

By Adams' account of divine command morality, it would apparently be inconsistent for God to command the murder of the innocent. However, the commands of God are themselves the ground of our moral obligations, and they could have been other than they are in various respects. For example, God gave certain commands to Abraham ("Pack your stuff and go to Canaan") that he might not have given or might have given to someone else. Once given, however, they create obligations. But what then happens to that *other* command God gave to Abraham, the command to sacrifice Isaac? Can we simply dismiss it on the grounds that such a command could not come from a good God? Are we forced to assume that Abraham was hallucinating or that he lived in a religious milieu so distant from ours that for him it would not have seemed obviously wrong to sacrifice a son to God? In either case there is a problem that does not go away, namely, how to answer the following questions.

1. Could God command us to kill an innocent child?
2. If God did, would we really be obligated to obey? (Recall Orienting Question 5.)

Adam's theory requires that he answer "yes" to question 2, since it is precisely God's commands that produce unqualifiedly moral obligations. But how do we know that "no" is the answer to question 1? Certainly *we* would consider it wrong to kill an innocent child, but part of the point of understanding moral obligation in terms of divine commands, according to Adams, is that what *we* think about morality is not likely to be good enough. After all, "we" have even thought that slavery is moral. How do we know that what *we* think about what is right or wrong is good enough here? Adams considers various cases where it has been considered right to "sacrifice" a child as an expression of obedience to God. Most of them are not like the command to Abraham in every respect, however. One involves a Jewish father who kills his son (who, unlike Isaac, voluntarily submits to being killed) rather than convert to Christianity. In that case there is at least some point to the "sacrifice." The sacrifice of Isaac, on the other hand, seems pointless. It is possible to respond with "I cannot see the point, but I trust God and believe that he has purposes I cannot see." Adams admits that this is a possible response but thinks it is not adequate. "A situation in which I would find it reasonable to believe that a good God had given such an abhorrent command [a command to kill an innocent child] seems to me so unimaginable, that I think it is at best a waste of spiritual energy to try to decide what one should do in that case" (p. 290).

**41. *Has Adams succeeded in making moral obligations dependent on God's commands while at the same time avoiding the "Abraham–Isaac" problem? Discuss pro and con.*

Double Effect, Abortion, Euthanasia (Matthews)

There is a principle that seems similar to Aquinas' as presented in the initial readings, which is often referred to in medical ethics and which is also called "the principle of double effect." A common formulation goes something like this (call this "formulation A" or simply "A" to contrast it with formulation Aq, given earlier):

Formulation A: An action that has both a good and a bad effect will be permissible just in case the following conditions are met:

1. The action is itself morally neutral or morally good.
2. The bad effect must not be the means by which the good effect is brought about.
3. The motive for the action must be the bringing about of the good effect only.
4. The good effect must be equivalent in importance to the bad effect.

42. *Are any of conditions 1–4 similar to the conditions laid down in Aq? Explain.*

One difficulty with formulation A lies in the notion of "the action itself." Actions can be described in many ways. If a surgeon cuts me open in order to remove my appendix, what is the "action itself"—cutting a person open? That doesn't sound like something morally neutral or good. Perhaps the action should be described as "cutting a person open in order to remove a ruptured appendix." But if I describe it that way, I have built the motive into the description of the act itself. Perhaps we could settle for something like "operating surgically on someone" as the best description of the act itself. Though the operation has bad effects, such as postoperative pain, this case clearly fits all four conditions. But it is rather trivial, since probably no one would even think to hold the doctor morally responsible for the postoperative pain.

Consider, on the other hand, two cases of abortion. In the first case, a pregnant woman has uterine cancer, and the only way to save her life is to remove the cancer, which also involves killing the fetus. This case seems to meet the conditions laid down in formulation A.

*43. *Show that it does. Here is how you could start: The first condition is met since the action of operating on the woman is morally neutral or good. Now show how the other three conditions are met.*

In a second case of abortion, a pregnant woman might be endangered if she carried a child to term, because of various physical weaknesses or defects. In this case, killing the fetus is the means to bringing about the good effect, namely, ensuring the woman's survival. Such an abortion could not be justified by appealing to the principle of double effect in its formulation A version, since condition 2 would be violated.

It is evident, then, that the principle can be used to rule out some abortions while some would be permissible.

Similar considerations apply to cases of euthanasia. Suppose a person is dying a very painful death due to incurable cancer. Suppose a doctor administers a high dose of morphine to reduce the pain, knowing that in doing so he will very probably shorten the patient's life by affecting the patient's respiration negatively. The action of administering the morphine seems to be morally neutral or even good (condition 1). The bad effect, namely, early death, is not the means by which the good effect (reduction of pain) is brought about (condition 2). The motive is, we are supposing, only to reduce the pain, not to shorten life (condition 3), and it could be argued that the good effect, namely, reduction of pain, is in these circumstances equivalent in importance to the bad effect, namely, a slightly earlier death (condition 4). So if this is a case of euthanasia, it is permissible under formulation A of the principle of double effect.

Consider a second contrasting case. A 90-year-old close to death has become a nuisance to herself and others. She wishes she could simply die and expresses that fact to her nurse. The nurse, feeling pity on her in her misery, turns her on her left side at night, which puts enough strain on her weak heart so that she is dead by morning.

> 44. *Analyze this second case to see if it fails any of conditions 1–4 of formulation A.*

Philosopher Gareth Matthews discusses formulation A and its relation to Aq. It certainly looks as though there is nothing like formulation A's conditions 1 and 2 in Aq. Go back and look at them if you doubt that. A3 and A4 do look something like Aq's conditions 1 and 3. So it looks as though Aquinas' account of double effect does not bear much of a relation to the modern version given by formulation A. However, Matthews thinks that what is called the "Pauline principle" may play a role in Aquinas's Aq and is also crucial to Formulation A. The Pauline principle is as follows: "One may not do evil that good may come" (St. Paul says in Rom. 3.8, "Shall I do evil that good may result? May it not be so!") Matthews comments:

> What could justify A3 ("The motive must be the achievement of the good effect only")? One plausible answer is that it is the Pauline principle that motivates A3 [which is like Aq 1], just as it is

the Pauline principle that gives plausibility to A2 ("The bad effect must not be the means by which the good effect is achieved"). In fact the Pauline principle can plausibly be thought to lie behind all four conditions of Formulation A.

> Thus, requiring that "the action itself must be morally indifferent or morally good" (A1) assures us that performing the action itself will not be, in itself, doing something evil. Insisting that "the bad effect must not be the means by which the good effect is achieved" (A2) assures us that the good effect is not contaminated by the bad affect. Adding that "the motive must be the achievement of the good effect only" (A3) guarantees that the agent will not be aiming to bring about evil. And the fourth condition, "the good effect must be equivalent in importance to the bad effect," certifies that fixing on the good, irrespective of the foreseen evil, does not undermine the proportionality of one's motivational structure. (from "St Thomas and the Principle of Double Effect" in *Aquinas' Moral Theory*, ed. MacDonald and Stump, 1999).

By Matthews' account, then, Aq is a kind of seedbed for more recent ideas about double effect and shares with it a commitment to the absolute wrongness of, for example, intentionally shedding innocent blood. *Absolute* here means "no matter what." No matter what consequences might ensue, it would always be wrong *intentionally* to shed innocent blood.

> *45. *Try to give an example, not contained in this text, of "shedding innocent blood" that would be acceptable according to the principle of double effect, formulation A. Make sure you check all four conditions.*

The Pauline principle and the principle of double effect prohibit any attempt to show that an action is right or morally permissible simply because the *consequences* of that action might be good, even if they were very, very good. For example, perhaps I could save the lives of 10,000 people by arranging for the judicial execution of an innocent person. The notion that an action is right if and only if it has or is reasonably believed to have better consequences than any alternative can be called *consequentialism*. The Pauline/double effect principles are thus *anti*-consequentialist.

> 46. *Does consequentialism still sound right to you? Why or why not?*

Double Effect, Warfare and Murder (Anscombe)

"The" principle of double effect has been invoked in warfare, particularly the principle as it appears in formulation A. Suppose that it is important to a war effort that a certain munitions factory be bombed, and it is fairly certain that some civilians in the neighborhood will be killed in the attack (collateral damage). On the views of Aquinas and Augustine, the act of bombing the factory could be considered morally permissible. Both of them argue that soldiers acting for the common good can kill without incurring guilt. So assume condition 1 is met. Condition 2 is also met, since the bad effect, the killing of a few civilians, is certainly not the means by which the good effect, the destruction of the factory (or shortening of the war) is achieved. Condition 3 is met since the motive is only the achieving of the good effect, and the bad effect is sincerely regretted and would be avoided if possible. And it might also be argued that condition 4 is met.

> 47. *Argue that it is met.*

British philosopher Gertrude Anscombe (1919–2001) gained public notice by openly accusing the U.S. president, Harry Truman, of murder when he authorized nuclear attacks on Hiroshima and Nagasaki. She wrote the essay cited here at the height of the Cold War, when Russia and the United States were prepared to destroy entire regions filled with innocent people. She discussed some of the problems with wartime applications of the principle of double effect (all quotes are from "War and Murder," in *War and Morality*, ed. Wasserstrom, 1970).

One problem in understanding and correctly applying the principle of double effect arises from misunderstanding of the concept of *intention*. If we think of intending as simply directing the mind toward something, then perhaps "it is all right for a servant to hold the ladder for his criminous master so long as he is merely avoiding the sack by doing so, or that a man might wish for and rejoice at his parent's death so long as what he had in mind was the gain to himself." That is to say, simply by thinking to myself "I am holding this ladder so as to avoid losing my job" I can avoid being morally guilty of aiding in a crime of theft by claiming that I did not intend the theft, but only intended to avoid losing my job. But Anscombe denies that intention consists in such an "interior act of the mind which could be produced at will." Rather, it has external criteria. "It is nonsense to pretend that you do not intend to do what is the means you take to your chosen end." In effect condition 4 in version A clarifies what it is for someone to intend or not intend some result. Thus, if I deliberately kill civilians as a means to ending a war, it cannot be said that I only intended the ending of the war but did not intend the killing of those civilians.

Anscombe agrees that there are "grey areas" where it may be difficult to decide whether the result of employing a given means (suppose the result is the death of an assailant by shooting in self-defense) could reasonably be said not to be intended. But the existence of twilight is no reason for denying the difference between day and night. There are clear-cut cases, and the obliteration bombing of cities in WW II is in her view an example. No one could argue that the fire bombing of Dresden or the bombing of Hiroshima and Nagasaki with atomic weapons was justified on the principle of double effect. One aim of the bombing of Hiroshima was of course a quick end to the war. That was one thing that was intended, or so it seems. But it would be nonsense to deny that the massive incineration of old women and children, servants in hotels, etc. was not also intended. It was in fact the means to achieving the intention of ending the war quickly. Anscombe mocks the attempted use of the principle of double effect as an excuse for such actions:

> The devout Catholic bomber secures by a "direction of intention" that any shedding of innocent blood that occurs is "accidental." I know a Catholic boy who was puzzled at being told by his schoolmaster that it was an *accident* that the

people of Hiroshima and Nagasaki were there to be killed; in fact, however absurd it seems, such thoughts are common among priests who know that they are forbidden by the divine law to justify the direct killing of the innocent. (from "Warfare and Murder" in Wasserstrom, ed., *War and Morality,* 1970)

These bombings certainly could not meet the requirements of version A. Could they have met the conditions laid down in Thomas' version, version Aq? Clearly that formulation is different. For example, it does not include the restriction that the bad effect must not be the means by which the good effect is brought about. It does include the idea of "proportionality," however. In the case of the bombing of Hiroshima, was the means chosen proportional to the good end that was being sought? (Assume, for the sake of discussion, that the good end sought was the saving of American lives by eliminating the need for an invasion of Japan.)

48. *Argue that it was not. Argue that it was.*
49. *Argue that even if it was, it still would not meet all the conditions of formulation Aq.*
50. *Argue that it does not meet all the conditions of formulation A.*

Stoicism and the *Bhagavad Gita*

Stoicism arose in the 4th century BCE and developed into a "school" that enjoyed great popularity throughout the Hellenistic/Roman era (roughly the 4th century BCE to the 5th century CE). The ethical teachings of stoicism continue to attract many thinkers. One of the most prominent Stoics was Epictetus (50–130 CE), who had been a slave to the emperor Nero's secretary. Epictetus draws a fundamental Stoic distinction in his "Manual," or *Enchiridion.*

Some things are in our control and others not. Things in our control are opinion, pursuit, desire, aversion, and, in a word, whatever are our own actions. Things not in our control are body, property, reputation, command, and, in one word, whatever are not our own actions. (Enchir. 1)

The Stoic view is that we should concern ourselves exclusively with the first group, things in our control.

We should be concerned, in effect, only with our own character. Thus I can control what I desire, but I cannot control whether or not I get what I desire, since that will depend on other people, natural events and the like. From that fact, the Stoic draws the conclusion that I should be *detached* from (not concerned about) the *results* of my actions, since I cannot control the results. I may do the right thing, for example, help an injured person, with a bad result (he or she is accidentally injured even more, even though I did my best). Such events should then not disturb me. These ideas are very much in the spirit of the *Bhagavad Gita*: "Your business is with actions only, and never with the fruits of your actions."

The Stoics draw the additional inference that we should be unattached to everything, even to those persons or things to which most people generally feel very strong attachments. Thus, I should not get upset if my wife dies, provided I have done my duty to her, since no one can control life and death. We can only control our *attitudes* toward life and death. "If you kiss your child, or your wife, say that you only kiss things that are human, and thus you will not be disturbed if either of them dies" (Enchir. 3). Again, this sounds like the *Gita*: "A sage of stable mind is free from anxiety when surrounded by pains, is indifferent when surrounded by pleasures, and is freed from passion, fear and anger. He is without attachments on every side."

The Stoics also stress the notion of duty. The notion of *duty* appears to include, or be, the notion of what *must* be done, no matter what the consequences or "fruit" of our actions. Neither the Stoic nor the pious Hindu is concerned with the consequences of action. But they are both very concerned with duty. The *Gita* says: "He who performs his actions as a duty, independent of the fruit of the action, is an ascetic."

But what determines our duties? The Stoic has more than one answer. Some duties are determined by our "station in life." For example, if I have a father, then it follows almost by definition that I have a duty to care for him, obey him, and so forth.

But duties also reflect a divine order, for both the Stoic and the Hindu. Epictetus asks whether duty to a father or a brother applies also to a *bad* father or brother and insists that what matters is not what "he does, but what you are able to do to keep your own will in a state conformable to nature." But the order in nature is a divine order, as it is also in the *Gita*: "The Yogi who harmonizes the self and puts away evil will enjoy the infinite bliss of unity with the eternal Brahman. I will never lose hold of the person who sees me everywhere, and sees everything in me, and that person will never lose hold of me." The Stoics speak of "nature" or the "logos" (principle of reason in the universe) or sometimes "the giver." Epictetus says:

> Never say of anything, "I have *lost* it"; but say instead that "I have *returned* it." Is your child dead? It is returned. Is your wife dead? She is returned. Is your estate taken away? Is that not also returned? [Don't say]"The person who took these away is bad." What difference is it to you who the giver assigns to take it back? While he gives it to you to possess, take care of it; but don't view it as your own, just as travelers view a hotel. (Enchir. 11)

Thus for the Stoic and the pious Hindu everything happens in accordance with the providence of God. Therefore we should stop thinking that what happens must conform to what *we* desire, and we should fit ourselves to the divine plan.

Stoic themes are found also in Christianity and scattered about elsewhere in Western culture. St. Paul says that those that are married should be as though not married, those that buy, as though they didn't (I Cor. 7.29). Thus he advocates a kind of inner detachment that is reminiscent of Stoicism. Likewise his references to what is according to nature (Rom. 1.28) suggest the influence of Stoic thought. The British philosopher the third Earl of Shaftesbury (1671–1713) insisted that we must learn to love whatever happens and see it all as fitting and orderly with respect to the whole, even when it included "the sack of cities and the ruin of mankind" (from *Philosophical Regimen* in *Life and Letters*). This severe advice fits the teachings of Epictetus as well as the advice given to Arjuna by Krishna on the field of battle. Or consider also the following epitaph from the tombstone of the great American poet Emily Dickenson, in light of the earlier quote from Epictetus about what is taken back or returned:

BORN DEC. 10, 1830. CALLED BACK MAY 15, 1886.

Stoicism shows religious undertones throughout its history. But it is also clearly an ethical view. Nonetheless it does not ground ethics in the commands of God (Scotus) or in the fulfillment of a God given nature (Aquinas). Rather, God is conceived as a kind of grand director of a theatrical production, assigning parts to all. The proper aim of living is thus to fit oneself to the divine plan by fulfilling one's role. Something similar to this thought also figures in the *Gita*. Thus the connections between ethics and religious belief in Stoicism and also in Hinduism appear to differ in important ways from many Western views of those relations.

51. *"Duty" in the Stoic view and the Hindu view requires doing what must be done, no matter what the _____ may be.*

52. *Does the Stoic ideal of nonattachment seem to you inhumane, with no place for normal human loving and caring? Does the Hindu view seem similar? Could you not feel great distress if you had to kill your own relatives in a war, as did Arjuna, or as many have had to do in civil wars?*

CHAPTER FIVE

Evil, Vice and Reason

Introduction

Just how great are the obstacles to living a good life in a good community? Do Plato and Aristotle or even Aquinas underestimate the power of evil in their accounts of the good? Consider Aristotle's account of the *akrates*, the incontinent person who seems to know what is good but nonetheless does what is destructive or evil. Aristotle wavers in his account, but it is not clear that he thinks people can commit deeply evil acts with full knowledge of what they are doing. Plato is even less inclined to admit that anyone could knowingly commit evil. Both of them trust that there is a durable power in the good that reason can identify and that draws people or to which they can be made to conform by those who are wise. Even the great tragedians, such as Sophocles, draw back from any description of humans as committing terrible evils entirely on their own volition. Rather, the evil that people do is at least in part the result of their entrapment in an impersonal fate or necessity as well as in ignorance, culpable or not culpable, or imprudence.

In the Christian era a notion of the will, and of the capacity to will evil for its own sake, gained credence. Augustine (354–430 CE) records in his *Confessions* a recollection from his youth of deliberate wrongdoing, doing evil for its own sake:

> There was a pear tree close to our vineyard, heavily laden with fruit, which was tempting neither for its color nor its flavor. To shake and rob this some of us wanton young fellows went, late one night (having, according to our disgraceful habit, prolonged our games in the streets until then), and carried away great loads, not to eat ourselves, but to fling to the very swine, having only eaten some of them; and to do this pleased us all the more because it was not permitted. Behold my heart, O my God; behold my heart, which Thou hadst pity upon when in the bottomless pit. Behold, now, let my heart tell Thee what it was seeking there, that I should be gratuitously wanton, having no inducement to evil but the evil itself. It was foul, and I loved it. I loved to perish. I loved my own error—not that for which I erred, but the error itself. (*Confessions* II iv)

Plato and Aristotle would have found this anecdote very puzzling indeed. It seems to conflict with their ideas about the powers of reason. But the idea that deliberate, willful evil is possible is not uncommon in the modern era.

Conflicting views on the extent and nature of evil and vice can generate or be generated by particular views on the possibility of a moral life, the religious basis of morality and the importance of ethics generally. Thus the notion that good will be rewarded and evil punished, a notion important to much thinking about ethics, might be abandoned in the face of great evil and cruelty that appears to go unpunished.

Great evil might also cause a person to give up belief in God altogether or in any transcendent source of goodness. In that case one could no longer ground morality in the will of God or rely on a cosmic order such as that postulated by Plato. Some people conclude that the world we live in is simply absurd or irrational, in the sense that reason cannot give a good account of moral concerns. Others argue that evildoing is inevitable, given the forms and limits of natural human life. Yet others argue that the nature of great evildoing has itself been widely misconstrued. Perhaps it is more a matter of being indifferent, empty and thoughtless than it is a matter of possessing (or being possessed by) some sort of demonic power.

ORIENTING QUESTIONS FOR DISCUSSION

1. Are evil and vice "natural" or somehow "unnatural"?
2. Would it be possible to overcome the evils of the world by education and a more scientific understanding of people? Or is evil inevitable?
3. Is it possible that the "moral" distinctions we think so important, including the basic distinction between good and evil, are a sham, a device used by the weak in an attempt to suppress those individuals who are strong enough to ignore those distinctions? Are good people just conformists who do out of weakness what those around them consider "right"?
4. Are those who commit great evils typically intent on doing so, or is it more typically the case that they are simply thoughtless conformists? (Check to see whether your answer to this question is consistent with your answer to the previous one).
5. Are there good explanations for evildoing, or do the usual explanations (for example, in terms of psychological deformity or a bad environment or even "God's plan") explain away rather than explain?

FEODOR DOSTOEVSKY

Dostoevsky (1821–1881), now regarded as one of the world's greatest novelists, focused in his works on philosophical, moral and religious themes. His reputation rests primarily on four long philosophical novels—Crime and Punishment (1866, excerpted in Chapter 9 of this book), The Idiot (1868–69), The Possessed, also known as The Devils (1871–72), and The Brothers Karamazov (1879–80)—and on one novella, Notes from Underground (1864). In his own lifetime Dostoevsky was as famous for his journalistic writing as for his fiction.

Dostoevsky rejected all attempts to fit human life and character into a theory, and thus he rejected any attempt to alleviate human misery by the imposition of theoretical and utopian schemes. Such schemes, in his view, always involve overlooking or underrating the capacity of humans to act freely both for evil and for good. He challenged the capacity of "reason," when abstracted from the unpredictable contingencies of life, to lead to good. The only hope for people, in his view, lay in the efforts of individual people to lead lives of kindness, hopefulness and faith. The resources for doing so could be found primarily in religion and ultimately only in religion.

As a young man Dostoevsky embraced socialist and utopian ideals himself, and he engaged in political activities that led to his arrest and imprisonment in a czarist prison camp in Siberia. There his views changed radically. He recovered religious faith and rejected all utopian ideas. His time in prison and his reflections on the criminal mind led him to emphasize the role of the irrational in human life. One must find resources for counteracting irrational cruelty, to take one example, that are much deeper than the appeal "Let's be reasonable about this" (cf. Orienting Question 2).

The Brothers Karamazov

In the following excerpt from *The Brothers Karamazov*, one of the brothers, Ivan, describes some cases of extreme cruelty. Ivan is putting the faith of his younger brother, Alyosha, to the test. Alyosha is a young monk, a novice, who greatly admires his superior, the saintly Zossima. Alyosha wants to believe that there is a power for good that can and will triumph somehow, the power of the God of Christianity. He wants to believe that the universe is ultimately good and that human beings can be redeemed. Ivan denies these ideas, and offers powerful evidence for the existence of meaningless and terrible evils that make life into a living hell. Dostoevsky has a vision of evil, which, it seems, Plato or Aristotle did not or could not have had. It is not clear how anything could compensate for the evils Ivan describes. It is not clear how any confidence in the triumph of a good God or some more impersonal "form of the good" can survive an honest admission of such facts as are recited here. And it is far from clear that what is needed, in order to come to grips with the kinds of facts described by Ivan, is "reason," however defined.

Ivan describes to Alyosha, in vivid and merciless detail, the kinds of evils that are committed against innocent children. There is evidence that Dostoevsky found some of the materials for this passage in newspaper accounts of actual cases.

Part II. Book V: Pro and Contra

CHAPTER 4: REBELLION (tr. GARNETT)

A well-educated, cultured gentleman and his wife beat their own child with a birch rod, a girl of seven. I have an exact account of it. The papa was glad that the birch was covered with twigs. "It stings more," said he, and so he began stinging his daughter. I know for a fact there are people who at every blow are worked up to sensuality, to literal sensuality, which increases progressively at every blow they inflict. They beat for a minute, for five minutes, for ten minutes, more often and more savagely. The child screams. At last the child cannot scream, it gasps, "Daddy, Daddy!" By some diabolical unseemly chance the case was brought into court. A counsel is engaged. The Russian people have long called a barrister "a conscience for hire." The counsel protests in his client's defense. : It's such a simple thing," he says, "an everyday domestic event. A father corrects his child. To our shame be it said, it is brought into court." The jury, convinced by him, give a favorable verdict. The public roars with delight that the torturer is acquitted. Ah, pity I wasn't there! I would have proposed to raise a subscription in his honor! Charming pictures.

"But I've still better things about children. I've collected a great, great deal about Russian children, Alyosha. There was a little girl of five who was hated by her father and mother, 'most worthy and respectable people, of good education and breeding.' You see, I must repeat again, it is a peculiar characteristic of many people, this love of torturing children, and children only. To all other types of humanity these torturers behave mildly and benevolently, like cultivated children, even fond of children themselves in that sense. It's just their defenselessness that tempts the tormentor, just the angelic confidence of the child who has no refuge and no appeal, that sets his vile blood on fire. In every man, of course, a demon lies hidden, the demon of rage, the demon of lustful heat at the screams of the tortured victim, the demon of lawlessness let off the chain, the demon of diseases that follow on vice, gout, kidney disease, and so on.

"This poor child of five was subjected to every possible torture by those cultivated parents. They beat her, thrashed her, kicked her for no reason till her body was one bruise. Then, they went to greater refinements of cruelty, shut her up all night in the cold and frost in a privy, and because she didn't ask to be taken up at night (as though a child of five sleeping its angelic, sound sleep could be trained to wake and ask), they smeared her face and filled her mouth with excrement, and it was her mother, her mother did this. And that mother could sleep, hearing the poor child's groans! Can you understand why a little creature, who can't even understand what's done to her, should beat her little aching heart with her tiny fist in the dark and the cold, and weep her meek, unresentful tears to dear, kind God to protect her? Do you understand that, friend and brother, you pious and humble novice? Do you understand why this infamy must be and is permitted? Without it, I am told, man could not have existed on earth, for he could not have known good and evil. Why should he know that diabolical good and evil when it costs so much? Why, the whole world of knowledge is not worth that child's prayer to 'dear, kind God'! I say nothing of the sufferings of grownup people, they have eaten the apple, damn them, and the devil take them all! But these little ones! I am making you suffer, Alyosha, you are not yourself. I'll leave off if you like."

"Never mind. I want to suffer too," muttered Alyosha.

"One picture, only one more, because it's so curious, so characteristic, and I have only just read it in some collection of Russian antiquities. I've forgotten the name. I must look it up. It was in the darkest days of serfdom at the beginning of the century, and long live the Liberator of the People! There was in those days a general of aristocratic connections, the owner of great estates, one of those men, somewhat exceptional, I believe, even then, who, retiring from the service into a life of leisure, are convinced that they've earned absolute power over the lives of their subjects. There were such men then. So our general, settled on his property of 2,000 souls, lives in pomp, and domineers over his poor neighbors as though they were dependents and buffoons. He has kennels of hundreds of hounds and nearly a hundred dog boys all mounted, and in uniform. One day a serf boy, a little child of eight, threw a stone in play and hurt the paw of the general's favorite hound. 'Why is my favorite dog lame?' He is told that the boy threw a stone that hurt the dog's paw. 'So you did it.' The general looked the child up and down. 'Take him.' He was taken from his mother and kept shut up all night. Early that morning the general comes out on horseback, with the hounds, his dependents, dog boys, and huntsmen, all mounted around him in full hunting parade. The servants are summoned for their edification, and in front of them all stands the mother of the child. The child is brought from the lock up. It's a gloomy, cold, foggy autumn day, a capital day for hunting. The general orders the child to be undressed; the child is stripped naked. He shivers, numb with terror, not daring to cry. . . . 'Make him run,' commands the general. 'Run! run!' shout the dog boys. The boy runs. . . . 'At him!' yells the general, and he sets the whole pack of hounds on the child.

"The hounds catch him, and tear him to pieces before his mother's eyes! . . . I believe the general was afterwards declared incapable of administering his estates. Well, what did he deserve? To be shot? To be shot for the satisfaction of our moral feelings? Speak, Alyosha!"

"To be shot," murmured Alyosha, lifting his eyes to Ivan with a pale, twisted smile.

"Bravo!" cried Ivan, delighted. "If even you say so . . . You're a pretty monk! So there is a little devil sitting in your heart, Alyosha Karamazov!"

"What I said was absurd, but . . ."

"That's just the point, that 'but'!" cried Ivan. "Let me tell you, novice, that the absurd is only too necessary on earth. The world stands on absurdities, and perhaps nothing would have come to pass in it without them. We know what we know!"

"What do you know?"

"I understand nothing," Ivan went on, as though in delirium. "I don't want to understand anything now. I want to stick to the fact. I made up my mind long ago not to understand. If I try to understand anything, I shall be false to the fact, and I have determined to stick to the fact."

"Why are you trying me?" Alyosha cried, with sudden distress. "Will you say what you mean at last?"

"Of course, I will; that's what I've been leading up to. You are dear to me, I don't want to let you go, and I won't give you up to your Zossima."

Ivan for a minute was silent, his face became all at once very sad.

"Listen! I took the case of children only to make my case clearer. . . . I must have justice, or I will destroy myself. And not justice in some remote infinite time and space, but here on earth, and that I could see myself. I have believed in it. I want to see it, and if I am dead by then, let me rise again, for if it all happens without me, it will be too unfair. Surely I haven't suffered simply that I, my crimes and my sufferings, may manure the soil of the future harmony for somebody else. I want to see with my own eyes the hind lie down with the lion and the victim rise up and embrace his murderer. I want to be there when everyone suddenly understands what it has all been for. All the religions of the world are built on this longing, and I am a believer. But then there are the children, and what am I to do about them? That's a question I can't answer. For the hundredth time I repeat, there are numbers of questions, but I've only taken the children, because in their case what I mean is so unanswerably clear. Listen! If all must suffer to pay for the eternal harmony, what have children to do with it, tell me, please? It's beyond all comprehension why they should suffer, and why they should pay for the harmony. Why should they, too, furnish material to enrich the soil for the harmony of the future?"

1. *Why might someone think that human life requires knowledge of good and evil? Consider whether nonhuman animals have such knowledge.*

At one point Ivan exclaims, "I understand nothing. . . . I don't want to understand anything now. I want to stick to the fact." Someone might think they "understand" why there are terrible evils in the world if they have an explanation of it, for example, an explanation in terms of free will, which was a good gift of God but has been put to evil use. Or someone might feel that a sociological explanation of terrible evils makes them more bearable. For example, if we can only get a sociological explanation of the actions of Nazi prison guards herding Jews into gas ovens, we may feel some relief when considering such otherwise-incomprehensible evils. (Recall Orienting Questions 2 and 5.)

2. *According to Ivan, what effect may such explanations have on our thinking? Is he right?*
3. *Suppose that vengeance is taken on all evildoers. Or suppose that those who do evil suffer for it eternally in hell. Would that take care of the problem of evil? Why or why not?*
4. *Alyosha's "solution" to the problem of evil, it turns out, is entirely religious in character. In his view people cannot, through the use of reason or any other faculty, escape from evil. Do you agree? If he is right, does "ethics" become irrelevant?*

Dostoevsky has presented a vision of human life in which the limits to moral endeavor are all too evident. But just exactly what are we talking about? What is "evil?" What is good? Plato only manages to allude to a transcendent good, and his account of evil as mere ignorance would certainly not satisfy Ivan. Aristotle's ethics includes some detailed accounts of vices, but once again it would surely not satisfy someone like Ivan, who dwells on the details of such terrible cases as are described here.

Our discussions so far seem to presuppose certain agreements about goodness and evil. Ivan assumes that we will find the cases he described morally abhorrent in the extreme. Aristotle appeals to common intuitions about right and wrong, vice and virtue. Plato assumes that his readers can come to see that justice would be desired by any rational person, the objections of Thrasymachus notwithstanding. Aquinas bases morality in God but largely agrees with Aristotle about what traits and actions are evil and that they all indicate failures of reason.

But do we have such agreements? If so, how did we arrive at them? Is there some sense of "reason" according to which we could, if fully rational, come to agreement about what is good and what is evil? What, finally is the nature of good and evil? Must we assume some transcendent standard or the requirements of a God? Or can we extract a sufficient account of these notions simply by thinking about life in more or less "natural" terms? Or is it perhaps the case that the distinction "good/evil" or "moral/immoral" is some kind of sham, tied to hypocrisy and weakness or to outmoded ways of thinking? (Compare with Orienting Question 3.) This last alternative is explored in the next selection.

Beyond Good and Evil

FRIEDRICH NIETZSCHE

Friedrich Nietzsche was born in 1844 in Lutzen, now in Germany, the son of a Lutheran pastor. His intellectual brilliance earned him a position as a university professor even before the completion of his doctoral dissertation, but physical ills led to his retirement at the age of 35. He claimed that the low point of his life was his 36th year, and he attributed that fact to a close connection to his "incomparable father," who had died at the age of 36. Although he apparently loved and admired his father, he came to reject Christianity completely. Toward the end of his life he became mentally ill. He died in 1900.

Nietzsche's dissertation, his first book, explores themes of suffering, madness and fate, which continued to concern him throughout his authorship. His treatment of these themes is similar in some ways to that of Dostoevsky, whom he had read sympathetically. Both Dostoevsky and Nietzsche are often credited with influencing the development of the 20th century philosophical movement called existentialism, *which stressed the moral anguish of individuals in an irrational world.*

Nietzsche was deeply concerned with suffering and cruelty. He was convinced that no explanation of tragic suffering was possible and that there is no way of ensuring ourselves against such suffering. People often try to explain tragic events in terms of morality (the sufferer was bad and deserved it) or religion (it is all part of God's plan or the ultimate "harmony" referred to by Ivan in the previous selection) or a combination of these, and they are often surprised and inconsolable when tragic suffering (e.g., the violent death of someone close to them, such as an innocent child) overtakes them. Religion and morality amount to ways of denying what is actually happening, they amount to saying "no" to life in all of its tragic complexity and absurdity. Religion and morality, with their sharp distinctions between good and evil, are expressions of a deep dissatisfaction with life as it actually is and are part of a dishonest attempt to escape it or interpret it in a way that makes it less terrible. Nietzsche wanted to be able to *affirm* life, even in the midst of absurd suffering.

In his first book, *The Birth of Tragedy,* Nietzsche argued that the Greek tragedians, Sophocles, for example, managed to affirm in just that way. Only in art and great literature, such as Sophocles' plays, is life faced as it truly is. Art represents life without distortion and at the same time enables us to accept it and even to celebrate it, as the Greeks did in their dramatic festivals, which were dedicated to Dionysius, the God of revelry, deep and irrational energies, intoxication. Logic and Science, on the other hand, gain the upper hand when people are afraid to face the absurdity of life and are becoming superficial and weak.

Madness and Reason

Nietzsche sees strength in the "Dionysian" attitudes of the Greek tragedies but only weakness in philosophical reason. In a later work, Preface to *The Birth of Tragedy,* Nietzsche reflected on his first book and summarized some of its themes.

Nietzsche hoped that something like the Greek tragic and Dionysian conception of art would be recovered in the musical dramas of his contemporary Richard Wagner. Later in life Nietzsche came to reject parts of his first book and to give up his hopes in Wagner, but the basic ideas just mentioned persist throughout his authorship.

Art Is Closer to Reality Than Is Morality

Metaphysics is the attempt to say what is really real. Nietzsche denied that metaphysics is possible, but the impulse that makes people ask what is real can be satisfied in art.

(from the Preface to *The Birth of Tragedy*)

Already in the foreword to Richard Wagner, art—and not morality—is set down as the properly metaphysical activity of man; in the book itself the piquant proposition recurs time and again, that the existence of the world is justified only as an aesthetic phenomenon. Indeed, the entire book recognizes only an artist—thought and artist—afterthought behind all occurrences—a "God," if you will, but certainly only an altogether thoughtless and unmoral artist—God, who, in construction as in destruction, in good as in evil, desires to become conscious of his own equable joy and sovereign glory; who, in creating worlds, frees himself from the anguish of fullness and overfullness, from the suffering of the contradictions concentrated within him. The world, that is, the redemption of God attained at every moment, as the perpetually changing, perpetually new vision of the most suffering, most antithetical, most contradictory being, who contrives to redeem himself only in appearance: This entire artist metaphysics, call it arbitrary, idle, fantastic, if you will—the point is, that it already betrays a spirit, which is determined some day, at all hazards, to make a stand against the moral interpretation and significance of life. Here, perhaps for the first time, a pessimism "Beyond Good and Evil" announces itself, here that "perverseness of disposition" obtains expression and formulation, against which Schopenhauer never grew tired of hurling beforehand his angriest imprecations and thunderbolts—a philosophy which dares to put, derogatorily put, morality itself in the world of phenomena, and not only among "Phenomena" (in the sense of the idealistic *terminus technicus* [technical term]), but among the "illusions," as appearance, semblance, error, interpretation, accommodation, art. Perhaps the depth of this antimoral tendency may be best estimated from the guarded and hostile silence with which Christianity is treated throughout this book—Christianity, as being the most extravagant burlesque of the moral theme to which mankind has hitherto been obliged to listen.

In fact, to the purely aesthetic world-interpretation and justification taught in this book, there is no greater antithesis than the Christian dogma, which is only and will be only moral, and which, with its absolute standards, for instance, its truthfulness of God, relegates—that is, disowns, convicts, condemns—art, all art, to the realm of falsehood. Behind such a mode of thought and valuation, which, if at all genuine, must be hostile to art, I always experienced what was hostile to life, the wrathful, vindictive counterwill to life itself; for all life rests on appearance, art, illusion, optics, necessity of perspective and error. From the very first Christianity was, essentially and thoroughly, the nausea and surfeit of Life for Life, which only disguised, concealed, and decked itself out under the belief in "another" or "better" life. The hatred of the "world," the curse on the affections, the fear of beauty and sensuality, another world, invented for the purpose of slandering this world the more, at bottom a longing for Nothingness, for the end, for rest, for the "Sabbath of Sabbaths"—all this, as also the unconditional will of Christianity to recognize only moral values, has always appeared to me as the most dangerous and ominous of all possible forms of a "will to perish"; at the least, as the symptom of a most fatal disease, of profoundest weariness, despondency, exhaustion, impoverishment of life—for before the tribunal of morality (especially Christian, that is, unconditional morality) life must constantly and inevitably be the loser, because life is something essentially unmoral—indeed, oppressed with the weight of contempt and the everlasting No, life must finally be regarded as unworthy of desire, as in itself unworthy.

5. *State three reasons why, in Nietzsche's view, morality, and especially Christian morality,*

involves saying "no" to life? Do you think he is right? Explain.

THE CRITIQUE OF MORALITY

Nietzsche attacks conventional and especially Christian morality, from several sides. It is part of a herd mentality, and it is rooted in the resentments and fears of the weak. The close connection between morality and custom practically annihilates individuality (cf. Orienting Question 4). These points are stressed in the following excerpts from *The Dawn of Day*.

In comparison with the mode of life which prevailed among men for thousands of years, we men of the present day are living in a very immoral age: The power of custom has been weakened to a remarkable degree, and the sense of morality is so refined and elevated that we might almost describe it as volatilized. That is why we latecomers experience such difficulty in obtaining a fundamental conception of the origin of morality: And even if we do obtain it, our words of explanation stick in our throats, so coarse would they sound if we uttered them! or to so great an extent would they seem to be a slander upon morality! Thus, for example, the fundamental clause: Morality is nothing else (and, above all, nothing more) than obedience to customs, of whatsoever nature they may be. But customs are simply the traditional way of acting and valuing. Where there is no tradition there is no morality; and the less life is governed by tradition, the narrower the circle of morality. The free man is immoral, because it is his will to depend upon himself and not upon tradition: In all the primitive states of humanity "evil" is equivalent to "individual," "free," "arbitrary," "unaccustomed," "unforeseen," "incalculable." In such primitive conditions, always measured by this standard, any action performed—not because tradition commands it, but for other reasons (e.g., on account of its individual utility), even for the same reasons as had been formerly established by custom—is termed immoral, and is felt to be so even by the very man who performs it, for it has not been done out of obedience to the tradition.

What is tradition? A higher authority, which is obeyed, not because it commands what is useful to us, but merely because it commands. And in what way can this feeling for tradition be distinguished from a general feeling of fear? It is the fear of a higher intelligence which commands, the fear of an incomprehensible power, of something that is more than personal—there is superstition in this fear. In primitive times the domain of morality included education and hygienics, marriage, medicine, agriculture, war, speech, and silence, the relationship between man and man, and between man and the gods—morality required that a man should observe her prescriptions without thinking of himself as individual. Everything, therefore, was originally custom, and whoever wished to raise himself above it had first of all to make himself a kind of lawgiver and medicine man, a sort of demigod—in other words, he had to create customs, a dangerous and fearful thing to do! Who is the most moral man? On the one hand, he who most frequently obeys the law, e.g., he who, like the Brahmins [Hindu priests], carries a consciousness of the law about with him wherever he may go, and introduces it into the smallest divisions of time, continually exercising his mind in finding opportunities for obeying the law. On the other hand, he who obeys the law in the most difficult cases. The most moral man is he who makes the greatest sacrifices to morality, but what are the greatest sacrifices? In answering this question several different kinds of morality will be developed, but the distinction between the morality of the most frequent obedience and the morality of the most difficult obedience is of the greatest importance. Let us not be deceived as to the motives of that moral law which requires, as an indication of morality, obedience to custom in the most difficult cases. Self-conquest is required, not by reason of its useful consequences for the individual, but that custom and tradition may appear to be dominant, in spite of all individual counterdesires and advantages. The individual shall sacrifice himself—so demands the morality of custom.

> 6. *Think of, or try to imagine, a case in which a person committed to the moral law might seem to be more of an individual than those who ignore morality. Would Socrates count as such a case?*

On the other hand, those moralists who, like the followers of Socrates, recommend self-control and

sobriety to the individual as his greatest possible advantage and the key to his greatest personal happiness are exceptions—and if we ourselves do not think so, this is simply due to our having been brought up under their influence. They all take a new path, and thereby bring down upon themselves the utmost disapproval of all the representatives of the morality of custom. They sever their connection with the community, as immoralists, and are, in the fullest sense of the word, evil ones. In the same way, every Christian who "sought, above all things, his own salvation" must have seemed evil to a virtuous Roman of the old school. Wherever a community exists, and consequently also a morality of custom, the feeling prevails that any punishment for the violation of a custom is inflicted, above all, on the community: This punishment is a supernatural punishment, the manifestations and limits of which are so difficult to understand, and are investigated with such superstitious fear. The community can compel any one member of it to make good, either to an individual or to the community itself, any ill consequences which may have followed upon such a member's action. It can also call down a sort of vengeance upon the head of the individual by endeavoring to show that, as the result of his action, a storm of divine anger has burst over the community—but, above all, it regards the guilt of the individual more particularly as its own guilt, and bears the punishment of the isolated individual as its own punishment. "Morals," they bewail in their innermost heart, "morals have grown lax, if such deeds as these are possible." And every individual action, every individual mode of thinking, causes dread. It is impossible to determine how much the more select, rare, and original minds must have suffered in the course of time by being considered as evil and dangerous, yea, because they even looked upon themselves as such. Under the dominating influence of the morality of custom, originality of every kind came to acquire a bad conscience, and even now the sky of the best minds seems to be more overcast by this thought than it need be.

> 7. *Why can a person not be both free and moral? Because being moral requires following custom, whereas being free requires being willing to act*

independently, without reference to what is customary. Does that sound like a good account of the relation between freedom and morality? Argue for your answer.

*8. *Socrates was considered evil and dangerous by many of his contemporaries. He was willing to stand apart. He was an individualist. But he was also a moralist. Why does this fact seem to contradict Nietzsche's view of morality? What does Nietzsche say about the morality of Socrates?*

SUSPICION OF MORALITY AND SELFLESSNESS

Nietzsche suspects that morality is a cover for weakness. What is needed is a study that uncovers the hidden motivations of morality and in particular of altruism or selflessness, rather than mere surveys of its history and problems (such as are found in this textbook!).

The following paragraphs are from Nietzsche's *Joyful Wisdom.*

"Selflessness" has no value either in heaven or on earth; the great problems all demand great love, and it is only the strong, well-rounded, secure spirits, those who have a solid basis, that are qualified for them. It makes the most material difference whether a thinker stands personally related to his problems, having his fate, his need, and even his highest happiness therein; or merely impersonally, that is to say, if he can only feel and grasp them with the tentacles of cold, prying thought. . . .

How is it that I have not yet met with anyone, not even in books, who seems to have stood to morality in this position, as one who knew morality as a problem, and this problem as his own personal need, affliction, pleasure, and passion? It is obvious that up to the present morality has not been a problem at all; it has rather been the very ground on which people have met, after all distrust, dissension, and contradiction, the hallowed place of peace, where thinkers could obtain rest even from themselves, could recover breath and revive. I see no one who has ventured to criticize the estimates of moral worth. I miss in this connection even the attempts of scientific curiosity, and the fastidious, groping imagination of psychologists and historians, which easily anticipates a problem and catches it on the wing, without rightly knowing what it catches. With difficulty I have discovered some scanty data for the purpose of furnishing a history of the origin of these feelings and estimates of value (which is something different from a criticism of them, and also something different from a history of ethical systems). In an individual case, I have done everything to encourage the inclination and talent for this kind of history—in vain, as it would seem to me at present. There is little to be learned from those historians of morality (especially Englishmen); they themselves are usually, quite unsuspiciously, under the influence of a definite morality, and act unwittingly as its armor-bearers and followers—perhaps still repeating sincerely the popular superstition of Christian Europe, that the characteristic of moral action consists in abnegation, self-denial, self-sacrifice, or in fellow feeling and fellow suffering. The usual error in their premises is their insistence on a certain consensus among human beings, at least among civilized human beings, with regard to certain propositions of morality, and from thence they conclude that these propositions are absolutely binding even upon you and me; or reversely, they come to the conclusion that no morality at all is binding, after the truth has dawned upon them that to different peoples moral valuations are necessarily different: Both of which conclusions are equally childish follies. The error of the more subtle amongst them is that they discover and criticize the probably foolish opinions of a people about its own morality, or the opinions of mankind about human morality generally; they treat accordingly of its origin, its religious sanctions, the superstition of free will, and such matters; and they think that just by so doing they have criticized the morality itself.

But the worth of a precept, "Thou shalt," is still fundamentally different from and independent of such opinions about it, and must be distinguished from the weeds of error with which it has perhaps been overgrown: just as the worth of a medicine to a sick person is altogether independent of the question whether he has a scientific opinion about medicine, or merely thinks about it as an old wife would do. A morality could even have grown out of an error, but with this knowledge the problem of its worth would not even be touched. Thus, no one has hitherto tested the value of that most celebrated of all medicines, called morality: for which purpose it is first of all necessary for one to call it in question. Well, that is just our work.

> 9. *Nietzsche has mentioned several mistakes that, in his opinion, people make when attempting to understand and criticize morality. Mention two of them. Do any of them seem correct to you? Discuss.*
> 10. *Nietzsche claims that certain "English" historians of morals are "unwittingly" under the influence of Christian ideas and are thus unable to criticize their own moral position. He undoubtedly is thinking of certain utilitarians (see Chapter 9). What are the "Christian superstitions" that he mentions?*

SLAVE MORALITY VS. ARISTOCRATIC MORALITY

Nietzsche's suspicion of morality leads him to the view that slavish values and resentments are at the base of moral beliefs and standards (from the *Genealogy of Morals*).

The revolt of the slaves in morals begins in the very principle of resentment becoming creative and giving birth to values—a resentment experienced by creatures who, deprived as they are of the proper outlet of action, are forced to find their compensation in an imaginary revenge. While every aristocratic morality springs from a triumphant affirmation of its own demands, the slave morality says "no" from the very outset to what is "outside itself," "different from itself," and "not itself": and this "no" is its creative deed. This turnabout [volte-face] of the valuing standpoint—this inevitable gravitation to the objective instead of back to the subjective is typical of "resentment": the slave morality requires as the condition of its existence an external and objective world, to employ physiological terminology, it requires objective stimuli to be capable of action at all—its action is fundamentally a reaction. The contrary is the case when we come

to the aristocrat's system of values: It acts and grows spontaneously, it merely seeks its antithesis in order to pronounce a more grateful and exultant "yes" to its own self; its negative conception, "low," "vulgar," "bad," is merely a pale, late-born foil in comparison with its positive and fundamental conception (saturated as it is with life and passion) of "we aristocrats, we good ones, we beautiful ones, we happy ones."

> 11. *Does it sound as though an aristocrat is a kind of "positive" thinker, a slave a "negative" thinker? Explain. What is the aristocrat positive about? What is the slave negative about?*

THE GREEKS AND ARISTOCRATIC MORALITY

Nietzsche thinks that in the ancient Greek writers we can find a conception of the "good" person as the proud person who is too far above ordinary folk to care what such people think or do. Only such Aristocrats, or noblepersons, are honest.

. . . Due weight should be given to the consideration that in any case the mood of contempt, or disdain, or superciliousness, even on the supposition that it falsely portrays the object of its contempt, will always be far removed from that degree of falsity which will always characterize the attacks—in effigy, of course, of the vindictive hatred and revengefulness of the weak in onslaughts on their enemies. In point of fact, there is in contempt too strong an admixture of nonchalance, of casualness, of boredom, of impatience, even of personal exultation, for it to be capable of distorting its victim into a real caricature or a real monstrosity. Attention again should be paid to the almost benevolent nuances which, for instance, the Greek nobility imports into all the words by which it distinguishes the common people from itself; note how continuously a kind of pity, care, and consideration imparts its honeyed flavor, until at last almost all the words which are applied to the vulgar man survive finally as expressions for "unhappy," "worthy of pity" . . . and how, conversely, "bad", "low," "unhappy" have never ceased to ring in the Greek ear with a tone in which "unhappy" is the predominant note: This is a heritage of the old noble aristocratic morality, which remains true to itself even in contempt. . . . The "well-born" simply felt themselves the "happy"; they did not have to manufacture their happiness artificially through looking at their enemies, or in cases to talk and lie themselves into happiness (as is the custom with all resentful men); and similarly, complete men as they were, exuberant with strength, and consequently necessarily energetic, they were too wise to dissociate happiness from action—activity becomes in their minds necessarily counted as happiness . . . all in sharp contrast to the "happiness" of the weak and the oppressed, with their festering venom and malignity, among whom happiness appears essentially as a narcotic, a deadening, a quietude, a peace, a "Sabbath," an enervation of the mind and relaxation of the limbs—in short, a purely passive phenomenon. While the aristocratic man lived in confidence and openness with himself (the term for "noble-born," emphasizes the nuance "sincere," and perhaps also "naive"), the resentful man, on the other hand, is neither sincere nor naive, nor honest and candid with himself.

12. *Mention four traits of the noble or aristocratic person. Mention four traits of the slavish person. Which do you admire? Which is most "moral" in the conventional sense?*

13. *Do you think Nietzsche is on to something in his criticism of morality? Give a brief statement of his main ideas.*

THE REAL REASON FOR HANGING ON TO MORALITY

Morality, as already indicated, is an expression of weakness. It is also a disguise, or clothing, to conceal our shame over the fact that we are willful immoral animals (from *Joyful Wisdom*).

Why We Can Hardly Dispense with Morality. The naked man is generally an ignominious spectacle—I speak of us European males (and by no means of European females!). If the most joyous company at table suddenly found themselves stripped and divested of their garments through the trick of an enchanter, I believe that not only would the joy-ousness be gone and the strongest appetite lost—it seems that we Europeans cannot at all dispense with the masquerade that is called clothing. But should not the disguise of "moral men," the screening under moral formulas and notions of decency, the whole kindly concealment of our conduct under conceptions of duty, virtue, public sentiment, honorableness, and disinterestedness, have just as good reasons in support of it? Not that I mean hereby that human wickedness and baseness, in short, the evil wild beast in us, should be disguised; on the contrary, my idea is that it is precisely as tame animals that we are an ignominious spectacle and require moral disguising—that the "inner man" in Europe is far from having enough of intrinsic evil "to let himself be seen" with it (to be beautiful with it). The European disguises himself in morality because he has become a sick, sickly, crippled animal, who has good reasons for being "tame," because he is almost an abortion, an imperfect, weak, and clumsy thing. . . . It is not the fierceness of the beast of prey that finds moral disguise necessary, but the gregarious animal, with its profound mediocrity, anxiety, and ennui. Morality dresses up the European—let us acknowledge it!—in more distinguished, more important, more conspicuous guise—in "divine" guise.

If we were strong, we would not have to disguise our "evil" behavior! And the disguise consists not only in our lip service to morality, but in our lip service to religion, the "divine" disguise.

14. *Nietzsche has been described as one of the "masters of suspicion." He is not suspicious of particular individuals, but of whole ways of living and thinking that are driven by unconscious motives. The way of living and thinking that we describe as "moral" or as concerned with morality is, he suspects, a subconscious cover-up for something. A cover-up (clothing) for what? Does it seem to you that there is something to this idea? Explain your answer.*

15. *If you studied Midgley, Chapter 1, recall her discussion of "amoralists" or antimoralists. She mentions Nietzsche as an example. Is Nietzsche*

passing a kind of moral judgment on those whom he considers to be "moralists"? Discuss.

The Human Crisis

ALBERT CAMUS

Camus was born in 1913 to a French-Algerian family from a poor, working-class district of Algiers. He seemed to be an outsider from the start, since he was not part of the Muslim majority in Algiers or a part of the wealthy and powerful French colonialist class. French literary culture attracted him, but he was at the same time repelled by the brutality of the colonial powers. He did move to France, and, when he was in his late 20s and early 30s, he participated in the underground resistance to the Nazi occupation of France during WW II. That experience marked his life deeply. He authored plays, novels and essays of cultural and philosophical criticism and was awarded the Nobel Prize for Literature in 1957 for having "illuminated the problems of the human conscience in our times." He refused to adopt any of the common religious, philosophical or political solutions to the problems of moral life. Thus the usual ways of "making sense" of life and morality were not available to him, with the result that life appeared to him as "absurd," beyond rational grasp. Like Nietzsche, he was important to the development of 20th century existentialism. Unlike Nietzsche, however, he clung to a notion of respect for ordinary humans and the value of simple human communities, even while denying any access to eternal ethical values. He died in an automobile accident in 1960.

The following remarks are excerpted from a lecture that Camus gave in the United States in 1946.

(from "The Human Crisis," in the journal *Twice a Year*, 1946–47)

The men of my age in France and in Europe were born just before or during the first great war, reached adolescence during the world economic crisis, and were 20 the year Hitler took power. To complete their education they were then provided with the war in Spain, Munich, the war of 1939, the defeat, and four years of occupation and secret struggle. I suppose

this is what is called an interesting generation. And so I thought that it would be more instructive if I spoke to you not in my own name but in the name of a certain number of Frenchmen who today are 30 years old, and whose minds and hearts were formed during the terrible years when, with their country, they were nourished on shame and learned to rebel.

Yes, this is an interesting generation, and first of all because, confronting the absurd world its elders had prepared for it, this generation believed in nothing and lived in revolt. The literature of their period was in revolt against clarity, narration, and even the phrase. Painting rejected the subject, reality, and even harmony. Music rejected melody. As for philosophy, it taught that there was no truth but only phenomena, that there could be Mr. Smith, M. Durand, Herr Vogel, but nothing common to these three particular phenomena. The moral attitude of this generation was even more categorical: Nationalism seemed to it a truth that had been transcended, religion a banishment, 25 years of international politics had taught it to doubt all the purities and to think that no one was ever wrong since everybody could be right. As for the traditional morality of our society, this was what it still seems to be to us, a monstrous hypocrisy.

Other generations in other countries had undergone this experience in other periods of history. But what was new was the fact that men, estranged from all values, should have had to adjust their personal position to the realities of murder and terror. It was at this point that they were led to think that there might be a Human Crisis, for they had to live the most heartbreaking contradictions. They entered the war as one enters Hell, if it is true that Hell is the denial of everything. They loved neither war nor violence; they had to accept war and exercise violence. They felt hatred only for hate. However, they had to apply themselves to the study of this severe discipline. In flagrant contradiction with themselves, without any traditional value to guide them, they had to confront the most grievous problems for men.

16. *Camus claims to be among those "estranged from all values." At the same time he rejects murder and violence, which seems to indicate that he certainly affirms certain "values." Is that*

the "contradiction" to which he refers? Is he be-ing inconsistent?

Camus goes on to provide four brief stories from the war that illustrate, he believes, some of the features of the "crisis in human consciousness" that humans are facing.

1. In an apartment rented by the Gestapo in a European capital, after a night of questioning, two accused, still bleeding and tightly bound, are discovered; the concierge of the establishment carefully proceeds to set the place in order, her heart light, for she had no doubt breakfasted. Reproached by one of the tortured men, she replies indignantly, "I never mix in the affairs of my tenants."
2. In Lyon, one of my comrades is taken from his cell for a third examination. In a previous examination his ears had been torn to shreds, and he wears a dressing around his head. The German officer who leads him, the very one who had taken part in the previous interrogation, asks in a tone of affection and solicitude: "How are your ears now?"
3. In Greece, after an action by the underground forces, a German officer is preparing to shoot three brothers he has taken as hostages. The old mother of the three begs for mercy and he consents to spare one of her sons, but on the condition that she herself designate which one. When she is unable to decide, the soldiers get ready to fire. At last she chooses the eldest, because he has a family dependent upon him, but by the same token she condemns the other two sons, as the German officer intends.
4. A group of deported women, among whom is one of our comrades, is being repatriated to France by way of Switzerland. Scarcely on Swiss soil, they see a funeral. The mere sight of which causes them to laugh hysterically: "So that is how the dead are treated here," they say.

The women described in the fourth case had probably witnessed mass murders and burials of people, perhaps Jews, gypsies or Poles, victims of genocide.

Camus goes on to describe how such dreadful acts impact human possibilities for relationship and care.

Men live and can only live by retaining the idea that they have something in common, a starting point to which they can always return. One always imagines that if one speaks to a man humanly, his reactions will be human in character. But we have discovered this: There are men one cannot persuade. It was not possible for an inmate of a concentration camp to hope to persuade the S.S. men who beat him that they ought not to have done so. The Greek mother of whom I spoke could not convince the German officer that it was not seemly for him to arrange her heartbreak. For S.S. men and German officers were no longer men, representing men, but like an instinct elevated to the height of an idea or a theory. Passion, even if murderous, would have been less evil.

Camus connects these evils to the prevalence of bureaucracy.

By means of paper, bureaus, and functionaries, a world has been created from which human warmth has disappeared, where no man can come in contact with another except across a maze of formalities. The German officer who spoke soothingly in the wounded ears of my comrade felt he could act thus because the pain he had inflicted was part of his official business, and, consequently, there was no real harm done. In short, we no longer die, love, or kill except by proxy. This is what goes by the name, if I am not mistaken, of "good organization."

Camus discerns a connection between bureaucratization and "the substitution of the political for the living man."

What counts now is not whether or not one respects a mother or spares her from suffering, what counts now is whether or not one has helped a doctrine to triumph. And human grief is no longer a scandal; it is only a cipher in reckoning, the terrible sum of which is not yet calculable. It is clear that all these symptoms may be summed up in the single tendency describable as the cult of efficiency and of abstraction. This is why

man in Europe today experiences only solitude and silence. For he cannot communicate with his fellows in
terms of values common to them all. And since he is
no longer protected by a respect for man based on the
values of man, the only alternative henceforth open to
him is to be the victim or the executioner.

17. *Camus thought that the Nazi regime provided
an example of the cult of efficiency and abstraction. On the basis of what you may know
or have heard about that regime, describe the
role in it of (a) efficiency and (b) abstraction.*

The response to such evils cannot, Camus claims,
be hope for a positive course to world history. The tyrants and murderers had precisely such a belief, and
they thought world history was on their side. Nor do
we, on his view, have access to the traditional moral
sources.

If the characteristics of this crisis are indeed the
will to power, terror, the replacement of the real by
the political and the historical man, the reign of ab-
stractions and of fate, solitude without a future, and
if we want to overcome this crisis, then these are the
characteristics we must change. And our generation
finds itself confronting this immense problem while
having nothing to affirm. It is in fact from its very ne-
gations that it has to draw the strength with which to
fight. It was perfectly useless to tell us: You must believe in God, in Plato, or in Marx, since the problem
was that we were without this type of faith. The only
question for us was whether or not to accept a world
in which there was no choice possible save whether
to be victim or executioner. And it goes without saying that we did not want to be the one or other, since
we knew deep in our hearts that even this distinction
was illusory, and that at bottom all were victims, and
that assassins and assassinated would in the end be
reunited in the same defeat. So the problem was no
longer merely whether or not to accept this condition and the world, but to determine what reasons we
could have for opposing them.

We had thought that the world lived and struggled without affirming any real value. And there we
were, fighting nevertheless against Germany. The
Frenchmen of the resistance whom I knew, and who

read Montaigne in the train transporting their pro-
paganda tracts, proved that it was possible, at least
among us, to understand the skeptics while at the
same time having a concept of honor. And all of us
consequently, by the mere fact of living, hoping , and
struggling, were affirming something.

But did this "something" have a general moral
significance—did it go beyond individual opinion—
could it serve others as a rule of conduct? The answer
is very simple. The men of whom I speak were willing
to die within the course of their revolt. And death so
met would prove that they had sacrificed themselves
for the sake of a truth transcending their personal
existence, beyond their individual destiny. What our
insurgents defended against a hostile fate was a value
common to all men. When men were tortured in the
presence of the concierge, when ears were hacked
with diligence, when mothers were obliged to condemn their children to death, when the dead were
buried like swine, these men, revolting, asserted that
something in them was being denied which did not
belong to them alone, but was a common good wherever men are truly ready for solidarity.

18. *There seems to be a tension in Camus' thought.
He refers to the skeptic Montaigne, whom he
read approvingly. Montaigne would agree with
Camus' earlier claim that there are no values
common to all people. At the same time Camus
claims to know something of general moral
significance. What is it that he claims to know?*
19. *Camus also refers to a "a truth transcending
personal existence." Are his earlier denials of
transcendent moral sources consistent with
this?*

As already pointed out, Camus associates politics with the evils of bureaucracy and the "cult of
abstraction." Politics may easily degenerate into
ideology, which belongs to the cult of "abstraction."
The abstraction in question consists largely in treating people as members of abstract classes or groups
(Jew, member of the superior race, "retarded" and so
forth), instead of thinking of people as individuals
with real lives of loving and hating, struggling and
suffering. The cult of efficiency is simply political bureaucracy in action. The abstractness of politics, as

Camus understands it, makes it unfit as a source for the struggle against evil.

Politics must, wherever possible, be put back in its rightful place, which is a secondary one. Its aim should not be to provide the world with a gospel, or a catechism, either political or moral. The great misfortune of our time is precisely that politics pretends to furnish us at once with a catechism, a complete philosophy, and at times even with a way of loving. But the role of politics is to set our house in order, not to deal with our inner problems. . . .

Finally, it is necessary to understand that this attitude requires that a universalism be created through which all men of good will may find themselves in touch with one another. In order to quit one's solitude it is necessary to speak, but to speak with candor, never to lie under any circumstances, and to tell all the truth that one knows. But one can speak the truth only in a world in which truth is defined and founded on values common to all men. It is not for a Hitler to decide that this is true and that false. No mortal man, today or tomorrow, can conclude that his truth is good enough to justify imposing it on others.

20. *Once again, Camus speaks of values common to all men. He suggests that these values are discovered, not invented at any individual's whim. What, then, does he mean when he says that no one can conclude that his truth is good enough to justify imposing it on others? Does he mean by "his truth" the personal views of someone (perhaps a "politician" like Hitler)? Does he imply that the values common to all men could not be "imposed" since they are already accepted?*

21. *Use your answer to the previous question to evaluate Camus' position. Answer the following three parts.*
    a. Is he consistent?
    b. Are his views plausible?
    c. What would he say to Thrasymachus, as portrayed in Plato's Republic *(see Chapter 2)?*

22. *Some contemporary educators complain that education has been "politicized." What sorts of things do you suppose they have in mind? Are they right? Would Camus have been troubled by such "politicization?"*

Toward the end of this essay, Camus says:

To sum up now, and to speak for myself for the first time, I would like to say just this: Whenever one judges France or any other country or question in terms of power, one aids and sustains a conception of man which logically leads to his mutilation, one encourages the thirst for domination and in the end one gives one's sanction to murder. As with real acts, so with thought. And he who says or writes that the end justifies the means, and he who says or writes that greatness is a question of power, that man is absolutely responsible for the hideous accumulation of crimes which disfigure contemporary Europe.

23. *Phillip Hallie, whose book* Lest Innocent Blood Be Shed *is excerpted in Chapter 10, tells of a letter he received after the publication of his book from a man who claimed that the defeat of the Nazis was made possible only by armies and nations and big political ideas. Individuals, he claimed, did not matter at all. Evaluate this claim from Camus' perspective.*

Further Discussion and Applications

Dostoevsky believed that evil is the result of rebellion against God and that goodness is only possible when people submit to God and humbly attempt to live according to God's revealed will. In particular, humans need certain virtues, such as humility, kindness, faith, hope and love, which they can only get from God as a gift.

Nietzsche, on the other hand, is suspicious of both religion and morality. The good/evil distinction is not, in his view, grounded in a divine ordering of the world or in any other transcendent source of goodness, nor can it be grounded in principles of reason or the notion of the "best kind of life" or self-interest. It is, instead, a distinction developed by the weak, to fend off the powerful. Thus what humans need is the will to power, the ability to assert themselves without any support from religion or any other "crutch."

Camus associates evil with ideological abstraction and the cult of efficiency.

Perhaps all of them are wrong about the nature of evil. Richard Taylor thinks they are.

Good and Evil as "Natural" (Taylor)

The American philosopher Richard Taylor would agree with Nietzsche that the good/evil distinction is not grounded in any transcendent source, but he argues that the good/evil distinction is grounded in facts of human nature, which make it a natural distinction rather than an artificial or conventional one, as Nietzsche supposed.

Taylor asks us to consider a universe in which there is no living thing. In such a universe it is clear, he thinks, that there could be no distinction between good and evil. In order for that distinction to arise, something must matter to a being, and nothing can matter to something dead, lifeless, incapable of feeling or sensation or enjoyment or pain.

Next Taylor asks us to imagine that we add to such a world beings or a being that is capable of perception and is perhaps rational, but that has no wants or desires or aversions or purposes (note that Aristotle would not agree that such beings could *be* rational). The beings in question would be "machine-like," and to them, also, nothing would matter. There could be no frustration of purposes, no pleasure taken in a sunset, no disgust at nauseous smells, and so forth. In such a world, once more there could be no distinction between good and evil. There would be facts of all sorts, the fact that it is cold, the fact that one of the beings is burning up or being run over. But since, by hypothesis, nothing matters to these beings, the notions of good and evil could not arise. Taylor admits that it may be somewhat difficult to imagine beings capable of perception, and thus sentient and alive, to whom nothing matters. If so, we can imagine them strictly as machines, and it will be clear then that the good/evil distinction cannot arise.

Finally, Taylor asks us to imagine a world in which there is one being of the type he calls *connative*. A connative being is one that has purposes, desires, aversions, aims of some sort. Such a being is capable of being frustrated in the pursuit of some goal or might possibly be able to fulfill a desire. With just one such being in the world, Taylor claims, the good/evil distinction becomes possible and exists only in relation to the wants and needs of that being. "Evil" would name things that frustrate that being's pursuits, and "good" would name the fulfillment of its purposes, desires, etc.

> 24. *By Taylor's account of the good/evil distinction there is nothing mysterious in it, nor is there any room for a sense of justice or injustice. All that is required for evil is the frustration of some being's desire or its inability to avoid something to which it is averse. Does this way of thinking about good and evil fit our intuitions about the kinds of evils described by Dostoevsky?*

Taylor then asks us to imagine a world that contains more than one such connative being. It is easy to imagine that with several such beings situations may arise where cooperation is valuable, insofar as it makes possible some good or avoidance of some evil. It might, for instance, be possible for two working together to kill an animal for food. Thus cooperation might bring about the good of satisfying hunger. Also, the possibility of conflict arises. One might have something the other needs or wants, and fighting may break out, fighting that might lead to injury or death to both and thus profit to none. Such a conflict would thus result in evil. In such a situation it is natural that "rules" should arise. By rules Taylor would have us mean no more than practices or agreed-on ways of doing things that introduce some regularity and predictability into behavior. Thus if one individual has a lot of food but is in need of clothing and another has lots of clothing and is in need of food, it would be natural that a regular way of trading would arise, which would advance the good of each. Likewise it would probably be to the good of each in the long run if they could rely on each other not to engage in violent attempts to get what they want. So a "rule" against such behavior might come into existence.

In this world, there is not only the possibility of good and evil, but the possibility of distinguishing right and wrong. Roughly, right actions will be those in accord with the rules, wrong actions those that violate the rules. Without rules, without some agreements and practices that enable me to expect others to behave in certain ways, there could be no right or wrong. If someone sneaks up on me and kills me in my sleep in order to get something of mine that he wants, then since my goal of living has been defeated, an *evil* has occurred, but absent any *rule* against such behavior, no one has done anything *wrong*. Thus, there is a clear distinction between some act being evil or producing evil and some act being wrong. Wrongness is only possible where there is a "rule," in Taylor's sense. And rules are only possible where there are two or more people and where the possibility of conflict and cooperation exists.

> With the multiplication of such beings, the possibilities of further goods and evils arise with the appearance of situations of cooperation and conflict. Thus, we can suppose that the multiplicity of sentient and purposeful beings by which our imaginary world is inhabited are men like ourselves, for we, too, are sentient and purposeful beings: We can suppose that those modes of behavior required for cooperation and the resolution of conflict situations become actual precepts, conveyed by one generation to the next, and that the most important of them come to be rules embodied in traditional literature for which men have a certain awe. They are, thus, passed from generation to generation, like the Ten Commandments of scripture. Others come to assume the form of written laws, and various practical means are hit on for securing, as nearly as possible, the adherence to them on the part of all. Groupings of men are formed for the attainment of the maximum of good for some or all and the minimization of evil. Thus do societies arise, by their common adherence to rules that become more elaborate as the societies themselves become larger and more complex. The behavior required by such rules rises, by some degree or other, to that level we call civilized conduct; but the basic principle of those rules remains exactly what it was from the outset: the minimization of conflict and its consequent evil, and the maximization of cooperation and its consequent good.
>
> All this is, of course, but a sketch, and a very superficial one, but no more is really needed for

our present purpose, which is to explain good and evil and moral right and wrong. (from *Good and Evil,* Part II, 1984)

It is worth noting that in the conception that Taylor is proposing, rationality is simply a name for an ability to find appropriate means to an end. If I want water in my camp and there is a stream a hundred yards away, it would be rational for me to take a vessel to the stream and fill it with water. That would be one effective way of getting what I want. If I have limited technical means, for example, nothing but a crude shovel, and the ground is mostly rock, it would be less rational under most circumstances to try to divert the stream to my dwelling. Rationality is simply a name for an ability to find more or less appropriate means to various ends. But the ends themselves are neither rational nor irrational. There is nothing "rational" in drinking water or in eliminating thirst. There is nothing irrational in them either. However, the frustration of a desire for water would be an evil, by Taylor's account. Similarly there is nothing irrational in killing someone to get what I want, though the result might be an evil for the victim. But it might nonetheless be rational to have a rule against killing people just to satisfy personal wants, since having such a rule might "minimize conflict and its consequent evil," including evils to me, which I, of course, want to avoid. Reason can tell me that such a rule might *work* as a means to the end of minimizing conflict. It cannot, however, tell me that such a rule is "good in itself," whatever that might mean. Taylor thinks of reason as an "instrument" for achieving nonrational ends. That conception of reason conflicts with the conceptions found in Plato, Aristotle and Aquinas.

In the subsequent chapters we will examine similar notions of the relation of moral distinctions to reason, as found in the writings of Hobbes and Mill.

25. *What does Taylor count as a "rule"? Give an example.*
26. *Suppose I shoot Bill dead in order to get his Porsche for myself. To the extent that doing that frustrates Bill's desire to keep on living and driving his Porsche, an "evil" has come into the world. But so far nothing has been done that is "wrong." What does it take to*

make my killing Bill not only evil but also wrong, according to Taylor? What do you think of Taylor's account?

**27. *Compare Taylor's notion of the character and role of rationality in morality to Aristotle's. Which seems more plausible to you, and why?*

**28. *Is there any way to account for Nietzsche's rejection of the good/evil distinction that would be consistent with Taylor's account? How or why not?*

Kinds of Evil and Wickedness (Benn)

Taylor's description of evil might provide a basis for distinguishing different kinds and levels of evil, but at first glance it does not. Also, his separation of the notions of right and wrong from the notions of evil and good seems initially plausible. But can it survive closer scrutiny? Ask, as you read the following discussion, whether Taylor's account can in fact do justice to all of our intuitions about the kinds and degrees of evil.

Australian philosopher Stanley Benn (1921–1986) distinguishes evils in nature and evils in persons. Evils in nature are what Taylor simply calls *evils*. They are the sort of thing that presuppose the existence of living, feeling beings with desires and purposes. Natural evil is, Benn claims, unproblematic, in just the way Taylor supposed. If a desire and need for water goes unmet long enough, a living being will die a terrible death from thirst. That is a terrible thing, an "evil."

But Benn wishes to focus on evil in human beings, which he calls *wickedness*. Wickedness is a characteristic of persons, not of acts. An evil act can be performed by someone who is not wicked, just weak. Also, someone who is full of hatred and malice, who spends his whole life wishing evil on others and rejoicing in other peoples' misfortunes, would be a wicked person even though he never managed, perhaps for reasons of disability, to do anything wrong.

Benn produces a categorization of types of wickedness and degrees of responsibility. He begins by considering cases of *self-centered forms of wickedness*. He includes in this category people who care only about their own group as well as those who care only about themselves, to the exclusion of others. Thus a chauvinist who proclaims "My country, right or wrong" would fit into this category. If in a given case the chauvinist's country is right and supporting its aims a good thing, it is nonetheless the case that the way the self-centered person pursues this good, without allowing the possibility of competing goods, is wicked.

The selfish person understands well enough that other people have interests and how the well-being of others could be a reason for doing or refraining from some action, but he simply disregards such reasons. In that respect he is unlike the psychopath, who does not even understand, in any but a conventional sense, that other people have interests and that their well-being counts in any way whatsoever. The psychopath cannot even be called wicked, though he is evil, for he does not genuinely recognize any moral constraints on his actions. The selfish person, on the other hand, is a wicked person even when he does not produce any great evils.

29. *Try to describe some feature of a person's life that explains, in Benn's account, how that person could be wicked even though he had never done anything wrong.*

30. *Does Taylor think there can be evil people? Does his account fail to explain our intuitive sense that someone who is spiteful and hateful is evil, no matter how much or how little damage (infliction of pain, etc.) he or she may cause? Justify your answers, and contrast Taylor to Benn.*

31. *Read the next paragraph with a view to answering this question: What is the difference between selfish wickedness and conscientious wickedness?*

Not all wickedness is selfish, however. What Benn calls *conscientious wickedness* consists in believing that one's ideals are universally valid and then seeking to implement them, even when doing so might bring great evils on many people. The ideal itself may be evil, as in the case of the committed Nazi's racist ideals. But it need not. Perhaps the ideals of some terrorists are not evil. They may even be good. For example, perhaps a united and truly Irish (and

Roman Catholic) Ireland would be a good thing. But the terrorist who pursues that ideal by slaughtering innocent men, women and children while feeling no pain in doing so is, according to Benn, wicked.

Politicians often make decisions that involve such evils. For example, President Harry Truman decided to use atomic bombs on Hiroshima and Nagasaki. That action indiscriminately destroyed innocent men, women and children. But he drew back from further bombings, reportedly out of pangs of conscience and a desire to avoid further evils of the same kind. He thus might escape the label *wicked* according to Benn.

32. *Do you think that Truman was wicked? Argue. Why might Benn think he was not?*
33. *Might Camus' concerns about the abstractness of politics have something to do with "conscientious wickedness"?*

The person who blindly follows orders, even though doing so involves great evils that he recognizes to be evils, is guilty of what Benn calls *heteronomous wickedness*. This sort of person is capable of acting rationally (like the psychopath) and also capable of acting autonomously. That is, she is capable of deciding for herself what to do, on the basis of principles she has acquired from moral and other kinds of training that have survived tests for coherence. The Nazi war criminal Adolph Eichmann might exemplify heteronomous wickedness. Eichmann apparently was capable of recognizing that, in following orders to slaughter Jews, he was acting in a way that did not cohere with his own moral convictions. He did in fact seek to rescue a few Jews at the request of a relative, though later he came to feel "guilty" for having done so. The later fact shows the extent to which such a person might become captive to the party, the ruler, the reigning ideology. But clearly there was a time when Eichmann could have, and should have, disobeyed orders.

It is worth noting that a person might be heteronomous, in the sense that he or she submits entirely to some external authority, without being wicked. If the authority in question was entirely benevolent, following its orders would always be a good thing to do. Nonetheless, the person who submits blindly, rather than submitting because he or she has seen that the authority in question is indeed benevolent, is a person who could easily be wicked, should they be unlucky enough to fall under the sway of some evil authority.

Further discussion of the distinction between heteronomy and autonomy can be found in the chapter on Kant (Chapter 8).

34. *Do you agree that someone who submits blindly to the authority of God or an apostle or prophet is potentially wicked simply because he submits in that way? Explain.*
35. *Huck Finn, in Mark Twain's novel* Adventures of Huckleberry Finn, *has a bad conscience about helping a slave escape. Would that be comparable to Eichmann's feeling guilty about helping out a few Jews? How do these two cases differ, if at all? (You can become familiar with Huck by reading the excerpt from Twain's novel in Chapter 7)*

There is, Benn believes, a kind of wickedness that consists in malignity . The *malignant* person desires some evil, say, the destruction of some person, *because* it is evil. Selfish wickedness, conscientious wickedness, and heteronomous wickedness all involve the idea that the wicked agent sees what she is doing as in some sense good, even though it may have evil effects. And it is the imagined good aspect that motivates the person. For example, the selfishly wicked person seeks his own good, though at the expense of others.

The malignant person, on the other hand, desires what he sees to be evil *because it is evil*. Socrates denied that there could be such a person. The Socratic position is that a person who does what is evil always does it because he mistakenly believes that it is good. Benn says,

> Socrates' paradox can be made plausible given a certain view of the motives of action. If we suppose that all intentional or voluntary action is undertaken with some aim, it must be supposed that what is aimed at must be desired; and if someone desires it, he must see it as a good thing to bring it about. Accordingly, for Socrates, whoever aims at

evil does so in ignorance of its true nature, under the misapprehension of it as good.

The trouble with Socrates' story is that it distorts the nature of true malignity. I said earlier that a malignant person recognizes the suffering of someone else as an evil and rejoices in it just because it is evil and that he would not rejoice in it were it not that he saw it as such. Even more perplexing, on Socrates' account, is the case of self-destructive action prompted by self-hatred. One must go a long and devious way round to find a good that such a person might believe that he was promoting in spiting himself. Clearly, if one aims at an outcome, then, in a rather weak sense, one must desire it; but it is not, even for the person desiring it, necessarily desirable on that account. For what is desirable is what it is appropriate to desire, and the malignant person desires things very often precisely because they are not appropriate. Consider the case of Claggart, the master-at-arms, in Herman Melville's story *Billy Bud*. Claggart conceives a hatred of "the Handsome Sailor," [Billy Budd] "who in Claggart's own phrase was 'the sweet and pleasant young fellow,'" and falsely charges him with sedition in order to destroy him. Claggart has no reason to hate Billy if by "reason" we mean reason of interest. There is no apparent good that can come to him, or anyone else, from the evil that will come about. So far from moving him to act for the sake of something he sees as a good, hatred moves him to spite and to destroy it. (from *Ethics,* 1985)

Some people might insist that Claggart sees and appreciates the good in Billy and is envious, wanting it for himself. He would thus be motivated by a frustration over the inability to achieve a good he recognizes, so in a sense he is still motivated by a perceived good. But such a view overlooks the actual details of the descriptions of Claggart that Melville supplies. Claggart hates the good in Billy and simply wants to destroy it rather than have it for himself. He is not envious. He is malignant. He takes as his "maxim" that goods he cannot have or embody are to be despised and that those who have them are to be hated, destroyed or made to suffer. If it is possible for

there to be such a person, then the Socratic position, which is that people always act for what they take to be their own good, will have been refuted by a counterexample. We could perhaps say that Socrates does not include "malignity" among the vices.

36. *Is it possible for there to be people like Claggart? Is the real motivation for Claggart's actions envy or spite after all? Argue pro and con.*
37. *Many people believe that there is at least one non-*human *being that is rightly described as malignant. Who might that be?*
38. *Briefly define each of the following:*
    Selfish wickedness
    Conscientious wickedness
    Malignancy

The Banality of Evil (Arendt)

A common assumption, in the discussions of evil so far in this section, is that evil actions are prompted by some vicious motivation, Benn's "wickedness" being an example. But perhaps some of the worst evils are committed by people who have no particularly vicious motivations but are simply meek conformists or thoughtless followers of an ideology or a leader. That was the view of Hannah Arendt (1906–1975), who was born in Germany but fled to the United States to escape Nazism. Arendt attended the trial of Adolph Eichmann, a Nazi war criminal who had supervised the transporting of millions of Jews to be murdered in prison camps. She claims that "except for an extraordinary diligence in looking out for his personal advancement, he had no motives at all." It would seem that if there is such a thing as "radical evil," Eichmann would exhibit it. But Arendt claims otherwise; it was "sheer thoughtlessness—that predisposed him to become one of the greatest criminals of that period. And if this is 'banal' and even funny, if with the best will in the world one cannot extract any diabolic or demonic profundity from Eichmann, that is still far from calling it commonplace." (*Eichmann in Jerusalem*, p. 288) It was, in fact, Arendt's avowed aim to undermine the sometimes-exciting or -titillating portrayals of demonic energy found in journalism and also in war films and fiction (Darth Vader might be a fictional example). That way of thinking of evil, as something positive and powerful, also makes it seem less commonplace, less likely to be found in ordinary citizens in their comfortable, ordinary homes. All such ways of thinking of evil are mistaken, in Arendt's view.

> It would have been very comforting indeed to believe that Eichmann was a monster. . . . The trouble with Eichmann was precisely that so many were like him, and that the many were neither perverted nor sadistic, that they were and still are terribly and terrifyingly normal. From the viewpoint of our legal institutions, and of our moral standards of judgment, this normality was much more terrifying than all the atrocities put together, for it implied that this new type of criminal, who is in actual fact *hostis generis humani,* commits his crimes under circumstances that make it well nigh impossible for him to know or to feel that he is doing wrong. (*Eichmann in Jerusalem,* p. 276)

Arendt's views here seem to come very close to those expressed by Camus in this chapter's selection. His focus on bureaucratic efficiency and an abstract indifference to the plight of actual human beings fits her account of Eichmann and the banality of evil.

There is another aspect to the critiques of both Camus and Arendt that deserves mention. Both of them note a kind of emptiness or vacuity on the part of the evildoers they describe. It is as though "no one is at home" in the case of such people. There is thus an implicit equation of goodness with substance, reality, being, and an equation of evil with nothingness. In an exchange with another Jewish scholar, Arendt wrote: "It [evil] is 'thought defying,' as I said, because thought tries to reach some depth, to go to the roots, and the moment it concerns itself with evil, it is frustrated because there is nothing. That is its banality. Only the good has depth and can be radical." ("Eichmann in Jerusalem," An Exchange of Letters between Gershom Sholem and Hannah Arendt, *Notes and Topics* 22 Jan. 1967, p. 56)

These remarks might bring to mind Plato's equation of Goodness with Being and of Evil with Nothingness. They are even more characteristic of Augustine, who understood evil as a privation, the absence of good. Thus it appears, despite Camus denial of the relevance of such traditional moral sources as Platonism or religion, that his own thinking, as well as Arendt's, comes close in spirit and sometimes in detail to those ancient thinkers.

39. *In what way is Arendt's account of the banality of evil similar to the accounts of each of the following?*
    a. Camus
    b. Plato/Augustine

The Vice of Self-Deception (Johnson)

Descriptions of extreme moral evil are shocking to most people. The behavior of the "well-educated, cultivated gentleman and his wife" who torments and murders a helpless child, described by Dostoevsky, or the actions of Claggart in Melville's story, or the actions of the Nazi doctor Franz Stangl, described by Stump in Chapter 4, or the German officer described by Camus may simply amaze "normal" people. And yet the people who perform such actions can also seem perfectly normal most of the time and may, as Arendt suggests, be almost comically banal. How do people who seem otherwise normal and even moral become evil? One vice in particular may help to explain this (unfortunately) common occurrence, namely, the vice of self-deception. Some of the ways of self-deception have already been described by Eleonore Stump in Chapter 4.

Samuel Johnson (1709–1784) provides a detailed account of the strategies people employ to deceive themselves about the evil in themselves. The vice of self-deception was certainly a concern of Socrates and many later writers. It is a vice because, among other things, it makes it easier for people to do what is evil or refrain from doing what is merely decent, not to mention what is positively good. Nietzsche castigates moralists in general for a kind of corrupt consciousness, in which the real motives for moral judgments are concealed. The sort of self-deception he has in mind is perhaps better described as "false consciousness," and it could infect entire cultures. However, even if Nietzsche has shown something important, his analysis does not tell us much about individuals or distinguish those who typically engage in self-deceptive strategies from those who do not.

Johnson would no doubt have considered that to be a defect in Nietzsche's work.

Johnson describes various "strategies" that enable people to think well of themselves even when they are wicked or vicious. He points out that a miser who performs one generous act may focus on that act and ignore the many times he has been stingy. He may even venture to be critical of others who are less "generous" than he. That is one strategy for avoiding the truth about oneself: Focus on any good deeds, however rare, and ignore the great mass of evil in oneself. On the other hand, a person who does evil frequently may take comfort in the fact that even the best of people act badly now and then and may construe his own *typical* nastiness as just like the occasional lapses of those who are more virtuous.

Another strategy consists in frequent verbal endorsement of goodness. A person who frequently praises virtue but seldom practices it may suppose that his verbal support for goodness actually makes him a good person too! One interesting version of this form of self-deception consists in thinking of oneself as a good person because one endorses humane causes and has correct and enlightened opinions about social matters, such as racism and poverty. The idea that one could be good by having good opinions was explicitly scoffed at by Aristotle. Johnson would scoff also.

Another strategy is to suppose that one is a good person simply because it is possible to find people who are worse. People who congratulate themselves for not having been Nazis or Stalinists or for not having lived like the Marquis de Sade would fall in this category. So would those who read Dostoevsky's descriptions of child abusers and congratulate themselves for not being one of those, or at least not so bad a one!

Johnson also considers possible remedies for self-deception. His comments on this matter run against Aristotle's claims about one of the values of friendship.

> For escaping these and a thousand other defects, many expedients have been proposed. Some have recommended the frequent consultation of a wise friend, admitted to intimacy, and encouraged to sincerity. But this appears a remedy by no means adapted to general use. For in order to secure the virtue of one, it presupposes more virtue in two than will generally be found. In the first, such a desire of rectitude and amendment, as may incline him to hear his own accusation from the mouth of him whom he esteems, and by whom, therefore, he will always hope that his faults are not discovered; and in the second such zeal and honesty, as will make him content for his friend's advantage to lose his kindness.
>
> A long life may be passed without finding a friend in whose understanding and virtue we can equally confide, and whose opinion we can value at once for its justness and sincerity. A weak man, however honest, is not qualified to judge. A man of the world, however penetrating, is not fit to counsel. Friends are often chosen for similitude of manners, and therefore each palliates the other's failings, because they are his own. Friends are tender and unwilling to give pain, or they are interested, and fearful to offend.
>
> These objections have inclined others to advise, that he who would know himself, should consult his enemies, remember the reproaches that are vented to his face, and listen for the censures that are uttered in private. For his great business is to know his faults, and those malignity will discover, and resentment will reveal. But this precept may be often frustrated; for it seldom happens that rivals or opponents are suffered to come near enough to know our conduct with so much exactness as that conscience should allow and reflect the accusation. The charge of an enemy is often totally false, and commonly so mingled with falsehood, that the mind takes advantage from the failure of one part to discredit the rest, and never suffers any disturbance afterward from such partial reports.
>
> Yet it seems that enemies have been always found by experience the most faithful monitors; for adversity has ever been considered as the state in which a man most easily becomes acquainted with himself, and this effect it must produce by

withdrawing flatterers, whose business it is to hide our weaknesses from us, or by giving loose to malice, and license to reproach; or at least by cutting of those pleasures which called us away from meditation on our conduct, and repressing that pride which too easily persuades us, that we merit whatever we enjoy.

Part of these benefits it is in every man's power to procure himself, by assigning proper portions of his life to the examination of the rest, and by putting himself frequently in such a situation by retirement and abstraction, as may weaken the influence of external objects. By this practice he may obtain the solitude of adversity without its melancholy, its instructions without its censures, and its sensibility without its perturbations.

The necessity of setting the world at a distance from us, when we are to take a survey of ourselves, has sent many from high stations to the severities of a monastic life; and indeed, every man deeply engaged in business, if all regard to another state be not extinguished, must have the conviction, tho', perhaps, not the resolution of Valdesso, who, when he solicited Charles the Fifth to dismiss him, being asked, whether he retired upon disgust, answered that he laid down his commission, for no other reason but because "there ought to be some time for sober reflection between the life of a soldier and his death."

There are few conditions which do not entangle us with sublunary hopes and fears, from which it is necessary to be at intervals disencumbered, that we may place ourselves in his presence who views effects in their causes, and actions in their motives; that we may, as Chillingworth expresses it, consider things as if there were no other beings in the world but God and ourselves; or, to use language yet more awful, "may commune with our own hearts, and be still."

40. *Give a label (you can use more than one word) to three of the strategies of the self-deceivers mentioned by Johnson and summarized in the preceding.*

41. *Does Aristotle's case for the value of friends as critics fall before Johnson's account? Why or why not? Remember that in Johnson's view self-deception may figure into our choice of friends.*

*42. *In Johnson's view, religious beliefs can play a very favorable role in the development of good character. Explain how that can work, and compare Johnson's view to Nietzsche's notion that religious beliefs and moral beliefs generally are themselves mired in self-deception. Which of them seems to you to have the more plausible view?*

The Qualities of Vice and Punishment (Augustine, Dante)

One advantage in an approach to ethics that focuses on virtues and vices, some philosophers claim, is that it brings us closer to the actual felt texture of moral life, with its many distinctions. *Right* and *wrong* are very general terms covering a host of different traits or actions. *Cruel, malignant, kind* and *generous,* on the other hand, are fairly specific; they provide "thicker" descriptions of actions and traits (see the discussion of "thick" moral concepts in Chapter 1). Most people know how to apply them, and they are, arguably, more central to daily thought about people, including oneself, than are the more abstract terms.

There is another factor that emerges from the following quotes. Some people hold that moral distinctions are grounded in the will of God, some hold they are grounded in self-interest, and others ground them in reason or in other ways. Nietzsche thought they were grounded primarily in self-deceiving weakness. But people who disagree in these ways are sometimes able to agree about how to describe someone who is cruel and also can often see the point in claiming that the virtuous are, as Aristotle argued, happy and the vicious miserable. Augustine, for example, who grounds moral distinctions in the will of God, provides a description of the miseries of living in vice, which can easily be recognized as accurate by people who do not even believe in God. In effect, both Augustine and Dante see that the punishment for vice can be construed as internal to vice. If virtue is its own reward, as people sometimes claim, vice is its own punishment.

(from Augustine, *On Free Choice of the Will*)

Surely the very fact that *disordered desire* rules the mind is itself no small punishment. Stripped by opposing forces of the splendid wealth of virtue, the mind is dragged by *disordered* desire into ruin and poverty; now taking false things for true, and even defending those falsehoods repeatedly; now repudiating what it had once believed and nonetheless rushing headlong into still other falsehoods; now withholding assent and often shying away from clear arguments; now despairing completely of finding the truth and lingering in the shadows of folly; now trying to enter the light of understanding but reeling back in exhaustion.

In the meantime cupidity* carries out a reign of terror, buffeting the whole human soul and life with storms coming from every direction. Fear attacks from one side and desire from the other; from one side, anxiety; from the other, an empty and deceptive happiness; from one side, the agony of losing what one loved; from the other, the passion to acquire what one did not have; from one side, the pain of an injury received; from the other, the burning desire to avenge it. Wherever you turn, avarice can pinch, extravagance squander, ambition destroy, pride swell, envy torment, apathy crush, obstinacy incite, oppression chafe, and countless other evils crowd the realm of *disordered* desire and run riot. In short, can we consider this punishment trivial—a punishment that, as you realize, all who do not cleave to wisdom must suffer?

43. *Give two everyday examples of the troubles Augustine mentions. For example, a covetous person who has got the lucrative job he coveted may very well worry a lot about losing it and, since he is covetous, will quickly become dissatisfied and want more.*

---

*cupidity = Extreme lust or desire, especially for the goods of others.

The Italian Dante Alighieri (1265–1321) is widely considered to be one of the greatest poets of all time and certainly one of the greatest Christian poets. One of the most vivid portrayals of the miseries of vice can be found in Dante's descriptions of those being punished in purgatory or damned in hell, included in his work *The Divine Comedy*. While it is possible to think of these descriptions as literal accounts of conditions suffered by the damned in a literal hell, it is also possible to see them as poetic renderings of what it is like even in this life to be trapped in various vices. Consider the following descriptions of those prone to excessive anger and of the slothful. (The "kind master" referred to is the Roman poet Vergil, whom Dante imagined as his guide through hell.)

(from *Inferno* Canto VII)

We crossed the circle, to the other bank, near a fount, that boils and pours down through a cleft, which it has formed.

The water was darker far than perse; and we, accompanying the dusky waves, entered down by a strange path.

This dreary streamlet makes a Marsh, that is named Styx, when it has descended to the foot of the grey malignant shores.

And I, who stood intent on looking, saw muddy people in that bog, all naked and with a look of anger.

They were smiting each other, not with hands only, but with head, and with chest, and with feet; maiming one another with their teeth, piece by piece.

The kind Master said: "Son, now see the souls of those whom anger overcame; and also I would have thee to believe for certain,

that there are people underneath the water, who sob, and make it bubble at the surface; as thy eye may tell thee whichever way it turns.

Fixed in the slime, they say: "Sullen were we in the sweet air, that is gladdened by the Sun, carrying lazy smoke within our hearts;

now lie we sullen here in the black mire." This hymn they gurgle in their throats, for they cannot speak it in full words."

Thus, between the dry bank and the putrid
  fen, we compassed a large arc of that loathly
  slough, with eyes turned towards those that
  swallow of its filth.

People who are, as we often say, "consumed" by
anger are prone to violence, even against themselves
in some cases. Dante's imagery brings out this consuming aspect and also alludes to the way in which
the whole body of an angry person is affected as he
seeks to strike out at the object of his anger.

Likewise the lazy, or slothful, cheat themselves of
"the sweet air." The slothful person is not someone
who habitually sleeps too much but when awake is
lively and alert to the joys life may offer. Rather, his
sloth pervades his entire life. Dante's description also
alludes to a kind of inarticulateness in slothful people.

It takes energy, effort, diligence to become articulate.
And being able to say what you mean, put thoughts
and feelings to words, can be immensely rewarding.
It is not a reward that is available to the slothful.

44. *Describe in some detail a vice that, in your
    view, makes a person miserable.*
*45. *Try to think of and describe an actual case of
    an angry or slothful person who fits Dante's
    description. Here is one example: In the 2006
    World Cup Soccer final, one player, seized
    with anger, butted another with his head,
    knocking him to the ground. Some people
    claimed that that angry action put the player
    in question into a kind of hell, and various
    facts about the case suggest that that descrip-
    tion is not overly dramatic.*

CHAPTER SIX

Egoism, Reason and Morality

Introduction

Plato and Aristotle no doubt had to lock their doors. They and other ancient as well as medieval thinkers obviously recognized that many people are trapped in vice and ignorance and given to evil deeds and are a threat to others and themselves. Nonetheless they also had some confidence in the power of reason and moral education to determine the content of a good life and to motivate people to seek wisdom. Many were confident that at least some people would be good by virtue of seeing the intrinsic value, and rationality, of being good. Only an ignorant fool lives unjustly, Socrates had claimed. Aristotle, Aquinas and others were also confident that a reasonable person would be motivated by an interest in the *common* good, since humans are profoundly "political," or social, animals.

That confidence was not universal in the ancient world, as the arguments of Glaucon (offered on behalf of Thrasymachus) in Plato's *Republic* indicate. But perhaps it was more common then than it is now. The kinds of connection between reason and goodness we found in Plato and Aristotle have been broken. Instead, in the modern era, reason has been construed as a morally neutral faculty, which can, at best, help to achieve our aims but cannot show which aims or goals are good or worth having. A common modern view is that stupid people can be morally

good (Forrest Gump) and that very rational or at least "smart" people can be evil (the evil scientists in many cartoons, for instance, or the infamous Dr. Hannibal Lecter).

Many modern thinkers have also questioned whether many people, however they may be motivated, are concerned with moral goodness at all. Moral pessimists argue that the belief in goodness to which many people cling would evaporate quickly were it not for the veneer of civilization that we take for granted but that could easily be stripped away. Deprived of that veneer and the sanctions against bad conduct it includes, we would all be exposed as barbarous and beastly, concerned only with personal survival. At the very least, if the support of police, the law and various social rules were stripped away, it would become apparent that we cannot be certain about the conduct of others. In such circumstances, a "reasonable" person would be careful to look out for number 1 and not rely on others. In such views there is no such thing as a genuine interest in the common good. Any appearance of concern for others is mere appearance, at best a device for pursing egoistic ends.

ORIENTING QUESTIONS FOR DISCUSSION

1. Do you think that everyone, including yourself, is basically selfish?
2. Political and economic arrangements seem to require that people cooperate to some extent. Does

that show that we really are interested in the welfare of others, or do we cooperate only for what we can get out of it for ourselves as individuals? State your view, and give some examples. (Here is one example: "I obey traffic rules only because of what I get out of doing so" or, on the contrary, "I obey traffic rules because life is better for all of us as a result and I want a good life for all.")

3. Is it more *reasonable or rational* to pursue self-interest and ignore the interests of others? For example, is it more reasonable for me to cheat rather than not to cheat on my income tax return or a philosophy exam when I know I can do so without getting caught? Consider some pros and cons.

4. Does your discussion in Orienting Question 3 show that a person who is immoral could be fully rational? Or does it instead show that being rational will usually make a person moral?

WILLIAM GOLDING

The British novelist William Golding (b. 1911) published his first and probably most famous novel, the one excerpted here, at the age of 43. Prior to achieving literary fame he graduated from Oxford university, worked as a schoolmaster and served in the British Navy during WW II. His wartime experiences of cruelty and suffering strongly influenced his ideas about human nature. His first novel remains his best known and most popular and was rendered as a film. Its pessimistic tone, its portrayal of human passions and the struggle to exert rational control, has marked most of his work since.

Lord of the Flies

The pessimistic way of thinking mentioned in the Introduction (people are by nature self-seekers who will stop at nothing to ensure their own survival) is illustrated very aptly in Golding's *Lord of the Flies*. In Golding's novel a group of schoolboys is stranded on a remote island after a plane crash. No adults survive. They quickly realize that in order to live decently and have some chance of being rescued, they will need rules and agreed-on procedures of various kinds. A fire is maintained on a hilltop as a beacon to any passing ship. An assembly is established where members may speak provided they hold the white conch, which the boys have adopted as a symbol of authority. Ralph, the son of a naval officer, is democratically elected as leader with limited powers. The older children take care of the "littluns," and various responsibilities are assigned to ensure that shelters will be built, food procured, the fire maintained, sewage disposed of properly. It is as though the children manage at first to draw from their civilized past. It is as though "Round the squatting child was the protection of parents and school and policemen and the law" (p. 78). Piggy, a chubby asthmatic with glasses, exhibits enough prudence to be counted as a kind of counselor. An epileptic boy, Simon, is credited with spiritual insight.

At the same time the children enjoy liberation from parental control, and before long problems arise. Rivalries develop, particularly between Ralph and Jack, the head choirboy. Responsibilities are shirked, the beach becomes filthy. Some try to free-load. Perhaps worst of all, the fire is neglected, so a chance for rescue by a passing ship is missed. We take up the narrative as some of those who should have maintained the fire return from hunting; Ralph vents his anger on them.

Ralph flung back his hair. One arm pointed at the empty horizon. His voice was loud and savage, and struck them into silence.

"There was a ship."

Jack, faced at once with too many awful implications, ducked away from them. He laid a hand on the pig and drew his knife. Ralph brought his arm down, fist clenched, and his voice shook.

"There was a ship. Out there. You said you'd keep the fire going and you let it out!" He took a step towards Jack, who turned and faced him.

"They might have seen us. We might have gone home—"

This was too bitter for Piggy, who forgot his timidity in the agony of his loss. He began to cry out, shrilly:

"You and your blood, Jack Merridew! You and your hunting! We might have gone home."

Ralph pushed Piggy on one side.

"I was chief; and you were going to do what I said. You talk. But you can't even build huts—then you go off hunting and let out the fire."

He turned away, silent for a moment. Then his voice came again on a peak of feeling.

"There was a ship."

One of the smaller hunters began to wail. The dismal truth was filtering through to everybody. Jack went very red as he hacked and pulled at the pig.

"The job was too much. We needed everyone."

Ralph turned.

"You could have had everyone when the shelters were finished. But you had to hunt—"

"We needed meat."

Jack stood up as he said this, the bloodied knife in his hand. The two boys faced each other. There was the brilliant world of hunting, tactics, fierce exhilaration, skill; and there was the world of longing and baffled common sense. Jack transferred the knife to his left hand and smudged blood over his forehead as he pushed down the plastered hair.

Piggy began again.

"You didn't ought to have let that fire out. You said you'd keep the smoke going—"

This from Piggy, and the wails of agreement from some of the hunters drove Jack to violence. The bolting look came into his blue eyes. He took a step, and able at last to hit someone, stuck his fist into Piggy's stomach. Piggy sat down with a grunt. Jack stood over him. His voice was vicious with humiliation.

"You would, would you? Fatty!"

Ralph made a step forward and Jack smacked Piggy's head. Piggy's glasses flew off and tinkled on the rocks. Piggy cried out in terror:

"My specs!"

He went crouching and feeling over the rocks, but Simon, who got there first, found them for him. Passions beat about Simon on the mountaintop with awful wings.

"One side's broken."

Piggy grabbed and put on the glasses. He looked malevolently at Jack.

"I got to have them specs. Now I only got one eye. Jus' you wait."

Jack made a move towards Piggy, who scrambled away till a great rock lay between them. He thrust his head over the top and glared at Jack through his one flashing glass.

"Now I only got one eye. Just you wait."

Jack mimicked the whine and scramble.

"Jus' you wait—yah!"

Piggy and the parody were so funny that the hunters began to laugh. Jack felt encouraged. He went on scrambling and the laughter rose to a gale of hysteria. Unwillingly Ralph felt his lips twitch; he was angry with himself for giving way.

He muttered.

"That was a dirty trick."

Jack broke out of his gyration and stood facing Ralph. His words came in a shout.

"All right, all right!"

He looked at Piggy, at the hunters, at Ralph.

"I'm sorry. About the fire, I mean. There. I—

He drew himself up.

"—I apologize."

The buzz from the hunters was one of admiration at this handsome behavior. Clearly they were of the opinion that Jack had done the decent thing, had put himself in the right by his generous apology and Ralph, obscurely, in the wrong. They waited for an appropriately decent answer.

Yet Ralph's throat refused to pass one. He resented, as an addition to Jack's misbehavior, this verbal trick. The fire was dead, the ship was gone. Could they not see? Anger instead of decency passed his throat.

"That was a dirty trick."

They were silent on the mountaintop while the opaque look appeared in Jack's eyes and passed away.

Ralph's final word was an ungracious mutter.

"All right. Light the fire."

With some positive action before them, a little of the tension died. Ralph said no more, did nothing, stood looking down at the ashes round his feet. Jack was loud and active. He gave orders, sang, whistled, threw remarks at the silent Ralph—remarks that did not need an answer, and therefore could not invite a snub; and still Ralph was silent. No one, not even Jack, would ask him to move and in the end they had to build the fire three yards away and in a place not really as convenient. So Ralph asserted his chieftainship and could not have chosen a better way if he had thought for days. Against this weapon, so indefinable and so effective, Jack was powerless and raged without knowing why. By the time the pile was built, they were on different sides of a high barrier.

When they had dealt with the fire another crisis arose. Jack had no means of lighting it. Then to his surprise, Ralph went to Piggy and took the glasses from him. Not even Ralph knew how a link between him and Jack had been snapped and fastened elsewhere.

"I'll bring 'em back."

"I'll come too."

Piggy stood behind him, islanded in a sea of meaningless color, while Ralph knelt and focused the glossy spot. Instantly the fire was alight. Piggy held out his hands and grabbed the glasses back.

Before these fantastically attractive flowers of violet and red and yellow, unkindness melted away. They became a circle of boys round a campfire, and even Piggy and Ralph were half drawn in. Soon some of the boys were rushing down the slope for more wood while Jack hacked the pig. They tried holding the whole carcass on a stake over the fire, but the stake burnt more quickly than the pig roasted. In the end they skewered bits of meat on branches and held them in the flames: and even then almost as much boy was roasted as meat.

Ralph dribbled. He meant to refuse meat but his past diet of fruit and nuts, with an odd crab or fish, gave him too little resistance. He accepted a piece of half-raw meat and gnawed it like a wolf.

Piggy spoke, also dribbling.

"Aren't I having none?"

Jack had meant to leave him in doubt, as an assertion of power; but Piggy by advertising his omission made more cruelty necessary.

"You didn't hunt."

"No more did Ralph," said Piggy wetly, "nor Simon." He amplified. "There isn't more than a ha'porth of meat in a crab."

Ralph stirred uneasily. Simon, sitting between the twins and Piggy, wiped his mouth and shoved his piece of meat over the rocks to Piggy, who grabbed it. The twins giggled and Simon lowered his face in shame.

Then Jack leapt to his feet, slashed off a great hunk of meat, and flung it down at Simon's feet.

"Eat! Damn you!" He glared at Simon. "Take it!"

He spun on his heel, center of a bewildered circle of boys.

"I got you meat!"

Numberless and inexpressible frustrations combined to make his rage elemental and awe-inspiring.

"I painted my face—I stole up. Now you eat—all of you—and I—"

Slowly the silence on the mountaintop deepened till the click of the fire and the soft hiss of roasting meat could be heard clearly. Jack looked round for understanding but found only respect. Ralph stood among the ashes of the signal fire, his hands full of meat, saying nothing.

Then at last Maurice broke the silence. He changed the subject to the only one that could bring the majority of them together.

"Where did you find the pig?"

Roger pointed down the unfriendly side.

"They were there—by the sea."

Jack, recovering, could not bear to have his story told. He broke in quickly.

"We spread round. I crept, on hands and knees. The spears fell out because they hadn't barbs on. The pig ran away and made an awful noise.

"It turned back and ran into the circle, bleeding—"

All the boys were talking at once, relieved and excited. "We closed in—"

The first blow had paralyzed its hind quarters, so then the circle could close in and beat and beat—

"I cut the pig's throat—"

The twins, still sharing their identical grin, jumped up and ran round each other. Then the rest joined in, making pig-dying noises and shouting.

"One for his nob!"

"Give him a fourpenny one!"

Then Maurice pretended to be the pig and ran squealing into the center, and the hunters, circling still, pretended to beat him. As they danced, they sang.

"Kill the pig. Cut her throat. Bash her in."

The barbarism of Jack and his followers increases, and the force of the agreements and symbols, such as the conch, that have tied the boys together in a community declines. The members of Jack's group begin painting themselves in savage colors.

One of the boys, frightened, reports seeing an unnatural beast. Piggy, always the source of common sense and science (and whose glasses represent one of the few remnants of civilization) denies the reality of ghosts and beasts. Such things do not fit into enlightened thinking, they fail to "make sense."

"'Cos things wouldn't make sense. Houses an' streets, an' TV—they wouldn't work."

But "sense" is declining, savagery is gaining the upper hand. Most of the boys abandon Ralph and form a wild band of hunters ruled by Jack. They set up their own camp. Only five, including Piggy, stay with Ralph. Piggy insists on confronting Jack and his followers. He declares his intentions:

I'm going to him with this conch in my hands. I'm going to hold it out. Look, I'm goin' to say, you're stronger than I am and you haven't got asthma. You can see, I'm going to say, with both eyes. But I don't ask for my glasses back, not as a favor. I don't ask you to be a sport, I'll say, not because you're strong, but because what's right's right. Give me my glasses, I'm going to say—you got to!

Led by Ralph he bears the conch, and they approach Jack's camp. Ralph blows the conch to call an assembly. "Savages appeared, painted out of recognition" and threaten Ralph and his group. They are challenged by Ralph.

"I've come to see about the fire," said Ralph, "and about Piggy's specs."

The group in front of him shifted and laughter shivered outwards from among them, light, excited laughter that went echoing among the tall rocks. A voice spoke from behind Ralph.

"What do you want?"

The twins made a bolt past Ralph and got between him and the entry. He turned quickly. Jack, identifiable by personality and red hair, was advancing from the forest. A hunter crouched on either side. All three were masked in black and green. Behind them on the grass the headless and paunched body of a sow lay where they had dropped it.

Piggy wailed.

"Ralph! Don't leave me!"

With ludicrous care he embraced the rock, pressing himself to it above the sucking sea. The sniggering of the savages became a loud derisive jeer.

Jack shouted above the noise.

"You go away, Ralph. You keep to your end. This is my end and my tribe. You leave me alone."

The jeering died away.

"You pinched Piggy's specs," said Ralph, breathlessly. "You've got to give them back."

"Got to? Who says?"

Ralph's temper blazed out.

"I say! You voted for me for Chief. Didn't you hear the conch? You played a dirty trick—we'd have given you fire if you'd asked for it."

The blood was flowing in his cheeks and the bunged-up eye throbbed.

"You could have had fire whenever you wanted. But you didn't. You came sneaking up like a thief and stole Piggy's glasses!"

"Say that again!"

"Thief! Thief!"

Piggy screamed.

"Ralph! Mind me!"

Jack made a rush and stabbed at Ralph's chest with his spear. Ralph sensed the position of the weapon from the glimpse he caught of Jack's arm and put the thrust aside with his own butt. Then he brought the end round and caught Jack a stinger across the ear. They were chest to chest, breathing fiercely, pushing and glaring.

"Who's a thief?"

"You are!"

Jack wrenched free and swung at Ralph with his spear. By common consent they were using the spears as sabers now, no longer daring the lethal points. The blow struck Ralph's spear and slid down, to fall agonizingly on his fingers. Then they were apart once more, their positions reversed, Jack towards the Castle Rock and Ralph on the outside towards the island. Both boys were breathing very heavily.

"Come on then."

"Come on."

Truculently they squared up to each other but kept just out of fighting distance.

"You come on and see what you get!"

"You come on."

Piggy, clutching the ground, was trying to attract Ralph's attention. Ralph moved, bent down, kept a wary eye on Jack.

"Ralph—remember what we came for. The fire. My specs."

Ralph nodded. He relaxed his fighting muscles, stood easily and grounded the butt of his spear. Jack watched him inscrutably through his paint. Ralph glanced up at the pinnacles, then towards the group of savages.

"Listen. We've come to say this. First you've got to give back Piggy's specs. If he hasn't got them he can't see. You aren't playing the game."

The tribe of painted savages giggled and Ralph's mind faltered. He pushed his hair up and gazed at the green and black mask before him, trying to remember what Jack looked like.

Piggy whispered.

"And the fire."

"Oh yes. Then about the fire. I say this again. I've been saying it ever since we dropped in."

He held out his spear and pointed at the savages. "Your only hope is keeping a signal fire going as long as there's light to see. Then maybe a ship'll notice the smoke and come and rescue us and take us home. But without that smoke we've got to wait till some ship comes by accident. We might wait years; till we were old—"

The shivering, silvery, unreal laughter of the savages sprayed out and echoed away. A gust of rage shook Ralph. His voice cracked.

"Don't you understand, you painted fools? Sam, Eric, Piggy, and me—we aren't enough. We tried to keep the fire going, but we couldn't. And then you, playing at hunting."

He pointed past them to where the trickle of smoke dispersed in the pearly air.

"Look at that! Call that a signal fire? That's a cooking fire. Now you'll eat and there'll be no smoke. Don't you understand? There may be a ship out there—"

He paused, defeated by the silence and the painted anonymity of the group guarding the entry. The chief opened a pink mouth and addressed Samneric, who were between him and his tribe.

"You two. Get back."

No one answered him. The twins, puzzled, looked at each other; while Piggy, reassured by the cessation of violence, stood up carefully. Jack glanced back at Ralph and then at the twins.

"Grab them!"

No one moved. Jack shouted angrily.

"I said 'grab them'!"

The painted group moved round Samneric nervously and unhandily. Once more the silvery laughter scattered.

Samneric protested out of the heart of civilization.

"Oh, I say!"

"—honestly!"

Their spears were taken from them.

"Tie them up!"

Ralph cried out hopelessly against the black and green mask.

"Jack!"

"Go on. Tie them."

Now the painted group felt the otherness of Samneric, felt the power in their own hands. They felled the twins clumsily and excitedly. Jack was inspired. He knew that Ralph would attempt a rescue. He struck in a humming circle behind him and Ralph only just parried the blow. Beyond them the tribe and the twins were a loud and writhing heap. Piggy crouched again. Then the twins lay, astonished, and the tribe stood round them. Jack turned to Ralph and spoke between his teeth.

"See? They do what I want."

There was silence again. The twins lay, inexpertly tied up, and the tribe watched Ralph to see what he would do. He numbered them through his fringe, glimpsed the ineffectual smoke.

His temper broke. He screamed at Jack.

"You're a beast and a swine and a bloody, bloody thief!"

He charged.

Jack, knowing this was the crisis, charged too. They met with a jolt and bounced apart. Jack swung with his fist at Ralph and caught him on the ear. Ralph hit Jack in the stomach and made him grunt.

Then they were facing each other again, panting and furious, but unnerved by each other's ferocity. They became aware of the noise that was the background to this fight, the steady shrill cheering of the tribe behind them.

Piggy's voice penetrated to Ralph.

"Let me speak."

He was standing in the dust of the fight, and as the tribe saw his intention the shrill cheer changed to a steady booing.

Piggy held up the conch and the booing sagged a little, then came up again to strength.

"I got the conch!"

He shouted.

"I tell you, I got the conch!"

Surprisingly, there was silence now; the tribe were curious to hear what amusing thing he might have to say.

Silence and pause; but in the silence a curious air-noise, close by Ralph's head. He gave it half his attention—and there it was again; a faint "Zup!" Someone was throwing stones: Roger was dropping them, his one hand still on the lever. Below him, Ralph was a shock of hair and Piggy a bag of fat.

"I got this to say. You're acting like a crowd of kids."

The booing rose and died again as Piggy lifted the white, magic shell.

"Which is better—to be a pack of painted niggers like you are, or to be sensible like Ralph is?"

A great clamor rose among the savages. Piggy shouted again.

"Which is better—to have rules and agree, or to hunt and kill?"

Again the clamor and again—"Zup!"

Ralph shouted against the noise.

"Which is better, law and rescue, or hunting and breaking things?"

Now Jack was yelling too and Ralph could no longer make himself heard—Jack had backed right against the tribe and they were a solid mass of menace that bristled with spears. The intention of a charge was forming among them; they were working up to it and the neck would be swept clear. Ralph stood facing them, a little to one side, his spear ready. By him stood Piggy still holding out the talisman, the fragile, shining beauty of the shell. The storm of sound beat at them, an incantation of hatred. High overhead, Roger, with a sense of delirious abandonment, leaned all his weight on the lever.

Ralph heard the great rock long before he saw it. He was aware of a jolt in the earth that came to him through the soles of his feet, and the breaking sound of stones at the top of the cliff. Then the monstrous red thing bounded across the neck and he flung himself flat while the tribe shrieked.

The rock struck Piggy a glancing blow from chin to knee: the conch exploded into a thousand white fragments and ceased to exist. Piggy, saying nothing, with no time for even a grunt, traveled through the air sideways from the rock, turning over as he went. The rock bounded twice and was lost in the forest. Piggy fell 40 feet and landed on his back across that square, red rock in the sea. His head opened and stuff came out and turned red. Piggy's arms and legs twitched a bit, like a pig's after it has been killed. Then the sea breathed again in a long, slow sigh, the water boiled white and pink over the rock; and when it went, sucking back again, the body of Piggy was gone.

This time the silence was complete. Ralph's lips formed a word but no sound came.

Suddenly Jack bounded out from the tribe and began screaming wildly.

"See? See? That's what you'll get! I meant that! There isn't a tribe for you anymore! The conch is gone."

He ran forward, stooping.

"I'm Chief."

Viciously, with full intention, he hurled his spear at Ralph. The point tore the skin and flesh over Ralph's ribs, then sheared off and fell in the water. Ralph stumbled, feeling not pain but panic, and the tribe, screaming now like the Chief, began to advance. Another spear, a bent one that would not fly straight, went past his face and one fell from on high where Roger was. The twins lay hidden behind the tribe and the anonymous devils' faces swarmed across the neck. Ralph turned and ran. A great noise as of seagulls rose behind him. He obeyed an instinct that he did not know he possessed and swerved over the open space so that the spears went wide. He saw the headless body of the sow and jumped in time. Then he was crashing through foliage and small boughs and was hidden by the forest.

The Chief stopped by the pig, turned and held up his hands.

"Back! Back to the fort!"

The original unity of the boys has been broken by theft, murder and a continuing rivalry between Ralph and Jack. Ralph is alone now, bruised, bloodied and hunted.

Ralph lay in a covert, wondering about his wounds. The bruised flesh was inches in diameter over his right ribs, with a swollen and bloody scar where the spear had hit him. His hair was full of dirt and tapped like the tendrils of a creeper. All over he was scratched and bruised from his flight through the forest. By the time his breathing was normal again, he had worked out that bathing these injuries would have to wait. How could you listen for naked feet if you were splashing in water? How could you be safe by the little stream or on the open beach?

Ralph listened. He was not really far from the Castle Rock, and during the first panic he had thought he heard sounds of pursuit. But the hunters had only sneaked into the fringes of the greenery, retrieving spears perhaps, and then had rushed back to the sunny rock as if terrified of the darkness under the leaves. He had even glimpsed one of them, striped brown, black, and red, and had judged that it was Bill. But really, thought Ralph, this was not Bill. This was a savage whose image refused to blend with that ancient picture of a boy in shorts and shirt.

The afternoon died away; the circular spots of sunlight moved steadily over green fronds and brown fiber but no sound came from behind the rock. At last Ralph wormed out of the ferns and sneaked forward to the edge of that impenetrable thicket that fronted the neck of land. He peered with elaborate caution between branches at the edge and could see Robert sitting on guard at the top of the cliff. He held a spear in his left hand and was tossing up a pebble and catching it again with the right. Behind him a column of smoke rose thickly, so that Ralph's nostrils

flared and his mouth dribbled. He wiped his nose and mouth with the back of his hand and for the first time since the morning felt hungry. The tribe must be sitting round the gutted pig, watching the fat ooze and burn among the ashes. They would be intent.

Another figure, an unrecognizable one, appeared by Robert and gave him something, then turned and went back behind the rock. Robert laid his spear on the rock beside him and began to gnaw between his raised hands. So the feast was beginning and the watchman had been given his portion.

Ralph saw that for the time being he was safe. He limped away through the fruit trees, drawn by the thought of the poor food yet bitter when he remembered the feast. Feast today, and then tomorrow.

He argued unconvincingly that they would let him alone; perhaps even make an outlaw of him. But then the fatal unreasoning knowledge came to him again. The breaking of the conch and the deaths of Piggy and Simon lay over the island like a vapor. These painted savages would go further and further. Then there was that indefinable connection between himself and Jack; who therefore would never let him alone, never.

He paused, sun-flecked, holding up a bough, prepared to duck under it. A spasm of terror set him shaking and he cried aloud.

"No. They're not as bad as that. It was an accident."

But they are as bad as that. Jack launches a hunt for Ralph. He even sets fire to the forest in an attempt to smoke him out. Jack is now fleeing for his life.

A nearer cry stood him on his feet and immediately he was away again, running fast among thorns and brambles. Suddenly he blundered into the open, found himself again in that open space—and there was the fathom-wide grin of the skull, no longer ridiculing a deep blue patch of sky but jeering up into a blanket of smoke. Then Ralph was running beneath trees, with the grumble of the forest explained. They had smoked him out and set the island on fire.

Hide was better than a tree because you had a chance of breaking the line if you were discovered. Hide, then.

He wondered if a pig would agree, and grimaced at nothing. Find the deepest thicket, the darkest hole on the island, and creep in. Now, as he ran, he peered about him. Bars and splashes of sunlight flitted over him and sweat made glistening streaks on his dirty body. The cries were far now, and faint.

At last he found what seemed to him the right place, though the decision was desperate. Here, bushes and a wild tangle of creeper made a mat that kept out all the light of the sun. Beneath it was a space, perhaps a foot high, though it was pierced everywhere by parallel and rising stems, perhaps a foot high. If you wormed into the middle of that you would be five yards from the edge, and hidden, unless the savage chose to lie down and look for you; and even then, you would be in darkness—and if the worst happened and he saw you, then you had a chance to burst out at him, fling the whole line out of step and double back.

Cautiously, his stick trailing behind him, Ralph wormed between the rising stems. When he reached the middle of the mat he lay and listened.

The fire was a big one and the drumroll that he had thought was left so far behind was nearer. Couldn't a fire outrun a galloping horse? He could see the sun-splashed ground over an area of perhaps 50 yards from where he lay: and as he watched, the sunlight in every patch blinked at him. This was so like the curtain that flapped in his brain that for a moment he thought the blinking was inside him. But then the patches blinked more rapidly, dulled and went out, so that he saw that a great heaviness of smoke lay between the island and the sun.

If anyone peered under the bushes and chanced to glimpse human flesh it might he Samneric, who would pretend not to see and say nothing. He laid his cheek against the chocolate-colored earth, licked his dry lips and closed his eyes. Under the thicket, the earth was vibrating very slightly; or perhaps there was a sound beneath the obvious thunder of the fire and scribbled ululations that was too low to hear.

Someone cried out. Ralph jerked his cheek off the earth and looked into the dulled light. They must be near now, he thought, and his chest began to thump. Hide, break the line, climb a tree—which was the best after all? The trouble was you only had one chance.

Now the fire was nearer; those volleying shots were great limbs, trunks even, bursting. The fools! The fools! The fire must be almost at the fruit trees—what would they eat tomorrow?

Ralph stirred restlessly in his narrow bed. One chanced nothing! What could they do? Beat him? So what? Kill him? A stick sharpened at both ends.

The cries, suddenly nearer, jerked him up. He could see a striped savage moving hastily out of a green tangle, and coming towards the mat where he hid, a savage who carried a spear. Ralph gripped his fingers into the earth. Be ready now, in case.

Ralph fumbled to hold his spear so that it was point foremost; and now he saw that the stick was sharpened at both ends,

The savage stopped 15 yards away and uttered his cry.

Perhaps he can hear my heart over the noises of the fire. Don't scream. Get ready.

The savage moved forward so that you could only see him from the waist down. That was the butt of his spear. Now you could see him from the knee down. Don't scream.

A herd of pigs came squealing out of the greenery behind the savage and rushed away into the forest. Birds were screaming, mice shrieking, and a little bopping thing came under the mat and cowered.

Five yards away the savage stopped, standing right by the thicket, and cried out. Ralph drew his feet up and crouched. The stake was in his hands, the stake sharpened at both ends, the stake that vibrated so wildly, that grew long, short, light, heavy, light again.

The ululation spread from shore to shore. The savage knelt down by the edge of the thicket, and there were lights flickering in the forest behind him. You could see a knee disturb the mold. Now the other. Two hands. A spear.

A face.

The savage peered into the obscurity beneath the thicket. You could tell that he saw light on this side and on that, but not in the middle there. In the middle was a blob of dark and the savage wrinkled up his face, trying to decipher the darkness.

The seconds lengthened. Ralph was looking straight into the savage eyes.

Don't scream.

You'll get back.

Now he's seen you. He's making sure. A stick sharpened.

Ralph screamed, a scream of fright and anger and desperation. His legs straightened, the screams became continuous and foaming. He shot forward, burst the thicket, was in the open, screaming, snarling, bloody. He swung the stake and the savage tumbled over; but there were others coming towards him, crying out. He swerved as a spear flew past and then was silent, running. All at once the lights flickering ahead of him merged together, the roar of the forest rose to thunder and a tall bush directly in his path burst into a great fan-shaped flame. He swung to the right, running desperately fast, with the heat beating on his left side and the fire racing forward like a tide. The ululation rose behind him and spread along, a series of short sharp cries, the sighting call. A brown figure showed up at his right and fell away. They were all running, all crying out madly. He could hear them crashing in the undergrowth and on the left was the hot, bright thunder of the fire. He forgot his wounds, his hunger and thirst, and became fear; hopeless fear on flying feet, rushing through the forest towards the open beach. Spots jumped before his eyes and turned into red circles that expanded quickly till they passed out of sight. Below him, someone's legs were getting tired and the desperate ululation advanced like a jagged fringe of menace and was almost overhead.

He stumbled over a root and the cry that pursued him rose even higher. He saw a shelter burst into flames and the fire flapped at his right shoulder and there was the glitter of water. Then he was down, rolling over and over in the warm sand, crouching with arm up to ward off, trying to cry for mercy.

He staggered to his feet, tensed for more terrors, and looked up at a huge peaked cap. It was a white-topped cap, and above the green shade of the peak was a crown, an anchor, gold foliage. He saw white drill, epaulettes, a revolver, a row of gilt buttons down the front of a uniform.

A naval officer stood on the sand, looking down at Ralph in wary astonishment. On the beach behind him was a cutter, her bows hauled up and held by two ratings [noncommissioned sailors]. In the stern-sheets another rating held a submachine gun.

The ululation faltered and died away.

The officer looked at Ralph doubtfully for a moment, then took his hand away from the butt of the revolver.

"Hullo."

Squirming a little, conscious of his filthy appearance, Ralph answered shyly.

"Hullo."

The officer nodded, as if a question had been answered.

"Are there any adults—any grownups with you?"

Dumbly, Ralph shook his head. He turned a half pace on the sand. A semicircle of little boys, their bodies streaked with colored clay, sharp sticks in their hands, were standing on the beach making no noise at all.

"Fun and games," said the officer.

The fire reached the coconut palms by the beach and swallowed them noisily. A flame, seemingly detached, swung like an acrobat and licked up the palm heads on the platform. The sky was black.

The officer grinned cheerfully at Ralph.

"We saw your smoke. What have you been doing? Having a war or something?"

Ralph nodded.

The officer inspected the little scarecrow in front of him. The kid needed a bath, a haircut, a nose wipe, and a good deal of ointment.

"Nobody killed, I hope? Any dead bodies?"

"Only two. And they've gone."

The officer leaned down and looked closely at Ralph.

"Two? Killed?"

Ralph nodded again. Behind him, the whole island was shuddering with flame. The officer knew, as a rule, when people were telling the truth. He whistled softly.

Other boys were appearing now, tiny tots some of them, brown, with the distended bellies of small savages. One of them came close to the officer and looked up.

"I'm, I'm . . ."

But there was no more to come. Percival Wemys Madison sought in his head for an incantation that had faded clean away.

The officer turned back to Ralph.

"We'll take you off. How many of you are there?"

Ralph shook his head. The officer looked past him to the group of painted boys.

"Who's boss here?"

"I am," said Ralph loudly.

A little boy who wore the remains of an extraordinary black cap on his red hair and who carried the remains of a pair of spectacles at his waist, started forward, then changed his mind and stood still.

"We saw your smoke. And you don't know how many of you there are?"

"No, sir."

"I should have thought," said the officer as he visualized the search before him, "I should have thought that a pack of British boys—you're all British aren't you?—would have been able to put up a better show than that—I mean—"

"It was like that at first," said Ralph, "before things—" He stopped.

"We were together then—" The officer nodded helpfully.

"I know. Jolly good show. Like the Coral Island."

Ralph looked at him dumbly. For a moment he had a fleeting picture of the strange glamour that had once invested the beaches. But the island was scorched up like dead wood—Simon was dead—and Jack had . . . The tears began to flow and sobs shook him. He gave himself up to them now for the first time on the island, great, shuddering spasms of grief that seemed to wrench his whole body. His voice rose under the black smoke before the burning wreckage of the island; and infected by that emotion, the other little boys began to shake and sob too. And in the middle of them, with filthy body, matted hair, and unwiped nose, Ralph wept for the end of innocence, the darkness of man's heart, and the fall through the air of the true, wise friend called Piggy.

The officer, surrounded by these noises, was moved and a little embarrassed. He turned away to give them time to pull themselves together; and waited, allowing his eyes to rest on the trim cruiser in the distance.

Golding's story is clearly allegorical. It might not be quite psychologically realistic. Perhaps a typical group of children would in fact have "stuck to-

gether," but certainly the dangers of rivalries breaking out are psychologically realistic. In any case, this allegory brings to consciousness in a vivid way a pessimistic view of human nature. Without the control of laws, police and other restraining influences, people might very well sink into barbarism, stealing, killing at random and seeking the maximum in self-indulgence. Golding implies that where external restraints are absent, people are revealed as murderous savages.

One only needs to watch the news to know how close to the surface the barbarism Golding describes really is and how frequently it breaks through. In the midst of such a world, what is the status of moral constraints and ideals of virtue? Recall that Piggy proclaims that he will confront Jack and demand the return of his glasses "because it is right." Piggy lacks power but he thinks he has the "right" on his side. Compare this to the argument between Thrasymachus and Socrates in the *Republic*. According to Thrasymachus, justice *is* power (might is right). So Piggy is deluded in thinking he has right on his side when he is so weak. An individual like Jack, who is able to impose his will on others, is able to make up "rules of justice" to suit himself and his appetites.

1. *What could Piggy appeal to in his claim that "it is right" that his glasses be returned? Consider some of the answers discussed so far in this text, and discuss whether any of them seem convincing to you.*
2. *Could any of them be made to seem convincing to Jack? Discuss.*

There are, however, constraints on even the most powerful individuals. Jack gets control of most of the boys, but he is a "loose cannon" who, in his desire to get rid of Ralph, destroys the means of his own subsistence by setting fire to the entire island. Now, it seems that any of the boys might kill, but it will be with a "stick sharpened at both ends," that is, with one end pointing at oneself. In fact, it is the heedless pursuit of self-centered interests that initiates the disintegration of the group. Once set loose, egoistic impulses stop at nothing, not even murder. The result is that no one is truly safe, except to the extent that they can get protection from a strong leader like Jack.

Even then they are not entirely safe, from either each other, themselves or Jack.

> 3. *Most of the boys follow the leader who will give them the most satisfactions and imposes the fewest rules. Are they all becoming dangerous to one another? Discuss.*

At the end of the story the boys are rescued by a British naval officer. As the officer stands on the beach with Ralph, he glances out to sea where his armed cruiser is anchored. He is part of an expedition that is hunting down enemies. He is part of war.

> *4. *The naval officer rescues Ralph. But does he bring him into a safe world, one unthreatened by any kind of barbarism? Explain your answer.*

The temporary "civilization" the boys manage to construct at the beginning of Golding's allegory depends on some willingness to give up egoistic claims, and it is made possible by institutions that are reinforced by symbols, such as the conch.

> 5. *Give some examples of symbolic objects or actions familiar to you. Think about civic institutions, the law, etc. For example, consider the symbols that are employed in courtrooms. In your opinion do these symbols contribute to social cohesion? Would their loss or destruction be a dangerous thing? Explain.*

Whether Human Nature Is Inherently Good or Evil: Mencius and Hsun-Tzu

Egoism and altruism, evil and goodness, seem to be inescapable concepts that we use in thinking about ourselves and others, so it should be no surprise that they have been discussed in philosophical traditions around the world. One of the more lively disputes took place among Confucian philosophers in China in the fourth and third centuries BCE. The specific issue under debate was whether human nature was inherently good or evil; but in the course of the de-

bate it is clear that selfishness is treated as a central component in an evil person's character.

People Are Inherently Good

MENCIUS

Mencius (390–305 BCE)—also called Mengzi—lived a century or so after Confucius, and, within the Confucian tradition, his writings are second in importance only to those of his great master. Mencius believed that human nature is inherently good. In the next selection, he debates the issue with the skeptical philosopher Kao-tzu (420–350 BCE), who holds that human nature is neither good nor evil but can be fashioned in either direction through environmental influences.

(From *The Mencius* Book 6)

[KAO:] Human nature is like a tree, and righteousness is like a wooden cup or a bowl. The fashioning of benevolence and righteousness out of a person's nature is like the making of cups and bowls from the tree.

[MENCIUS:] Without touching the nature of the tree, can you make it into cups and bowls? You must do violence and injury to the tree before you can make cups and bowls with it. If you must do violence and injury to the tree in order to make cups and bowls with it, on your principles you must in the same way do violence and injury to humanity in order to fashion from it benevolence and righteousness. Thus, your words would certainly lead all people on to consider benevolence and righteousness to be calamities.

[KAO:] Human nature is like water whirling around in a corner. Open a passage for it to the east, and it will flow to the east. Open a passage for it to the west, and it will flow to the west. Human nature is indifferent to good and evil, just as water is indifferent to the east and west.

[MENCIUS:] Water indeed will flow indifferently to the east or west, but will it flow indifferently up or down? The tendency of human nature to do good is like the tendency of water to flow downwards. All people have this tendency to good, just as all water flows downwards. Now, by striking water and causing it to leap up, you may make it go over your forehead, and, by damming and leading it, you may force it up a hill. But are such movements according to the nature of water? It is the force applied which causes them. When people are made to do what is not good, their nature is dealt with in this way.

6. *Mencius believes that water naturally flows downward but can be forced to leap up by striking it. What does the act of striking water represent in this analogy?*

What precisely does it mean to say that human nature is inherently good? According to Mencius, this means that we all have certain emotions that direct us to follow moral principles.

[KUNG-TU:] The philosopher Kao says that human nature is neither good nor bad. Some say that human nature may be made to practice good and it may be made to practice evil. . . . Others say that the nature of some is good, and the nature of others is bad. . . . And now you say that human nature is good. Are all those other views, then, wrong?
[MENCIUS:] From the feelings proper to it, human nature is constituted for the practice of what is good. This is what I mean in saying human nature is good. If people do what is not good, the blame cannot be placed on their natural powers. The feeling of commiseration belongs to all people. So do that of shame and dislike, and that of reverence and respect, and that of approving and disproving. The feeling of commiseration implies the principle of humanity. The feelings of shame and dislike imply the principle of righteousness. The feelings of reverence and respect imply the principle of social custom. The feelings of approving and disapproving imply the principle of knowledge. Humanity, righteousness, social custom, and knowledge are not infused into us from outside factors. We are certainly furnished with them. Any different view simply owes to an absence of reflection. Hence it is said, "Look and you will find them. Neglect and you

will lose them." People differ from one another in regard to them: some have twice as much as others, some five times as much, and some to an incalculable amount. This is because they cannot fully carry out their natural powers. The *Book of Poetry* states that "In producing humankind, heaven gave people their various faculties and relations with their specific laws. These are the invariable rules of nature for everyone to hold; all love this admirable virtue." Confucius said, "The writer of this ode indeed knows the principle of our nature." We may thus see that every faculty and relation must have its law, and since there are invariable rules for all to hold, they consequently love this admirable virtue.

7. *Explain why, in your view, feelings of "shame" imply the "principle of righteousness" (you will have to try to figure out what that principle is).*

Mencius/Confucius claim that "heaven" gave humans "rules" of nature to guide behavior. Some scholars argue that Confucius was a purely secular thinker, but others stress his debt to traditional Chinese religion, in which "heaven" is practically equivalent to God.

8. *If the latter view is correct, would Mencius/ Confucius agree with Aquinas (Chapter 4) that humans have a built-in ability to recognize a single pattern of life, which when followed leads to human fulfillment and conformity to a kind of "natural law"?*

People Are Inherently Evil

HSUN-TZU

Even more skeptical than Kao-tzu, the Confucian philosopher Hsun-tzu (298–238 BCE) held the more extreme view that human nature is inherently bad—principally because of our selfish tendencies. Like Kao-tzu and Mencius, Hsun-tzu too recognized the importance of environmental influence in altering conduct, but he stresses the importance of positive environmental influence, given the naturally evil tendencies in people. We should not take this need lightly if we hope to live in a civilized society.

(from *The Hsun-Tzu*, Chapter 17)

Human nature is evil and the good that we show is artificial. Even at birth human nature includes the love of gain. Since we act according to our desires, conflict and robberies emerge. We will not find self-denial and altruism. Human nature includes envy and dislike, and as actions are in accordance with these, violence and injuries spring up, whereas loyalty and faith do not. Human nature includes the desires of the ears and the eyes, leading to the love of sounds and beauty. And as the actions are in accordance with these, lewdness and disorder spring up, whereas righteousness and social custom, with their various orderly displays, do not. It thus appears that following human nature and yielding to its feelings will surely create strife and theft. It will lead to violation of everyone's duties and disruption of all order, until we are in a state of savagery. We must have the influence of teachers and laws, and the guidance of social custom and righteousness. For, from these we get self-denial, altruism, and an observance of the well-ordered regulations of conduct, which results in a state of good government. From all this it is plain that human nature is evil; the good which it shows is artificial.

Consider some illustrations. A crooked stick must be submitted to the pressing-frame to soften and bond it, and then it becomes straight. A blunt knife must be submitted to the grindstone and whetstone, and then it becomes sharp. Similarly, human nature, being evil, must be submitted to teachers and laws, and then it becomes correct. It must be submitted to social custom and righteousness, and then it is capable of being governed. If people were without teachers and laws, our condition would be one of deviation and insecurity, and would be entirely wrong. If we were without social custom and righteousness, our condition would be one of rebellious disorder and we would reject all government. The sage kings of old understood that human nature was evil, in a state of hazardous deviation, improper, rebellious, disorderly, and resistant to governance. Accordingly, they set up the principles of righteousness and social custom, and framed laws and regulations. These efforts served to straighten and embellish our natural

feelings. They correct them, tame them, change them and guide them. By this means we might proceed on a path of moral governance which is in agreement with reason. Now, the superior person is the one who is transformed by teachers and laws. He takes on the distinction of learning, and follows the path of social custom and righteousness. The inferior person is the one who follows his nature and its feelings, indulges its resentments, and walks contrary to social custom and righteousness. Looking at the subject in this way, we see clearly that human nature is evil, and the good that it shows is artificial.

9. *According to Hsun-tzu, what are the main environmental influences that shape people toward moral goodness?*

Hsun-tzu believes that in order to resolve the dispute over human nature we must understand precisely what it means for a quality to be natural or artificial. Mencius, he contends, failed to do that.

Mencius said, "Man has only to learn, and his nature appears to be good"; but I reply, It is not so. To say so shows that he had not attained to the knowledge of human nature, nor examined into the difference between what is natural in people and what is artificial. The natural is what the constitution spontaneously moves to: It does not need to be learned, it does not need to be followed hard after. Propriety and righteousness are what the sages have given birth to: It is by learning that people become capable of them, it is by hard practice that they achieve them. That which is in people—not needing to be learned and striven after—is what I call natural. That in people which is attained to by learning, and achieved by hard striving, is what I call artificial. This is the distinction between those two. By human nature, eyes are capable of seeing and ears are capable of hearing. But the power of seeing is inseparable from the eyes, and the power of hearing is inseparable from the ears. It is plain that the faculties of seeing and hearing do not need to be learned.

Mencius says, "The nature of man is good, but all lose and ruin their nature, and therefore it becomes bad." But I say that this representation is erroneous. People being born with their nature, when they thereafter depart from its simple constituent elements, must lose it. From this consideration we may see clearly that human nature is evil. What might be called the nature's being good, would be if there were no departing from its simplicity to beautify it, no departing from its elementary dispositions to sharpen it. Suppose that those simple elements no more needed beautifying, and the mind's thoughts no more needed to be turned to good, than the power of vision, which is inseparable from the eyes, and the power of hearing, which is inseparable from the ears, need to be learned. Then we might say that human nature is good, just as we say that eyes see and ears hear. It is human nature, when hungry, to desire to be filled; when cold, to desire to be warmed; when tired, to desire rest. These are the feelings and nature of people.

10. *According to Hsun-tzu, what does it mean to say that a particular human tendency is natural?*

Imagine, for example, that a person is hungry in the presence of an elder, but does not dare to sit before him. He instead yields to that elder; tired with labor, he nevertheless does not dare to ask for rest. Imagine similarly a son's yielding to his father and a younger brother to his elder; or, a son's laboring for his father and a younger brother for his elder. These examples illustrate conduct that is contrary to nature and against one's feelings. However, these actions are in accord with the course laid down for a filial son, and to the refined distinctions of propriety and righteousness. It appears, then, that if feelings and nature were in accord with each other, there would be no self-denial and yielding to others. Self-denial and yielding to others are simply contrary to the feelings and the nature. In this way we come to see how clear it is that human nature is evil, and the good which it shows is artificial.

One might ask, "If human nature is evil, what is the source of social custom and righteousness?" I reply, all social custom and righteousness are the artificial productions of the sages, and should not be thought of as growing out of human nature. It is just as when a potter makes a vessel from the clay. The vessel is the product of the workman's art, and

should not be thought of as growing out of human nature. Or it is as when another workman cuts and hews a vessel out of wood; it is the product of his art, and is not to be considered as growing out of human nature. The sages pondered long in thought and gave themselves to practice, and so they succeeded in producing social custom and righteousness, and setting up laws and regulations. In this way social custom and righteousness, laws and regulations, are artificial products of the sages, and should not be seen as growing properly from human nature.

11. *What, for Hsun-tzu, is the ultimate source of all social custom and righteousness? Does his view seem plausible to you? Explain.*

Social Rules, Egoism and Morality: Hobbes' *Leviathan*

THOMAS HOBBES

Thomas Hobbes (1588–1679) was born in Wiltshire, England, at a time when conflicts between royalists and antiroyalists of various kinds were beginning to heat up. He spent most of his life as a tutor, traveling companion, business agent and political consultant to English aristocrats. His travels brought him into contact with major continental thinkers who were developing a groundwork for the new science and a materialistic theory of nature. It is possible that on one journey to Italy he met the great astronomer and physicist Galileo. His interest in the new science increased throughout his career and led to the development of views about human psychology that played an important role in his ethical views. In particular he gave up the Aristotelian notions of virtue and emotion that had dominated much of the intellectual landscape in the 17th century. Those views stressed that people can shape themselves and educate their emotions. In place of those views he developed mechanistic ideas of desire and fear as forces propelling people into conflict.

Hobbes' views on the need for strong centralized authority in government made him a natural ally of the royalists. When the English King Charles I was de-

posed and executed in 1640, Hobbes joined other exiles with royalist sympathies in Paris. In England civil war between royalists and puritans raged. Although he favored the kind of strong rule that Charles had tried to impose, Hobbes did not favor a strong role for the established church that many royalists cherished. He acquired a reputation as an atheist, and when the monarchy was restored, after years of civil war, Hobbes was nearly condemned as a heretic, even though he continued to enjoy royal favor and the support of the aristocracy.

Hobbes saw what can happen when central authority is lost, namely, civil war and danger for all. The events that transpired in England during his mature years must have seemed like a verification of his rather grim view of humanity. People are, he thinks, simply unable to live in community without virtually dictatorial power enforcing conformity.

Hobbes had a conception of human nature similar in many respects to that expressed in Golding's story. Hobbes supposed that without the restraining influences of a strong leader, people would be at each other's throats constantly, and no one would be safe. The starting point for Hobbes' moral theory is the psychological position that humans are essentially machinelike, unable to operate on any other motive than the desire to survive. Even supposedly charitable acts are, in his view, motivated by self-interest and the desire for power over others. In his book *Leviathan* (1651) Hobbes speculates about how people would behave in a state of nature, prior to the formation of any government.

The State of Nature: Equality, Quarrel and War

Hobbes begins with the observation that humans are essentially equal, both mentally and physically, insofar as even the weakest person has the strength to kill the strongest.

(From Thomas Hobbes, *Leviathan*, Chapters 13–15)

Nature has made men so equal in the faculties of body and mind, as that though there be found one man sometimes manifestly stronger in body or of quicker mind than another, yet when all is reckoned together, the difference between man and man is not so considerable as that one man can thereupon claim to himself any benefit to which another may not pretend as well as he. For as to the strength of body, the weakest has strength enough to kill the strongest, either by secret machination or by confederacy with others that are in the same danger with himself.

As to the faculties of the mind . . . I find yet a greater equality among men than that of strength. For prudence is but experience, which equal time equally bestows on all men in those things they equally apply themselves to. That which may perhaps make such equality incredible, is but a vain conceit of one's own wisdom which almost all men think they have in a greater degree than the vulgar, that is, than all men but themselves and a few others whom by fame, or for concurring with themselves, they approve. For such is the nature of men, that howsoever they may acknowledge many others to be more witty, or more eloquent, or more learned, yet they will hardly believe there be many so wise as themselves; for they see their own wit at hand, and other men's at a distance. But this proves rather that men are in that point equal, than unequal. For there is not ordinarily a greater sign of the equal distribution of anything, than that every man is contented with his share.

From this equality of ability arises equality of hope in the attaining of our ends. And therefore if any two men desire the same thing, which nevertheless they cannot both enjoy, they become enemies. And in the way to their end (which is principally their own conservation, and sometimes their own delectation only), [they] endeavor to destroy or subdue one another. And from hence it comes to pass that where an invader has no more to fear than another man's single power, if one plants, sows, builds, or possesses a convenient seat, others may probably be expected to come prepared with forces united, to dispossess and deprive him, not only of the fruit of his labor, but also of his life or liberty. And the invader again is in the like danger of another.

And from this diffidence [or distrust] of one another, there is no way for any man to secure himself so reasonably as [through] anticipation. That is, by force or wiles, to master the persons of all men he can, so long till he sees no other power great enough to endanger him. And this is no more than his own conservation requires, and is generally allowed. Also because there be some, that taking pleasure in contemplating their own power in the acts of conquest (which they pursue farther than their security requires); if others, that otherwise would be glad to be at ease within modest bounds, should not by invasion increase their power, they would not be able [for a] long time (by standing only on their defense) to subsist. And by consequence, such augmentation of dominion over men, being necessary to a man's conservation, it ought to be allowed him.

Again, men have no pleasure (but on the contrary a great deal of grief) in keeping company where there is no power able to overawe them all. For every man looks that his companion should value him at the same rate he sets upon himself. And upon all signs of contempt or undervaluing, [he] naturally endeavors, as far as he dares . . . to extort a greater value from his contemners [or scorners] by damage, and from others by example.

So that in the nature of man, we find three principle causes of quarrel. First, competition; secondly, diffidence [or distrust]; thirdly, glory. The first makes men invade for gain, the second for safety, and the third for reputation. The first uses violence to make themselves masters of other men's persons, wives, children, and cattle; the second to defend them; the third for trifles, [such] as a word, a smile, a different opinion, and any other sign of undervalue, either direct in their persons, or by reflection in their kindred, their friends, their nation, their profession, or their name.

12. *Give an example of each of the three principle causes of quarrel.*

Because of the natural causes of quarrel, Hobbes argues, the natural condition of humans is a state of perpetual war of all against all, where no morality exists and everyone lives in constant fear.

Hereby it is manifest, that during the time men live without a common power to keep them all in awe, they are in that condition which is called war; and such a war as is of every man against every man. For war consists not in battle only, or the act of fight-

ing, but [also] in a tract of time, wherein the will to contend by battle is sufficiently known; and therefore the notion of time is to be considered in the nature of war, as it is in the nature of weather. For as the nature of foul weather lies not in a shower or two of rain, but in an inclination thereto of many days together; so the nature of war consists not in actual fighting, but in the known disposition thereto, during all the time there is no assurance to the contrary. All other time is peace.

Whatever therefore is consequent to a time of war, where every man is enemy to every man, the same is consequent to the time wherein men live without other security, than what their own strength and their own invention shall furnish them withal. In such condition, there is no place for industry, because the fruit thereof is uncertain; and consequently no culture of the earth, no navigation, nor use of the commodities that may be imported by sea; no commodious building, no instruments of moving and removing such things as require much force; no knowledge of the face of the earth, no account of time, no arts, no letters, no society; and which is worst of all, continual fear and danger of violent death; and the life of man, solitary, poor, nasty, brutish, and short.

13. *State Hobbes' definitions of war and peace.*
*14. *Explain why in the state of nature there would be no industry, agriculture, imports or building.*

PROOF OF THE STATE OF NATURE

Hobbes continues offering proofs that the state of nature would be as brutal as he describes.

It may seem strange to some man, that has not well weighed these things, that nature should thus dissociate, and render men apt to invade and destroy one another. And he may therefore (not trusting to this inference made from the passions) desire perhaps to have the same confirmed by experience. Let him therefore consider with himself [that], when taking a journey, he arms himself and seeks to go well accompanied. When going to sleep, he locks his doors. When even in his house, he locks his chests, and this when he knows there be laws and public officers armed, to revenge all injuries [which] shall be done [to] him. [Consider] what opinion he has of his fellow subjects when he rides armed; of his fellow citizens when he locks his doors; and of his children and servants when he locks his chests. Does he not there as much accuse mankind by his actions as I do by my words? But neither of us accuse man's nature in it. The desires, and other passions of man, are in themselves no sin. No more are the actions, that proceed from those passions, till they know a law that forbids them; which till laws be made they cannot know, nor can any law be made till they have agreed upon the person that shall make it.

It may perhaps be thought [that] there was never such a time nor condition of war as this, and I believe it was never generally so over all the world. But there are many places where they live so now. For the savage people in many places of America (except the government of small families the concord whereof depends on natural lust) have no government at all and live at this day in that brutish manner, as I said before. However, it may be perceived what manner of life there would be, where there were no common power to fear; [and] by what manner of life, which men that have formerly lived under a peaceful government, . . . [would] degenerate into in a civil war.

But though there had never been anytime wherein particular men were in a condition of war one against another; yet in all times, kings and persons of sovereign authority (because of their independence) are in continual jealousies and in the state and posture of gladiators, having their weapons pointing and their eyes fixed on one another. That is, their forts, garrisons, and guns [are fixed] upon the frontiers of their kingdoms, and continual spies [are fixed] upon their neighbors, which is a posture of war. But because they uphold thereby the industry of their subjects, there does not follow from it that misery which accompanies the liberty of particular men.

15. *Mention five things that people normally do that tend to confirm Hobbes' account of the state of nature.*
16. *Do you think that present relations between nations, as opposed to relations within a nation, illustrate Hobbes' ideas? Does an institu-*

tion like the United Nations count against his view? Argue pro and con.

To this war of every man against every man, this also is consequent, that nothing can be unjust. The notions of right and wrong, justice and injustice have there no place. Where there is no common power, there is no law; where no law, no injustice. Force and fraud are in war the two cardinal virtues. Justice and injustice are none of the [instinctive] faculties, neither of the body nor mind. If they were, they might be in a man that were alone in the world, as well as his senses and passions. They are qualities that relate to men in society, not in solitude. It is consequent also to the same condition, that there be no propriety, no dominion, no mine and thine distinct; but only that to be every man's that he can get, and for so long as he can keep it. And thus much for the ill condition which man by mere nature is actually placed in; though with a possibility to come out of it consisting partly in the passions [and] partly in his reason.

17. *Hobbes claims that "justice" and more generally moral goodness and badness count for nothing without social control. Is that the view of Jack in Golding's story? Is it your view? Explain.*
**18. *If you studied the section on Taylor's discussion of evil (Chapter 5), compare Hobbes' account of justice, right and wrong, to Taylor's. How are they alike?*

Further on in Chapter 13 (not included here), Hobbes notes that humans have three motivations for ending this state of war: the fear of death, the desire to have an adequate living, and the hope to attain this through one's labor. Nevertheless, until the state of war ends, each person has a right to everything, including another person's life.

FIRST LAW OF NATURE

Hobbes next explores the process by which we get out of the state of nature. The first step involves making contracts with others to secure peace. In articulating this peace-securing process, Hobbes draws on the language of the natural law tradition of his time, according to which all particular moral principles derive from immutable principles of reason. Since these moral mandates are fixed in nature, they are thus called *laws of nature*. By using the jargon of natural law theory, Hobbes is suggesting that, from human self-interest and social agreement alone, one can derive the same kinds of laws that more traditional natural law theorists believed were immutably fixed in nature, usually because God put them there. Throughout his discussion of morality, Hobbes continually redefines traditional moral terms (such as *right, liberty, contract* and *justice*) in ways that reflect his account of self-interest and social agreement and his materialist views of nature.

The passions that incline men to peace are fear of death, desire of such things as are necessary to commodious living, and a hope by their industry to obtain them. And reason suggests convenient articles of peace, upon which men may be drawn to agreement. These articles are they which otherwise are called the laws of nature, whereof I shall speak more particularly in the two following chapters.

The right of nature, which writers commonly call *jus naturale*, is the liberty each man has to use his own power as he will himself, for the preservation of his own nature (that is to say, of his own life, and consequently of doing anything which, in his own judgment and reason, he shall conceive to be the aptest means thereunto).

By liberty is understood, according to the proper signification of the word, the absence of external impediments; which impediments may often take away part of a man's power to do what he would, but cannot hinder him from using the power left him, according as his judgment and reason shall dictate to him.

A Law of Nature (*lex naturalis*) is a precept, or general rule, found out by reason, by which a man is forbidden to do that which is destructive of his life, or takes away the means of preserving the same; and to omit that by which he thinks it may be best preserved. For though they that speak of this subject use to confound *jus*, and *lex*, right and law; yet they ought to be distinguished. Because, right consists in the liberty to do or to forbear, whereas law determines and binds to one of them, so that law and right differ as

much as obligation and liberty, which in one and the same matter are inconsistent.

Hobbes continues by listing specific laws of nature, all of which aim at preserving a person's life. He derives his laws of nature deductively, modeled after the type of reasoning used in geometry. That is, from a set of general principles, more specific principles are logically derived. Hobbes' general principles are (1) that people pursue only their own interest, (2) that people are roughly equal in most respects, (3) that there are invariable causes of quarrel, (4) that there is a natural condition of war and (5) that there are inevitable motivations for peace. From these he derives at least 15 specific laws. The first three are the most important, since they establish the overall framework for putting an end to the state of nature. Since we desire to get out of the state of nature, and thereby to preserve our lives, we should seek peace. This for Hobbes is the first law of nature.

And because the condition of man (as has been declared in the precedent chapter) is a condition of war of everyone against everyone, in which case everyone is governed by his own reason (and there is nothing he can make use of that may not be a help to him in preserving his life against his enemies), it follows that in such a condition, every man has a right to everything, even to one another's body. And therefore, as long as this natural right of every man to everything endures, there can be no security to any man (how strong or wise soever he be) of living out the time which nature ordinarily allows men to live. And consequently it is a precept, or general rule of reason, that every man ought to endeavor peace as far as he has hope of obtaining it; and when he cannot obtain it, that he may seek and use all helps and advantages of war; the first branch of which rule contains the first and fundamental Law of Nature, which is, To seek peace and follow it; the second, the sum of the right of nature, which is, By all means we can, to defend ourselves.

SECOND LAW OF NATURE
The reasonableness of seeking peace, indicated by the first law, immediately suggests a second law of

nature, which is that we mutually divest ourselves of certain rights (such as the right to take another person's life) so as to achieve peace. The mutual transferring of these rights is called a *contract* and is the basis of the notion of moral obligation. For example, I agree to give up my right to steal from you, if you give up your right to steal from me. We thereby become obligated not to steal from each other. From selfish reasons alone, we are both motivated mutually to transfer these and other rights, since this will end the dreaded state of war between us.

From this fundamental Law of Nature, by which men are commanded to endeavor peace, is derived this second Law, That a man be willing, when others are so too (as far-forth as for peace and defense of himself he shall think it necessary), to lay down this right to all things; and be contented with so much liberty against other men, as he would allow other men against himself. For so long as every man holds this right of doing anything he likes, [then] so long are all men in the condition of war. But if other men will not lay down their right as well as he, then there is no reason for anyone to divest himself of his. For that were to expose himself to prey (which no man is bound to) rather than to dispose himself to peace. This is that law or the gospel: Whatever you require that others should do to you, that do you to them. And that law of all men: Do not do to others what you would not want done to yourself.

To lay down a man's right to anything, is to divest himself of the liberty of hindering another of the benefit of his own right to the same. For he that renounces or passes away his right, gives not to any other man a right which he had not before. Because, there is nothing to which every man had not [a] right by nature; but [a person] only stands out of his way, that he may enjoy his own original right, without hindrance from him, [though] not [necessarily] without hindrance from another [person]. So that the effect which redounds [or accrues] to one man by another man's defect of right, is but so much diminution of impediments to the use of his own right original.

19. *According to Hobbes' second law of nature, of what rights do we divest ourselves in the peace process?*

The second law of nature consists of a contract between the agreeing parties. Hobbes takes this notion of contract somewhat literally, and he describes at length the validity of certain contracts. For example, contracts made in the state of nature are not generally binding, for if I fear that you will violate your part of the bargain, then no true agreement can be reached. No contracts can be made with animals, since animals cannot understand an agreement. Most significantly, I cannot contract to give up my right to self-defense, since self-preservation is my sole motive for entering into any contract.

THIRD LAW OF NATURE

Simply making contracts will not in and of itself secure peace. We also need to keep the contracts we make, and this is Hobbes' third law of nature.

From that Law of Nature, by which we are obliged to transfer to another such rights as, being retained, hinder the peace of mankind, there follows a third, which is this: That men perform their covenants made, without which, covenants are in vain, and but empty words. And the right of all men to all things remaining, we are still in the condition of war.

And in this Law of Nature consists the fountain and original of justice. For where no covenant has preceded, there has no right been transferred, and every man has right to everything, and consequently no action can be unjust. But when a covenant is made, then to break it is unjust. And the definition of injustice is no other than the not performance of covenant. And whatever is not unjust, is just.

*20. *Suppose I contract with someone, A, to kill my boss. Would it be a case of injustice if A failed to kill my boss, according to Hobbes? Is there any sense in which killing my boss would also be unjust, according to Hobbes? What do you think of his view?*

Hobbes goes on to note a fundamental problem underlying all contracts: Each of us will have an incentive to violate a contract when it serves our best interests. For example, it is in the mutual interest of Jones and myself to agree not to steal from each other. However, it is also in my best interest to break this contract and steal from Jones if I can get away with it. And of course Jones is aware of this fact, just as I am of the fact that he has an incentive to break the contract also. So it seems that no contract can ever get off the ground. This problem can only be solved, according to Hobbes, by giving unlimited power to a political sovereign who will punish us if we violate our contracts. Again, it is for purely selfish reasons—that is, in order to end the condition of war and to escape the state of nature—that I agree to a policing power that will punish me if I violate a contract.

But because covenants of mutual trust [are invalid] where there is a fear of not performance on either part, ... though the original of justice be the making of covenants; yet injustice actually there can be none, till the cause of such fear be taken away, which while men are in the natural condition of war, cannot be done. Therefore before the names of just and unjust can have place, there must be some coercive power to compel men equally to the performance of their covenants, by the terror of some punishment greater than the benefit they expect by the breach of their covenant. And [this coercive power serves] to make good that propriety, which by mutual contract men acquire, in recompense of the universal right they abandon. And such power there is none before the erection of a commonwealth. And this is also to be gathered out of the ordinary definition of justice in the schools: for they say that Justice is the constant will of giving to every man is own. And therefore where there is no own, that is, no propriety, there is no injustice. And where there is no coercive power erected (that is, where there is no commonwealth), there nothing is unjust. So that the nature of justice consists in [the] keeping of valid covenants. But the validity of covenants begins not but with the constitution of a civil power, sufficient to compel men to keep them. And then it is also that propriety begins.

The fool has said in his heart, there is no such thing as justice ... [and that] to make or not make, keep or not keep covenants [is] not against reason when it conduces to one's benefit. ... This specious

reasoning is nevertheless false. ... [H]e that breaks his covenant, and consequently declares that he thinks he may with reason do so, cannot be received into any society that unite themselves for peace and defense, but by the error of them that receive him. Nor [can he] be retained in it when he is received, without seeing the danger of the error, which errors a person cannot reasonably reckon upon as the means of his security. And therefore if he be left or cast out of society, he perishes. And if he lives in society, it is by the errors of other people which he could not foresee, nor reckon upon, and consequently against the reason of his preservation. ... Justice, therefore (that is to say, keeping of covenant), is a rule of reason by which we are forbidden to do anything destructive to our life, and consequently a law of nature.

As noted, Hobbes' first three laws of nature establish the overall framework for putting an end to the state of nature. The remaining laws give content to the earlier ones by describing more precisely the kinds of contracts that will preserve peace. For example, the fourth law is to show "gratitude" toward those who comply with contracts. Otherwise people will regret that they complied when someone is ungrateful. Similarly, the fifth law is that we should be accommodating to the interests of society. For if we quarrel over every minor issue, this will interrupt the peace process. Briefly, the remaining laws have to do with: (6) cautious pardoning of those who commit past offenses; (7) punishment only for the purpose of correcting the offender, not "an eye for an eye" retribution; (8) avoidance of direct or indirect signs of hatred or contempt of another; (9) avoidance of pride; (10) retaining of only those rights you would acknowledge in others; (11) impartiality; (12) sharing in common that which cannot be divided, such as rivers; (13) assigning by lot those items that cannot be divided or enjoyed in common; (14) safe conduct for mediators of peace; (15) resolution of disputes through an arbitrator. Hobbes explains that there are other possible laws that are less important, such as those against drunkenness, which is a threat to particular people.

Concluding Comments About the Laws of Nature

At the close of his account of the laws of nature, Hobbes states that morality consists entirely of those laws that are arrived at through the social contract.

The Laws of Nature are immutable and eternal.

And the science of them is the true and only moral philosophy. For moral philosophy is nothing else but the science of what is good and evil in the conservation and society of mankind. Good and evil are names that signify our appetites and aversions, which in different tempers, customs, and doctrines of men, are different. And diverse men differ not only in their judgment on the senses of what is pleasant and unpleasant to the taste, smell, hearing, touch, and sight, but also of what is conformable or disagreeable to reason in the actions of common life. Nay, the same man in diverse times differs from himself, and one time praises (that is, calls good) what another time he dispraises and calls evil, from whence arise disputes, controversies, and at last war. And therefore so long a man is in the condition of mere nature (which is a condition of war) as private appetite is the measure of good and evil.

*21. *Hobbes denies that the basis of morality is in some objective Platonic good, or in the commands or creative design of God. Does he also reject Aristotle's notion that morality is based in the requirements for flourishing, or being happy, that are built into human nature? In thinking about this question, consider any similarities or differences between* eudaimonia *and* peace *as Hobbes defines it.*

**22. *In Hobbes' account, reason can determine what is necessary for survival, but it cannot determine that murder or theft are wrong per se. Do you agree? Can you provide an account of reason that would show how any reasonable person would avoid theft or murder, even apart from a "commonwealth"? Feel free to draw on thinkers already studied in this text.*

Hobbes adds that moral virtues are relevant to ethical theory only insofar as they promote peace. Outside of this function, virtues have no moral significance.

And consequently all men agree on this, that peace is good, and therefore also the way or means of peace (which, as I have shown before, are justice, gratitude, modesty, equity, mercy, and the rest of the Laws of Nature) are good. That is to say, moral virtues [are good], and their contrary vices evil. Now, the science of virtue and vice is moral philosophy, and therefore the true doctrine of the Laws of Nature is the true moral philosophy. But the writers of moral philosophy, though they acknowledge the same virtues and vices (yet not seeing wherein consisted their goodness, [and] not [seeing] that they come to be praised, as the means of peaceable, sociable, and comfortable living), place them in a mediocrity of passions. [Thus, they treat virtue] as if, not the cause but the degree of daring made fortitude—or, not the cause but the quantity of a gift made liberality.

23. *In the preceding paragraph, Hobbes alludes to the Aristotelian view that virtue is a disposition to choose the mean ("mediocrity"), which is between "too much" and "too little," as though virtue were a matter of "quantity." Does his criticism apply to Aristotle? Review Chapter 3.*

*24. *In Hobbes' view, a virtue such as generosity is not determined by how* much *a person gives, but by what causes the person to give. If I give in order to maintain peace, then I have the virtue of generosity. What might Aristotle say to that? Does Aristotle think of virtues as means to an end that can be specified independently of the virtue itself?*

Hobbes claims that humans always act out of self-interest or a desire to preserve life. Just what does that mean? Is that equivalent to saying that humans are always acting selfishly, or in a self-centered way, and always ignore the interests of others? Is it then psychologically impossible for people to act with a genuine concern for others?

25. *What do you think? Defend your answer.*

Self–Love and Altruism

JOSEPH BUTLER

Butler was born in May 1692 in Wantage, Berkshire (England). Although his father was a dissenter from the established church (the Church of England), Butler eventually converted to it and attended Oxford university, where he developed friendships with influential men and important thinkers of his time. After he took his degree in 1718, Butler's supporters secured his appointment as Preacher at the Rolls Chapel in London, and his rise in the Church began. He eventually became Bishop of Bristol, then Dean of St. Paul's (London's great church) and finally Bishop of Durham. He enjoyed royal favor and in 1747 was appointed as a "clerk" to George II himself. Shortly after becoming Bishop of Durham in 1750, Butler fell ill. He died in June 1752. He was one of a group of thinkers who responded critically both to Hobbesian egoism and to Deism (the belief that there is a god but that revealed religion should be rejected).

In the next selection, from "Sermon 11" of Butler's *Fifteen Sermons Preached at the Rolls Chapel* (1726), he argues that egoism is conceptually confused. This sermon, titled "Upon the Love of Our Neighbor," is based on Romans 13.9: "And if there be any other commandment, it is briefly comprehended in this saying, namely, You shall love your neighbor as yourself."

Against Egoism
Butler argues that the various common and theoretical defenses of *egoism* (the theory that all actions are dictated by self-love and thus that real concern for others is impossible) are mistaken and confused.

Since there is generally thought to be some peculiar kind of contrariety between self-love and the love of our neighbor, between the pursuit of public and of private good, insomuch that when you are recommending one of these, you are supposed to be speaking against the other; and from hence arises a secret prejudice against and frequently opens scorn of all talk of public spirit and real goodwill to our fellow creatures; it will be necessary to inquire what respect benevolence has to self-love, and the pursuit of private interest to the pursuit of public; or whether there be anything of that peculiar inconsistency and contrariety between them, over and above what there is between self-love and other passions and particular affections, and their respective pursuits.

> 26. *Butler is here alluding to the common view that if I am acting out of self-love, then I cannot be acting out of _____.*

General Desires and Particular Affections
Butler's crucial point emerges in what follows: Self-love is not a "particular affection."

Every man has a general desire of his own happiness, and likewise a variety of particular affections, passions, and appetites to particular external objects. The former proceeds from or is self-love, and seems inseparable from all sensible creatures who can reflect upon themselves and their own interest or happiness, so as to have that interest an object to their minds; what is to be said of the latter is that they proceed from, or together make up, that particular nature according to which man is made. The object the former pursues is something internal—our own happiness, enjoyment, satisfaction, whether we have or have not a distinct particular perception what it is or wherein it consists; the objects of the latter are this or that particular external thing which the affections tend towards, and of which it has always a particular idea or perception. The principle we call "self-love" never seeks anything external for the sake of the thing, but only as a means of happiness or good; particular affections rest in the external things themselves. One belongs to man as a reasonable creature reflecting upon his own interest or happiness. The others, though quite distinct from reason, are as much a part of human nature.

If, because every particular affection is a man's own, and the pleasure arising from its gratification his own pleasure, or pleasure to himself, such particular affection must be called self-love, according to this way of speaking no creature whatever can possibly act but merely from self-love, and every action and every affection whatever is to be resolved up into this one principle. But then this is not the language of mankind; or if it were, we should want words to express the difference between the principle of an action proceeding from cool consideration that it will be to my own advantage, and an action, suppose of revenge or of friendship, by which a man runs upon certain ruin to do evil or good to another.

26. *Self-love, Butler says, is a general desire for happiness and belongs to man as a rational creature. Particular affections, on the other hand, rest in external things and are distinct from reason. Which of the following would be a "particular affection" by Butler's account: a love of tennis; a desire for revenge; the desire for a good life; the desire for a warm bath?*

*27. *The "language of mankind" makes a distinction between actions motivated by self-love and those done from some* particular *motive, such as friendship or revenge. The idea that all actions proceed from self-love therefore ignores that distinction. What is the reason some people nonetheless claim that all actions proceed from self-love?*

Happiness does not consist in self-love. The desire of happiness is no more the thing itself than the desire of riches is the possession or enjoyment of them. People may love themselves with the most entire and unbounded affection, and yet be extremely miserable. Neither can self-love anyway help them out, but by setting them on work to get rid of the causes of their misery, to gain or make use of those objects which are by nature adapted to afford satisfaction. Happiness or satisfaction consists only in the enjoyment of those objects which are by nature suited to our several particular appetites, passions, and affections. So that if self-love wholly engrosses us, and leaves no room for any other principle, there can be absolutely no such thing at all as happiness, or enjoyment of any kind whatever, since happiness

consists in the gratification of particular passions, which supposes the having of them. Self-love then does not constitute this or that to be our interest or good; but, our interest or good being constituted by nature and supposed, self-love only puts us upon obtaining and securing it.

Acting out of self-love cannot be "gratifying a particular passion," since there is no such particular passion. Sit in a corner and try doing nothing at all but just loving yourself. You will not succeed in doing anything whatsoever! Rather, if I want to love myself, I need to engage those particular passions or interests I do have. There will be many of them, and reason tells me which ones to pursue, and when, and which ones to ignore or postpone.

28. *It follows that if one of my particular passions is tennis, then if I want to love myself I should arrange to play some tennis. Thus, self-love tells me to pay attention to various particular affections or interests. However, if I spent all my time playing tennis, that would be irrational, and I would be miserable. Why?*

Butler has here touched on what is sometimes called the *hedonistic paradox*. Suppose that a hedonist is a person who lives *entirely* for pleasure and does not care about anything else. The only thing he is *interested* in is pleasure. So if he plays tennis, he plays it not because he is interested in tennis, but because he is interested in the pleasure he may get from playing. But of course, if he is not interested in tennis, he will not get any pleasure out of it! There is a practical side to this paradox: If you try too hard to enjoy something, you will not enjoy it much. That is the hedonistic paradox. This is true for all sorts of enjoyments.

Egoism and Happiness

Butler argues that egoism as usually understood actually conflicts with self-love, as we can see from the way it conflicts with happiness. Just as overfondness for a child may lead a parent to indulge that child in a way that will make it spoiled and eventually unhappy, so overfondness for oneself may result in unhappiness and thus conflict with the goal of self-love.

Overfondness for a child is not generally thought to be for its advantage; and if there be any guess to be made from appearances, surely that character we call selfish is not the most promising for happiness. . . . Immoderate self-love does very ill consult its own interest; and how much soever a paradox it may appear, it is certainly true that even from self-love we should endeavor to get over all inordinate regard to and consideration of ourselves.

In other words, if you really want to love yourself, you should not "love yourself" too much. Pursuit of what immediately gratifies me often leads to much misery. If I am "interested" in being a rock star, that is a particular interest. Whether it contributes or detracts from self-love is an open question. I might fulfill that interest and still be a miserable person who treats himself very badly.

It might be argued, however, that even though self-love does not conflict with various particular affections (such as a love of tennis), it does nevertheless conflict with benevolence, or love of neighbor. For benevolence is by definition an interest in the welfare of others, and benevolent people often act in sacrificial ways and give up some of their own interests or "particular affections" in order to benefit others. Butler considers, and rejects, this argument. He argues that there is not necessarily any conflict between love of self and love of others. The reason is that if I have an "interest" in helping others, that is also a particular interest, and whether it leads to happiness or not is an open question. Butler remarks that there is a verbal dispute going on here. We can call ambition "interested" and the interest in helping others "disinterested" if we like, but logically the two are on a par.

Benevolence Is a Particular Affection

Butler argues that benevolence cannot, logically, conflict with self-love, since benevolence is itself one particular affection among others, whereas the latter is not a particular affection.

Self-love and interestedness was stated to consist in or be an affection to ourselves, a regard to our own private good; it is therefore distinct from benevo-

lence, which is an affection to the good of our fellow creatures. But that benevolence is distinct from, that is, not the same thing with self-love, is no reason for its being looked upon with any peculiar suspicion; because every principle whatever, by means of which self-love is gratified, is distinct from it; and all things which are distinct from each other are equally so.

Does the benevolent man appear less easy with himself, from his love to his neighbor? Does he less relish his being? Is there any peculiar gloom seated on his face? Is his mind less open to entertainment, to any particular gratification? Nothing is more manifest than that being in good humor, which is benevolence while it lasts, is itself the temper of satisfaction and enjoyment.

29. *The fact that benevolence is distinct from self-love is no more reason for thinking it conflicts with self-love than is the fact that love of tennis is distinct from self-love is a reason for thinking that love of tennis conflicts with _____.*
30. *Suppose that one of my "particular affections," i.e., one of the things I enjoy, is helping other people have a good time. Does the fact that I increase their enjoyment in any way take away from my enjoyment?*
31. *Butler claims that a benevolent person is even more likely to be happy than a person who is "selfish," ambitious and the like. Argue that he is right about that.*

Butler speculates that the mistaken notion that benevolence is in conflict with self-love may arise from confusing happiness with property. If I give you some of my property (in the form of money, say), then I have less; and if property is happiness, then I have less happiness. But surely property and happiness are not identical, even though having wealth may conduce to happiness.

For if property and happiness are one and the same thing, as by increasing the property of another, you lessen your own property, so by promoting the happiness of another, you must lessen your own happiness. But whatever occasioned the mistake, I hope it has been fully proved to be one, as it has been proved that there is no peculiar rivalship or competition between self-love and benevolence; that as there may be a competition between these two, so there may also between any particular affection whatever and self-love; that every particular affection, benevolence among the rest, is subservient to self-love by being the instrument of private enjoyment; and that in one respect benevolence contributes more to private interest, that is, enjoyment or satisfaction, than any other of the particular common affections, as it is in a degree its own gratification.

32. *In Butler's view, could an act of genuine self-sacrifice for the sake of my neighbor be an expression of love for myself? What do you think of his answer?*

Further Discussion and Applications

The Unselfishness Trap (Browne)

Harry Browne is a New York journalist. He argues that real freedom requires putting my own interests first. He argues for one kind of egoism, a kind that Butler would have rejected as confused.

(from "How I Found Freedom in an Unfree World," 1973)

The Unselfishness Trap is the belief that you must put the happiness of others ahead of your own.

Unselfishness is a very popular ideal, one that's been honored throughout recorded history. Wherever you turn, you find encouragement to put the happiness of others ahead of your own—to do what's best for the world, not for yourself.

If the ideal is sound, there must be something unworthy in seeking to live your life as you want to live it.

So perhaps we should look more closely at the subject—to see if the ideal *is* sound. For if you attempt to be free, we can assume that someone's going to consider that to be selfish.

Each person always acts in ways he believes will make him feel good or will remove discomfort from his life. Because everyone is different from everyone else, each individual goes about it in his own way.

One man devotes his life to helping the poor. Another one lies and steals. Still another person tries to create better products and services for which he hopes to be paid handsomely. One woman devotes herself to her husband and children. Another one seeks a career as a singer.

In every case, the ultimate motivation has been the same. Each person is doing what he believes will assure his happiness. What varies between them is the means each has chosen to gain his happiness.

We could divide them into two groups labeled *selfish* and *unselfish*, but I don't think that would prove anything. For the thief and the humanitarian each have the same motive—to do what he believes will make him feel good.

In fact, we can't avoid a very significant conclusion: Everyone is selfish. Selfishness isn't really an issue, because everyone selfishly seeks his own happiness.

What we need to examine, however, are the means various people choose to achieve their happiness. Unfortunately, some people oversimplify the matter by assuming that there are only two basic means: sacrifice yourself for others or make them sacrifice for you.

33. Browne clearly argues as follows:
   a. Everyone acts to assure his own happiness.
   b. Therefore, everyone acts selfishly.
   Butler would deny that (a) follows from (b). Explain why.

Browne thinks that the mark of being caught in the "unselfishness trap" is that one feels *required* to be unselfish, even though one would rather look out for oneself. He does not deny that someone might get pleasure from giving to another person, but one should never feel obligated to "make sacrifices" for others.

Suppose however that you *desire* to make sacrifices for someone else. If you act on that desire, then you are still, in Browne's view, acting selfishly. You are still following your *own* desires.

34. *Does the mere fact that you are doing what you desire to do show that you are selfish? Butler would say "no." Why? What do you say, and why?*

Reason and Morality (Baier)

Kurt Baier taught philosophy in Australia and at the University of Pittsburgh. He presents a careful case for a view of reason in ethics that is closely related to Hobbes'.

Hobbes' account of moral distinctions is based on factual claims about human nature. Rules of justice, enforced by a strong ruler, are grounded in the fact that without such rules people will do anything to survive, including killing and stealing. Thus without those enforced rules life would be "solitary, poor, nasty, brutish and short." So people usually submit to rules of justice in order to escape such bad results.

The idea that moral distinctions can be grounded in facts and that moral judgments refer to or in some way depend on those facts has been contested. The opposing view, that moral claims express evaluations or attitudes but not facts, has been widespread in moral philosophy since Hume (see Chapter7). But Baier argues that something like Hobbes' view is defensible. Moral rules, Baier thinks, can be shown to be "rational" in the sense that a reasonable being can see that it is in her own interest to have such rules.

(from *The Moral Point of View*)

On [the view propounded in this book], judgments to the effect that a certain course of action is morally right or morally wrong express "natural," if complicated, facts. They state that the course of action in question has the weight of moral reasons behind or against it. Since this theory belongs in the group which construes moral judgments as fact-stating, the main task confronting this view is to explain how such facts can guide a moral agent in his conduct. The answer is that knowledge of the fact that a certain course of action is morally right or morally wrong can guide a moral agent, because by *moral agent* we mean a person who is already determined to do whatever is morally right and to refrain from doing whatever is morally wrong. . . . If my case is to be more than an empty definition of *moral agent*, I must mention a reason why any and every agent should be a moral and not an immoral agent, why everybody should do what has the weight of moral reasons behind it and refrain from doing what has the weight of

moral reasons against it. The reason is that a general acceptance of a system of merely self-interested reasons would lead to conditions of life well described by Hobbes as "poor, nasty, brutish, and short." These unattractive living conditions can be improved by the general adoption of a system of reasoning in which reasons of self-interest are overruled, roughly speaking, when following them would tend to harm others. Such reasons are what we call *moral reasons*, and we rightly regard them as overruling reasons of self-interest, because the acceptance of self-interested reasons as overruling moral ones would lead to the undesirable state of affairs described by Hobbes. This is the reason why moral reasons must be regarded as superior to self-interested reasons and why everyone has an excellent reason for so regarding them.

Suppose someone who "has the ring of Gyges" (see Plato's *Republic,*) objects that while anyone has a good reason to want others to behave morally, no one has a good reason to suppose he himself should, provided he can get along without being caught doing evil and can thereby "freeload," so to speak, on the goodness of others. Imagine, for example, that I steal, *knowing I can get away with it*. My reason for stealing is that it will put me in a better position financially and thus increase life enjoyments more than anything else open to me to do. So I have a reason to steal, I also have a reason not to steal, the reason cited by Baier and by Hobbes. Which reason should have the most weight? The answer is already contained in Baier's account. Moral reasons by their very nature override reasons of self-interest. A reasonable person can see on reflection that moral reasons just are the best reasons, since only by following them do we get to what we want, namely, peace. Therefore the only way out for the immoralist is for him to deny that he needs to follow reason or be reasonable. But Baier objects that no one could sensibly ask, "Why should I bother to be reasonable?" To be reasonable is to give reasons, the best one can, for doing anything. And in that sense all but the insane are reasonable (and even they?), for all people find it natural to give reasons for doing whatever they do. So to ask, "Why should I be reasonable?" is equivalent to asking "What reason do I have for being reasonable?" And that is nonsense.

35. *Is it nonsense because it amounts to asking "What reason do I have for having reasons?"*

There are a few important differences between Baier and Hobbes. Baier does not suppose that the only hope for escape from a state of nature is a dictator who forces people to follow moral rules. He thinks that other kinds of government or institutional arrangements can do the job. Also, Baier does not suppose that the state exists primarily to restrain potential evildoers. It also can play a positive role. It can be the means to achieving social goods that could not be achieved without it. Hobbes recognizes that fact also, but he tends to stress the importance of self-preservation.

**36. *Compare Baier, Hobbes and Aristotle on the role of community in human life.*

Rational Choice, Ethics and the Prisoner's Dilemma

A reasonable person, according to Hobbes and to Baier, will always do what is in his own interest, and sometimes he will see that it is in his own interest to submit to social (moral) rules that may override immediate or lower-level self-interest. Sometimes it pays to cooperate. In Hobbes' view it pays only if you can be sure that others will cooperate.

We can think of our interactions with other people on the model of games. Imagine games between two people, A and B. In some games any strategy that has a positive payoff for A will have a negative one for B, and vice versa (chess or poker are examples). But in some games there are strategies that are better for *both* A and B than any strategy that is good for one of them and not the other, *provided that* they cooperate (this would not be unusual in games involving more than two people). Many social interactions are like such games. A problem arises, however, with the "provided that" clause. How can we have any confidence that people *will* cooperate? What if cooperating involves risks? The problem has been illustrated by the so called *prisoner's dilemma*.

THE PRISONER'S DILEMMA

Imagine that two men, A and B, have been arrested on the basis of incriminating evidence. There is not enough evidence to convict either one of them of the crime suspected (theft, for example), but there is enough to convict them on a lesser charge (suppose both possessed stolen goods). But if A would tell on B, or vice versa, they could be convicted of a greater charge (theft). Imagine that the police separate A from B and do not allow any communication between them. They offer A the following deal: If you confess to the greater crime and implicate B and B doesn't confess, you will be given a 1-year sentence and B a 10-year sentence (see box I in the nearby matrix). If you do not confess and B doesn't either, you will both get 2 years (see box II). If both confess, both will get a 5-year sentence (see box III). If you don't confess and B does, you get 10 years (see box IV). They offer the same kind of deal to B. But neither A nor B can be sure the other will not confess (they cannot communicate and make a deal, nor could they rely on promises, since neither could be sure that the other would keep the promise). The "choices" or "strategies" available to A and B can be represented by the following matrix:*

You can see that B's order of preferences would be square I (he gets only a 1-year sentence), II (a 2-year

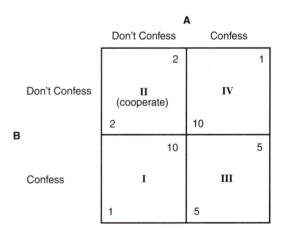

---

*The numbers in the upper right-hand corner of each box denote the number of years, or length of sentence, A gets under that strategy or choice. The numbers in the lower left-hand corner denote the years B gets. For example, in box I, under A's "Don't confess" column, A gets 10 years, whereas B, who is in the "Confess" row, gets just 1 year.

sentence), III (a 5-year sentence), and IV(a 10-year sentence). A's will be IV, II, III, I.

37. *Is it the case, then, that both A and B would prefer II to III?*

What would a rational person do when presented with such choices or strategy options? Suppose you are A. You reason that if you confess and B does not, you get only 1 year. If you confess and B confesses also, you both get 5 years. If you do *not* confess, you risk getting 10 years. There is no way you can be sure of what B is doing. It occurs to you that he will be thinking the same as you. Not confessing is too risky for B also, *unless* he can be sure that you will not confess also (if neither of you confesses, you both land in II). But he can't be sure. In fact, the rational thing for you to do is to confess no matter what. And the rational thing for B to do is confess no matter what. Not confessing exposes each to the possibility of a sentence of 10 years, whereas the worst that can happen as a result of confessing is a 5-year sentence. So if A and B are both rational, they both confess, that is, end up in square III. And that is so even though both would prefer square II to square III. You can see then that being rational in this "game" makes it impossible to choose in a way that maximizes preferences. To echo Hobbes, A could maximize (get to square II) only if he could be sure that B would "cooperate," and vice versa. But there is no Hobbesian dictator around to make sure they do cooperate. So both of them should "defect" (opt out of cooperation).

Rational choice theory operates on the assumption that being rational enables people to choose the best strategy or option available to them rather than the second best. But the prisoner's dilemma illustrates a kind of game or circumstance in which that is not so. In other words, given the payoff structure of the prisoner's dilemma, the very fact that A and B *attempt* to achieve the best or most rational alternative makes it impossible to achieve the best alternative.

Rational Choice, Ethics and Egoism

The prisoner's dilemma might look like a puzzle arising only in very unusual circumstances, but in fact the structure of the dilemma is very common. Here is an example. When pollution control devices began to appear on automobiles, the owners had an incentive to disconnect them (which was easy to do). Keeping them connected lowered mileage and thus raised fuel costs to the individual owner. The chances of getting caught for disconnecting were extremely low. And the benefit aimed at, namely, better air to breathe, would not be affected by disconnecting one such device. Now consider Albert, who is wondering whether to disconnect or not. If other owners do not disconnect and Albert does, then he will get the benefit (cleaner air) without the cost (higher fuel costs), since just a few disconnected devices are not going to affect air quality. He would be a "free rider," like A in the position of square IV (or B in I), who gets the other party to bear (almost all of) the "cost." On the other hand, suppose other people do disconnect their devices. Then Albert will get no benefit from keeping his connected. One auto with a connected pollution device will not make any significant difference to air quality. So if he keeps the device connected, he is a sucker, like B in square IV or A in square I. If he thinks other people are mostly rational choosers, he figures they are thinking like he is, either trying to be free riders or at least avoiding being suckers. So either way the rational thing to do is to disconnect the pollution device. He would of course like cleaner air. But as a rational chooser he is unable to make the choice that would give him cleaner air so long as other people are rational choosers also. He cannot rationally get into square II, anymore than the rational prisoner can. So he ends up in III, along with all the other rational folk, choking on the same old polluted air.

Now, disconnecting a pollution device is cheating and/or violating the law. Some people would say it shows a scorn for the public good or that it is unfair or unjust. Yet it looks like the rational thing to do, and it looks like any other action is simply stupid. So it seems to follow that being honest, fair or just is not (always or ever) compatible with being rational. That was the position of Thrasymachus/Glaucon in Plato's *Republic*. Unless of course we redefine *justice* as "what you can get away with." It looks as though what is needed to solve this dilemma is a Hobbesian dictator.

But it is difficult to imagine even the most vigilant dictator enforcing *all* of the rules that are needed for optimal social relations. Would such a dictator check *every car* to make sure its pollution control device was connected, for example? That would be impracticable in any sizeable society. The dilemma underscores the need for a Hobbesian dictator to enforce rules. But the common occurrence of dilemma-like circumstances makes it unlikely that even a dictator could produce "justice" as Hobbes defines it. For these and other reasons, many have doubted that we can base morality on the operation of self-interested rationality in the way that Hobbes and many after him have supposed.

Various attempts to solve or soften the impact of the prisoner's dilemma have been proposed. One of them stresses the fact the people get into prisoner's dilemma–like games repeatedly, round after round, so to speak. If A decides to cooperate in round 1 and gets taken for a sucker by B, A is unlikely to cooperate with B in future rounds. But if he plays with someone who does cooperate, he is likely to cooperate with that person again in the future. After many rounds, cooperators will begin to come out ahead, even though they have been taken for suckers a few times. "Defectors," on the other hand, will eventually get left out in the cold.

This and other "solutions" to the prisoner's dilemma involve questionable assumptions and are widely disputed. Thus it is argued that it is unlikely that agents who guide their conduct by nothing more than enlightened self-interest will succeed in being moral or just or succeed in getting the benefits of justice. Many thinkers still argue that the tight connection between morality, morally neutral reason and self-interest that Hobbes claimed founders on the prisoner's dilemma.

It is, however, an obvious fact that there is a great deal of social cooperation even without Hobbesian dictators to enforce it and that people often end up in square II, where the costs and benefits of cooperation are shared quite evenly. Are such people irrational? Or is it, rather, the case that a commitment to morality and justice is precisely what makes cooperation and justice possible in the first place, so that kind of commitment *is* rational?

*38. *If the answer to the immediately preceding question is "yes," does it follow that Hobbes is wrong when he argues that the rules of justice are grounded in a morally neutral use of "reason"?*

**39. *Suppose that you and your neighbor would both like sidewalks in your new subdivision, but you can get them only if you pay the city to put them in. Show that this situation has the makings of a prisoner's dilemma. Draw a matrix like the one earlier. Hint: Box I will have in it that you (A, let us suppose) bear almost all of the cost and your neighbor (B) bears hardly any (he held out longer than you, or convinced you he was too poor, or whatever, and is now a "free rider" on your generosity).*

Egoism, Altruism and Biology

Rational choice theory, and Hobbes' conception of "laws of nature" both depend on the idea that in the struggle to preserve life and make it as good as possible, people reason themselves into a certain amount of cooperation and even "altruism." To avoid the very great disadvantages of a "state of nature," a person might even see that it makes sense to have to serve in an army and to get killed for the sake of preserving "society"! The soldier who sacrifices his life is commonly credited with altruism, sacrifice of personal advantage for the sake of others. But in Hobbes' view he is only doing what he has to do, as ordered by a ruler who enforces such behavior, and in doing so brings about society, justice, peace, a better life. Even the soldier can see that submission to authority is reasonable, despite the burden placed on him.

In the last half century or so some biologists have sought for clues to the basis for human society, justice and altruism in something purportedly more basic than "rationality." According to Darwin, the most "fit" organisms are those that can produce more offspring. Darwin's idea has combined with knowledge of genetics to produce the idea of a "gene derby," in which those organisms are most fit that pass on more of their genes to succeeding generations, thereby winning a kind of "gene" race or derby.

Genes don't have much. They don't have blue eyes or brown, intelligence or stupidity, kindness or cruelty. Genes do not have consciousness and thus do not have aims or interests, but if they did it would be right to say that they are interested in only one thing, namely, survival. They would be very much like Hobbesian rational agents in that respect! However, even though they do not *have* much, they *do* a great deal. They determine eye color and, within limits, kinds of intelligence.

40. *Could genes also determine behavioral or character traits? If not, why not?*

NATURAL SELECTION

As environments change, the traits needed for survival change. Suppose, for the sake of discussion, that a single gene controls the color of an insect. Any color that makes good camouflage in that insect's environment, that is, makes it difficult for predators to spot that insect, will make it more "fit." To speak of an organism's *fitness* is to speak of the degree to which its genes are likely to turn up in future generations. The longer it lives, the more chances it will have to reproduce and thus make its genes turn up in future generations; and the better the camouflage, the longer it lives.

Now suppose the dominant color of vegetation in that insect's environment changes. In that case an insect that used to be fit may no longer be fit. But in any large population, occasional members will mutate. A random throw of the genetic dice occasionally produces an insect with somewhat different coloring, for instance. Suppose that a mutation makes an insect more fit by making it a color that camouflages better than its parents' color. It will live longer and reproduce more. It will tend to win in the "gene derby." Its color has in effect been "selected" by the new environment.

When some biologists try to explain such things as adaptive behavior in humans, they may try to use a model along the lines just laid out. Certain behavioral traits or tendencies will be selected by certain environments. If certain group behaviors are adaptive, we might expect them to be selected also. To say they are adaptive is to say they help to ensure the survival of that group or society. However, since only individuals have genes, it is not immediately evident how any behavior that does not contribute to the sur-

vival of the *individual* that emits it could be selected. For instance, the altruistic behavior of the soldier who sacrifices for his country may lead to his early death and thus cause him to lose in the gene derby. He dies young and misses chances to produce many offspring as a result. One might expect, then, that altruistic behavior or in fact any behavior that puts an individual at risk in order to benefit others would be "selected against." Eventually there should be no altruists. They would all be "weeded out" by natural selection (it might take a long time of course).

But there are altruists. And the ethical values that motivate them, or the "reasoning" that guides them, need some kind of explanation. Can a biological explanation be given? Doesn't the fact of altruism, behavior devoted to the interest of others or to a common good, require a kind of explanation that *cannot* be given by natural selection and survival of the fittest?

41. *At this point, what is your answer to the immediately preceding question?*

SOCIOBIOLOGY (WILSON)

The discipline called *sociobiology* has devoted itself to answering such questions and to showing that there can be a biological basis for altruism. Strictly speaking, the notion of rationality need play no role in explanations of socially useful behavior even of the most extraordinary sort, such as the sacrifice of life for another person or group of persons. A leader in the development of sociobiology is E. O. Wilson (b. 1929), who became a professor of zoology at Harvard in 1956. In his book *Sociobiology* (1975) Wilson argued that, in fact, altruistic behavior would be selected in some societies. Wilson does not make any fundamental distinction between human societies and societies of insects or other animals. In all sorts of "societies," the key to understanding altruism (as well as other behavioral tendencies) lies in "kin selection." (from *Sociobiology: The New Synthesis*):

> Imagine a network of individuals linked by kinship within a population. These blood relatives cooperate or bestow altruistic favors on one another in a way that increases the average genetic fitness of the members of the network

as a whole, even when this behavior reduces the individual fitnesses of certain members of the group. The members may live together or be scattered throughout the population. The essential condition is that they jointly behave in a way that benefits the group as a whole, while remaining in relatively close contact with the remainder of the population. This enhancement of kin-network welfare in the midst of a population is called kin selection. . . .

The modern genetic theory of altruism, selfishness, and spite was launched instead by William D. Hamilton. Hamilton's pivotal concept is inclusive fitness: the sum of an individual's own fitness plus the sum of all the effects it causes to the related parts of the fitnesses of all its relatives. When an animal performs an altruistic act toward a brother, for example, the inclusive fitness is the animal's fitness (which has been lowered by performance of the act) plus the increment in fitness enjoyed by that portion of the brother's hereditary constitution that is shared with the altruistic animal. The portion of shared heredity is the fraction of genes held by common descent by the two animals and is measured by the coefficient of relationship.

Consider the following simple illustration. Albert shares half of his genes with his brother Bob (all humans share half their genes with their full siblings). Suppose, acting on altruistic tendencies, Albert gives up resources (money, time, property, etc.) to Bob that make it possible for Bob to prosper and start a family at a young age, but with the result that it impossible for Albert to start a family of his own. Suppose that if Albert had not done so he could have eventually married in time to have one child. Then half of Albert's genes would have "survived" in that child had Albert behaved "selfishly." But he has altruistically sacrificed for Bob. To be sure, that might mean less personal happiness for Albert. But what might be the end result, so far as the gene derby goes? Genes, after all, are not "interested" in happiness. Well, suppose that Bob, married young, has three children. Each of them has half of Bob's genes and thus one-quarter of Albert's. So the result of Albert's altruistic act is that

three-quarters of his genes survive, which is better than under the proposed "selfish" alternative, where only half survived. This is an example of *kin selection*. Although Albert's altruistic behavior does not benefit him, it does, in this very simplified scenario, enhance "fitness," that is, it increases the proportion of his genes that get "represented" in future generations. Wilson and Hamilton's way of putting it is to say that Albert's "inclusive fitness," the sum of his own fitness plus the sum of all the effects it causes to the fitness of his relatives, has been increased by altruism.

*42. *If I sacrificed my life to save the life of my nephew, how many children would he have to have in order for me to remain as "inclusively fit" as I would have been had I let him die and I had lived to have one child? (A quarter of my genes show up in my nephew).*

Kin selection could perhaps explain altruistic acts directed toward relatives. But what about altruism directed toward unrelated persons, for example, the altruism of the soldier who sacrifices his life, the altruism of the parent who cares for an adopted child, or the altruism of a Mother Teresa, whose actions did nothing to increase inclusive fitness? These are the kinds of altruism that interest us most. They are examples of altruism in the strictest sense. How could they be explained biologically?

One reply suggested by Wilson and others exploits some already familiar notions. The situation in relation to unrelated persons could be like a repeated prisoner's dilemma. If A behaves altruistically toward B in round 1 and B responds in kind, we have something like square II, the best outcome of cooperation. Suppose that A risks his life to save B from drowning and that B reciprocates by sacrificing something for A on some other occasion. Both of them are likely to do better than they would operating egoistically, so far as the gene derby goes. B is still alive and reproducing, for instance. Suppose, however, that B does not reciprocate. He "free rides" on A's generosity. In round 1, A has lost, has been suckered. But let us suppose that A's cooperative or altruistic behavior is limited by a "tit for tat" rule, according to which if B does not reciprocate in round 1, A does not cooperate with B in round 2. It turns out that given a sufficient number of rounds, "selfish" behaviors will be weeded out, or "selected against," just so long as there are at least two "players" who are willing to cooperate at least once. Computer simulations of such iterated games show that cooperative behavior tends to produce the best outcome (as measured by money, say) for rational players, or the greatest *fitness* where the measure is fitness in the biological sense.

Although it seems that sociobiological accounts of altruism are theoretically possible, many thinkers find the enterprise strained and conceptually insensitive. Some object that what sociobiologists call *altruism* is simply not what is usually designated by that term. Mother Teresa's behavior was generated by complex religious and moral loyalties that she had learned, or so it seems. One can only understand *what* altruism comes to in her case by understanding the moral and religious concepts that informed her behavior. One would have to understand her "training" or religious "nurture" in order to get her actions rightly described and explained. Also, explanations of human behavior in sociobiological terms seem heavily weighted in favor of "nature" and against "nurture." But the disputes over the relative roles of nature and nurture in human life are certainly not settled at this point, and it will not do simply to assume "Nature is all" as a premise.

One thing at least is clear: If nature is "Hobbesian," so that every "player" never cooperates but always defects, then the process that weeds out those who defect will never get started. In order for the sociobiological account to be even theoretically plausible, we must thus make the assumption that there are at least a few people (or organisms) who spontaneously act out of "an impulse to cooperate" or "altruistic impulses" or some other motive that is not individually self-serving. Otherwise the process that will supposedly select the altruist and weed out the egoist will never get going.

43. *Does it seem plausible to you to suppose that Mother Teresa participated in a process that weeded out those who defected, a process of repeated interactions between players or agents?*

An Aristotelian Account of Reason, Egoism and Justice (Broadie)

Aristotle's account of ethical life stresses practical reason and the role of upbringing and training in acquiring it. Good practical reasoning is a necessary condition for leading a good life, a life that is *eudaimon* and virtuous. It is Aristotle's commonsense view that people are not born good, practical reasoners. We are just as dependent on those who raise us for our ideas of how best to get on in life and of what the good of life is as we are for our bodily needs. Even if we expand the population of those around us to include God or Gods, our dependency seems to be a fact, except in some very special views (such as, perhaps, Plato's).

Now we must ask, would those who raise us teach us to be rational egoists who consider "justice" as merely a means to an end? Suppose we start from the Hobbesian "state of nature." Would anyone in that state or condition raise her children so that they would tell the truth or refrain from stealing *only when* they saw that it was to their personal advantage to do so, but otherwise would raise them to lie and steal if it suited them? If I were *deliberately* to raise a child that way, I would be rearing a potential enemy, one who would take *my* interests into account only when doing so served *his* interests. Consider that practical reason, in the egoist's view, consists in taking into account and finding ways to further his own interests and not, except incidentally, the interests of others. It follows that if I am a rational egoist, I would not rear a child to be a rational egoist, but would try to keep her stupid, by, for instance, encouraging her to believe that truthfulness is intrinsically valuable and that the interests of others should be taken into account, sometimes even at the sacrifice of her own immediate interests.

44. *Why would a rational egoist not raise her children to become rational egoists?*

Suppose I do raise my children in the way just suggested. How did I ever become so smart as to do that? After all, someone reared me. I did not spring full blown from the brain of a God. If the people who raised me were rational egoists, they would not have raised *me* to be a rational egoist, according to the argument just given. If they reared me to be stupid or if they were themselves foolish and thus raised me foolishly, how do I know I am not now being stupid in the way I raise my child and that I am generally wrong in my egoist views? Princeton philosopher Sarah Broadie describes Aristotle's view of the situation in the following way:

If, when others were rearing me and showing me how to be and behave, I had already been able to exercise reason, I might have reasoned that I ought not to absorb their lessons and examples unless I could see that accepting these would conduce to what I saw to be my own good; and I might have cautioned myself to be vigilant about this, on the ground that the others would be imparting those lessons only to forward their own advantage and not for the sake of mine at all except incidentally. But as things actually were, I could engage in and act on no such reasonings, partly because I was too unformed to be under my own rational control, and partly because I had no sustainable conception of my own good independent of what I gained by simply accepting to do what I was encouraged by others to do. (from *Ethics with Aristotle*, 1991)

Someone might object that I could have equated what is "good for me" with the satisfaction of whatever desires I happen to have at any moment. But that conception of the good would very soon lead me to a great deal of trouble.

*45. *Try to imagine a life governed entirely by impulse. What would such a life be like for the child? How long would such a child last once it was on its own?*

In fact, the best any child can do is to fall in with the ways taught by others. What are some minimal elements in a viable conception of the good, one that would enable individuals and communities to survive? Could they be the sort that Hobbes supposed? But Hobbes imagines that in the state of nature *every* individual is looking out for himself. Would that include young people? Would young people even be able to reason as Hobbes supposes? A negative answer emerges, according to Broadie.

As one who started life amongst others unable to reason on my own behalf, I was unable to regard others as either means or obstacles to ends of mine that looked beyond ends of theirs. Consequently, I lacked the capacity to see others in their dealings with me as working through me, round me or past me towards ends that are theirs and in no way mine. On the contrary, if I absorbed their teaching at all, a kind of practical natural logic will have sustained me in the trust that what they impart to me they seek to impart for my own good. In accepting what is imparted I accept it as being for my good.

46. *Given that I get my ideas of how to live from others, and given that I naturally think that the aim of living is to do well in some sense, would it be possible for me to accept some teaching from, say, a parent, without *accepting it as being for my good? Explain.*

It might seem that those who raised me could have been manipulating me for their own purposes and that later I "find them out" by applying a standard independent of the standards I learned from them. However, to have any standards at all I would have had to trust *someone,* since I have no access to standards that are independent of all training whatsoever. Moreover, *examples* are more important for learning how to live than are moral lectures. I watch what others do and trust that what I see is good for creatures such as ourselves. Could it be typically the case that such trust is mistaken? Could it be the *rule* that people, in giving the kind of training or upbringing that is required by human dependence, provide examples for those in their care that, for example, encourage them (stupidly) to be concerned about the interests of others, *all* such examples being a charade? The difficulties of imagining such "training" are enormous. One difficulty is that when parents, teachers and the like supply examples of how to behave, they do not usually do so with much deliberation or with a clear view of what they are doing. In any case, neither Hobbes nor Thrasymachus apparently even tries to imagine such a thing. Rather, what is wrong with views such as theirs is that they could be true only of beings who need no upbringing whatsoever to be at their best. Aristotle takes it to be pretty obvious that human beings are not such beings. Human beings are essentially dependent.

> ****47.** *Try to state in a brief outline Aristotle's main reasons for rejecting the idea that people are all rational egoists and that justice is thus no more than a name for devices that further egoistic interests.*

It is not possible to infer any particular account of justice from the points just made about the general human need for training and good examples. What can be inferred is that some considerable degree of trust between people is a necessary condition for a good life and that such trust cannot in general be simply a mistake that could be discovered by better reasoning. There could be no such better reasoning. We learn to reason from others. That is most manifestly so where reasoning about how to live is concerned—or so Aristotle argued. It follows that there can be no basis for justice, nor any basis for viable social life generally, in "reason," where reason is understood merely as a tool for furthering egoistic needs. A richer conception of reason, in which reason plays a role in determining what is good, seems required.

Hopefully it is clear that Aristotle's position does not entail that all people be raised well or that there be no parents who are egoists and whose influence turns their children into selfish people. There would be very little injustice to worry about if everyone had been well raised and had "taken" to their training!

CHAPTER SEVEN

Feeling, Reason and Morality

Introduction

I sometimes think or say such things as the following about myself or others:

That was cruel!
That was dishonest.
That was wrong.
That was brave.

When I make judgments like these sincerely, I always have negative or positive feelings, feelings of revulsion or admiration, or various other kinds of approval or disapproval. The sorts of actions or circumstances that evoke such judgments seem to be emotionally loaded. For example, people are sometimes so emotionally upset and repelled after witnessing films depicting what appears to be extreme and gratuitous cruelty to farm animals that they become vegetarians. The judgment "That is cruel" is not simply a statement of fact. It is also, it seems, an expression of revulsion or distress of some kind. Similarly I have positive feelings when I judge that an action is kind or courageous.

These obvious facts about moral judgments set them apart from many of the judgments made elsewhere. When I judge that the angles of a triangle equal 180 degrees or that the French Revolution began in 1789 or that water is H_2O, there are no typical feelings, negative or positive, that I am likely to

have. I might feel good about having mastered a bit of history or science, but that feeling is not regularly or typically associated with the judgment itself (e.g., "Water is H_2O") but with the judgment "I am good at chemistry." Judgments about math or science or history or many aspects of daily life are the result of applying our "thinking powers," or *reason*, and we often think of reason as "cool" and objective. Emotions, on the other hand, are "warm" and might even get in the way of clear thinking or reasoning. The notion of reason or rationality as "cool" and unemotional has contributed to the idea that women are less rational than men, since women are supposedly more emotional.

Some people have concluded that so-called moral judgments are in fact *nothing but* expressions of feeling. Perhaps moral principles are used in arguments and reasoning, but a person with good principles and good reasoning could still be bad or immoral if she *lacks the appropriate feelings*, such as feelings of revulsion on witnessing cruelty or feelings of sympathy for a starving child. These ideas are the focus of this chapter.

ORIENTING QUESTIONS FOR DISCUSSION

1. Does getting very emotional about actions or behavior (come up with your own examples) tend to get in the way of thinking clearly and making correct judgments about that behavior?

2. Can you think of a moral judgment or term that does not have *any* emotional force or connotations?

3. Would it be really odd to say, "That was wrong (cruel, dishonest), but I have no feelings about it one way or the other"? .

4. If emotions tend to cancel out reason, and if moral judgments are always "emotional" to some degree, would it follow that moral judgments are somehow irrational?

MARK TWAIN

Samuel Clemens (1835–1910), better known by his pen name, "Mark Twain," was an American humorist, novelist, writer and lecturer. He was born in Missouri, which had become a slave state by the time of the Missouri Compromise (1821), so Twain grew up surrounded by slaveholders. His humor and often-satirical wit made him one of the most popular American writers of his time. He had many famous friends, including William Dean Howells, Booker T. Washington and Helen Keller. American author William Faulkner called him "the first truly American writer," and continued, "and all of us since are his heirs." His popularity continues to the present day.

Perhaps his most famous novel is Adventures of Huckleberry Finn, *excerpted next. In it Twain portrays pre–Civil War southern culture and the beliefs and mores of slaveholders and those who condoned slavery. The novel recreates dialects and speech mannerisms of the day and freely employs racial epithets that would have been used casually in the racist culture that Twain encountered as a young man in Missouri.*

Adventures of Huckleberry Finn

The main characters in this novel are young Huckleberry, who runs away to avoid an abusive father, and a slave named Jim, owned by a neighbor of Huck's named Mrs. Watson. Jim is trying to flee northward to freedom. Huck and Jim accidentally encounter one another "on the run" and raft together down the Mississippi, with the intention of reaching Cairo, Illinois, where they hope to take a riverboat north on the Ohio. Huck is thought to be dead, so he is not worried about anyone looking for him, and since he is white he can travel freely. Jim, on the other hand, is a runaway slave who is being hunted and will bring a good reward to anyone who finds him and turns him in. Huck, by helping Jim, is in the position of breaking the law and helping someone who is breaking the law.

Huck takes seriously a moral code that includes typical elements such as Don't steal. Don't lie. Do unto others as you would have them do unto you. But the code is combined with racist mores within which slaves are regarded as property, so it seems natural to him to think that helping Jim escape is a kind of theft. Despite the "naturalness" of that thought, he also has, and further develops, a fellow feeling with Jim, and he has the same sorts of reactions that he would have with any friend. For example, he feels bad when he hurts Jim or seems to betray him in any way. At one point Huck tricks Jim into thinking he has left, thus causing Jim a lot of anxiety.

Jim is speaking to Huck when Huck returns:

When I got all wore out wid work, en wid de callin' for you, en went to sleep, my heart wuz mos' broke bekase you wuz los', en I didn' k'yer no' mo' what become er me en de raf'. En when I wake up en fine you back agin, all safe en soun', de tears come, en I could a got down on my knees en kiss yo' foot, I's so thankful. En all you wuz thinkin' 'bout wuz how you could make a fool uv ole Jim wid a lie. Dat truck dah is TRASH; en trash is what people is dat puts dirt on de head er dey fren's en makes 'em ashamed."

Then he got up slow and walked to the wigwam, and went in there without saying anything but that. But that was enough. It made me feel so mean I could almost kissed HIS foot to get him to take it back.

It was 15 minutes before I could work myself up to go and humble myself to a nigger; but I done it, and I warn't ever sorry for it afterwards, neither. I didn't do him no more mean tricks, and I wouldn't done that one if I'd a knowed it would make him feel that way.

We slept most all day, and started out at night, a little ways behind a monstrous long raft that was as long going by as a procession. She had four long sweeps at each end, so we judged she carried as many as 30 men, likely. She had five big wigwams aboard, wide apart, and an open camp fire in the middle, and a tall flagpole at each end. There was a power of style about her. It amounted to something being a raftsman on such a craft as that.

We went drifting down into a big bend, and the night clouded up and got hot. The river was very wide, and was walled with solid timber on both sides; you couldn't see a break in it hardly ever, or a light. We talked about Cairo, and wondered whether we would know it when we got to it. I said likely we wouldn't, because I had heard say there warn't but about a dozen houses there, and if they didn't happen to have them lit up, how was we going to know we was passing a town? Jim said if the two big rivers joined together there, that would show. But I said maybe we might think we was passing the foot of an island and coming into the same old river again. That disturbed Jim—and me too. So the question was, what to do? I said, paddle ashore the first time a light showed, and tell them pap was behind, coming along with a trading-scow, and was a green hand at the business, and wanted to know how far it was to Cairo. Jim thought it was a good idea, so we took a smoke on it and waited.

There warn't nothing to do now but to look out sharp for the town, and not pass it without seeing it. He said he'd be mighty sure to see it, because he'd be a free man the minute he seen it, but if he missed it he'd be in a slave country again and no more show for freedom. Every little while he jumps up and says:

"Dah she is?"

But it warn't. It was Jack-o'-lanterns, or lightning bugs; so he set down again, and went to watching, same as before. Jim said it made him all over trembly and feverish to be so close to freedom. Well, I can tell you it made me all over trembly and feverish, too, to hear him, because I begun to get it through my head that he WAS most free—and who was to blame for it? Why, ME. I couldn't get that out of my conscience, no how nor no way. It got to troubling me so I couldn't rest; I couldn't stay still in one place. It hadn't ever come home to me before, what this thing was that I was doing. But now it did; and it stayed with me, and scorched me more and more. I tried to

make out to myself that I warn't to blame, because I didn't run Jim off from his rightful owner; but it warn't no use, conscience up and says, every time, "But you knowed he was running for his freedom, and you could a paddled ashore and told somebody." That was so—I couldn't get around that noway. That was where it pinched. Conscience says to me, "What had poor Miss Watson done to you that you could see her nigger go off right under your eyes and never say one single word? What did that poor old woman do to you that you could treat her so mean? Why, she tried to learn you your book, she tried to learn you your manners, she tried to be good to you every way she knowed how. THAT'S what she done."

I got to feeling so mean and so miserable I most wished I was dead. I fidgeted up and down the raft, abusing myself to myself, and Jim was fidgeting up and down past me. We neither of us could keep still. Every time he danced around and says, "Dah's Cairo!" it went through me like a shot, and I thought if it WAS Cairo I reckoned I would die of miserableness.

Jim talked out loud all the time while I was talking to myself. He was saying how the first thing he would do when he got to a free State he would go to saving up money and never spend a single cent, and when he got enough he would buy his wife, which was owned on a farm close to where Miss Watson lived; and then they would both work to buy the two children, and if their master wouldn't sell them, they'd get an Ab'litionist to go and steal them.

It most froze me to hear such talk. He wouldn't ever dared to talk such talk in his life before. Just see what a difference it made in him the minute he judged he was about free. It was according to the old saying, "Give a nigger an inch and he'll take an ell." Thinks I, this is what comes of my not thinking. Here was this nigger, which I had as good as helped to run away, coming right out flatfooted and saying he would steal his children—children that belonged to a man I didn't even know, a man that hadn't ever done me no harm.

I was sorry to hear Jim say that, it was such a lowering of him. My conscience got to stirring me up hotter than ever, until at last I says to it, "Let up on me—it ain't too late yet—I'll paddle ashore at the first light and tell." I felt easy and happy and light as a feather right off. All my troubles was gone. I went to looking out sharp for a light, and sort of singing to myself. By and by one showed. Jim sings out:

"We's safe, Huck, we's safe! Jump up and crack yo' heels! Dat's de good ole Cairo at las', I jis knows it!"

I says:

"I'll take the canoe and go and see, Jim. It mightn't be, you know."

He jumped and got the canoe ready, and put his old coat in the bottom for me to set on, and give me the paddle; and as I shoved off, he says:

"Pooty soon I'll be a-shout'n' for joy, en I'll say, it's all on accounts o' Huck; I's a free man, en I couldn't ever ben free ef it hadn' ben for Huck; Huck done it. Jim won't ever forgit you, Huck; you's de bes' fren' Jim's ever had; en you's de ONLY fren' ole Jim's got now."

I was paddling off, all in a sweat to tell on him; but when he says this, it seemed to kind of take the tuck all out of me. I went along slow then, and I warn't right down certain whether I was glad I started or whether I warn't. When I was 50 yards off, Jim says:

"Dah you goes, de ole true Huck; de on'y white genlman dat ever kep' his promise to ole Jim."

Well, I just felt sick. But I says, I GOT to do it—I can't get OUT of it. Right then along comes a skiff with two men in it with guns, and they stopped and I stopped. One of them says:

"What's that yonder?"

"A piece of a raft," I says.

"Do you belong on it?"

"Yes, sir."

"Any men on it?"

"Only one, sir."

"Well, there's five niggers run off tonight up yonder, above the head of the bend. Is your man white or black?"

I didn't answer up prompt. I tried to, but the words wouldn't come. I tried for a second or two to brace up and out with it, but I warn't man enough—hadn't the spunk of a rabbit. I see I was weakening; so I just give up trying, and up and says:

"He's white."

"I reckon we'll go and see for ourselves."

"I wish you would," says I, "because it's pap that's there, and maybe you'd help me tow the raft ashore where the light is. He's sick—and so is mam and Mary Ann."

"Oh, the devil! we're in a hurry, boy. But I s'pose we've got to. Come, buckle to your paddle, and let's get along."

I buckled to my paddle and they laid to their oars. When we had made a stroke or two, I says:

"Pap'll be mighty much obleeged to you, I can tell you. Everybody goes away when I want them to help me tow the raft ashore, and I can't do it by myself."

"Well, that's infernal mean. Odd, too. Say, boy, what's the matter with your father?"

"It's the—a—the—well, it ain't anything much."

They stopped pulling. It warn't but a mighty little ways to the raft now. One says:

"Boy, that's a lie. What IS the matter with your pap? Answer up square now, and it'll be the better for you."

"I will, sir, I will, honest—but don't leave us, please. It's the—the—Gentlemen, if you'll only pull ahead, and let me heave you the headline, you won't have to come a-near the raft—please do."

"Set her back, John, set her back!" says one. They backed water. "Keep away, boy—keep to looard. Confound it, I just expect the wind has blowed it to us. Your pap's got the smallpox, and you know it precious well. Why didn't you come out and say so? Do you want to spread it all over?"

"Well," says I, a-blubbering, "I've told everybody before, and they just went away and left us."

"Poor devil, there's something in that. We are right down sorry for you, but we—well, hang it, we don't want the smallpox, you see. Look here, I'll tell you what to do. Don't you try to land by yourself, or you'll smash everything to pieces. You float along down about 20 miles, and you'll come to a town on the left-hand side of the river. It will be long after sunup then, and when you ask for help you tell them your folks are all down with chills and fever. Don't be a fool again, and let people guess what is the matter. Now we're trying to do you a kindness; so you just put 20 miles between us, that's a good boy. It wouldn't do any good to land yonder where the light is—it's only a wood-yard. Say, I reckon your father's poor, and I'm bound to say he's in pretty hard luck. Here, I'll put a 20-dollar gold piece on this board, and you get it when it floats by. I feel mighty mean to leave you; but my kingdom! it won't do to fool with small-pox, don't you see?"

"Hold on, Parker," says the other man, "here's a 20 to put on the board for me. Goodbye, boy; you do as Mr. Parker told you, and you'll be all right."

"That's so, my boy—goodbye, goodbye. If you see any runaway niggers you get help and nab them, and you can make some money by it."

"Goodbye, sir," says I; "I won't let no runaway niggers get by me if I can help it."

They went off and I got aboard the raft, feeling bad and low, because I knowed very well I had done wrong, and I see it warn't no use for me to try to learn to do right; a body that don't get STARTED right when he's little ain't got no show—when the pinch comes there ain't nothing to back him up and keep him to his work, and so he gets beat. Then I thought a minute, and says to myself, hold on; s'pose you'd a done right and give Jim up, would you felt better than what you do now? No, says I, I'd feel bad—I'd feel just the same way I do now. Well, then, says I, what's the use you learning to do right when it's troublesome to do right and ain't no trouble to do wrong, and the wages is just the same? I was stuck. I couldn't answer that. So I reckoned I wouldn't bother no more about it, but after this always do whichever come handiest at the time.

I went into the wigwam; Jim warn't there. I looked all around; he warn't anywhere. I says:

"Jim!"

"Here I is, Huck. Is dey out o' sight yit? Don't talk loud."

He was in the river under the stern oar, with just his nose out. I told him they were out of sight, so he come aboard. He says:

"I was a-listenin' to all de talk, en I slips into de river en was gwyne to shove for sho' if dey come aboard. Den I was gwyne to swim to de raf' agin when dey was gone. But lawsy, how you did fool 'em, Huck! Dat WUZ de smartes' dodge! I tell you, chile, I 'spec it save' ole Jim—ole Jim ain't going to forgit you for dat, honey."

1. *What does Huck's conscience tell him he should do?*

2. *If Huck had completely ignored his feelings about Jim, what would he have done?*

*3. *It appears that "conscience" can be corrupted in various ways. Could a person's feelings also be corrupted so that he would not feel bad about stealing, for example?*

*4. *In Twain's story, are the duties to tell the truth, not steal, etc. merely social conventions used to support a slave culture? Imagine several different contexts in which Huck might feel bound to tell the truth.*

DAVID HUME

Hume (1711–1776) was born in Edinburgh. Scotland. He left a brief account of his life, where he describes the "good family" he came from (lawyers and landowners on both sides of the family), his dislike for the study of law (which was considered suitable for him as younger son) and his "passion for literature."

He began the study of law at Edinburgh University and then started working on what became the Treatise of Human Nature *while living with his mother, brother and sister near Berwick, Scotland. He traveled abroad in 1734 and completed the* Treatise *in La Flèche, "a country retreat" in France, where he had the use of the library of the Jesuit college where Descartes had been educated. Later he served as a military and diplomatic secretary, as a librarian and as an Under-secretary of State in London, 1767–69. While serving as Secretary to the British Ambassador in Paris he met many French intellectuals and earned the title "le bon David" (the good David). In 1769 he retired to Edinburgh, built a house in the new St. Andrews Square and lived well on his earnings. He and his sister entertained numerous Scottish friends (including Adam Smith and many ministers of the Church of Scotland) and occasional guests from overseas, such as Benjamin Franklin. As was dying he was visited by James Boswell. Hume joked with Boswell about death and the possibility of an afterlife (Hume was an atheist and did not believe in immortality), and Boswell was left "with impressions which disturbed me for some time."*

Hume's reputation as a religious skeptic may have led to some neglect of his writings. However, Thomas

*Reid, Immanuel Kant, Jeremy Bentham and John Stuart Mill all paid close attention to his work. Hume continually engaged in what he called "a cautious observation of human life . . . men's behavior in company, in affairs, and in their pleasures" (*Treatise: xix*). His discussions of ethics and his denial that reason can play any substantive role in moral judgment have been much discussed up to the present day, as have his views on knowledge and religion.*

(From *An Enquiry Concerning the Principles of Morals*, 1751)

Moral Distinctions Not Derived from Reason

Hume opens his *Enquiry* arguing that the role of reason in moral decisions is very limited and that moral approval is essentially a feeling. Hume sees the relationship between reason and feeling as the key problem in moral theory. Hume uses the term *sentiment* to refer to feelings of all sorts.

There has been a controversy started of late . . . concerning the general foundation of morals: whether they be derived from reason or from sentiment; whether we attain the knowledge of them by a chain of argument and induction, or by an immediate feeling and finer internal sense; whether, like all sound judgment of truth and falsehood, they should be the same to every rational intelligent being; or whether, like the perception of beauty and deformity, they be founded entirely on the particular fabric and constitution of the human species.

The ancient philosophers, though they often affirm that virtue is nothing but conformity to reason, yet, in general, seem to consider morals as deriving their existence from taste and sentiment. On the other hand, our modern inquirers (though they also talk much of the beauty of virtue and deformity of vice, yet) have commonly endeavored to account for these distinctions by metaphysical reasonings, and by deductions from the most abstract principles of the understanding. Such confusion reigned in these subjects, that an opposition of the greatest consequence could prevail between one system and another, and even in the parts of almost each individual system. And yet nobody, till very lately, was ever sensible of it.

It must be acknowledged that both sides of the question are susceptible of specious arguments. Moral distinctions, it may be said, are discernible by pure *reason*. Else, whence the many disputes that reign in common life as well as in philosophy with regard to this subject: the long chain of proofs often produced on both sides, the examples cited, the authorities appealed to, the analogies employed, the fallacies detected, the inferences drawn, and the several conclusions adjusted to their proper principles? Truth is disputable, not taste. What exists in the nature of things is the standard of our judgment, [but] what each man feels within himself is the standard of sentiment. Propositions in geometry may be proved, systems in physics may be controverted. But the harmony of verse, the tenderness of passion, the brilliance of wit must give immediate pleasure. No man reasons concerning another's beauty, but frequently concerning the justice or injustice of his actions. In every criminal trial the first object of the prisoner is to disprove the facts alleged, and deny the actions imputed to him. The second [is] to prove that, even if these actions were real, they might be justified as innocent and lawful. It is confessedly by deductions of the understanding that the first point [of alleged facts] is ascertained. How can we suppose that a different faculty of the mind is employed in fixing the other [point regarding moral justification]?

On the other hand, those who would resolve all moral determinations into *sentiment* may endeavor to show that it is impossible for reason ever to draw conclusions of this nature. To virtue, say they, it belongs to be *amiable*, and [to] vice *odious*. This forms their very nature or essence. But can reason or argumentation distribute these different epithets to any subjects, and pronounce beforehand that this must produce love, and that hatred? Or what other reason can we ever assign for these affections but the original fabric and formation of the human mind, which is naturally adapted to receive them?

The end of all moral speculations is to teach us our duty, and (by proper representations of the deformity of vice and beauty of virtue) beget correspondent habits, and engage us to avoid the one, and embrace the other. But is this ever to be expected from, which, of themselves, have no hold of the affections nor set in motion the active powers of men? They discover truths. But where the truths which they discover are indifferent, and beget no desire or aversion, they can have no influence on conduct and behavior. What is honorable, what is fair, what is becoming, what is noble, what is generous, takes possession of the heart and animates us to embrace and maintain it. What is intelligible, what is evident, what is probable, what is true, procures only the cool assent of the understanding, and gratifying a speculative curiosity, puts an end to our researches.

It is not contrary to reason to prefer the destruction of the whole world to the scratching of my finger. It is not contrary to reason for me to choose my total ruin, to prevent the least uneasiness of an *Indian* or person wholly unknown to me. It is as little contrary to reason to prefer even my own acknowledged lesser good to my greater, and have a more ardent affection for the former than the latter. A trivial good may, from certain circumstances, produce a desire superior to what arises from the greatest and most valuable enjoyment. Nor is there anything more extraordinary in this than in [the field of] mechanics to see [a] one-pound weight raise up a hundred by the advantage of its situation [such as by a lever]. In short, a passion must be accompanied with some false judgment in order to its being unreasonable. [This paragraph is from the *Treatise*, 2.3.3.]

Extinguish all the warm feelings and prepossessions in favor of virtue, and all disgust or aversion to vice; render men totally indifferent towards these distinctions, and morality is no longer a practical study, nor has any tendency to regulate our lives and actions.

5. *How do criminal trials support the claim that moral distinctions and judgments are based on reason? Illustrate*

6. *Give an example that supports the view that moral distinctions arise only from feelings.*

7. *Hume makes some remarkable claims in the preceding paragraphs. Wouldn't most people think that preferring the destruction of the whole world to the scratching of one's finger was*

a sign of insanity, the total loss of reason? What is your view?

8. *Hume claims that the "inferences and conclusions of the understanding" have no influence on conduct " where the truths which they discover are indifferent," that is, where we do not personally care about them. An example might be "2 + 2 = 4," which is a truth that does not move people much. Give two more examples (not from math) of "conclusions of the understanding," one of which would influence how you act.*

These arguments on each side (and many more might be produced) are so plausible, that I am apt to suspect they may, the one as well as the other, be solid and satisfactory, and that *reason* and *sentiment* concur in almost all moral determinations and conclusions. The final sentence, it is probable, which pronounces characters and actions amiable or odious, praiseworthy or blamable; that which stamps on them the mark of honor or infamy, approbation or censure; that which renders morality an active principle and constitutes virtue our happiness, and vice our misery; it is probable, I say, that this final sentence depends on some internal sense or feeling which nature has made universal in the whole species. For what else can have an influence of this nature?

But in order to pave the way for such a *sentiment*, and give a proper discernment of its object, it is often necessary, we find, that much *reasoning* should precede, [so] that nice distinctions be made, just conclusions drawn, distant comparisons formed, complicated relations examined, and general facts fixed and ascertained.

[First,] some species of beauty, especially the natural kinds, on their first appearance, command our affection and approbation. And where they fail of this effect, it is impossible for any reasoning to redress their influence, or adapt them better to our taste and sentiment. But in many orders of beauty, particularly those of the finer arts, it is requisite to employ much reasoning in order to feel the proper sentiment. And a false relish may frequently be corrected by argument and reflection. There are just grounds to conclude that moral beauty partakes much of this latter species, and demands the assistance of our intellectual faculties, in order to give it a suitable influence on the human mind.

> *9. *Hume usefully compares the judgments we make about beauty to moral judgments. If I claim that a certain song is really beautiful and moving and you deny it and claim that it leaves you cold, does that show that one of us has made a mistake in reasoning? What does Hume say? Be careful!*

[Second,] one principal foundation of moral praise being supposed to lie in the *usefulness* [or beneficial consequences] of any quality or action, it is evident that *reason* must enter for a considerable share in all decisions of this kind. [This follows] since nothing but that faculty can instruct us in the tendency of qualities and actions, and *point out their beneficial consequences* to society and to their possessor. In many cases, this is an affair liable to great controversy. Doubts may arise, opposite interests may occur, and a preference must be given to one side [versus the other side] from very nice views, and a small overbalance of utility [or benefit which is in its favor]. This is particularly remarkable in questions with regard to justice (as is, indeed, natural to suppose from that species of utility, which attends every virtue). Were every single instance of justice, like that of benevolence, useful to society, this would be a more simple state of the case, and seldom liable to great controversy. But as single instances of justice are often pernicious in their first and immediate tendency (and as the advantage to society results only from the observance of the general rule, and from the concurrence and combination of several persons in the same equitable conduct) the case here becomes more intricate and involved. The various circumstances of society, the various *consequences* of any practice, the various interests which may be proposed; these, on many occasions, are doubtful and subject to great discussion and inquiry. The object of municipal laws is to fix all the questions with regard to justice. The debates of civilians, the reflections of politicians, the precedents of history and public records, are all directed to the same purpose. And a very accurate *reason* or *judgment* is often requisite to give the true determination,

amidst such intricate doubts arising from obscure or opposite utilities.

But though reason, when fully assisted and improved, be sufficient to instruct us in the pernicious or useful tendency of qualities and actions, it is not alone sufficient to produce any moral blame or approbation. Utility is only a tendency to a certain end. And were the end totally indifferent to us, we should feel the same indifference towards the means. It is requisite [that] a *sentiment* should here display itself, in order to give a preference to the useful above the pernicious tendencies. This sentiment can be no other than a feeling for the happiness of humankind, and a resentment of their misery, since these are the different ends which virtue and vice have a tendency to promote. Here, therefore, *reason* instructs us in the several tendencies of actions, and *humanity* [or sentiment] makes a distinction in favor of those which are useful and beneficial.

Hume makes some important points here which may need additional clarification.

1. First, Hume speaks of "utility." An action or a character trait has utility if it is useful. Useful for what? Take an example of an action: Bill spends Saturday morning helping to construct a house for Habitat for Humanity. In doing this he helps to make a house available to a low-income family that could otherwise not afford to own a home. How does he know it will do that? Well, presumably he knows something about housing costs, he knows something about how much money a person needs to afford a house, he has good reason to believe that the family in question does not have that much money, he knows a little bit about the value of the labor he is contributing and so forth. All of this knowledge has been acquired through the exercise of reason, through inferences from known facts and "conclusions of the understanding." That "reason" in that sense has been required to produce what Bill knows can hardly be disputed. But now the question we want answered is, has Bill done something useful or beneficial or, to put it another way, will the result of his activity be a useful state of affairs? Most people would say "yes." Why? Here comes Hume's second point.

2. We think of a state of affairs as useful when it pleases us. Many of us have positive feelings about a poor family owning their own home. If Bill did not have such positive feelings he probably would not be spending Saturday morning helping to build a house for someone he hardly even knows. This does not rule out other possible motives, but probably most typically someone like Bill simply likes to see poor people do better. (If that claim seems implausible, go back to Butler in Chapter 6 for further discussion.)

Now, Hume is claiming that what motivates Bill is a desire to produce something pleasing (to himself and/or others). Without such a motivation he would stay home and watch TV on Saturday morning. So it is the desire to produce what is useful (has utility or is pleasing), and that alone, that provokes Bill to act. However, he would not know what to do on Saturday morning to bring about a pleasing result if he did not know any relevant facts or make any relevant inferences. If he thought, mistakenly, that someone with an annual income below the poverty line could afford to buy a house without assistance, then he would not be working for Habitat for Humanity on Saturday. So the use of reason to acquire relevant facts is necessary for the action he takes, but it is not sufficient. Only a feeling, a positive attitude, toward the prospering of poor people can get him to act. Other people might know all the facts Bill knows about housing and poverty and never do anything to help. They have and use "reason," but they lack sufficient feeling, or "sentiment." Their attitudes of approval and disapproval are different from Bill's.

What then is the relation between feeling and reason in morality? Well, the morally good person, the person who acts well and/or has character traits that tend to result in acting well is simply the person who has positive feelings toward "utility" and negative feelings toward disutility, suffering etc. and knows enough (has enough reason) to be able to bring about the actual useful results. Thus, both reason and feeling play a crucial role in morality, but reason by itself will never produce utility. It merely tells us *how* to get results that we approve of. Reason is thought of as a value-neutral faculty that can link means to ends but can tell us nothing about what ends to pursue. We could say that Hume thinks of reason as merely instrumental. In Hume's view, a thoroughly rational person could be completely immoral. He could prefer the destruction of the whole world to the scratching of his own finger!

> ****10.** *Aristotle also claimed that reason by itself will not move anyone to act. But Aristotle would not agree with Hume that the only function of reason is to tell us how to link means to ends. Aristotle does not think of reason as simply a morally neutral instrument. How does what Aristotle says about the "uncontrolled man" (the* akrates, *see Chapter 3) make this point clear?*

Thus, the distinct boundaries and offices of *reason* and of *taste* are easily ascertained. The former conveys the knowledge of truth and falsehood. The latter gives the sentiment of beauty and deformity, vice and virtue. The one discovers objects as they really stand in nature, without addition or diminution. The other has a productive faculty and (gilding or staining all natural objects with the colors borrowed from internal sentiment) raises in a manner a new creation. Reason, being cool and disengaged, is no motive to action, and directs only the impulse received from appetite or inclination, by showing us the means of attaining happiness or avoiding misery. Taste, as it gives pleasure or pain (and thereby constitutes happiness or misery), becomes a motive to action, and is the first spring or impulse to desire and volition. From circumstances and relations known or supposed, the former leads us to the discovery of the concealed and unknown. After all circumstances and relations are laid before us, the latter makes us feel from the whole a new sentiment of blame or approbation. The standard of the one, being founded on the nature of things, is eternal and inflexible, even by the will of the Supreme Being. The standard of the other, arising from the internal frame and constitution of animals, is ultimately derived from that Supreme will, which bestowed on each being its peculiar nature, and arranged the several classes and orders of existence.

Hume has just used an important metaphor to clarify the respective roles of sentiment and reason in morality, though here he is using the word *taste* to include sentiment. Reason, he says, "discovers objects as they really stand in nature." Reason properly employed give us facts, tells us what is true and false, tells how things are in themselves, quite apart from how we might feel about them.

Taste, or sentiment, on the other hand, "gilds," or colors, natural objects with feelings, thus producing a "new creation," something that is not there at all prior to the ways of thinking and feeling typical of human subjects. Taste does not tell us, he implies, what is true or false. It does not reflect how the world is, but only how we feel about it. We might put it this way: Moral and aesthetic judgments involve projecting our own attitudes and feelings onto the world. Thus, in Hume's view, when someone says, "It is cruel to torture animals," they are not stating a fact about anything, and, strictly speaking, what they say is neither true nor false. Rather, in uttering "It is cruel to torture animals" I am simply projecting my feelings onto a morally neutral action or situation. I "color" the cruel action a certain way. Someone with different feelings or sentiments, a sadist, for instance, might color the very same action differently.

Nonetheless when I make such a moral judgment I usually do think that the "cruelty" is really out there in the world, it is part of what I actually experience when I see someone torturing an animal, just as the colors and shapes and movements that I experience when I witness an act of torture are out there, are part of the world. In Hume's view, on the other hand, when I see someone joyfully pushing a lighted cigarette into a cat's eye, what I see is the cigarette, the cat's eye, etc., but I do not actually see something that is "objectively" cruel!

11. *Do you think Hume is right about that? Defend your answer.*

Given Hume's view on the respective roles of reason and feeling (sentiment, taste) in morality, we can perhaps begin to appreciate the following famous and much-discussed (but not perfectly clear) passage.

I cannot forbear adding to these reasonings an observation, which may, perhaps, be found of some importance. In every system of morality which I have hitherto met with, I have always remarked that the author proceeds for some time in the ordinary way of reasoning, and establishes the being of a God, or makes observations concerning human affairs. When of a sudden, I am surprised to find that, instead of the usual copulations of propositions, *is* and *is not*, I meet with no proposition that is not connected with an *ought* or an *ought not*. The change is imperceptible, but is, however, of the last [and greatest] consequence. For as this *ought* or *ought not* expresses some new relation or affirmation, it is necessary that it should be observed and explained. And at the same time, [it is necessary] that a reason should be given for (what seems altogether inconceivable) how this new relation can be a deduction from others, which are entirely different from it. But as authors do not commonly use this precaution, I shall presume to recommend it to the readers. And [I] am persuaded that this small attention would subvert all the vulgar systems of morality, and let us see that the distinction of vice and virtue is not founded merely on the relations of objects nor is perceived by reason. [This paragraph is from the *Treatise*, 3.1.1.]

First a note on "reasoning." Reasoning often involves constructing arguments with premises and a conclusion. The premises and conclusions must be statements, that is, either true or false.

Here is a rather mundane example of a possible argument in ethics:

(1) Poor people cannot afford to buy their own homes.
(2) People with a little time to spare can (often) help to build homes for poor people.
(3) Therefore people with the time to spare ought (other things being equal) to spend time helping to build homes for poor people.

In this "argument" or piece of reasoning, premises 1 and 2 are examples of what Hume calls "observations concerning human affairs." They are either true or false. They are true if the world is as they say it is, false otherwise. Conclusion 3 is thought to follow from 1 and 2. It is treated as a "deduction" from 1 and 2. Now, Hume objects that conclusion 3 has in it a "new relation or affirmation" that differs completely from anything found in premises 1 and 2. There is, he thinks, a major disconnect between the premises (1 and 2) and the conclusion (3). In a good or valid argument there will not be such a disconnect. In a good deductive argument the conclusion will not contain anything that is not already implicit in the premises. So Hume wants to know why so many smart people have been taken in by this sort of argument (the smart people he had in mind included the "rationalist" philosophers of his own day, who thought that moral distinctions arise from reasoning alone. They might not have liked this particular argument, but they would have used arguments that were similar in crucial respects).

Perhaps you think you can patch this up easily. Just add a few obvious premises. For example, add the following:

1a. It would be a good thing for all people to own their own homes.
2a. Good people ought to help bring about good things.
2b. Everyone ought to be good.

Now we have a six-premise argument. And the conclusion seems to follow. But of course in Hume's view this will never do. For one thing, statements 1a and 2a are, he seems to think, expressions of feeling or sentiment, and strictly speaking they are neither true nor false and thus cannot be premises in any argument. They do not arise from observations concerning human affairs. Rather, they express how some people feel about certain states of affairs. And premises 2a and 2b contain "ought" already. Ultimately Hume claims that "ought" statements are themselves simply expressions of preference. When I say, " You ought to help the poor," I am indicating that I believe helping the poor has high utility and thus that it is, or leads to, something I (and others) approve of or find pleasing. The value of helping the poor, or my belief that it has value, is not based on any observations or reasonings. It amounts to a projection of my feelings on what I have observed.

12. *Consider the following argument:*
    1. God exists
    2. God commands that I give aid to the poor.
    3. I ought to aid the poor.
    Assume that we can prove that God exists and that he does command that we aid the poor. Would Hume still object to this argument? If so, why exactly?

In the late 18th and early 19th century Hume was regarded as the founder of the "theory of utility." We have already shown most of what such a theory involves. Any action, or personal trait, that is "useful" in the sense already described, useful either to ourselves or to others or both, will attract approval, and traits that have disutility will attract disapproval of various sorts. The idea that "utility" in some such sense is the basis of value is developed further by the "utilitarians" of the 19th century, particularly Mill (see Chapter 9).

Many people have wondered whether any attempt to base morals in feelings of approval and disapproval will lead to some kind of relativism. For it seems that such feelings can vary quite a bit from person to person and perhaps from culture to culture. Hume's comparison of moral to aesthetic judgments seems to support this point. Most people in the 16th and 17th centuries would not have agreed with "She is beautiful" said of a thin woman. Look at the "beautiful" women portrayed by Rembrandt or Titian, and ask yourself how many of them could win a beauty contest now. Not many. Feelings about beauty vary quite a bit from time to time and place to place. Isn't it the same way with judgments about what is morally good or fine? Hume would point out that where there are variations, some of them may be due to different assessments of the facts. That is true even in aesthetics. But apart from such differences he seems to think that people everywhere tend to approve and disapprove of pretty much the same character traits and types of actions. So his view about morals does not entail any kind of relativism. His own discussion may cast some doubt on this optimistic view, however. In discussing what he calls "monkish virtues" he has the following to say.

And as every quality, which is useful or agreeable to ourselves or others, is, in common life, allowed to be a part of personal merit; so no other will ever be received, where men judge of things by their natural, unprejudiced reason, without the delusive glosses of superstition and false religion. Celibacy, fasting, penance, mortification, self-denial, humility, silence, solitude, and the whole train of monkish virtues, for what reason are they everywhere rejected by men of sense, but because they serve to no manner of purpose; neither advance a man's fortune in the world, nor render him a more valuable member of society; neither qualify him for the entertainment of company, nor increase his power of self-enjoyment? We observe, on the contrary, that they cross all these desirable ends, [that they] stupefy the understanding and harden the heart, obscure the fancy and sour the temper. We justly, therefore, transfer them to the opposite column, and place them in the catalogue of vices; nor has any superstition force sufficient among men of the world, to pervert entirely these natural sentiments. A gloomy, harebrained enthusiast, after his death, may have a place in the calendar; but will scarcely ever be admitted, when alive, into intimacy and society, except by those who are as delirious and dismal as himself.

13. *Hume was an Enlightenment thinker who took a dim view of religion. If he had lived 300 years earlier he probably would have thought that the monkish virtues are indeed virtues. Does that fact, if it is a fact, show that Hume's account of morality is vulnerable to relativism? Discuss pro and con.*

14. *Hume's claim that humility and self-denial "serve no manner of purpose" seems false. Try to think of cases where these "virtues" would serve a good purpose, a purpose that most people, whether religious or not, would find pleasing and approve of.*

Further Discussion and Applications

Emotivism, Prescriptivism, Noncognitivism, the Open-Question Argument (Ayer, Moore)

As discussed earlier, Hume thinks that (1) "You ought to help the poor" and (2) "It is wrong to torture animals" and similar "moral" claims are not really statements of fact but expressions of emotion or more generally of approval or disapproval. A "statement of fact" is simply something that can be true or false. So in his view it appears that neither (1) nor (2) is either true or false.

Now, most people, on reflection, would agree that to know that *P*, where *P* is any statement (of fact), is, at the very least, and by definition, to believe *P* when *P* is true. So if neither (1) nor (2) is true or false, then they certainly are not true, so nobody can know them. What appear to be moral truths that can be known are more like shouts of "hurrah" where we express approval but do not make a statement. (Someone next to you at the game jumps up and shouts, "Hurrah!" You say, "How do you know that's true?" This sounds like a joke.) The view that moral utterances are neither true nor false thus entails *noncognitivism*, the view in ethics that there is no such thing as moral knowledge, and could not be, given the nature of moral language.

In the 20th century the view that sentences like (1) and (2) are not used to make statements but are merely expressions of emotion has been dubbed *emotivism*. Some 20th century philosophers, such as A. J. Ayer, claimed that (1) and (2) serve not only to express emotions but also to "prescribe" behavior for others. To prescribe is to command, more or less. Ayer puts it like this:

> It is worth mentioning that ethical terms do not serve only to express feeling. They are calculated also to arouse feeling, and so to stimulate action. Indeed some of them are used in such a way as to give the sentences in which they occur the effect of commands. Thus the sentence "It is your duty to tell the truth" may be regarded both as the expression of a certain sort of ethical feeling about truthfulness and as the expression of the command "Tell the truth." (From *Language, Truth and Logic*, Chapter 6)

It is of course obvious that commands, or prescriptions, are also neither true nor false. The view that ethical judgments are "prescriptive" is called *prescriptivism*.

Problems with Emotivism

Emotivism (and also noncognitivism and prescriptivism) have been attacked in the following ways, among others. To understand the first attack, you must understand what an *equivocation* is. The following argument illustrates what an equivocation is:

1′. I am standing on the bank of a river.
2′. All the banks are charging 6% on auto loans.
3′. Therefore, the bank I am standing on is charging 6%.

This is silly of course. The argument is obviously invalid. It involves an equivocation. The word *bank* means something different in premise 2′ than it does in premise 1′: financial institution in 2, and edge of a river in 1.

The argument is silly because it depends on using *bank* in one way in one premise, another way in another premise.

Now consider this argument:

1. If it is wrong to cause harm and torturing animals causes harm, then it is wrong to torture animals.
2. It is wrong to cause harm.
3. Torturing animals causes harm.
4. Therefore, it is wrong to torture animals.

This certainly looks like a valid argument. But it is valid only if "It is wrong to cause harm" means the same thing in premises 1 and 2. Otherwise we have an equivocation, and the argument is invalid. Does "It is wrong to cause harm" mean the same thing in 1 as in 2? Not according to the emotivist, it seems! According to him, in premise 2 I am using the words simply to express my disapproval of, or hostility toward, causing harm. They have only "emotive" meaning. But clearly I am not doing any such thing in premise 1. A person could assert 1 who had no negative feelings or any other feelings toward causing harm or torturing animals. Right?

So in the emotivist way of looking at things, an obviously valid argument must be invalid. The emotivist cannot give an account of the use of "It is wrong to cause harm" in premise 1. So there must be something wrong with emotivism. It is true that the emotivist denies that 2 is a statement at all (and can thus be part of an argument), but he still owes us an account of "It is wrong to cause harm" in statement 1, and it is not clear that he has any.

Here is another problem, originally brought up in a somewhat different form by British philosopher

G. E. Moore. Suppose I define *good* in this emotivist fashion:

good = "something I approve of"

If that is a good definition, than anywhere the word *good* occurs I should be able to replace it with "something I approve of," and vice versa. That is how definitions work. So in the sentence "Eating pizza is good," I should be able to replace the word *good* with "something I approve of." But Moore objects: Is it not possible to approve of something that is not good? It might be true that eating pizza is something I approve of, but false that it is something good. It is, Moore said, always an *open question* whether what I approve of is good. But it is never an open question whether what is good is good, anymore than it is an open question whether what is round is round. If it is true that eating pizza is good, then, of course, it must be true that eating pizza is good.

15. *If* good = *"pleasurable," then you can replace* good *with "pleasurable," and vice versa, in any context. So if it is true that "Eating pizza is pleasurable," then it must also be true that "Eating pizza is good." Right? So far that seems just fine. But now, suppose you are a sadist. In your case it is true that "Torturing people is pleasurable." If you accept the definition, what follows (write it down)? Do you see the problem? Moore's argument might apply to utilitarianism (see Chapter 9) as well as to emotivism.*

Moore inferred that the property of goodness was "indefinable." But it would also be possible to infer that emotivism must be mistaken.

Sympathy, Moral Judgment and Morality (Bennett)

Often people must act against their feelings in order to act well or morally. I may feel deep sympathy for my child, who is crying and pleading for relief as she undergoes a painful medical procedure. But if the procedure is necessary to life or long-term health, it may be my duty to set aside those feelings and allow the pain to be inflicted and even continue for some time, even though I could prevent it. Only by doing so could I follow the principle or judgment that parents should give the best care possible to their children.

In other cases I act out of sympathy and there is no conflict with any principles I hold. If my child is crying from a badly scraped knee, my feelings for her may be the entire and sufficient motivation for my actions, which will consist in doing all I can to remove the pain.

Sometimes my feelings, such as feelings of sympathy, motivate me to act. Sometimes my principles do. Sometimes these two sources of motivation coincide or at least are not in conflict. That seems to be so in the case of the scraped knee. But sometimes they conflict, and I must go with one or the other.

16. What does Huck go with, feelings or principles?

Now, in Hume's view it is always feelings, in particular the "sentiment of humanity," that move us to act. If it appears that I am impelled to act by a "principle" or judgment, that can only mean that the judgment carries with it some feeling, one that might win out over other feelings, as in our first case.

American philosopher Jonathan Bennett thinks that moral judgments can be an independent source of motivation, lacking any significant "feeling" component. My judgment that it is wrong to give handouts to beggars can simply be a principle I have learned, instilled by my parents, for instance. It may typically conflict with sympathetic feelings I have for beggars. It may go against all my feelings or sentiments, as Kant thought moral judgments typically do (unless we are to count among feelings a "feeling of respect for the moral law" or for "duty"). Thus Bennett does not entirely agree with Hume. In his view, principles as well as sentiments can motivate to action. But he does agree that sympathy in itself has no "judgment component." "My sympathy for someone in distress may lead me to help him. . . . But in itself it is not a judgment about what I ought to do, but just a feeling for him."

Bennett argues that our feelings should often be allowed to correct our judgments. The problem with Huck Finn, he claims, is twofold: First, his "moral principles" are bad principles; and second, they are so ingrained that his feelings cannot, so to speak, "get

to them" and thus aid in correcting them. The result is that Huck simply acts on impulse and gives up on his (bad) morality. But then he feels like a morally weak person who has failed to do his duty.

Bennett cites another case in which sympathetic feelings failed to correct a bad morality. Heinrich Himmler, who supervised the slaughter of Jews for Hitler, felt queasy about what he was doing. He felt some sympathy for the people he was killing, but he also felt it was his duty to kill them and "cleanse the soil" so that the nation could prosper. In Himmler's case the conflict between duty and sympathy is decided in favor of duty (as he conceived it), so he ends up feeling like a morally strong person rather than a weak person, as did Huck. Strong but queasy.

A third possibility is supposedly illustrated by the puritan preacher and theologian Jonathan Edwards. According to Bennett, Edwards simply squelched or stamped out all natural feelings of sympathy for sufferers, particularly those suffering in Hell. He overcame the conflict between what he conceived as right or just, on the one hand, and what normal sympathetic feelings would require, by purging himself of the feelings. The inhabitants of Heaven, he claims, "will have no love or pity" for the damned. They may even "rejoice" at the sight of the damned in torment.

Here then are some possible types of people:

A. People whose morality coincides with their feelings, for the most part: Their motivational structures are relatively smooth. Such would be the Aristotelian wise man, whose feelings and principles necessarily work together.
B. People whose morality typically or in very significant cases conflicts with their feelings of sympathy.

Type B people divide into the following groups:

B1. People who give up their morality in favor of feelings (like Huck Finn).
B2. People who give up feelings in favor of their morality (like Himmler).
B3. People who stamp out feelings that conflict with morality by becoming cold and unsympathetic or "unfeeling" (like Edwards).

Bennett thinks that B3 are the worst type. When their morality is bad, it cannot be corrected by sympathetic feelings or replaced by sympathetic feelings. It follows from Bennett's account that Himmler's morality is better than Edwards', even though Himmler arranged the slaughter of millions of people and Edwards never harmed a flea! At least Himmler felt very uncomfortable with his job. His natural sympathies worked against his sense of duty, but not enough to get him to stop killing. Edwards, on the other hand, felt no sympathy at all for the sufferers in Hell.

17. *What do you think? Is Himmler's "morality" actually better than Edwards'? Defend your answer. Consider your response to Orienting Question 3 when answering.*

Sentiment and Sentimentality (Carroll)

How important are feelings, such as feelings of sympathy, to morality? Certainly how we feel about things sometimes motivates us to act, and obviously actions are important. Morality is a matter of actions, or of character traits that produce actions. But actions take place outside our heads, so to speak, and it seems to many that what we actually do matters much more than how we feel. That is because feelings can so easily be disconnected from actions. Like Himmler, a person may feel bad about what he is doing but do it anyway.

Sentimental people are people in whom there is such a disconnection between feeling and action. Here are some quotations from the *Oxford English Dictionary*, chosen to illustrate the meaning of *sentimental*:

SIR W. SCOTT: "Dropping a sentimental tear when there was room for effective charity."
J. GALSWORTHY: "Fleur was not sentimental, her desires were ever concrete and concentrated."

The first quotation conveys a contrast between feelings that are effective, on the one hand, and sentimentality on the other. The second contrasts feelings that are focused and produce real results and feelings that are vague and ineffective. It appears that the con-

cept *sentimental* applies well to Himmler. It also applies to the Walrus in the following poem by Lewis Carroll. Tweedledum relates the poem to Alice, and both comment on it.

Lewis Carroll: The Walrus and the Carpenter (from Through the Looking Glass*)*

"Oysters, come and walk with us!"
    The Walrus did beseech.
"A pleasant walk, a pleasant talk,
    Along the briny beach:

We cannot do with more than four,
    To give a hand to each."
The eldest Oyster looked at him,
    But never a word he said;

The eldest Oyster winked his eye,
    And shook his heavy head—
Meaning to say he did not choose
    To leave the oyster-bed.

But four young Oysters hurried up
    All eager for the treat:
Their coats were brushed, their faces washed,
    Their shoes were clean and neat—

And this was odd, because, you know,
    They hadn't any feet.
Four other Oysters followed them,
    And yet another four;

And thick and fast they came at last,
    And more, and more, and more—
All hopping through the frothy waves,
    And scrambling to the shore.

The Walrus and the Carpenter
    Walked on a mile or so,
And then they rested on a rock
    Conveniently low:

And all the little Oysters stood
    And waited in a row.
"The time has come," the Walrus said,
    "To talk of many things,

Of shoes—and ships—and sealing-wax—
   Of cabbages—and kings—
And why the sea is boiling hot—
   And whether pigs have wings."

"But wait a bit," the Oysters cried,
   "Before we have our chat;
For some of us are out of breath,
   And all of us are fat!"

"No hurry!" said the Carpenter,
   They thanked him much for that.
"A loaf of bread," the Walrus said,
   "Is what we chiefly need:

Pepper and vinegar besides
   Are very good indeed—
Now if you're ready, Oysters dear,
   We can begin to feed."

"But not on us!" the Oysters cried,
   Turning a little blue.
"After such kindness, that would be
   A dismal thing to do!"

"The night is fine," the Walrus said,
   "Do you admire the view?"
"It was so kind of you to come!
   And you are very nice!"

The Carpenter said nothing but
   "Cut us another slice:
I wish you were not quite so deaf—
   I've had to ask you twice!"

"It seems a shame," the Walrus said,
   "To play them such a trick,
After we've brought them out so far,
   And made them trot so quick!"

The Carpenter said nothing but
   "The butter's spread too thick!"
"I weep for you," the Walrus said:
   "I deeply sympathize."

With sobs and tears he sorted out
   Those of the largest size,
Holding his pocket-handkerchief
   Before his streaming eyes.

"O Oysters," said the Carpenter,
   "You've had a pleasant run!
Shall we be trotting home again?"
   But answer came there none—

And this was scarcely odd, because
   They'd eaten every one."

"I like the Walrus best," said Alice: "because you see he was a little sorry for the poor oysters."

"He ate more than the Carpenter, though," said Tweedledee. "You see he held his handkerchief in front, so that the Carpenter couldn't count how many he took: contrariwise."

"That was mean!" Alice said indignantly. "Then I like the Carpenter best—if he didn't eat so many as the Walrus."

"But he ate as many as he could get," said Tweedledum.

This was a puzzler. After a pause, Alice began: "Well! They were both very unpleasant characters—"

It seems that Alice at first adopts a position like Bennett's. Since the Walrus shows some sympathy for his victims, she likes him better. But in fact his "sympathy" is worthless sentimentality. It has no effect on his actions, and he devours as many victims as does the supposedly less humane carpenter. Her concluding judgment is that they are both bad characters. Her focus turns outward, to what is actually being done, and to the actual victims.

Such a perspective would give Edwards higher marks than Himmler. Edwards did not harm anyone. He did not encourage anyone to harm anyone. As a puritan he was strictly bound by a duty of charity to his neighbors. We may dislike or even be shocked by some of his attitudes. But no sane person would prefer Himmler to Edwards as a neighbor or, say, a babysitter. In Alice's final perspective, Himmler's sentimentality has no redeeming value.

18. *What is your view on Himmler vs. Edwards? Which one do you consider to be morally superior, or are they both equally bad?*

The Education of the Feelings

How should we think of the contrast between reason and feeling that is central to Hume and the ethical reflection of his time? Something seems to be amiss. Aristotle would not have claimed that feelings are judgments, but he would not have separated them from knowledge the way Hume or the emotivists or the projectivists, have done. Some modern philosophers might insist that feelings are "intentional," that is, are directed on something. When I feel fear or anger, there is something objective that I fear. Some fears are, however, directed on things that are not, objectively, fearful, such as being in a confined space. Some feelings of anger are "out of whack" with the way things are objectively in the world. It "makes sense," we say, to be angry at someone who has openly insulted me, but not at someone who inadvertently stepped on my toe or played a harmless practical joke. Feelings, or "sentiments" insofar as they are a topic in ethics, are not simply "raw feels" that have no content, no correctness or incorrectness. They are not like a can of paint that could be splashed anywhere, coloring the world in all sorts of ways.

Perhaps the contrast that needs to be explored, then, is not that between reason and feelings, but between well-educated feelings and miseducated or uneducated feelings. Perhaps, too, *feeling* and *sentiment* are excessively vague and general terms. A careful probing of the (fictional) life of Huck or of the real-world lives of monsters like Himmler and the Nazi doctors may show a complex motivational structure in which trained and untrained emotions and attitudes, self-deception, bad habits, cowardice, greed and much else are interwoven.

Consider Huck again, just briefly. It hardly seems that the contest within Huck is between feeling and reason or between acting on principle and acting from emotion, though Bennett seems to think so. Huck's negative feelings about stealing are visceral, perhaps even stronger than his feelings of friendship toward Jim. On the other hand, his feelings about Jim have a strong cognitive dimension. It is obvious that Jim is a human being, that he can feel resentment and hurt, joy and hope, and concern for others, in a way that no nonhuman animal could. As such he evokes certain attitudes that are, arguably, appropriate to the facts. Those who lack such attitudes and feelings, such as, presumably, slave owners, are, on the other hand, probably mired in complex forms

of self-deception that require false beliefs or involve beliefs that are not fully spelled out and so forth. It seems unlikely that the difference between Huck and Mrs. Watson is that she is simply missing a range of feelings that he has or that she has only a very weak version of those feelings.

Would a full and detailed analysis of human motivation, or of what might be called "moral psychology," support a sharp contrast between reason (knowledge, objectivity, fact), on the one hand, and feeling (sentiment, the subjective), on the other? The Aristotelian answer has always been "no!" But the idea that there must be some such contrast has been very deep seated in modern philosophy, and a form of it emerges also in Kant, discussed in the next chapter.

Projectivism (Blackburn)

Hume claims that in making moral judgments we "gild and stain" natural objects with "colors" taken from "internal sentiment." He thinks the same thing applies to aesthetic judgments, and as we attempt to understand and evaluate Hume's claim here it might pay to take a look first at aesthetic judgments. Suppose Bill responds to oval-shaped faces and long noses with appreciation, as did the painter Modigliani. Bill says, "How lovely!" when he sees such a face. That would be one kind of aesthetic judgment. Now suppose Bob finds such features repellent in some way. He responds to the same face with "Yuck!" or "That is a very ugly face." Has one of these persons seen something that the other had missed? Are they not both presented with the same data, the same "natural objects" as Hume would say? It seems that they are. Let us call the natural object (the oval face, say) *X*. What we have is this:

> Bill: *X* is lovely.
> Bob: *X* is ugly (it is not the case that *X* is lovely).

Clearly Bill and Bob disagree. How come? Could it be that Bob actually fails to see something that Bill does see? Perhaps Bob doesn't see that the face is oval, for instance? That seems very unlikely. Rather, what we are inclined to say is that they have different "attitudes" toward the same object. Attitudes are subjective. They are in people, not in the world apart from people. Suppose Bill insists that the face is itself beautiful, even if no one thinks it is. That seems odd.

The best explanation of this disagreement, Hume thinks, is that people "project" various properties (beauty, ugliness) onto the world, properties that are "borrowed from inner sentiment." For some reason Bill feels that oval faces are beautiful, and he projects that feeling onto the object itself and thus thinks that the object itself is beautiful. But the object itself, or in itself, is neither beautiful nor ugly. Bob has negative feelings about oval faces and "projects" those feelings on them. A third person might have no feelings at all about oval faces. That is at least one way to understand Hume's remarks about "gilding natural objects with colors taken from internal sentiment."

*19. *Moral and aesthetic judgments are sometimes compared to perceptual judgments. "X is red" is a perceptual judgment. Is the "redness" in X, or is it only in the perceiver? Explain your view.*

Similarly, in the projectivist view, moral judgments, such as "That was kind," are used to "gild" a natural object or event or state of affairs with a moral quality, the quality of kindness. Spending time on a Habitat for Humanity home consists in nailing together floor joists and wall studs, pushing insulation in certain spaces, etc. Saying of all of that that it is a "kind" thing to do is simply to express a certain attitude toward it. The kindness is obviously not objectively present in the nails, the hammering, etc. By calling what is done "kind" we project a certain "color" onto it.

Isn't all of this just common sense? Perhaps, but there are some objections. One of them is that if we accept the "projectivist" theory, we lose the commitment involved in moral judgment and action. If I come to think of the kindness as just an attitude that I project onto my building activities or, to put it another way, if I come to think that there is nothing existing apart from my attitudes and my will that demands a certain response from me, then we might expect the pressure to act morally to diminish. You might think it very important to be kind, or keep your promises, or eschew cruelty, but once you realize, with Hume, that that feeling of importance is

just "you," might not those things cease to seem important? If you believe Hume's theory, will that belief conflict with moral concern? To some it will seem to have explained away, rather than explained, moral life. Contemporary philosopher Simon Blackburn puts it this way:

> From the inside, the objects of our passions are their immediate objects: it is the loved one, the sunset, that matters to us. It is not our own state of satisfaction or pleasure. Must projectivism struggle with this fact, or disown it? Is it that we projectivists, at the crucial moment when we are about to save the child, throw ourselves on the grenade, walk out into the snow, will think, "Oh, it's only me and my desires or other connative pressures—forget it"? (from "How to Be an Ethical Anti-Realist" in *Essays in Quasi-Realism*, 1993)

But Blackburn thinks this worry is misplaced. One way the worry arises is this: When I learn about Hume's theory, I may begin to believe that what happens when people make moral judgments, or engage in moral acts, is that they think what they are doing is dependent on their desires and attitudes. But that is a mistake. My responses will not necessarily be any weaker or less immediate just because I learned Hume's theory. Blackburn says:

> The lover who hears that the beloved is present and feels he must go . . . has no thoughts of the form "If I desire her I must go." The news comes in and the emotion goes out. Nothing in human life could be or feel more categorical.

Likewise in the witnessing of a cruel act, "the news comes in and the emotion [revulsion etc] goes out." No thought about the possibility that I am "projecting" need intervene.

Another, related worry about projectivism is that it will lead to relativism. If moral judgments and reactions are just projections of feelings I have, then there is going to be a lot of variation in moral judgments, it seems. Think about how quickly feelings can change about all sorts of things, such as how to dress. But this overlooks the nature of moral feelings, according to Blackburn. They are not like feelings about how people dress. A teen might think that the way her parents dressed when they were teens was ugly and wrong. But that is a mistake, and one that is usually found out, when people discover how quickly fashion can change. The teen gets older and sees that she is mistaken. The judgment that torturing an animal is cruel is not, however, like that. A person might cease to make that judgment, might cease to react with horror to torture, due to some very unusual, perhaps degrading, circumstances in his life. That is something to be regretted. In the variations in fashion there is normally not anything to be regretted. Moral remarks are made from within a moral perspective of course, but then that is the only place to make them, in the projectivist view.

20. *Is Blackburn claiming that moral feelings do not change much, whereas matters of taste do change quite quickly? If so, does he agree with Hume? Do you think he is right?*

The plausibility of projectivism seems to vary with the sorts of examples used. Consider the following statements:

1. That dance was graceful.
2. That act was cruel.
3. That dance was beautiful.
4. That act was wrong.

Statements 3 and 4 can probably be accounted for with projectivist assumptions. We even say that beauty is in the eye of the beholder, which of course implies that it is not in the beautiful thing. *Wrongness* is a very general term used to condemn actions, and it often seems easy to describe a wrong action informatively without any reference to its wrongness. A case of ignoring the needs or even the rights of another person, for instance, might be described in behaviorist or evolutionary terms, as a piece of behavior with a certain causal history or as behavior that has been "selected against" in the gene derby (see the discussion of sociobiology in Chapter 6). Things are not so easy with statements 1 and 2, however. On exactly what features of a person's movements do we "project" the property of gracefulness? What descriptions of the dance could we give that would not employ the notion of gracefulness or closely allied "evaluative" concepts? And how do we

describe a cruel piece of behavior without showing its cruelty? Suppose the cruel behavior consists in forcing a lit cigarette into an animal's eyeball. That description and the description of it as cruel are "glued together," so to speak. Someone who treated that action as a "natural object" on which various attitudes could be projected might seem alienated, even crazy. Whether these "thick" descriptive properties require some other account than that given by projectivism continues to be hotly debated.

21. *Which of the following descriptions obviously involve "projection"?*
    a. That is beautiful (said of a dress).
    b. That is flowing (said of a gown).
    c. That is yellow.

Is/Ought, Facts and Values, and Institutional Facts (Searle)

The contrast between reason and feeling is, as we have seen in Hume, linked to another contrast that is very commonly taken for granted, both in philosophy and outside of it, between facts and values. We say, "That is just a value judgment, not a fact." Reason is on the fact side, feeling on the value side. Philosophers also distinguish *descriptive* from *prescriptive* statements. Hume's claim that it is not possible to derive "ought" statements from "is" statements sounds a lot like the claim that there is a gap between facts, or description, and values, or prescription. "Is" statements are statements of fact. "Ought" statements are statements of value.

In contemporary philosophy there has been a good deal of discussion of the "is/ought" problem. Some philosophers have argued that Hume has a mistaken view about what makes anything a fact. There are different kinds of facts, and some of them are such that it is possible to derive ought statements from them.

One of the important discussions of these issues is by the American philosopher John Searle (b. 1932). In his essay "How to Derive 'Ought' from 'Is,'" he recasts the is/ought problem in contemporary language:

It is often said that one cannot derive an "ought" from an "is." This thesis, which comes from a famous passage in Hume's *Treatise*, though not as clear as it might be, is at least clear in broad out-line: There is a class of statements of fact which is logically distinct from a class of statements of value. No set of statements of fact by themselves entails any statement of value. Put in more contemporary terminology, no set of descriptive statements can entail an evaluative statement without the addition of at least one evaluative premise.

Searle agrees that many descriptive statements, or statements of fact—such as "Poor people cannot afford to buy houses"—cannot directly imply evaluative statements or statements of obligation, such as "One ought to donate time to help build houses for poor people." However, he argues, there is a special set of facts—which he calls *institutional facts*—that can imply statements of obligation:

> [S]tatements containing words such as "married," "promise," "home run," and "five dollars" state facts whose existence presupposes certain institutions: a man has five dollars, given the institution of money. Take away the institution and all he has is a rectangular bit of paper with green ink on it. A man hits a home run only given the institution of baseball; without the institution he only hits a sphere with a stick. Similarly, a man gets married or makes a promise only within the institutions of marriage and promising. Without them, all he does is utter words or make gestures. We might characterize such facts as institutional facts, and contrast them with noninstitutional, or brute, facts. (from "How to Derive Ought from Is")

The *fact* that Bob hit a home run is a fact only within a set of rules and agreements. If Bob is standing all by himself in Fenway park and hits a ball over the left field fence, he does not then hit a home run. And no one is obligated to register a score. Only where certain rules and conventions are operative can it be a fact that Bob hits a home run, with all that that may entail. Most people know those rules (for example, it is not a home run unless it is "fair," there is another team present, etc.). If it is a fact that Bob hit a home run, that fact logically implies other facts, for instance, that Bob's team "ought" to get additional points. In exactly the same way, the fact that

Bob made a promise to return a car is a fact only within a set of rules and agreements. If no one else is present when he utters the words "I promise . . . ," or if he utters them while playing a part in a theatre production, he has not actually made a promise. But if it is a fact that he has made a promise (i.e., the right conditions for doing so obtained), that fact logically implies further facts, such as that Bob is obligated to return the car. The institution of promise keeping provides a good illustration of Searle's point. When we make promises, we step inside a framework of rules and legitimate expectations. Thus we can derive an "ought" from an "is" like this (this is a very simplified version of Searle's derivation):

> *Statement of institutional fact*: Smith promised to return Bob's car.
> *Ought statement*: Smith is morally obligated to return Bob's car.

Searle's solution to the is/ought problem focuses on obvious institutional facts, such as promising. In this case, there is a particular verbal act by which we participate in the institution of promising, namely, the utterance, under appropriate circumstances, of "I promise to do such and such." Aside from these more obvious institutions, there may be less obvious ones surrounding other kinds of moral behavior. This is so with the rules and expectations we have about stealing. Here, the institutional fact might be something like this: "Society mandates that its members do not steal." This, then, would lead to the ought statement "Smith, who is a member of society, is morally obligated not to steal," given that Smith is indeed committed to membership in that society. Following Searle, we might be able to uncover institutional facts surrounding all of our basic moral obligations, such as prohibitions against lying, adultery and murder.

*22. *Is the statement "I paid the rent by check" a statement of institutional fact? If it is true, does it imply any statement about what ought or ought not to be done? If so, give an example.*

23. *Are there any institutional facts that might imply the claim that we ought not commit murder?*

CHAPTER EIGHT

Reason, Duty and Dignity

Introduction

Many people have the sense that there are certain things that absolutely must or must not be done, no matter what. For example, the deliberate torture of an innocent child would, many people think, be "absolutely" wrong. Nothing could justify such an act.

This idea of a moral "must" captures much of what is meant by *duty*. To say that it is my duty to do *X* is often taken to mean that *X* must be done, no matter what. Theories that stress the centrality of duty are called *deontological* theories (from Greek words for an account of necessity or what must be). Many moral theories seem to have difficulty accounting for this "must." Aristotle, it seems, has nothing to say about it. Divine command theories, on the other hand, typically stress the absoluteness of God's commands. One must obey them no matter what. But even such theories seem not to explain what many people feel, namely, that there is something in certain actions themselves, apart from their being commanded, that makes them right or wrong. Is there any way to account for the sense that many people have (including many atheists) that there are things that absolutely, categorically must or must not be done?

The idea of a moral "must" can be connected to the belief, or feeling, that human beings should never, under any circumstances, be treated with disrespect. Perhaps the sense that we should not lie, harm the in-nocent or enslave others is traceable to this sense that we should not manipulate or abuse people but should always respect their freedom and dignity. The following selections explore some deontological themes.

ORIENTING QUESTIONS, INITIAL REACTIONS

1. Suppose you have promised to take your daughter to a ballet performance on Tuesday that she very much wants to attend (though you personally do not care for ballet). Tuesday comes and you have a chance to go on a very exciting trip with some friends. But you have an *obligation* to take your daughter to the ballet, since you *promised*. Doesn't this obligation, or *duty*, run completely against what you want (in this case, to go on the trip)? Is this case typical of duties? That is, do they typically have no basis in what people want or feel and even *typically* interfere with what people want?

2. Is there something especially *rational* about doing ones duty and something irrational about following appetites, feelings or desires? Or is it the other way around?

3. Is there something absolutely wrong with treating a person as a mere "thing," to be used as a means to an end, somewhat like a tool?

4. Are there ethically significant things you ought to do that are not duties? For example, if a friend is in the hospital, you might think you ought to visit her, but do you have a *duty* to visit her?

5. The notions of *respect* for others and of human *dignity* play a large role in much contemporary moral discourse. What do you understand by human dignity?

6. We may criticize a person who cheats on his taxes by saying "What if everyone did that?," to which he might reply, "Not everyone will." Does that seem like a relevant reply to you? State why or why not.

ANTHONY TROLLOPE

Trollope (1815–1882) was a major English novelist of the Victorian era. He worked many years in the postal service in England and Ireland until his resignation in 1867. By that time he had already attained fame with his novel The Warden *(1855), the first in the series of Barsetshire novels . He traveled over much of the globe, a fact that is evident even in the novel cited here,* Dr. Wortle's School. *His insights into the self-deception and hypocrisies that infect daily life are important to this late novel. He is indeed a kind of moralist. The following remarks, from another, late novel, are typical:*

> *Needless to deny that the normal London plumber is a dishonest man. We do not even allow ourselves to think so. That question, as to the dishonesty of mankind generally, is one that disturbs us greatly;—whether a man in all grades of life will by degrees train his honesty to suit his own book, so that the course of life which he shall bring himself to regard as soundly honest shall, if known to his neighbors, subject him to their reproof. We own to a doubt whether the honesty of a bishop would shine bright as the morning star to the submissive ladies who now worship him, if the theory of life upon which he lives were understood by them in all its bearings." (The "Plumber", 1880)*

The notion of duty, as what must or must not be done no matter what, figured prominently in the morality, at least the public morality, of Victorian ladies and gentlemen (the Victorian era coincides roughly with the second half of the 19th century and the beginning of the 20th, during which time Queen Victoria ruled the British empire). Although Trollope sees that "duty" can become a cover for meanness and inhumanity, he seems to accept that the notion has genuine moral importance, if not always absolute centrality. There are, after all, legitimate and non-negotiable demands on people; certainly not all of those demands are simply rigid social conventions. But what are those demands, and how non-negotiable are they? Most people shrink at the thought of certain deeds, such as the torture of an innocent child. Some would insist that such a thing should not be done, *no matter what*. It would be a violation of an absolute duty. But there are other duties that might not be so non-negotiable. Might it even be wrong to fulfill certain duties, if doing so caused great suffering? There are times when doing one's duty seems cruel. Cruelty is wrong. But how can something that is genuinely a duty, and thus must be done or avoided, be at the same time wrong? Furthermore it sometimes seems that there are conflicts between duties. If doing one's duty can sometimes be cruel, and if there is a duty not to be cruel, it seems that there can be real conflicts between duties.

The topic of *Dr. Wortle's School* is bigamy. Trollope presumably shares the view, still widely held, that bigamy is simply impermissible. Yet in this novel it seems that the rule must be bent to avoid great cruelty.

One of the principle characters, Mr. Peacocke, a clergyman and president of the College of St. Louis, has unwittingly married a woman who is already married. Mrs. Peacocke (Ella Beaufort at the time) had married the elder of two brothers, Ferdinand Lefroy, who attempted to take her with him to Mexico to seek a fortune with desperadoes conducting raids along the Texas border. Ferdinand's cruel treatment of his wife becomes known, and when he attempts to force her to join him in a life of crime, certain clergymen of St. Louis, including Mr. Peacocke, intervene. Ella's husband and his brother leave for Mexico anyway, and she is left to support herself. Mr. Peacocke, in a perfectly honorable way, provides her with help. After a few years a rumor is circulated that Ferdinand is dead. Mr. Peacocke, who is in love with the beautiful Mrs. Lefroy, sets out to determine whether the rumor is true. He finds the younger brother, Robert, who assures him that Ferdinand was indeed killed by U.S. troops. Peacocke returns to St. Louis elated, and he proposes marriage to the "widow," who accepts him "with a full and happy heart." But after only six very happy months of marriage, Ferdinand shows up quite alive. He accuses them (correctly) of bigamy. What should they do? (Ferdinand disappears almost immediately and, as it eventually turns out, is never heard from again).

(From *Dr. Wortle's School*)

Should they part? There is no one who reads this but will say that they should have parted. Every day passed together as man and wife must be a falsehood and a sin. There would be absolute misery for both in parting—but there is no law from god or man entitling a man to escape from misery at the expense of falsehood and sin. Though their hearts might have burst in the doing of it, they should have parted. Though she would have been friendless, alone, and utterly despicable in the eyes of the world, abandoning the name which she cherished, as not her own, and going back to that which she utterly abhorred, still she should have done it. And he, resolving, as no doubt he would have done under any circumstances, that he must quit the city of his adoption—he should have left her with such material sustenance as her spirit would have enabled her to accept, should have gone his widowed way, and endured as best he might the idea that he had left the woman whom he loved behind, in the desert, all alone! That he had not done so the reader is aware. That he had lived a life of sin—that he and she had continued in one great falsehood—is manifest enough.

In fact Mr. Peacocke decides to leave the country. He travels with his "wife" to England, where he takes a position in Dr. Wortle's school, a typical English private church school, a preparatory school for boys. But the fact of their bigamous relationship becomes known, and, with the assistance of various spiteful gossips such as Mrs. Stantiloup, the gossip is likely to destroy the school. Dr. Wortle himself wants to stand by his assistant, whom he admires and respects. But his "conscience" conflicts with what he feels (his "inclination"). And if he supports his friend the price will be high.

For an hour or two before his dinner, the Doctor went out on horseback, and roamed about among the lanes, endeavoring to make up his mind. He was hitherto altogether at a loss as to what he should do in this present uncomfortable emergency. He could not bring his conscience and his inclination to come square together. And even when he counseled himself to yield to his conscience, his very conscience—a second conscience, as it were—revolted against the first. His first conscience told him that he owed a primary duty to his parish, a second duty to his school, and a third to his wife and daughter. In the performance of all these duties he would be bound to rid himself of Mr. Peacocke. But then there came that other conscience, telling him that the man had been more "sinned against than sinning,"—that common humanity required him to stand by a man who had suffered so much, and had suffered so unworthily. Then this second conscience went on to remind him that the man was preeminently fit for the duties which he had undertaken—that the man was a God-fearing, moral, and especially intellectual assistant in his school—that were he to lose him he could not hope to find anyone that would be his equal, or at all approaching to him in capacity. This second conscience went further, and assured him that the man's excellence as a schoolmaster was even increased by the peculiarity of his position. Do we not all know that if a man be under a cloud the very cloud will make him more attentive to his duties than another? If a man, for the wages which he receives, can give to his employer high character as well as work, he will think that he may lighten his work because of his character. And as to this man, who was the very phoenix of school assistants, there would really be nothing amiss with his character if only this piteous incident as to his wife were unknown. In this way his second conscience almost got the better of the first.

But then it would be known. It would be impossible that it should not be known. He had already made up his mind to tell Mr. Puddicombe, absolutely not daring to decide in such an emergency without consulting some friend. Mr. Puddicombe would hold his peace if he were to promise to do so. Certainly he might be trusted to do that. But others would know it; the Bishop would know it; Mrs. Stantiloup would know it. That man, of course, would take care that all Broughton, with its close full of cathedral clergymen, would know it. When Mrs. Stantiloup should know it there would not be a boy's parent through all the school who would not know it. If he kept the man he must keep him resolving that all the world should know that he kept him, that all the world should know of what nature was the married life of the assistant in whom he trusted. And he must be prepared to face all the world, confiding in the uprightness and the humanity of his purpose.

In such case he must say something of this kind to all the world: "I know that they are not married. I know that their condition of life is opposed to the law of God and man. I know that she bears a name that is not, in truth, her own; but I think that the circumstances in this case are so strange, so peculiar, that they excuse a disregard even of the law of God and man." Had he courage enough for this? And if the courage were there, was he high enough and powerful enough to carry out such a purpose? Could he beat down the Mrs. Stantiloup? And, indeed, could he beat down the Bishop and the Bishop's phalanx— for he knew that the Bishop and the Bishop's phalanx would be against him? They could not touch him in his living, because Mr. Peacocke would not be concerned in the services of the church; but would not his school melt away to nothing in his hands, if he were to attempt to carry it on after this fashion? And then would he not have destroyed himself without advantage to the man whom he was anxious to assist?

To only one point did he make up his mind certainly during that ride. Before he slept that night he would tell the whole story to his wife. He had at first thought that he would conceal it from her. It was his rule of life to act so entirely on his own will, that he rarely consulted her on matters of any importance. As it was, he could not endure the responsibility of acting by himself. People would say of him that he had subjected his wife to contamination, and had done so without giving her any choice in the matter. So he resolved that he would tell his wife.

"Not married," said Mrs. Wortle, when she heard the story.

"Married; yes. They were married. It was not their fault that the marriage was nothing. What was he to do when he heard that they had been deceived in this way?"

"Not married properly! Poor woman!"

"Yes, indeed. What should I have done if such had happened to me when we had been six months married?"

"It couldn't have been."

"Why not to you as well as to another?"

"I was only a young girl."

"But if you had been a widow?"

"Don't, my dear; don't! It wouldn't have been possible."

"But you pity her?"

"Oh yes."

"And you see that a great misfortune has fallen upon her, which she could not help?"

"Not till she knew it," said the wife, who had been married quite properly.

"And what then? What should she have done then?"

"Gone," said the wife, who had no doubt as to the comfort, the beauty, the perfect security of her own position.

"Gone?"

"Gone away at once."

"Whither should she go? Who would have taken her by the hand? Who would have supported her? Would you have had her lay herself down in the first gutter and die?"

"Better that than what she did do," said Mrs. Wortle.

"Then, by all the faith I have in Christ, I think you are hard upon her. Do you think what it is to have to go out and live alone—to have to look for your bread in desolation?"

"I have never been tried, my dear," said she, clinging close to him. "I have never had anything but what was good."

"Ought we not to be kind to one to whom Fortune has been so unkind?"

"If we can do so without sin."

"Sin! I despise the fear of sin which makes us think that its contact will soil us. Her sin, if it be sin, is so near akin to virtue, that I doubt whether we should not learn of her rather than avoid her."

"A woman should not live with a man unless she be his wife." Mrs. Wortle said this with more of obstinacy than he had expected.

"She was his wife, as far as she knew."

"But when she knew that it was not so any longer—then she should have left him."

"And have starved?"

"I suppose she might have taken bread from him."

"You think, then, that she should go away from here?"

"Do not you think so? What will Mrs. Stantiloup say?"

"And I am to turn them out into the cold because of a virago such as she is? You would have no more charity than that?"

"Oh, Jeffrey! what would the Bishop say?"

"Cannot you get beyond Mrs. Stantiloup and beyond the Bishop, and think what Justice demands?"

"The boys would all be taken away. If you had a son, would you send him where there was a schoolmaster living—living—. Oh, you wouldn't."

It is very clear to the Doctor that his wife's mind was made up on the subject; and yet there was no softer-hearted woman than Mrs. Wortle anywhere in the diocese, or one less likely to be severe upon a neighbor. Not only was she a kindly, gentle woman, but she was one who always had been willing to take her husband's opinion on all questions of right and wrong. She, however, was decided that they must go.

On the next morning, after service, which the schoolmaster did not attend, the Doctor saw Mr. Peacocke, and declared his intention of telling the story to Mr. Puddicombe. "If you bid me hold my tongue," he said, "I will do so. But it will be better that I should consult another clergyman. He is a man who can keep a secret." Then Mr. Peacocke gave him full authority to tell everything to Mr. Puddicombe. He declared that the Doctor might tell the story to whom he would. Everybody might know it now. He had, he said, quite made up his mind about that. What was the good of affecting secrecy when this man Lefroy was in the country?

In the afternoon, after service, Mr. Puddicombe came up to the house, and heard it all. He was a dry, thin, apparently unsympathetic man, but just withal, and by no means given to harshness. He could pardon whenever he could bring himself to believe that pardon would have good results; but he would not be driven by impulses and softness of heart to save the faulty one from the effect of his fault, merely because that effect would be painful. He was a man of no great mental caliber—not sharp, and quick, and capable of repartee as was the Doctor, but rational in all things, and always guided by his conscience. "He has behaved very badly to you," he said, when he heard the story.

"I do not think so; I have no such feeling myself."

"He behaved very badly in bringing her here without telling you all the facts. Considering the position that she was to occupy, he must have known that he was deceiving you."

"I can forgive all that," said the Doctor vehemently. "As far as I myself am concerned, I forgive everything."

"You are not entitled to do so."

"How—not entitled?"

"You must pardon me if I seem to take a liberty in expressing myself too boldly in this matter. Of course I should not do so unless you asked me."

"I want you to speak freely—all that you think."

"In considering his conduct, we have to consider it all. First of all there came a great and terrible misfortune which cannot but excite our pity. According to his own story, he seems, up to that time, to have been affectionate and generous."

"I believe every word of it," said the Doctor.

"Allowing for a man's natural bias on his own side, so do I. He had allowed himself to become attached to another man's wife; but we need not, perhaps, insist upon that." The Doctor moved himself uneasily in his chair, but said nothing. "We will grant that he put himself right by his marriage, though in that, no doubt, there should have been more of caution. Then came his great misfortune. He knew that his marriage had been no marriage. He saw the man and had no doubt."

"Quite so; quite so," said the Doctor, impatiently.

"He should, of course, have separated himself from her. There can be no doubt about it. There is no room for any quibble."

"Quibble!" said the Doctor.

"I mean that no reference in our own minds to the pity of the thing, to the softness of the moment—should make us doubt about it. Feelings such as these should induce us to pardon sinners, even to receive them back into our friendship and respect—when they have seen the error of their ways and have repented."

"You are very hard."

"I hope not. At any rate I can only say as I think. But, in truth, in the present emergency you have nothing to do with all that. If he asked you for counsel you might give it to him, but that is not his present position. He has told you his story, not in a spirit of repentance, but because such telling had become necessary."

"He would have told it all the same though this man had never come."

"Let us grant that it is so, there still remains his relation to you. He came here under false pretenses, and has done you a serious injury."

"I think not," said the Doctor.

"Would you have taken him into your establishment had you known it all before? Certainly not. Therefore I say that he has deceived you. I do not advise you to speak to him with severity; but he should, I think, be made to know that you appreciate what he has done."

"And you would turn him off—send him away at once, out about his business?"

"Certainly I would send him away."

"You think him such a reprobate that he should not be allowed to earn his bread anywhere?"

"I have not said so. I know nothing of his means of earning his bread. Men living in sin earn their bread constantly. But he certainly should not be allowed to earn his here."

"Not though that man who was her husband should now be dead, and he should again marry—legally marry—this woman to whom he has been so true and loyal?"

"As regards you and your school," said Mr. Puddicombe, "I do not think it would alter his position."

With this the conference ended, and Mr. Puddicombe took his leave. As he left the house the Doctor declared to himself that the man was a straitlaced, fanatical, hard-hearted bigot. But though he said so to himself, he hardly thought so; and was aware that the man's words had had effect upon him.

This story forces us to ponder a conflict of duties, or perhaps a conflict of entire moralities. One morality is based in principles that are non-negotiable. We might disagree about what principles those should be, but many people will concede that there are at least some principles that are non-negotiable.

Another morality is based in sentiment or feeling: We feel pity for Mr. and Mrs. Peacocke, we feel admiration for their goodness, we may also have negative feelings toward those who seem cold toward them and who insist too much on "principles" or "rules" that cannot be bent. What is the status of principles vs. the status of feelings or inclinations? We dealt with this question in Chapter 7. Here it arises again.

1. *Do you think it is ever right for a woman to have two husbands? What is the basis for your view?*
2. *Even if you answered "no" to the previous question, do you think that in the very special circumstances of the Peacockes, they should continue to live as husband and wife?*

Trollope is also exploring impure motives in this work. Various characters, such as Mrs. Wortle, at first, and then Puddicombe, seem to be motivated by a concern for appearances. They consider bigamy wrong in itself, but they also worry about how they will look to various prominent people or how their school will look with a bigamist as a teacher. And Dr. Wortle, though he wants to defend Peacocke out of affection, also is motivated by the fact that Wortle is an exceptionally good assistant. It may appear that what is presented as a concern for duty (what is required "no matter what the consequences") is actually often a concern for the social and other consequences of violating certain duties.

3. *Does the fact that Puddicombe has mixed or just plain rotten motives for wanting to get rid*

of Peacocke show that there is no substantive moral objection to Peacocke's behavior?

4. Do you agree that "there is no law from god or man entitling a man to escape from misery at the expense of falsehood and sin?" What, in your opinion, might happen to laws if people readily broke them in order to "escape misery"?

*5. The strictness respecting sexual behavior that makes it unthinkable, for the characters in this novel, that Mr. Peacocke might continue living with his nonwife might seem quaint to some people today. Does that suggest that the "social rules" are just conventions, with no basis in anything permanent? What would a relativist say? Aquinas? Scotus?

6. Dr. Wortle finds that he "could not bring his conscience and his inclination to come square together." But he also speaks of a "second conscience" that squares with, but actually seems to arise from, his inclinations (feelings). Does it seem to you that conscience and inclination do often conflict? Recall your answer to Orienting Question 1.

**7. Does it also seem to you that genuine morality might arise from inclination rather than be opposed to it? How do you think Aquinas would have answered these questions? Aristotle? Hume? Hobbes?

IMMANUEL KANT

Kant was born in 1724 in Königsberg, the capital of East Prussia. His parents were followers of Pietism, a Lutheran revival movement stressing love and good works and individual access to God. Kant was recognized as a promising student, and he received a free education at the Pietist gymnasium (high school). At 16, Kant entered the University of Königsberg, where he studied mathematics, physics, philosophy and theology. He published several works dealing with philosophical and scientific topics, some of which eventually earned him the position of professor at the university. He read the works of David Hume and was much influenced by him, but Kant's mature works constitute an attempt to overcome what he saw as the defects of Hume's views. Those mature works are among the most famous and important works in the history of modern philosophy. Kant was a product of the 18th century Enlightenment in many ways, and the focus on "reason alone" in his writings on religion and ethics sounds like typical Enlightenment thinking, although Kant's account of reason also stresses its limits.

Kant never married, and he never traveled more than 40 miles from Königsberg. Nearly his entire life was spent in concentrated thought and writing and in teaching. He died in 1804.

The Categorical Imperative

Kant stated that he wanted to "proceed from common knowledge [of morality] to its supreme principle." That is, he wanted, like most moralists before him, to do justice to ordinary intuitions about right and wrong, virtue and vice. And he wanted to find some single principle standing behind those ordinary intuitions.

Kant employs a somewhat technical vocabulary in his ethical writings, and the structure of his arguments is not easily displayed. In preparing you to read his texts, it may help to present some of his ideas in a more intuitively natural way.

GETTING WHAT YOU WANT, DOING WHAT YOU OUGHT, AND THE GOLDEN RULE

Ethics is a practical discipline for Kant just as much as for Aristotle. It is a study of actions, for example, lying or refraining from lying. Since both are things people *do*, let's call both doings and refrainings *actions*.

Often when people act, they are acting to get something they want or need. You want an A in philosophy and see that you must study to get one, so you study. You want your friend to feel comfortable at your party, so you refrain from saying something embarrassing about him. Kant thinks of human actions as arising from the application of principles. In the first example, the principle would be "When you want an A and see that getting one requires studying, study." The principle gives the reason for studying, it rationalizes it. Only rational beings can operate on principles in this way, Kant claims.

Now, sometimes, perhaps even quite often, it seems you can get what you want or need only by doing something you ought not to do. Kant uses the following example: Suppose you are desperately in need of money and see that the only feasible way to get what you need is by borrowing from a friend. But let us suppose that you know you will not be able to repay the loan, and you know you will not get the loan unless you promise to repay. So to get it, you will have to make a lying promise. But you feel that you ought not to lie. It is morally wrong.

If you decide not to make the lying promise, what explains your action? Well, there are many possible explanations, many kinds of reasons that might be given or "principles" that you might be following. You might refrain from lying because you are afraid of what other people will think of you if they find you out (cf. the mixed motives discussed earlier). Or you might think it is important to establish trust with someone for some purpose, so you avoid lying (at least for the time being). To many people those do not sound like *moral* reasons, however.

On the other hand, suppose the reason you refrain from lying is that you think to yourself, "I would not want anyone to do that to me, so I should not do it to anyone either." In this case you are following a *moral* principle. It is in fact the moral principle called "the Golden Rule." It is easy to see that following this principle may obstruct your attempt to get what you want or need. So if the Golden Rule motivates me to act a certain way, it cannot be that it does so because I see that by following it I will be better able to get what I need. Kant often gives the impression that moral rules or principles *always* conflict with what we want or need. That might be an exaggeration, but it is clear that sometimes when we follow such principles as the Golden Rule, we thereby prevent ourselves from getting what we want.

These facts reveal something fundamental about human beings, in Kant's view. Humans, like other animals, have a desiring, needing, feeling side to them. Kant uses the term *inclination* to refer to that side. But humans (unlike other animals) also have a rational side to them. I think about how to act, how to get what I want, what it would make sense to do, given that I want something. What Kant calls *hypothetical*

imperatives are principles of reason that tell me to do X if I want A. For example, if I want an "A" in philosophy, I should study.

But the crucial element in Kant's view is his belief that our rational side extends beyond operating on such hypothetical principles. Kant thinks moral principles arise from reason, and acting on moral principles may *not* get us what we want. Following such principles may not make us happy or admired or rich. But in Kant's view all such things are only conditionally good. For example, it is good to be rich only *on the condition* that you got rich honestly. Willing to act on moral principles *because they are moral* is, however, unconditionally good. It is good *in itself*. In fact Kant claims that the good will is the only thing that is good in itself. Thus the goodness of moral actions does not appeal to our desiring, wanting, needing nature. It appeals to something else in us. Let us try to understand why Kant thinks that the "something else" is reason, understood in a very particular way.

(From *Groundwork of the Metaphysics of Morals*, First Section, tr. T. K. Abbott)

MORALITY NOT BASED ON VIRTUE, HAPPINESS OR CONSEQUENCES

Nothing can possibly be conceived in the world, or even out of it, which can be called good, without qualification, except a good will. Intelligence, wit, judgment, and the other *talents* of the mind, however they may be named, or courage, resolution, perseverance, as qualities of temperament, are undoubtedly good and desirable in many respects; but these gifts of nature may also become extremely bad and mischievous if the will which is to make use of them, and which, therefore, constitutes what is called *character*, is not good. It is the same with the *gifts* of *fortune*. Power, riches, honor, even health, and the general well-being and contentment with one's condition which is called *happiness*, inspire pride, and often presumption, if there is not a good will to correct the influence of these on the mind, and with this also to rectify the whole principle of acting and adapt it to its end. The sight of a being who is not adorned with a single feature of a pure and good will, enjoying unbroken prosperity, can never give pleasure to an impartial rational spectator. Thus a good will appears to constitute the indispensable condition even of being worthy of happiness.

There are even some qualities which are of service to this good will itself and may facilitate its action, yet which have no intrinsic unconditional value, but always presuppose a good will, and this qualifies the esteem that we justly have for them and does not permit us to regard them as absolutely good. Moderation in the affections and passions, self-control, and calm deliberation are not only good in many respects, but even seem to constitute part of the intrinsic worth of the person; but they are far from deserving to be called good without qualification, although they have been so unconditionally praised by the ancients. For without the principles of a good will, they may become extremely bad, and the coolness of a villain not only makes him far more dangerous, but also directly makes him more abominable in our eyes than he would have been without it.

A good will is good not because of what it performs or effects, not by its aptness for the attainment of some proposed end, but simply by virtue of the volition; that is, it is good in itself, and considered by itself is to be esteemed much higher than all that can be brought about by it in favor of any inclination, nay even of the sum total of all inclinations. Even if it should happen that, owing to special disfavor of fortune, or the niggardly provision of a stepmotherly nature, this will should wholly lack power to accomplish its purpose, if with its greatest efforts it should yet achieve nothing, and there should remain only the good will (not, to be sure, a mere wish, but the summoning of all means in our power), then, like a jewel, it would still shine by its own light, as a thing which has its whole value in itself. Its usefulness or fruitfulness can neither add nor take away anything from this value. It would be, as it were, only the setting to enable us to handle it the more conveniently in common commerce, or to attract to it the attention of those who are not yet connoisseurs, but not to recommend it to true connoisseurs, or to determine its value.

8. *Kant mentions that certain qualities of character, such as moderation, have been praised unconditionally by "the ancients." What ancient philosopher praised moderation, or temperance, as a fundamental virtue?*

9. *Whether I am stupid or smart may be due to facts of nature, such as genetic inheritance. Some people are dealt a bad deck, so to speak, when conceived. That is what Kant describes, quite vividly, as "the niggardly provision of a stepmotherly nature." According to him, do such facts have any bearing on whether a person can or cannot be morally good? Compare Kant and Aristotle on this point.*

10. *Suppose I decide (or "will") to help George, who is poor, weak and hungry, to get some food. Now, there are stupid ways of doing that and ways that are not so stupid. Just handing George some cash without first determining whether he is likely to spend it on food rather than drugs would be foolish. If I do that he may not get what I intended, namely, food. But if I do that, could that action of giving him the cash nonetheless be good and in fact be good without qualification, according to Kant?*

11. *If I will with all my heart and act with all my abilities to get George some food, then, even if I fail to get him some food (because I pick a stupid means or for some other reason), according to Kant I have a good will, and only a good will is good without qualification. Does it follow that my chances for being morally good or bad are unaffected by my intelligence? What is your own view?*

We can think of the principles that we adopt to govern our actions as commands or imperatives. When I study for my course, it is as though I am obeying the command "Study for your course!" Sometimes it is as though, when acting, I am giving orders to myself. Kant observes that there are two basic kinds of imperatives or commands.

RATIONALITY AND HYPOTHETICAL VS. CATEGORICAL IMPERATIVES

The conception of an objective principle, insofar as it is obligatory for a will, is called a command (of reason), and the formula of the command is called an imperative.

Now all *imperatives* command either *hypothetically* or *categorically*. The former represent the practical necessity of a possible action as means to something else that is willed (or at least which one might possibly will). The categorical imperative would be that which represented an action as necessary of itself without reference to another end, i.e., as objectively necessary.

Since every practical law represents a possible action as good and, on this account, for a subject who is practically determinable by reason, necessary, all imperatives are formulae determining an action which is necessary according to the principle of a will good in some respects. If now the action is good only as a means *to something else*, then the imperative is *hypothetical*; if it is conceived as good *in itself* and consequently as being necessarily the principle of a will which of itself conforms to reason, then it is *categorical*.

Thus the imperative declares what action possible by me would be good and presents the practical rule in relation to a will which does not forthwith perform an action simply because it is good, whether because the subject does not always know that it is good, or because, even if it know this, yet its maxims might be opposed to the objective principles of practical reason.

When I conceive a hypothetical imperative, in general I do not know beforehand what it will contain until I am given the condition. But when I conceive a categorical imperative, I know at once what it contains. For as the imperative contains besides the law only the necessity that the maxims shall conform to this law, while the law contains no conditions restricting it, there remains nothing but the general statement that the maxim of the action should conform to a universal law, and it is this conformity alone that the imperative properly represents as necessary.

12. *"If you want to be happy, tell the truth"* is what Kant calls
   a. *a hypothetical imperative*
   b. *a categorical imperative*
13. *Kant calls a principle that depends on what you need or want a* subjective *principle.*
   a. *Is the principle stated in Question 12 subjective?*
   b. *Is it "necessary"?*

Unlike hypothetical imperatives, "Never tell a lie" and "Keep your promises" are both categorical imperatives. They do not say, "Do *X* if you want *A*." They simply say, "Do *X*. Period." Kant thinks particular categorical imperatives or principles, such as "Keep your promises" are all based in a single fundamental moral imperative, *the* categorical imperative.

There is therefore but one categorical imperative, namely, this: Act only on that maxim whereby you can at the same time will that it should become a universal law.

Now if all imperatives of duty can be deduced from this one imperative as from their principle, then, although it should remain undecided what is called duty is not merely a vain notion, yet at least we shall be able to show what we understand by it and what this notion means.

This supreme principle of morality, the categorical imperative, mentions *maxims* of actions. The maxim of an action of mine is a statement describing what I intend to do and the motive for my doing it. Consider the case mentioned earlier of the lying promise made to get some cash. In a case like that one, the maxim of my action might be:

> "When in need of money and unable to get it except by making a lying promise, make a lying promise."

I will refer to this maxim as the *lying promise maxim*.

14. *If I am tired and decide to take a nap, what might the maxim of my action be?*

Kant claims that some maxims (like the lying promise maxim) are immoral, others are moral, others are at least not inconsistent with morality. How do we tell which are which? By asking, Kant claims, whether we could consistently will the maxim as a law of nature. If it can be willed consistently, then the action is moral or at least compatible with morality. If not, then it is immoral. What does that mean?

Kant uses some examples to illustrate his idea. Two of them are cases of perfect duties, i.e., duties that clearly require or prohibit some specific act. The first of these is a duty to oneself, the other a duty to others.

Since the universality of the law according to which effects are produced constitutes what is properly called *nature* in the most general sense (as to form), that is, the existence of things so far as it is determined by general laws, the imperative of duty may be expressed thus:

Act as if the maxim of your action were to become by your will a universal law of nature.

We will now enumerate a few duties, adopting the usual division of them into duties to ourselves and to others, and into perfect and imperfect duties.

1. A man reduced to despair by a series of misfortunes feels wearied of life, but is still so far in possession of his reason that he can ask himself whether it would not be contrary to his duty to himself to take his own life. Now he inquires whether the maxim of his action could become a universal law of nature. His maxim is: "From self-love I adopt it as a principle to shorten my life when its longer duration is likely to bring more evil than satisfaction." [We will call this the "suicide maxim"]. It is asked then simply whether this principle founded on self-love can become a universal law of nature. Now we see at once that a system of nature of which it should be a law to destroy life by means of the very feeling whose special nature it is to impel to the improvement of life would contradict itself and, therefore, could not exist as a system of nature; hence that maxim cannot possibly exist as a universal law of nature and, consequently, would be wholly inconsistent with the supreme principle of all duty.

To will a maxim is to try to actualize it. If I will the "suicide maxim" then, under the conditions it specifies, I do what I can to kill myself. I might not succeed, but I "willed" it nonetheless. Now suppose it were a law of nature that people (all people) try to kill themselves under those conditions (the condition where they love themselves and think that continued existence will bring more evil than good), just as it is a law of nature that every object attracts every other object with a certain force (the gravitational "law of

nature"). Could I consistently (that is, without getting into a contradiction) will a world that operates according to the gravitational law? Sure, what would be the problem? In fact the world we live in *is* just such a world. There are, however, maxims that I can't will, simply because they are impossible to will without contradiction. The suicide maxim is one such.

You can consistently will a world in which you sometimes move around. You cannot consistently will a world in which you sometimes move around and also never move around. Could I consistently will a world where *everyone* follows the suicide maxim? Kant thinks not. Why not? Because I would be willing a world where (a) each person who loves himself tries to keep himself alive and prospering (since that is what loving one's self amounts to, that is its "nature") and (b) each person who loves himself tries to kill himself when the going gets tough. It looks like you cannot have a world where both (a) and (b) are true. They contradict each other, Kant thinks. In fact, (b) is itself logically self-contradictory, if you spell it out.

Kant assumes that it is the "special nature" of self-love to "impel" to self-improvement. But what if that isn't the nature of self-love? Perhaps the way to love yourself is to do what you can to improve your life, except when things get really bad, in which case the loving thing would be to kill yourself. Perhaps that is the nature of self-love.

15. *If that were the nature of self-love, could you consistently will the suicide maxim?*

If Kant is right in thinking that no one can consistently will the suicide maxim, then it follows that anyone who acts on that maxim is violating the categorical imperative. And since, by his account, the categorical imperative is the supreme principle of morality, to violate it is to be immoral. We could put it another way; moral maxims are maxims I can *universalize*, i.e., I can consistently will them to be universally true, true for everyone. He claims I cannot do that with the suicide maxim. Therefore suicide is immoral.

2. Another finds himself forced by necessity to borrow money. He knows that he will not be able to repay it, but sees also that nothing will be lent to

him unless he promises stoutly to repay it in a definite time. He desires to make this promise, but he has still so much conscience as to ask himself: "Is it not unlawful and inconsistent with duty to get out of a difficulty in this way?" Suppose, however, that he resolves to do so: then the maxim of his action would be expressed thus: "When I think myself in want of money, I will borrow money and promise to repay it, although I know that I never can do so." Now this principle of self-love or of one's own advantage may perhaps be consistent with my whole future welfare; but the question now is, "Is it right?" I change then the suggestion of self-love into a universal law, and state the question thus: "How would it be if my maxim were a universal law?" Then I see at once that it could never hold as a universal law of nature, but would necessarily contradict itself. For supposing it to be a universal law that everyone when he thinks himself in a difficulty should be able to promise whatever he pleases, with the purpose of not keeping his promise, the promise itself would become impossible, as well as the end that one might have in view in it, since no one would consider that anything was promised to him, but would ridicule all such statements as vain pretenses.

Let us consider this particular example in more detail. I need money. I formulate a "maxim," a description of a possible action, including the reasons for it, namely, "In order to get needed money, make a lying promise." I ask whether the lying promise would work as a means to my end, namely, getting money. Suppose it would. Then this maxim passes the test of rationality posed by a hypothetical imperative. On the condition that I want money, cannot get it any other way, etc., making a lying promise would be just the thing to do.

Next, I check this maxim against the categorical imperative. I ask, "Could this maxim be a universal law of nature?" Well, suppose that everyone, as if by natural necessity, should, when needing money, borrow it and lie when promising to repay it. In that case it seems that there would be no promising to pay back money. "The promise itself would become impossible" because no one would ever believe such a promise. I would be *willing* a world in which (a) ev-

eryone makes lying promises in order to get money and (b) no one ever gets money by making lying promises, since promises to repay money are never believed, or, more exactly, never *count as* promises (which they obviously would not if *everyone always* lied in such circumstances).

With such a maxim universalized, I could no longer rationally will it, even as hypothetical. Lying would not be a viable means to the end I seek. In fact I cannot even consistently *imagine* a world in which the lying promise maxim becomes a universal law, like a law of nature. There is a kind of contradiction that arises when I try to "universalize" such a maxim. Kant thinks that that is one mark of an immoral maxim. To say I cannot *universalize* such a maxim is to say that I cannot will that everyone act on it. Some people could act on it in some cases, but not everyone any time there is an opportunity. *I* could do it, for example, but I could not consistently will that everyone do it. This is very close to the Golden Rule. Kant says I can't lie like this to other people unless I can will that they lie also in similar circumstances to me, and in fact to anyone, whenever they are in those circumstances.

*16. *Suppose that people make lots of promises and generally keep them, and very rarely make lying promises in order to acquire money through a loan and never keep those promises. Would such a world be impossible? Might not people be able to get money when acting under the lying promise maxim in such a world? Remember, that would still be a world where it is always the case that people in certain circumstances make a lying promise.*

*17. *Even if Kant's argument here shows that lying promises are wrong by his test of wrongness, does he have a similar argument to show that all lying is wrong? Suppose I lie to avoid taxes. What would the "maxim" of my action be? Could I universalize it? See if you can give a description of a world in which everyone, by a kind of necessity, always cheats on his or her taxes.*

Kant is trying to show that immorality involves a kind of irrationality. Whether he has succeeded so far is not clear. But it is clear that the categorical imperative has nothing to do with producing good consequences. The badness of making a lying promise does not consist in the fact that it produces bad consequences. It might well produce very nice consequences, even for the person lied to, and Kant would have insisted on that fact! And the badness of making a lying promise would not be due to the bad consequences that would result if *everyone always* made them, since it is not even possible that everyone always make them.

18. *Try to think up an example of lying to someone that could have the result that both the person lied to and the liar are better off as a result.*

WHAT IF EVERYONE DID THAT?

If Bill cheats on his income tax and we criticize him by saying "What if everyone did that?," he could respond with "But not everyone will." That reply makes it sound as though what we are interested in is the *actual consequences* that would result if Bill cheats. In fact the actual consequences are likely to be completely harmless, since the government will not miss Bill's payment and since there does not seem to be any reason to think that just because Bill cheats, others will too. Only if everyone, or a very large number, cheated, would the consequences be bad (and then, of course, the disaster would be the result of what everyone does, and thus no single individual could be entirely blamed for it).

However, most people will not accept Bill's reply. The point is not that his failure to pay will lead to disaster, nor is it that everyone will cheat just because Bill does. Rather, the point is that there is something unfair about Bill's not paying when most other people do. What makes him so special? Why should he get to be an exception? The desire to make an exception of oneself is, in Kant's view, the very essence of immorality. Thus Kant's notion of what is right or obligatory in actions is also, this suggests, tied to something like an *idea of fairness in conduct*.

3. A third finds in himself a talent which with the help of some culture might make him a useful man in many respects. But he finds himself in comfort-

able circumstances and prefers to indulge in pleasure rather than to take pains in enlarging and improving his happy natural capacities. He asks, however, whether his maxim of neglect of his natural gifts, besides agreeing with his inclination to indulgence, agrees also with what is called duty. He sees then that a system of nature could indeed subsist with such a universal law although men (like the South Sea Islanders) should let their talents rest and resolve to devote their lives merely to idleness, amusement, and propagation of their species—in a word, to enjoyment; but he cannot possibly will that this should be a universal law of nature, or be implanted in us as such by a natural instinct. For, as a rational being, he necessarily wills that his faculties be developed, since they serve him and have been given him, for all sorts of possible purposes.

This is an example of an imperfect duty to oneself. Kant admits that we can conceive a world in which nobody bothers to develop her talents (such a world "could subsist"), whereas he denies that we can even conceive a world in which everyone, in certain circumstances, makes lying promises. Now, since you cannot even conceive the "lying promise world," obviously you cannot will it, anymore than you can will to be moving and be sitting motionless at one and the same moment.

However, Kant thinks that even though you *can* conceive a world in which no one develops her talents, you cannot rationally *will* such a world. A rational being "necessarily wills" that his abilities be developed. Clearly, no one can consistently will to develop his talents and also not will to develop his talents. But a person could simply not will to develop his talents at all, and indeed not everyone does.

Thus Kant claims that the South Sea Islanders don't will to develop theirs. They supposedly adopt a "laziness maxim." Are they involved in some sort of inconsistency then? Not, it seems, a logical inconsistency. It is not clear why Kant thinks there is any kind of inconsistency in willing the "laziness maxim" as a universal law of nature. Thus it is not clear that people who are lazy in that way are immoral (though they may be disgusting or repellent somehow). Yet there might seem to be something irrational in, so to speak, not using what you have and ignoring your own needs. Your natural faculties have after all been "given for all sorts of possible purposes." You cannot rationally will the realization of those purposes while at the same time willing that no one will the means to them. But you could will that you remain lazy and profit from those who are not. So you would still be making an exception of yourself.

4. A fourth, who is in prosperity, while he sees that others have to contend with great wretchedness and that he could help them, thinks: "What concern is it of mine? Let everyone be as happy as Heaven pleases, or as he can make himself; I will take nothing from him nor even envy him, only I do not wish to contribute anything to his welfare or to his assistance in distress!" Now no doubt if such a mode of thinking were a universal law, the human race might very well subsist and doubtless even better than in a state in which everyone talks of sympathy and goodwill, or even takes care occasionally to put it into practice, but, on the other side, also cheats when he can, betrays the rights of men, or otherwise violates them. But although it is possible that a universal law of nature might exist in accordance with that maxim, it is impossible to *will* that such a principle should have the universal validity of a law of nature. For a will which resolved this would contradict itself, inasmuch as many cases might occur in which one would have need of the love and sympathy of others, and in which, by such a law of nature, sprung from his own will, he would deprive himself of all hope of the aid he desires.

Let us consider this example, an example of an imperfect duty to others, a little further too. In this case my maxim is something like this: "When in prosperity, ignore the needs of others." Suppose now that all people should at all times, by a kind of natural necessity, never help anyone who is in need of their assistance. Now, unlike the "lying promise world," Kant admits that there could be such a world as the "Ignore the needs of others" world (it could "subsist"). There could be such a world, although it would not be a very nice one to live in, given what life is like. But could I consistently *will* it? Only if I cease to will that

I should sometimes be helped. But there are a great many ends I can pursue only with the help of others. For example, if I accidentally get trapped with a broken arm under a fallen tree limb, it is very likely that the only way I can pursue the end of keeping myself alive is through the help of others. So if I am a rational being, I shall will that others sometimes help me. But if I universalize my maxim ("Ignore the needs of others"), I will be willing that *I* not be helped. So here there is a contradiction in *willing*. I cannot, being the sort of vulnerable being I am, consistently will this maxim as a universal law of nature while continuing to will the sorts of things I naturally do will (such as staying alive). So "Ignore the needs of others" does not pass the test imposed by the categorical imperative, for that imperative says, "Act as if the maxim of your action were to become by your will a universal law of nature."

Notice that what makes refusing to help those in need wrong is not that failing to do so would bring bad consequences. Sometimes it doesn't bring bad consequences. Attempting to help someone, on the other hand, could produce a bad consequence, such as further injury to him. But even then, Kant insists, it would still be to my credit that I tried to help, and it would still be the case that the kind of action I attempted *must* be willed by anyone deserving to be called good. Note also that the moral law does not tell me how much help I should give others. It certainly does not tell me that I have a duty to maximize benefit for others.

There is another thing to notice in connection with this example. It may seem that Kant's categorical imperative, the "supreme principle of morality," is only a negative principle, it only tells us what *not* to do. And that seems pretty odd. Surely some of our duties must be duties actually to do certain things. But this duty to help those in need is in fact a duty to do something, as opposed to merely avoiding some immoral act.

*19. *Suppose someone wills the maxim "Ignore the needs of others" to be a universal law of nature while hoping that he will never be in need of aid from others, and it turns out that he never is in need. Has he gotten involved in*

any contradiction in willing? (Remember that it is possible to will something that never in fact happens.)

20. Would there be anything irrational or self-contradictory in willing that no one ever help anyone and then, when in a jam and in need of help to survive, saying to oneself, "Well, that is how it is; if the only way to survive is through the help of others, then I guess it is time to die"? Discuss.

THE FORMULA OF THE END ITSELF

Kant proposes a second formulation of the categorical imperative. He claims that it is equivalent to the formulation discussed earlier, but it is not obvious that it is. In any case, this new formulation is more appealing to many people than is the previous one. In brief, the formula is this: Always treat people as an end and never only as means. We might express this by saying that one should never exploit or use any person.

Supposing, however, that there were something whose existence has *in itself* an absolute worth, something which, being *an end in itself*, could be a source of definite laws; then in this and this alone would lie the source of a possible categorical imperative, i.e., a practical law.

Now I say: man and generally any rational being *exists* as an end in himself, *not merely as a means* to be arbitrarily used by this or that will, but in all his actions, whether they concern himself or other rational beings, must be always regarded at the same time as an end. All objects of the inclinations have only a conditional worth, for if the inclinations and the wants founded on them did not exist, then their object would be without value. But the inclinations, themselves being sources of want, are so far from having an absolute worth for which they should be desired that on the contrary it must be the universal wish of every rational being to be wholly free from them. Thus the worth of any object which is *to be acquired* by our action is always conditional. Beings whose existence depends not on our will but on nature's have nevertheless, if they are irrational beings, only a relative value as means, and are therefore called *things*;

rational beings, on the contrary, are called *persons*, because their very nature points them out as ends in themselves, that is, as something which must not be used merely as means, and so far therefore restricts freedom of action (and is an object of respect). These, therefore, are not merely subjective ends whose existence has a worth *for us* as an effect of our action, *but objective ends*, that is, things whose existence is an end in itself; an end moreover for which no other can be substituted, which they should subserve *merely* as means, for otherwise nothing whatever would possess *absolute worth*; but if all worth were conditioned and therefore contingent, then there would be no supreme practical principle of reason whatever

If then there is a supreme practical principle or, in respect of the human will, a categorical imperative, it must be one which, being drawn from the conception of that which is necessarily an end for everyone because it is *an end in itself*, constitutes an *objective* principle of will, and can therefore serve as a universal practical law. The foundation of this principle is: *Rational nature exists as an end in itself*. Man necessarily conceives his own existence as being so; so far then this is a *subjective* principle of human actions. But every other rational being regards its existence similarly, just on the same rational principle that holds for me: so that it is at the same time an objective principle, from which as a supreme practical law all laws of the will must be capable of being deduced. Accordingly the practical imperative will be as follows:

> So act as to treat humanity, whether in your own person or in that of any other, in every case as an end, never as means only.

We will now inquire whether this can be practically carried out.

To abide by the previous examples: Firstly, under the head of necessary duty to oneself: He who contemplates suicide should ask himself whether his action can be consistent with the idea of humanity as *an end in itself*. If he destroys himself in order to escape from painful circumstances, he uses a person merely as a *means* to maintain a tolerable condition up to the end of life. But a man is not a thing, that is to say, something which can be used merely as means, but must in all his actions be always considered as an end in himself. I cannot, therefore, dispose in any way of a man in my own person so as to mutilate him, to damage or kill him. (It belongs to ethics proper to define this principle more precisely, so as to avoid all misunderstanding, e.g., as to the amputation of the limbs in order to preserve myself, as to exposing my life to danger with a view to preserve it, etc. This question is therefore omitted here.)

Secondly, as regards necessary duties, or those of strict obligation, towards others: He who is thinking of making a lying promise to others will see at once that he would be using another man *merely as a means,* without the latter containing at the same time the end in himself. For he whom I propose by such a promise to use for my own purposes cannot possibly assent to my mode of acting towards him and, therefore, cannot himself contain the end of this action. This violation of the principle of humanity in other men is more obvious if we take in examples of attacks on the freedom and property of others. For then it is clear that he who transgresses the rights of men intends to use the person of others merely as a means, without considering that as rational beings they ought always to be esteemed also as ends, that is, as beings who must be capable of containing in themselves the end of the very same action.

TREATING PEOPLE AS A MEANS TO AN END

What might be meant by "treating a person merely as a means"? If I hire someone to mow my lawn, I am treating him as a means to getting the lawn mowed. But since he is free to decide whether to do it or not, I am not in such a case treating him only as a means. The person I hire can "contain the end of this action in himself." He is not a mere tool in my hands. He adopts the action and its ends as his own, subject to being paid. Thus I respect his freedom when I hire him. I do not treat him as a *thing* or object. Respect for the freedom of others, and the refusal to treat them as things or objects, seems to be the essence of Kant's notion that I should treat people always as ends in themselves and never merely as means.

DIGNITY AND UNIQUE VALUE

Kant's idea that we should treat people always also as an end is still not as clear as it might at first seem to be. Part of Kant's thought is that each person is uniquely valuable. Only persons have what he calls *dignity.*

> Everything has either a price or a dignity. If it has a price, something else can be put in its place as an equivalent; if it is exalted above all price and so admits of no equivalent, then it has a dignity. (*Lectures on Ethics*)

Kant seems to hold that individual persons are not replaceable by others. I cannot get "equivalent value" for the loss of a person in the way that I could for the loss of a house or my wallet. Perhaps to treat someone as an end is somehow to acknowledge this elevation of persons above any kind of exchange value. If so, the "buying and selling" of persons, *even with their consent,* would violate the categorical imperative. In order to see what this means, we would, it seems, have to be able to distinguish between cases where someone sells a service to others (I mow your law for a price) and cases where what I sell is actually myself, my own body, or my entire self, body and soul, so to speak.

21. *Would a prostitute be violating the categorical imperative even when she regards her activities as simply a job or a business transaction? Would her work differ in some important way from the work of other people who are hired to perform various services? Try to give a good account of Kant's argument. Think about your answer to Orienting Question 6 here.*

22. *Does it seem to you that there are other things besides human persons that are "without price" and that cannot be replaced by a supposed equivalent? Try to give some examples.*

Why Is It So Important to Be Rational?

There may be a question that has been nagging many readers through all of this. Suppose someone were to say, "Well, maybe I would be inconsistent and irrational when behaving immorally, but so what? Why should I care whether I am rational or not, so long as I get what I want? Sometimes it will pay to be rational (consistent), other times not." It seems that the fact that acting a certain way would be rational is not by itself much, or any, motivation for acting that way. This question would be in line with the claims of both Aristotle and Hume, since both insist that reason, or reason all by itself, cannot motivate a person in any case. Why bother being rational, except when doing so "pays," that is, gets me what I want or satisfies my "inclinations"?

How does reason motivate, in Kant's view? He thinks that reason arouses "respect" and that respect is what motivates. Here he differs from previous moral theorists. The dominant view and, you might think, the commonsense view is that actions, including morally right ones, are motivated by desire for some good or avoidance of some evil. A good person is one who is motivated by a desire for what is indeed good (as opposed to what he merely thinks is good). All actions, in this view, aim at some good end (as Aristotle put it). Kant denies this. Respect is not directed toward the ends or aims of action, but toward the "form" of action, its conformity with law. A good person, in Kant's view, is a person with a good will, a will that conforms itself to law, in the sense of rational consistency. Thus Kant's view breaks with a deeply entrenched traditional view.

Other differences follow. For example, particular motives, such as love, greed, fear, desires of various kinds, are sometimes present, sometimes absent. If these are the only sorts of motives I have, I will be motivated to do something kind for someone whom I love only when in fact I do love them, and that might change tomorrow. The motive of respect, on the other hand, can always be present in every person, no matter how he may feel about others, according to Kant.

Moreover, only the motive of respect can guarantee that a person acts rightly. My love for someone might well lead me to do something wrong, such as lying in order to protect her. But respect for others, based on the fact they are rational beings who operate according to principle or law, could never lead me to do something wrong, Kant thinks.

Furthermore, some of us may be supplied by nature with more generous or loving natures or have the good fortune of being brought up in such a way that it becomes easy for us to be helpful and not selfish, or to be brave, or patient. Others may not be so lucky in their upbringing or natural temperament. But Kant's view is that the gifts of nature or a good upbringing are irrelevant to moral worth. We all have equal access to the motive of respect, so no matter how nature or the environment has treated us, we all have an equal motivation and an equal chance of achieving moral worth. Kant's view is, you might say, very democratic.

23. *What is the main way Kant's view on morals differs from most traditional views?*
24. *Suppose I visit someone in the hospital simply because I am motivated by love for him or by a generous and caring temperament. Would Kant think that such an action has moral worth? Explain.*
25. *Suppose I visit someone, say, my brother, in the hospital just out of a sense of duty, even though I feel no love for him and even though I lack any generous or caring tendencies. Would Kant think such an action does have real moral worth?*
26. *Do the two previous questions suggest that there is something counterintuitive in Kant's view? Explain.*

IS KANT RIGHT?

Kant has claimed that the supreme principle of morality is the categorical imperative. But he has not proved this claim. He needs to show that a rational will acts only on maxims that can be universalized.

There is no problem with prudential rationality. If a person is rational, then if that person wants x and reason tells him that M is the only means of getting x, he will use M, other things being equal. That is trivially true. Someone who claimed to want x but didn't will the means to it would not really want x after all (or would want something else more, or fear something, and the like). But couldn't someone be rational without willing to act according to the categorical imperative?

One way Kant thinks he can answer this is to show that a rational will must be free, and vice versa.

After all, if my will is determined by my desires and fears, which are themselves determined by factors over which I have no control (or so it seems), then I would not be free. Suppose, for example, that I have a desire or craving for sex. That desire arises in people due to secretions of hormones and other "natural" factors over which people have no control. If I act on that desire, then even though I chose to act that way, my motive for acting is something that arises in me without my "say-so." In that case, acting on desire *cannot be acting freely*, Kant claims. Also, if my will is determined by the desires and commands of others, then, too, I would not be free but would be enslaved to those others. In all such cases Kant says that I am operating *heteronomously*, that is, under the influence of factors I do not control or that do not truly originate in me. Finally, if my will is not determined by anything at all, then the result would be merely meaningless chaotic movements, uncaused by anything. That would not be real freedom either. A will that is free must be bound by *something*, something essentially connected to the agent, to me, to who I am.

Here then are three possible ways to describe someone who is doing *X*: He is doing *X* because he desires to; he is doing *X* because someone else is making him do it; he is doing *X* without desiring anything, without being commanded, or for any other reason. All of these describe someone who is *not free*. A fourth possible way is this: He is doing *X* out of respect for the moral law. This fourth way, and *only* it, describes a *free* action. This fourth way needs further explanation.

Since a rational will is not determined by desires and similar natural factors, when I act simply in accord with my rational nature, perhaps I am free. But what is meant by "acting in accordance with my rational nature"? It means that a person's will is bound by a law or rational command, but one that comes from *within*, not from without. What is needed is a will that gives the law to itself, or is *autonomous* (self-ruling, rather than *heteronomous*, ruled by another). The categorical imperative is such a law, a law that we give to ourselves. It does not arise from anything or anyone (including God) other than ourselves. Rather, it arises directly from our rational, not our desiring,

nature. It is thus a principle of freedom. Kant thinks the only plausible candidate for such a law given to oneself is the categorical imperative, which is itself the supreme principle of morality. Thus freedom entails the moral law, as Kant understands the moral law. To act freely is to act autonomously, so autonomy is essential to morality. Heteronomy, on the other hand, is inconsistent with true morality.

Now, even to a non-Kantian it does seem that there is some important connection between freedom and morality, for only if I am free can I be held responsible for what I do. Only if I am free can I be morally blamed or praised. Moral concepts are tied to these ideas of praise and blame, and thus they are tied to freedom. Kant thinks his notion that the categorical imperative is the supreme principle of morality gives us the only way of doing justice to these facts.

The obvious question now is "Are we free?" Is it really possible to act purely out of respect for the form of law, or rational consistency, without any motivating force coming from our inclinations, all of which are, according to Kant, determined by something like heredity and environment (nature)? Kant does not believe it is possible to give a theoretical, that is, scientific, proof that we are free in this sense, though we cannot disprove it theoretically either. But he does think we can have a kind of practical proof. He does think that *practically* we cannot avoid thinking of ourselves as free. To think of all our actions as determined is to think of ourselves as beings that never should be praised or blamed for anything whatsoever, and we cannot really, practically, do that. If we are not free, we cannot be either moral or immoral. Freedom entails the moral law. It is worth noting that Kant has a very strong notion of freedom. He does not think freedom is compatible with any kind of determination other than "determination" by the moral law.

One consequence of this view creates a problem for Kant. If I am free only when I am rational and following rational moral rules, then it would seem that when I am not following those rules, that is, when I am being immoral, I am not free. And if I am not free, then I am not responsible and should not be blamed. Thus I can be praised when I follow the moral law and have a good will, but I cannot be blamed when I fail to follow it. That seems very counterintuitive. In his later writings Kant tried to repair this problem by distinguishing *choice* and *freedom*. We will not discuss his attempts here, but it should be noted that in Kant's ethics some kind of freedom or ability to choose is quite central.

27. *Define the following: categorical imperative; hypothetical imperative; autonomy; heteronomy; inclination; deontology.*

*28. *How, according to Kant, does the idea of actions motivated by "law" or consistency imply freedom? (Hint: Think of how* other *motivations, such as a desire, might be "determined.")*

29. *Could an action, such as visiting my brother in the hospital, be motivated* both *by respect for the moral law* and *by my love for my brother? Would the one motive have to interfere with, or cancel out, the former? Argue pro and con.*

MORALITY, MORAL PERFECTION AND HAPPINESS

As we have seen, Kant denies that the pursuit of happiness could ever provide a moral motivation. Nonetheless it is worth noting that in Kant's later writings he stresses the idea that we must believe not only in freedom (otherwise the moral law could have no practical bearing) but must also believe in God and the eternal rewards of heaven. Our ethical ideals lead to the notion of *moral perfection*. Moral perfection must be our goal, but we can never achieve it in this life. So there must be life beyond this one. And since only a good will merits happiness, it must be that the moral life is rewarded with happiness, which obviously is not typically the case in this life.

Kant does not believe, however, that theoretical proofs of the existence of God or an afterlife are possible. They are, rather, requirements of practical reason. Theoretical reason, which operates within the domain of the empirical, cannot, on the other hand, actually disprove the existence of either God or an afterlife.

30. *In your opinion would there be no motivation to be a moral person if being moral resulted in absolutely no reward and even in much suffering? Discuss.*

Further Discussion and Applications

Prima Facie Duties and Conflict Between Duties (Ross)

Kant is a deontologist. He stresses that we have duties, that is, requirements on our actions that have no exceptions. One such duty is the duty to keep promises. Another is to avoid doing things that would harm innocent people. Suppose that you borrow a gun from your neighbor and promise to return it when he needs it. Suppose that he gets depressed and decides to kill himself and needs the gun to do so. He comes asking for it. What should you do? It seems that in such a case there is a conflict between duties. You cannot possibly observe both duties. It is not clear how Kant thinks such cases should be handled. But most people will say right off that the gun should not be returned. How can they be so sure about that? British philosopher William David Ross (1877–1971), who, like Kant, approached ethics from a deontological stance, addressed this issue. Ross wants to do justice to the common belief that there can be conflicts between duties and that we can often know pretty well how to resolve them.

THE NATURE AND NUMBER OF OUR DUTIES

Like many earlier duty theorists, Ross believes that understanding our duties is an intuitive process and that we can morally intuit which of two duties is the stronger in a particular situation. He begins by distinguishing between *prima facie* duties and *actual* duties. The term *prima facie* is Latin for "on first appearance" or "on the face of it"; it is an expression borrowed from the legal profession: We presume some contention to be *prima facie* true unless it is disproved by a fact to the contrary. In the context of moral obligations, Ross holds that *prima facie* duties are those that we are presumed to have—such as keeping promises—unless they are outweighed by stronger duties—such as the duty to avoid endangering the lives of others. Once we pinpoint the stronger duty, it becomes our *actual* duty, and the weaker one thereby becomes no duty at all.

When I am in a situation, as perhaps I always am, in which more than one of these *prima facie* duties is incumbent on me, what I have to do is to study the situation as fully as I can until I form the considered opinion (it is never more) that in the circumstances one of them is more incumbent than any other; then I am bound to think that to do this *prima facie* duty is my duty *sans phrase* [or actual duty] in the situation.

"*Prima facie*" suggests that one is speaking only of an appearance which a moral situation presents at first sight, and which may turn out to be illusory; whereas what I am speaking of is an objective fact involved in the nature of the situation, or more strictly in an element of its nature, though not, as duty proper does, arising from its *whole* nature. (from *The Right and the Good*, 1930)

Ross thinks there are seven basic duties that we intuit. We have duties that arise from previous actions of our own, such as promises we have made, which he calls *duties of fidelity*. Some also depend on previous wrongful actions, in which case we may owe reparation for the wrong (duties of reparation). Thus if I have gotten something that belongs to you in an immoral way, by stealing, for instance, I have a duty to return it and perhaps to make further restitution. Some duties rest on previous acts of others, such as services done to me. These might be called *duties of gratitude*. Some duties are rooted in fairness or justice, such as the duty to see to it that people do not get rewards they do not deserve (duties of justice). Some duties arise from the mere fact that there are "beings in the world whose condition we can make better in respect of virtue, or intelligence, or of pleasure." Ross calls these *duties of beneficence*. Other duties are to ourselves. We must care for and improve ourselves (duties of self improvement). And we also have duties not to injure others, which are distinct from our duties to make others better. These last duties are *duties of nonmaleficence* and take priority over duties of beneficence. Ross claims that a "duty of nonmaleficence is recognized as a distinct one and as *prima facie* more binding. We should not

in general consider it justifiable to kill one person in order to keep another alive, or to steal from one in order to give alms to another."

31. *If the duties just listed are indeed basic, then more particular duties should be included in them. Under which of these seven basic duties should we include the duty to tell the truth? Argue.*

REASON AS AN INTUITING FACULTY

Ross contends that our apprehension of duties involves two distinct intuitions. The first entails our initial apprehension of the seven principal *prima facie* duties, which, he contends, are self-evident. Like some previous duty theorists, he believes that we intuitively apprehend these, in the same way that we do mathematical principles. Thus mature persons can see, without needing any proof, that it is wrong to harm innocent people, just as they can see, without proof, that if $a = b$ and $b = c$, then $a = c$. Such claims are self-evident. Ross claims that

> the moral order expressed in [moral] propositions is just as much part of the fundamental nature of the universe (and, we may add, of any possible universe in which there were moral agents at all) as is the spatial or numerical structure expressed in the axioms of geometry or arithmetic. In our confidence that these propositions are true there is involved the same trust in our reason that is involved in our confidence in mathematics.

However, our ability to intuit these basic duties does not by itself help solve the problem of conflicting duties. So we need another range of intuitions capable of resolving moral dilemmas and determining which of two competing duties is our actual one. These intuitions do not, however, rise to the level of self-evident certainty. In fact, in Ross's view, we can never be completely certain that a given *prima facie* duty is our actual duty. Though we can know with rational certainty that we have a *prima facie* duty to help those in need, we cannot know that we have an actual duty to help George, who is in need. Helping George might require ignoring Mary's more urgent need or might require breaking a strict promise. The best we can do then, in Ross's view, is to make an "all things considered" probable judgment that, say, helping George is our actual duty.

32. *Do you think you can directly intuit a "moral order" in the universe? Argue pro and con.*

33. *Ross tries to address an issue that Kant supposedly leaves hanging, namely, what to do when duties conflict. Do you think his claim that we have intuitions about these matters is true to life? Does he really solve the problem?*

*34. *Kant and Ross agree that reason can tell us what our duty is, but Ross thinks reason intuits several basic duties. Would Kant agree? Do Kant and Ross think of reason in the same way? Discuss and illustrate.*

Personal Goodness and Kantian Good Will (Sorell)

As we have seen, Kant insists that (a) only a good will is unconditionally good, and only it confers moral worth, and (b) a person might be kind, fun to be with, compassionate and generous and still fail to have a good will. Thus all of those characteristics mentioned in (b) would not suffice to make a person morally good and might even exist in a person who completely lacked moral goodness. It is of course possible that a person might do what the categorical imperative requires, even though that person is motivated by his own natural kindness, not by the moral law. But that would be a mere coincidence in Kant's view, and a person who acts on such "natural" motives cannot be relied on to act morally. Feelings of kindness can disappear in a hurry.

Kant's refusal to grant moral worth to people on the basis of such personal qualities as kindness seems counterintuitive to many people, and since Kant claims that he is doing justice to intuitive notions about morality, it looks as though there is a problem in the neighborhood.

British philosopher Tom Sorell thinks Kant's view may not be so counterintuitive after all. Sorell argues that a certain kind of moral exemplar will be approved by most people and that the kind in question is a Kantian kind.

It is helpful, in thinking about this matter, to compare Aristotle's views on moral exemplars. Aristotle holds that noble people who act out of virtue are admired for their goodness and can rightly serve as moral exemplars. We hold them up to young people and say, "Be like that." However, such people may not be common, and the route to becoming such a person is not always open to just anyone. Aristotle notes that people who are poor or ugly are unlikely to become "great-souled" individuals, which suggests that moral exemplars are people lucky enough to be fairly well off and fairly good-looking! Moreover, perhaps other psychological qualities that are simply gifts of nature and good upbringing should be included in the Aristotelian great-souled person, such as dispositions of kindness and generosity.

But now a problem arises: If such people are what they are partly as a result of good fortune or luck (*tuche*, see Chapter 3But it is even more important to ask whether or not the Aristotelian great-souled man can inspire genuine *respect*. We do not normally respect a person simply because he or she is *lucky*. But if we do not truly respect someone (though we may admire that person), how can she or he be a *moral exemplar*?

Perhaps we can retrieve a more palatable exemplar from Hume's writings on morals. Hume disavows the "aristocratic" tendencies in Aristotle and insists that there is a very widespread natural distribution of positive feelings and sympathetic attitudes toward others, a "sentiment of humanity" found in most people, rich, poor, old, young, smart, stupid, etc. But even the Humean "peasant," the ordinary man who is endowed with a generous, benevolent, sympathetic nature, does not inspire the kind of respect that a truly moral exemplar should, according to Kant. Kant admits that it is a "beautiful thing to do good to men because of love and a sympathetic good nature." But such "beauty" produces a kind of aesthetic pleasure in those who behold it. A genuine moral exemplar, on the other hand, may actually produce pain in the beholder, who may feel humiliated by an example that brings to mind his own failings and his own lack of single-minded struggle for holiness.

Sorell describes a typical reaction to the Humean exemplar in this way:

> The Humean exemplar allows us to indulge in pure spectatorship, and so gives us unwonted relief from the struggle against self-conceit. We are momentarily arrested by the charm of good nature, but not goaded by it. On the contrary, the example of good nature can actually encourage us to take it easy by encouraging us to think that nature itself sees to the development of the good will. (from "Kant's Good Will and Our Good Nature," *Kant Studien* 78, 1987)

But nature does *not* see to it, in Kant's view. *We* must see to it. We are moral agents, not mere moments in a natural process. Reminders of that fact may make us uncomfortable, due to our own moral deficits, and "goad" us into attempting self-reform.

Kant does not deny that we can take pleasure in or admire people who seem naturally good. What he does deny is that such pleasure or admiration is a moral reaction or that it fits our idea of what it is to be morally inspired. Morally inspiring people are attractive in a way, since they excite respect, but that respect is directed not toward pleasant personal qualities, but toward the discipline through which a person subjects himself to the moral law, whether or not his natural tendencies are pleasing. What people sense intuitively is that *moral* goodness is not the sort of thing that just flows out of people. It must be actively *willed*. The Humean good person or even the Aristotelian great-souled man may be pleasing to behold and arouse a kind of admiration. But to the extent that who that person is is the result of natural tendencies or the fortune of a good upbringing, that person does not inspire moral respect.

Sorell thinks that in fact these points show that Kant's position is not so counterintuitive after all. Take the case of the person who visits a brother in the hospital out of a sense of duty but not because of any warm feelings. Kant does not need to deny that we may feel a kind of displeasure when encountering a person who so lacks natural affection. And he is quite clear that we can feel a kind of pleasure and admiration when we meet someone who does exhibit such "human" qualities. We will probably like such a person. What Kant insists on, however, is that *moral* admiration is produced by a sense that a person's behavior is the result of something actively willed. Insisting on that does not require that we think a person who overcomes selfish inclinations and visits her brother is somehow better than the one who has warm feelings for her brother. Morally speaking, she is neither better nor worse.

35. *Does your admiration for people who are naturally kind and generous seem like the same kind of thing as your respect for someone who overcomes a temptation to lie and sticks to the truth? Discuss this in relation to Kant's notion of moral respect.*

36. *It seems that a person could be motivated both by respect for the moral law and by a naturally good disposition. Would that make him or her more suitable, or less suitable, as a moral exemplar than a person motivated only by respect for the moral law, in your view? In Kant's view?*

Kant on Sex and Using Persons Merely as Means (Singer)

Kant claims that using persons merely as means violates our most fundamental duty. That claim seems to resonate with many people, particularly in the area of sexual conduct. Rape can be construed as an extreme case of using another person as a means (it might also be simply a species of violence against others). As we have seen, using a person merely as a means involves overriding that person's freedom or consent, and rape obviously does that. A less extreme case of the same thing might be getting somebody drugged or extremely drunk so as to do with him or her as one pleases without his or her consent. But even cases of more subtle manipulation are wrong in the same way. If Bill can get Mary to agree to sex by falsely vowing that he truly loves her or by falsely promising to marry her or in any number of other ways, simply in order to satisfy his own lust, then he has used her merely as a means to that satisfaction. In all of these cases the indication that a person is being used merely as means is that his or her freedom is bypassed or overridden.

So far Kant's idea seems to confirm and perhaps clarify some basic moral intuitions that people have. But Kant also thinks, as we have seen, that using another merely as a means involves treating that person as a "thing" or object. That also fits with a common feeling that most people have, that persons should not be treated as mere objects, even if they *do* consent to being so treated. The violation of the supreme principle of morality must thus involve more than ignoring another person's free decision (assuming that people really can give themselves up freely to being treated as mere objects).

Now, it is possible to wonder whether there is *any* "use" of a person as a means to sexual satisfaction that does not somehow involve treating him or her as an object. In fact, Kant thinks that there is only one circumstance in which such "use" can be avoided or at any rate made legitimate. Kant thinks that sexual love "taken in itself" is always nothing more than appetite. As such the satisfaction it seeks is not basically different from the kind of satisfaction sought when I am hungry. The beefsteak I seize on to satisfy hunger is obviously a mere object. Must the seeking of sexual satisfaction be the same sort of thing? Does the person through whom I seek such satisfaction necessarily become nothing more than a mere piece of meat to me? Kant seems to think so: "As soon as a person becomes an object of appetite for another, all motives of moral relationship cease to function, because as an object of appetite for another a person becomes a thing" (*Lectures on Ethics*). Kant thinks that sexual relationships are unique among all the sorts of relationships that people have, because they alone involve in their very nature this reduction of persons to things.

It is worth noting here that Kant thinks that it is just as immoral to allow oneself to be treated as a thing as it is to treat someone else as a thing. We cannot treat ourselves as a piece of property (even our own property) or allow others to do so without degrading ourselves and violating the categorical imperative. Thus prostitution is always wrong, both for the prostitute and for the person who uses him or her (cf. the preceding quote).

While many people would resonate to many of the claims Kant makes here, not many would agree that *all* sexual relationships are by their very nature tainted with treating another as an object. When faithful married people come together in true affection and self-giving, must the mere fact that in doing so they may also satisfy an appetite make their action immoral? In fact, Kant thinks that only in monogamous marriage can there be sex that is not immoral, but his reasons for thinking so are rather unusual. They are not the ones most people would give.

Kant stresses that persons are unities. I cannot take one part of a person and use it without taking the whole person along with it. If I hire someone to mow the lawn, I use his arms, legs, feet, shoulders and the like. But in Kant's view I cannot do that without using the whole person, body and soul, since people cannot be in actuality, or practically, separated into parts (though we might do so for theoretical or medical purposes). Consequently I cannot use another person's sexual organs without using the whole person. Under what conditions might I do that? Only under the condition that a person has given him- or herself over to me completely, body and soul, *and* I have likewise given myself over entirely to that person. Kant argues that

> if I yield myself completely to another, and obtain the person of the other in return, I will win myself back; I have given myself up as the property of another, but in turn I take that other as my property, and so win myself back again in winning the person whose property I have become. In this way the two persons become a unity of will. (*Lectures on Ethics*)

In this way, Kant thinks, I can avoid using another person or the objectifying of another person. To quote again from an earlier passage, in such circumstances the person whom I "use" is in fact able to "himself contain the end of this [sexual] action" since he or she has become "I" in a "unity of will." The complete giving up of oneself that is required is only possible in marriage because of the full legal and social as well as personal implications of marriage.

It is interesting to note that on this basis (which is admittedly not entirely clear) Kant thinks he is able to rule out all sex as immoral that does not take place in a monogamous marriage. All extramarital sex, masturbation, concubinage and polygamy (or poly-andry) are wrong. For example, bigamy and polyandry are wrong because it is impossible to give oneself up completely to more than one person. To do so would require that a person actually be two or more persons, which is nonsense.

37. *In brief, what is it that makes prostitution wrong, according to Kant? Do you agree? Why or why not?*

38. *Does Kant's description of the marriage contract as "taking a person as property and giving oneself up as property" seem to clash with the claim that one should not treat others or oneself as things? Doesn't property consist of things, normally?*

SINGER'S RESPONSE TO KANT

American philosopher Irving Singer takes seriously Kant's concerns about the abuse or degradation of persons that may be all too common in sexual relationships. But he thinks that Kant's attempt to address this matter is defective in many ways.

Singer notes that sexual relations need not and often are not "appetitive" in the way Kant supposes. Sexual attraction and satisfaction are quite different in all sorts of ways from the hungry person's attraction to and enjoyment of a piece of meat. Sexual attraction is very often attraction to a person, who may have pleasing bodily features but who may also attract through his or her intelligence, charm, wit, kindness, respectfulness and a host of other qualities. Bodily beauty (sexual attractiveness) may be enhanced by such personal qualities or may be diminished to zero through their absence. The sexual element in attraction to others cannot be neatly separated from the other attractions. Moreover, even rather crudely lustful sexual relations are sometimes transformed. Singer quotes Hume, who remarked that even one "who is enflamed by lust, feels at least a momentary kindness towards the object of it." Nothing similar takes place in connection with other appetites (do people feel a momentary kindness toward the piece of chicken they are consuming?). And surely it is often the case that unmarried lovers may feel respect for one another's personhood.

However, Singer is particularly critical of Kant's account of marriage. Marriage is not, as Kant imagines, the uniting of two persons into one. That is an extravagantly romantic notion. And it is not a description of very many, if any, marriages. Typically in marriages, people maintain much, often a great deal, of their individuality and do not give it up as though it were "owned" by someone else. But even if there were that kind of union in marriage, there is no reason to think that it would follow from the mere fact of the marriage contract. Kant claims that simply by entering into marriage, a person gives him- or herself over completely to another. Singer thinks that is a crudely legalistic notion, which cannot account for the features of married sex that may in fact make it moral.

By Singer's account, Kant would not have been driven to such a view of marriage if he had not started with the assumption that sex is intrinsically manipulative and can be moralized only by a contract.

> Once we free ourselves from the notion that sex is always and ineluctably manipulative, once we recognize that frequently it is a gratifying search for someone we do not wish to manipulate, and may even want to strengthen as an autonomous person, there can be no valid reason to think that its ethical potentiality resides within the dictates of a contract. ("The Morality of Sex: Contra Kant" in Alan Soble, ed., *The Philosophy of Sex*, p. 271)

This point might be reinforced by the fact that a spouse who is overly submissive, dependent or lacking in distinctive personal resources and autonomy may actually, for those reasons, make sex itself unsatisfying or even impossible.

39. *Does it seem to you that sex is intrinsically manipulative? Don't say "no" simply because it might be* mutually *manipulative! Argue pro and con.*

40. *Do you think Singer's critique of Kant's conception of marriage is on the mark? Summarize his critique, and say why you do or do not agree. Can you add anything to it?*

41. *Despite any possible defects in Kant's argument, is he nonetheless right in thinking that*

sex can only be moral within a monogamous marriage? Explain your answer.

Duties Toward Animals (Kant and Regan)

Duty theorists (*deontologists*) have tried to distinguish *direct* from *indirect* duties. For example, I have a direct duty to avoid slandering you because of the harm I would directly cause you by doing so. On the other hand, I have only an indirect duty to avoid slandering your deceased grandfather. My obligation cannot be connected with your grandfather himself, since he is no longer alive; my obligation, instead, is based on the harm that I would cause you and his other surviving relatives. By slandering your grandfather I do not harm you directly.

Kant argued that duties toward animals are only indirect. Animals themselves are not the subjects of direct duties, since they are irrational and are at best only items of property. The duties we owe animals are based only on how our treatment of them affects human beings and not on any pain or other problem the animal itself might experience. Animal behavior, according to Kant, exhibits some similarities with human behavior, and, by being cruel to animals, we desensitize ourselves to human decency. Thus by being cruel to animals (not in itself wrong) we may become cruel to people.

> [S]o far as animals are concerned, we have no direct duties. Animals are not self-conscious and are there merely as a means to an end. That end is man. We can ask, "Why do animals exist?" But to ask, "Why does man exist?" is a meaningless question. Our duties towards animals are merely indirect duties towards humanity. Animal nature has analogies to human nature, and by doing our duties to animals in respect of manifestations which correspond to manifestations of human nature, we indirectly do our duty towards humanity. Thus, if a dog has served his master long and faithfully, his service, on the analogy of human service, deserves reward, and when the dog has grown too old to serve, his master ought to keep him until he dies. Such action helps to support us in our duties towards human beings, where they are bounden duties.

> If then any acts of animals are analogous to human acts and spring from the same principles, we have duties towards the animals because thus we cultivate the corresponding duties towards human beings. If a man shoots his dog because the animal is no longer capable of service, he does not fail in his duty to the dog, for the dog cannot judge, but his act is inhuman and damages in himself that humanity which it is his duty to show towards mankind. If he is not to stifle his human feelings, he must practice kindness towards animals, for he who is cruel to animals becomes hard also in his dealings with men. (Kant, "Duties Towards Animals," 1775)

42. *How, according to Kant, does cruelty to animals damage a person's humanity? In your view, is that the* only *reason for not being cruel to animals?*

Contemporary philosopher Tom Regan believes that views such as Kant's are horribly misguided. They presume that animals are not conscious creatures and thus are not capable of experiencing pain.

> Suppose your neighbor kicks your dog. Then your neighbor has done something wrong. But not [according to Kant] to your dog. The wrong that has been done is a wrong to you. After all, it is wrong to upset people, and your neighbor's kicking your dog upsets you. So you are the one who is wronged, not your dog. . . . How could someone try to justify such a view? Someone might say that your dog doesn't feel anything and so isn't hurt by your neighbor's kick, doesn't care about the pain since none is felt, is as unaware of anything as is your windshield. Someone might say this, but no rational person will, since, among other considerations, such a view will commit anyone who holds it to the position that no human being feels pain either—that human beings also don't care about what happens to them. (Tom Regan, "The Case for Animal Rights," 1985)

43. *According to Regan, we must dismiss the view that animals are incapable of feeling pain. What is his argument? Think about how you can tell that a human being is in pain. And*

remember, most people probably think animals experience pain because they have witnessed the behavior of injured animals. What is that behavior like?

According to Regan, we have direct duties to many animals for the same reasons that we have direct duties toward humans; that is, humans and many animals have psychological capacities, such as having preferences, beliefs, feelings, recollections and expectations. And surely they are capable of feeling pain. These are features that give any creature a direct moral standing, Regan claims.

Moral Development, Moral Education and Autonomy (Kohlberg)

Kant places great stress on the notion of duty and the notion that duty consists in the strict following of principles that admit of no exceptions. He analyzes the notion of duty in such a way that autonomy, the characteristic of making decisions independently without relying on the commands or advice of others, is absolutely central. A genuinely moral agent wills the good out of respect for the moral law and apart from all influences from both without and within. That would include influences from one's own natural feelings, such as sympathetic feelings for others. The notions of fairness and impartiality also figure centrally in Kant's account. The very notion of a moral principle is the notion of something that applies impartially and universally, apart from all specific differences between people.

Kant believes that his account squares with what people commonly think about morality and how it is acquired or developed in a person. Do empirical studies of moral development confirm Kant's ideas about what people normally think?

MORAL EDUCATION AND UNIVERSAL MORAL PRINCIPLES

Important studies of moral development have been undertaken by psychologist Lawrence Kohlberg (1927–87), who taught at Harvard university for many years. Kohlberg was concerned with the problem of moral education. Some of the issues in moral education discussed by Sher and Bennett (Chapter 3) were

important to him also. How can moral education avoid indoctrination that *violates autonomy*? How can it avoid the problems posed by relativism? For example, if I educate someone into showing respect for other people's religious beliefs, am I not depriving them of the moral insights that might come from someone like Marx or Nietzsche, who despised all religion? What gives me the right to do that?

These are real practical problems for many teachers. Some teachers openly wonder how they can make a convincing case against cheating when they feel required to stress acceptance of moral "differences" and avoid indoctrination. How can they respond when students say, "Who's to say?" or "You can't make moral judgments"? (Compare with your response to Orienting Question 1 in Chapter 1.) How can they possibly respond to the student who says, "Your idea that cheating is wrong is just your opinion. You cannot force it on me." (See all of Chapter 1 of this text for a discussion of precisely these sorts of issues.) The various solutions that educators have proposed to these problems are described by Kohlberg as being, for the most part, "copouts."

Kohlberg came to the conclusion that the fear of violating autonomy is *unjustified*. In fact people everywhere develop morally in pretty much the same way, or so he claimed. The moral teacher is simply someone who encourages the kind of development that will take place anyway under more or less normal conditions. Kohlberg based his claims on cross-cultural studies of moral development. He did surveys in the United States, in Taiwanese villages, Atayal (Malaysian aboriginal) villages, Mexico and elsewhere. Although these studies did not supply warrant for the claim that there are no moral differences whatsoever between cultures, Kohlberg thought they did warrant the claim that people everywhere operate with the same basic moral principles. An example of a basic moral principle would be "Treat people equally."

LEVELS AND STAGES OF MORAL THINKING AND DEVELOPMENT

Kohlberg thought that his studies revealed "levels" of moral thinking, with "stages" within the levels. The first, or lowest, level is *preconventional*, the second is *conventional*, and the third is *postconventional* or autonomous. Each level breaks down into two stages, for a total of six stages. For example, at the first stage of the preconventional level, which is where we find most children ages 4–10, ideas about good and bad are learned from parents and other authority figures in the culture (that is, they are the moral conventions of the culture), but they are interpreted in terms of punishment and reward. Something is good that leads to reward, bad if it leads to punishment. This stage of moral thinking always comes before a stage in which what is good is what the person himself approves, rather than what others approve. The sequence is universal, though of course people move at slightly different rates and can be partly in one stage and partly in the next, and some people get stuck at a certain stage.

The stages are understood by reference to responses children and young adults give to various "moral dilemmas" posed in Kohlberg's surveys and studies. Some of the dilemmas have to do with the value of human life. For example, children at various ages were asked whether a man should steal food that he could not possibly afford to buy, if he needed it to save the life of his wife. The changes through time in their responses to this question were tabulated. Here is how Kohlberg describes the stages (*Essays on Moral Development*).

1. The value of human life is confused with the value of physical objects and is based on the social status or physical attributes of the possessor.
2. The value of human life is seen as instrumental to the satisfaction of the needs of its possessor or of other people.
3. The value of human life is based on the empathy and affection of family members and others toward its possessor.
4. Life is conceived as sacred in terms of its place in a categorical moral or religious order of rights and duties.
5. Life is valued both in terms of its relation to community welfare and in terms of life being a universal human right.
6. Human life is sacred—the universal human value of respect for the individual.

To illustrate: Children at stages 1 and 2 might claim that the man who steals the food is justified because the cost of the funeral for his wife would be too great (Taiwanese) or because the man needs her to cook for him (Atayal). The variations in response have something to do with varying funeral expenses, so there is that much "cultural relativity." But both responses fall more or less into Stage 2.

Kohlberg argues that the "higher" stages show greater rationality or cognitive maturity. Cognitive maturity is registered partly in the way concepts correctly differentiate (for example, differentiate the value of life from the value of property), integrate and increase in scope or universality. Thus

> When one's concept of human life moves from Stage 1 to Stage 2, the value of human life becomes more differentiated from the value of property, more integrated (the value of life enters an organizational hierarchy where it is "higher" than property so that one steals property in order to save life), and more universalized (the life of any sentient being is valuable regardless of status or property). The same advance is true at each stage in the hierarchy. (*Essays on Moral Development*)

Since, according to Kohlberg, all kinds of intellectual development progress through increasing differentiation and increasing integration, moral thought is not fundamentally different from scientific or other kinds of thought.

Kohlberg claims that the role of cultural differences decreases with maturity. The preconventional and conventional levels may be bound by culturally specific emphases, such as an emphasis on courage in battle in one culture (perhaps a warrior culture) or honesty in another. But "in the higher postconventional levels, Socrates, Lincoln, Thoreau and Martin Luther King tend to speak without confusion of tongues, as it were." Otherwise put, relativism is only a problem at lower levels of moral development. At the higher levels there is agreement on the fundamental importance of "respect for the individual."

In light of these studies, Kohlberg thinks that the problem of moral education can be solved without involving teachers in indoctrinating students. His studies show that young people understand the stage they are at and the next highest and are drawn to the next-highest level without any special encouragement or indoctrination. So the educator simply encourages reflection on various examples, with a view to bringing a higher level into focus. The students will want to move to it on their own.

Those familiar with Kant will notice a Kantian flavor in Kohlberg's stages 5 and 6. In his view the highest moral development involves a focus on individual rights and respect for the individual and downplays feelings, such as empathy, love for family and the like, that play a prominent role in stage 3.

44. *Briefly, how does Kohlberg solve the problem of "indoctrination," or violation of autonomy, that seems to many to result from directive moral education?*

45. *Does Kohlberg's account of moral development square with your own experiences? What stage do you think* you *are at? Discuss and give examples.*

*46. *Does Kohlberg's belief that the higher-numbered stages are* morally *higher actually follow from the empirical data, or is that belief the result of his own moral (perhaps Kantian) biases? In answering this, try to be open to the possibility that children or younger people might actually be more moral than adults in many crucial respects.*

*47. *If Kantian moral theory should prove to be significantly defective as compared to, say, Aristotle's virtue theory, would that cast doubt on Kohlberg's claims about what constitutes moral development? How might Aristotle describe the highest stage of moral development?*

Moral Principles and the Moral Focus of Women (Gilligan and Homiak)

Carol Gilligan (b. 1936) has been professor of education at Harvard. In her widely discussed book *In A Different Voice* she takes issue with the picture of moral maturity derived from the studies of scholars like Kohlberg. Her own studies have focused on women, and she thinks they show that women tend to have a way of thinking about morality that Kohlberg would classify at a low or immature level, such

as stage 3 in his scheme. It is indeed a striking fact that Kohlberg's conclusions are based on interviews with boys and young men *only*.

Women, Gilligan argues, typically focus on interdependence, care and responsibility within particular personal relationships, and attention to particular individuals and contexts, just the sort of thing that would seem important in families. Men typically focus on autonomy or independence, rights, impartiality and general "impersonal" principles, such as principles of fairness, like the Golden Rule. This focus might seem more appropriate to the workplace and public or civic life, at least as they are often conceived.

Gilligan thinks that the view of moral maturity proposed by Kohlberg and other male psychologists simply begs the question regarding(stet) women and their typical perspectives on life. In Kohlberg's view, women are typically morally immature!

Some of Gilligan's reasons for thinking that Kohlberg's analysis is defective, apart from its obvious ignoring of women, come out in the following interview with a woman about her changing moral views. This woman was 25 and a law student at the time of the interview.

[Is there really some correct solution to moral problems, or is everybody's opinion equally right?]

No, I don't think everybody's opinion is equally right. I think that in some situations there may be opinions that are equally valid, and one could conscientiously adopt one of several courses of action. But there are other situations in which I think there are right and wrong answers, that sort of inhere in the nature of existence, of all individuals here who need to live with each other to live. We need to depend on each other, and hopefully it is not only a physical need but a need of fulfillment in ourselves, that a person's life is enriched by cooperating with other people and striving to live in harmony with everybody else, and to that end, there are right and wrong, there are things which promote that end and that move away from it, and in that way it is possible to choose in certain cases among different courses of action that obviously promote or harm that goal. (from *In a Different Voice*, 1982)

48. *Think of and discuss an example of something that is right because it promotes living in harmony with others. Then consider a case of something that is wrong because it interferes with that harmony.*

As the interview continues, this woman admits that when she was younger she thought morality was "pretty relative" but that now she has changed her thinking.

[When did that change occur?]

When I was in high school. . . . Now I think even when it is only the person himself who is going to be affected, I say it is wrong to the extent it doesn't cohere with what I know about human nature and what I know about you, and just from what I think is true about the operation of the universe, I could say I think you are making a mistake.

[What led you to change, do you think?]

Just seeing more of life. . . . There are certain things that you come to learn promote a better life and better relationships and more personal fulfillment than other things that in general tend to do the opposite, and the things that promote these things, you would call morally right.

49. *What would Kant say about the claim that what is right is what promotes a better life, better relationships, etc.? What would Kohlberg say?*

Gilligan observes that this woman is more concerned about responsibility to and care for others than she is about their right not to suffer interference from others. She is concerned about "the possibility of omission, of your not helping others when you could help them."

50. *By and large, and with due allowance for particular situations, who would you rather have around you, someone who focuses on not interfering or someone who will try to help when trouble appears? Consider various kinds of cases.*

Gilligan's account allows for a different conception of autonomy than that proposed by the Kohlbergian kinds of analyses. She mentions the views of another women writer, Jane Loevinger.

The autonomous stage in Loevinger's account witnesses a relinquishing of moral dichotomies and their replacement with "a feeling for the complexity and multifaceted character of real people and real situations."

Whereas the rights conception of morality that informs Kohlberg's principled level (stages 5 and 6) is geared to arriving at an objectively fair or just resolution to moral dilemmas upon which all rational persons could agree, the responsibility conception focuses instead on the limitations of any particular resolution and describes the conflicts that remain.

Women, by this account, are likely to be more attentive to particular contexts requiring distinctive decisions and judgments. Objective fairness is not always best.

*51. *Describe a family conflict in which an objectively fair resolution would be possible, and say what it would be. Then describe a family conflict in which an objectively fair resolution would not be possible, and say what you think would be the best approach in that case.*

Gilligan makes this recommendation:

Only when life-cycle theorists divide their attention and begin to live with women as they have lived with men will their vision encompass the experience of both sexes and their theories become correspondingly more fertile.

Gilligan sees the following as characteristic of women and also as morally important and mature: personal relationships; caring and the promotion of flourishing; interdependence; attention to particular cases and contexts.

Kohlberg sees the following as morally most important and as evidence of moral maturity: general reasoned principles; impartiality or fairness; disregard for loyalty to particular groups or cultures and a cultivation of universality in ethics.

*52. *In your opinion, are the differences between Kohlberg's and Gilligan's views on morality determined more by differences in philosophical ethical theories than by differences between men and women?*

The women interviewed by Gilligan make remarks that may sound familiar if you have studied Chapter 3, on Aristotle. Those remarks emphasize the need to learn what is required for human fulfillment and the importance of communities of various kinds to such fulfillment. They explicitly connect what is right and wrong to such learning and stress the objectivity of ethical knowledge. They clearly indicate that the "moral focus" of women is reasonable or rational, rooted in accurate assessments of such things as who needs what and when. Aristotle also stresses that the aim of human life is to develop a kind of practical wisdom or rationality that is necessary and sufficient for flourishing and that flourishing requires relationships or community. Perhaps what Gilligan has shown is, in effect, that Aristotelian approaches to ethics are particularly agreeable to women in our current historical situation. But she may not have shown that there is anything essentially "feminine" in such approaches (obviously, Aristotle was male).

Unfortunately, in *The Nichomachean Ethics*, Book VIII, and elsewhere in his writings, Aristotle classifies women in many respects with children and slaves. He thinks they are not capable of the kind of development that is necessary for the best kind of life. It is thus understandable that some contemporary feminists have written off Aristotle as a source of useful ethical insights. But Marcia Homiak, a contemporary feminist with detailed knowledge of Aristotle, finds such a dismissal to be ill-advised.

Homiak makes interesting applications of basically Aristotelian ideas that would, admittedly, never have occurred to Aristotle. She considers ways in which the care of women for men may become corrupted. In particular, bad kinds of dependency may corrupt the care women show for men. Now, Aristotle is quite aware that there are forms of dependency that interfere with the free deliberation required for virtue and a good life. Even a skilled sculptor like Phidias (a famous Greek sculptor) could not fully control his own activity through deliberation on what he saw to be best, Aristotle claims. Why? Simply because he was dependent on patrons and state institutions to make a living. Thus, in Aristotle's view, he would have been hindered in the pursuit of the best kind of life. And he certainly would have been unable to enter into that

productive relationship called "friendship," at least with respect to his patrons. Friends are able to show genuine care for each other because of the freedom inherent in their relationship. Such care does not involve false dependencies or any lack of self-esteem. It is based on an accurate assessment of the true nature and needs of the friend, and that assessment is internally connected to correct self-development, since the friend is "another self."

Homiak sees in these Aristotelian ideas a clear application to certain feminist concerns. For instance, they rule out forms of kindness toward or love for others based in dependency and lack of self-development. Thus the person with the virtue of kindness does not always do what other people want her to do. Homiak remarks:

> Aristotle's virtuous citizen knows that another's good is not equivalent simply to what another wants. He knows that another's good includes the performance of activities that will nurture and sustain the other's self-love. So Aristotle's virtuous citizen recognizes that showing concern for another's good for the other's own sake may take all sorts of forms, only some of which will look like mere behavioral niceness.
>
> I have been suggesting that if compassion and a concern for relationships constitutes some kind of model or ideal, it is not a simple one according to which we simply act to preserve the relationship or act to help another achieve what he might want. If compassion and concern are directed toward another's good for that person's sake, then for them to be proper objects of an ideal, they must operate against the background of some sound recognition of what another's good consists in. If not, compassion and concern can serve to promote oppressive or destructive relationships. Moreover, if the compassionate person is an ideal, she must be someone whose concern for another is ungrudging and noninstrumental. Aristotle's virtuous person is most likely to offer that kind of concern. (from "Feminism and Aristotle's Rational Ideal," in *Aristotle's Ethics*, ed. Nancy Sherman, 1999)

Homiak undoubtedly has in mind women who show compassion or concern for their husbands or male companions because they fear losing the relationship or because they need to get something from their male companions, who may be better situated than they are to control who gets what. She considers such forms of concern to be unhealthy, and indeed it seems that they are. But there is nothing particularly rational, and thus nothing truly virtuous, about such concerns. The emotions that motivate unhealthy concern are not properly integrated with reason.

If Aristotle's fundamental conceptions are neither inherently sexist nor inherently exploitative, and if as Homiak argues Aristotle provides an analysis of reason, emotions and friendship that can be invoked in support of feminist concerns, then Aristotle's conception of ethical life is, she concludes, "worthy of emulation by both men and women."

> 53. *Homiak implies in her remarks just quoted that the kind of care women show (for men particularly) may often be corrupt. In what way might it be corrupt?*
> *54. What is there in Gilligan's account of the moral focus of women that could be associated with Aristotle's account of virtue and self-development?*

Kantian Ethical Concepts and Discursive Reason (Habermas)

Kant's contrast between hypothetical imperatives and categorical imperatives is strongly connected to competing notions of reason. On the one hand, reason can be thought of as an "instrument" that is used to achieve certain ends, while the ends themselves are not subject to rational assessment (instrumental reason). Thus "reason" may tell me to build divided highways to enhance rapid movement of traffic, but it is not clear how it could tell me that a social organization requiring such rapid movement is itself "reasonable." But according to Kant moral "reason" is nothing like that; it is brought to bear directly on actions themselves, not on the ends sought. Actions that proceed from a good will are good in themselves, quite apart from any other ends that they may achieve, and are supremely rational. Someone who keeps a promise for no other reason than that it is required by the moral law is "reasonable" in that second sense. And

Kant insists that real *freedom* consists in the ability to be reasonable in that way. Instrumental reason, on the other hand, does not contribute to freedom, but leaves us under the control of "inclinations." It is also clear that Kant believes that his account of morality avoids subjectivism and relativism.

Jürgen Habermas (b. 1929), a German philosopher and social theorist, argues that something like the Kantian distinctions must be recovered. Failure to do so explains some of the worst features of our technological societies, in which freedom is constrained by the progress of technology. Thus someone who objects to the use or dominance of certain technologies (for example, divided highways or computers) might be dismissed as irrational, unfit for "reasonable" discussion. Instrumental reason dominates the social world and represses those who take a morally critical stance toward dominant forms of social life. Their voices are unheard because morality is thought to be merely subjective (and thus not subject to "reason") or is itself assimilated to "the done thing" (the dominant conventions, which by definition exclude protestors) or to some form of instrumental reasoning. This sidelining of those who fail to conform to the "technological imperative" is of course unjust. Justice requires that all be given equal voice. Justice is by definition "egalitarian." Kant's notion that genuinely moral maxims must be *universalizable* (acceptable to all) registers that sense of justice. Only where there is that kind of universality are the relations between people rightly ordered.

> 55. *What is it about Kant's rejection of the moral significance of "hypothetical imperatives" that makes that rejection ethically important in the contemporary world, according to Habermas?*

But Habermas does not think that Kant has given a convincing account of the basis or "grounds" of moral reason. That is why many contemporary moral theorists have rejected Kant in favor of utilitarian theories (Chapter 9) or subjectivist/emotivist theories (Chapter 7) or conventionalist (morality as determined by local conventions) theories. Moreover, the increased awareness in the (post)modern world of the great diversity of cultures and moral perspectives (Chapter 1) makes Kant's universalism implausible to many.

Habermas, on the other hand, argues that we can preserve something similar to Kantian universality and objectivity by showing that the very possibility of discourse (discussion, argument) assumes universal agreement on how discussion and argument should, ideally, proceed. Without that universalism, freedom and autonomy will be lost. The key to a better understanding of (noninstrumental) reason and thus of ethics is in *language*.

> The human interest in autonomy and responsibility is not mere fancy, for it can be apprehended a priori. What raises us out of nature is the only thing whose nature we can know: language.
> (*Truth and Justification*, Chapter 6, p. 314)

By understanding discourse (those verbal interchanges called *discussion* or *argument* or *debate*) we can justify our Kantian intuitions about the objectivity of morals, freedom or autonomy, and universality. Thus Habermas developed what is called a *discourse ethics,* which, he believed, could avoid relativism, subjectivism etc.

> The normative validity of moral statements [is grounded in] the regulative idea of the mutual inclusion of the other [other persons] in an inclusive—and to that extent universal—world of well-ordered interpersonal relationships. This projection of a single moral world is rooted in the communicative presuppositions of rational discourse. For under the conditions of the modern pluralism of worldviews, the idea of justice has been sublimated into the concept of the impartiality of a discursively attained agreement. . . . The key to this account lies in the demanding conditions of communication that attribute to participants in practical discourses the ability of generating a shared perspective of self-critical impartiality. (*Truth and Justification*, p. 247)

We can perhaps get a sense for the ideal that Habermas is promoting (namely, striving to achieve the "ideal speech situation") by contrasting it with something not so ideal. Consider a classroom discussion in which the teacher, by virtue of his power and his presumed expertise, manages to override or marginalize the arguments offered by some students

regarding some controversial issue (say, the permissibility of abortion). The students' arguments might be just as good as or better than the teacher's, but the teacher is in a good position to make it *look as though* his arguments are better. He can employ unfamiliar concepts, take advantage of the students' lack of advance preparation on the particular issue, and in other ways manipulate an unfair conclusion to the "debate."

The ideal speech situation, on the other hand, would require the elimination of all such unfair (and nonrational) advantages so that the discussion would proceed according to standards to which everyone can freely subscribe. Habermas' ideal can thus be seen to do homage to another formulation of Kant's view, namely, that it is always wrong to "use" (manipulate) other persons.

56. *Describe an example of a less-than-ideal "speech situation" (a discussion, for example) that you have witnessed or in which you have been involved.*

Habermas claims that even in a less-than-ideal speech situation, standards of discourse that are *inclusive*, i.e., to which everyone can freely subscribe, are implicit or "presupposed." If they were not, we could not even have discussions or even understand one another. If, for example, I did not generally assume that any good relevant reason should be admitted to a discussion, there would be no discussion. If there were no distinction between good reason, bad reason, and no reason at all or between manipulation and fairness or between what follows from a claim and what does not, there would be no point to *communication*. (It is worth observing that the *co* in *communication* means "with" and that the *muni* refers originally to strengthening, thus "strengthening with" others). People might still push each other around, of course, and some kind of language might play a role in that, but there would be no communication or discussion. Words and sentences would be more like sticks used by people to beat each other. Thus the very fact of communication, Habermas argues, with its intrinsic inclusivity or universality, grounds the objectivity of moral judgments.

But of course the ideal speech situation is an *ideal*, which we must continually strive to realize. That striving requires an ability to take up the perspectives of people with whom we may disagree.

Recall my earlier observation that the validity of moral judgments is *assessed* in terms of how *inclusive* the normative agreement is that has been reached among conflicting parties. By directing ourselves toward the goal of a "single right answer" even in moral controversies, we presuppose that a valid morality applies to a single social world that includes all claims and persons equally. Of course, like Kant's "kingdom of ends," this world is not so much a given for us as it is a mandate. . . . Participants in the social dimension have to bring about an inclusive We-perspective by means of mutually taking one another's perspectives. (*Truth and Justification*)

Habermas has tried to do justice to certain Kantian themes, centering on the idea of freedom and fairness. However, Kant thought that an individual, all by herself and simply by virtue of possession of "reason," could arrive at a correct answer to any question about right and wrong. Habermas thinks that it is only in interaction with *other* people in discourse situations that correct answers can be found.

*57. *Habermas thinks, as did Kant, that there should ideally be a single right answer in*

moral controversies. *Thus he does not give in to the idea that "anyone's view is as good as anyone else's" or that one person's moral beliefs can be incommensurable with another person's. Yet there are some obvious advantages to Habermas' approach in a pluralistic world, such as ours appears to be. State what some of the advantages are.*

**58. *Depending on which of the previous readings you have completed, try to figure out what Habermas would say about each of the following:*

Relativism (Chapter 1)
Natural law theory (Chapter 4)
Hobbesian "realism" (Chapter 6)
Humean "emotivism" (Chapter 7)
Rawls' notion of justice as fairness
  (Chapter 9)
Baier's "best reasons" approach (Chapter 6)

*59. *Habermas' conception of justice is proceduralist. That means that a just law, for example, is one that has been decided on through a correct (open, fair, inclusive etc.) procedure. Do you think his conception would be of any help in legislative debates about (a) slavery, (b) stem cell research, (c) gay marriage? Argue pro and con for each one.*

Rightness, Reason and Consequences

Introduction

When we deliberate on what would be the right thing to do, we often try to calculate the consequences of various options. In some situations I will have the option of either telling the truth or telling a lie. Would it ever be right to tell a lie? Perhaps. Suppose my wife is interviewing this morning for a new job. She has been worrying about it, did not sleep well and is now looking tired. She asks me how she looks. In fact she does not look good, and there is no time to do anything about it. But she very much needs some esteem building, so I tell her, with as much enthusiasm and appearance of sincerity as I can muster, that she really looks great. With a big smile she heads off confidently to the interview. I lied. Was that the right thing to do? Many people would think so, probably for reasons such as the following: The *consequences* of telling the truth would have been mostly bad; she would have felt very bad; she probably would have done poorly in the interview. Moreover it appears that nothing is to be gained from telling the truth. No good consequences would ensue. The good consequences are all, it seems, on the side of lying. Lying would also be the kind thing to do, since it produces the most pleasurable and satisfying consequences, given the particular situation. So lying would be best, even morally best, in those circumstances, assuming that consequences are what count morally.

We might be tempted to generalize from this case. We might think that *whenever* we must choose a course of action, the right thing to do is to choose the action that produces the best overall consequences or, at least, avoids the worst consequences. This way of thinking seems to be both moral and reasonable. What reason could there be for telling my wife how she really looks? And since it would be harmful, how could it be morally right? So telling the truth in such a situation would be both *unreasonable* and *morally bad* or wrong.

Utilitarians are people who argue that those actions (or action types) are right that can reasonably be expected to produce the best overall consequences. Utilitarianism is thus a kind of *consequentialism*. The goodness of consequences may be measured in various ways. For example, those consequences might be counted as good that do most to maximize happiness (or preferences or something else) or at least minimize unhappiness or pain. Maximize happiness for whom? Perhaps for *everyone* who would be affected by the action. "Altruistic utilitarians" argue that we are morally required to act in ways that are likely to maximize happiness for the greatest number of those affected by our action. We should not think just about how our actions may affect *us*.

Utilitarianism seems to many people to suggest a morally good approach to addressing social issues, such as poverty. Tax policies, for instance, should be chosen that produce the greatest happiness for the greatest number. Higher taxes for the rich and lower taxes for the poor might be justified on the grounds that the higher taxes for the rich do not hurt them very much, if at all, and can help the poor quite a bit. Even though the rich might be a little bit unhappy with that policy, their unhappiness may be more than outweighed by the increased happiness of the poor. The overall result is better than with a flat tax policy or high taxes for the poor. The morally right policy is the one that has the best overall consequences. So higher taxes for the rich would usually be morally right, in the utilitarian view.

However, there are obvious problems with utilitarianism and with consequentialism generally. To some people it looks suspiciously like the idea that the end justifies the means. For example, if many lives could be saved by executing one innocent person, it may seem that, in the utilitarian view, executing that person could be the morally right thing to do. But many people cringe at this idea. Recall the question raised by Ivan Karamazov (Chapter 5) and the response of his brother, Alyosha:

> Imagine that you are creating a fabric of human destiny with the object of making men happy in the end, giving them peace and rest at last, but that it was essential and inevitable to torture to death only one tiny creature, that baby beating its breast with its fist, for instance, and to found that edifice on its unavenged tears, would you consent to be the architect?
>
> "No, I wouldn't consent," said Alyosha softly.

What could be morally worse than deliberately torturing an innocent child? Even if doing so would "make men happy in the end," it ought not to be contemplated. This is often regarded as a fundamental challenge to utilitarian and some other consequentialist views, and that would be so even if we thought of God himself as a consequentialist! Other problems are discussed in the selections that follow.

ORIENTING QUESTIONS FOR DISCUSSION

1. It seems obvious to most people that sometimes consequences should be taken into account when deciding what is the right thing to do. Is it obvious that consequences should always be taken into account? Try to think of a case where they should and a case where they should not.
2. Would there be something stupid about not cheating on your tax return, provided you know that you will not get caught and that your family is in need? After all, the government will not miss a few dollars, and you and your family might miss them quite a bit. It is reasonable to think overall happiness will increase if you cheat. (If you studied Plato's *Republic*—Chapter 2—try to recall what Thrasymachus would say.)
3. Do your intuitions about *justice* square with utilitarianism as you now understand it? Try to think of some action or policy that would produce good overall results but would not be just or fair.
4. Some people argue that the consequences of keeping a person alive who is in a "persistent vegetative state" are not good for the person (or subpersonal "being") involved or for anyone else. If that is correct, what would a utilitarian probably recommend should be done with such a person? What would you recommend? Why?
5. Any action can have a great many consequences. Some of them may be very remote, that is, far away from the present time or situation. Try to think of some possible bad but remote consequences of removing a feeding tube from someone in a persistent vegetative state.
6. If we have somehow determined that some result, for example, the removal of a tyrannical or oppressive or racist regime, is morally mandated, should we do "whatever it takes" to remove that regime? Argue pro and con.

(From *Crime and Punishment*)

Reason, Morality and Social Engineering

Dostoevsky's biography was given earlier (Chapter 5). As mentioned there, he endorsed utopian ideas as a young man. Like other Russian radicals, he thought that a better society could be produced by casting aside irrational traditions and prejudices and using reason to figure out a good structure for society. Later he became skeptical about the powers of reason, and he questioned what kind of goodness would likely result from *social engineering*, i.e., attempts to develop policies on the basis of a calculation of the greatest good for the greatest number. He was not confident that the use of "reason" would enable anyone to plan the future and map consequences so as to produce happiness for all. More significantly, he thought such attempts often involve what he referred to as the "Jesuit" principle, that the end justifies the means. That, he thought, was an evil principle. Violent revolutions are themselves often justified in precisely that way. The slogan "by whatever means necessary" has figured in the rhetoric of more than one revolutionary. The revolutions that come out of such thinking may spread murder and misery.

A kind of critique of reason and of the supposed morality of actions that might improve overall happiness figure importantly in several of Dostoevsky's works, including, notably, the novel *Crime and Punishment*.

The main character in the novel is Raskolnikov, a highly reflective young man who is caught up in the idea that common morality might be cast aside in order to achieve some higher end. Raskolnikov's motives are complex, but one thing, at least, that drives him is the belief that he can master his own life and actions through sheer intelligence or reason, the same reason that leads him to consider casting aside normal moral scruples. In particular, he is considering whether murder might be justified by some higher end. Murder might be the rational and perhaps therefore the moral thing, in certain circumstances.

At the beginning of the novel he is in a state of mental and physical disarray. He is living in poverty, unable to navigate daily life in a "normal" way, and chagrined by the fact that the very reason or rationality that he wants to rely on to achieve his ends seems so easily upset by trivial circumstances and his own temperament. Even as he tries to plot the murder of an old pawnbroker, Alyona Ivanovna, he finds himself making what are, or seem to be, stupid mistakes. He is planning a trip to her apartment to look over the situation as this selection begins.

(tr. Constance Garnett)

PART I, CHAPTER I

On an exceptionally hot evening early in July a young man came out of the garret in which he lodged in S. Place and walked slowly, as though in hesitation, towards K. bridge.

He had successfully avoided meeting his landlady on the staircase. His garret was under the roof of a high, five-storied house and was more like a cupboard than a room. The landlady, who provided him with garret, dinners, and attendance, lived on the floor below, and every time he went out he was obliged to pass her kitchen, the door of which invariably stood open. And each time he passed, the young man had a sick, frightened feeling, which made him scowl and feel ashamed. He was hopelessly in debt to his landlady, and was afraid of meeting her.

This evening, however, on coming out into the street, he became acutely aware of his fears.

"I want to attempt a thing like that and am frightened by these trifles," he thought, with an odd smile. "Hmm . . . yes, all is in a man's hands and he lets it all slip from cowardice, that's an axiom. It would be interesting to know what it is men are most afraid of. Taking a new step, uttering a new word is what they fear most. . . . But I am talking too much. It's because I chatter that I do nothing. Or perhaps it is that I chatter because I do nothing. I've learned to chatter this last month, lying for days together in my den thinking . . . of Jack the Giant-killer. Why am I going there now? Am I capable of that? Is that serious? It is not serious at all. It's simply a fantasy to amuse myself, a plaything! Yes, maybe it is a plaything."

The "thing like that" that Raskolnikov is contemplating is in fact murder. It occurs to him that even though people have it in their power to do just about anything, they shrink back in cowardice. The greatest cowardice shows up in the refusal to "take a new step," i.e., do something that violates conventional religious or moral or social codes, such as murder. He wants to view himself as a bold, young intellectual who has the courage to do such new things, to rise above "the crowd" and do whatever must be done to improve the lot of humankind.

The heat in the street was terrible: and the airlessness, the bustle and the plaster, bricks, and dust all about him, and that special Petersburg stench, so familiar to all who are unable to get out of town in summer—all worked painfully upon the young man's already overwrought nerves. The insufferable stench from the pot-houses, which are particularly numerous in that part of the town, and the drunken men whom he met continually, although it was a working day, completed the revolting misery of the picture. An expression of the profoundest disgust gleamed for a moment in the young man's refined face. He was, by the way, exceptionally handsome, above the average in height, slim, well-built, with beautiful dark eyes and dark brown hair. Soon he sank into deep thought, or more accurately speaking into a complete blankness of mind; he walked along not observing what was about him and not caring to observe it. From time to time, he would mutter something, from the habit of talking to himself, to which he had just confessed. At these moments he would become conscious that his ideas were sometimes in a tangle and that he was very weak; for two days he had scarcely tasted food.

He was so badly dressed that even a man accustomed to shabbiness would have been ashamed to be seen in the street in such rags. In that quarter of the town, however, scarcely any shortcoming in dress would have created surprise. Owing to the proximity of the Hay Market, the number of establishments of bad character, the preponderance of the trading and working-class population crowded in these streets and alleys in the heart of Petersburg, types so various were to be seen in the streets that no figure, however queer, would have caused surprise. But there was such accumulated bitterness and contempt in the young man's heart, that, in spite of all the fastidiousness of youth, he minded his rags least of all in the street. It was a different matter when he met with acquaintances or with former fellow students, whom, indeed, he disliked meeting at any time. And yet when a drunken man who, for some unknown reason, was being taken somewhere in a huge wagon dragged by a heavy dray horse, suddenly shouted at him as he drove past: "Hey there, German hatter" bawling at

the top of his voice and pointing at him—the young man stopped suddenly and clutched tremulously at his hat. It was a tall, round hat from Zimmerman's, but completely worn out, rusty with age, all torn and bespattered, brimless and bent on one side in a most unseemly fashion. Not shame, however, but quite another feeling akin to terror had overtaken him.

"I knew it," he muttered in confusion, "I thought so! That's the worst of all! Why, a stupid thing like this, the most trivial detail might spoil the whole plan. Yes, my hat is too noticeable. . . . It looks absurd and that makes it noticeable. . . . With my rags I ought to wear a cap, any sort of old pancake, but not this grotesque thing. Nobody wears such a hat, it would be noticed a mile off, it would be remembered. . . . What matters is that people would remember it, and that would give them a clue. For this business one should be as little conspicuous as possible. . . . Trifles, trifles are what matter! Why, it's just such trifles that always ruin everything."

Raskolnikov fears that he will not be able to keep track of all the details that must be attended to in order to commit a murder without being detected. The ability to predict or anticipate everything that must be taken into account is, he fears, above him. But that ability is precisely what he assumes as the basis for his decision to commit the murder in the first place. The murder is to be justified by utilitarian considerations, which assume an ability to predict consequences, even to anticipate "trifles." Utilitarianism is in fact a kind of consequentialism, and if it should prove impossible to predict all the relevant consequences of any action, the practicality of utilitarianism will of course be in doubt.

Later, when Raskolnikov enters a restaurant, the utilitarian character of his thought becomes evident. He has been visiting the old pawnbroker in order to get clear about the physical layout of her flat and other relevant facts that have a bearing on how he should carry out the murder. In the restaurant he overhears a conversation.

Almost beside him at the next table there was sitting a student, whom he did not know and had never seen, and with him a young officer. They had played a game of billiards and began drinking tea. All at once he heard the student mention to the officer the pawn-broker Alyona Ivanovna and give him her address. This of itself seemed strange to Raskolnikov; he had just come from her and here at once he heard her name. Of course it was a chance, but he could not shake off a very extraordinary impression, and here someone seemed to be speaking expressly for him; the student began telling his friend various details about Alyona Ivanovna.

"She is first-rate," he said. "You can always get money from her. She is as rich as a Jew, she can give you 5,000 rubles at a time and she is not above taking a pledge for a ruble. Lots of our fellows have had dealings with her. But she is an awful old harpy. . . ."

And he began describing how spiteful and uncertain she was, how if you were only a day late with your interest the pledge was lost; how she gave a quarter of the value of an article and took five and even seven percent a month on it and so on. The student chattered on, saying that she had a sister Lizaveta, whom the wretched little creature was continually beating, and kept in complete bondage like a small child, though Lizaveta was at least six feet high.

"There's a phenomenon for you," cried the student and he laughed.

They began talking about Lizaveta. The student spoke about her with a peculiar relish and was continually laughing and the officer listened with great interest and asked him to send Lizaveta to do some mending for him. Raskolnikov did not miss a word and learned everything about her. Lizaveta was younger than the old woman and was her half-sister, being the child of a different mother. She was 35. She worked day and night for her sister, and besides doing the cooking and the washing, she did sewing and worked as a charwoman and gave her sister all she earned. She did not dare to accept an order or job of any kind without her sister's permission. The old woman had already made her will, and Lizaveta knew of it, and by this will she would not get a farthing; nothing but the movables, chairs and so on; all the money was left to a monastery in the province of N—, that prayers might be said for her in perpetuity. Lizaveta was of lower rank than her sister, unmarried

and awfully uncouth in appearance, remarkably tall with long feet that looked as if they were bent outwards. She always wore battered goatskin shoes, and was clean in her person. What the student expressed most surprise and amusement about was the fact that Lizaveta was continually with child.

"But you say she is hideous?" observed the officer.

"Yes, she is so dark-skinned and looks like a soldier dressed up, but you know she is not at all hideous. She has such a good-natured face and eyes. Strikingly so. And the proof of it is that lots of people are attracted by her. She is such a soft, gentle creature, ready to put up with anything, always willing, willing to do anything. And her smile is really very sweet."

"You seem to find her attractive yourself," laughed the officer.

"From her queerness. No, I'll tell you what. I could kill that damned old woman and make off with her money, I assure you, without the faintest conscience-prick," the student added with warmth. The officer laughed again while Raskolnikov shuddered. How strange it was!

"Listen, I want to ask you a serious question," the student said hotly. "I was joking of course, but look here; on one side we have a stupid, senseless, worthless, spiteful, ailing, horrid old woman, not simply useless but doing actual mischief, who has not an idea what she is living for herself, and who will die in a day or two in any case. You understand? You understand?"

"Yes, yes, I understand," answered the officer, watching his excited companion attentively.

"Well, listen then. On the other side, fresh young lives thrown away for want of help and by thousands, on every side! A hundred thousand good deeds could be done and helped, on that old woman's money which will be buried in a monastery! Hundreds, thousands perhaps, might be set on the right path; dozens of families saved from destitution, from ruin, from vice, from the Lock hospitals—and all with her money. Kill her, take her money and with the help of it devote oneself to the service of humanity and the good of all. What do you think, would not one tiny crime be wiped out by thousands of good deeds? For one life thousands would be saved from corruption and decay. One death, and a hundred lives in exchange—it's simple arithmetic! Besides, what value has the life of that sickly, stupid, ill-natured old woman in the balance of existence! No more than the life of a louse, of a black-beetle, less in fact because the old woman is doing harm. She is wearing out the lives of others; the other day she bit Lizaveta's finger out of spite; it almost had to be amputated."

"Of course she does not deserve to live," remarked the officer, "but there it is, it's nature."

"Oh, well, brother, but we have to correct and direct nature, and, but for that, we should drown in an ocean of prejudice. But for that, there would never have been a single great man. They talk of duty, conscience—I don't want to say anything against duty and conscience;—but the point is, what do we mean by them? Stay, I have another question to ask you. Listen!"

"No, you stay, I'll ask you a question. Listen!"

"Well?"

"You are talking and speechifying away, but tell me, would you kill the old woman yourself?"

"Of course not! I was only arguing the justice of it. . . . It's nothing to do with me . . ."

"But I think, if you would not do it yourself, there's no justice about it. . . . Let us have another game."

Raskolnikov was violently agitated. Of course, it was all ordinary youthful talk and thought, such as he had often heard before in different forms and on different themes. But why had he happened to hear such a discussion and such ideas at the very moment when his own brain was just conceiving . . . the very same ideas? And why, just at the moment when he had brought away the embryo of his idea from the old woman, had he dropped at once upon a conversation about her? This coincidence always seemed strange to him. This trivial talk in a tavern had an immense influence on him in his later action; as though there had really been in it something preordained, some guiding hint.

1. *The student argues that the murder of the old pawnbroker would be morally justified. What would justify it? Do you find his reasoning convincing? Look at it again carefully, and say what exactly is wrong with it, if you think anything is. Otherwise, defend it.*

On a hot dusty evening Raskolnikov finally does carry out his plan. He murders Alyona Ivanovna. But something that he did not at all predict does indeed happen. The young woman Lizaveta, kind and gentle, shows up immediately after the murder. Raskolnikov has to kill her also, in order to eliminate a witness. He began with the intention of killing off a "bug," a nasty old woman who was not at all "useful" and in fact was positively harmful. He ends up having to kill an innocent and gentle girl. Obviously the "simple arithmetic" referred to by the student in the café did not work out very well in practice. The attempt to base action on the calculation of supposedly good consequences went astray due to unforeseeable or at any rate unforeseen contingencies. At the same time Dostoevsky suggests that people are subject to something "preordained" that can foil the best-laid plans and calculations.

Dostoevsky's view is that life is too complex to encourage attempts to "engineer" the good. Allegiance to "ordinary morality," on the other hand, might have prevented Raskolnikov's actions. Of course, the case imagined by Dostoevsky is extreme. There might, it seems, be many cases where the application of utilitarian reasoning would in fact lead to a result that is best for all and *also* consistent with normal moral beliefs. That is in fact the view of Jeremy Bentham and J. S. Mill.

The Calculation of Pleasures and Pains

JEREMY BENTHAM

Bentham (1748–1832) was an important moral and political philosopher of the late 18th and early 19th centuries. He studied law but never practiced it. Instead he devoted much of his life to writing on issues of legal reform. Influenced by early discussions of moral theory, particularly Hume's, he developed one of the first systematic expositions of the utilitarian moral theory.

Bentham hoped to produce a "groundwork" for morals (cf. Kant) that would be empirical, based in observation and clear facts about human beings. One of the obvious facts about humans, and many other organisms, is that they are capable of experiencing pleasure and pain. Those are, he says, *organical* facts, i.e., are what they are as a result of the kinds of nervous systems that humans and other animals have. Bentham argues that organical facts provide a sufficient basis for moral judgments. He proposes a way of determining the rightness or wrongness of an action by a calculation of the pleasures or pains it is likely to produce. There is no need to take into account any transcendent or nonempirical source of obligation (Platonic forms, God, Kantian "reason" etc.).

(from Jeremy Bentham, *Principles of Morals and Legislation*, Chapters 1 and 4)

1.1. Nature has placed humankind under the governance of two sovereign masters, *pain* and *pleasure*. It is for them alone to point out what we ought to do, as well as to determine what we shall do. On the one hand the standard of right and wrong, on the other the chain of causes and effects, are fastened to their throne. They govern us in all we do, in all we say, in all we think: every effort we can make to throw off our subjection, will serve but to demonstrate and confirm it. In words a man may pretend to abjure their empire: but in reality he will remain subject to it all the while. The *principle of utility* recognizes this subjection, and assumes it for the foundation of that system, the object of which is to rear the fabric of felicity by the hands of reason and of law.

1.3. By utility is meant that property in any object, whereby it tends to produce benefit, advantage, pleasure, good, or happiness, or to prevent the happening of mischief, pain, evil, or unhappiness to the party whose interest is considered: if that party be the community in general, then the happiness of the community: if a particular individual, then the happiness of that individual.

1.4. The community is a fictitious body, composed of the individual persons who are considered as constituting as it were its members. The interest of the community then is, what?—the sum of the interests of the several members who compose it.

1.5 A thing is said to promote the interest, or to be for the interest, of an individual, when it tends to add to the sum total of his pleasures: or, what comes to the same thing, to diminish the sum total of his pains.

1.6. An action then may be said to be conformable to the principle of utility, or, for shortness sake, to utility (meaning with respect to the community at large), when the tendency it has to augment the happiness of the community is greater than any it has to diminish it.

Bentham claims that seven factors are involved when calculating the total amounts of pleasure and pain resulting from any action.

4.2. To a person considered *by himself*, the value of a pleasure or pain considered *by itself*, will be greater or less, according to the four following circumstances: (1) Its *intensity*; (2) Its *duration*; (3) Its *certainty* or *uncertainty*; (4) Its *propinquity* or *remoteness*.

4.3. These are the circumstances which are to be considered in estimating a pleasure or a pain considered each of them by itself. But when the value of any pleasure or pain is considered for the purpose of estimating the tendency of any act by which it is produced, there are two other circumstances to be taken into the account; these are, (5) Its *fecundity*, or the chance it has of being followed by sensations of the same kind: that is, pleasures, if it be a pleasure: pains, if it be a pain. (6) Its *purity*, or the chance it has of not being followed by, sensations of the *opposite* kind: that is, pains, if it be a pleasure: pleasures, if it be a pain.

4.4. To a *number* of persons, with reference to each of whom the value of a pleasure or a pain is considered, it will be greater or less, according to seven circumstances: to wit, the six preceding ones; viz. (1) Its *intensity*; (2) Its *duration*; (3) Its *certainty* or *uncertainty*; (4) Its *propinquity* or *remoteness*; (5) Its *fecundity*; (6) Its *purity*. And one other; to wit: (7) Its *extent*; that is, the number of persons to whom it extends; or (in other words) who are affected by it.

Consider the case of either lying or telling the truth to my wife, discussed earlier. In order to evaluate such an alternative, I have to consider the intensity of the pleasure or pain it would produce (the pain might be quite intense if I told the truth, the pleasure just average if I tell the lie), how long it would last (the pain might last a long time), the certainty or uncertainty (that pain would ensue seems quite certain if I tell the truth), the propinquity (nearness in time) or remoteness (the effects of either one would be immediate), the fecundity (telling the truth would tend to produce a pain, which would in turn produce further pains, such as the pain of failing at the interview, telling the truth would also be "fecund," in that it might produce a pleasure that would lead to further pleasures, such as the pleasure that might ensue following a good interview) and the extent (in fact many people would be affected by both the truth and the lie). Bentham seems to think that I could assign definite values to each option on the basis of this "calculation" and that the one that could be expected to produce the greatest balance of pleasure over pain or the least overall pain would be the morally right act.

> 2. *As you think about this example, how do your calculations come out? Should I lie, or should I tell the truth?*

Bentham apparently thinks that all pleasures and pains are *commensurable*, i.e., can be, as it were, "weighed on the same scale." His view is thus quite like the view proposed by Socrates in the *Protagoras* (see Chapter 2). Suppose that I feel some pain (a pain of conscience) over telling a lie. Bentham apparently thinks that that pain is no different in *quality* from the pain I might feel at seeing my wife very unhappy if I told the truth. If it differs at all, it would be only in the more or less quantitative ways Bentham has enumerated (it might last more or less long, and so forth).

> **3. *If Bentham were to assign a higher value (greater importance) to the pain of conscience than to the pain of seeing someone I care about being unhappy simply because it is a pain of conscience (i.e., is, we might say, a "moral" pain), his attempt to base morality on something empirical might fall apart. State why. Ask yourself whether pains of conscience could be "organical."***
> 4. *Is it plausible to think of a pain of conscience as "organical" or as traceable somehow to what is organical? Argue pro and con. Does how this question should be answered matter to the viability of Bentham's approach to ethics?*

> 5. *Would you agree that the pleasure a sadist feels in torturing someone is qualitatively on the same level as the pleasure of enjoying ice cream and differs from it only with respect to the six criteria Bentham mentions? Argue pro and con.*

Utilitarianism and Higher Pleasures

JOHN STUART MILL

Mill (1806–1873) was a brilliant child, whose father started him in the study of Greek at age three and Latin at eight. He was a member of parliament from 1865 to 1868 and wrote on a variety of philosophical and political subjects. By Mill's time, utilitarianism was a comparatively popular moral theory, due largely to the writings of the earlier British utilitarian philosophers, particularly Bentham, who was Mill's godfather. The political interests of the utilitarians show up in the title of Bentham's major work, cited earlier. In 1861 Mill published a short defense of utilitarianism, which quickly became the principal articulation of that theory. Mill does not claim originality for his theory and, in fact, maintains that he is restating many of the views of Epicurus (347–271 BCE) and Bentham.

INDUCTIVE VS. INTUITIVE SCHOOL OF ETHICS

Mill argues that moral theories are divided between two distinct approaches: the intuitive and inductive schools—that is, duty theories and consequentialist theories. By Mill's day, Kant had achieved a preeminent status among duty theorists. Mill observed that duty theorists and consequentialists both agreed that there is a single and highest moral principle. They only disagreed about what that principle is and whether we have knowledge of it *intuitively* (without appeal to experience) or *inductively* (through experience and observation).

(from J.S. Mill, *Utilitarianism*, Chapters 1 and 2)

The intuitive, no less than what may be termed the inductive, school of ethics, insists on the necessity of general laws. They both agree that the morality of an individual action is not a question of direct perception, but of the application of a law to an individual case. They recognize also, to a great extent, the same moral laws, but differ as to their evidence, and the source from which they derive their authority. According to the one opinion, the principles of morals are evident *a priori*; requiring nothing to command assent, except that the meaning of the terms be understood. According to the other doctrine, right and wrong, as well as truth and falsehood, are questions of observation and experience. But both hold equally that morality must be deduced from principles; and the intuitive school affirms, as strongly as the inductive, that there is a science of morals. Yet they seldom attempt to make out a list of the *a priori* principles which are to serve as the premises of the science; still more rarely do they make any effort to reduce those various principles to one first principle, or common ground of obligation. They either assume the ordinary precepts of morals as of *a priori* authority, or they lay down as the common groundwork of those maxims some generality much less obviously authoritative than the maxims themselves, and which has never succeeded in gaining popular acceptance. Yet, to support their pretensions, there ought either to be some one fundamental principle or law at the root of all morality; or, if there be several, there should be a determinate order of precedence among them; and the one principle, or the rule for deciding between the various principles when they conflict, ought to be self-evident.

It is not my present purpose to criticize these thinkers; but I cannot help referring, for illustration, to a systematic treatise by one of the most illustrious of them—the "Metaphysics of Ethics," by Kant. This remarkable man, whose system of thought will long remain one of the landmarks in the history of philosophical speculation, does, in the treatise in question, lay down a universal first principle as the origin and ground of moral obligation. It is this: "So act, that the rule on which thou actest would admit of being adopted as a law by all rational beings." But, when he begins to deduce from this precept any of the actual duties of morality, he fails, almost grotesquely, to show that there would be any contradiction, any logical (not to say physical) impossibility, in the adoption by all rational beings of the most outrageously immoral rules of conduct. All he shows is that the *consequences* of their universal adoption would be such as no one would choose to incur.

On the present occasion, I shall, without further discussion of the other theories, attempt to contribute something towards the understanding and appreciation of the Utilitarian or Happiness theory, and towards such proof as it is susceptible of.

6. *Mill criticizes what he calls the "intuitive" school (which he believed included Kant), because it does not provide a rule for deciding between conflicting duties. If you have studied Kant, do you think that is a valid criticism?*
7. *According to Kant's categorical imperative, wrong actions, such as lying promises, are those falling under maxims that cannot be willed universally without contradiction. According to Mill, Kant is actually (without realizing it) making the following claim: If everyone were to make lying promises, the actual consequences would be very bad, so that is what makes lying promises wrong. Has Mill understood Kant correctly? Support your view.*

Having rejected the theories of the intuitive school and, specifically, Kant's categorical imperative, Mill defends the inductive utilitarian approach.

The creed which accepts, as the foundation of morals, Utility, or the Greatest Happiness Principle, holds that actions are right in proportion as they tend to promote happiness, wrong as they tend to produce the reverse of happiness. By happiness is intended pleasure and the absence of pain; by unhappiness, pain and the privation of pleasure. To give a clear view of the moral standard set up by the theory, much more requires to be said; in particular, what things it includes in the ideas of pain and pleasure, and to what extent this is left an open question. But these supplementary explanations do not affect the theory of life on which this theory of morality is grounded—namely, that pleasure, and freedom from pain, are the only things desirable as ends; and that all desirable things (which are as numerous in the utilitarian as in any other scheme) are desirable either for the pleasure inherent in themselves, or as means to the promotion of pleasure and the prevention of pain.

Now, such a theory of life excites in many minds, and among them in some of the most estimable in feeling and purpose, inveterate dislike. To suppose that life has (as they express it) no higher end than pleasure—no better and nobler object of desire and pursuit—they designate as utterly mean and groveling; as a doctrine worthy only of swine, to whom the followers of Epicurus were, at a very early period, contemptuously likened: and modern holders of the doctrine are occasionally made the subject of equally polite comparisons by its German, French, and English assailants.

When thus attacked, the Epicureans have always answered, that it is not they, but their accusers, who represent human nature in a degrading light, since the accusation supposes human beings to be capable of no pleasures except those of which swine are capable. If this supposition were true, the charge could not be gainsaid, but would then be no longer an imputation; for, if the sources of pleasure were precisely the same to human beings and to swine, the rule of life which is good enough for the one would be good enough for the other. The comparison of the Epicurean life to that of beasts is felt as degrading, precisely because a beast's pleasures do not satisfy a human being's conceptions of happiness. Human beings have faculties more elevated than the animal appetites; and, when once made conscious of them, do not regard any thing as happiness which does not include their gratification. I do not, indeed, consider the Epicureans to have been by any means faultless in drawing out their scheme of consequences from the utilitarian principle. To do this in any sufficient manner, many Stoic as well as Christian elements require to be included.

Epicurus (341–270 BCE) was a Greek philosopher who claimed that the only intrinsically good things are pleasure and the absence of pain. Epicurus himself tended to downplay the value of "lower" pleasures, but his name became associated with the pursuit of sensual indulgence.

8. *How have Epicureans responded to the accusation that they propose a doctrine worthy only of swine?*

As discussed earlier, Mill's predecessor Bentham thought that pleasures differed only with respect to such traits as duration, intensity, "fecundity" and the like (for example, the pleasures of conversation with friends might not be very intense, but they might be long-lasting). This view is of considerable importance in Bentham's thought. He derides "philosophers" who want to discard gross pleasures "that is, such as are organical, or of which the origin is easily traced up to the organical" (*Principles*, Chapter 2, paragraphs 5, 6). This is important to Bentham because he wants a "natural" basis for ethics, and the physiological or organical is certainly "natural," that is, there is no element in it of convention or of any other moral source (God etc.). Mill, on the contrary, thinks that some "organical" pleasures, for example, the pleasure of a warm bath on a cold evening, are more or less animalistic and intrinsically less valuable than "higher" pleasures that are unique to humans, such as the pleasures of solving a problem in geometry (!). A good utilitarian, Mill claims, will recognize the difference and try to maximize the higher pleasures in particular without necessarily ignoring the lower ones.

But there is no known Epicurean theory of life which does not assign to the pleasures of the intellect, of the feelings and imagination, and of the moral sentiments, a much higher value as pleasures than to those of mere sensation. It must be admitted, however, that utilitarian writers in general have placed the superiority of mental over bodily pleasures chiefly in the greater permanency, safety, uncostliness, &c., of the former—that is, in their circumstantial advantages rather than in their intrinsic nature. And, on all these points, utilitarians have fully proved their case; but they might have taken the other, and, as it may be called, higher ground, with entire consistency. It is quite compatible with the principle of utility to recognize the fact, that some kinds of pleasure are more desirable and more valuable than others. It would be absurd, that while, in estimating all other things, quality is considered as well as quantity, the estimation of pleasures should be supposed to depend on quantity alone.

If I am asked what I mean by difference of quality in pleasures, or what makes one pleasure more valuable than another, merely as a pleasure, except its being greater in amount, there is but one possible answer. Of two pleasures, if there be one to which all or almost all who have experience of both give a decided preference, irrespective of any feeling of moral obligation to prefer it, that is the more desirable pleasure. If one of the two is, by those who are competently acquainted with both, placed so far above the other that they prefer it, even though knowing it to be attended with a greater amount of discontent, and would not resign it for any quantity of the other pleasure which their nature is capable of, we are justified in ascribing to the preferred enjoyment a superiority in quality, so far outweighing quantity, as to render it, in comparison, of small account.

9. *State as fully as you can Mill's test for distinguishing higher from lower pleasures. Do you think Mill's test would work? Try to imagine some objections to it.*

*10. *Why does Mill insist that a valid test for the superiority of pleasure A over pleasure B must include the fact that people who have experienced both must prefer A "irrespective of any feeling of moral obligation to prefer it"? Remember, Mill is trying to tell us what it is that makes morally right actions morally right, or obligatory.*

Now, it is an unquestionable fact, that those who are equally acquainted with and equally capable of appreciating and enjoying both [types of pleasures] do give a most marked preference to the manner of existence which employs their higher faculties. Few human creatures would consent to be changed into any of the lower animals, for a promise of the fullest allowance of a beast's pleasures: no intelligent human being would consent to be a fool, no instructed person would be an ignoramus, no person of feeling and conscience would be selfish and base, even though they should be persuaded that the fool, the dunce, or the rascal is better satisfied with his lot than they are with theirs. They would not resign what they possess more than he for the most complete satisfaction of any of the desires which they have in common with him. If they ever fancy they would, it is only in cases of unhappi-

ness so extreme, that, to escape from it, they would exchange their lot for almost any other, however undesirable in their own eyes. A being of higher faculties requires more to make him happy, is capable probably of more acute suffering, and certainly accessible to it at more points, than one of an inferior type; but, in spite of these liabilities, he can never really wish to sink into what he feels to be a lower grade of existence. We may give what explanation we please of this unwillingness; we may attribute it to pride, a name which is given indiscriminately to some of the most and to some of the least estimable feelings of which mankind are capable; we may refer it to the love of liberty and personal independence—an appeal to which was with the Stoics one of the most effective means for the inculcation of it; to the love of power, or to the love of excitement, both of which do really enter into and contribute to it: but its most appropriate appellation is a sense of dignity, which all human beings possess in one form or other, and in some, though by no means in exact, proportion to their higher faculties, and which is so essential a part of the happiness of those in whom it is strong, that nothing which conflicts with it could be, otherwise than momentarily, an object of desire to them.

Whoever supposes that this preference takes place at a sacrifice of happiness; that the superior being, in any thing like equal circumstances, is not happier than the inferior—confounds the two very different ideas of happiness and content. It is indisputable, that the being whose capacities of enjoyment are low has the greatest chance of having them fully satisfied; and a highly endowed being will always feel that any happiness which he can look for, as the world is constituted, is imperfect. But he can learn to bear its imperfections, if they are at all bearable; and they will not make him envy the being who is indeed unconscious of the imperfections, but only because he feels not at all the good which those imperfections qualify. It is better to be a human being dissatisfied, than a pig satisfied; better to be Socrates dissatisfied, than a fool satisfied. And if the fool or the pig are of a different opinion, it is because they only know their own side of the question. The other party to the comparison knows both sides.

11. *Mill states that it is better to be Socrates dissatisfied than a fool satisfied. What does he mean? Do you agree? Why?*

WHY PEOPLE REJECT HIGHER PLEASURES

Although Mill thinks that qualified judges will usually choose higher pleasure over lower ones, he admits that often that is not the case. He tries to explain why many people in fact reject higher pleasures for lower ones.

It may be objected, that many who are capable of the higher pleasures, occasionally, under the influence of temptation, postpone them to the lower. But this is quite compatible with a full appreciation of the intrinsic superiority of the higher. Men often, from infirmity of character, make their election for the nearer good, though they know it to be the less valuable, and this no less when the choice is between two bodily pleasures than when it is between bodily and mental. They pursue sensual indulgences to the injury of health, though perfectly aware that health is the greater good. It may be further objected, that many who begin with youthful enthusiasm for everything noble, as they advance in years sink into indolence and selfishness. But I do not believe that those who undergo this very common change voluntarily choose the lower description of pleasures in preference to the higher. I believe, that, before they devote themselves exclusively to the one, they have already become incapable of the other. Capacity for the nobler feelings is in most natures a very tender plant, easily killed, not only by hostile influences, but by mere want of sustenance; and, in the majority of young persons, it speedily dies away if the occupations to which their position in life has devoted them, and the society into which it has thrown them, are not favorable to keeping that higher capacity in exercise. Men lose their high aspirations as they lose their intellectual tastes, because they have not time or opportunity for indulging them; and they addict themselves to inferior pleasures, not because they deliberately prefer them, but because they are either the only ones to which they have access, or the only ones which they are any longer capable of enjoying. It may be questioned, whether anyone, who has remained

equally susceptible to both classes of pleasures, ever knowingly and calmly preferred the lower; though many in all ages have broken down in an ineffectual attempt to combine both.

From this verdict of the only competent judges, I apprehend there can be no appeal. On a question, which is the best worth having of two pleasures, or which of two modes of existence is the most grateful to the feelings, apart from its moral attributes and from its consequences, the judgment of those who are qualified by knowledge of both, or, if they differ, that of the majority among them, must be admitted as final. And there needs be the less hesitation to accept this judgment respecting the quality of pleasures, since there is no other tribunal to be referred to even on the question of quantity. What means are there of determining which is the acutest of two pains, or the intensest of two pleasurable sensations, except the general suffrage of those who are familiar with both? Neither pains nor pleasures are homogeneous, and pain is always heterogeneous with pleasure. What is there to decide whether a particular pleasure is worth purchasing at the cost of a particular pain, except the feelings and judgment of the experienced? When, therefore, those feelings and judgment declare the pleasures derived from the higher faculties to be preferable *in kind*, apart from the question of intensity, to those of which the animal nature, disjoined from the higher faculties, is susceptible, they are entitled on this subject to the same regard.

12. *What are some reasons why people often choose lower pleasures over higher ones?*
13. *Suppose we want to compare the pleasures a sadist experiences to the pleasures of enjoying Mozart. In order to know which was the "highest," what would we have to do, according to Mill? Might there be a problem with this?*

HIGHER AND LOWER PLEASURES AND THE UTILITARIAN PROGRAM

As discussed earlier, Mill's distinction between higher and lower pleasure does not fit with some fundamental features of the utilitarian program. But there is another lack of fit that emerges here. As noted already, the utilitarians, Mill included, were interested in social reforms. They wanted to find a moral principle that could be invoked in attempts to legislate away many of the miseries, so evident all around them, of the poor or marginalized. They proposed, for example, that wealth should be "redistributed" by government so that there would not be such great disparities between rich and poor. That would be morally right since it would supposedly increase overall happiness.

It is worth asking just how well Mill's desire to distinguish higher from lower pleasure fits with these ideas about social reform. The problem that arises can be illustrated from Henry James' novel *The Princess Casamassima*. The main characters in the novel are people interested in social reform and advocacy for the poor (referred to here as "the sacred cause" and "the great redistribution"). One of them, Hyacinth, has been in Venice, and he writes a letter to the Princess, from whom he has learned some "higher" tastes. In this letter he mentions one of their radical associates, Hoffendahl, who apparently has little time for the "higher pleasures."

> Dear Princess, . . . I may have helped you to understand and enter into the misery of the people (though I protest I don't know much about it), but you have led my imagination into quite another train. However, I don't mean to pretend that it's all your fault if I have lost sight of the sacred cause almost altogether in my recent adventures. It is not that it has not been there to see, for that perhaps is the clearest result of extending one's horizon—the sense, increasing as we go, that want and toil and suffering are the constant lot of the immense majority of the human race. I have found them everywhere, but I haven't minded them. Excuse the cynical confession. What has struck me is the great achievements of which man has been capable in spite of them—the splendid accumulations of the happier few, to which, doubtless, the miserable many have also in their degree contributed. The face of Europe appears to be covered with them, and they have had much the greater part of my attention. They seem to me inestimably precious and beautiful, and I have become conscious, more than ever before, of how

little I understand what, in the great rectification, you and Poupin propose to do with them. Dear Princess, there are things which I shall be sorry to see you touch, even you with your hands divine; and—shall I tell you *le fond de ma pensée*, as you used to say?—I feel myself capable of fighting for them. You can't call me a traitor, for you know the obligation that I recognize. The monuments and treasures of art, the great palaces and properties, the conquests of learning and taste, the general fabric of civilization as we know it, based, if you will, upon all the despotisms, the cruelties, the exclusions, the monopolies and the rapacities of the past, but thanks to which, all the same, the world is less impracticable and life more tolerable—our friend Hoffendahl seems to me to hold them too cheap and to wish to substitute for them something in which I can't somehow believe as I do in things with which the aspirations and the tears of generations have been mixed. You know how extraordinary I think our Hoffendahl (to speak only of him); but if there is one thing that is more clear about him than another it is that he wouldn't have the least feeling for this incomparable, abominable old Venice. He would cut up the ceilings of the Veronese into strips, so that everyone might have a little piece. I don't want everyone to have a little piece of anything, and I have a great horror of that kind of invidious jealousy which is at the bottom of the idea of a redistribution. (from Chapter 30)

Hyacinth wonders whether the higher pleasures available from the great works of artistic genius are not perhaps worth the sufferings and dullness of the lives of the many poor people who make "civilization," and thus such works, possible. He also comes to the conclusion that the motives of reformers are corrupted by a kind of jealousy of those geniuses who produced all those things that give us "higher" pleasures. Hyacinth is even ready to "fight for" those higher things, despite his supposed commitment to social reform.

Perhaps Mill cannot have it both ways. Perhaps he cannot be both a social reformer and someone who thinks that Socrates dissatisfied is better than a pig satisfied. If he really thinks that it is the "higher plea-sures" that should be maximized, then as a reformer he should think it possible, and necessary, to educate the masses into an appreciation for Mozart and Mi-chelangelo, Plato and Isaac Newton. How possible is it? And even if it were possible, what would happen if *everyone* spent lots of time cultivating his or her higher capacities? What time would be left for all the ordinary tasks, done by ordinary people, that are es-sential to a high civilization?

In contrast, the utilitarian project as conceived by Bentham did not make any distinctions between higher and lower pleasures. According to Bentham, pushpin (a popular sport) was just as good as poetry. The task of a just legislator, in his view, was to get the greatest total of pleasure. All pleasures were for him "commensurable." Pleasures are distinguished from each other only in terms of "quantitative" factors. It follows that government support for vulgar enter-tainment that gives pleasure to many people might be more justified than support for fine art, education in the history of civilization and so forth.

It turns out, for these reasons and others, that Mill's attempt to distinguish higher from lower plea-sures, and his recommendation that we seek to maxi-mize the higher ones, has far-reaching implications for utilitarianism.

14. *State briefly, in your own words, the difference between Mill and Bentham on the nature of pleasure.*

15. *Do you have any sympathy for the views of Hyacinth expressed in the excerpt from his letter to the Princess? Are there some things so intrinsically beautiful and elevated that their preservation and enjoyment trumps even the relief of poverty? Discuss.*

16. *Is the federal government justified in spend-ing money on artists, musicians etc. via grants from the National Endowment for the Arts or the National Endowment for the Humanities? Should the government have a National Endowment for Popular Entertain-ments that would give grants to bars that install pool tables? What would Bentham say? Mill?*

THE HAPPINESS OF THE GREATEST NUMBER

According to Mill, an essential feature of utilitarian-ism is the fact that we judge an action according to the general happiness it produces rather than merely the agent's private happiness.

I have dwelt on this point, as being a necessary part of a perfectly just conception of Utility or Happiness, considered as the directive rule of human conduct. But it is by no means an indispensable condition to the acceptance of the utilitarian standard; for that standard is not the agent's own greatest happiness, but the greatest amount of happiness altogether: and, if it may possibly be doubted whether a noble char-acter is always the happier for its nobleness, there can be no doubt that it makes other people happier, and that the world in general is immensely a gainer by it. Utilitarianism, therefore, could only attain its end by the general cultivation of nobleness of character, even if each individual were only benefited by the no-bleness of others, and his own, so far as happiness is concerned, were a sheer deduction from the benefit. But the bare enunciation of such an absurdity as this last renders refutation superfluous.

According to the Greatest Happiness Principle, as above explained, the ultimate end, with reference to and for the sake of which all other things are desir-able (whether we are considering our own good or that of other people), is an existence exempt as far as possible from pain, and as rich as possible in en-joyments, both in point of quantity and quality; the test of quality, and the rule for measuring it against quantity, being the preference felt by those, who in their opportunities of experience, to which must be added their habits of self-consciousness and self-observation, are best furnished with the means of comparison. This, being, according to the utilitarian opinion, the end of human action, is necessarily also the standard of morality: which may accordingly be defined, the rules and precepts for human conduct, by the observance of which an existence such as has been described might be, to the greatest extent pos-sible, secured to all mankind; and not to them only, but, so far as the nature of things admits, to the whole sentient creation.

Mill suggests that even if nobleness of character (for example) did not make the person who had it happy, we should still seek to develop it in people, since the practical effect of such nobleness is to increase over-all happiness.

> 17. *Does that amount to claiming that in the utilitarian view it would be morally right, and even required, to make one person unhappy if doing so would make 100 people (to choose an arbitrary number) happier then they ever could have been without the unhappiness of that one person?*

These remarks about "nobleness of character" lead naturally to a discussion of virtue theories, which would include Aristotle's views.

REJECTION OF VIRTUE THEORY

The principle of utility requires exclusive attention to an action's consequences and not to the motives or character traits of the agent performing the action. The latter, on the other hand, are the primary concern of classical virtue theory. Mill speculates about what an advocate of virtue theory might say about utilitarianism.

It is often affirmed, that utilitarianism renders men cold and unsympathizing; that it chills their moral feelings towards individuals; that it makes them regard only the dry and hard consideration of the consequences of actions, not taking into their moral estimate the qualities from which those actions emanate. If the assertion means that they do not allow their judgment respecting the rightness or wrongness of an action to be influenced by their opinion of the qualities of the person who does it, this is a complaint, not against utilitarianism, but against having any standard of morality at all: for certainly no known ethical standard decides an action to be good or bad because it is done by a good or a bad man; still less because done by an amiable, a brave, or a benevolent man, or the contrary. These considerations are relevant, not to the estimation of actions, but of persons; and there is nothing in the utilitarian theory inconsistent with the fact, that there are other things which interest us in persons besides the rightness and wrongness of

their actions. The Stoics indeed, with the paradoxical misuse of language which was part of their system, and by which they strove to raise themselves above all concern about anything but virtue, were fond of saying, that he who has that, has everything; that he, and only he, is rich, is beautiful, is a king. But no claim of this description is made for the virtuous man by the utilitarian doctrine. Utilitarians are quite aware that there are other desirable possessions and qualities besides virtue, and are perfectly willing to allow to all of them their full worth. They are also aware that a right action does not necessarily indicate a virtuous character; and that actions which are blamable often proceed from qualities entitled to praise. When this is apparent in any particular case, it modifies their estimation, not certainly of the act, but of the agent. I grant that they are, notwithstanding, of opinion, that, in the long run, the best proof of a good character is good actions; and resolutely refuse to consider any mental disposition as good, of which the predominant tendency is to produce bad conduct. This makes them unpopular with many people: but it is an unpopularity which they must share with everyone who regards the distinction between right and wrong in a serious light; and the reproach is not one which a conscientious utilitarian need be anxious to repel.

If no more be meant by the objection than that many utilitarians look on the morality of actions, as measured by the utilitarian standards, with too exclusive a regard, and do not lay sufficient stress upon the other beauties of character which go towards making a human being lovable or admirable, this may be admitted. Utilitarians who have cultivated their moral feelings, but not their sympathies nor their artistic perceptions, do fall into this mistake; and so do all other moralists under the same conditions. What can be said in excuse for other moralists is equally available for them; namely, that, if there is to be any error, it is better that it should be on that side. As a matter of fact, we may affirm that among utilitarians, as among adherents of other systems, there is every imaginable degree of rigidity and of laxity in the application of their standard: some are even puritanically rigorous, while others are as indulgent as can possibly be desired by sinner or by sentimentalist. But, on the whole, a doctrine which brings prominently forward the interest that mankind have in the repression and prevention of conduct which violates the moral law, is likely to be inferior to no other in turning the sanctions of opinion against such violations. It is true, the question, What does violate the moral law? is one on which those who recognize different standards of morality are likely now and then to differ. But difference of opinion on moral questions was not first introduced into the world by utilitarianism; while that doctrine does supply, if not always an easy, at all events a tangible and intelligible, mode of deciding such differences.

18. *Mill claims that actions that are blamable could arise from a good character trait. For example, a bad action could follow from courage. Think up an example of an action motivated by kindness that would have bad consequences.*

Mill claims that "no known ethical standard decides an action to be good or bad because it is done by a good or a bad man." But isn't that exactly what Aristotle does when he claims that the actions of the wise person, the "*phronimos*," are the only standard of rightness? For more on this issue, see the discussion by Williams that follows later in the "Further Discussions" section.

19. *Virtue theorists may criticize utilitarianism because it does not take into account the motives behind peoples actions, but instead focuses only on the consequences of those actions. What is Mill's response to this criticism?*

*20. *One of the advantages of utilitarianism just cited by Mill is that it gives a "tangible and intelligible mode of deciding" moral differences. Suppose that A and B disagree on the morality of abortion. Illustrate, in outline, how this disagreement could supposedly be resolved by using the utilitarian approach.*

RULE UTILITARIANISM

We have seen that Mill departs from Bentham and other earlier utilitarians in his distinction between higher and lower pleasures. That, as was suggested, is a significant departure. A second feature of Mill's approach that sets him against Bentham is his *rule utilitarianism* (as it is now called). Bentham suggested an approach that has been dubbed *act utilitarianism,* since he advocates tallying the consequences of each act that we perform. Mill, on the other hand, argues that we cannot and should not try to calculate the consequences of every action. Sometimes, he claims, the rightness of particular actions can be determined by the conformity of the action in question to some accepted moral rule. But doesn't that simply eliminate consequentialism and thus utilitarianism itself? Not so, according to Mill.

Moral rules, Mill argues, constitute a summary of what the human race has learned about the kind of actions that tend to promote overall happiness. For example, Mill would say that a car thief's action was immoral, since he broke a major social prohibition against stealing. That social prohibition against stealing is a valid moral rule because societies with that rule are presumably better off (happier overall) than societies that lack such a rule. That is, the *consequences* of having such a rule and of having people generally follow it are better than the consequences of not having such a rule. So the rule's justification is consequentialist in nature.

This idea is used by Mill to deflect a criticism. Critics of utilitarianism sometimes argued that it is a useless theory since we simply don't have time to calculate all the relevant consequences of an action. Mill's response follows.

Again: defenders of Utility often find themselves called upon to reply to such objections as this—that there is not time, previous to action, for calculating and weighing the effects of any line of conduct on the general happiness. This is exactly as if anyone were to say that it is impossible to guide our conduct by Christianity, because there is not time, on every occasion on which anything has to be done, to read through the Old and New Testaments. The answer to the objection is, that there has been ample time; namely, the whole past duration of the human species. During all that time, mankind have been learning by experience the tendencies of actions, on which experience all the prudence as well as all the morality of life are dependent. People talk as if the commencement of this course of experience had hitherto been put off, and as if, at the moment when some man feels tempted to meddle with the property or life of another, he had to begin considering for the first time whether murder and theft are injurious to human happiness. Even then, I do not think that he would find the question very puzzling; but, at all events, the matter is now done to his hand. It is truly a whimsical supposition, that, if mankind were agreed in considering utility to be the test of morality, they would remain without any agreement as to what is useful, and would take no measures for having their notions on the subject taught to the young, and enforced by law and opinion.

There is no difficulty in proving any ethical standard whatever to work ill, if we suppose universal idiocy to be conjoined with it: but, on any hypothesis short of that, mankind must by this time have acquired positive beliefs as to the effects of some actions on their happiness; and the beliefs which have thus come down are the rules of morality for the multitude, and for the philosopher, until he has succeeded in finding better. That philosophers might easily do this, even now, on many subjects; that the received code of ethics is by no means of divine right; and that mankind have still much to learn as to the effects of actions on the general happiness—I admit, or, rather, earnestly maintain. The corollaries from the principle of utility, like the precepts of every practical art, admit of indefinite improvement; and, in a progressive state of the human mind, their improvement is perpetually doing on. But to consider the rules of morality as improvable is one thing; to pass over the intermediate generalizations entirely, and endeavor to test each individual action directly by the first principle, is another. It is a strange notion, that the acknowledgment of a first principle is inconsistent with the admission of secondary ones.

Mill thinks ordinary moral rules, such as prohibitions against stealing or murder, represent the cumulative experience of the human race respecting what sorts of consequences come from what sorts of actions. It is as though people had tried both telling lies and telling the truth and gradually came to the conclusion that telling the truth produced better consequences overall. They then made it a rule that everyone should tell the truth (normally). Why should each individual have to learn for himself the "general tendencies of actions" when he can rely on the experience of his ancestors? And the experience of the ancestors is "summed up" in common moral codes. This is not to say that we need to rely blindly on the past. We may be able to make improvements in moral codes. But it would be impractical and unwise simply to ignore what the past experience of the group can teach us.

At the same time we can still calculate the consequences of particular acts in the light of the utilitarian standard when we face a moral dilemma or a conflict of rules. Recall the problem that appears to arise in the Kantian view, between, say, telling the truth and protecting the lives of the innocent. Utilitarians supposedly have a way of resolving such conflicts: Simply tote up the consequences of each of the two acts, and pick the one that produces the greater overall happiness, or "utility." But Mill admits that doing that may not be so simple after all. Still, it is the best thing going.

If utility is the ultimate source of moral obligations, utility may be invoked to decide between them [moral rules] when their demands are incompatible. Though the application of the standard may be difficult, it is better than none at all: while in other systems, the moral laws all claiming independent authority, there is no common umpire entitled to interfere between them; their claims to precedence one over another rest on little better than sophistry; and unless determined, as they generally are, by the unacknowledged influence of considerations of utility, afford a free scope for the action of personal desires and partialities. We must remember that only in these cases of conflict between secondary principles is it requisite that first principles should be appealed to. There is no case of moral obligation in which some secondary principle is not involved; and, if only one, there can seldom be any real doubt which one it is, in the mind of any person by whom the principle itself is recognized.

21. *Mill is claiming that the rule "Do not tell lies" applies most of the time but not always. Should*

*we generally assume that it does apply? Why?
When should we question that assumption?*

One of the most common objections to utilitarianism is that it cannot account for our intuitions about justice. For example, enslaving a few people might in some situations be useful, in that it would greatly increase overall happiness, but it would not be just. Justice is clearly not the same as what is useful or what is expedient, or so it seems. Mill responds to this criticism in Chapter 5.

Utility and the Two Elements of Justice

There are two essential elements in the notion of justice: punishment and the notion that someone's rights were violated. Punishment derives from a combination of vengeance and social sympathy. Vengeance alone has no moral component, and social sympathy is the same thing as social utility. The notion of rights violation also derives from utility, for rights are claims we have on society to protect us, and the only reason society should protect us is because of social utility. Thus, both elements of justice (i.e., punishment and rights) are based on utility.

ON THE CONNECTION BETWEEN JUSTICE AND UTILITY

In all ages of speculation, one of the strongest obstacles to the reception of the doctrine that Utility or Happiness is the criterion of right and wrong, has been drawn from the idea of justice. The powerful sentiment, and apparently clear perception, have seemed to the majority of thinkers to point to an inherent quality in things; to show that the just must have an existence in Nature as something absolute . . . inasmuch as the subjective mental feeling of justice is different from that which commonly attaches to simple expediency, and, except in the extreme cases of the latter, is far more imperative in its demands, people find it difficult to see, in justice, only a particular kind or branch of general utility, and think that its superior binding force requires a totally different origin.

To throw light upon this question, it is necessary to attempt to ascertain what is the distinguishing character of justice, or of injustice; what is the quality, or whether there is any quality, attributed in common to all modes of conduct designated as unjust (for justice, like many other moral attributes, is best defined by its opposite), and distinguishing them from such modes of conduct as are disapproved, but without having that particular epithet of disapprobation applied to them. . . . To find the common attributes of a variety of objects, it is necessary to begin by surveying the objects themselves in the concrete. Let us therefore advert successively to the various modes of action, and arrangements of human affairs, which are classed, by universal or widely spread opinion, as Just or as Unjust. The things well known to excite the sentiments associated with those names are of a very multifarious character. I shall pass them rapidly in review, without studying any particular arrangement.

In the first place, it is mostly considered unjust to deprive anyone of his personal liberty, his property, or any other thing which belongs to him by law [unless he may] have forfeited the rights which he is so deprived of.

Secondly; the legal rights of which he is deprived, may be rights which ought not to have belonged to him; we may say, therefore, that a second case of injustice consists in taking or withholding from any person that to which he has a moral right.

Thirdly, it is universally considered just that each person should obtain that (whether good or evil) which he deserves, and unjust that he should obtain a good, or be made to undergo an evil, which he does not deserve.

Fourthly, it is confessedly unjust to break faith with anyone: to violate an engagement, either express or implied, or disappoint expectations raised by our conduct, at least if we have raised those expectations knowingly and voluntarily.

Fifthly, it is, by universal admission, inconsistent with justice to be partial—to show favor or preference to one person over another, in matters to which favor and preference do not properly apply.

Nearly allied to the idea of impartiality is that of equality, which often enters as a component part both into the conception of justice and into the practice of it, and, in the eyes of many persons, constitutes its essence. But in this, still more than in any other case, the notion of justice varies in different persons, and always conforms in its variations to their notion of utility. Each person maintains that equality is the dictate of justice, except where he thinks that expediency requires inequality. The justice of giving equal protection to the rights of all, is maintained by those who support the most outrageous inequality in the rights themselves. Even in slave countries it is theoretically admitted that the rights of the slave, such as they are, ought to be as sacred as those of the master; and that a tribunal which fails to enforce them with equal strictness is wanting in justice; while, at the same time, institutions which leave to the slave scarcely any rights to enforce, are not deemed unjust, because they are not deemed inexpedient.

Among so many diverse applications of the term "justice," which yet is not regarded as ambiguous, it is a matter of some difficulty to seize the mental link which holds them together, and on which the moral sentiment adhering to the term essentially depends. Perhaps, in this embarrassment, some help may be derived from the history of the word, as indicated by its etymology.

In most, if not in all, languages, the etymology of the word which corresponds to "just," points distinctly to an origin connected with the ordinances of law. *Justum* is a form of *jussum*, that which has been ordered. *Dikaion* comes directly from *dike*, a suit at law. Recht, from which came right and righteous, is synonymous with law. The courts of justice, the administration of justice, are the courts and the administration of law. [Those] who knew that their laws had been made originally, and still continued to be made, by men, were not afraid to admit that those men might make bad laws; might do, by law, the same things, and from the same motives, which if done by individuals without the sanction of law, would be called unjust. And hence the sentiment of injustice came to be attached, not to all violations of law, but only to violations of such laws as ought to exist, including such as ought to exist, but do not, and to laws themselves, if supposed to be contrary to what ought to be law. In this manner the idea of law and of its injunctions was still predominant in the notion of justice, even when the laws actually in force ceased to be accepted as the standard of it.

The above is, I think, a true account, as far as it goes, of the origin and progressive growth of the idea of justice. But we must observe, that it contains, as yet, nothing to distinguish that obligation from moral obligation in general. For the truth is, that the idea of penal sanction, which is the essence of law, enters not only into the conception of injustice, but into that of any kind of wrong. We do not call anything wrong, unless we mean to imply that a person ought to be punished in some way or other for doing it—if not by law, by the opinion of his fellow-creatures; if not by opinion, by the reproaches of his own conscience. This seems the real turning point of the distinction between morality and simple expediency. It is a part of the notion of Duty in every one of its forms, that a person may rightfully be compelled to fulfill it. Duty is a thing which may be exacted from a person, as one exacts a debt. Unless we think that it may be exacted from him, we do not call it his duty. Reasons of prudence, or the interest of other people, may militate against actually exacting it; but the person himself, it is clearly understood, would not be entitled to complain. There are other things, on the contrary, which we wish that people should do; which we like or admire them for doing, perhaps dislike or despise them for not doing, but yet admit that they are not bound to do; it is not a case of moral obligation; we do not blame them, that is, we do not think that they are proper objects of punishment.

This, therefore, being the characteristic difference which marks off, not justice, but morality in general, from the remaining provinces of Expediency and Worthiness; the character is still to be sought which distinguishes justice from other branches of morality. Now it is known that ethical writers divide moral duties into two classes, denoted by the ill-chosen expressions, duties of perfect and of imperfect obligation; the latter being those in which, though the act is obligatory, the particular occasions of performing it are left to our choice, as in the case of charity or beneficence, which we are indeed bound to practice, but not towards any definite person, nor at any prescribed time. In the more precise language of philosophic jurists, duties of perfect obligation are those duties in virtue of which a correlative right resides in some person or persons; duties of imperfect obligation are those moral obligations which do not give birth to any right. I think it will be found that this distinction exactly coincides with that which exists between justice and the other obligations of morality. In our survey of the various popular acceptations of justice, the term appeared generally to involve the idea of a personal right—a claim on the part of one or more individuals, like that which the law gives when it confers a proprietary or other legal right. Whether the injustice consists in depriving a person of a possession, or in breaking faith with him, or in treating him worse than he deserves, or worse than other people who have no greater claims—in each case the supposition implies two things—a wrong done, and some assignable person who is wronged. Injustice may also be done by treating a person better than others; but the wrong in this case is to his competitors, who are also assignable persons. It seems to me that this feature in the case—a right in some person, correlative to the moral obligation—constitutes the specific difference between justice, and generosity or beneficence. Justice implies something which it is not only right to do, and wrong not to do, but which some individual person can claim from us as his moral right. No one has a moral right to our generosity or beneficence, because we are not morally bound to practice those virtues towards any given individual. And it will be found with respect to this, as to every correct definition, that the instances which seem to conflict with it are those which most confirm it. For if a moralist attempts, as some have done, to make out that mankind generally, though not any given individual, have a right to all the good we can do them, he at once, by that thesis, includes generosity and beneficence within the category of justice. He is obliged to say, that our utmost exertions are due to our fellow creatures, thus assimilating them to a debt; or that nothing less can be a sufficient return for what society does for us, thus classing the case as one of gratitude; both of which are acknowledged cases of justice. Wherever there is right, the case is one of justice, and not of the virtue of beneficence; and whoever does not place the distinction between justice and morality in general, where we have now placed it, will be found to make no distinction between them at all, but to merge all morality in justice.

22. *Mill claims that anyone who insists that we have a strict obligation to be beneficent, for example, a strict obligation to help feed remote starving persons, has merged all morality into justice. Isn't that what a utilitarian should do? Why or why not?*

For further light on this question, study the upcoming discussion, from Singer, on feeding the hungry.

Having thus endeavored to determine the distinctive elements which enter into the composition of the idea of justice, we are ready to enter on the inquiry, whether the feeling, which accompanies the idea, is attached to it by a special dispensation of nature, or whether it could have grown up, by any known laws, out of the idea itself; and in particular, whether it can have originated in considerations of general expediency.

I conceive that the sentiment itself does not arise from anything which would commonly, or correctly, be termed an idea of expediency; but that though the sentiment does not, whatever is moral in it does.

We have seen that the two essential ingredients in the sentiment of justice are, the desire to punish a person who has done harm, and the knowledge or belief that there is some definite individual or individuals to whom harm has been done.

Now it appears to me, that the desire to punish a person who has done harm to some individual is a spontaneous outgrowth from two sentiments, both in the highest degree natural, and which either are or resemble instincts; the impulse of self-defense, and the feeling of sympathy.

It is natural to resent, and to repel or retaliate, any harm done or attempted against ourselves, or against those with whom we sympathize.

To recapitulate: the idea of justice supposes two things—a rule of conduct, and a sentiment which sanctions the rule. The first must be supposed common to all mankind, and intended for their good. The other (the sentiment) is a desire that punishment may be suffered by those who infringe the rule. There is involved, in addition, the conception of some definite person who suffers by the infringement, whose rights (to use the expression appropriated to the case) are violated by it. And the sentiment of justice appears to me to be, the animal desire to repel or retaliate a hurt or damage to oneself, or to those with whom one sympathizes, widened so as to include all persons, by the human capacity of enlarged sympathy, and the human conception of intelligent self-interest. From the latter elements, the feeling derives its morality; from the former, its peculiar impressiveness, and energy of self-assertion.

When we call anything a person's right, we mean that he has a valid claim on society to protect him in the possession of it, either by the force of law, or by that of education and opinion. If he has what we consider a sufficient claim, on whatever account, to have something guaranteed to him by society, we say that he has a right to it. If we desire to prove that anything does not belong to him by right, we think this done as soon as it is admitted that society ought not to take measures for securing it to him, but should leave him to chance, or to his own exertions.

To have a right, then, is, I conceive, to have something which society ought to defend me in the possession of. If the objector goes on to ask, why it ought? I can give him no other reason than general utility. If that expression does not seem to convey a sufficient feeling of the strength of the obligation, nor to account for the peculiar energy of the feeling, it is because there goes to the composition of the sentiment, not a rational only, but also an animal element—the thirst for retaliation; and this thirst derives its intensity, as well as its moral justification, from the extraordinarily important and impressive kind of utility which is concerned. The interest involved is that of security, to everyone's feelings the most vital of all interests. All other earthly benefits are needed by one person, not needed by another; and many of them can, if necessary, be cheerfully foregone, or replaced by something else; but security no human being can possibly do without; on it we depend for all our immunity from evil, and for the whole value of all and every good, beyond the passing moment; since nothing but the gratification of the instant could be of any worth to us, if we could be deprived of anything the next instant by whoever was momentarily stronger than ourselves. Now this most indispensable of all

necessaries, after physical nutriment, cannot be had, unless the machinery for providing it is kept unintermittedly in active play. Our notion, therefore, of the claim we have on our fellow-creatures to join in making safe for us the very groundwork of our existence, gathers feelings around it so much more intense than those concerned in any of the more common cases of utility, that the difference in degree (as is often the case in psychology) becomes a real difference in kind. The claim assumes that character of absoluteness, that apparent infinity, and incommensurability with all other considerations, which constitute the distinction between the feeling of right and wrong and that of ordinary expediency and inexpediency.

There are few if any clearer instances of injustice than the enslaving of a person or the torturing of the innocent. Utilitarianism supposedly cannot account for this sense of what is just and unjust. After all, enslaving someone might be "useful," and torturing an innocent person might be a means to saving many lives (cf. the statement of Caiaphas, the high priest at the trial of Jesus: "It is expedient that one should die, so that the people might be saved"). So how can utilitarians account for the extremely strong feeling that such things *must not* be done, no matter what (recall Kant and the idea of *deontology*.)

Now, Mill has here attempted to provide a utilitarian reason why we should not enslave or torture one person for the benefit of many. To do so would violate the need for security or "immunity from evil," which Mill considers to be so fundamental that our feelings about that need or any violation of it outweigh virtually all other feelings respecting how people may treat one another. Thus feelings about justice *seem* to be distinct from feelings about what is useful or has utility. But in fact even those feelings are rooted in utility, the utility of security.

23. *It certainly seems that a person could have security, say, security from assault, arbitrary arrest, or enslavement, in a society that was not just by typical modern standards. Thus a woman might be perfectly secure in all of these respects, even though she did not have the right to vote, or even the right to go out without cov-*

*ering her face. Is there some kind of "security"
that such a woman lacks? Does Mill simply
count anything that has come to be regarded as
unjust as a violation of "security"? If so, would
that damage his argument?*

24. *If we grant that people feel as strongly about
the need for security as Mill claims they do,
does that show that a utilitarian could not
still in some circumstance condone slavery or
torture of an innocent person? Argue pro and
con, keeping Mill's points in mind.*

25. *Just how important, in utilitarian calculations,
should feelings be, particularly feelings that do
not point us to what is useful?*

If the preceding analysis, or something resembling it,
be not the correct account of the notion of justice—if
justice be totally independent of utility, and be a standard per se, which the mind can recognize by simple
introspection of itself—it is hard to understand why
that internal oracle is so ambiguous, and why so
many things appear either just or unjust, according
to the light in which they are regarded.

We are continually informed that Utility is an uncertain standard, which every different person inter-
prets differently, and that there is no safety but in the
immutable, ineffaceable, and unmistakable dictates
of justice, which carry their evidence in themselves,
and are independent of the fluctuations of opinion.
One would suppose from this that on questions of
justice there could be no controversy; that if we take
that for our rule, its application to any given case
could leave us in as little doubt as a mathematical
demonstration. So far is this from being the fact, that
there is as much difference of opinion, and as much
discussion, about what is just, as about what is useful
to society. Not only have different nations and individuals different notions of justice, but in the mind of
one and the same individual, justice is not some one
rule, principle, or maxim, but many, which do not
always coincide in their dictates, and in choosing between which, he is guided either by some extraneous
standard, or by his own personal predilections.

For instance, there are some who say, that it is
unjust to punish anyone for the sake of example to
others; that punishment is just, only when intended

for the good of the sufferer himself. Others maintain
the extreme reverse, contending that to punish persons who have attained years of discretion, for their
own benefit, is despotism and injustice, since if the
matter at issue is solely their own good, no one has
a right to control their own judgment of it; but that
they may justly be punished to prevent evil to others, this being the exercise of the legitimate right of
self-defense. Mr. Owen, again, affirms that it is unjust
to punish at all; for the criminal did not make his
own character; his education, and the circumstances
which surrounded him, have made him a criminal,
and for these he is not responsible. All these opinions
are extremely plausible; and so long as the question is
argued as one of justice simply, without going down
to the principles which lie under justice and are the
source of its authority, I am unable to see how any of
these reasoners can be refuted.

Utilitarianism's critics sometimes claim that it is
too flexible and allows competing and incompatible
notions of what is useful. Thus, they say, we need to
focus not on what is *useful* but on what is *just*. Mill
responds by pointing out that we also have competing and incompatible notions of justice.

26. *Recall two examples of such incompatible notions of justice.*

Is, then, the difference between the just and the expedient a merely imaginary distinction? Have mankind been under a delusion in thinking that justice
is a more sacred thing than policy, and that the latter
ought only to be listened to after the former has been
satisfied? By no means. The exposition we have given
of the nature and origin of the sentiment, recognizes
a real distinction; and no one of those who profess
the most sublime contempt for the consequences of
actions as an element in their morality, attaches more
importance to the distinction than I do. While I dispute the pretensions of any theory which sets up an
imaginary standard of justice not grounded on utility,
I account the justice which is grounded on utility to
be the chief part, and incomparably the most sacred
and binding part, of all morality. Justice is a name
for certain classes of moral rules, which concern the

essentials of human well-being more nearly, and are therefore of more absolute obligation, than any other rules for the guidance of life; and the notion which we have found to be of the essence of the idea of justice—that of a right residing in an individual—implies and testifies to this more binding obligation.

> 27. *By placing a very high utilitarian value on justice, Mill hopes to deflect any claim that utilitarianism might allow for violations of justice. That high value is due, he says, to the fact that justice concerns the "essentials of human well-being." Has he proved what those essentials are? Recall the difference between Hoffendahl and Hyacinth. Would Mill agree with Hyacinth? Argue pro and con. If not, should he, given his theory of justice?*

All persons are deemed to have a right to equality of treatment, except when some recognized social expediency requires the reverse. And hence all social inequalities which have ceased to be considered expedient, assume the character not of simple inexpediency, but of injustice, and appear so tyrannical, that people are apt to wonder how they ever could have been tolerated—forgetful that they themselves perhaps tolerate other inequalities under an equally mistaken notion of expediency, the correction of which would make that which they approve seem quite as monstrous as what they have at last learnt to condemn. The entire history of social improvement has been a series of transitions, by which one custom or institution after another, from being a supposed primary necessity of social existence, has passed into the rank of a universally stigmatized injustice and tyranny. So it has been with the distinctions of slaves and freemen, nobles and serfs, patricians and plebeians; and so it will be, and in part already is, with the aristocracies of color, race, and sex.

It appears from what has been said, that justice is a name for certain moral requirements, which, regarded collectively, stand higher in the scale of social utility, and are therefore of more paramount obligation, than any others; though particular cases may occur in which some other social duty is so important, as to overrule any one of the general maxims of justice. Thus, to save a life, it may not only be allow-

able, but a duty, to steal, or take by force, the necessary food or medicine, or to kidnap, and compel to officiate, the only qualified medical practitioner. In such cases, as we do not call anything justice which is not a virtue, we usually say, not that justice must give way to some other moral principle, but that what is just in ordinary cases is, by reason of that other principle, not just in the particular case. By this useful accommodation of language, the character of indefeasibility attributed to justice is kept up, and we are saved from the necessity of maintaining that there can be laudable injustice.

The considerations which have now been adduced resolve, I conceive, the only real difficulty in the utilitarian theory of morals. It has always been evident that all cases of justice are also cases of expediency; the difference is in the peculiar sentiment which attaches to the former, as contradistinguished from the latter. Justice remains the appropriate name for certain social utilities which are vastly more important, and therefore more absolute and imperative, than any others are as a class (though not more so than others may be in particular cases); and which, therefore, ought to be, as well as naturally are, guarded by a sentiment not only different in degree, but also in kind; distinguished from the milder feeling which attaches to the mere idea of promoting human pleasure or convenience, at once by the more definite nature of its commands, and by the sterner character of its sanctions.

> 28. *Mill concludes that "justice remains the name for certain social utilities," which are vastly more important than other utilities, though "not more so than others may be in a particular case." Suppose I promise to meet you for lunch tomorrow. Suppose that when tomorrow comes I have an opportunity to lunch with my boss, who is extremely important to me, but I know you will not let me off my promise to you so that I can pursue that opportunity. So I break my promise to you. Could I argue that the social utility of promise keeping is not greater than the utility of lunching with my boss in this "particular case"? What is your view? Is there any way to tell what Mill's view would be?*

Some of the common criticisms of utilitarianism are addressed by Mill. For example, the claim that utilitarianism is impractical because the calculation of consequences requires more time than people usually have has, he thinks, been dealt with. He also attempts to deal with the criticism that his theory cannot account for what we understand by (or "feel" about!) justice.

Here are some other obvious criticisms, some of which are not addressed by Mill in the previous selections: It is, more often than not, impossible to have much certainty about what the consequences of any action will actually be; all sorts of things could happen that would prevent good outcomes, so it is, more often than not, impossible to improve life by the utilitarian method; the notion of a good outcome is itself hopelessly vague, and controversial to boot, and Mill's attempt to distinguish higher and lower pleasures shows it; the idea that moral rules are mere summaries of what the human race has learned about the "general tendencies of actions" is absurd when applied, for example, to such rules as "Keep your promises," since (as Kant more or less suggested) there would be no such thing as making and accepting promises if that rule had not been in place right at the start; rule utilitarianism is actually antiutilitarian in spirit, since it advocates a kind of "rule worship" and gives no guidelines for when to follow and when not to follow any give rule.

Some of these criticisms have been dealt with by further modifications in formulations of utilitarianism. For example, the vagueness in the notion of good outcomes might be repaired by simply giving up the notion that there is some one value, such as pleasure or reduction of pain, that moral persons seek to maximize. Instead, some modern utilitarians advocate maximizing preferences without making any attempt to rank them in terms of some overriding "values." Some further criticisms, and replies to them, are explored in the following discussions.

29. *Which of the criticisms just mentioned seems to you to have the greatest force? Which has the least (or no) force?*

Further Discussion and Applications

Criticisms of Utilitarianism (Williams)

Imagine the following scenarios (both are versions of examples invented by Bernard Williams).

1. Jim is an American on a botanical expedition through the jungles of a "banana Republic" in South America. He comes to a village that has just been taken over by government troops who are hunting for guerilla insurgents. The commander of the troops is about to order the execution of 20 men picked at random, as a warning to the village not to get involved in aiding or sheltering the guerrillas. But when Jim happens on the scene, the commander, who looks on him as an honored guest, offers him a "guests privilege": shoot one of the men, and he will let the other 19 go. Everyone in the village is pleading for Jim to take the offer. What should he do?

2. George, a recent Ph.D. in chemistry, is desperately in need of a job to support his family. His wife has had to work to keep the family going, and that has put a lot of strain on her, the children and himself. The only job that opens up for him is one with a manufacturer of chemical weapons. George feels he cannot accept this job. For years he has been strongly opposed to the development of such weapons. A friend who found him the job points out that if he does not take it, someone else will, so the end result as far as the production of the weapons goes will be the same whether he takes the job or does not. Moreover his wife is not particularly opposed to his taking such a job. What should he do?

A superficial acquaintance with utilitarianism would lead to the conclusion that in the utilitarian view Jim should shoot one villager and George should take the job. Jim and George might be very upset over having to do these things, both of them might be made very "unhappy" by them; but that unhappiness has to be weighed against the increased happiness of many other people (in the one case, practically everyone in the village, in the other, George's entire family). If Mill is committed to the idea that a greater happiness for many could sometimes be purchased at the price of some unhappiness for a few, it seems particularly clear what the utilitarian answer to these dilemmas must be.

Bernard Williams (see Chapter 1) thinks that utilitarian analyses of situations like these are deeply defective. It is not so much that the specific answers recommended would always be disputed by non-utilitarians. But the considerations that are thought important in deciding what to do are not, many will think, what the utilitarian claims they are. Nor are our moral reactions in such situations accounted for by a utilitarian analysis.

The utilitarian must hold that in Jim's case the fact that it is Jim that does the shooting (even if he shoots only one native) is not important. What matters is the overall results, no matter who brings them about. The results will be much better if Jim does shoot one man. Of course the utilitarian has to take into account all the consequences of each alternative action, and the consequences of Jim's killing an innocent man might include that for the rest of his life Jim feels terrible about having done it, has nightmares, etc. But that consequence cannot have too much weight, since such a reaction on Jim's part would be, according to the utilitarian, irrational. As such it should be discouraged. Rationally Jim ought to be glad that he got to save 19 lives! And he should not feel responsible for the death of one man who would have ended up dead anyway. In any case his (irrational) bad feelings are just the feelings of one man. How much weight can they have compared to the weight of terrible distress afflicting 19 entire families if he refuses to shoot?

30. *If you were in Jim's situation: (a) Would you think that the best thing you could do would be to shoot one of the men? (b) If so, would you nonetheless feel terrible about having to kill an innocent person? (c) If you (or anyone in your situation) would feel terrible, would you regard that feeling as irrational? Consult your answer to Orienting Question 6 in thinking about this.*

Williams thinks utilitarians distort the nature of moral thinking. The utilitarian must think of Jim's subsequent sufferings as mere squeamishness. There are things a man must sometimes do that are very unpleasant. Face up to that fact, the utilitarian says to Jim. Be a man!

But why should Jim think of his feelings about this situation as mere squeamishness, unless he has already accepted the utilitarian stance? In that stance, Jim will feel that his negative feelings are just feelings, nothing more. In particular they are not indications that what he is doing is wrong. But prior to accepting that stance he is likely to view those feelings precisely as an indication that it is wrong, evil, to shoot to death an innocent man.

Another feature of moral thinking that may seem to play no role in utilitarian analyses is what we call *integrity*. The fact that it is I who shoot someone, even if that someone would end up dead anyway, rightly weighs on me, since I am an agent, my own self is involved in such an action. I am not a mere impersonal link in one causal chain that leads to a man's death. Jim's feelings are an indication of that fact. Williams remarks:

> Because our moral relation to the world is partly given by such feelings, and by a sense of what we can and cannot "live with," to come to regard those feelings from a purely utilitarian point of view, that is to say, as happenings outside one's moral self, is to lose a sense of one's moral identity, to lose, in the most literal way, one's integrity. (from "A Critique of Utilitarianism" in *Utilitarianism: For and Against*, ed. J. J. C. Smart and Bernard Williams, 1973)

The notion of integrity assumes that people have commitments. Integrity is a kind of following through on one's deepest commitments and convictions. In the case of George we can imagine that he has ordered an important part of his life around his opposition to the development of chemical weapons. He considers them evil, and his opposition to them is not just an opinion he happens to have. He has invested himself, his life, in toiling against such evils. For him to take the job in question would require that he set *himself*, in an important sense, aside or that he be willing to violate himself in order to achieve a greater aggregate "happiness." When asked to do so he might find himself wondering whether it is not important to happiness, whatever that is, that people have commitments and projects that absorb them and give definition to their lives. Thus the utilitarian requirement that a person be prepared to set aside such commitments, when doing so will purportedly increase the "happiness" of the greatest number, may well seem to him to be shallow or even nonsense.

> 31. *In your own view: (a) How important is integrity? (b) Can people have integrity if nothing has very great or overriding importance for them?*

Williams' critique amounts to the claim that important facts about the way people think about moral demands and character cannot be accounted for by utilitarians. Is that a bad thing? Is it possible that utilitarianism is still the best theory of morality, even if it conflicts now and then with how many people think about morality? Utilitarians might be willing to accept that possibility, but generally they seem as concerned as most other moralists with finding a theory of morality that does not conflict with too many deeply entrenched moral beliefs.

A Defense of Utilitarianism (Hare)

We can see something that is quite common to many attacks on utilitarianism in Williams' critique. The critic begins by imagining various scenarios that pose moral dilemmas. He then tries to show that the utilitarian way of resolving those dilemmas conflicts with what most people think about right and wrong. The British utilitarian philosopher R. M. Hare thinks that this tactic works only when people fail to insist that the scenarios in question be fully spelled out and the actual teachings of utilitarianism be accurately represented. When that is done, he claims, most people will accept the utilitarian verdict after all.

Utilitarians are often criticized for being unable to account for ordinary intuitions about "special obligations," such as my obligation to care for my children but not necessarily for yours and my obligations to my country but not to someone else's country. To illustrate this supposed defect in utilitarianism, consider the following case: Bill and his young son are traveling by plane. On the flight Bill has conversed with the woman next to him and discovered that she is an emergency room doctor, with special expertise in treating burns. There is a forced emergency landing and the plane crashes and begins to burn. His son

and the doctor are trapped in the burning wreckage, but Bill is able to free himself and he has time to rescue just one other person. If he rescues the doctor he may in effect save many people, since the doctor has the skills to care for other crash victims who are injured but still able to survive, provided they get quick help. If he rescues his son instead, the doctor, and his skills, and perhaps the lives of many other passengers will be lost. What should Bill do? No doubt most people, if put into Bill's situation, would instantly work to save their own children. Most people feel special obligations to their own children. If Bill rescues his son and as a result has to watch the doctor perish, he will no doubt feel very bad, but he will not feel that he has done the wrong thing, and indeed he may suppose that he did exactly what he ought to have done. But according to the utilitarian it is (supposedly) obvious that he should have saved the doctor instead. Overall utility is clearly served when the person who is saved is able to save many others. So this is a case where what the utilitarian claims is morally required conflicts with most people's intuitions.

Hare responds to this criticism on several fronts. He points out how much the example depends on doubtful claims about what Bill knows and could do and about how much the rescued doctor could do. How does Bill know the woman really is a doctor? And even if it is certain that she is, how much could she do without his drugs and equipment? Hare thinks it is difficult to make this example truly realistic. But a more central point is that both act utilitarians and rule utilitarians fully recognize that in such a situation, where one must act quickly, one relies on dominant family loyalties and, further, that it is good to do so. If Bill was brought up by a critical utilitarian, his upbringing still would not have prepared him for handling such statistically improbable cases (what are the chances of being in a plane crash at all, not to mention one in which you can escape and *also* happen to be able to rescue a doctor, etc.?). Utilitarians recognize that the tendency to care for one's own has high utility normally. What would happen if mothers, for instance, felt no special obligation to their own children? Thus it misrepresents utilitarian thinking to suppose that it would be obvious that Bill should rescue the doctor.

Bill's natural tendency to care for his own is a good tendency that would be encouraged by a utilitarian upbringing, so it would not be inconsistent with the utilitarian's view that Bill save his son. Hare proposes a distinction between *critical thinking* about morality and, on the other hand, following moral intuitions. Hare comments:

> Insofar as the intuitions are desirable ones, they can be defended on utilitarian grounds by critical thinking, as having a high acceptance-utility; if they can be so defended, the best bet, even for an utilitarian, will be to cultivate them and follow them in all normal cases; [utilitarianism], unlike intuitionism, is actually able to *justify* the intuitions, where they can be justified. (from "Loyalty and Evil Desires," in *Moral Thinking*, 1981)

Suppose, on the other hand, that Bill had plenty of time to think it over critically and could be sure that he could save many lives by rescuing the doctor, could reasonably believe that allowing his son to die would not deprive the world of even greater benefits (if, for example, he could see that his son was on the way to being a great doctor or researcher himself), was confident in his own strength and so forth. In that case, though the case is so unlikely as to be of just about zero significance, Bill might well decide to rescue the doctor, and we might even agree. Thus Hare contends that most people would actually agree with utilitarian analyses when situations are properly described. Thus the usual strategy in attacking it does not succeed.

32. *Recall, from* Crime and Punishment, *the speech of the student overheard by Raskolnikov. It seems that the student justifies murder by utilitarian considerations. What might Hare have to say to this speech? Does the speech involve distortions of utilitarian thinking? If so, what are they?*

33. *Does the response of Hare, as briefly described here, to utilitarianism's critics answer the claim of Williams that utilitarians cannot account for the moral importance of integrity? Argue.*

Utilitarianism and Feeding the Hungry (Singer)

Utilitarians have been criticized for sometimes allowing or recommending actions that are commonly regarded as morally impermissible, such as the murder of the nasty old woman committed by Raskolnikov, Thus utilitarianism, it is claimed, is inconsistent with ordinary moral intuitions. But there is another way to be inconsistent with those intuitions, which consists in treating actions or policies as *required* or obligatory that are normally regarded as *not* required.

Consider the following principle, as stated by the utilitarian philosopher Peter Singer: "If it is in our power to prevent something bad from happening, without thereby sacrificing anything of comparable moral importance, we ought, morally, to do it." This principle implies that if I see a child drowning in a shallow muddy pond and am able to prevent the drowning without sacrificing anything more than the cleanness of my clothing, I ought to do it. And who would argue with that? But analogously, if I know that somewhere in the world there is a child who is starving to death and I am able to prevent it without sacrificing anything of comparable moral importance, I should do it. Now, Singer thinks that most people from affluent Western countries are in precisely such a situation. There are in fact, in various places in the world, children starving to death, and their distance is no longer a factor; there are ways that I, an affluent American, can render aid and prevent the death, and I can even do so on quite a large scale by sufficient "sacrifice" of such things as expensive stereos, luxurious vacations, many new changes of clothes and other such items not essential to my own well-being. So I ought to do so.

But what is meant by "I ought to do so"? Sometimes all it means is that it would be kind or benevolent of me to do so. To say "You ought to be kind to poor old Aunt Sadie" is just to say that it would be good of you, that it is what a good person would do. If it is a duty at all, it is a duty of beneficence. But in other cases, to say that I ought to do something, such as feeding the hungry, is (perhaps) to say that I am morally *required* to do so. It is not to say that it would merely be good or benevolent or charitable of me to do so. If I refrain from charitable giving, I have not thereby failed in a duty, that is, failed to do what is *required* of me. But by failing to help the starving child, I fail to do something that clearly *is* required of me, just as saving the drowning child in the nearby pond is required of me. That is Singer's claim. Perhaps he thinks of that claim as actually consistent with our all-things-considered moral views. That seems unlikely, however. Most people do think of charitable aid as exactly that, charitable, and do not think of failure to be charitable as a failure to observe a strict duty. So in cases like these, most people have a lower moral standard than that implied by utilitarianism. So perhaps once again utilitarianism requires a significant revision in our moral intuitions, though in this case the revision is upward, so to speak (*requiring* aid to the starving), rather than downward (*permitting* murder).

34. *What is your view on aid to starving people? Given that it really is possible to render such aid effectively, is the failure to do so actually as wrong as ignoring the drowning child next door? Is it as wrong as* killing *the child?*

35. *The notion of rights plays an important part in contemporary moral thinking. People have a right to life, for instance. Children have a right to be cared for (fed and clothed) by their parents. Do they also have a right to be fed by people who are not their parents when the parents are unable to feed them (cf. the* UN Universal Declaration of Human Rights, *Chapter 1 of this book)?*

36. *Common ways of moral thinking allot a central role to the notion of justice or fairness. Is it fair to require (force) someone to part with hard-earned and honestly acquired wealth in order to increase overall happiness? (Some taxes do exactly that!) Or is it rather the case that people are entitled to what they have earned and should only part with it of their own free will and out of motives of charity?*

Under What Description? (Schick)
One of the purported advantages of early formulations of utilitarianism was a kind of "naturalism."

Bentham took pleasures and pains to be "natural" occurrences, the stimulation of certain parts of the nervous system in a certain way. When choosing what to do, one ought to look to the consequences and seek to maximize total pleasure over pain. That could mean more than one thing. It could mean that a person ought, morally, to choose that course of action that he foresees will have consequences as good as or better than any open alternative; or it could mean that a person ought morally to choose that course of action that has the best foreseeable consequences (whether he actually foresees them is another matter). Either way, we could think of actions as causing their consequences, and the question of what actions contribute causally to what states of the nervous system is a matter for natural science to determine. We thus could have a "science" of ethics comparable to that sought by Socrates in the *Protagoras*.

Some of the problems with thinking of consequences in terms of pleasure/pain are already bothering Mill, otherwise he would not have tried to distinguish higher from lower pleasures. More recent utilitarians have largely given up on the Benthamite type of analysis and recommend thinking in terms of maximizing preferences. Suppose Albert has the following order of preferences:

A1. Eating meat (because he thinks it is healthy, not because it gives pleasure)
A2. Eating vegetables

Suppose Bill has the following order of preferences:

B1. Protecting all animals from slaughter
B2. Eating vegetables (he may actually dislike them)

Suppose for the sake of simplicity these are all the preferences they have and that we ignore my preferences. Now, obviously these preferences do not have a lot to do with simple pleasures and pains. So we will ignore pleasure and pain and simply accept Albert's and Bill's say-so on how to rank their preferences.

Suppose, then, that by supporting an animal rights group I can help Bill to maximize his preferences (cause an increase in vegetable eating while reducing animal slaughter) and that by supporting the cattlemen's association I can help Albert maximize his. In that case I ought to support animal rights, since then Bill gets B1 and B2 and Albert gets A2 (one rank-1 preference and two rank-2 preferences are realized), whereas under the other alternative, where I support the cattlemen's association, Albert gets A1 (one rank-1 preference is realized, and that is all). The "utility sums" are such that supporting animal rights is the moral thing for me to do.

In this way of thinking the difficulties of comparing different sorts of pleasures or pains, and trying to figure out which should have the most weight, simply disappear.

However, there are other difficulties that arise. The utility sums reflect how consequences are evaluated by those affected by an agent's actions. But how we evaluate any state of affairs, for example, the state of affairs in which eating meat is no more, depends on how that state of affairs is described. Any state of affairs can be described many different ways. For example, if Jane is Bill's wife, then the state of affairs that consists in Norman kissing Jane could also be described as the state of affairs in which Norman kisses Bill's wife. Likewise, the state of affairs in which eating meat is no more could also be described as the state of affairs in which all meat producers are out of business or as the state of affairs in which many formerly employed people are unemployed. Albert might prefer (set a very high utility on) the state of affairs described as "eating meat is no more" but a much lower utility on the state of affairs of many formerly employed people being unemployed, even though those could be, in a certain historical situation, simply two descriptions of one and the same state of affairs.

How does all of this bear on utilitarianism? If we want to maximize utility sums, we must know what description of an outcome to use in order to compare its utility to the utility of other outcomes. Under one description, the causal result of an action might have high utility, under another a low utility. So which description is relevant? Perhaps we can avoid this problem by simply asking George which description he is using. Call this *agent-relativizing*. But perhaps George simply does not know what all the different descriptions of a certain state of affairs are. If the

right action for him is the one with the best foreseeable consequences, what if he simply does not foresee certain consequences? If he does not foresee them at all, then he cannot foresee them under any particular description. So we are left in the dark in calculating utilities. Or suppose he acknowledges that many different descriptions apply to a given outcome and that different utilities result. Do we add the different resultant utilities together, or what?

Frederick Schick illustrates the difficulty with the following example.

> Consider the British and French appeasement of Germany in the 1930s. A utilitarian may be convinced that the appeasers were shortsighted. They knew enough to tell which way the wind was blowing. What they were doing led to disaster, and this effect was foreseeable by them. He would then judge their conduct in terms of the utilities set on this consequence. But, again, under what description? We typically report the disaster by saying that Europe was engulfed in a war. But why is that the way to describe it? Why not say instead that the peace arranged at Versailles collapsed—most people cared much less about this. (Most people didn't know that the war undid that particular peace.) We cannot hope here to pass the buck by agent-relativizing. The politicians did not see what would follow under any description. ("Under Which Descriptions" in *Utilitarianism and Beyond*, 1982).

A utilitarian judgment on what one of these appeasers, say, Neville Chamberlain, did would be that what he did was wrong. But in this case the appeasers did not foresee certain foreseeable consequences. Since they didn't see them at all, we cannot compute the utilities of those consequences as they saw them (we cannot rely on agent-relativizing.) If we compute them under the descriptions that *we* see apply, we have to choose which way of seeing them does apply in order to get our utilitarian computations going. But the utilitarian does not tell us how to choose one way of seeing them over another.

37. *In terms of Schick's example, the consequence of the appeasers' actions was nothing less than*

World War II, European theater. But that consequence could also be described as the collapse of the Versailles treaty. . But the utility of the given consequence is lower under the _____ description, and higher under the _____. So we need to know which description to use in order to get a utilitarian judgment on whether the appeasers did the _____. But utilitarians cannot tell us what _____ to use. So we cannot use utilitarianism to determine whether the appeasers did the _____.

Social Justice and Utility (Rawls)

We have already seen that utilitarians may have particular difficulties in explaining justice. Just actions and practices are presumably fair, and many critics have thought utilitarianism, since it emphasizes aggregate or overall benefit, cannot account for the importance of fairness, which requires that we pay attention to each individual, no matter what the consequences may be for the aggregate.

There is another major approach to ethics that does focus quite definitely on fairness. Kant's categorical imperative could be thought of as a principle of fairness, insofar as it identifies acting for the sake of duty as a refusal to make an exception of oneself. In effect Kant thinks that morality rules out "bias" in favor of oneself. He also sees the tendency toward bias as irrational, since the biased person cannot, by definition, give a reason why he should enjoy special treatment.

A Theory of Justice (1971), by Harvard University philosophy professor John Rawls (b. 1921), combines Kantian insights with a notion of the "social contract" that is quite different from Hobbes' (see Chapter 6). Rawls envisions a contractual arrangement in which people are impartial. In what he calls the *original position*, a group of people could establish fair principles as the foundation for regulating all rights, duties and distributions of rewards and responsibilities. The first step in determining such principles requires imagining that we contract with one another (the "social contract") in an *original position* of complete equality, behind a *veil of ignorance* (all quotations from John Rawls, *A Theory of Justice*).

Among the essential features of this situation is that no one knows his place in society, his class position or social status, nor does anyone know his fortune in the distribution of natural assets and abilities, his intelligence, strength, and the like. . . . The principles of justice are chosen behind a veil of ignorance. This ensures that no one is advantaged or disadvantaged in the choice of principles by the outcome of natural chance or the contingency of social circumstances.

38. *a. Name three things that we must imagine people do not know behind the veil of ignorance.*
    b. Pick one of them and argue that if a person did know that fact, he or she would tend to be biased in thinking about which social rules or policies (for example, tax policies) would be right or just.
    c. Explain why he or she might be biased.

The *veil of ignorance* is an imagined condition in which bias or unfairness would be eliminated. Try imagining forming a real (not just hypothetical) *social contract* between yourself and all of your classmates. You are about to form a small society or club, with all of you as the sole members. You must eliminate from your thoughts all that you know about yourself (how healthy you are, how rich or poor, how advantaged or disadvantaged by race or gender or even what you think is good). Doing so will supposedly prevent you from picking principles governing the contract that would unfairly favor the rich or the poor, the sick or the healthy, etc.

39. *Is it really possible to imagine yourself in such a position? Mention any difficulties that you encounter in attempting this experiment.*

Rawls believes that this conception of justice may conflict with utilitarian views of justice.

It may be observed, however, that once the principles of justice are thought of as arising from an original agreement in a situation of equality, it is an open question whether the principle of utility would be acknowledged. Offhand it hardly seems likely that persons who view themselves as equals, entitled to press their claims upon one another, would agree to a principle which may require lesser life prospects for some simply for the sake of a greater sum of advantages enjoyed by others. Since each desires to protect his interests, his capacity to advance his conception of the good, no one has a reason to acquiesce in an enduring loss for himself in order to bring about a great net balance of satisfaction. In the absence of strong and lasting benevolent impulses, a rational man would not accept a basic structure merely because it maximized the algebraic sum of advantages irrespective of its permanent effects on his own basic rights and interests. Thus it seems that the principle of utility is incompatible with the conception of social cooperation among equals for mutual advantage. It appears to be inconsistent with the idea of reciprocity implicit in the notion of a well-ordered society.

Rawls argues that there are two basic principles that would be arrived at in the original position, behind the veil of ignorance:

I shall maintain that persons in the initial situation would choose two rather different principles: The first requires equality in the assignment of basic rights and duties, while the second holds that social and economic inequalities, for example, inequalities of wealth and authority, are just only if they result in compensating benefits for everyone, and in particular for the least advantaged members of society. These principles rule out justifying institutions on the grounds that the hardships of some are offset by a greater good in the aggregate. It may be expedient but it is not just that some should have less in order that others may prosper.

The social/political character of Rawls' conception of justice is clear. Not much thought is required to realize that we live in a social order in which there are, and have to be, various roles and tasks. Some people build skyscrapers, some are doctors, some work on assembly lines and others own or run the companies with the assembly lines. However, even in a complex society certain basic rights apply to all, such as the right not to be enslaved. That is Rawls' first principle. But we would not expect that everyone has a right to the same compensation for his work. If a doctor was not paid more than a worker on an assembly line, very few people would become doctors. Even the most generous would not be able to bear the expense or expend the years of effort required to become a doctor if they earned a low wage in the end. But if there should not be enough doctors to go around, that would be to *everyone's* disadvantage. After all, everyone is subject to illness and injury and may need medical services at some point. It follows logically that some significant difference in compensation between doctors and assembly line workers would be to *everyone's* advantage. That difference is thus an inequality that everyone, both doctors and nondoctors, could accept as fair according to the second of the principles that Rawls has stated.

It follows that in a just society there will be no difference between people with respect to basic rights such as political liberty, freedom of speech, freedom from arbitrary arrest and so forth. But a just society *can* contain inequalities in wealth, social power and so on.

40. *Give an example of an inequality in wealth that would be just and an example of one that would not be just, according to Rawls' account.*
41. *Look again at Rawls' two principles and then answer the following:*
    a. *Would the difference in social power and wealth between a senator and a sanitation worker, for instance, be unfair?*
    b. *Would it matter, according to Rawls, if only people from certain classes were allowed by law to become senators?*

Rawls believes that his account of justice is incompatible with utilitarian accounts of justice. His preceding remarks indicate that he thinks that utilitarians are willing, in principle, to allow "some to have less in order that others might prosper." But Mill has argued that the utilitarian can account for all our usual intuitions about what is or is not just.

42. *Is Rawls' utilitarian a straw man? Argue pro and con. Has Mill successfully met the objec-*

tion that utilitarianism could allow some to have less in order that others might prosper?

43. *Does Mill's discussion of justice really deal with the issues of distribution of wealth that concern Rawls, or is Mill thinking primarily of something like "criminal justice"?*

Justice and the Allocation of Medical Resources (Veatch)

One of the vexing problems facing most modern societies has to do with the distribution of increasingly expensive medical resources. A utilitarian might argue that inequalities in access to health care could be justified if the result were the greatest possible *aggregate* benefit. In this view, issues of efficiency would be considered important. If the most efficient distribution of medical resources was one in which some people, perhaps those with congenital health problems, were left with less help than they needed, that might be considered just, provided net aggregate benefit were maximized.

In opposition to such a utilitarian view, medical ethicist Robert Veatch endorses a view similar to Rawls'. Equality is more important than efficiency, from a moral point of view. An equal amount of "net welfare" is always morally desirable, in Veatch's view. There can of course be various kinds of inequality. One person might suffer more unhappiness than another, but that should be offset by a greater amount of benefit. Gross inequalities poison relationships; even if they do not produce envy in the poor and resentment in the rich, they tend to make genuinely moral relationships between rich and poor impossible.

Veatch points out that certain basic needs, such as the need for food, clothing and shelter, do not vary much from person to person. There is, for example, no reason to think that one person needs 5,000 square feet of living space and another needs only 500, all other things being equal. So with respect to meeting such basic needs, rough equality of distribution would be just, and whatever inequalities there may be should be the result primarily of trade-offs. One person might wish to spend more for food and get less in the way of fine clothing, another might prefer the opposite. The differences that would result

are surely compatible with justice. Net welfare is not disturbed. It is, however, not obvious how to apply this "egalitarian" ideal to the issue of allocating medical resources.

The main reason is that the need for health care, unlike the need for food or shelter, obviously varies a great deal from person to person. Some people, through no fault of their own, may need a great deal of it, while others may need none at all. Thus if the distribution of health care started out with initial equality, those who need a great deal of it might be forced to trade *basic* goods, such as adequate food, for health care. Although limited trading would seem fair (someone might prefer a better suit of clothes to an annual checkup), Veatch argues that the *need* for health care should be the primary thing that determines initial distributions. An equal distribution, say, of a health allowance or the resources of a public health system, would result in some people exhausting their resources quickly and others spending pointlessly. Those worst off in terms of health could, along with all others, bargain for health care by trading something else for it, and the result might be that everyone gains something from the bargaining, But those worst off would have to bargain away goods that the more fortunate take for granted. That, Veatch thinks, would not be just.

> I see justice not just as a way to efficiently improve the lot of the least well off by permitting them trades (even though those trades end up increasing the gap between the haves and the have-nots). That might be efficient and might preserve autonomy, but it would not be justice. If I were an original contractor I would cast my vote in favor of the egalitarian principle of justice, applying it so that there would be a right to health care equal in proportion to health care need. The principle of justice for health care could, then, be stated as follows: People have a right to needed health care to provide an opportunity for a level of health equal as far as possible to the health of other people. (from *A Theory of Medical Ethics*, 1983)

44. *Imagine that a friend of yours gets in a bad accident, due to no fault of her own, and must spend the next 20 years of her life receiving*

expensive medical care, costing millions of dollars, in order to bring her back to a level of health that is as close as possible to "normal." Would social policies or arrangements that ensure that she gets that care be just, even if this required heavily taxing people like yourself who, let us suppose, never need any health care? Explain your view in light of Veatch's position. How might a utilitarian argue in this case?

CHAPTER TEN

Virtues, Narrative and Community: Some Recent Discussions

Introduction

In the medieval period, Aristotle's ideas about ethics and a focus on virtues and character continued to have a deep hold on the thinking of most philosophers. Aristotelian ideas could be combined with ideas about divine law, as they were in Aquinas. What Aristotle and Aquinas shared was a belief that there is a human nature that has a built-in *telos* and that the realization of that nature would be a life of virtue. It would also be a flourishing, even "happy" life. Reason itself showed that there is such a nature, even though divine revelation might be required to fully grasp what its fulfillment required.

Discussions of the virtues continued up through Kant, but the understanding of the virtues changed dramatically, and the focus of ethical analysis was increasingly the individual act. This development reached a characteristic modern expression in Mill, who rejects virtue theory explicitly. Mill thinks of moral rightness as a property of actions that accord with his utilitarian criterion of rightness. Kant thought of moral goodness as a property of the will, which is shown in actions done for the sake of duty. Hume denied cognitive significance to moral judgments. The influence of these three figures was pervasive in much moral philosophy up through the first half or two-thirds of the 20th century. But problems

with their views led some philosophers to turn back to Aristotle or to broadly Aristotelian ideas.

ORIENTING QUESTIONS, INITIAL REACTIONS

1. Among the various approaches to ethics discussed in this text, are there any that seem to you to have definite advantages over the virtues approach of Aristotle? If so which, and what are the advantages?

2. Most people would grant that courage is a good quality in a person. Does that fact imply anything about how to act in specific cases?

3. Modern ethics seems to focus on disputes about abortion, euthanasia, racial and gender equality, genetic engineering, treatment of animals and the environment, and the like. Does thinking clearly about such issues require thinking about virtues or character?

4. Aristotle argued that the development of good character requires a good community. That is the meaning of his claim that the highest science is "political." What would some of the features of a community have to be in order to encourage the development of good character?

5. The psychologist Robert Coles discovered that the students in a certain southern high school who were considered by all those around them to have the best character were also those who came from

families that upheld strong religious and other communal traditions. Why might there be such a connection? Would there have to be such a connection?

One reason the virtues approach was sidelined in much modern moral philosophy was a seemingly broad consensus that there could be no rationally compelling account of what is involved in flourishing or happiness or "living well." One reason for a bit more optimism on that matter may reside in the fact that a good deal of literature appeals to a great variety of people precisely by appealing to common intuitions about what it is to live well or not so well. The following excerpt from *The House of Mirth* may illustrate this point.

EDITH WHARTON

Wharton (1862–1937) was born into a wealthy New York family at the beginning of the "gilded age," a period in American history of a rapidly expanding economy that brought wealth and lives of aesthetic splendor to an elite class. She entered into an unhappy marriage at the age of 23 and tried to take on the role of a wealthy society matron. But her exceptional creativity and literary ambitions made that impossible in the long run. She lived much of the latter part of her life in France, where she came to know many of the artistic and literary notables of her era. She won the Pulitzer prize in 1921 for The Age of Innocence, *one of over 40 novels that she produced. She was a perceptive social critic, a literary moralist who exposed the hypocrisies and superficialities of the wealthy classes and the artificial and sometimes destructive mores that governed their lives. She was not, however, a moral cynic. Her moral seriousness is evident in the work cited here,* The House of Mirth *(1905).*

The focus on character in ethics and on the notion of a good life and *eudaimonia* naturally invites consultation of literary sources, where character is examined, rendered and evaluated, sometimes in subtle and telling detail. Novels in particular may exhibit failures and achievements in the struggle for an authentic or "*eudaimon*" life, with detail and vividness that are usually missing in philosophical discussion. In the following excerpt we see how a life fails through the lack of certain virtues and how the failures in virtue are related to social structures that fail to provide sufficient context for human flourishing. If a good life requires a good community, as Aristotle stressed, then a good life in the "high" society described here would be a very rare achievement.

The House of Mirth

A Shallow Society and a Failed Life

Lily Bart, the principal character in this novel, is a young and beautiful New York socialite with limited family wealth. In order to remain within the privileged classes, she must contract a socially favorable marriage and/or stay on the right side of her wealthy aunt, Mrs. Peniston. She fails at both. Given her charms, the first would not have been difficult. But she is unable to identify herself fully with the role of a social ornament that seems to be the principal expectation of a married woman of her type and class. And she offends her aunt by failing to keep up all of the appearances required of a gentlewomen (she gambles, in particular, though she is also honorable in ways that her aunt seems unable to recognize).

Lily passes up or sabotages some promising marital possibilities, and she becomes entangled in relations with various men and women who are unable or unwilling to acknowledge her worth and in some cases are positively harmful or exploitative. Part of her is so accustomed to the superficial manners she has learned that she accepts them as givens, as the standard norms for how to live. But another part of her desires a humane life and a marriage in which she can develop her higher possibilities. Unfortunately that desire is not widely honored. What does get results in her world is a willingness to sacrifice honor and integrity to social conventions that are mostly a dead substitute for real moral norms that might enhance life. Her upbringing has not provided her with the means to achieve a worthy and happy self, since her upbringing has been tailored to the superficial norms of her age and class.

Lily gradually descends into poverty. The customary props—the beautiful dresses, the lavish parties, the company of the wealthy and influential—gradually become a thing of the past. She does have a means to regain her position, for she has letters that reveal damning secrets about the powerful and unscrupulous Bertha Dorset. Since Bertha was instrumental in Lily's downfall, Lily has strong motivation to use the letters against Bertha and a financial incentive to use them to blackmail her way back into money and society. But she has just enough virtue to avoid such low tactics, and in the scene excerpted here from Chapter XIII she throws the letters into the fire. She also finally receives a bequest from her aunt, but it is just enough to pay off her debts to the manipulative Gus Trenor, who had attempted to get her in his power by providing her with financial assistance. She could, of course, have gotten out of those debts without too much loss of honor or by capitulating to the advances of another wealthy man who desires her. Again, her sense of honor prevents her from employing such means to restoring her fortune. She takes a job as a seamstress but is unable to meet its demands. Nearly penniless, she ends up living alone in a boarding house, frail, anxious, unable to sleep. She has managed to get a prescription for Chloral, a sleeping aid, and uses it regularly.

There was one possibility of fulfillment that Lily missed precisely because of her attachment to the superficial glitter of high society. She loves (without really admitting it to herself) and is loved by a lawyer, Laurence Selden, who is well enough off but hardly able to live in splendor. He is himself an ironical observer of the foibles of high society, but like Lily he follows the social conventions of his class, almost as though unable to do otherwise. So their feeble attempts to come together fail. Nonetheless, toward the end of this story (and her story) she returns to him, vaguely hoping to express her real feelings or establish a significant contact. He fails to reciprocate at the crucial moment.

Selden continued to stand near her, leaning against the mantelpiece. The tinge of constraint was beginning to be more distinctly perceptible under the friendly ease of his manner. Her self-absorption had not allowed her to perceive it at first; but now that her consciousness was once more putting forth its eager feelers, she saw that her presence was becoming an embarrassment to him. Such a situation can be saved only by an immediate outrush of feeling; and on Selden's side the determining impulse was still lacking.

The discovery did not disturb Lily as it might once have done. She had passed beyond the phase of well-bred reciprocity, in which every demonstration must be scrupulously proportioned to the emotion it elicits, and generosity of feeling is the only ostentation condemned. But the sense of loneliness returned with redoubled force as she saw herself forever shut out from Selden's inmost self. She had come to him with no definite purpose; the mere longing to see him had directed her; but the secret hope she had carried with her suddenly revealed itself in its death-pang.

Here it is clear how "well-bred reciprocity" actually cuts off the possibility of real friendship rather than encouraging it. It even works against a virtue, the virtue of generosity. Lily and Selden have some of that virtue, but they cannot entirely escape the social rule; the rule is: "Do not show deep feelings, it is inappropriate 'ostentation' [showing off]." Although Selden seems unable to respond fully to Lily's appeals, she presses on, trying to reveal her true feelings.

Whether he wished it or not, he must see her wholly for once before they parted.

Her voice had gathered strength, and she looked him gravely in the eyes as she continued. "Once—twice—you gave me the chance to escape from my life, and I refused it: refused it because I was a coward. Afterward I saw my mistake—I saw I could never be happy with what had contented me before. But it was too late: you had judged me—I understood. It was too late for happiness—but not too late to be helped by the thought of what I had missed. That is all I have lived on—don't take it from me now! Even in my worst moments it has been like a little light in the darkness. Some women are strong enough to be good by themselves, but I needed the help of your belief in me. Perhaps I might have resisted a great temptation, but the little ones would have pulled me down. And then I remembered—I remembered your saying that such a life could never satisfy me; and I was ashamed to admit to myself that it could. That is what you did for me—that is what I wanted to thank you for. I wanted to tell you that I have always remembered; and that I have tried—tried hard . . .'"

She broke off suddenly. Her tears had risen again, and in drawing out her handkerchief her fingers touched the packet in the folds of her dress. A wave of color suffused her, and the words died on her lips. Then she lifted her eyes to his and went on in an altered voice.

"I have tried hard—but life is difficult, and I am a very useless person. I can hardly be said to have an independent existence. I was just a screw or a cog in the great machine I called life, and when I dropped out of it I found I was of no use anywhere else. What can one do when one finds that one only fits into one hole? One must get back to it or be thrown out into the rubbish heap—and you don't know what it's like in the rubbish heap!"

Her lips wavered into a smile—she had been distracted by the whimsical remembrance of the confidences she had made to him, two years earlier, in that very room. Then she had been planning to marry Percy Gryce—what was it she was planning now?

The blood had risen strongly under Selden's dark skin, but his emotion showed itself only in an added seriousness of manner.

"You have something to tell me—do you mean to marry?" he said abruptly.

Lily's eyes did not falter, but a look of wonder, of puzzled self-interrogation, formed itself slowly in their depths. In the light of his question, she had paused to ask herself if her decision had really been taken when she entered the room.

"You always told me I should have to come to it sooner or later!" she said with a faint smile.

"And you have come to it now?"

"I shall have to come to it—presently. But there is something else I must come to first." She paused again, trying to transmit to her voice the steadiness of her recovered smile. "There is someone I must say goodbye to. Oh, not you—we are sure to see each other again—but the Lily Bart you knew. I have kept her with me all this time, but now we are going to part, and I have brought her back to you—I am going to leave her here. When I go out presently she will not go with me. I shall like to think that she has stayed with you—and she'll be no trouble, she'll take up no room."

She went toward him, and put out her hand, still smiling. "Will you let her stay with you?" she asked.

He caught her hand, and she felt in his the vibration of feeling that had not yet risen to his lips. "Lily—can't I help you?" he exclaimed.

She looked at him gently. "Do you remember what you said to me once? That you could help me only by loving me? Well—you did love me for a moment; and it helped me. It has always helped me. But the moment is gone—it was I who let it go. And one must go on living. Goodbye."

She laid her other hand on his, and they looked at each other with a kind of solemnity, as though they stood in the presence of death. Something in truth lay dead between them—the love she had killed in him and could no longer call to life. But something lived between them also, and leaped up in her like an imperishable flame: it was the love his love had kindled, the passion of her soul for his.

In its light everything else dwindled and fell away from her. She understood now that she could not go forth and leave her old self with him: that self must indeed live on in his presence, but it must still continue to be hers.

Selden had retained her hand, and continued to scrutinize her with a strange sense of foreboding. The external aspect of the situation had vanished for him as completely as for her: he felt it only as one of those rare moments which lift the veil from their faces as they pass.

"Lily," he said in a low voice, "you mustn't speak in this way. I can't let you go without knowing what you mean to do. Things may change—but they don't pass. You can never go out of my life."

She met his eyes with an illumined look. "No," she said. "I see that now. Let us always be friends. Then I shall feel safe, whatever happens."

"Whatever happens? What do you mean? What is going to happen?"

She turned away quietly and walked toward the hearth.

"Nothing at present—except that I am very cold, and that before I go you must make up the fire for me."

She knelt on the hearth-rug, stretching her hands to the embers. Puzzled by the sudden change in her tone, he mechanically gathered a handful of wood from the basket and tossed it on the fire. As he did so, he noticed how thin her hands looked against the rising light of the flames. He saw too, under the loose lines of her dress, how the curves of her figure had shrunk to angularity; he remembered long afterward how the red play of the flame sharpened the depression of her nostrils, and intensified the blackness of the shadows which struck up from her cheekbones to her eyes. She knelt there for a few moments in silence; a silence which he dared not break. When she rose he fancied that he saw her draw something from her dress and drop it into the fire; but he hardly noticed the gesture at the time. His faculties seemed tranced, and he was still groping for the word to break the spell. She went up to him and laid her hands on his shoulders. "Goodbye," she said, and as he bent over her she touched his forehead with her lips.

Lily's image of herself as merely part of a machine registers her sense of being without individual significance, subordinated to a larger entity that reflects no interest of hers. Unlike a genuine community, in which the good of each member is fostered, her "society" is a depersonalized system devoted to nothing more than the perpetuation of undeserved social status and the exclusion of anyone who fails to "fit in."

It is evening as Lily returns to her boardinghouse. She encounters a young woman, Nettie Struther, whom she had once helped by providing her with the money for a trip to a spa where she was able to recover from an illness. The grateful Nettie, who admires and looks up to Lily as her benefactor and "social better," invites her to her poor tenement home, where she lives with her husband and their infant. The community of this little family is formed by acceptance and generosity. The social norms that are used to judge and exclude in Lily's world play no role here. In this world it is not "ostentation" to show deep feelings. Lily holds the infant for a few moments:

> As she continued to hold it the weight increased, sinking deeper, and penetrating her with a strange sense of weakness, as though the child entered into her and became a part of herself.

She looked up, and saw Nettie's eyes resting on her with tenderness and exultation.

Lily has sensed the unaffected bonds of family, of real "human fellowship," and the kind of happiness that does not require wealth or social status. But Nettie's world is not Lily's.

As she reached the street she realized that she felt stronger and happier: the little episode had done her good. It was the first time she had ever come across the results of her spasmodic benevolence, and the surprised sense of human fellowship took the mortal chill from her heart.

It was not till she entered her own door that she felt the reaction of a deeper loneliness. It was long after seven o'clock, and the light and odors proceeding from the basement made it manifest that the boardinghouse dinner had begun. She hastened up to her room, lit the gas, and began to dress. She did not mean to pamper herself any longer, to go without food because her surroundings made it unpalatable. Since it was her fate to live in a boardinghouse, she must learn to fall in with the conditions of the life. Nevertheless she was glad that, when she descended to the heat and glare of the dining room, the repast was nearly over.

In her own room again, she was seized with a sudden fever of activity. For weeks past she had been too listless and indifferent to set her possessions in order, but now she began to examine systematically the contents of her drawers and cupboard. She had a few handsome dresses left—survivals of her last phase of splendor, on the Sabrina and in London—but when she had been obliged to part with her maid she had given the woman a generous share of her cast-off apparel. The remaining dresses, though they had lost their freshness, still kept the long unerring lines, the sweep and amplitude of the great artist's stroke, and as she spread them out on the bed the scenes in which they had been worn rose vividly before her. An association lurked in every fold: each fall of lace and gleam of embroidery was like a letter in the record of her past. She was startled to find how the atmosphere of her old life enveloped her. But, after all, it was the life she had been made for: every dawning tendency in her had been carefully directed toward it, all her interests and activities had been taught to center around it. She was like some rare flower grown for exhibition, a flower from which every bud had been nipped except the crowning blossom of her beauty.

Last of all, she drew forth from the bottom of her trunk a heap of white drapery which fell shapelessly across her arm. It was the Reynolds dress she had worn in the Bry tableaux. It had been impossible for her to give it away, but she had never seen it since that night, and the long flexible folds, as she shook them out, gave forth an odor of violets which came to her like a breath from the flower-edged fountain where she had stood with Lawrence Selden and disowned her fate. She put back the dresses one by one, laying away with each some gleam of light, some note of laughter, some stray waft from the rosy shores of pleasure. She was still in a state of highly wrought impressionability, and every hint of the past sent a lingering tremor along her nerves.

She had just closed her trunk on the white folds of the Reynolds dress when she heard a tap at her door, and the red fist of the Irish maidservant thrust in a belated letter. Carrying it to the light, Lily read with surprise the address stamped on the upper corner of the envelope. It was a business communication from the office of her aunt's executors, and she wondered what unexpected development had caused them to break silence before the appointed time. She opened the envelope and a check fluttered to the floor. As she stooped to pick it up the blood rushed to her face. The check represented the full amount of Mrs. Peniston's legacy, and the letter accompanying it explained that the executors, having adjusted the business of the estate with less delay than they had expected, had decided to anticipate the date fixed for the payment of the bequests.

Lily sat down beside the desk at the foot of her bed, and spreading out the check, read over and over the $10,000 written across it in a steely business hand. Ten months earlier the amount it stood for had represented the depths of penury; but her standard of values had changed in the interval, and now visions of wealth lurked in every flourish of the pen. As she continued to gaze at it, she felt the glitter of the visions mounting to her brain, and after a while she lifted the lid of the desk and slipped the magic formula out of sight. It was easier to think without those five figures dancing before her eyes; and she had a great deal of thinking to do before she slept.

She opened her checkbook, and plunged into such anxious calculations as had prolonged her vigil at Bellomont on the night when she had decided to marry Percy Gryce. Poverty simplifies bookkeeping, and her financial situation was easier to ascertain than it had been then; but she had not yet learned the control of money, and during her transient phase of luxury at the Emporium she had slipped back into habits of extravagance which still impaired her slender balance. A careful examination of her checkbook, and of the unpaid bills in her desk, showed that, when the latter had been settled, she would have barely enough to live on for the next three or four months; and even after that, if she were to continue her present way of living, without earning any additional money, all incidental expenses must be reduced to the vanishing point. . . .

It was no longer, however, from the vision of material poverty that she turned with the greatest shrinking. She had a sense of deeper impoverishment—of an inner destitution compared to which outward conditions dwindled into insignificance. It was indeed miserable to be poor—to look forward to a shabby, anxious middle age, leading by dreary degrees of economy and self-denial to gradual absorption in the dingy communal existence of the boardinghouse. But there was something more miserable still—it was the clutch of solitude at her heart, the sense of being swept like a stray uprooted growth down the heedless current of the years. That was the feeling which possessed her now—the feeling of being something rootless and ephemeral, mere spin-drift of the whirling surface of existence, without anything to which the poor little tentacles of self could cling before the awful flood submerged them. And as she looked back she saw that there had never been a time when she had had any real relation to life. Her parents too had been rootless, blown hither and thither on every wind of fashion, without any personal existence to shelter them from its shifting gusts. She herself had grown up without any one spot of earth being dearer to her than another: there was no center of early pieties, of grave endearing traditions, to which her heart could revert and from which it could draw strength for itself and tenderness for others. In whatever form, a slowly accumulated past lives in the blood—whether in the concrete image of the old house stored with visual memories, or in the conception of the house not built with hands, but made up of inherited passions and loyalties—it has the same power of broadening and deepening the individual existence, of attaching it by mysterious links of kinship to all the mighty sum of human striving.

Such a vision of the solidarity of life had never before come to Lily. She had had a premonition of it in the blind motions of her mating instinct; but they had been checked by the disintegrating influences of the life about her. All the men and women she knew were like atoms whirling away from each other in some wild centrifugal dance: her first glimpse of the continuity of life had come to her that evening in Nettie Struther's kitchen.

The poor little working-girl who had found strength to gather up the fragments of her life, and build herself a shelter with them, seemed to Lily to have reached the central truth of existence. It was a meager enough life, on the grim edge of poverty, with scant margin for possibilities of sickness or mischance, but it had the frail audacious permanence of a bird's nest built on the edge of a cliff—a mere wisp of leaves and straw, yet so put together that the lives entrusted to it may hang safely over the abyss.

Yes—but it had taken two to build the nest: the man's faith as well as the woman's courage. Lily remembered Nettie's words: I knew he knew about me. Her husband's faith in her had made her renewal possible—it is so easy for a woman to become what the man she loves believes her to be! Well—Selden had twice been ready to stake his faith on Lily Bart; but the third trial had been too severe for his endurance. The very quality of his love had made it the more impossible to recall to life. If it had been a simple instinct of the blood, the power of her beauty might have revived it. But the fact that it struck deeper, that it was inextricably wound up with inherited habits of thought and feeling, made it as impossible to restore to growth as a deep-rooted plant torn from its bed. Selden had given her of his best; but he was as incapable as herself of an uncritical return to former states of feeling.

There remained to her, as she had told him, the uplifting memory of his faith in her; but she had not reached the age when a woman can live on her memories. As she held Nettie Struther's child in her arms the frozen currents of youth had loosed themselves and run warm in her veins: the old life-hunger possessed her, and all her being clamored for its share of personal happiness. Yes—it was happiness she still wanted, and the glimpse she had caught of it made everything else of no account. One by one she had detached herself from the baser possibilities, and she saw that nothing now remained to her but the emptiness of renunciation.

It was growing late, and an immense weariness once more possessed her. It was not the stealing sense of sleep, but a vivid wakeful fatigue, a wan lucidity of mind against which all the possibilities of the future were shadowed forth gigantically. She was appalled by the intense cleanness of the vision; she seemed to have broken through the merciful veil which intervenes between intention and action, and to see exactly what she would do in all the long days to come. There was the check in her desk, for instance—she meant to use it in paying her debt to Trenor; but she foresaw that when the morning came she would put off doing so, would slip into gradual tolerance of the debt. The thought terrified her—she dreaded to fall from the height of her last moment with Lawrence Selden. But how could she trust herself to keep her footing? She knew the strength of the opposing impulses—she could feel the countless hands of habit dragging her back into some fresh compromise with fate. She felt an intense longing to prolong, to perpetuate, the momentary exaltation of her spirit. If only life could end now—end on this tragic yet sweet vision of lost possibilities, which gave her a sense of kinship with all the loving and foregoing in the world!

She reached out suddenly and, drawing the check from her writing desk, enclosed it in an envelope which she addressed to her bank. She then wrote out a check for Trenor, and placing it, without an accompanying word, in an envelope inscribed with his name, laid the two letters side by side on her desk. After that she continued to sit at the table, sorting her papers and writing, till the intense silence of the house reminded her of the lateness of the hour. In the street the noise of wheels had ceased, and the rumble of the "elevated" came only at long intervals through the deep unnatural hush. In the mysterious nocturnal separation from all outward signs of life, she felt herself more strangely confronted with her fate. The sensation made her brain reel, and she tried to shut out consciousness by pressing her hands against her eyes. But the terrible silence and emptiness seemed to symbolize her future—she felt as though the house, the street, the world were all empty, and she alone left sentient in a lifeless universe.

But this was the verge of delirium . . . she had never hung so near the dizzy brink of the unreal. Sleep was what she wanted—she remembered that she had not closed her eyes for two nights. The little bottle was at her bedside, waiting to lay its spell upon her. She rose and undressed hastily, hungering now for the touch of her pillow. She felt so profoundly tired that she thought she must fall asleep at once; but as soon as she had lain down every nerve started once more into separate wakefulness. It was as though a great blaze of electric light had been turned on in her head, and her poor little anguished self shrank and cowered in it, without knowing where to take refuge.

She had not imagined that such a multiplication of wakefulness was possible: her whole past was re-enacting itself at a hundred different points of consciousness. Where was the drug that could still this legion of insurgent nerves? The sense of exhaustion would have been sweet compared to this shrill beat of activities; but weariness had dropped from her as though some cruel stimulant had been forced into her veins.

She could bear it—yes, she could bear it; but what strength would be left her the next day? Perspective had disappeared—the next day pressed close upon her, and on its heels came the days that were to follow—they swarmed about her like a shrieking mob. She must shut them out for a few hours; she must take a brief bath of oblivion. She put out her hand, and measured the soothing drops into a glass; but as she did so, she knew they would be powerless against the supernatural lucidity of her brain. She had long since raised the dose to its highest limit, but tonight

she felt she must increase it. She knew she took a slight risk in doing so—she remembered the chemist's warning. If sleep came at all, it might be a sleep without waking. But after all that was but one chance in a hundred: the action of the drug was incalculable, and the addition of a few drops to the regular dose would probably do no more than procure for her the rest she so desperately needed.

Lily finally sinks into a sleep from which she never wakes. She has taken too large a dose. Her physical existence dissolves in a dreamlike state, just as her existence as a person had dissolved, unsustained by any meaningful traditions and early pieties, any deep human bonds and inherited passions and loyalties. She has not been part of a coherent story that could broaden and deepen her existence and attach her with "mysterious links of kinship" to other human beings. Rather, her days are like a "shrieking mob" that swarms over her. The people in her world have been like "atoms whirling away from each other" rather than members of a community coming together in solidarity with one another.

Lily Bart has been unable to acquire sufficient courage to break with her stifling world and turn to real community with Selden. She lacks that cardinal virtue, and that is not surprising given the meager resources provided by her family, her social class, her world. A good life, a life that develops toward a fulfilled state over time, requires, Aristotle insisted, a good community. The only community she has known, apart from a few glimpses of fragile alternatives such as the community of Nettie Struther's family, has not been good.

1. *Is their anything similar to Lily's world in your world? Describe similarities and differences.*

ALASDAIR MACINTYRE: TRADITIONS AND VIRTUES

Alasdair MacIntyre (b. 1929) has been a professor at several British and American universities, and he is currently professor of philosophy at Notre Dame. In his book After Virtue *(1981), he argues that the dominant modern ethical theories rely on a largely incoherent tra-*

dition initially forged by Hume and others during the 18th and 19th centuries. Thus he accepts, at least in its main outlines, the diagnosis of modern ethics given by Gertrude Anscombe, who argued in an essay of 1958 that the principal traditions in philosophical ethics from Hume through Kant and into the first half of the 20th century had run aground. Anscombe proposed a return to certain aspect of Aristotle's virtue ethics. MacIntyre's own proposed solution stresses the importance of participation in particular familial, religious, professional, civic and other forms of community. A person who is shut out from a deep participation in a viable and healthy community must perforce be lonely, fragmented, unfulfilled. She lacks a point of reference, a "script" without which she will be a "stutterer in words and actions." That might in fact be a good description of Lily Bart! MacIntyre has continued to explore these themes in subsequent works, including Dependent Rational Animals, *a title that should bring to mind Aristotelian ideas about human nature and vulnerability.*

The Virtues, the Unity of a Human Life, and Narrative

MacIntyre stresses, as did Aristotle, that the good for human life is the good for a whole life, not just for life next Monday. The virtues, which are long-term dispositions, are what are needed for such a "whole life" good. But contemporary society and currently dominant modes of thought provide social and philosophical obstacles to conceiving life "as a whole."

One obstacle arises from the common notion that life consists of strongly demarcated stages, such as childhood, adolescence, old age, each with its "special" problems. Another obstacle is rooted in the notion of the self as a function of "roles," so that I am one person at work, another at home, another when out on the town. Moreover, the tendency among many contemporary philosophers to thinking atomistically about human action creates, according to MacIntyre, obstacles to appreciating the fact that actions make sense only in a context, particularly a narrative context. The kind of unity a life needs in order for the virtues to be possible is like the unity of stories or of characters in stories.

The unity of a virtue in someone's life is intelligible only as a characteristic of a unitary life, a life that can be conceived and evaluated as a whole. . . . So now, in defining the particular premodern concept of the virtues with which I have been preoccupied, it has become necessary to say something of the concomitant concept of selfhood, a concept of a self whose unity resides in the unity of a narrative which links birth to life to death as narrative beginning to middle to end.

It is a conceptual commonplace, both for philosophers and for ordinary agents, that one and the same segment of human behavior may be correctly characterized in a number of different ways. To the question "What is he doing?" the answers may with equal truth and appropriateness be "Digging," "Gardening," "Taking exercise," "Preparing for winter" or "Pleasing his wife." Some of these answers will characterize the agent's intentions, others unintended consequences of his actions, and of these unintended consequences some may be such that the agent is aware of them and others not.

> 2. *In your judgment, which of the five answers just mentioned to the question "What is he doing?" would most likely characterize an unintended consequence?*

What is important to notice immediately is that any answer to the questions of how we are to understand or to explain a given segment of behavior will presuppose some prior answer to the question of how these different correct answers to the question "What is he doing?" are related to each other. For if someone's primary intention is to put the garden in order before the winter and it is only incidentally the case that in so doing he is taking exercise and pleasing his wife, we have one type of behavior to be explained; but if the agent's primary intention is to please his wife by taking exercise, we have quite another type of behavior to be explained and we will have to look in a different direction for understanding and explanation.

In the first place [instance] the episode has been situated in an annual cycle of domestic activity, and the behavior embodies an intention which presupposes a particular type of household-cum-garden setting with the peculiar narrative history of that setting in which this segment of behavior now becomes an episode. In the second instance the episode has been situated in the narrative history of a marriage, a very different, if related, social setting. We cannot, that is to say, characterize behavior independently of intentions, and we cannot characterize intentions independently of the settings which make those intentions intelligible both to agents themselves and to others.

For example, if your behavior includes regular class attendance, and you explain it in terms of your intention to get an "A," I will only understand this "intention" to the extent that I understand such things as what a university is, what a class is, how they are conducted, how work in them is evaluated, how university courses and success in them is related to the kinds of work available in a society, the kinds of responsibilities which must be met for personal and social existence, the kinds of institutional settings within which those responsibilities arise, and so forth. Moreover my understanding will be deepened when I learn something about the unfolding of your unique life, the place that academic achievement has assumed, perhaps something about your family and its values, and so forth.

In my earlier example the agent's activity may be part of the history both of the cycle of household activity and of his marriage, two histories which have happened to intersect. The household may have its own history stretching back through hundreds of years, as do the histories of some European farms, where the farm has had a life of its own, even though different families have in different periods inhabited it; and the marriage will certainly have its own history, a history which itself presupposes that a particular point has been reached in the history of the institution of marriage. If we are to relate some particular segment of behavior in any precise way to an agent's intentions and thus to the settings which that agent inhabits, we shall have to understand in a precise way how the variety of correct characterizations of the agent's behavior relate to each other first by identifying which characteristics refer us to an inten-

tion and which do not and then by classifying further the items in both categories.

Consider what the argument so far implies about the interrelationships of the intentional, the social and the historical. We identify a particular action only by invoking two kinds of context, implicitly if not explicitly. We place the agent's intentions, I have suggested, in causal and temporal order with reference to their role in his or her history; and we also place them with reference to their role in the history of the setting or settings to which they belong. In doing this, in determining what causal efficacy the agent's intentions had in one or more directions, and how his short-term intentions succeeded or failed to be constitutive of long-term intentions, we ourselves write a further part of these histories. Narrative history of a certain kind turns out to be the basic and essential genre for the characterization of human actions.

3. *Could the "actions" of a dog constitute a narrative history, in the sense expounded here by MacIntyre? How or why not?*

A central thesis then begins to emerge: man is in his actions and practice, as well as in his fictions, essentially a story-telling animal. . . . I can only answer the question "What am I to do?" if I can answer the prior question "Of what story or stories do I find myself a part?" We enter human society, that is, with one or more imputed characters-roles into which we have been drafted, and we have to learn what they are in order to be able to understand how others respond to us and how our responses to them are apt to be construed. It is through hearing stories about wicked stepmothers, lost children, good but misguided kings, wolves that suckle twin boys, youngest sons who receive no inheritance but must make their own way in the world and eldest sons who waste their inheritance on riotous living and go into exile to live with the swine, that children learn or mislearn both what a child and what a parent is, what the cast of characters may be in the drama into which they have been born and what the ways of the world are. Deprive children of stories and you leave them unscripted, anxious stutterers in their actions as in their words.

4. *Give an example of a shared story that has func-tioned importantly in your life or has shaped your behavior in some way—a family story, bible story, national story, work of fiction.*

Narratives and Quests

MacIntyre argues that human lives can be understood as attempts, successful or not, to achieve some ideal. The literary equivalent would be a narrated quest that describes people—and heroes—in the pursuit of a highest-value goal.

It is now possible to return to the question from which this enquiry into the nature of human action and identity started: In what does the unity of an individual life consist? The answer is that its unity is the unity of a narrative embodied in a single life. To ask "What is the good for me?" is to ask how best I might live out that unity and bring it to completion. To ask "What is the good for man?" is to ask what all answers to the former question must have in common. But now it is important to emphasize that it is the systematic asking of these two questions and the attempt to answer them in deed as well as in word which provide the moral life with its unity. The unity of a human life is the unity of a narrative quest. Quests sometimes fail, are frustrated, abandoned or dissipated into distractions; and human lives may in all these ways also fail. But the only criteria for success or failure in a human life as a whole are the criteria of success or failure in a narrated or to-be-narrated quest. A quest for what?

5. *Name three things that can happen on a quest that can cause it to fail.*
6. *Lily Bart could be thought of as on a "quest." A quest for what? What frustrates her quest?*

It is in looking for a conception of the good which will enable us to order other goods, for a conception of the good which will enable us to extend our understanding of the purpose and content of the virtues, for a conception of the good which will enable us to understand the place of integrity and constancy in life, that we initially define the kind of life which is a quest for the good.

A life that is a quest for the good cannot just be a life in which I try to develop those traits necessary to be a better chess player, cook or banker; these might be examples of "practices" or consist of various subpractices. Suppose I were all three. If I spent too much time on chess, the rest of my life might fall apart. I need to be able to order the various goods in my life, and doing that requires more than just having the traits and abilities necessary for chess or banking. A quest must be a search for a way to order a whole life and, thus, the search for the good of a whole life. The virtues are specifications of the practical wisdom required for a more or less successful quest, and the virtue of constancy or integrity, the virtue that "ties a person's life together," would figure prominently in any account of life as a quest.

7. *Suppose that a person had all the skills neces-sary to cook, bank and play chess. How might that person still lack "constancy"? Think about particular virtues, such as courage, in answering this.*

The Virtues and Community

My idea of the good, MacIntyre contends, cannot be independent of the particular social order of which I am a part.

For I am never able to seek for the good or exercise the virtues only qua individual. . . . I am someone's son or daughter, someone else's cousin or uncle; I am a citizen of this or that city, a member of this or that guild or profession; I belong to this clan, that tribe, this nation. Hence what is good for me has to be the good for one who inhabits these roles. As such, I inherit from the past of my family, my city, my tribe, my nation, a variety of debts, inheritances, rightful expectations and obligations. These constitute the given of my life, my moral starting point. This is in part what gives my life its own moral particularity.

This thought is likely to appear alien and even surprising from the standpoint of modern individualism. From the standpoint of individualism I am what I myself choose to be. . . . The young German who believes that being born after 1945 means that what Nazis did to Jews has no moral relevance to his relationship to his Jewish contemporaries [thinks that] the self is detachable from its social and historical roles and statuses. . . . The contrast with the narrative view of the self is clear. For the story of my life is always embedded in the story of those communities from which I derive my identity. I am born with a past; and to try to cut myself off from that past, in the individualist mode, is to deform my present relationships. The possession of a historical identity and the possession of a social identity coincide. Notice that rebellion against my identity is always one possible mode of expressing it.

Notice also that the fact that the self has to find its moral identity in and through its membership in communities such as those of the family, the neighborhood, the city and the tribe does not entail that the self has to accept the moral limitations of the particularity of those forms of community. Without those moral particularities to begin from there would never be anywhere to begin; but it is in moving forward from such particularity that the search for the good, for the universal, consists. Yet particularity can never be simply left behind or obliterated. The notion of escaping from it into a realm of entirely universal maxims which belong to man as such, whether in its eighteenth-century Kantian form or in the presentation of some modern analytical moral philosophies, is an illusion.

What I am, therefore, is in key part what I inherit, a specific past that is present to some degree in my present. I find myself part of a history and that is generally to say, whether I like it or not, whether I recognize it or not, one of the bearers of a tradition. It was important when I characterized the concept of a practice to notice that practices always have histories and that at any given moment what a practice is depends on a mode of understanding it which has been transmitted often through many generations.

8. *Why will it not do for an American to say, "I never owned any slaves"? (What would be the point of saying that, in the first place?)*

The concept of a "practice" that MacIntyre refers to can be illustrated by reference to a sport, such as basketball. At any given time in its history the rules and penalties and strategies and skills that define this game have varied to some extent, but it is obvious that, however different this game may be now from what it was in, say, 1950, there is historical continuity. Thus a non-free-throw basket made from anywhere on the floor used to count two points, and that is no longer the case. But of course points are still accumulated only by making baskets! That has not changed. The traditions that have formed the game and the aims in playing it have altered somewhat but can only be fully understood historically. We should add that the "goods" provided by such practices are "internal" to the game or practice. You cannot have what is good about playing and watching basketball in some other way than by playing and watching basketball. There is no generic, nonhistorical "good," such as the good of "entertainment" that can be had in playing and in other ways enjoying various games and other structured activities.

Now consider the practice of medicine or law or politics. All of these are what they are as a result of long traditions constituted by rules or standards and ideals of various kinds. The point of such practices can only be fully understood in terms of a history, and the goods they provide are largely, perhaps entirely, internal to the practices in the sense just proposed. What are some of the traditions that are constitutive for those practices? And how does the history of practices bear on the history or stories of individual lives?

And thus; insofar as the virtues sustain the relationships required for practices, they have to sustain relationships to the past—and to the future—as well as in the present. . . . Once again the narrative phenomenon of embedding is crucial: the history of a practice in our time is generally and characteristically embedded in and made intelligible in terms of the larger and longer history of the tradition through which the practice in its present form was conveyed to us; the history of each of our own lives is generally and characteristically embedded in and made intelligible in terms of the larger and longer histories of a number of traditions. I have to say "generally and characteristically" rather than "always," for traditions decay, disintegrate and disappear. What then sustains and strengthens traditions? What weakens and destroys them?

The answer in key part is: the exercise or the lack of exercise of the relevant virtues.

> *9. *What virtues might be required for the practice of law? What traditions have constituted the practice of law? Have "lawyer jokes" become popular because certain virtues once considered important to the practice of law have been neglected? Explain. In your opinion, has the practice of law decayed? Of medicine?*

The virtues find their point and purpose not only in sustaining those relationships necessary if the variety of goods internal to practices are to be achieved and not only in sustaining the form of an individual life in which that individual may seek out his or her good as the good of his or her whole life, but also in sustaining those traditions which provide both practices and individual lives with their necessary historical context. Lack of justice, lack of truthfulness, lack of courage, lack of the relevant intellectual virtues—these corrupt traditions, just as they do those institutions and practices which derive their life from the traditions of which they are the contemporary embodiments. To recognize this is of course also to recognize the existence of an additional virtue, one whose importance is perhaps most obvious when it is least present, the virtue of having an adequate sense of the traditions to which one belongs or which confront one.

> **10. *It is not possible, in MacIntyre's view, for a person to lead a good life without paying any attention to the history of her own family, religious and civic communities or the professional, moral, aesthetic and other traditions that shape her world. Try to state his reasons for his view.*
> *11. *Is MacIntyre a utopian, someone who imagines a good life in the sort of community that could not exist? Explain your answer.*
> **12. *Could we account for the failed life of Lily Bart in terms provided by MacIntyre? Try to give a brief account of her that illustrates his claims. Look for relevant quotes from Wharton's novel.*

Further Discussion and Applications

Problems with Virtue Theory

The revival of interest in a virtue ethics has, as might be expected, met a lot of resistance. Varieties of contract theory (Hobbes), Kantian, Humean and utilitarian ideas have developed into refined and subtle theories that continue to command the loyalty of many thinkers. At the same time, there are many complaints about the shortcomings of virtue theory. Here are a few of them.

1. One common complaint is that the virtues approach is unable to help in the resolution of actual moral dilemmas. When asked what to do in some difficult situation, such as making a decision about withdrawing life support from a terminally ill patient, the virtue theorist purportedly has nothing more to say than "Do what the virtuous person, the practically wise person, would do." But that is thought to be uninformative or completely useless.

2. This complaint amounts to the very general complaint that virtue theory reduces all moral questions to questions about the good moral agent. Virtue theory is *mononomic*, with the notion of a virtuous agent taken as the primitive notion, just as the notion of the greatest happiness is the single primitive moral notion for utilitarianism.

3. Another complaint has already been discussed in presenting Aristotle's ideas: It seems that some virtues could produce evil acts. The courageous Nazi and the patient plotter of an assassination are examples.

4. It also seems that the virtues are culture-bound. What counts as a virtue varies from one set of cultural circumstances to another. The virtues celebrated in a harsh frontier culture differ from those desired in a highly civilized urban culture. In the former, self-reliance and a willingness to deal quickly with horse thieves might be prized, whereas in the latter cooperation and respect for the law might be virtues. This difficulty is connected to another.

5. Both differences in circumstances and differences in ideological commitments can, it appears, produce different views on the virtues. The Christian list of virtues differs in some important ways from Aristotle's list (in fact, pride is high on Aristotle's list, whereas it can actually be a vice for Christians). We might say that the Christian and Aristotle "look at the world" differently and consequently prize different character traits. Even where the same term (*courage*, for instance) is used in different cultures, it can mean different things.

6. A related difficulty: If the virtues are culture-bound, then the virtue theorist seems more threatened by relativism than are competing theories. MacIntyre's stress on the building of character through local stories and traditions seems even more threatened by relativism than does, say, Aristotle's approach.

7. It may appear doubtful whether communitarians, like MacIntyre, can account for intuitions about fairness. The Aristotelian background to MacIntyre reinforces this worry, for Aristotle wrote in an illuminating way about the "good community" and its role in producing virtuous people, and yet he lived in a slave-based society.

8. Virtue theory does not tell us how to decide who is a virtuous agent and who is not. And it is supposedly unable to account for cases where two people who are both considered virtuous disagree about what to do in a given situation. It is certainly possible that virtuous people might disagree about disconnecting a respirator from a comatose person. So using the virtuous person as a standard for right action will be useless. We will have to find some criteria for right *actions* (as opposed to good character) to get around such difficulties.

9. One of the supposed strengths of a focus on virtues is that it requires attention to "moral psychology," to the nature of motivation and the psychological features of those who act well or badly. But some critics point out that in fact virtue theorists may distort facts about agents. In the next section an example of that

problem is discussed, as well as the problem of the courageous thief.

13. *Pick one of the listed objections to virtue theory and discuss it carefully. Which of these objections seems most important to you, and why?*

Virtue and the Will (Roberts)

Aristotle supposed that since virtues are something like habits, something like a "second nature," we might expect that the virtuous person would typically practice her virtues easily and even with enjoyment. But that seems psychologically unrealistic for most cases of courage or patience. Presumably Charlemagne's lieutenant, Roland, was not enjoying himself or finding things easy as he faced the prospect of being crushed by enemy forces while protecting Charlemagne's retreat from Spain. He rose to the occasion magnificently, but one does not easily imagine him as free of inner struggle or pain. Yet Roland is a paradigm of courage whose actions were celebrated in a famous poem. Aristotle's claim also conflicts with the commonsense intuition, so stressed by Kant, that actions that are difficult deserve more praise. If things are generally easy for a virtuous person, we might question how much praise her virtuous character deserves.

Robert Roberts develops a distinction between virtues of will power and motivational virtues that may help us through the difficulties just mentioned. Courage, he argues, is an example of a virtue of will power, not a motivational virtue. That distinction can be explained as follows.

If I were to ask a person who is courageous why she acts as she does, she would not say, "in order to be courageous." The motivation for courageous acts is not courage but something else that requires courage, such as the defense of one's retreating master or defense of the truth or of one's honor. Generosity, on the other hand, is a motivational virtue. Generous people are motivated by their generosity to act as they do. If I were to ask a generous person why he acted generously (as is typical for him), he might answer, "It was the generous thing to do" or "I saw that so and so could use some of my time (money, etc.)."

Now, sometimes it requires patience or courage to act generously. Thus we might think of virtues of the will, like courage and patience, as aids to motivational virtues such as generosity, truthfulness, kindness. Another illustration may help here. Consider the motivational virtue of truthfulness.

Suppose that my commitment to the truth requires that I speak out against a tyrant. It is of course my concern for the truth that motivates me. But it may take courage to do such a thing. I might even be putting my own life on the line. If all I had was concern for the truth (the virtue of truthfulness), that concern might be overcome by fear, so that I would not speak out, though I would feel guilty and ashamed as a result. But if in addition to the virtue of truthfulness I have the virtue of courage, that virtue will enable me to manage my fear properly, and it thus may "come to the aid" of my concern for the truth. Truthfulness will not always be easy. I may, by virtue of training or disposition, find truthfulness in myself and others a very good thing and be very repelled by dishonesty of any kind. So other things being equal, I will find it easy to be truthful. But when other things are not equal, when, for instance, truthfulness requires facing something very fearful, my concern for the truth might not be strong enough to override my fears. Thus, Roberts argues, the motivational virtue of truthfulness or of others, such as generosity and kindness, might often come easily, but in some circumstances they will not, and then I may need virtues of the will as well.

Courage itself, on the other hand, does not ever have to be easy, contrary to Aristotle's claim. That is not to rule out that there might sometimes be cases of courageous people acting fearlessly and easily. But it is certainly not definitive of the virtue of courage that all cases of courageous action are easy, let alone "enjoyed." And indeed, we are likely to praise the more difficult cases more highly. Where great fears are overcome, we feel great admiration. That is common sense, and it is central to Kant's account.

14. *In Roberts' account, to call a virtue, such as kindness, a "motivational virtue" is to say that a kind person's motivation for acting in a kindly way is, simply, their _____.*

15. *In Roberts' account, to call a virtue, such as courage, a "virtue of will power" is to say that a courageous person who performs a courageous act in order to be kind to someone uses _____ to overcome contrary impulses or feelings (such as fear of injury or loss of some other kind), which would get in the way of their being kind.*

Roberts' distinction can be employed to address another difficulty. Virtue moralists from ancient times up to the present have struggled with this question:

Is it possible to have one or several of the virtues without having all of them or at least all of the most important ones?

That is called *the problem of the "unity of the virtues."* Many major representatives of the classical tradition have answered "no" to this question. They have thought that the various virtues require each other. You can probably see why if you recall why it might be difficult to have the virtue of truthfulness without also having the virtue of courage. Perhaps other virtues would be needed too.

Suppose, then, that we take the position that it is impossible to have just one or two of the virtues. What, then, are we to say about the courageous thief or the patiently plotting murderer? Couldn't the thief have just the virtue of courage while lacking all other virtues? Some might simply deny that the "courage" of the thief is genuine courage. But it is difficult to find convincing grounds for that idea.

Roberts' distinction can be applied to this problem. In his view it *would* be possible for a vicious person, such as a thief or murderer, to have the virtue of courage, for that virtue is a "will power" virtue. There are two senses of *will* to be considered. On the one hand, a person who does *whatever he wants* without regard for anything or anyone else might be described as *willful*. But in another sense of *will*, a person is exercising his will only when he is fighting *against* what he wants or against other "inclinations" (as Kant called them). It is in this second sense that courage involves the will, for courage will usually involve fighting against feelings I naturally have, primarily fear in the face of real dangers. Since the thief also may have to fight off fears in order to go through with a given theft, he also may have the virtue of courage, provided that such actions are characteristic of him.

16. *In what sense of* will *is courage a virtue of the will?*
17. *What is Roberts' account of the courageous thief? Does his account seem intuitively right to you?*

There is, however, some truth in the idea of the unity of the virtues. It does seem that I will often need courage, patience and temperance in order to be kind, just or helpful. Question 15 shows how that works. I do often need the virtues of will in order to be genuinely and completely in possession of the motivational virtues, such as kindness and justice. It is, however, possible to have those same virtues of will power without being just. The courageous thief is an example. Perhaps not every virtue requires every other, but many of the motivational virtues might require virtues of the will.

There is a further and perhaps more significant truth to the idea of the unity of the virtues that Roberts' analysis brings out. The indispensability of virtues of will power testifies to the fact that the acquisition of character involves struggle and that only those who have struggled deserve to be thought of as agents, as persons with a definite moral identity. Even if it were possible, by giving an injection or fiddling with his or her genes, to produce a person who acts in accordance with courage or kindness, we would not be inclined to praise such a person, and he or she would give us nothing to emulate. Roberts remarks:

> Struggles are an important part of the way we become centers of initiation of actions and passions. They are the contexts in which the shape of our personality takes on that toughness and independence that we call "autonomy," and that seems to be a basic feature of mature personhood. Thus, powers of will are a logically and psychologically necessary part of our development as persons. (from "Will Power and the Virtues" in *Virtue and Vice in Everyday Life*, ed. Christina Hoff Sommers, 1993)

18. *Do you think that a person who has not struggled with temptations to cowardice or impatience or other "vices of the will" could be considered "mature"? Discuss.*

Applying Virtue Ethics (Hursthouse)

It is often claimed that virtue theory does not tell us what we ought or ought not to do. Various deontological theories, including natural law and divine command theories, and consequentialist theories, on the other hand, claim to give us specific rules for conduct or at least definite principles from which we can derive specific rules. Even if those theories are themselves subject to various criticisms, they are at least trying to do the thing we supposedly want ethics to do, namely, give us guidance with respect to specific actions and moral dilemmas. It seems that virtue theory cannot be *applied* in the ways required for medical ethics, business ethics and other areas of applied ethics. Moreover, critics of virtue theory allege that it *cannot* give the appropriate applications, not merely that most virtue theorists have not actually done so. American philosopher Rosalind Hursthouse has attempted to respond to these criticisms.

There are in fact some applications of virtue ethics. Critics complain, however, that these exceptional cases still do not give us the definite answers we need to questions about our obligations. Phillipa Foot, a major representative of virtue theory, produced a well-known discussion of euthanasia. But according to some critics she merely leaves our various and sometimes conflicting intuitions about euthanasia roughly where they were to begin with. We agree that taking a life is a serious matter, we agree that in some cases it nonetheless seems the best of the alternatives available (all of them being unsavory), we realize there are many different sorts of cases, for example, those that would involve giving lethal injections as opposed to those that merely allow a person to die by removal of a respirator or feeding tube. Sometimes we feel inclined to say, "Yes, do it," other times "Absolutely not"; and still other times we are utterly unsure what to say. Some people believe that a moral theory should straighten up this messy situation, show where ordinary intuitions go wrong, if they do, and otherwise satisfy a need to get beyond the conflicting intuitions with which we start. But Foot, some claim, does not do that, whereas others have at least attempted to. For example, in a famous article, James Rachels (see his bio in Chapter 1) tried to show that the distinction between killing and letting die had no moral significance. If our ordinary intuitions are to the effect that that distinction is important, then Rachels, if he is right, has cleared up some confusions rather than simply letting them stand. That is the sort of thing we hope to get from a philosophical ethicist.

19. *In brief, what is the objection to virtue theory stated in the preceding paragraph?*

These objections could amount to a request for an ethical algorithm or decision procedure. But hardly any moral theory can seriously claim to provide an algorithm for such complex cases. The quandaries are just that, quandaries. To expect a simple and straightforward rule for resolving them is to act as though something is simple that clearly is not. But the objection could be more general: The claim may be that virtue theory offers no rules at all, not just no clear rules, for resolving difficult cases. But that too is a mistake; the virtues imply rules. To value truthfulness is to endorse the rule "Tell the truth." A truthful person will follow that rule, with proper allowances for unusual and conflicted circumstances.

Perhaps the objection really has to do with the *kind* of rules derivable from virtue-centered approaches. "Tell the truth," "Help those in need" and their like are relatively banal. What we need, critics may claim, are rules that tell us what to do in the complicated situations.

It is easy to imagine an Aristotelian response to such a complaint. In Aristotle's view it is clearly appropriate that there be no such precise rules. Modern virtue ethicists will echo that idea and point out that a theory that recognizes the truly baffling nature of some moral dilemmas should be *credited* for doing so, rather than criticized. Hursthouse thus claims that it should be "a condition of adequacy on a [moral] theory that it leave some cases unresolved." Virtuous people are, in her account, likely to be the first to admit that sometimes they do not know what should be done. That is certainly not, however, an ad-

mission that some rule is needed to supplement the virtues approach.

Nor is admitting the unresolvability of some moral dilemmas equivalent to admitting that one virtuous person might consider a certain act clearly right and another equally virtuous person might think the same act wrong. Two virtuous persons might *act* differently in the face of a difficult situation; one might opt for removing a feeding tube, another might refuse to do so. But they will share a great deal. In particular, we might expect that the virtuous person who takes the first option will feel distress, a sense of having had to act in a way that goes against the grain and may always be regretted. The person who takes the second option will also feel the tug of the alternative and a recognition that on the matter at hand equally virtuous persons might disagree about what the *best* (as opposed to the *right*) action would be. In fact, if we understand *choice* in an Aristotelian way, this barely qualifies as a case of choice. Sometimes the capacity for genuine agency is defeated by terrible circumstances. And it is characteristic of the virtuous person that she recognize *that* fact also. And *that* is once again to the credit of virtue theory.

20. *Hursthouse admits that two virtuous people might act differently when confronted with a moral dilemma, such as that posed by the euthanasia case. What sorts of agreements are likely to still exist between two such people? Describe them.*

It might still seem, however, that the sorts of rules that can be garnered from virtue ethics are of little or no use. The person with the virtue of truthfulness may follow the rule "Tell the truth" because lying is a type of action he cannot stomach. But the rules we need, critics may claim, are not related to character in that way. Lying certainly is out of keeping with a virtue or character trait, namely, truthfulness. But is disconnecting a feeding tube an act that is inconsistent with some virtue? And if so, which virtue? There is not generally a certain type of person, a person of a certain kind of character, who "goes in for" that type of act, in the way that a truthful person "goes in for" telling the truth and the way a liar ignores it. Virtue ethics, critics may claim, cannot give us rules for these sorts of practical dilemmas, and such rules are the ones we really need in ethics.

However, while it is true that the virtuous person may be unable to provide us with a rule for such a case, it is not true that she has nothing to say about it or about closely related cases. Hursthouse considers the case, discussed by Judith Jarvis Thompson, of a woman who gets an abortion late in term in order not to miss a vacation.

> There is lots she could say about why it would be wrong of the woman in Thompson's case to have the abortion. For instance, she could say that it would be wrong because it would be callous, wrong because it would be stunningly light-minded, very likely (pending further details) to be wrong because it was very selfish, or self-centered, or cruel. She could also say it was wrong because it was folly. And all such claims universalize in the required way; any abortion which is similarly callous, or light-minded, or cruel, is wrong. So, in a way, virtue ethics can produce "rules governing abortion"—not of course the sort which the deontic theorist expected, but nevertheless rules which rebut the claim "virtue ethics can't say anything about the rights and wrongs of acts such as abortion, and hence needs to be supplemented by rules governing them."

Will this reply suffice? One might wonder why it is callous for the woman to act as she does. The answer seems to be "because killing babies is wrong," and that would be a rule of a sort that deontologists take as basic. This worry may reflect the idea that virtue ethics tries to reduce all moral concepts to virtues, and fails. But, in fact, virtue ethicists typically rely on the concepts of the good, a good life, happiness. And those concepts are not reducible to virtue concepts.

> 21. *Do you find any of the replies to the critics of virtue theory unsatisfying? If so, state why. If not, which reply do you think is weakest?*

Hursthouse concludes with a suggestion about what motivates philosophers' searches for something "better" than a virtues approach.

Perhaps what philosophers, as a body of professionals, tend to find uncomfortable about virtue ethics is that it makes all too explicit a fact we would like to think was not so; that we are not, qua philosophers, thereby fitted to say anything true or even enlightening on real moral issues. It requires that we give up the pretence that all we bring to bear on them is the expertise of our trade—our oft-claimed clarity and rigor in argument, our detachment, our skill in working out inconsistencies and dreaming up counter-examples. It reveals that, if we are to say anything true about them, we must also bring our knowledge of the correct application of the virtue-vice terms—about which actions are, say, charitable or dishonest—and, moreover, our knowledge of what is truly good and bad, of what is worthwhile, of what counts as a good, mature, developed human life, and what as a wasted, perverted, or childish one. (from "Applying Virtue Ethics" in *Virtues and Reasons*, ed. Rosalind Hursthouse, Gavin Lawrence, and Warren Quinn, 1998)

Virtue and Care for Natural Environments (Hill)

Much of the debate between environmentalists, antienvironmentalists and those with mixed views and loyalties has stressed the rightness or wrongness of certain actions rather than focusing on character traits. Thus, actions such as strip mining are sometimes condemned for reasons such as the following: Their purported good economic consequences are outweighed by various bad consequences, such as depriving people of certain kinds of enjoyments "in the wild"; they destroy something that is intrinsically valuable; they violate some religious precept, such as the need to be good stewards of the gifts of God in nature; they violate something's rights (say, the rights of animals that needed the destroyed environment or possibly even the rights of plants).

However, arguments along these lines often fail because people can differ so much in their calculations of consequences, can disagree about what has intrinsic value in ways that do not seem resolvable by rational persuasion or do not share religious frameworks, or they deny rights to the items in question and so forth.

22. *Which of the reasons people have used to argue that we should respect natural environments strikes you as most plausible? If none of them seem plausible, say why.*

However, as the classical virtues tradition testifies, we are by no means limited in our ethical thinking to the evaluation of acts. T. E. Hill asks us to consider the case of a grandson who pretends devotion to his grandmother in order to ensure a sizable inheritance and then secretly spits on her grave after she dies. Secretly spitting on a grave will not have undesirable consequences, nor does it appear to violate anyone's rights or destroy anything intrinsically valuable. Yet we would have good reason to evaluate such a person negatively. Evaluation of agents is important and indeed may be logically prior to evaluation of acts.

Now, there is little evidence that Plato or Aristotle would be concerned with virtues that did not have to do with our relationships with other people or to the development of our own proper natures. But it may well be that Aristotelian ways of thinking about character can be brought to bear on environmental concerns. Might there be something about the character of persons who are willing to destroy natural environments that deserves rebuke? Hill thinks there may be. His strategy is to try to show that lack of concern for nonsentient nature (natural environments apart from the interests of human and other animals) may be connected in some way with character traits that would generally be considered bad.

Hill suggests that "ignorance of the natural world and their place in it; an inability to see things as important apart from themselves; and reluctance to accept themselves as natural beings" may account for the heedlessness regarding nature exhibited by some strip miners or others who appear to lack concern for or appreciation of nature. And such concern may be necessary for proper humility. Moreover, that heedlessness may also be rooted in lack of aesthetic sensitivity and/or a diminished capacity to care about things that have enriched one's own life. And such traits, though perhaps not in themselves necessarily

bad, may be necessary for other character traits, such as gratitude, which are good or at least are topics for moral evaluation.

Consider, for instance, the reluctance to accept oneself as a natural being. What does this mean? Hill comments:

> Self-acceptance of this sort has long been considered a human excellence, under various names, but what has it to do with preserving nature? There is, I think, the following connection. As human beings we are part of nature, living, growing, declining, and dying by natural laws similar to those governing other living beings; despite our awesomely distinctive human powers, we share many of the needs, limits, and liabilities of animals and plants. These facts are neither good nor bad in themselves, aside from personal preference and varying conventional values. To say this is to utter a truism which few will deny, but to accept these facts, as facts about oneself, is not so easy—or so common. Much of what naturalists deplore about our increasingly artificial world reflects, and encourages, a denial of these facts, an unwillingness to avow them with equanimity.
>
> Like the Victorian lady who refuses to look at her own nude body, some would like to create a world of less transitory stuff reminding us only of our intellectual and social nature, never calling to mind our affinities with "lower" living creatures. The "denial of death," to which psychiatrists call attention, reveals an attitude incompatible with the sort of self-acceptance which philosophers, from the ancients to Spinoza and on, have admired as a human excellence. (From "Ideals of Human Excellence and Preserving Natural Environments," *Environmental Ethics* 5, 1983)

23. *What, according to Hill, is one important vulnerability we share with much of "nature"?*

The relevance of these remarks to remarks in previous sections about the place of human vulnerability in ancient thought generally and Aristotle in particular, should be obvious.

Consider also how attitudes toward nature might bear on the virtue of gratitude. Hill asks us to consider things, even inanimate things, that we value apart from their usefulness.

> One simply wants the thing to survive and (when appropriate) to thrive, and not simply for its utility. We see this attitude repeatedly regarding mementos. They are not simply valued as a means to remind us of happy occasions; they come to be valued for their own sake. Thus, if someone really took joy in the natural environment, but was prepared to blow it up as soon as sentient life ended, he would lack this common human tendency to cherish what enriches our lives. While this response is not itself a moral virtue, it may be a natural basis of the virtue we call "gratitude." People who have no tendency to cherish things that give them pleasure may be poorly disposed to respond gratefully to persons who are good to them. Again the connection is not one of logical necessity, but it may nevertheless be important. A nonreligious person unable to "thank" anyone for the beauties of nature may nevertheless feel "grateful" in a sense; and I suspect that the person who feels no such "gratitude" toward nature is unlikely to show proper gratitude toward people.

> Suppose these conjectures prove to be true. One may wonder what is the point of considering them. Is it to disparage all those who view nature merely as a resource? To do so, it seems, would be unfair. But when we set aside questions of blame and inquire what sorts of human traits we want to encourage, our reflections become relevant in a more positive way. The point is not to insinuate that all antienvironmentalists are defective, but to see that those who value such traits as humility, gratitude, and sensitivity to others have reason to promote the love of nature.

24. *Why, according to Hill, might someone who lacks an appreciation for the value of nature also lack the virtue of gratitude?*

The People of Le Chambon (Hallie, Sauvage)

MacIntyre's claim that virtuous lives logically require communal resources, such as family traditions, commemorations, historical stories, narratives and ethi-

cal teachings, is aptly illustrated and supported by accounts of the actions of the people of Le Chambon during the Nazi occupation of France during WWII. This little village in southern France sheltered and otherwise assisted some 5,000 Jews at a time when to do so was a crime that could have provoked terrible reprisals. The villagers and farmers from the surroundings hid Jews in their homes, led them to hide in the woods when "roundups" were taking place and became involved in the production and distribution of false identity papers that enabled the Jews to move about to some extent. Some were led along mountains paths to neutral Switzerland.

Jews under Hitler's regime were not simply slaughtered. They were systematically degraded and humiliated. Phillip Hallie argues that the opposite of this degrading cruelty is not kindness. Even cruel Nazi prison guards could occasionally be kind. Moreover, when we are kind to people who are at our mercy, the kindness can simply add to the sense of powerlessness and degradation that oppressed people may feel. Rather, Hallie claims, the opposite of cruelty is *hospitality*. This realization dawned on him when he learned about Le Chambon. The people of this village did not simply shelter Jews. They welcomed them. The "Chambonais" were almost all protestant (French Huguenot ancestry), and religious life was important to them. The Jews were religious aliens as well as a persecuted minority, yet the Chambonais welcomed them as brothers and sisters. In doing so they showed great openness to others as well as such virtues as courage, generosity, practical wisdom, the ability to get dangerous tasks done effectively and without flinching and a single-minded determination. However, they did not see themselves as doing anything unusual or heroic. Rather, they assumed that they were simply doing what had to be done. It was "the natural thing," one of them said. In other words, their actions were the output of formed dispositions, or *virtues*, and they sometimes showed the "ease" that Aristotle claims as characteristic of virtuous agents.

What could account for such extraordinary courage, such an outpouring of generosity and hospitality? Obviously this little community did not contain some "hospitality gene"! Most French villages and cities did little or nothing to protect the Jews, and the Vichy regime that governed southern France in the first years of the occupation, although supposedly an independent French government, actively collaborated with the Nazis. What made the Chambonais different?

Filmmaker Pierre Sauvage, who was himself born in Le Chambon to Jewish refugee parents during the Nazi occupation of France, produced a documentary in which he explored that question. The documentary, titled *Weapons of the Spirit*, is available in some libraries. In it various individuals, both Chambonais and those whom they sheltered, were interviewed and filmed, and the history of the war years was recounted.

It is clear that a shared history, shared stories and narratives and songs, and a deep commitment to their own Protestant type of Christianity had shaped this little community. The old folk of the community are shown singing an old hymn recalling the resistance of their ancestors to the persecution of Protestants by the Roman Catholic government of France at the beginning of the 18th century, a hymn that both commemorates the ancestors and urges to imitation of them. They had kept alive the memory of what it is to be persecuted to such an extent that they could readily identify with any person being hunted down by oppressors. They also kept alive a memory of the particular *kind* of resistance practiced by their ancestors from Le Chambon and another nearby village, namely, quiet, nonviolent but skillful resistance.

Biblical resources were also powerfully formative. Issue after issue of the parish paper, from the time of the occupation, quoted, in the margins, biblical passages with a very pointed application to the contemporary situation: "He who does not love his brother whom he has seen, how can he love God whom he has not seen?"; "One must obey God rather than man"; One woman accounts for the actions of the community in terms of the parable of the good Samaritan, who rescued a man who had been set upon by thieves and was lying by the road beaten and bloody. The Jews, she says, were lying along the road beaten and bloody. As the narrator describes how the SS finally came to the door of the Protestant pastor of Le Chambon to demand that he reveal where Jews were being hidden, we hear an ancient sung lament that describes how French dragoons came to the door of the Protestant pastor hundreds of years before, demanding that he reveal the names of the members of the (illegal) Protestant community. In both cases, the interrogators are met with a stiff refusal. In both cases, the pastor was dragged away in the middle of the night and imprisoned.

MacIntyre's remarks about the role of shared stories and "scripts" come easily to mind on viewing this documentary. The ancient lament almost literally produced a script that the modern pastor of Le Chambon knew how to follow. He was himself a solid inhabitant of a tradition, one in which resistance to tyranny was the "done thing" and protection of the innocent was considered "normal." It certainly appears that he did not need to struggle over what to do when interrogated. He did not need to calculate the consequences of various options or figure out what maxim described his action. He acted securely, solidly. He had been prepared and schooled by traditions, stories, songs and other ancient texts that reminded him of who he was and gave him strength for the occasion.

In fact, one of the adjectives prominent in the refugees' descriptions of the Chambonais was *solid*. There was a security in their actions that contrasts with those "unscripted stutterers in words and actions" that MacIntyre thinks will be produced by societies that are meager or lacking in shared narrative resources.

25. *Does the society you live in (or any of its social groups) provide you with the sort of narrative resources available to the people of Le Chambon? Does it seem to matter whether it does or not?*

26. *It is often remarked that the United States is a "pluralistic" society. Does that imply that the people who live here have no shared stories or traditions at all? If there are some, name them.*

27. *It is sometimes claimed that people from small, close-knit communities are necessarily closedminded, provincial, bigoted. Yet the Chambonais showed little sign of being any of those things. Is that to be explained, at least in part,*

by the actual content *of their traditions and beliefs? Discuss.*

Although the communal resources of Le Chambon were crucial to the great mission they carried out over four difficult years, they certainly did not operate automatically. As MacIntyre observes, "Lack of justice, lack of truthfulness, lack of courage, lack of the relevant intellectual virtues—these corrupt traditions, just as they do those institutions and practices which derive their life from the traditions of which they are the contemporary embodiments." What is required to keep traditions and powerful communal institutions and norms alive and effective is those virtues that are in part made possible by those same traditions; there must be a lively circular interchange between them, and in the process the importance of individual effort becomes apparent.

The most notable individual in the case of Le Chambon was the chief pastor, André Trocmé. It was he above all who galvanized the latent energies of nearly all the Chambonais, made alive to them the resources they needed to possess forcefully in order to act as they did. He was both spiritually and intellectually engaged with the resources of his own religious traditions—but not uncritically. As Hallie describes him, Trocmé had to fight his way free from certain aspects of his own family of origin, which had hardened in various ways. And he was also in conflict with the particular embodiment of Huguenot theological and ethical traditions of his own time, particularly with regard to questions of violence. Church officials advised Trocmé that his strict pacifism was not part of that church's ethical understanding. These conflicts, so far from detracting from the importance of the particular familial and more broadly communal traditions to the life of such a man, are in fact part of their vitality. MacIntyre remarks that "traditions, when vital, embody continuities of conflict."

In summing up what took place at Le Chambon, Hallie anticipates many of the themes developed by MacIntyre:

> The classic conception of good and evil as inward conditions of the mind or the soul is not totally wrong. It points up one of the important forces in ethical action: respect for the demands of ethics

despite fear, despite indifference, and despite all the other passions that tend to debilitate and destroy action. [Nonetheless] in Le Chambon, at least, there was more to being good than this deep inward respect for the demands of ethics. . . . The study of ethics must not be a way of trying, by a use of abstract, traditional terms, to cast a fitful light within the inward world of men's souls. It must illuminate the great, rich regions of plainly visible human history. It must concern itself with the story of what individuals do in the context of the *story* of their times. . . . Narrative, plot, and character, especially when the characters involved in the action are surrounded and pervaded by a world intimately involved in their deeds and passions, can help us to understand "good" and "evil" in large, clear, and concrete terms. And narrative can show us the many grey areas between good and evil, as well as the many differences of opinion about what kind of person or action *is* good or evil.

> Because all of this is so, the story of André Trocmé and Le Chambon tells us a great deal about the ethical meaning of Darcissac's term *wonderful*, when he applied it to the Chambonais during the German occupation of France. Rich regions of human history as revealed in narrative illuminate ethics as much as ethics illuminates those regions. (from *Lest Innocent Blood Be Shed*, 1994)

28. *Critically discuss the following, keeping in mind what you have learned from MacIntyre and Hallie:*

The demands of ethics, the requirements of duty and goodness, are personal, individual. They require the ability to evaluate individually one's inherited systems of value or belief. They require a strong will and individual commitment. Therefore, it cannot matter much what community a person is born into, how a person is raised, what stories are heard as a child or what the adults around him or her value. After all, what adults value is itself often corrupt, and the traditions they hand on to their children can actually be immoral.

WORKS CITED

Given here is a list of works cited, in order of appearance. In some cases information on alternative editions or translations has been provided.

CHAPTER I
Relativism, Skepticism and the Possibility of Moral Judgment

Tolstoy, Leo, After the Ball (1911), trans. Hans Lillegard. Used by permission.

Montaigne, Michel, Essays (1580). A recent translation, by D. M. Frame, is included in The Complete Works of Montaigne (Stanford, CA: Stanford University Press, 1957).

Rachels, James, Elements of Moral Philosophy, 3rd ed. (New York: McGraw-Hill, 1999). Reprinted by permission of the publisher.

Midgley, Mary, Can't We Make Moral Judgments? (New York: St. Martin's Press, 1993). Reprinted by permission of the publisher and author.

Stoppard, Tom, Every Good Boy Deserves Favor and Professional Foul (Grove Press 1994)

Williams, Bernard, "Ethics," in Philosophy, ed. A. C. Grayling (New York: Oxford University Press, 1995).

Glendon, Mary Ann, "Rights Talk" (Commonweal, October 2001).

CHAPTER II
The Good Life, Reason and Tragic Conflict

Sophocles, Antigone, trans. R. C. Jebb, revised, Norman Lillegard. A recent translation, by E. Wyckoff, is included in Sophocles I (Chicago: University of Chicago Press), 1954.

Plato, Apology, Phaedo, Euthyphro, Protagoras, Republic, trans. B. Jowett. Many recent translations can be found in John Cooper, ed. Plato: The Complete Works (Indianapolis, IN: Hackett, 1997).

Annas, Julia, "Understanding and the Good: Sun, Line and Cave," in Plato's Republic: Critical Essays, ed. Richard Kraut (Lanham, MD: Rowman & Littlefield, 1997).

Murdoch, Iris, The Sovereignty of Good (London: Routledge and Kegan Paul, 1970).

Taylor, Charles, Sources of the Self (Cambridge, MA: Harvard University Press, 1989).

Popper, Karl, The Open Society and Its Enemies, vol. I (New York: HarperTorch, 1963).

CHAPTER III
The Good Life, Reason and Virtue

Aristotle, The Nichomachean Ethics, trans. N. Lillegard. The Greek text with English translation by H. Rackham on facing pages can be found in the Loeb Classical Library, Aristotle: The Nichomachean Ethics (Cambridge, MA: Harvard University Press, 1923).

Kraut, Richard, "Aristotle on the Human Good: An Overview," in Nancy Sherman, ed., Aristotle's Ethics: Critical Essays (Lanham, MD: Rowman & Littlefield, 1999).

Nussbaum, Martha, Love's Knowledge (Oxford: Oxford University Press, 1990).

Sher, George, and William Bennett, "Moral Education and Indoctrination," Journal of Philosophy, November 1982.

Cooper, John, "Friendship and the Good in Aristotle," in Philosophical Review, 86, (1977).

Sherman, Nancy, ed., Aristotle's Ethics: Critical Essays (Lanham, MD: Rowman & Littlefield, 1999).

Wallace, James D., Virtues and Vices (Ithaca, NY: Cornell University Press, 1978).

Confucian School, The Analects (5th century BCE), The Great Learning (3rd century BCE), The Doctrine of the Mean (2nd century BCE). Recent translations in Wang-tsit Chan's A Source Book in Chinese Philosophy (Princeton, NJ: Princeton University Press, 1963).

CHAPTER IV
Morality and Religion

Psalm 1, Psalm 19

Aquinas, Thomas, Summa Theologica: "The Treatise On Law" and "On Wisdom and Folly" (Benziger Bros. edition, 1947), trans. Fathers of the English Dominican Province.

The Story of Abraham and Isaac (Gen. 22)

Duns Scotus, Excerpts from the Ordinatio and the Reportatio, trans. Thomas Williams, (used by permission).

Rupp, E. Gordon, and Watson, P. S., eds., Luther and Erasmus: Free Will and Salvation (Louisville, KY: Westminster John Knox Press, 1978).

The Bhagavad Gita (3rd century CE). A recent translation is by Juan Mascaro (London: Penguin, 1962).

Rachels, James, The Elements of Moral Philosophy (New York: McGraw-Hill, 1999).

Adams, Robert, Finite and Infinite Goods (Oxford: Oxford University Press, 1999).

Stump, Eleonore, "Wisdom: Will, Belief, and Moral Goodness," in Aquinas' Moral Theory, ed. Scott MacDonald and Eleanor Stump (Ithaca, NY: Cornell University Press, 1999).

Matthews, Gareth, "St. Thomas and the Principle of Double Effect," in Aquinas' Moral Theory, ed. Scott MacDonald and Eleanor Stump (Ithaca, NY: Cornell University Press, 1999).

Anscombe, G. E. M, "Warfare and Murder" in War and Morality, ed. Richard Wasserstrom (Belmont, CA: Wadsworth, 1970).

Epictetus, Enchiridion. A recent translation by George Long can be found at Digireads.com (January 1, 2005).

CHAPTER V
Evil, Vice and Reason

Dostoevsky, Feodor, The Brothers Karamazov (1879). A more recent translation by Sidney Monas is in a Signet Classic edition, 2006.

Nietzsche, Friedrich, Genealogy of Morals (1887). A recent translation, with an introduction and notes, is by Douglas Smith (Oxford: Oxford University Press, 1996). Joyful Wisdom (1882). A recent translation is by Walter Kaufmann, The Gay Science (New York: Vintage, 1974). The Dawn of Day (1881). A recent translation is by R. J. Hollingdale, Daybreak: Thoughts on the Prejudices of Morality, with an introduction by Michael Tanner (New York: Cambridge University Press, 1982).

Camus, Albert, "The Human Crisis," in Twice a Year, edited and published by Dorothy Norman, Fall–Winter 1946–47.

Taylor, Richard, Good and Evil, rev. ed. (Amherst, NY: Prometheus Books, 1999).

Benn, Stanley, Ethics (Chicago: University of Chicago Press, 1985).

Arendt, Hannah, Eichmann in Jerusalem: A Report on the Banality of Evil (Penguin Classics, 2006).

Johnson, Samuel, in The Rambler, ed. W. J. Bate and A. B. Strauss, vol. 3 (New Haven, CT: Yale University Press, 1969).

Augustine, On Free Choice of the Will, trans. T. Williams (Indianapolis, IN: Hackett, 1993).

Dante, Alighieri, Inferno. A useful Italian/English edition is Dante's Inferno: Italian text with English Translation and Comment by John D. Sinclair (New York: Oxford University Press, 1939).

CHAPTER VI
Egoism, Reason and Morality

Golding, William, Lord of the Flies (Wideview/Perigee Books, 1954). Used by permission.

Mencius, The Mencius (4th century BCE). A recent translation is by D. C. Lau (New York: Penguin Books, 1970).

Hsun-Tzu, The Hsun-Tzu (3rd century BCE). A recent translation is by J. Knoblock, Xunzi: A Translation and Study of the Complete Works (Stanford, CA: Stanford University Press, 1988–1994).

Hobbes, Thomas, Leviathan (1651). A recent edition is by Edwin Curly (Indianapolis, IN: Hackett, 1994).

Butler, Joseph, Fifteen Sermons (1726). A recent edition of the central sermons is Five Sermons (Indianapolis, IN: Hackett, 1983).

Browne, Harry, How I found Freedom in an Unfair World (Great Falls, MT: Liamworks, March 1998).

Baier, Kurt, The Moral Point of View (Ithaca, NY: Cornell University Press, 1958).

Wilson, Edward O., Sociobiology: The New Synthesis (Cambridge, MA: Harvard University Press, 1975).

Broadie, Sarah, Ethics with Aristotle (New York: Oxford University Press, 1991).

CHAPTER VII
Feeling, Reason and Morality

Twain, Mark, Adventures of Huckleberry Finn. A recent edition is available from Prestwick House (Clayton, DE, January 1, 2005).

Hume, David, Enquiry Concerning the Principles of Morals (1751). The standard edition is by Tom L. Beauchamp (Oxford: Clarendon Press, 1998).

Hume, David, Treatise of Human Nature (1739–1740). The standard edition is by David Fate Norton and Mary J. Norton (Oxford: Clarendon Press, 2000).

Carroll, Lewis, Alice's Adventure in Wonderland. Many editions.

Bennett, Jonathan, "The Conscience of Huckleberry Finn" in Virtue and Vice in Everyday Life, ed. F. Sommers (Orlando, FL: Harcourt Brace Jovanovich, 1993).

Blackburn, Simon, Essays in Quasi Realism (New York: Oxford University Press, 1993).

Searle, John, "How to Derive Ought from Is," Philosophical Review (1964), Vol. 73.

CHAPTER VIII
Reason, Duty and Dignity

Trollope, Anthony, Dr. Wortle's School. A recent edition is in Penguin Classics (December 1, 1999), ed. Mick Imiah.

Kant, Immanuel, Groundwork of the Metaphysics of Morals (1785). A recent translation is by Mary Gregor (Cambridge: Cambridge University Press, 1998).

Ross, William David, The Right and the Good (Oxford: Clarendon Press, 1930).

Sorell, Tom, "Kant's Good Will and Our Good Nature" in Kant's Groundwork of the Metaphysics of Morals: Critical Essays, ed. Paul Guyer (Lanham, MD: Rowman & Littlefield, 1998).

Singer, Irvin, "The Morality of Sex: Contra Kant" in Alan Soble, ed., The Philosophy of Sex: Contemporary Readings, 5th ed. (Lanham, MD: Rowman & Littlefield, 2007).

Kant, Immanuel, "Duties Towards Animals" in Lectures on Ethics (1775–1794). A recent translation is by Peter Heath (Cambridge: Cambridge University Press, 1997).

Reagan, Tom, "The Case for Animal Rights" in In Defense of Animals, ed. Peter Singer (Oxford: Basil Blackwell, 1985), pp. 13–26.

Kohlberg, Lawrence, Essays on Moral Development (New York: Harper & Row, 1981).

Gilligan, Carol, In a Different Voice (Cambridge, MA: Harvard University Press, 1982).

Homiak, Marcia, "Feminism and Aristotle's Rational Ideal," in Aristotle's Ethics: Critical Essays, ed. Nancy Sherman (Lanham, MD: Rowman & Littlefield, 1999).

Habermas, Jürgen, Truth and Justification (Cambridge, MA: MIT Press, 2005).

CHAPTER IX
Rightness, Reason and Consequences

Dostoevsky, Fyodor, Crime and Punishment. Many editions. A recent translation is by Richard Pevear and Larissa Volokhonsky (New York: Vintage, 1993).

Bentham, Jeremy, Principles of Morals and Legislation (1789). The standard edition is by J. H. Burns (Oxford: Clarendon Press, 1996).

Mill, John Stuart, Utilitarianism (1861). The standard edition is included in J. M. Robson, ed., Essays on

Ethics, Religion and Society (Toronto: University of Toronto Press, 1969).

Williams, Bernard, "A Critique of Utilitarianism" in Utilitarianism: For and Against, ed. J. J. C. Smart and Bernard Williams (Cambridge: Cambridge University Press, 1973.)

Hare, Richard, "Loyalty and Evil Desires," in Moral Thinking (Oxford: Oxford University Press, 1981).

Schick, Frederick, "Under Which Descriptions" in Utilitarianism and Beyond, ed. Amartya Sen and Bernard Williams (Cambridge: Cambridge University Press, 1982).

Singer, Peter, "Famine, Affluence, and Morality," in Virtue and Vice in Everyday Life, ed. Christina Hoff Sommers (Orlando, FL: Harcourt Brace Jovanovich, 1993).

Rawls, John, A Theory of Justice (Cambridge, MA: Belknap Press, 2005).

Veatch, Robert, A Theory of Medical Ethics (New York: Basic Books, 1983).

CHAPTER X
Virtues, Narrative and Community: Some Recent Discussions

Wharton, Edith, The House of Mirth. Many editions.

MacIntyre, Alasdair, After Virtue (1981). There is a second, revised edition (Notre Dame, IN: University of Notre Dame Press, 1984). Used by Permission.

Hursthouse, Rosalind, "Applying Virtue Ethics" in Virtues and Reasons, ed. Rosalind Hursthouse, Gavin Lawrence and Warren Quinn (Oxford: Clarendon Press, 1998).

Roberts, Robert, "Will Power and the Virtues" in Virtue and Vice in Everyday Life, ed. Christina Hoff Sommers (Orlando, FL: Harcourt Brace Jovanovich, 1993).

Hill, Thomas, "Ideals of Human Excellence and Preserving Natural Environments," Environmental Ethics, vol. 5, 1983.

Hallie, Phillip, Lest Innocent Blood Be Shed, (New York: Harper Perennial, 1994).

TOPICAL INDEX